Monetary Economics

Monetary Economics
Policy and its Theoretical Basis

Second Edition

Keith Bain
Formerly Principal Lecturer, University of East London

and

Peter Howells
*Professor of Monetary Economics, Centre for Global Finance,
Bristol Business School*

First edition 2003
Reprinted four times
Second edition 2009
Published by
PALGRAVE MACMILLAN

Palgrave Macmillan in the UK is an imprint of Macmillan Publishers Limited, registered in England, company number 785998, of Houndmills, Basingstoke, Hampshire RG21 6XS.

Palgrave Macmillan in the US is a division of St Martin's Press LLC, 175 Fifth Avenue, New York, NY 10010.

Palgrave Macmillan is the global academic imprint of the above companies and has companies and representatives throughout the world.

Palgrave® and Macmillan® are registered trademarks in the United States, the United Kingdom, Europe and other countries.

ISBN-13: 978–0–230–20599–4   hardback
ISBN-10: 0–230–20599–2   hardback
ISBN-13: 978–0–230–20595–6   paperback
ISBN-10: 0–230–20595–X   paperback

This book is printed on paper suitable for recycling and made from fully managed and sustained forest sources. Logging, pulping and manufacturing processes are expected to conform to the environmental regulations of the country of origin.

A catalogue record for this book is available from the British Library.

A catalog record for this book is available from the Library of Congress.

Designed and typeset by Sarum Editorial Services.

10 9 8 7 6 5 4 3 2 1
18 17 16 15 14 13 12 11 10 09

Printed and bound in China

Contents

List of tables, boxes and figures

Preface

Two major things have happened in the world of monetary economics since our first edition.

The first has been the dramatic events of the credit crunch with the associated collapse or rescue by governments of major banks, the large reductions in the official interest rates of many countries and the revival of the idea that fiscal policy might have a part to play in the avoidance of recession. Monetary economics textbooks have seldom had to cope with such rapid changes in the policy landscape. No matter what we did, the book on publication would have been 'out of date' in terms of events. Since this is a textbook on the theory and practice of monetary policy, not a journalistic account of events, we did not see this as a major problem but we have added an appendix which relates the credit crunch and its causes to the theory outlined in the book and points out the likely impact of events on the future practice of monetary policy.

The second major change has been the general acceptance of the view that the money supply is endogenous. The first edition had set out to redress the imbalance in monetary economics textbooks and courses, most of which had continued to retain the assumption that the money supply was exogenous, when clearly it was not. This was no small thing, since the assumption of endogenous money changes entirely one's attitude to the nature of monetary policy and elevates the importance of the supply of money far above that of the demand for money. This involved a reversal of an imbalance indeed — a three-volume set edited by David Laidler published in 1999 under the title *The Foundations of Monetary Economics* contained 17 papers on the demand for money and none on its supply!

We knew in 2001 that our view that the money supply was endogenous was correct. However, many economists were not then prepared to drop the assumption exogeneity, much less to admit the consequences that followed. Hence we included two rather long chapters on the demand for money and much of the two chapters on the transmission mechanism of monetary policy assumed an exogenous money supply.

The widespread move to the acceptance of endogenous money has allowed us to remove most of the empirical material on the demand for money and all traces of the *IS/LM* model of transmission. We have replaced this with a model which makes the obviously correct assumption that the principal instrument of monetary policy is the short-term interest rate set by the central bank. We trust also that the fact that we do not, in this edition, feel such a strong need to justify our stance, has allowed us produce a work that cannot easily be accused of academic imbalance.

Other changes reflect comments that we received on the first edition. Our belief that monetary economics is a very important subject which should be studied by all students of economics, has been reinforced by recent events. This explains why we have felt no need to change the balance of the book, which continues to favour the theory and practice of monetary policy. This is what we believe students should know about *and* are likely to find interesting.

KB

PGAH

Acknowledgements

The authors and publishers are grateful to the following for permission to reproduce copyright material:

Oxford U P for the definitions of money on pp. 2 and 10, taken from their *Oxford English Dictionary Online*; the US Federal Reserve for the money supply data on p. 33 and for the extracts from policy statements on pp. 400-405, all taken from their web-site, www.federalreserve.gov; the European Central Bank for the money supply data on p. 33 taken from their *Annual Report, 2006*, extracts from *The Monetary Policy of the ECB* (2001) on pp. 262 and 358 and the data on pp. 366 and 368 taken from their 'statistical warehouse' at sdw.ecb.europa.eu/ We are also grateful to John Wiley and Sons for the quotations: on p. 1 from Boulding's paper in the *Journal of Money, Credit and Banking*, vol. 1, 1969; on p. 95 from Goodhart's paper in the *Economic Journal*, vol. 104, 1994; and from Laidler's paper in *Manchester School*, vol. 56, 1988 on p.177. We are grateful to Princeton U P for the quotations from Woodford's *Interest and Prices* (2003) which appear on pp. 99 and 100; to Palgrave Macmillan for the quotation from J M Keynes's *Treatise on Money* (1930) on p. 99; to Pearson for extracts from the *Financial Times* on pp. 99, 143, 271 and 274; the Bank of England for the quotations from articles in the *Bank of England Quarterly Bulletin* on pp. 96, 105, 297 and 305 and the data on p. 331, taken from the website, www.bankofengland.co.uk/statistics; the Association of Payment Clearing Systems for the statistics on p. 42 from their website www.apacs.org.uk/resources_publications/documents/; the Queen's Printer and HMSO for the quotations on pp. 258 (from www.bankofengland.co.uk/monetary policy), on p. 280 (from the evidence given to the Treasury and Civil Service Select Committee on *Monetary Policy* in 1980 and on p. 300 from the Report of the *Committee on the Working of the Monetary System* (1959); the US Bureau of Labor Statistics for the data on p. 399 and to Elsevier Science B V for the quotation on p. 31 from William Poole's paper in *Carnegie-Rochester Series on Public Policy*, 34 (1991).

Every effort has been made to trace rights holders but if any have been over-looked the publishers would be pleased to make the necessary arrangements at the first opportunity.

Like the first edition, this book is largely the product of our teaching experience. Our thanks, therefore go to those many students who, at UWE, Bristol and at the University of Bath, have taken courses in some combination of banking, finance, money and monetary economics in recent years.

But we are also indebted to numerous colleagues in the UK and overseas who have made useful suggestions and sometimes, by critical comments, spurred us to make improvements. The extent of our debt (and the identity of our creditors) can be seen in the references.

Perhaps, after many years of working together, we should principally be grate-ful for each other's forbearance.

KB
PGAH

1 The meaning of money

'We must have a good definition of Money,
For if we do not, then what have we got,
But a Quantity Theory of no-one-knows-what,
And this would be almost too true to be funny.'

Kenneth Boulding, *Journal of Money, Credit and Banking*, Vol I, Aug 1969 p 555.

1.1 Introduction

Monetary economics is the branch of economics dealing with money and monetary relationships in the economy. This is a broad definition which can include topics such as the reasons for the existence of money, the roles money performs in economic exchange, the transfer of wealth or models of economic growth. However, as the sub-title makes clear, this book is interested principally in monetary policy and hence on the macroeconomic aspects of monetary economics - on the links between money and the general level of prices, output, and employment both in the short- and long-term. Within this, monetary economists have been particularly concerned with the relationship between the rate of growth of the money supply and the rate of inflation and the question of the 'neutrality' of money — whether changes in the quantity of money in an economy have an impact on the 'real' values of output and employment or influence only the general level of prices.

This has led to a great deal of theory but we should always recall that a major aim of monetary economics is to produce a better understanding of the operation and impact of monetary policy: what, if anything, governments and/or central banks can do to improve the way in which economies perform through the use of the instruments of monetary policy or, at least, to avoid damaging the performance of the real economy.

Monetary policy is now regarded as central to the welfare of households and the profitability of firms. The regular decisions of central banks on interest rates are major news items. Changes in exchange rates are part of every day journalism. The question of whether the UK should give up sterling to join a monetary union has been one of the principal political decisions of our day. Monetary policy has become so sensitive that over recent years many countries have made major constitutional decisions regarding its operation, notably in granting their central banks independence from the political process in interest rate decisions.

Despite this, the study of monetary economics is generally regarded as esoteric — a specialist area tackled by a relatively small proportion of undergraduate economics students. This occurs at least partly because of the controversial nature of the material. The subject is full of disagreements and conflict. The standard throw away line, that on any subject two economists will have three opinions, seems to apply to monetary economics par excellence. Even the reasons for the existence of money, the role it plays in economies and its definition have been controversial. It is clear that people talking and writing about 'money' are not always dealing with the same thing. The word 'money' is used in everyday speech in a number of ways, often in different senses from its meaning within monetary economics. *Oxford Reference Online* (Oxford University Press, http://www.oxfordreference.com/) lists over 100 quotations using the word 'money', ranging from the Bible to the Beatles — from 'the love of money is the root of all evil' (*Epistle of St Paul to the Ephesians*, vi. 10) to 'For I don't care too much for money, For money can't buy me love' (John Lennon). Many everyday usages do not correspond to definitions of money used by monetary economists. For example, in many of the quotations, 'money' means 'income' or 'wealth'. This is not new. Adam Smith noted in 1776 that 'wealth and money ... are, in common language, considered as in every respect synonymous' (Smith, 1776, IV, I). In economics, on the other hand, income and wealth can be expressed in money terms but are certainly not synonymous with 'money'.

A greater problem is that even within monetary economics 'money' can be viewed in a variety of ways and different definitions of money follow. Thus, we must begin by examining carefully what money is and why it exists.

Pause for thought 1.1

What does the word 'money' mean in the following quotation from Shakespeare's *The Merchant of Venice*, Act I Scene III?

'Hath a dog money? Is it possible a cur can lend three thousand ducats?'

1.2 The functions and forms of money

Money exists in all modern economies and it clearly plays a major role in the exchange of goods and services. One way, then, to explain why it exists is to analyse the process of exchange. The conventional approach to this is through an explanation of individual behaviour, asking why individual people ('economic agents') engage in exchange. The first problem we face is that we face a complex world with a past which has determined endowments and institutions and with interactions and reactions which are difficult to decipher and which may occur with very long time lags. People have unclear and conflicting motivations and many variables that influence decisions change at the same time. The degree of complexity is such that analysis of economic behaviour requires us to make many simplifying assumptions. Economists, typically, have approached this by excluding from consideration history, taking existing capital and labour endowments and wealth as given, and assuming that the distribution of these endowments does not change.

Since the utility-maximising individual is assumed to be central to economic analysis, the simplest beginning of all is with a single person (Robinson Crusoe) on a desert island.[1] He is self-sufficient and no exchange is possible. There is clearly no need for money. The Robinson Crusoe of economic models has no history. When he has any human characteristics at all, these are allocated to him on an ad hoc basis which suits the particular story being told. For example, one story begins with two Robinson Crusoes on the same island. Both are old and with poor memories. They meet occasionally but only to have dinner with each other.

However, their memories are so bad that they both forget who provided the most recent dinner. From here develops an account of money as a device for keeping records.

If we extend the model to many individuals, each agent remains, in effect, a Robinson Crusoe, acting as if no one else existed.[2] Even in such a world, however, agents soon realise that utility can be much increased through the division of labour, specialisation and participation in exchange. Within a family in a traditional society, a certain degree of specialisation is possible — one member of the family catches fish, a second tends the family's animals, a third weaves cloth and so on — but a more thorough exploitation of specialisation requires exchange and this implies the establishment of markets.

All exchange proceeds through markets, which are treated as a logical construct without institutional and social detail. The only available basis for judging welfare in this abstract world is through consumption and the dominant economic aim becomes the maximisation of individual utility through the most efficient use of scarce resources. The performance of the economic system is, then, judged in 'real terms'. This is still true in modern economic analysis. We know that, in practice, people often make judgements in money terms. For example, the rich occasionally gain utility by engaging in extravagant consumption with the purpose being to demonstrate to others how much they can afford to spend. Such ideas form a part of specific areas of economic analysis but do not influence the general presumption that the aim of all economic agents is to maximize utility with utility being judged in terms of real consumption. Indeed, in orthodox economics, any decision based on money rather than real values must be an example of money illusion — a confusion of money and real values and can occur only in the short-run when the system is in disequilibrium. Thus, it is inadvertent and temporary.

Pause for thought 1.2

To what extent do you make economic judgements in real terms? Can you think of occasions when you have been subject to 'money illusion'?

We can then attempt to explain such things as the determination of prices of different goods and services through the use of demand and supply analysis. To do this we need a starting point at which everyone is currently maximising his or her utility and the economy is, thus, in equilibrium. We can then assume an exogenous change that disturbs equilibrium positions and causes behaviour to change as agents seek to maximize utility under the changed circumstances. We do not know how long this will take but we can define the new equilibrium position (whenever it is reached) as the long-run and the period during which agents are changing their behaviour (when the system is in disequilibrium) as the short-run. Since, in our simplified model, a new equilibrium is always reached, the short-run is just an inconvenient period of adjustment. Equilibrium models may be either partial (with only one variable allowed to change at a time) or general, acknowledging the existence of a much more intricate set of interactions among variables. However, to make general equilibrium models amenable to analysis and mathematical logic, they too need to be hedged around with assumptions.

The best-known general equilibrium model is that developed by the Belgian mathematician/economist, Léon Walras.[3] This was a formidable intellectual exercise which described the world as if it consisted of a large number of markets in which agents acted to bring about the set of prices that caused demand to be equal to supply in all markets simultaneously. As a mathematical exercise this was unexceptionable but it was difficult to understand how anything like Walras' result could come about in practice. To help with this, Walras created a god/auctioneer who collected all information regarding demand and supply at existing prices from all agents, calculated excess demands and supplies and formulated a new set of prices. He (naturally) then repeated the exercise over and over again until the equilibrium set of prices was achieved. To make things work, however, two other assumptions had to be made. Firstly, no trading could take place until the final, market-clearing set of prices was arrived at. That is, trade only occurred when people had full knowledge of all prices, including future prices. Secondly, there were no costs involved in this vast information-collecting exercise.

When we talk of prices here, we are talking of relative prices and these can be expressed entirely in terms of goods. Exchange can take place through barter and there is no immediately apparent need for money. How then is the universal presence of money explained?

The standard approach concentrates on efficiency with the advantages of a monetary economy being considered in terms of the costs involved in the process of exchange and the extent to which a movement from barter to the use of money in exchange reduces those costs.

One clear assumption here is that exchange through markets preceded money and took place entirely through barter.

Barter is, however, inefficient because of the need for the *double coincidence of wants* for exchange to occur — that a person who catches fish and wishes to exchange them for pots needs to find a maker of pots who happens to want fish at precisely the same time. This implies very large search and information costs. In other words, people spend a lot of time in the process of exchange that could be used in a more efficient system for producing additional goods and services. The model suggests that the first development was for economies to pass through stages of increasingly efficient systems of barter, notably *fairground barter* and *trading post barter*. Fairground barter occurs when a fair is held for the sale of a particular good in the same place at regular intervals. A common example around Europe was the horse fair. Trading post barter occurs when someone sets up a trading post at which a specified set of goods are bought and sold and advertises the location and opening hours. People know that if they were to go to the trading post during its opening hours, they would have a good chance of meeting other people who wished to buy the good they wished to sell or *vice versa*. Thus, both fairs and trading posts considerably reduced search costs involved in the process of exchange.[4]

Nonetheless, a major problem remains because, however it is organised, a barter system requires knowledge of a large number of price ratios: how many fish exchange for one pot; how much maize or fish for one cow, and so on. If there are only two goods to be exchanged (fish and pots), there is only one price ratio. With three goods (fish, pots, and maize), however, there are three price ratios (fish/pots; fish/maize; pots/maize). As Visser (1974, pp. 2 and 3) shows, the number of price ratios can be calculated as the number of combinations of two elements from a set of n elements. The formula for this calculation is:

$$\frac{1}{2}n(n-1) \tag{1.1}$$

where n is the number of goods and services. Thus, in an economy with 4 goods, there will be 6 price ratios; with 100 goods there will be 4,950; and with 1,000 goods 499,500. Clearly, barter is a very inefficient system for this reason. It takes a good deal of time to collect information about such a large number of price ratios and so barter involves high transaction costs.

Money, then, enters the story as a way of dramatically reducing the number of price ratios with which people had to cope. This could be done by the adoption of one of the goods as a unit of account in which the price of all other goods could be expressed. The great reduction in information costs resulting from the use of a unit of account (money) allows people to spend a greater proportion of their time producing goods and services, thus improving their standard of living.[5] In analysing this role, Goodhart (1989a) describes money as one of the social artefacts (along with the distribution network and organised markets) that have evolved to economise on the use of time, which is seen as the ultimate scarce resource.

This idea can be extended in a number of ways. For instance, the high information costs in a barter economy would mean that many decisions would be made on the basis of incomplete information, creating uncertainty for market participants. The use of money, then, reduces uncertainty for market participants and allows a more efficient use of resources (see, for example, Brunner and Meltzer, 1989).

We may have an explanation of money as a unit of account but this is not sufficient to explain why money actually needs to change hands. That is, why did money develop as a means of payment? Goodhart (1989a) accounts for this by stressing another informational problem associated with market exchange - the lack of information about the trustworthiness and/or creditworthiness of the counter-party to the exchange. This, he says, truly makes money essential. If everyone in a market could be fully trusted, all exchange could be based on credit and with multilateral credit and a complete set of markets, money would not be needed. An unwillingness of traders to extend credit or to accept other goods as a means of payment means that money is required if some goods are to be purchased. This has become known as a liquidity or cash in advance constraint.

There are two major criticisms of this examination of a movement from a barter to a monetary economy. Firstly, the barter/money distinction proposes a static view of economies — all are classed as one of two simple possibilities even though exchange is a social process and money a social invention. The role of money in exchange differs from one economy to another and changes over time. In any modern economy, monetary exchange and barter both occur, sometimes in a single transaction. The tendency to think in terms of simplified models can lead to a failure to consider the way in which economic change and the nature of exchange interact. We are more likely to interpret the complex real world in terms of our model — as static societies confronted by occasional exogenous shocks. For example, problems with the testing of demand for money functions in the 1970s and 1980s led to the apparent discovery by monetary economists of financial innovation as if this had not always been a part of the development of the process of exchange.

Pause for thought 1.3

What forms of uncertainty can you identify in an act of exchange of goods and services involving delivery at a future date? How does the existence of money help to overcome these?

Secondly, the barter/monetary exchange distinction is ahistorical and implies that money came into existence solely to facilitate exchange. However, there is no evidence that barter preceded money anywhere other than in pre-economic societies in which exchange was only ceremonial. Indeed, Wray (1990) argues that money evolved before markets developed and that its use grew more quickly than the growth of markets. This is not a matter of pedantry since the ahistorical approach leads to the view that it is possible to analyse a barter economy in which money does not exist and then simply add money. This remains a powerful idea in modern economics and is at the heart of views that 'money is a veil' over the real economy (Pigou, 1949, p.24) and that money has no impact on the functioning of the real economy.

We can summarise the argument to this point by saying that money exists in modern economies because:

- exchange encourages the division of labour and specialisation and the more efficient use of time;

- money reduces the cost of exchange by acting as a unit of account;

- money is needed as a means of payment because of the existence of inadequate information and uncertainty in markets.[6]

This does not help us much, however, in any attempt to specify exactly what money is. We have a descriptive definition of money that fits the first part of definition 1 in the *Oxford English Dictionary's* latest definition of money (see box 1.1)

> Any generally accepted medium of exchange which enables a society to trade goods without the need for barter, any objects or tokens regarded as a store of value and used as a medium of exchange.

Indeed that definition takes us a little further than our explanation above by introducing the notion of money as a store of value. This can also be accounted for in terms of a lowering of transactions costs as well as helping us to understand what types of asset might serve as money. As long as money is a durable asset, its existence allows the separation of the decision to buy sell in the market from the decision to buy. In other words, it greatly reduces the problem associated with the double coincidence of wants and gives sellers of products time to collect the information needed to make wise purchases.

We can easily make other points about the nature of assets that might serve as money. For it to be easily used in exchange it would need to be easily transportable and easily divisible into small parts and be able to be used in units of a standard value. Finally, for it to be generally acceptable it would need to be an asset whose value was not subject to sharp changes. That implies that the conditions of supply of the asset would need to be relatively stable.

Although we now have an outline of the characteristics needed for an asset to act as money, we are still faced with the problem that money can take many forms and indeed has done so.[7] We can perhaps make a little more progress by looking in general terms at the forms money has taken. This begins with 'commodity moneys' — assets with an intrinsic value but with sufficient of the characteristics needed to make them generally acceptable in exchange — but it is easy to understand from our listing of these characteristics why commodity moneys were quickly replaced by coins of predetermined weight struck from precious metals. The problem with coinage was that people saw very quickly the possibility of reducing the amount of precious metal in coins, for example by shaving off a small amount of metal and keeping the shavings for their own use ('sweating the coinage'). This allowed the same amount of precious metal to exchange for more goods than previously. The value of the goods the coins exchanged for became greater than the value of the metal in the coins. This difference between the value of the coins in exchange and their production cost ('seigniorage')[8] was often put to use by princes and kings, to finance, among other things, the fighting of foreign wars.

Because of such practices as the sweating of the coinage, people saving (or 'hoarding') coins for their future use would hoard those coins containing the highest weight of metal and would seek to use in exchange the coins that had been interfered with. Thus, coins whose metal content was lower than the stated weight were the most likely to stay in circulation.[9] The possibility of making a profit from reducing the amount of metal in coins led to an important development in banking. As Galbraith (1975, pp. 25-6) explains, public banks were set up in the seventeenth century, initially in the Netherlands, to guarantee the value of coins by weighing them and assessing the true value of metal in the coins. At the same time, as nation states became more important, governments began to take over the responsibility for the minting of coins, reducing considerably the variety of coins in circulation.

Financial intermediaries initially issued notes as receipts for coin and gold deposited with them. Thus, initially, issued notes were backed by an equivalent amount of gold in reserves. However, as banks realised that their notes were willingly held and accepted in exchange for goods and services, they were able safely to lend on the gold they held on deposit and the modern fractional reserve banking system developed. The issue of notes, too, ultimately became the preserve of the central bank, which held the official reserves of gold. Later, the precious metal content disappeared entirely from coins and the gold backing of the central bank note issue was removed. The currency became *fiat* money with its acceptability in exchange supported by legislation through the specification of legal tender.

Fiat money is also known as outside money because it is issued outside the private sector by the monetary authorities, or as 'high-powered' money because it is seen as the monetary base from which the rest of the money supply derives. Definition 1a. in box 1.1 includes coins and banknotes but adds:

> ...any written, printed, or electronic record of ownership of the values represented by coins and notes which is generally accepted as equivalent to or exchangeable for these.

This introduces the familiar idea that exchange can occur on the basis of a transfer of entitlements to notes and coin, notably the transfer of bank deposits. Cheques drawn on bank deposits became a means of effecting such transfers to the extent that they were accepted as a correct record of ownership of a bank deposit of the required amount. Goodhart's problem of lack of information about the trustworthiness and/or creditworthiness of the counter-party was partially overcome by the issue of cheque cards. Debit cards, telephone and internet banking allow bank deposits to be transferred without the exchange of a paper instrument. Thus, definition 1 and 1a. admits all the elements of modern 'narrow' definitions of money in economics — notes and coin plus sight or chequable deposits held with banks.

However, the phrase 'any generally accepted medium of exchange' allows other possibilities and leaves us with the problem that to decide which assets are 'money' and which are not, we need to say what precisely we mean by 'generally accepted' and this can vary from place to place and over time. As Goodhart (1989a) notes, money is a social phenomenon that exists in all societies but that is everywhere different.

Box 1.1: Dictionary definitions of money

The *Oxford English Dictionary* (draft revision, Dec. 2007) provides the following in its definition of 'money':

1. Any generally accepted medium of exchange which enables a society to trade goods without the need for barter; any objects or tokens regarded as a store of value and used as a medium of exchange.

   a. Coins and banknotes collectively as a medium of exchange. Later also more widely: any written, printed, or electronic record of ownership of the values represented by coins and notes which is generally accepted as equivalent to or exchangeable for these.

   b. Any other objects or materials which serve the same purpose as coins or banknotes....

2. a. Means of payment considered as representing value or purchasing power; the power of purchase or means of exchange represented by coins, banknotes, cheques, etc. Hence: property, possessions, resources, etc., viewed as having exchangeable value or a value expressible in terms of monetary units; liquid assets, funds.

   b. With demonstrative or possessive adjective, or the. A monetary amount or sum applied to a particular purpose or in the possession of a particular person.

   c. spec. Money treated as a marketable commodity that can be bought, borrowed, etc.

   d. Wealth, esp. inherited wealth; a person or class possessing wealth.....

   f. Wages, salary; a person's pay or remuneration; profit....

4. A particular coin; a coinage (now rare). Also (more fully money of account): a denomination or unit of value used in records and for accounting purposes, sometimes representing a particular (current or obsolete) coin or other means of payment.

(extracted from *The Oxford English Dictionary* (draft revision, Dec. 2007),
Oxford English Dictionary Online (2008). http://dictionary.oed.com/

More importantly, we need to say something about the meaning of 'exchange' in the phrase 'medium of exchange'. This is particularly because the exchange of products in a modern economy is frequently based not on the transfer of notes and coin or bank deposits but on the promise to pay later. That is, the purchaser goes into debt, usually being granted credit by the seller or a financial intermediary. Why, then, is not credit a 'generally accepted medium of exchange'? Monetary economics accepts the importance of credit but has always sought to distinguish between 'money' and 'credit'. The standard way of doing so has been to define the act of exchange such that it is only completed when the debt incurred by the purchase is settled and for this to happen there has to be a transfer of 'money'.

The consequent definition of 'money' as any asset that is generally acceptable as a medium of exchange and is acceptable in final settlement of debt is a common one but this is radically different from the idea that only money allows exchange to occur. The debt incurred, for example, in the purchase of a motor car may not be settled for some years but the act of exchange occurs when the purchaser acquires the legal right to make use of the car. The later settlement of the debt is a consequence of the exchange but is not needed to allow it to happen. Further, many of the broader economic consequences of the exchange follow from the exchange of contracts rather than from any subsequent settlement of the debt — cars purchased with debt enter into sales figures and these influence production and hence employment decisions in following periods. Some purchasers fail to pay the debt but companies allow in their calculations for a certain level of bad debts. Naturally, there will be a later economic impact if more people than expected do not repay the debt they have taken on, but it remains that the ability to obtain credit permits a high proportion of the exchange in a modern economy. Things become more complex when we consider the use of credit cards to buy a number of different products. The seller of each product is paid by the transfer of a deposit from the bank issuing the credit card. Exchange occurs when the credit card is accepted. In this case, the bank determines the ability to enter into exchange by the limit that it allows on each credit card. A purchaser's debt no longer corresponds directly to any particular good he has bought. Indeed, the bank to which he is in debt might sell that debt on to another firm or the purchaser might repay the debt by borrowing from another bank or finance company or by re-mortgaging his house. Yet again, the debt might be passed on to subsequent generations or be extinguished by bankruptcy or death. In such ways, the final settlement of the debt becomes almost totally detached from any particular act of exchange.

We can still accept a logical distinction between money and credit based on the notion that an exchange remains 'incomplete' until the debt has been settled and that this, by definition, requires 'money' — assets that are legally and/or customarily accepted in settlement of debt. However, this is to look at matters entirely from the point of view of the creditor. From the point of view of the purchaser, we can think of 'money' as 'spending resources' — anything that allows him to enter immediately into exchange. This, in turn, is dependent on two things:

(a) currently-held real and financial assets plus the amount that can be borrowed;

and

(b) the ease and speed with which currently-held assets can be converted into forms accepted by sellers (the degree of liquidity of assets).

(a) gives us a broad definition of wealth, including Milton Friedman's (1957) idea of 'human wealth' — abilities and skills that enable people to borrow against expected future income. The importance of 'liquidity' means, of course, that, even from the point of view of the purchaser, not all wealth can be used to make immediate purchases — not, at least, without considerable risk of associated loss. Consequently, even from the purchaser's point of view, 'money' is only one part of total wealth. However, it is clear that any definition of money from the point of view of the purchaser will be much broader than a definition from the point of view of the seller. It is also clear that neither approach leads to a precise definition that tells one exactly which assets must be included and which excluded. This is more so in the case of broader definitions of money (taken from the purchaser's point of view) since purchasers may be more or less willing to suffer some loss in converting assets into a form allowing them finally to settle debt. That is, there is no precise notion of how liquid assets must be before we include them in a broad definition of money.

Pause for thought 1.4

We have suggested that:

(a) sight deposits are 'money' because they can be used to settle debt through the writing of cheques, the use of debit cards or electronic transfer; but

(b) credit is not 'money' because its use creates a debt.

What, then, should one make of agreed overdraft limits on current accounts? They can be used to settle other debts but their use creates a debt to the bank. Are they 'money'?

This uncertainty as to precisely which assets we should include in a definition of money gives us a particular problem concerning the notion of a demand for money. We can say that people have a demand for money because they need it to allow them to purchase goods and services and we can see that the lack of money in this sense acts as a constraint on expenditure and to the extent that it does this it is important in analysing expenditure in the economy.

However, we have seen that goods and services can be acquired through going into debt or by liquidating other assets. Thus, at the level of the individual economic agent, holdings of 'narrow money' do not act as a constraint on expenditure. People who have assets and/or are able to borrow will almost always be able to obtain funds in the form necessary to undertake expenditure. From the point of view of exchange, it is difficult to see why they should be particularly concerned with the proportion of their assets that they hold in the form of narrow money. Yet, even if we exclude credit but widen our definition of money to include relatively liquid assets, we muddy the waters by including assets that people might choose to hold for reasons that have nothing to do with the desire to enter into exchange.

1.3   Money in the aggregate

We saw at the beginning of the chapter that we are particularly interested in the relationship between money and expenditure in an economy. However, we have seen that at the level of the individual agent, there is no reason to believe in a close relationship between money, *narrowly defined*, and expenditure since transactions can be undertaken through borrowing or by converting other assets into a form that allows expenditure to take place. That is, at a microeconomic level, there is little significance to be attached to an excess demand for or supply of narrow money.

We can only hope, therefore, to defend an interest in narrow money at the aggregate level.

This requires us to say something about the supply of narrow money at an aggregate level. If we were to assume that the monetary authorities had direct control over the supply of money (if the money supply were exogenous), we could imagine the aggregate supply of narrow money in an economy being held temporarily fixed or, at least, being allowed to grow only at a pre-determined rate. Then, an unanticipated increase in the demand for goods and services, and the consequent increase in the demand for money to allow the additional exchanges to take place, might produce a shortage of narrow money in the aggregate. Such a shortage would not occur through a shortage of notes and coin since these are supplied by the central bank and the mint on demand in exchange for deposits, but would result from bank deposits growing insufficiently rapidly. Since bank deposits are created when banks make loans, we need to ask why banks might be unable or unwilling to meet fully the increased borrowing requirements of customers.

The view that the authorities have direct control over the supply of narrow money sees this as occurring through control over the size of the monetary base (high-powered money).[10] As banks tried to increase their lending to meet the increased demand for loans, they would become short of monetary base. The price of borrowing (the interest rate) would very likely rise and the excess demand for money would be eliminated as the increase in interest rate persuaded people to borrow and hence spend less. That is, we are adding 'willingness to borrow' as a constraint on expenditure not just the 'ability to borrow' we included in the notion of 'spending power'. Under certain circumstances, banks might respond by tightening the conditions on which they are willing to lend. People's ability to borrow and hence their spending resources would be restricted — they would be credit-constrained. This would change our view regarding the likely effects of the unanticipated increase in the demand for goods and services but we would still be interested in the demand for narrow money and would wish to be able to predict how the demand for money would change. This would apply too if we told the story beginning with a decision of the central bank to reduce the size of the monetary base (or the rate at which it was growing). Note that this involves the type of partial equilibrium model we discussed earlier — begin by assuming an equilibrium and then compare it with the new equilibrium following an exogenous change.

If, however, the authorities could not control the monetary base or changes in the monetary base did not have a predictable impact on the money supply, banks might go on meeting the increased demand for credit as people sought to borrow more in order to increase their spending. The stock of bank deposits, and hence of money, would increase (the money supply would be endogenous). In other words, the supply of money might simply increase to meet the increased demand for it and an excess demand for narrow money might never arise. Thus, whether an increase in the demand for narrow money, even at an aggregate level, is of much significance depends on the nature of the money supply process in the economy.

Let us for the moment accept the exogenous money version and assume that the monetary authorities seek to reduce inflationary pressure by restricting the rate of growth of the monetary base in the expectation that this will restrict the ability of banks to lend, force up the rate of interest and deter people from borrowing. For the monetary authorities to follow such a policy, they would need to believe that the relationship between the supply of money and the level of spending in the economy was close and stable. To put it another way, they would need to believe that the demand for money was stable. This, in turn, would imply a stable technical relationship between the amount of money in the economy at any particular time and the total amount of spending able to be undertaken: the velocity of money would need to be stable. To test for this, we need a clear definition of money and the argument above suggests that this should be a narrow definition. However, if the supply of money is endogenous, the demand for money loses much of its importance and our need for a precise definition of money is also much diminished.

Pause for thought 1.5

Can you explain why a stable demand for money implies a stable velocity of money?

In fact, for much of its history, monetary economics has been dominated by the combined assumptions of an exogenous money supply and a stable demand for money. This was not because very many economists thought that it provided an accurate description of economies in practice. Rather it derived from the view that the economic system could best be analysed by assuming well-informed economic agents and markets that tend towards equilibrium. In such a world, current real income is always at its equilibrium level and this level is known. Savings decisions reflect the long-term choice between the present and future consumption (of goods and services), a real not a monetary decision. All savings are invested and the level of investment determines the rate of growth of capital stock, which in turn ensures the desired future level of output. The real rate of interest is determined by the actions of savers and investors. The plans of economic agents are always fulfilled. There is no uncertainty and no scope for purely financial transactions. The monetary authorities determine the rate of growth of the money supply. Given the stable demand for money, the control of the money supply provides control over the rate of growth of aggregate demand and, with the rate of growth of output determined by real factors, the price level and the rate of inflation. In such a model, money is neutral. We can see this as another form of the notion that money acts as a veil over the real economy.

How can this be defended when the world we see is not at all like this? There are two types of answer. The first plays down the role of theory and suggests that if tests of empirical relationships developed from such a model hold, the economy can be assumed to act as if it were always in equilibrium. The second uses the distinction between the short run and the long run that we made in section 1.2. The 'short run', remember, is equivalent to 'disequilibrium' and implies that economic agents make mistakes and confuse real and monetary values.

One problem with this, is that there can be no calendar-time equivalent to these definitions of the short run and long run. The length of time a complex economic system might take to a single change in an important variable might be very long. Add to this the following features of real world economies:

- economies are subject to frequent shocks and are never in equilibrium positions;

- shocks are likely to cause other elements within the system to change;

- these changes may well interact with the initial shock to produce further changes;

- shocks and the subsequent changes generate expectations about future changes.

We can then easily to see that no actual economy will ever reach a position of long-run equilibrium. We might then choose to think of monetary policy as always taking place within the short run and seek to look at monetary relationships in a world characterised by uncertainty and disequilibrium. In such a world, money has value in itself since (in periods without inflation) there is no risk of loss from holding it. Consequently, savers may choose to hold part of their savings in the form of money and increases in the quantity of money may be held idle as an asset rather than used in the purchase of goods and services. Market agents often make mistakes. Indeed, in the absence of clear and reliable information about the future values of real variables, it may be wisest for people to base decisions on current nominal values. Money illusion may be a reflection of rational behaviour in an uncertain world. It would seem highly unlikely that we could find a definition of money that would reliably and consistently be associated with a stable income velocity of money. We might conclude that we do not need a definition of money at all. If we did, out of a general interest, seek to measure the supply of money as distinct from credit, we would opt for a broad definition that included a range of highly liquid financial assets.

1.4   Formal definitions of money

So far, we have said that money takes a variety of forms — it is anything that circulates among economic agents in the process of exchange and which provides a common unit for expressing the price of goods and services exchanged. This stresses the narrow approach to defining money based on the point of view of the creditor and the idea of final settlement of debt. It is obviously important for individuals to know what is acceptable in exchange but this is a matter of national, and sometimes local, practice and might change over time. People also need to know how easily and speedily, and at what cost, they can convert illiquid assets into money and how likely they are to be able to obtain liquid resources through borrowing. For none of this do people need either a formal definition of 'money' or an appreciation of how much 'money' exists in the economy. At an individual level, people are seldom prevented from engaging in the exchange of goods because of a lack of money in the sense that we are using it here, although they may be so prevented because of a lack of spending power or by the cost of borrowing against their assets or their expected future income.

Pause for thought 1.6

Keynes is widely quoted as having said: 'In the long run we are all dead'. Is this an accurate quotation? (Hint: check *The Tract on Monetary Reform*, 1923). In the light of the discussion in this chapter and the context of the original statement, what do you think he meant?

We have seen, however, that things may be different at an aggregate level. Much depends on whether we accept the notion that the authorities could and should operate on the interest rate by attempting to control the stock of money. In this case, we would need a clear idea of what constitutes the money supply and some ability to measure it. If, however, the authorities attempt to control spending directly by adjusting the interest rate, we do not need to define or to measure 'money' even at an aggregate level. We might still choose to attempt to do so but only perhaps as one of a number of indicators of the desirability of adjusting the interest rate. The fact that we might only have a very limited and specific need for a definition of 'money' in economics may well influence the definition we use, although we should bear in mind that the interest of economists in money is not limited to the macroeconomic relationship between the aggregate money supply and aggregate demand. Let us look, next, at various ways in which economists have responded to the various problems associated with the definition of money.

Descriptive definitions of money

Most definitions of money in the economics literature follow the path we have followed above, stressing money's role as a medium of exchange, unit of account and store of value with the principal emphasis being on its function as a medium of exchange. Any asset that performs the role of a medium of exchange is generally held to be able also to act as a store of value and a unit of account. Hicks (1967) denied this, arguing that money could be a medium of exchange without being a store of value as long as, over the course of a day's trading, no individuals have sold more than they have bought and vice versa. However, this would be a very special case and the usual view is that all forms of money are stores of value, whereas the reverse is not true (see Harris, 1985). Thus, acting as a medium of exchange is taken as the only role that clearly sets money apart from other assets.

Our discussion above, however, alerted us to a problem with the notion of 'money' as a medium of exchange since credit acts as a medium of exchange but is almost always excluded from definitions of 'money'. One way out is to follow Shackle (1971) and distinguish between the medium of exchange (which includes credit) and a means of payment, in the sense of a means of final settlement of debt. It is this latter idea that most writers have in mind. Expressions along these lines commonly used in textbooks include:

- a temporary store of purchasing power;

- an asset that gives immediate command over goods and services;

- a property right generally acceptable in exchange..

These are descriptive or *a priori* definitions of money which do not give a precise idea of which assets should be included in a measure of the economy's money stock. Everything depends on what is 'generally acceptable'. Nonetheless, the concentration on the role of money as a means of payment led to the common acceptance of the 'narrow' view of money as an asset that would be held only temporarily and not as a form of savings. That is, economic agents will not choose to hold money for any reason other than to participate in exchange.

This, in turn, led to the distinction between narrow money and other financial assets based on whether or not interest was paid on them. Banks were assumed not to need to pay interest on deposits that were only being held to allow people to purchase goods and services in the immediate future. Interest-bearing assets might relatively easily be converted into money but might also be held as part of savings. Until the middle 1980s, this gave a neat set of assets consisting of notes and coin (outside money or the monetary base) plus non-interest bearing deposits with banks ('sight' or chequable deposits). Sight deposits with banks are part of 'inside money' because they are both created by and held within the private sector.

We have seen two obvious problems with the narrow definition of money. Firstly, its justification is that all other assets must be converted into notes and coin or sight deposits in order to carry out exchange. However, other types of bank deposits and deposits with non-bank financial institutions can be converted so quickly (and at virtually no cost) into narrow money that the distinction is hardly worth maintaining. This has been true for many years but is all the more true when funds can be moved from one account to another through the internet or by telephone at any time of the day or night. Indeed, some banks now offer 'sweep' facilities that transfer funds automatically between low interest current accounts and other higher-interest accounts. Equally, other assets do not need to be sold to obtain narrow money but can be used as collateral for a loan that takes the form of narrow money. Under these circumstances, many types of asset are as good as narrow money for the purpose of exchange. Certainly, if our interest lies in the notion of a lack of money acting as a constraint on expenditure or as influencing expenditure plans, the distinction between narrow money and other highly liquid assets is not worth maintaining.

This justifies the widening of the standard definition to include bank deposits other than sight deposits. However, once one moves away from the strict interpretation of means of final settlement of debt and includes liquidity as a criterion it becomes impossible to draw a line between assets that are money and those that are nearly money but not quite.

The issue was slightly complicated by the move to the payment of interest on sight deposits in the 1980s since that raised the question of whether some sight deposits might be savings rather than being held because of the function of sight deposits as means of payment. In fact, this merely emphasised a problem that had always existed in the distinction between deposits held for transactions purposes (money) and those held as savings. One only has to acknowledge that people do not know with certainty either the total future value of their wealth or the precise value of the transactions they will be undertaking to realise that the distinction is dubious. Some assets provide convenience because they are acceptable as means of payment or can be easily converted into means of payment. Banks offer a lower rate of interest on these assets because they are more likely than other types of deposit to be withdrawn at no notice and so banks are less able to make profits from funds deposited with them in this form. Depositors are prepared to accept a lower rate of interest on these assets because of their convenience. What is important is the interest rate differential between assets of differing degrees of liquidity. The attribution in the past of some special significance to the fact that sight deposits paid no interest simply gave a false security to the distinction between them and other kinds of bank deposits.

The second obvious problem with the narrow definition of money is that it ignores the significance of the idea that to be a means of payment, an asset must be generally acceptable. Since acceptability depends on custom and the nature of financial institutions, what is and is not 'money' differs from economy to economy and changes over time.

This leaves us in the position that the narrow definition of money is too limited and does not reflect the complexity of influences on decisions regarding the form in which to hold wealth. However, broader definitions of money are insufficiently precise because there are no clear criteria for deciding what should be included and what left out. Milton Friedman is widely quoted as saying 'money is what money does', implying that anything can be counted as 'money' that performs the role of money. This does not take us very far as a descriptive definition of money.

There have been attempts to resolve this issue by making use of the 'revealed preferences' of money-holders. This is a microeconomic approach that works on the principle that the best way to find out which assets are 'money' is to discover which assets people treat as money. We start with a narrow definition including only assets that everyone would agree form part of the money stock (notes and coins) and then seek to discover by studying household economic behaviour which other assets are treated as sufficiently close substitutes for the original set that they are, to all intents and purposes, equivalent to money. This leaves open what is meant by a 'sufficiently close substitute' and so remains subjective.

Prescriptive definitions of money

An entirely different approach is to decide on the theoretical nature of the relationship of money with other important variables in the economy and then to define money so as to show that this relationship exists in practice. In other words, one starts with a model of the economy in which 'money' plays a clear role, with the nature of that role depending on the assumptions underlying the model. Once we have the model, we seek a definition of money that validates it. Let us assume that we believe money to be neutral. That is, 'money' is a set of assets changes in the value of which have no impact on real variables such as output and employment. We then hope to define money in such a way that empirical tests show this neutrality. Alternatively, we might begin with the view that inflation is caused by a too rapid growth of the money supply. A corollary of this is that the demand for money is stably related to real income. Thus, a demand for money function is constructed, using what seems to be the most likely definition of money for the purpose. However, if the function turns out not to be stable, the definition of money may be changed until a definition of money is found for which demand does appear to be stable. This extremely pragmatic approach is strongly supported by Milton Friedman and reflects the statement quoted above that 'money is what money does'. The underlying belief is that there must be something, the rate of growth of which is closely linked to the rate of inflation, and we may call this something 'money'. The only problem is the practical one of finding an empirical counterpart to the theoretical idea. Money is thus defined in the way that yields the most accurate predictions. This is an example of a general approach to economics that sees the predictive power of models as all-important. We are told not to worry unduly if the assumptions made in the construction of models that predict accurately appear to be unrealistic.

It remains that this approach to defining money can lead to frequent ad hoc adjustments to the definition in an attempt to produce the correct answer. Given the problems associated with definitions of other variables in the functions, the dubious quality of many of the statistics being employed and the complexity of the time lags involved, there is a danger of exercises of this kind becoming more interesting for the range of econometric techniques used than for any light shed on important economic relationships. It follows naturally that economists who do not start by believing in the theory that inflation is caused by excess growth of an exogenous money supply regard all such empirical exercises with scepticism. In any case, there is a potential practical difficulty. No simple combination of assets might produce the desired results. Alternatively, a particular definition may seem to give favourable results when applied to the data for one period but the apparent relationships may break down in later periods. One reason for difficulties of this kind might be that the different assets included in a definition of money may have different relationships with income. For example, notes and coins, sight bank deposits and other bank deposits may each have a stable relationship with nominal income but the relationship may be different in each case. Then, if our definition of money includes all three of these assets and the proportion each forms of the money supply changes over time, the relationship between money as a whole and nominal income will change. Thus, a development of the empirical approach has been to weight the various types of deposit to try to take account of different velocities of circulation. Alternatively, as in the case of Divisia indexes, different degrees of liquidity are measured by rates of interest (the lower the interest rate payable on an asset, the more liquid it is assumed to be). These are discussed in section 1.5 below.

1.5   Official measures of money

In the last section we have suggested that the way in which one chooses, or would like, to define money is influenced by the way in which one thinks that money works: theoretical perceptions predispose us towards particular definitions. In practice, when it comes to defining monetary aggregates for policy purposes, the authorities have no such luxury. Debates surrounding inside and outside money may require, for example, a measure of non-interest bearing money, but if banks make no distinction between interest bearing and non-interest bearing sight deposits, there will be no such data. Official measures of money have to reflect the behaviour and practices of deposit-taking institutions. This leads us to two rather obvious consequences and an important conclusion. Firstly, pragmatism plays a significant role in the compilation of official monetary aggregates with the authorities having to accept what they can get from the banking system, albeit sometimes with pressure applied. Secondly, the aggregates will change because of changes in banking practice and banking products, as a result, in other words, of innovation. Both of these characteristics are strongly present in the history of UK aggregates, as we shall see in a moment. Before that though we might just pause to note that this is our first encounter in this book with a fundamentally important principle for monetary policy (as opposed to theory), namely that the creators of money are private sector institutions whose responsibilities to their shareholders, and even to their clients, come before their responsibilities as agents of monetary policy. In most economies, the official definitions of money as well as the development of appropriate instruments of monetary control are the out-come of a continuous dialectic between the monetary authorities and the banking system.

Table 1.1 gives a complete listing of all the official monetary aggregates for which data have been recorded in the UK in recent years. It also gives their com-position and their status at various times. The latter point needs careful interpre-tation. The Bank of England has published data for each series at some time. The column headed 'first published' gives the date of first appearance in the *Bank of England Quarterly Bulletin*. Quite often, however, a short back-run of data was also compiled, so date of first publication may not coincide with the beginning of the data series. 'Discontinued' means publication ceased at that date. 'Targeted' is a rather elastic term. It may mean targeted explicitly or implicitly and it may also mean targeted by the authorities even though no series was published, as in the early days with DCE, or targeted according to published ranges — in the hey-day of monetary targeting. We have also indicated in the final column those series that have been subject to 'monitoring' rather than 'targeting'. 'Monitoring' means that they were closely observed for the information they might contain about future developments in the economy and thus as an aid to setting the level of interest rates.

The table is laid out so that aggregates are listed in increasingly 'broad' order, although M4 and M5 are replacements for PSL1 and PSL2 rather than further extensions of them. DCE, 'domestic credit expansion', and the Divisia indexes are rather different categories and we discuss them separately below.

Leaving aside the changes in definitions for a moment, what the table shows for the UK is similar to what we would find in any other system, namely that the authorities record data (published or not) for several series. At the narrowest end, all central banks are interested in the magnitude of the monetary base or 'high-powered money'. The reason that is usually given is that base is an essen-tial input into the money-creation process since banks must hold a minimum quantity of base in relation to deposits in order to ensure convertibility of their deposits into cash. This ratio lies at the centre of the deposit-multiplier models of money supply determination (see section 2.3). The components of the base are all liabilities of the central bank and it is therefore suggested that officially determined changes in the quantity of the base could create multiple expansions/contractions of the money supply, a technique known as 'monetary base control'. For many years, this series was known in the UK as the wide monetary base and was given an identity M0, which indicated its very narrow nature, in relation to other aggregates. However, in 2006, the Bank of England changed the way in which it dealt with the money markets. The essential change here is that the Bank of England decided to pay interest on deposits held at the Bank by banks and building societies. These balances were, at the same time, re-christened 'reserves'. Previously, they were known as 'operational balances' and were not remunerated. Inevitably, the payment of interest led to a large jump in the balances held at the Bank of England and when added to the notes and coin series this would have caused a large jump in M0 in turn. Rather than leave the M0 series with a large break a new series was created called 'notes and coin and reserves', although it contains the same components as M0.

NIBM1, M1, and M2 are progressively wider definitions of what is generally termed 'narrow money'. The first two are narrow in the sense that they focus upon notes and coin plus 'sight' or 'demand' or 'chequable' deposits — the media that one would expect to be used primarily for transactions purposes. The appearance of M2 in 1982 illustrates the point we made earlier about institutional changes. If one were interested in money for transactions purposes, it seemed illogical to leave out many building society deposits since, although they were not at that time generally chequable, cash for transactions could be drawn on demand and there was evidence that many such deposits were used by the less wealthy who did not have bank accounts. The same argument applied to National Savings (a government department) accounts. On the other hand, some large building society deposits were clearly savings (as indeed might have been some bank interest-bearing sight deposits) and so M2 was an attempt to cut across both bank and building society deposits to provide another measure of transactions money.

M3 is a measure of 'broad' money in the sense that it includes sight and time deposits, including certificates of deposit (CDs). The components of M3 come closest to providing a universal definition of money — important if one wishes to do comparative empirical work — as the authorities in most countries publish a series very similar to this (in Germany and the USA the series are actually denoted M3 as well).

PSL1 and PSL2 are even broader definitions. The terms stand for 'private sector liquidity — definitions 1 and 2' and indicate a tendency at the time to think of some components as reaching beyond the limits of 'money'. Bank time deposits with long maturities, treasury bills, and certificates of tax deposit could none of them be used for transactions. On the other hand they could be turned, quickly, into sight deposits. It is worth noting that as late as 1979, building society deposits were not only thought of as non-money assets; they were included only in PSL2. This explains why when, in the heyday of monetary targeting, only three years later, it was PSL2 that was chosen rather than PSL1.

The 1986 Building Society Act permitted societies for the first time to make unsecured loans up to a small maximum proportion of their total assets. This was enough, however, to allow them to issue their own cheque books and guarantee cards. This made their deposits virtually indistinguishable from bank deposits as a means of payment. The exclusion of building society deposits from mainstream monetary aggregates (symbolised by the M3/PSL2 distinction) became unsustainable and so M4 developed alongside M3 as a rival broad money aggregate. The same Act enabled building societies to convert to plc status, in other words to become banks. When the Abbey National Building Society did so in June 1989, this produced a sharp upward break in all those series (excluding NIBM1), which contained only bank deposits. From July 1989, therefore, M3 was discontinued and building society deposits became officially, as many holders had regarded them for years unofficially, 'money'. NIBM1 survived until 1991 because it was unaffected, the Abbey National Building Society having virtually no non-interest-bearing deposits.

1991 also saw major changes in the recording and classification of liquid (non-money) assets. Part of the revision involved discontinuing the publication of M4c and transferring the foreign currency component to M5. But the assets in M5 itself were dramatically supplemented to include, amongst other items, UK-owned off-shore sterling deposits; the overseas sector's holdings of sterling deposits (in the UK and offshore); UK-owned commercial paper, short-dated gilts and, reminiscent of a suggestion first made over seventy years ago by J M Keynes, unused sterling credit facilities such as agreed (but unused) overdraft agreements.

The traditional approach to defining money, as table 1.1 shows, involves identifying an appropriate subset of financial assets. Measuring the quantity of money then involves the simple aggregation of all those assets in the subset at their nominal value. While this may be an obvious (and straightforward) approach it suffers from both a theoretical and an empirical weakness. At the theoretical level, simple aggregation implies that we are dealing with homogeneous assets. We seem to be saying, for example, that from a monetary point of view, £1bn of CDs is the same as £1bn of notes and coin. The mere fact that CDs pay interest while notes and coin do not, however, indicates some degree of differentiation since otherwise no one would hold notes and coin. At the empirical level, as we saw in section 1.3, economists are usually interested in the closeness of the relationship between a monetary aggregate and income. This is likely to increase with the extent to which the aggregate is dominated by assets used for transactions. As we also saw in 1.3, however, it is difficult to know exactly where to draw the line between whole classes of assets for this purpose. Notes and coin and sight deposits are all perfectly liquid and are obvious transactions media but we know that time deposits can be switched to sight deposits quickly and cheaply and that other, apparently less liquid, assets have sufficient liquidity that they could still be relevant to transactions, albeit to a lesser degree.

Table 1.1: UK official definitions of money

Name	Components	First published	Discontinued	Targeted
DCE (Domestic credit expansion)	Change in £ bank lending to the non-bank public and private sectors	Dec. 1972	March 1986	1967-9 1976-9
Notes and coin and reserves	Notes and coin outside the Bank of England + banks' reserve balances at the Bank of England.	May 2006		
M0 (Wide monetary base)	Notes and coin outside the Bank of England + banks' operational deposits at the Bank of England	June 1981	May 2006	1984-2006[1]
NIBM1 (Non-interest bearing M1)	Notes and coin in circulation + NBPS[2] holdings of non-interest bearing £ sight deposits	June 1975	Feb. 1991	
M1	NIBM1 + NBPS holdings of interest-bearing £ sight deposits	Dec. 1970	July 1989	1982-4
M2	NIBM1 + NBPS holdings of interest bearing retail £ deposits with banks and building societies + National Savings ordinary accounts	Sept. 1982[3]		
M3 (£M3 until May 1987)	M1 + NBPS holdings of £ bank time deposits and certificates of deposits (CDs)	March 1977[4]	July 1989	1976-86
M3c (M3 until May 1987)	M3 + NBPS holdings of foreign currency bank deposits	Dec. 1970[4]	July 1989	

	Definition			
PSL1	M3 - NBPS £ bank time deposits with original maturity >2 years + NBPS holdings of bank bills, treasury bills, local authority deposits and certificates of tax deposit	Sept. 1979	May 1987	1982-4
PSL2	PSL1 + NBPS building society £ deposits (excl. term shares) + short-term National Savings instruments	Sept. 1979	May 1987	
M4	M3 + M4PS holdings of building society £ shares, deposits and CDs	May 1987		
M4c	M4 + M4PS holdings of bank and building society foreign currency deposits	May 1987	May 1991	
M3H[6]	M4c + public corporations' holdings of £ and foreign currency bank and building society deposits	August 1992		
M5	M4 + M4PS holdings of bank bills, treasury bills, local authority deposits and certificates of tax deposit + short term National Savings instruments	May 1987	May 1991	
'Liquid assets outside M4'	M5 + M4PS holdings of bank and building society foreign currency deposits + further £ liquid assets of M4PS and £ assets of the overseas sector	May 1991		
Divisia	Liquidity-weighted components of M4 (see text)			

Notes: 1 'monitored'; 2 'non-bank private sector'; 3 not to be confused with an earlier version of M2 (Dec. 1970 - Dec. 1971) which was roughly midway between M1 and M3; 4 £M3 and M3 included public sector; 5 'M4 private sector' or non-bank, non-building society private sector; 6 a harmonised measure of broad money, consistent across the EU.

The Divisia approach involves weighting each of the component assets according to the extent to which they provide transactions services. If this could be done accurately, then the resulting index should measure the quantity of money available in the economy for transactions purposes and should be more closely linked to expenditure and income.

The weights given to each asset are often said to represent the 'user cost' of the asset. To measure the user cost, we must first choose a benchmark asset which provides no transactions services. For example, the Bank of England has published a Divisia index going back to 1977 based upon the components of M4 and using the rate on three-month local authority deposits (the 3mLA rate) as the benchmark. In order to construct the index, we subtract the rate of interest on the component asset from the rate on the benchmark asset. Notes and coin are given a weight of one representing the difference between the 3mLA rate and zero. Each other asset, a_i, is then given a lesser weight, w_i, equal to the difference between the benchmark rate and its own rate, i_i, as a fraction of the benchmark-notes and coin differential. In symbols:

$$w_i = (3\text{mLA rate} - i_i)/(3\text{mLA rate} - 0)$$

The index, D, is then the sum of the nominal value of each asset adjusted for its appropriate weight:

$$D = \sum a_i w_i \qquad (1.2)$$

If it is the transactions services of money in which we are primarily interested, then Divisia clearly possesses numerous attractions. There are some problems though. Firstly, it is still not clear that such an index is measuring transactions services alone since bank accounts give access to other banking services for their holders. Secondly, in using interest rate differentials to measure user cost we are assuming that interest rates are equilibrium rates in a perfectly competitive system. A characteristic of the UK monetary sector in the 1980s, however, was a marked increase in competition especially between banks and building societies. For earlier periods, therefore, it seems unlikely that this condition holds. Thirdly, unless we assume that portfolio adjustments are instantaneous, and this is not suggested by evidence, then the weighted components are unlikely to have equilibrium values. For example, if the rate on an asset increases, the differential with the benchmark asset (and thus the weight) diminishes. But until holdings of that asset have adjusted to its new own rate, the re-calculated weight will be attached to an asset quantity which is too small. Since we are dealing with an index derived from numerous assets and interest rates and since the latter are frequently changing, this is more than just a theoretical objection. Lastly, though more a complication than an objection, there is the question of which index to construct and what interest rates to use in its construction. We noted above that the Bank of England has an index based upon the components of M4, but such an index could be computed for any of the simple-sum aggregates (excepting M0) and indeed for any other set of assets that we might think relevant. The choice of interest rate for each asset is unlikely to be ambiguous but the choice of the benchmark rate is often more difficult and will depend upon institutional features of the monetary system. The benchmark asset has to be capital certain (to be comparable with other assets in the index) and yet offer no transactions services (if it did, it should be in the index). In most cases, the problem will be one of finding any such asset (there must not be a secondary market, for example). Where there is more than one, and if differentials between the benchmark assets change over time, the logical resolution is to select always the highest benchmark rate.

1.6 Summary

Monetary economics is concerned with monetary relationships in the economy. Monetary policy is central to government economic policy and the interest rate decisions of central banks are everywhere seen to be very important. However, monetary economics is still often seen as an esoteric subject and is less widely studied than many other areas of economics. This is partly due to the controversial nature of the subject. This, in turn, derives in part from debates over the role of money in the economy and views of precisely what money is.

The existence of money may be explained by analysing the process of exchange through barter and then considering the gains in efficiency and the reduction of transaction costs through the adoption of money. This can easily explain money's role as a unit of account. Lack of information about the trustworthiness of the counter-party to an exchange can explain the role of money as a means of payment. The use of money as a store of value also reduces transaction costs in exchange. However, this leaves open the question of precisely what money is. Clearly, it can take different forms in different places and has taken a variety of forms at different times ranging from commodity moneys to bank deposits that may be transferred electronically.

Much exchange in modern economies occurs through the use of credit rather than definitions of money that concentrate on assets that act in final settlement of debt. Credit is not classed as money because it creates debt rather than finally settling it. However, from the point of view of the individual economic agent, the lack of narrow money seldom acts as a constraint on exchange since exchange can proceed through borrowing or through the conversion of other assets into assets acceptable in settlement of debt. The demand for narrow money has little significance at an individual level.

Even in the aggregate, the demand for money is only of real importance if we assume the money supply to be exogenous and the demand for money to be a stable function of a small number of variables. For a long time, monetary economics was dominated by the assumption of exogenous money and so much time was spent on the question of whether the demand for money in the aggregate is indeed stable. Since it is now clear that the money supply is not exogenous, there is a strong argument that the demand for money is not of great importance.

Nonetheless, the debate over this issue has been so central to much of monetary economics that economists have spent much time trying to produce definitions of money that overcome the various conceptual problems. There have also been many official definitions of money and these have changed frequently over the years.

Key concepts used in this chapter

money	liquidity
unit of account	exogenous money
store of value	endogenous money
medium of exchange	narrow money
means of payment	broad money
inside money	divisia indexes
outside money	benchmark asset
credit	benchmark rate

Questions and exercises
Answers at the end of the book

1. The text refers to the importance of the interest rate decisions of central banks. How often and when are interest rate announcements made by:
   • the Bank of England Monetary Policy Committee?
   • the European Central Bank?
   • the Federal Reserve Board of the United States?

2. For a short time, in the early years of the British settlement of Australia (the 1790s), rum was used as a currency. What advantages and disadvantages would rum have as a commodity money?

3. What limits currently exist on the amount of credit that can be obtained by households? Is there any attempt by the monetary authorities to control the amount of credit available?

4. There is a distinction made in the economics literature between 'consumption' and 'consumption expenditure'. This distinction implies different definitions of

'saving'. What are these different definitions and how do they relate to the discussion in the text about information and uncertainty?

5. Distinguish between:
    (a) means of payment and medium of exchange;
    (b) inside money and outside money.

6. Distinguish between 'monitoring' and 'targeting' in the context of money supply measures.

... and also to think about

7. The words 'exogenous' and 'endogenous' are used widely in economics — not just referring to money. What precisely do they mean? Provide other examples of their use.

8. Provide examples of transactions in our modern monetary economy that take place through barter or through a combination of barter and money.

9. Would it be sensible always to act as if the weather forecast for the following day were always correct if, on average, weather forecasts were correct:

    10 per cent of the time?
    50 per cent of the time?
    90 per cent of the time?

Does this question provide a reasonable analogy with the notion of analysing an economy as if it were always in equilibrium? If not, why not?

Further reading

Discussions of the meaning of 'money' in economics are often limited to definitions or standard roles of money. For more discursive treatment, you are likely to need to consult older books such as Visser (1974) — but these are not now easy to find. By far the most entertaining book on what money is and how it developed is Galbraith (1975). The early story of money is also told in Glyn Davies (1994). L Randall Wray (1990) provides useful criticism of the simplistic approach to the history of money, often taken by economists, in the first chapter. Many older monetary economics books have also spent time on definitions of money. Examples included J Struthers and H Speight (1986) and D Fisher (1989). However, the *New Palgrave Dictionary of Economics* (2008, also available online) contains articles on inside and outside money, commodity money and fiat money. Official measures of money, too, are less dealt with now than during the brief period in which the money supply was set as an intermediate target. For a discussion of broad measures of money including a comparison of definitions of broad money used in the UK, the USA, the euro area and Japan, see Burgess and Jansen (*BEQB*, 2007).

2 The money supply process

'Central banks almost everywhere usually implement their policies through tight control of money market interest rates. Academic monetary economists almost everywhere discuss monetary policy in terms of the monetary stock. These facts say something about either central bankers or academic monetary economists, or both.'

W Poole, 'Interest rates and the conduct of monetary policy: a comment', *Carnegie-Rochester Series on Public Policy,* 34 (1991).

2.1   Introduction

In the last chapter we saw that we encounter many problems when trying to define money, especially if we are looking for a definition which actually specifies the assets that should be included rather than simply specifying money's functions. However, we also saw that if the authorities wish to conduct any sort of monetary policy they have to decide which assets they are going to monitor, even if this involves a degree of arbitrariness and requires the frequent redrawing of boundaries.

In practice, most monetary authorities work with three measures of money. These are the *monetary base*, and some measure of *narrow* and *broad* money. For convenience, these are usually identified by numbers. Starting from the narrowest measure, M0 is sometimes used to denote the monetary base. This consists only of notes and coin outside the central bank plus banks' deposits held with the central bank. In April 2006, the Bank of England began paying interest on these deposits with the predictable result that this led to a jump in these holdings and a break in the M0 series. For this reason, the M0 series was discontinued. The size of the monetary base can still be seen, however, by looking at a new series, titled 'notes and coin and bank reserves'.

Next is a measure of 'narrow money', often called M1, which consists of notes and coin in circulation outside the banking system together with the non-bank public's holdings of bank sight deposits. M0 and M1 have pretty much the same meaning in all monetary systems. However, the same cannot be said of the measure of broad money. In the majority of countries this is denoted M3, while in the UK it is denoted M4 and, while we can say that the difference between broad and narrow money is that the former includes time deposits and maybe other assets, exactly which assets are included will vary from one system to another. This merely reflects what we said in chapter 1, namely that different monetary systems have different institutional structures and these structures change over time. What is accepted as money in one system is not necessarily treated in the same way in another. To illustrate the point, we show the components of broad and narrow monies in the UK, the Eurozone and the USA in Box 3.1. The box also gives an indication of the relative magnitudes of the three measures.

In this chapter, we are going to explore how changes in the quantity of money occur. For this purpose, 'money' consists of notes and coin in circulation outside the banking system plus a comprehensive range of bank deposits. It corresponds roughly, therefore, to the national measures of broad money in Box 3.1 and is dominated by bank deposits. The magnitude of bank deposits is important for two reasons. Firstly, it should alert us to the fact that changes in the quantity of money are the outcomes of an interaction between the preferences of banks, their customers and the monetary authorities: the quantity of deposits will not expand (for example) unless banks can find a profitable return from marginal additions to loans and deposits and clients wish to add to loan and deposit portfolios on

Box 2.1: Official measures of money - end 2006

USA Name: components	Size $bn	UK Name: components	Size £bn	Eurozone Name: components	Size €bn
Currency outside Federal Reserve banks + bank deposits at FR banks	818	Notes and coin and reserves: Currency outside the Bank of England + banks' operational deposits with the Bank of England	68	M0: Currency outside national central banks + banks' deposits with NCBs	801
M1: Currency in circulation + check-able deposits + travellers cheques + NOW deposits	1366	M4: Currency in circulation + sterling sight and time deposits of the non-bank private sector at banks and building societies	1498	M1: Currency in circulation + sight deposits	3677
M2: M1 + savings and time deposits <£100,000	7031			M3: M1 + time deposits + money market funds + bills and bonds with less than 2 years residual maturity	7732

Sources: www.bankofengland.co.uk/statistics/ms/current/index.htm;   www.federalreserve.gov/releases/h3/ ;   ECB, *Annual Report*, 2006 current terms. Secondly, it should alert us to the likely difficulties that monetary authorities will face when they try to constrain the growth of money and credit. It is not a simple question of modifying their own actions but of modifying the actions of other agents who have no particular interest in co-operating in order to further the authorities' objectives: indeed, these agents may well feel that the authorities' actions are designed to frustrate their own self-interest.

Before we begin, it is worth noting that what we are describing here is a particular set of institutional arrangements which, while their familiarity may give them a sense of permanence, have not always prevailed. Money has not always consisted of bank deposits and its quantity has not always involved the interaction between the income-expenditure decisions and portfolio preferences of non-bank agents, and the profit-seeking behaviour of banks. Over the years, the importance of a correct understanding of monetary institutions as an essential prerequisite for the understanding of how money 'works' has been stressed by a number of writers (Hicks 1967, Dow 1988, 1996, Niggle 1990, 1991, Goodhart, 2002). The best results from consistently applying this principle are revealed in the work of Victoria Chick (for example, Chick 1986, 1993, 1996).

There are broadly speaking two approaches to the analysis of money supply changes and both involve the manipulation of a series of (related) identities. The reason for manipulating these identities is that they can provide insights, or useful ways of looking at things, which may not be apparent at the outset. The fact that two parallel approaches exist, therefore, suggests that there are rival insights: there are differences of opinion about which insights are worth having. And this brings us to another important issue which is that is that there are different views about how the quantity of money changes, different views, we might say, about the underlying reality. The insights generated by one approach are useful if one thinks the underlying system has one set of characteristics, while the insights of the other are useful if the system behaves in a different way. This will become clearer as we proceed, but it should be stressed at the outset that either approach could be used to analyse changes in the quantity of money in any regime. The fact that each is identified with a particular state of affairs is simply that the insights it gives are more appropriate to those circumstances.

Since 'money' consists overwhelmingly of bank deposits, in order to make any progress at all, we need to be familiar with the balance sheet of commercial banks and of the central bank and we also need to understand how flows of funds between commercial banks themselves, and between commercial banks and the central bank, cause changes in the quantity of deposits and in the liquidity of the banking system. Thus, in section 2.2 we shall look at stylised versions of commercial banks' and a central bank's balance sheets, look at the effect of flows of funds and introduce some notation which will be used throughout the remainder of this book. In section 2.3 we shall analyse money supply changes through the 'base-multiplier approach', giving a simple summary first and then looking at it more formally. In section 2.4 we shall do the same using the 'flow of funds' identity. In section 2.5 we shall show how the two can be formally reconciled and try to explain why the latter approach has generally been favoured in the UK. Section 2.6 summarises. Throughout the discussion we shall point out the nature of the underlying monetary regime which the insights seem to suggest.

2.2 Bank balance sheets

Box 2.2 shows the stylised balance sheets of commercial banks and a central bank.

Box 2.2: Commercial and central bank balance sheets

Commercial bank

Assets		Liabilities	
Cb	banks' holdings of notes and coin	Fs	capital and shareholders' funds
Db	banks' deposits with the central bank	Dp	customer deposits
MLb	banks' holdings of loans to the money market		
Gb	banks' holdings of securities		
Lp	loans (advances) to the general public		
Lg	loans to the government or public sector		

Central bank

Assets		Liabilities	
$BLcb$	central bank loans to the banking system	Db	commercial banks' deposits with central bank
$GLcb$	central bank loans to government	Cb	notes and coin with commercial banks
Gcb	central bank holdings of government debt	Cp	notes and coin with the non-bank public
		Dg	government deposits

Notice that the assets of commercial banks are arranged in descending order of liquidity. Cb and Db, which we shall later call 'reserves' (R), are generally low or even non-interest bearing but are essential nonetheless because confidence in the banking system depends upon the instant convertibility of deposits into notes and coin, and because payments between clients of different banking companies will require corresponding transfers between commercial banks' deposits at the central bank. The immediate determinant of the size of these reserves will be the volume and composition of customer deposits, time deposits requiring a smaller reserve ratio than sight deposits. Because of their low rate of interest (in the UK they paid no interest at all until April 2006) we can be reasonably sure that banks will hold minimum quantities, either as specified by the monetary authorities (a 'mandatory' reserve ratio) or as dictated by their own experience of what provides a safe level of liquidity (a 'prudential' reserve ratio). This reserve ratio we can denote as R/Dp. These reserves will be supplemented by 'money market loans', that is to say lending in the interbank market and holdings of money market instruments, much of which can be liquidated on demand or at very short notice. There is also a ready market for securities (mainly short-dated government bonds). The most illiquid assets are of course loans and advances (to the public and private sectors). These are generally non-marketable and, in the latter case, can only be called for repayment at the risk of bankrupting the borrowers.

Notice that the 'reserve' component of bank *assets* appear as *liabilities* of the central bank. This has the effect of interlocking the two sets of balance sheets. Using the symbols introduced in box 2.2, tables 2.1 and 2.2 show how two different disturbances in commercial bank balance sheets (i) communicate themselves to the central bank and (ii) affect the money supply and (iii) the liquidity of the banking system.

In the first case, we assume a sale of government bonds to the non-bank public (an example of what is often called 'open-market operations').

Table 2.1: An open market sale of government bonds

Commercial bank				Central bank			
Assets		*Liabilities*		*Assets*		*Liabilities*	
Cb		Fs		BLcb		Cb	
Db	(-)	Dp	(-)	GLcb		Cp	
MLb				Fx		Db	(-)
Gb				Gcb		Dg	(+)
Lp							
Lg							

The non-bank public pays for the sale of government bonds by drawing on its deposits at commercial banks (shown by (-)). At the central bank, commercial bank deposits are transferred (shown (-)) to the government's account (shown (+)). Notice that balance sheets must always balance. For commercial banks there is a matching change (-) on opposite sides of the balance sheet; for the central bank there are compensating changes (-,+) on the same side.

What of the money supply and bank liquidity? Since we define the money stock to include bank deposits of the non-bank private sector, the money stock is reduced (by Db (-)). The effect on liquidity is not perhaps so obvious until we remember that 'reserves' ($Cb + Db$) are a small fraction of assets while deposits dominate liabilities. (The reserve ratio, R/Dp, is very small in other words). Since the reduction on both sides of the balance sheet is equal in absolute size, the effect on R is much more pronounced than the effect upon Dp and the reserve ratio falls. The reverse can be easily demonstrated for the case of an open market purchase of government bonds.

For the second example, it helps if we remember that a monetary system is usually a multi-bank system and that what is commercially attractive to one bank is likely to be attractive to many. In this case we shall assume that banks wish to increase their lending and to make the illustration more realistic we must introduce a second commercial bank in order to simulate a multi-bank system.

Table 2.2: Commercial banks increase their lending

Commercial bank A		Central bank		Commercial bank B	
Assets	Liabilities	Assets	Liabilities	Assets	Liabilities
Cb	Fs	BLcb	Cb	Cb	Fs
Db (-) [+]	Dp [+]	GLcb	Cp	Db (+) [-]	Dp (+)
MLb		Gcb	Db	MLb	
Gb			Dg	Gb	
Lp (+)				Lp [+]	
Lg				Lg	

We begin with commercial bank A which decides that it will increase its lending to its clients. This is shown as Lp (+). Strictly speaking, the additional loans come into existence only when the clients of A make payments. Let us suppose that they make payments exclusively to clients of bank B. Customer deposits in bank B increase by the same amount (shown as Dp (+))as the increase in lending in bank A. These payments are matched by a transfer between the accounts of banks A and B at the central bank. Thus in A we have Db (-) and in B we have Db (+). What is attractive to bank A, however, is also attractive to other banks in the system, including bank B. Thus, bank B makes additional loans to its customers who (we assume) make payments exclusively to bank A. The process repeats itself, in reverse. We show the changes this time in square brackets. Loans to customers in bank B increase, Lp [+]. Customers in bank A receive the payments as additional deposits, Dp [+]. At the central bank, deposits are transferred from bank B, Db [-] to bank A, Dp [+]. Notice that at the end of the sequence changes in the two banks' deposits at the central bank cancel (i.e. they remain unchanged) while in each bank loans have increased matched by a corresponding increase in deposits.

What can we say about the money supply and bank liquidity in this second case? Remember that we define money as notes and coin (Cp) plus bank deposits (Dp). In both banks, A and B, Dp have increased and there is thus a corresponding increase in the money stock. As for bank liquidity, measured by the reserve ratio R/Dp, it is clear that with Dp increased and R ($= Cb + Db$) unchanged, liquidity is reduced.

Equipped with this basic knowledge of bank balance sheets and how flows of loans and deposits affect the money supply, we can now turn to the two main approaches to aggregate money supply determination.

2.3 The base-multiplier approach to money supply determination

The first characteristic of the base-multiplier (B-M) approach is that it focuses upon stocks. The stocks in question are the stock of monetary base (which we shall call M0) and the stock of money (e.g. M4). It points out that the latter is a multiple of the former and that this multiple is likely to be stable because of two underlying behavioural relationships. Since the components of the monetary base are liabilities of the central bank, the quantity can be varied at the bank's discretion and, given the stable relationship between M0 and M4, central bank action on M0 will produce a corresponding (multiple) reaction in M4.

The latter is certainly a powerful insight. After all, it says that the stock of money is given by the size of the base and *in the absence of any deliberate decision on the part of the central bank, the money stock remains constant*. It encourages the impression that the monetary authorities are central and all-powerful in the determination of the money stock because banks' ability to acquire non-reserve assets (e.g. loans and advances) are reserve constrained.

But we can also see from this simple summary that this insight depends upon some crucial assumptions about the underlying system. Firstly it assumes the stability of two behavioural relationships: indeed, in its simplest version the B-M approach is sometimes presented as though these relationships are fixed. But this is an empirical question which needs to be examined. (Remember what we said in 2.2 about agents' having their own preferences). Secondly, while it is true that the monetary base consists of central bank liabilities, it does not automatically follow that the central bank either can or even desires to control these liabilities. Finally, there is a question about whether concentrating on stock equilibrium is very useful when the underlying variables are subject to continuous change. Put briefly, a monetary system in which the money supply changes only as the result of the central bank's deliberate adjustment of the monetary base, is a system in which the money supply is *exogenous* — exogenous at least with respect to the preferences of other agents in the economic system. We turn now to a more formal examination of the base multiplier approach.

We begin by defining the two stocks:

$$M \equiv Cp + Dp \tag{2.1}$$

and

$$B \equiv Cp + Cb + Db \tag{2.2}$$

M is (broad) money and consists of notes and coin in circulation with the non-bank public (Cp) plus their holdings of bank deposits (Dp). In practice, M corre-

---

Box 2.3: Bank loans, deposits and money

Imagine a monetary system with just two commercial banks. Their simplified balance sheets are shown below.

Bank A		Bank B	
Assets	Liabilities	Assets	Liabilities
Cb = 50	Dp = 2000	Cb = 150	Dp = 5000
Db = 30		Db = 50	
Lp = 1920		Lp = 4800	

In addition, the non-bank public holds notes and coin (Cp) of 400.

1. What is the current stock of broad money?
2. What is the reserve ratio for each individual bank and for the system as a whole?

Suppose now that bank A makes additional loans of 50 to a subset of its customers and that some of these customers use 20 to make payments to other depositors of the same bank and 30 to make payments to clients of bank B.

3. Draw up new balance sheets for each bank.
4. What is the total money stock now?
5. What is the reserve ratio for each individual bank and for the system as a whole?

Suppose now that bank B makes additional loans of 100 to a subset of its customers and that some of these customers use 50 to make payments to other depositors of the same bank and 50 to make payments to clients of bank A.

6. Draw up new balance sheets for each bank.
7. What is the total money stock now?
8. What is the reserve ratio for each individual bank and for the system as a whole?

Suppose that the non-bank public now decides to hold 50 of additional notes and coin.

9. What effect does this have upon the total money stock?
10. What effect has it had upon the aggregate reserve ratio?

---

sponds to one of the broad money measures in Box 2.1. B, the monetary base, consists of those same notes and coin plus also now notes and coin held by banks (Cb) and banks' own deposits at the central bank (Db). In practice, B corresponds to M0 in Box 2.1. If we now refer to $Cb + Db$ as bank reserves and denote them R, then 2.2 can be rewritten as:

$$B \equiv Cp + R \tag{2.3}$$

At any particular time, there will be a monetary base of given value and similarly a given quantity of broad money and it is a simple task to create a ratio of money to base:

$$\frac{M}{B} \equiv \frac{Cp + Dp}{Cp + R} \tag{2.4}$$

The first insight comes when we divide through by the non-bank public's holdings of deposits.

$$\frac{M}{B} \equiv \frac{Cp/Dp + Dp/Dp}{Cp/Dp + R/Dp} \tag{2.5}$$

For convenience, let $Cp/Dp = \chi$, and let $R/Dp = \rho$, then we can rewrite 2.5 as:

$$\frac{M}{B} \equiv \frac{\chi + 1}{\chi + \rho} \tag{2.6}$$

The insight is that the volume of broad money, in relation to the base, depends upon the two ratios χ, which is the public's cash ratio, and ρ which is the banks' reserve ratio. Let us suppose for a moment that these ratios are stable (not necessarily fixed) then we can *predict* that:

$$M = B.\frac{\chi + 1}{\chi + \rho} \tag{2.7}$$

and

$$\Delta M = \Delta B.\frac{\chi + 1}{\chi + \rho} \tag{2.8}$$

Notice that in a fractional reserve system, ρ will have a value less than one and the term $(\chi + 1)/(\chi + \rho)$, let us call it m, will be a multiplier. Recall that the base consists of liabilities of the central bank then, if we assume that the central bank is both willing and able to manipulate these liabilities at its discretion, then we get a second, more dramatic, insight, namely that the size of the money stock is determined by the central bank's willingness to supply assets comprising the monetary base. These assumptions amount to a description of a monetary system where the money supply is exogenously determined and we can immediately see why the B-M model tends to be favoured as a way of describing and analysing changes in the money stock in an exogenous regime: by rearranging two simple definitions we are quickly led to this conclusion.

In an unrealistically simple world, χ and ρ might be treated as fixed. But they are both portfolio decisions about which the public and banks respectively are likely to have preferences depending upon relative prices and other constraints.

We cannot throw away the standard economic axioms of maximising behaviour just because we are dealing with money. That said, we do not promise an exhaustive account of how maximisation might be achieved, but we can offer some illustration of relevant factors which will bear upon preferences. If we take χ, the public's cash ratio, we can say firstly that the decision to divide money holdings between notes and coin ('cash') and bank deposits must surely depend upon any rate of interest paid on deposits, money's 'own rate', which we might denote i_m. The higher the rate paid on deposits (and the wider the range of deposits on which it is paid), the less willing, *ceteris paribus*, people will be to hold cash.

Furthermore, one of the reasons for holding deposits is to have access to the payments mechanism. Just how attractive deposits are as a means of payment depends upon current usage — many fewer transactions involved bank deposits a hundred years ago than they do now — and this depends to some extent upon technological considerations. The widespread use of deposits as means of payment requires the development of an efficient cheque clearing system. Since the mid-1960s the big developments in the payments system have involved electronic payments — automating them first of all so that customers could set up standing order or direct debit instructions and then making electronic transfers possible, most recently in the form of debit cards. As the services offered by deposits increase and improve, so they become more attractive relative to cash.

Technology has almost certainly affected the cash/deposit split through other routes. For a given level of money's own rate and a given level of 'services' from deposits, the decision about how much cash to hold must depend to some extent upon the difficulties of switching between cash and deposits, the so-called 'shoe leather costs' based on the idea that replenishing cash balances involved walking to the bank and standing in a queue. But one of the many achievements of banking technology has been the development of the cash machine or automated teller machine ('ATM') to give it its proper name. These machines now allow a wide range of routine banking transactions to be carried out at remote sites like supermarkets, filling stations, shopping malls and even educational institutions. Given that these facilities make cash replenishment easier, they encourage people to hold smaller cash balances. The effect is likely to be more marked in periods of rapid inflation and high nominal interest rates when the protection of purchasing power offered by interest-bearing deposits will be greatest.

The two examples of technological change we have given, both tend to reduce the public's cash ratio: χ gets smaller. This need not be the case *a priori*. It is conceivable that future technological changes will push in the opposite direction. This means that we cannot give a definite sign to the partial derivative of technology (as we could with money's own rate, for example). In practice, however, it is very likely that technological changes have acted over the years towards a reduction in the public's need to hold cash.

Recent changes in payment preferences are shown in Table 2.3. The figures are consistent with our remarks about technology in so far as they show a dramatic increase in automated payments (45 per cent in five years) and a rapid growth in the use of plastic cards (up by 39 per cent in the same period). On the other side of the picture, the clearing of paper-based payments has declined by 25 per cent and the use of cash by about 14 per cent.

As regards influences upon the public's cash ratio, therefore, we can surmise that χ will depend to some extent upon at least two factors, money's own rate and technological conditions.

$$\chi \equiv \frac{Cp}{Dp} = f(\underset{-}{i_m}, \underset{?}{T}) \tag{2.9}$$

Table 2.3: Total transaction volumes in the UK by medium

Millions	2001	2002	2003	2004	2005	Annual rate of change 2001-05
Paper payments	2,567	2,394	2,251	2,089	1,931	-5.9%
Automated payments	3,706	3,930	4,271	4,827	5,378	+7%
Plastic cards	4,387	4,821	5,318	5,739	6,094	+6.8%
Cash (>£1)	27,684	26,622	25,859	24,916	23,968	-2.9%
Other	3,076	3,025	3,049	3,009	3,061	0%
Total	41,420	40,792	40,748	40,580	40,432	-0.5%

Source: www.apacs.org.uk/resources_publications/documents/Paymenttrendstable2.doc

When it comes to banks' decisions about their reserve ratios, therefore, there are numerous influences at work. Remember that banks are profit-seeking firms, that the cash element of reserves yields no interest and that, in most systems deposits at the central bank are also low-interest bearing. This means that holding reserves acts like a tax on banking.

Pause for thought 2.1

Some operators charge for the use of ATMs. If this practice were to become general, how do you think it would affect the public's cash ratio and why?

Banks' decisions to hold reserves will depend firstly upon their cost. Where reserves pay no interest then the cost can be proxied by the return on alternative liquid assets, which might be proxied by the bond rate, i_b. Where reserves do pay interest, then the cost will be the return on reserves, i_r relative to the bond rate.

The quantity of reserves held will depend also on the cost of being short, that is upon the rediscount rate charged for lender of last resort facilities, i_d. This is the rate of interest announced periodically, usually monthly, by the central bank. In the UK and the eurozone it is a rate of interest charged by the central bank on short-dated repurchase deals with banks, using government bonds as the underlying security. Reserve holdings will also depend upon any mandatory reserve requirement, RR, and, lastly, upon the variability of inward and outward flows to which banks are subject, σ. This last factor is relevant because the primary purpose of reserves is to enable individual banks to meet demands for cash or, more importantly, for transfers of deposits as customers make payments to customers of other banks or to the government. The majority of payments are offsetting (payments from bank A to bank B will roughly cancel); reserves are necessary to meet the balance. Provided this balance is predictable, the need for reserves will be limited to the predicted net flow. If it is unpredictable, then additional funds have to be held. The greater the variance (or standard deviation) of the flows, the greater the margin that will be necessary.

In summary, then:

$$\rho \equiv \frac{R}{Dp} = f(\underset{+}{i_r}, \underset{-}{i_b}, \underset{+}{i_d}, \underset{+}{RR}, \underset{+}{\sigma}) \qquad (2.10)$$

Given that we now have some idea of the sorts of influences, and the direction of their effect, upon the ratios χ and ρ, the next obvious question is what effect will changes in χ and ρ have upon the size of the multiplier expression in 2.7 and 2.8. From there, we can see their effect on the money supply.

The answer to the first question lies in the value '1'. Because the values of χ and ρ are fractions (in practice, very small fractions) it is the '1' which gives the expression a multiplier value: the numerator is bound to be larger than the denominator. Consider now what happens if we change χ and ρ.

If we increase (for example) χ, we increase the numerator and denominator simultaneously and the outcome may therefore appear indeterminate at first glance. But with the numerator already larger than the denominator by virtue of the '1', any change in a must have a bigger effect proportionate effect upon the denominator. If we are looking at an increase, therefore, a given change in a must have a bigger effect upon the denominator than the numerator and the value of the multiplier will fall.

With ρ, the effect is obvious since it appears only in the denominator. Any change in ρ must lead to an inverse change in the value of the multiplier.

Since the money supply depends upon both the base and the multiplier we can write:

$$M = f(\underset{+}{B}, \underset{-}{\chi}, \underset{-}{\rho}) \qquad (2.11)$$

and since we know (from 2.9 and 2.10) how χ and ρ are likely to respond to a number of influences, we can substitute into (2.11), to yield a money supply determined as follows:

$$M = f(B, i_m, T, i_r, i_b, i_d, RR, \sigma) \qquad (2.12)$$

A change in B is a change in the multiplicand; changes in all other variables cause a change in the size of the multiplier itself.

Box 2.4: The multiplier

1. Suppose that $\chi = 0.05$ while $\rho = 0.01$, calculate a value for the multiplier.

2. Suppose that the public's cash preferences change such that α falls to 0.04. Recalculate the multiplier value.

3. Calculate a new value for the multiplier if banks increase their reserve ratio to 0.012 (α remaining at 0.04).

We turn now to how this account of money supply determination can be presented diagrammatically. The account of money supply determination which we have just given is more familiar than it may seem since it is what is assumed, but rarely spelt out, in money market diagrams where a vertical money supply curve intersects a downward sloping money demand curve. This is what we have drawn in figure 2.1, though we have given the money supply curve a positive slope for reasons we return to at the end of this section. Before we do that, let us be clear how changes in the variables listed in 2.12 will be reflected in the diagram.

Pause for thought 2.2:

Making explicit use of the B-M analysis, explain how you would expect the money supply to be affected by a rise in interest rates announced by the central bank.

The horizontal axis depicts the quantity of money as a stock. In this space, a money supply curve intersects the horizontal (money) axis at a point where $M = m.B$ (where m is the multiplier). A change in B changes the point of intersection (the supply curve shifts). The same results from a change in any of RR, i_d i_r, i_m, σ, T since these cause a change in the value of the multiplier.

Notice that we have omitted the bond rate, i_b, from this list. This is because the bond rate must appear on the vertical axis. This is because the purpose of drawing the money supply curve in interest-money space at all is ultimately to discuss money market equilibrium, the interaction of supply and demand. With a downward sloping demand curve in the diagram, the rate on the vertical axis must be the opportunity cost of holding money. Strictly, in a modern monetary system, one might argue that this rate ought to be a spread term, representing the difference between the bond rate (appearing as a proxy for the return on 'non-money financial assets' which agents could hold as an alternative) and money's own rate (effectively the weighted average rate on cash and deposits). This is true but does not change the point we are about to make. If we put a spread term on the vertical axis it remains the case that a rise in bond rate increases the opportunity cost of holding money. As the size of the spread increases the quantity of money demanded declines. The crucial point is that it is the bond rate which *must* appear on the vertical axis, either on its own (if money is non-interest bearing) or as part of a spread term.

Figure 2.1: The money supply curve

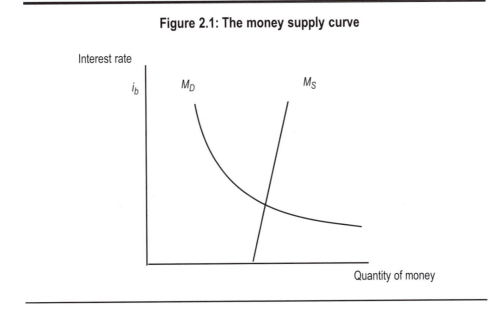

Now we can see why the money supply curve is drawn with a positive slope. In our discussion of ρ, we saw that banks would economise on reserves if returns on other assets increased; this would reduce the value of their reserve ratio (2.10) and this in turn (2.12) increases the money supply. In short, the money supply shows some degree of elasticity with regard to the bond rate *and since the bond rate appears in the diagram on the vertical axis*, the effect of changes in the bond rate must be captured by giving a positive slope to the money supply curve.

If as seems reasonable, banks' behaviour towards reserves is dependent upon non-reserve interest rates, the 'vertical' money supply curve must have some positive slope and one might argue that the money supply has acquired some degree of endogeneity, contrary to what we said at the beginning of this section about the B-M approach being associated with exogenous money regimes. Davidson (1988 p.156) does indeed refer to this aspect of the money supply as 'interest-endogeneity'. This form of endogeneity is, however, extremely limited. In a fully-endogenous monetary regime, it is generally accepted that continuous expansion of the money stock, with little, if any, effect upon interest rates is the norm. Clearly that is not compatible with what we see in figure 2.1 where a continuous expansion of the money supply is possible, ceteris paribus only if the level of interest rates i_b rises without limit. But the more normal case of course is that the authorities have some range within which they wish to see ib remain. In circumstances of full-endogeneity continuous expansion requires the authorities to change one of the other variables in 2.12 and this has to be the monetary base, B.

Pause for thought 2.3:

How would you expect the money supply curve in figure 2.1 to be affected by an increase in the coefficient on the bond rate?

2.4 The flow of funds approach

Where the base-multiplier approach focused upon stocks, the flow of funds (FoF) approach concentrates upon changes in stocks, i.e. on *flows*. There is a connection with the B-M approach in that one of the flows is the change in money stock; but the other flow which dominates the FoF approach is the flow of bank *lending* to the non-bank public. This is strictly speaking the net change in the stock of bank loans — the difference over time in the stock of loans taking account of both new loans made and loans repaid. The flow of money is shown as ΔM, the flow of new loans is shown as ΔLp (for new lending to the *non-bank private sector*) and ΔLg (for new lending to the *public sector*).[1] Because it focuses upon flows of new lending and their ability to create deposits, the FoF approach is sometimes known as the 'credit-counterparts' approach.

As with the B-M approach, we begin with the money supply identity:

$$M \equiv Cp + Dp \qquad\qquad (2.13/2.1)$$

and then rewrite it in flows:

$$\Delta M \equiv \Delta Cp + \Delta Dp \qquad\qquad (2.14)$$

We next concentrate on the deposit element and use the bank balance sheet identity to remind ourselves that since deposits (liabilities) must be matched by loans (assets) then the same must be true about changes.[2] On the asset side, loans can be decomposed into loans to the private and to the public sector.

$$\Delta Dp \equiv \Delta Lp + \Delta Lg \qquad\qquad (2.15)$$

Concentrate now on bank loans to the public sector. These are just one way of financing the public sector and, because of its monetary implications and short-term nature, it tends to be a residual source of financing — something to be resorted to after all other forms of finance. So it follows that we can locate the flow of new bank lending to the public sector (PSBR) within the public sector's total borrowing requirement:

$$\Delta Lg \equiv \text{PSBR} - \Delta Gp - \Delta Cp \pm \Delta\text{ext} \qquad (2.16)$$

where ΔGp represents net sales of government bonds to the general public. Notice that Δext can take a positive or negative value. Δext refers to the monetary implications of external flows. For example, if the public sector buys foreign currency assets with sterling (as it might if it were trying to hold a fixed exchange rate) this adds to the public sector's borrowing requirement. Selling foreign currency assets for sterling reduces the need for sterling borrowing.

We can then substitute 2.16 into 2.15 to show all the sources of change in deposits:

$$\Delta Dp \equiv \Delta Lp + \text{PSBR} - \Delta Gp - \Delta Cp \pm \Delta\text{ext} \qquad (2.17)$$

and then substitute 3.17 into 3.14 to show all sources of monetary change. In making the substitution we have tidied up (notice that ΔCp cancels because it enters twice, with opposite signs) and reordered the terms to give 3.18, which is often referred to as the 'flow of funds identity'.

$$\Delta M \equiv \text{PSBR} - \Delta Gp \pm \Delta\text{ext} + \Delta Lp \qquad (2.18)$$

What insights do we gain from the FoF approach? The explicit message is that changes in the money stock are inextricably linked to lending/borrowing behaviour. But behind this are three implications. The first of these is that changes themselves are what matters — one would not use the FoF approach to analyse a system where stocks dominate everyone's interest. It is an implication of the FoF approach that our interest in money supply is an interest in monetary growth. The second implication is that the monetary base is of little interest. We shall see in the next section that we can rewrite the flow of funds identity so as to include changes in the monetary base, but the fact that the FoF identity is not normally written in that way is significant. One does not adopt a method of analysis which deliberately omits variables which one thinks are important. It points to flows as the important variables and by omitting references to the monetary base it hints that the authorities might need to find some non-base-orientated way of influencing these flows. Equally, one does not normally adopt a mode of analysis which gives a key position to variables of little interest. The third implication of the FoF analysis, therefore, is that if/when the authorities become interested in the magnitude of flows, they should pay attention to lending/borrowing. While the B-M approach creates the impression that bank lending is reserve (*supply*) constrained, the FoF creates the impression that it is (*demand*) constrained by the non-bank private sector's desire for additional credit.

Pause for thought 2.4:

According to the FoF approach, what is the relevance to monetary growth of government debt sales to the non-bank private sector?

2.5 The two approaches compared

While the B-M and FoF approaches are different ways of analysing the quantity of monetary assets, both consist of rearranging identities at least one of which — the money stock and its components — is common to both. In fact, even though each approach offers a different range of insights and highlights different features of the monetary system as being significant, it is possible to reconcile the two approaches. Indeed it is perfectly possible to analyse money supply changes or flows by using an identity which features the monetary base while one could, if one were so inclined, analyse the existing stock of money in terms of the amount of lending. Each approach is, strictly speaking, agnostic as regards the underlying behavioural characteristics of the monetary system, but each furnishes insights which are more relevant to a certain type of regime and has thus become associated with it. We shall see more of this in a moment, but let us firstly see that the two approaches are formally equivalent.

Pause for thought 2.5:

Using the FoF approach, explain the likely effect on the rate of monetary expansion of a central bank's decision to raise interest rates. (Compare your answer with your reaction to PfT 2.2).

The B-M approach consists of a statement about the monetary base and two behavioural relations (see equation. 2.6). We can write the FoF approach in exactly the same terms if we remember that the monetary base consists of cash held by the non-bank public (Cp) together with bank lending to the public sector in the form of reserve assets ($Db + Cb$). Bank lending to the public sector in the form of reserve assets must be equal to total bank lending to the public sector minus bank holdings of non-reserve assets (e.g. bank holdings of government bonds, Gb). So (in changes):

$$\Delta B \equiv \Delta Cp + (\Delta Lg - \Delta Gb) \tag{2.19}$$

and, substituting 2.16 and rearranging:

$$\Delta B \equiv \Delta Cp - \Delta Gb + (\text{PSBR} - \Delta Gp \pm \Delta\text{ext} - \Delta Cp) \qquad (2.20)$$

From 2.18 and 2.20 we can obtain:

$$\Delta M \equiv \Delta B + \Delta Gb + \Delta BLp \qquad (2.21)$$

What 2.21 shows is that we can make control of changes in the money stock appear to depend upon control of the base together with two behavioural relationships, in this case the banks' demand for government debt (ΔGb) and lending to the non-bank private sector (ΔLp), almost as easily as making it depend upon flows of new lending.

In the UK, monetary analysis has tended to follow the FoF rather than the B-M approach. Some of the reasons for this are historic. These encouraged the FoF approach years ago and thus ensured a lasting role if only through inertia. But the FoF also has one overwhelming contemporary advantage that we come to in a moment, but which really forms the theme of the next chapter. We look at four older reasons first.

In the UK, analysis for policy purposes has often focused on the broad money aggregates — M3 until 1989 and M4 thereafter. This does not require but it does permit the FoF approach which puts the whole of bank lending on the right hand side. Such an approach cannot be applied to a monetary aggregate containing only a subset of deposits (e.g. M1) since the balance sheet identity requires only that *total* lending is matched by total deposits, and there is no way in which a subset of loans can be linked to any subset of deposits. In other policy regimes, in the US for example, the policy emphasis has often been upon these narrower aggregates and the FoF approach does not work.

We noted earlier that the B-M approach emphasises the availability of reserves as a constraint on bank lending while the FoF approach focuses upon the general public's desire for bank credit. The tradition in the UK is for much short-term bank lending to be based upon the overdraft system whereby a maximum credit limit is agreed in advance and the borrower then uses (and is charged for) only that fraction of the loan that is required on a day-to-day basis. Clearly in these circumstances, a proportion of bank lending is done at the discretion of the borrower. Furthermore, it cannot be reserve-constrained. A bank that enters into overdraft contracts must guarantee to meet 100 per cent of the commitment if called upon.

Thirdly, the FoF approach allows all the credit counterparts to monetary growth to be identified separately. This was particularly important in the days when UK governments frequently ran large budget deficits some of which had to be financed by monetary means. With the independence of the Bank of England and the separation of monetary from fiscal policy (since 1997) and a policy of fully-funding budget deficits, this is a less compelling argument than it once was.

Another compelling reason for the popularity of the FoF in the UK involves 'credit rationing'. The literature began with Stiglitz and Weiss in 1981 who advanced a number of reasons why it might be rational for banks to ration the volume of their lending in order to screen out some unsafe borrowers who would be willing and able to pay the going price. The rationality of apparently forego-ing profitable opportunities derives from the presence of asymmetric informa-tion. It is argued that borrowers have a much better idea about the risks attached to the projects for which they take out loans than do the providers of the loans. It is very difficult for banks to assess the creditworthiness of borrowers and their projects, this gives rise to moral hazard and adverse selection problems. The bor-rower characteristics that banks might use in the screening are discussed in Leland and Pyle (1977) and Diamond (1984) but the important point from the FoF perspective is that variations in the flow of lending are partly the outcome of banks' lending decisions (Stiglitz and Weiss, 1981) and while this is the case there is little point in focusing upon changes in the availability of reserves.

The final and by far the most powerful reason for the widespread adoption of the FoF framework is that it is easier to apply to the way in which the UK author-ities have, in practice, tried to influence monetary conditions. The FoF approach gives a central role to flows of new bank lending and it is the flow of bank credit that the UK authorities have focused on, albeit in differing ways, since 1945. Up until 1971, this control consisted of an evolving collection of direct interventions — 'moral suasion' imposed on banks to discriminate by type of borrower, then by specifying minimum deposits and maximum payback periods for consumer loans. The first of these was a supply-side constraint but the latter were intend-ed to work on the demand for loans as potential borrowers ruled themselves in or out depending upon the severity of the conditions.

In 1971 the Competition and Credit Control arrangements swept away all direct controls and stated the intention of relying upon variations in the price of credit, the short term rate of interest, to regulate the demand for credit. In the inflationary years of the 1970s, the authorities had occasional failures of nerve when it was clear that interest rates needed to be held in double figures, and there were occasional outbursts of direct control in the form of supplementary special deposits (a reversion to supply-side control). But in 1981, market methods were restored and the last twenty years have seen a steady convergence in central bank operating procedures towards adjustment of short-term interest rates (Borio, 1997). The short-term rate over which central banks have direct control is the lender of last resort or rediscount rate which we have already met as i_d in 2.10. But in the B-M approach the purpose of raising (for example) i_d would be explained as an attempt to increase the reserve ratio and reduce the size of the multiplier. In practice, raising i_d is assumed to cause banks to raise their lending and borrowing rates and thus to reduce the *demand* for net new bank lending and thus to slow the creation of new deposits. The quantity of reserves and the result-ing size of reserve ratios has nothing to do with it. In spite of the occasional appearance of 'ratios' in UK monetary regulations, none of them have been ratios of deposits to reserve assets under the control of the central bank. Monetary regulation has always targeted bank lending and never the quantity of reserves.

Furthermore, it is the *rate* of money (or credit) expansion that has exercised monetary authorities the world over. Nowhere is the stock of any particular interest. A rise in interest rates (today) or a tightening of credit terms (in the past) was never intended to produce an absolute reduction in the stock of monetary assets or their credit counterparts. This is quite difficult to deal with in a B-M framework. Recall that we began by saying that the major 'insight' of the approach was that if the authorities did nothing (by way of changing the quantity of reserve assets) then the money stock would be unchanged. But in practice, the money stock *expands* continuously at the going rate of interest. If the authorities do nothing (to change the level of interest rates), in the real world the money stock expands at its current rate. Thus, the real reason why the FoF approach to money supply determination has been so attractive in the UK over the years is that the Bank of England has targeted the flow of new lending and sought to control it through the demand side by changing interest rates.

2.6 Summary

In this chapter we have seen that there are two ways of analysing changes in the quantity of money. One focuses upon stocks and looks at the multiple relationship between the monetary base and broad measures of money; the other focuses on flows of new loans and new deposits. Although either can be used to analyse changes in money in any monetary system and under any policy regime, each approach carries with it unstated assumptions about the nature of the regime it is analysing and each is easier to use and provides more relevant insights when applied to the type of regime which it is assuming. Thus the B-M approach, through its emphasis upon the stock of monetary base is most helpful in analysing monetary change in a system where the central bank can and does control the quantity of base directly and where the cash/deposit preferences of banks and their clients are stable. The flow of funds or credit-counterparts approach is more helpful in looking at a system where the monetary authorities are more concerned with the rate of monetary expansion and try to influence it through the flow of new bank loans.

It should be apparent by now that the FoF approach to the analysis of the money supply has been widely-adopted in the UK for the simple reason that the Bank of England has, for many years, chosen to set the level of interest rates and then allow private sector preferences to determine the growth rate of money and credit. In fact, this is true for most central banks as we shall see in chapter 4 where we include some comments from those closely involved in the day to day conduct of policy.

It is curious, therefore, that mainstream monetary economics has persisted with the mistaken notion that the money supply *is* exogenously determined by a central bank which uses the monetary base as the policy instrument and is there-fore able to create policy 'shocks' which take the form of unsolicited changes in the stock of money. At the pedagogic level this has led to the continued focus upon the rather unhelpful *IS/LM* model as the principle vehicle of instruction. At the research level, the result has been little short of disastrous in leading a whole generation of economists to devote their efforts to understanding the demand for money in order to be able to explain how agents respond to these unsolicited (but non-existent) shocks. We take a brief look at some of this misplaced effort in the next chapter before returning to the real world of policy in chapter 4.

Key concepts used in this chapter

monetary base	the bond rate
narrow money	money's own rate
broad money	prudential reserve ratio
reserve ratio	mandatory reserve ratio
cash ratio	open market sales and purchases
flow of funds	credit counterparts
stocks	credit rationing
flows	

Questions and exercises
Answers at the end of the book

1. In the B-M approach, explain the effects of the following and show them dia-grammatically:

a) an introduction of a mandatory reserve ratio in excess of the prudential ratio currently in force;
b) the development of new deposit liabilities with zero reserve requirements;
c) a dramatic increase in the number and distribution of cash machines.

2. Using figure 2.1, show the difference in impact on money market equilibrium of a given reduction in reserve assets when (a) the money supply curve shows some positive elasticity with respect to the bond rate and (b) when the money supply curve is completely inelastic with respect to the bond rate.

3. In the flow of funds analysis, explain the effect of an increase in the government's budget deficit, *ceteris paribus*.

...and also to think about

4. What steps might the authorities take to offset the monetary effects of events in question 3?

5. Why, according to the flow of funds approach, does the choice of exchange rate regime make monetary control more, or less, difficult for the authorities?

6. The money supply curve in figure 2.1 is one component in the derivation of the *LM* curve. What effect does changing the slope of the money supply curve have on the *LM* curve?

Further reading

The base-multiplier account of money supply determination can be found in most intermediate macroeconomic textbooks. To see it presented as the definitive account of the money supply process in specialist textbooks we need to go to the USA. Mishkin (2006), especially ch.13, is a good and typical example. Though now rather old, Cuthbertson (1985) provides one of the clearest expositions of the approach, together with the flow of funds approach and a comparison of the two. Lewis and Mizen (2000) also discuss the two approaches and make an explicit comparison, in ch.13. Handa (2000) ch.10 is devoted entirely to 'the money supply process' and treats the money supply as a stock determined as a multiple of reserves.

The flow of funds (or 'credit counterparts') approach with its implicit message that 'loans create deposits' is the obvious framework within which to analyse a regime in which the money supply is endogenously determined. As such, it is central to the post-Keynesian treatment of monetary economics. This has spawned a vast literature, though little of it in textbook form. One of many post Keynesian accounts of money supply determination which brings out the importance of the demand for loans is Moore (1983).

A fascinating essay, which shows that the approaches are neither of them 'right' or 'wrong' but each appropriate for a different type of monetary regime, was written many years ago by Victoria Chick (1986). It deserves wider recognition.

The *Bank of England Quarterly Bulletin* (1997) explains that monetary policy in the UK consists of setting interest rates and letting quantities adjust to demand while the *BEQB* (1999) contains a box explaining how interest rates are set. Together they show the Bank thinking in terms of the flow of funds approach. Blinder (1998) gives the central banker's view of the appropriate instrument of monetary policy.

3 The demand for money

'It is not any scarcity of gold and silver, but the difficulty which such people find in borrowing, and which
their creditors find in getting payment, that occasions
the general complaint of scarcity of money.'

Adam Smith, *Wealth of Nations* (1776) IV. I

3.1   Introduction

We talked in chapter 1 of the difficulties associated with the concept of the
demand for money, pointing out that if we accept the standard definition of
money as a set of assets generally acceptable in exchange for goods and services,
money is only demanded indirectly — to allow acts of exchange. We also pointed out that from the point of view of individual economic agents there would
rarely be a problem of excess demand for or supply of money and went on to suggest that, even at an aggregate level, the demand for money was only of much significance if we made particular assumptions about the money supply process and
the nature of the demand for money — that the money supply was exogenous
and that the demand for money was stably related to real income. But, we then
showed in chapter 2, that the supply of money is not exogenous and that central
banks do not even attempt to control it through control of the monetary base, conducting monetary policy rather through the impact they have on short-term interest rates in the economy. And yet, we have also said that a very high proportion
of research activity in monetary economics has been devoted to the theory of the
demand for money and to the testing of the demand for money function.

We have argued that this has been so because of the approach that has dominated many areas of economic analysis — the assumption that an economy can
be best analysed as if it were in equilibrium, responding to the argument that
economies are not in equilibrium with the argument that it is only in the long run,
under equilibrium conditions, that economic agents can be seen to be maximising
utility with full information. In other words, disequilibrium models are only special cases of the more general equilibrium model. Clearly, the reverse position can
be argued — that economic agents act under conditions of uncertainty and imper-
fection information and that, therefore, disequilibrium models are more general
and better explain the real world. From this perspective, an equilibrium model
requires particular assumptions and is just a special case of a more general model.
We would also add that economic policy-makers necessarily make their decisions
in economies that are not in equilibrium and are not characterised by full information.

The relevance of this to the demand for money becomes clear in section 5.4
when we shall see that the transmission mechanism from short-term interest rates
(the chosen instrument of central banks) to aggregate demand has no place for the
demand for money. There is, thus, a temptation to leave out the demand for
money altogether from a book such as this in which monetary policy is the principal interest. Yet, the theoretical disputes about the nature of the demand for
money have been of great importance in the controversies over monetary policy,
notably whether monetary policy is weak or strong, especially in times of depression. This, in turn, has led to judgements about the relative importance of monetary and fiscal policies.

Consequently, we need to examine the various views of the demand for
money, looking as we do at contributions that have relevance beyond the

attempts to identify a demand for money that might be stable. We shall not, however, spend much time on the vast literature on the testing of demand for money
functions. This has been of considerable interest to econometricians and has
involved the development of econometric techniques, but it has had little significance for economic policy.

We deal with the theory of the demand for money historically, beginning in
section 3.2 with an outline of the Quantity Theory of Money. Although the
Quantity Theory was not a theory of the demand for money, dealing with the use
of money in transactions rather than with the decision to hold money, there are
compelling reasons to start our account here. From the Quantity Theory of
Money, we move to the Cambridge cash balance approach to the demand for
money. This, in turn, leads us into the treatment of the demand for money in
Keynes's *General Theory*, which we consider in section 3.3. Section 3.4 to 3.6 treat
theories arising from Keynes's work — later views of the transactions demand for
money (3.4) and of the precautionary demand (3.5) and, then, Tobin's alternative
to the speculative demand (3.6). The monetarist approach to the demand for
money is the subject of 3.7. We look briefly at some other theoretical approaches
in section 3.8, especially at buffer stock models of the demand for money. Section
3.9 attempts to tie together a number of the points raised in the chapter and in earlier chapters. In section 3.10, we look briefly at empirical work on the demand for
money.

3.2   The Quantity Theory of Money

There are three compelling reasons for commencing with the Quantity Theory of
Money.

- The Quantity Theory stresses the connection between changes in the economy's money stock and changes in the general price level - the issue at the heart
  of the monetary debate.

- Many writers on the subject thereafter have seen themselves as opponents
  or inheritors of the Quantity Theory tradition.

- The varying views on the demand for money can be easily compared using
  the Quantity Theory equation.

The Quantity Theory of money can be traced back at least as far as the eighteenth
century and can be seen as a reaction to the mercantilist identification of money
with wealth.[1] In its early days the theory was expounded with varying degrees
of rigour but it was generally held that an increase in the quantity of money
would:

(a) lead to a proportional increase in the price level and

(b) not have a permanent impact on real income.

Some versions of the theory did not require exact proportionality and admitted the possibility of a time lag between the increase in the money stock and the change in the price level.[2]

The Quantity Theory is most familiar to modern readers through Fisher's (1911) version in which it is approached through the equation of exchange:

$$MV_t \equiv P_t T \tag{3.1}$$

where M is the stock of money, $P_t T$ is the value of all transactions undertaken with money and V_t, is the transactions velocity of money. We next assume that V_t, T and M are all exogenous and can be taken as constant. We also assume that the monetary authorities can change the size of M at will. Then, causality runs from the supply of money to prices. We now have:

$$M\overline{V}_t \equiv P_t\overline{T} \tag{3.2}$$

This expresses the proposition that an exogenous increase in the quantity of money leads to a proportional increase in the price level and has no impact on real income (money is neutral). It is common to say that T is constant because the economy is making full use of all available resources (including labour). But we should note that this is not just a simple assumption that we can easily relax. The model accepts the classical view of a clear division between the monetary and real sectors of the economy. T is determined in the real sector and cannot be influenced by changes in M. In other words, money neutrality does not follow from the analysis of the role that money plays in an economy. Rather, the monetary sector is merely added on to an already-existing real sector and does not modify it in any way.

Irving Fisher's approach was more complex than this suggests since he distinguished between transactions related to national income and those related to financial transactions:

$$MV = P_y Y + P_f F \tag{3.3}$$

where Y and F are income and financial transactions respectively. If we accept this, and still require T to be exogenous and entirely unrelated to M, we must assume that financial transactions only take place in the pursuit of real ends. That is, there are no purely financial transactions — a difficult assumption to maintain even in the 18th century and clearly impossible amidst the speculative behaviour in modern financial markets. This distinction has largely been ignored since Fisher's time. Indeed, most textbook versions of Fisher's statement have replaced T with Y, excluding the financial sector from consideration.

A further complexity arises if we pay attention to the precise meaning of M.

M was initially limited to currency (in modern terms, the monetary base or high-powered money) but was later extended to include bank deposits:

$$M_C \overline{V_C} + M_D + \overline{V_D} = P\overline{T} \tag{3.4}$$

where the subscripts C and D indicate currency and bank deposits respectively. M_C is the monetary base. V_C and V_D are assumed to have different values and so variations in M_C / M_D lead to changes in P. As long as M_C/M is constant (people hold a constant proportion of their money holdings in the form of currency), the extension to bank deposits does not change the result. Although this formulation allows us to consider the possibility of a change in M undesired by the authorities, even if they were totally in control of M_C, the Quantity Theory has not been used as a vehicle for the examination of the relationship between the monetary base and the money stock. According to Fisher, an increase in M_C caused prices to rise and hence real interest rates to fall. This led to an increase in demand for bank loans and an increase in M_D. Nominal interest rates were pushed up until the real rate of interest returned to its initial level.

Although V is usually written as a constant, it is affected by changes in the financial system, in particular by changes in the form in which income is received and payments are made. Thus, V changes over time (and is different from one economy to another) but if we accept that the financial system changes only gradually, we should expect changes in V to happen only slowly. We should also be able to predict quite accurately the direction in which V is likely to move. A standard list of the factors likely to influence velocity in the Quantity Theory approach is provided in box 3.1. As we stress there the most important assumption is that the nature of the financial system is not influenced by changes in M.

Since T is determined in the real sector, it is influenced by changes in the availability of resources, technology and the skills of the labour force, and grows steadily over time.

Pause for thought 3.1

Does it matter, within the Quantity Theory, how rapidly V and T change?

The Quantity Theory is, in essence, a long-run theory. We can accept that changes in M might cause short-run changes in V and T during the transition to a new equilibrium without disturbing the central message of the approach. All this requires is that V and T are independent of M in the long run and that M is fully controlled by the monetary authorities.

There is no need within the theory to analyse the demand for money since it is clear that the only reason for holding money balances is to undertake transactions. There is also no role for interest rates except during the period of transition to the new equilibrium. The interest rate, like T, is determined in the real sector of the economy. What can we say about the meaning of M in the theory? Plainly, it assumes the existence of a clearly defined set of assets (currency and bank deposits), which can be used to undertake transactions but has no other role in the economy. But we know nothing else except that it is fully controlled by the monetary authorities.

Box 3.1: Velocity in the Quantity Theory of Money (QTM)

We are concerned in the QTM with the transactions velocity of money — the relationship between the flow of goods and services exchanged in a period and the stock of money. We can write this

as: $\dfrac{P\bar{T}}{M}$

We have said that V changes slowly over time as the financial system changes. But what types of changes in the financial system are relevant to the size of V? A standard list of such changes reads:

   (a)   the frequency with which income is received;
   (b)   expenditure patterns and the timing of payments;
   (c)   the degree of vertical integration of industry; and
   (d)   the extent to which credit is used.

We wish to know how much money people need to hold on average over a period in order to finance the exchange of a given quantity of goods and services. The more money they need to hold, the lower velocity will be. How does each of the points listed above fit in with this?

(a)   We assume people receive income in the form of money — either cash or direct payments into a sight deposit at a bank. Much depends on what alternatives are available for the holding of wealth in relatively liquid but income-earning form. Can people easily move part of their income from money balances into income-earning assets and be able to convert those assets into money when they wish to enter into exchange? The frequency with which income is received is only a small part of what is involved here. Still, other things being equal, we might expect that people are more likely to hold lower average balances of money if they receive their incomes in larger amounts less frequently. Issues of this kind are discussed in section 3.4. Of course, much depends on the definition we use of M (see section 1.5 on official definitions of money).

(b)   Given the possibility of moving from money to income-earning assets and back, the amount of money people need to hold on average is influenced by the frequency with which they undertake transactions or have to pay for them — *ceteris paribus*, the less often they spend, the less money they need to hold on average.

(c)   Some transactions occur for which money is not needed because they take place *within* a firm — the firm is vertically integrated. The exchange is recorded in the books of the various parts of the firm but settlement in money might never occur or occur only infrequently as a net figure.

(d)   This follows on from the second part of (b) — the frequency of payment. The greater availability of credit allows exchange to occur but payment to be postponed.

The replacement of T by Y in the Quantity Theory equation implied that real income was a constant proportion of transactions and, as we mentioned above, excluded financial transactions from consideration. This undermined much of the logic of the original Quantity Theory,[3] accepting, as we shall see, the same logic as the Cambridge approach and the later portfolio models of the demand for money. In these, the central question is why people wish to hold part of their real resources (real income, wealth) in the form of money, a question which did not arise in Fisher's version of the Quantity Theory.

Endogenous money and the Quantity Theory

From one point of view, it makes little sense to talk of endogenous money in conjunction with the Quantity Theory since exogenous money was one of its central assumptions. However, it is worth recalling here the point we made in section 2.4 that if M is not controlled by the authorities, the causal direction of the relationship is reversed. Changes occur in the economy that lead to a change in the demand for bank loans. This, in turn, changes the level of bank deposits and, hence, M. Endogenous money is one, but as we shall see below not the only, way of undermining the conventional conclusions of the Quantity Theory.

Pause for thought 3.2:

Answer the following questions (based on box 3.1):

What is likely to happen to the size of V if:

(a)   people start to make much greater use of credit cards?

(b)   there is a wave of mergers among firms leading to greater vertical integration of industry?

(c)   many people who used to pay gas, electricity and telephone bills each quarter, now do so by monthly direct debit payments?

(d)   instead of buying fresh food daily from their local markets, people buy frozen food in major shopping expeditions once a month?

(e)   people, who used to receive their salaries once a week in cash are now paid monthly directly into their bank accounts?

The Quantity Theory and rates of change

We have told the story here in the traditional way in terms of the money stock and price levels. In a growing economy, however, it makes more sense to talk of rates of change. None of the argument is altered thereby. The central message of the

Quantity Theory is then that changes in the rate of growth of the money supply determine the rate of inflation. Putting a dot over a variable to represent the percentage rate of change, in growth rates the QTM appears as:

$$\dot{M} + \dot{V} = \dot{P} + \dot{Y} \tag{3.5}$$

The Cambridge cash balance approach

The Cambridge cash balance approach, which first appeared in the UK towards the end of the 19th century, attempted to cast the Quantity Theory into the form of demand and supply analysis, which was becoming prominent in other areas of economics. An assumption of a change in an exogenous money supply clearly prompted a question about the demand for money. An increase in the money supply, *ceteris paribus*, disturbs the equilibrium in the money market and the consequent change must continue until the demand for money increases to the new level of the money supply. It then becomes natural to ask why people choose to hold money.

One might still answer this question in terms of the role played by money in exchange, but demand is essentially a subjective concept and the analysis of demand allows psychological factors as well as institutional arrangements to be considered. In all of the several versions of the Cambridge approach, people wish to hold a part of their real resources in the form of money (thus the concern is with the real value of money demanded):

$$\frac{M_d}{P} = kw \tag{3.6}$$

where M_d is the demand for money; w = real resources (wealth); and k (the Cambridge k) expresses the relationship between them. That is, it is a relationship between two stocks (of money and of resources) rather than a relationship between a stock and a flow as in the Fisher version of the Quantity Theory.

The definition of real resources varied but was always a long run concept, retaining an important element of the Classical model.[4] In long-run equilibrium, savings, rather than being held as money, are invested leading to an increase in the economy's resources. The individual's demand for money depends on:

(a) the convenience and feeling of security obtained from holding money;

(b) the expectations and total resources of the individual; and

(c) the opportunity costs of holding money.

The nature of the financial system, which determines V in the Quantity Theory appears here only as an element in (a) and (c).

Since the convenience obtained from holding money derives from its functions as a medium of exchange and store of value, it was still possible to think of k as a constant and to draw the same policy message as that coming from the Fisher version of the Quantity Theory. This can be seen by formally comparing the two. We begin with the Cambridge equation:

$$M_d = kPw \qquad (3.7)$$

Firstly, we need to convert the stock of resources into a flow of output. Since output is produced from the economy's stock of resources and since both theories related to long-term equilibrium, we can assume w/T constant. Thus, let

$$w = c\bar{T} \qquad (3.8)$$

giving us
$$M_d = kPc\bar{T} \qquad (3.9)$$

and
$$Md.\frac{1}{ck} = P\bar{T} \qquad (3.10)$$

With c and k both constant, we can define Fisher's V as the inverse of ck and write:

$$M_d\bar{V} = P\bar{T} \qquad (3.11)$$

Finally, we assume the money market to be in equilibrium with $M_d = M_s$. Thus,

$$M\bar{V} = P\bar{T} \qquad (3.12)$$

The two versions of the Quantity Theory appear very similar. In both, as long as money is exogenous, increases in the price level result from an excess supply of money. The demand for money function in the Cambridge version is stably related to w and, hence, to T.

Nonetheless, there are important differences between the Quantity Theory and the Cambridge approach.[5] Firstly, the Cambridge approach makes use of marginal analysis and extends the general neo-classical model to the money market. It is, thus, a forerunner of the later portfolio models of Milton Friedman and James Tobin dealt with below.

Secondly, the factors influencing V in the Fisher version are only a subset of those influencing k in the Cambridge version. The inclusion of the opportunity cost in the Cambridge version makes k potentially more subject to short-term change than is V. The possibility at least exists that people might choose to hold money for purposes other than engaging in the exchange of goods and services. Crucially, it gave a potential role to the rate of interest. Keynes, as early as 1923 in *A Tract on Monetary Reform* (JMK Vol IV), showed how the incorporation of inflationary expectations could produce changes in the price level, in the absence of changes in the money stock. In *A Treatise on Money* (1930 and JMK Vols V and VI), he argued that changing expectations regarding security prices might cause changes in nominal interest rates. In *A Treatise*, his price equation did not include the money stock at all. The opportunity cost of holding money was assuming greater importance.

3.3   *The General Theory* and the demand for money

Keynes's (1936) theory of the demand for money as treated in macroeconomic text books is widely known. It is a part of his general model, which deals with the determination of short-run income, output, and employment. In terms of the Fisher equation, T is replaced by Y (income), but Y is subject to change since it is endogenous - the real and monetary sectors of the economy are interdependent. The assumption that money is neutral is removed.

The analysis of the monetary sector dealt only with financial assets and was limited to two such assets: money and non-maturing, fixed-interest-rate bonds (consols). This limited choice of assets arises because, in a simple Keynesian model, savers (households) and investors (firms) are separate: households do not own firms and do not invest. Saving is defined as the difference between current disposable income and consumption expenditure. The purchase of real assets by households is part of consumption expenditure rather than a form of saving. Savings are held in the form of money or other financial assets. The plans of investors, on the other hand, are typically long-term. They seek to raise funds for investment by selling fixed-interest long-term bonds to households. The bond market acts as a vital link between the money market and the goods market.

> ## Pause for thought 3.3:
>
> Why might Keynes have assumed only two types of financial assets when we all know that there are many others? Does this form of simplification seriously damage a model in the analysis of events in real world economies?

Three motives are distinguished for holding money: the transactions, precautionary and speculative motives. The first two are related to current consumption expenditure and, following on from Keynes's theory of the consumption function, their principal determinant is current income.

There is a precautionary demand for money because people do not know exactly what their consumption expenditure in the current period will be. The transactions demand for money depends on their consumption expenditure plans, but, in an uncertain world, their plans may not be fulfilled. *Ex-post* (actual) consumption and saving may differ from their *ex-ante* (planned) values, requiring the quantity of money needed for transactions ex-post to differ from the planned level. When planned saving is less than planned investment, income rises, causing actual saving and consumption to be higher than planned. The quantity of money needed to undertake consumption is higher than if people's plans had been fulfilled. Equally, when planned investment is lower than planned saving, actual consumption is less than planned consumption and money held for transactions purposes will lie idle. However, the costs of holding too little money are likely to be greater than those of holding too much money, causing people to hold precautionary balances.

Pause for thought 3.4:

What are the likely costs of holding lower money balances than those needed for transactions purposes?

There are, thus, two effects of lack of certainty about the level of consumption on the income velocity of money: (a) more money will be held on average to finance a given value of transactions, causing V to be lower on average than it would otherwise be; and (b) in a recession, V will be lower still. The precautionary demand for money alone allows us to predict that the income velocity of money will move pro-cyclically, rising during booms and falling as income falls in recessions.

Despite its importance, the precautionary demand for money is usually elided with the transactions demand for money as:

$$L_1 = kY \qquad (3.13)$$

where L_1 stands for the demand for money for transactions and precautionary motives (active money balances), Y is nominal income, while k expresses the relationship between active money balances and nominal income and is assumed constant. Figure 3.1 shows the demand curve for active money balances. There is no particular role for the rate of interest here. It could be one of many parameters underlying the demand for active money balances and, thus, changes in the interest rate might cause shifts in the curve.

In *The General Theory*, the principal relationship between the demand for money and interest rates derived from the third motive — the speculative demand for money (the demand for idle balances). This provides an argument for an inverse and unstable relationship between interest rate and the demand for money and hence an inverse and unstable relationship between the money stock and the income velocity of money. To understand this relationship, we must consider the choice households face in allocating their savings between money and bonds. Money pays no interest but is free of risk; the reverse is true for bonds. In deciding whether to hold bonds, market agents must compare the interest rate payable on bonds with the risk of capital loss in holding them. This requires a decision regarding the likely future bond price. In the case of bonds that never mature, this depends entirely on the relationship between the rate of interest payable on bonds currently held and the expected interest rate on bonds to be issued in the future.

Figure3.1: Demand for active money balances

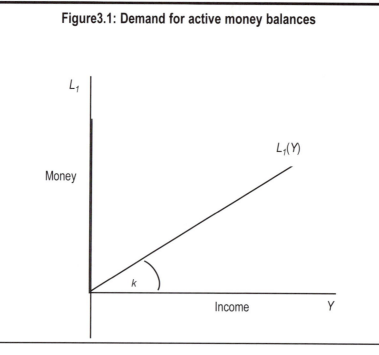

Keynes assumed that at any time each person held a view of the likely interest rate in the economy; that is, of the interest rate he regarded as 'normal'. When the interest rate was at this normal rate, a person would be happy with his present holdings of bonds and money and have no incentive to switch from one to the other. When a person thought the current interest rate to be below the normal rate, he would anticipate a rise in interest rates and a fall in bond prices and would switch from bonds to money. The reverse would apply when the current rate was thought to be above the normal rate. In other words, people were assumed to hold regressive expectations.

At any time, the current rate would be below the normal rate of some people and above the normal rate of others. Thus, some people would be switching from bonds to money, some would be moving in the opposite direction, while others would be content with their existing position. For the market as a whole, the average view of the normal rate was important since if the current rate were below this average view, more people would wish to switch from bonds to money than the reverse. The bond price would fall and the interest rate rise until equilibrium was restored.

Pause for thought 3.5:

How important is the expected future interest rate in the explanation of the price of bonds that mature:
(a) in 2028?
(b) in 2018?
(c) in 2013?
(d) at the end of 2009?
How does your answer to (a) differ from that to (d)?

It would also be true that, given an existing set of individually-held views of the normal rate, a fall in the current rate of interest would lead to an increase in the proportion of people believing the current interest rate to be too low and would increase the number of people wishing to switch into money. That is, falls in interest rate, *ceteris paribus*, cause an increase in the demand for money.

We can now complete the picture. Starting from a position of equilibrium in the money and bonds markets, an unanticipated increase in the supply of money causes interest rates to fall and this causes the demand for money to increase. That is, part of the increased supply of money is held in the form of increased speculative money balances. Let us consider this in terms of a modified form of the Fisher equation:

$$\bar{M}V_Y = PY \tag{3.14}$$

where V_Y is the income velocity of money. M is under the control of the monetary authorities as before. An increase in the money supply pushes down the rate of interest and causes an increase in speculative money balances. Since this is unrelated to current income, V_Y falls. This weakens the impact of the increase in M on the left-hand side of the equation. By how much does V_Y fall? This is difficult to say since we do not have any information about the views held by people of the normal rate of interest. However, when interest rates were low, V_Y might fall considerably - the interest elasticity of the demand for money would be high — since few people would think it likely that they would fall further. Many people would, indeed, anticipate a rise in interest rates and a fall in bond prices. The demand for speculative or idle balances (L_2) can be written as:

$$L_2 = f(i) \tag{3.15}$$

where i is the rate of interest. This negative relationship between the interest rate and the demand for money is shown in figure 3.2.

Of even greater importance than the existence of a perhaps powerful negative relationship between the interest rate and the demand for money is the question of the *stability* of the curve. Although each person holds his own view of the normal rate of interest, this must be heavily influenced by his estimate of the views held by other people in the market. Although he might see no objective reason for interest rates to rise, he will know that if sufficient people believe it is going to rise, bond sales will increase and bond prices fall. The most important information to have about a market is what other market participants think and are likely to do. Views of the normal rate of interest are, thus, highly subjective and open to change.

Consider the impact of a change in the average view of the normal rate. We start with the current rate of interest equal to the average view of the normal rate and assume that the average view changes in favour of a higher normal rate. This would cause many people to believe that the current rate was likely to rise and to seek to switch out of bonds into money. Since the current rate has not changed, we can only represent this in figure 3.2 by shifting the curve to the right. With an unchanged money supply, the demand for idle balances would increase and V_Y would fall, causing a fall in P_Y. If views regarding the normal rate were at all volatile, the speculative demand for money curve would be unstable.

Figure 3.2: The demand for idle balances

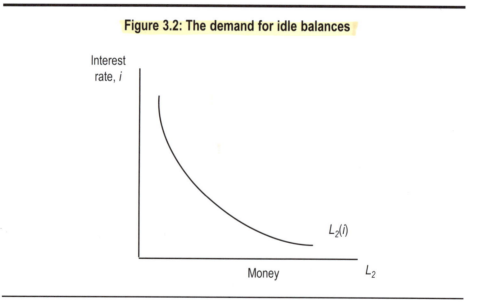

Even without this possible instability, the theory of the speculative demand suggests that the supply of money and the demand for money are not independent of each other. An increase in the supply of money pushes interest rates down and this encourages an increase in the quantity of money demanded because of the movement of the current rate away from the normal rate.

Keynes's motives approach was for many years the standard theory of the demand for money, although there were important differences from the version given here. In the standard version, the demand curve for speculative balances was linear, which does not allow for the possibility that the demand for money might be much more interest elastic at low rates of interest. In addition, the normal rate of interest was assumed constant, removing the possibility of unpredictable shifts in the demand for idle balances. Thirdly, the role of the bond market in providing investment funds for firms was ignored. Falls in interest rates were assumed to increase investment but the question of how this investment was to be financed was not tackled.

This accounts for a fourth motive for demanding money (the *finance motive*), which Keynes did not include in *The General Theory* but proposed later. The finance motive applies to any large, non-routine expenditure but the need to finance investment projects is crucial. The demand for money to meet such expenditure is only temporary and may be met by the sale of liquid assets or by borrowing from banks. It is of some importance because it provides an additional argument for instability in the demand for money since Keynes argued that investment plans were volatile, being much influenced by the level of confidence of firms.[6]

In summary, Keynes's writings suggest that the demand for money varies inversely with the rate of interest (or, if interest is paid on money balances, with the difference between the interest payable on financial assets and that payable on money balances). In addition, the demand for money curve might shift with changes in expectations about future interest rates and with the need to meet unpredictable expenditure including the financing of investment projects.

Keynes's approach to the demand for money was, then, radically different from anything that preceded it, however much its origins can be traced in the works of earlier writers or in his own earlier ideas. Firstly, we are concerned with nominal money balances. Secondly, we have an analysis of short-term *disequilibrium*. Because of this, the demand for money may be highly interest elastic (especially in periods of falling interest rates) and the demand for money function might be unstable.

In *The General Theory*, Keynes continued to assume an exogenous money supply but his approach to the demand for money produced quite different views about the usefulness of monetary policy, especially for an economy experiencing a depression. An expansion of the money supply causing interest rates to fall might cause the demand for money to rise rather than leading to an increase in income in the economy. With an unstable demand for money, the monetary authorities could not have a clear idea of the impact of an increase in the exogenous monetary policy. It followed that fiscal policy might be a much more effective way than monetary policy for governments to pull economies out of depression. This appeared to justify a much larger direct role for governments in the management of the economy. It is hardly surprising that the theory was much criticised. The most common criticisms are summarised in box 3.2.

Box 3.2: Common criticisms of Keynes's speculative demand for money

1. The theory of portfolio choice is incorrect - the speculative demand implies that people hold all money or all bonds, depending on what they believe is likely to happen to the rate of interest in the future. They do not do this in practice.

2. The assumption of regressive expectations is unrealistic.

3. The normal rate of interest is exogenous and no explanation is given of what determines it.

4. The restriction to only two assets - money and consols - is too limiting.

5. The liquidity trap is a logical impossibility since not everyone can switch from bonds to money - someone must hold the existing stock of bonds.

6. Savings deposits should not be included in the money stock.

The first criticism concentrates on portfolio choice. In Keynes's theory, any expectation that the interest rate is about to change causes people to hold either all money or all bonds. A belief that the interest rate is about to rise (and bond prices to fall) causes a switch entirely out of bonds into money. The reverse case, an expectation of an interest rate fall, causes people to switch entirely into bonds in order to make the expected capital gain. But rational behaviour dictates portfolio diversification and the holding of a mixture of bonds and money. It is clearly unrealistic, at a microeconomic level, for a fear of a fall in bond prices to cause a switch entirely from bonds to money (and *vice versa*).

This is particularly objectionable to economists who wish to construct macroeconomic models on microeconomic foundations, a view that implies that the behaviour of the economy as a whole can be analysed only as the sum of individual activity. However, treating the economy as the sum of a set of microeconomic decisions might cause us to misunderstand important aspects of the macro economy.

It is certainly possible to construct a macroeconomic model that has unrealistic microeconomic assumptions but still produces an accurate analysis of the behaviour of households as a group. In this case, since people hold different views of the normal rate of interest, at any time some people will be moving to holding all bonds, others to holding all money. Yet, as we have seen, a fall in the rate of interest causes a net increase in the demand for money. As long as this increased preference for money over bonds as interest rates fall happens in practice, Keynes's model produces the correct macroeconomic outcome, even if it fails to describe accurately what individual agents do. In any case, the criticism can be handled by increasing the number of financial assets in the model, a point we consider below.

Pause for thought 3.6:

Why does rational portfolio behaviour lead to the holding of a mixture of bonds and money rather than all bonds or all money?

The second criticism concerns the assumption of regressive expectations and the lack of explanation of how each agent forms his view of the normal rate of interest. In practice, many examples can be found in markets of extrapolative expectations — where a change in price causes people to believe that the price will continue to move in the same direction. Thus, the assumption of regressive expectations may seem unreasonable. More importantly, since there is no explanation of how people decide on the normal rate, there is no way of analysing the factors that might cause it to change. Again, since people hold different views of the normal rate, we cannot distinguish a clear set of market expectations other than to say, as we have above, that the lower the current interest rate is, the more people are likely to think that the next move will be up. This provides an explanation of the negative relationship between interest rates and the demand for money but gives no indication of the steepness of that slope or of whether the money demand curve is likely to be stable.

However, the assumption of exogenous expectations is important since it explains why market participants can only guess at what other market participants might do in response to a change in interest rates. This unpredictability of the market lies at the heart of the argument for an unstable demand for money. If we knew how market participants formed their views of the normal rate of interest, we would be able to predict accurately how the market was going to behave and the speculative element in the demand for money would disappear.

Thus, the criticism of the normal rate of interest ignores the world to which Keynes's theory applies — one of disequilibrium in which uncertainty is endemic, with knowledge of the future being 'fluctuating, vague and uncertain'.[7] It is not a world in which meaningful probabilities can be assigned to all possible outcomes. Since expectations are subject to sudden change from panic fears and rumours, they cannot be modelled formally as an endogenous variable. Thus, changes in expectations regarding interest rates cause changes in the demand for money (and the demand for bonds), and produce shifts in the demand for money curve.

Further, in the complex world of market psychology, in which much depends on how people think other people will act, many possibilities arise. For example, the majority feeling in the market following an interest rate fall may temporarily be that the interest rate will continue to fall (extrapolative expectations). Nonetheless, everyone will be aware that at some point people will begin to sell bonds in order to realise their capital gains. This is more likely the lower the rate of interest currently is. Everyone will wish to sell out before the market turns, although the attempt to do this will cause bond prices to stop rising and the interest rate to stop falling. Indeed, the fact that the interest rate is changing may, in itself, cause expectations regarding the future rate to change. The idea of regressive expectations based on a normal rate of interest provides a shorthand way of expressing the macroeconomic outcome of a complex set of market interactions. To criticise it as an inadequate theory of microeconomic behaviour is to misjudge its purpose.

Pause for thought 3.7:

In football programmes on television, viewers are sometimes asked to choose the best three goals of the month in order. In fact, to win, a viewer must guess correctly what the judges think were the best three goals. Does this provide a good analogy with market behaviour — that what people in markets do is to try to guess what other people think rather than to attempt to understand underlying real forces?

Another common criticism relates to the limitation of choice to two types of asset leaving us with only one rate of interest. Gowland (1991) points to the existence of a large number of capital-certain assets, such as building society deposits, whose value does not vary with interest rates. He argues that people not wishing to hold bonds may hold these assets instead of money and that Keynes's theory is a theory of the demand for short-term capital-certain assets in general rather than a theory specifically of the demand for money.

However, Keynes's choice of two assets at the extremes of the spectrum of degrees of liquidity of financial assets was not intended as a realistic description of financial markets but as a means of clarifying important issues. In particular, we have seen that the two-asset model derives in part from the separation of households from firms. In relation to these issues, the inclusion of a variety of financial assets lying between money and bonds on the liquidity spectrum does not change the analysis.

UK firms no longer raise a significant proportion of investment funds through the long-term bond market. Allowing for this merely transfers some of the uncertainty associated with changing interest rates from households to firms. Assume, for instance, that firms borrow investment funds short-term from banks at variable interest rates. Now, any fear of future interest rate rises increases firms' estimates of the likely costs of investment funds and reduces their demand for them. As the government increases the monetary base of the economy, banks may be more willing to lend, but firms become less willing to borrow. Firms accumulating profits for future investment are influenced in their decisions regarding the deployment of their savings in the same way as are households.

Fear of a rising interest rate leads them to prefer greater liquidity and they are more likely to hold funds in the form of money or short-term securities than to invest in plant and equipment.

The final criticism is aimed not at the theory as a whole but at the *liquidity trap* — the extreme state in which any increase in the money stock is held as specula-tive (idle) balances. In a liquidity trap, therefore, any increase in the money sup-ply has no impact on the interest rate and hence no impact on aggregate demand. A liquidity trap, then, implies the existence of a minimum rate of interest for the economy — a rate that is so low that everyone thinks the next interest rate move must be up.

Therefore, everyone believes that bond prices will fall and no one wishes to hold bonds. Everyone switches from bonds to money; but this must involve a fal-lacy of composition because it is not possible for everyone to hold money rather than bonds. Someone must hold the existing stock of bonds. Gowland (1991) argues further that the bond market will always be in equilibrium (because of low transactions costs and zero storage costs) and that, in the aggregate, it will not be possible for investors to exchange bonds for money. A general expectation that interest rates will fall causes an increased demand for bonds, a rise in bond prices and a fall in interest rates but, at the end of the process, the same quantity of bonds is held as before. Thus, the theory of the speculative demand for money explains who holds money not the quantity of money held. However, this prob-lem also disappears if we assume an uncertain world in which disequilibrium is the normal state of affairs. Then, we could imagine a situation in which all bond-holders were *attempting* to sell but could not find buyers. In any case, the liquid-ity trap represents the extreme theoretical position of the model rather than being a position likely to be reached by any economy.

3.4   Interest rates and the transactions demand for money

The criticisms of Keynes's theory led economists to find other ways of justifying some of Keynes's message, in particular the inverse relationship between interest rates and the demand for money. One approach was to return to the transactions demand for money and to show how this could be influenced by changes in inter-est rates. The best-known model of this kind is the Baumol/Tobin *inventory-theo-retic model* (Baumol, 1952; Tobin, 1956).

In this model, balances set aside for transactions purposes are held temporar-ily in the form of securities, which may be converted into money when needed to purchase goods and services. The demand for money is then influenced nega-tively by changes in the interest rate payable on short-term securities and posi-tively by changes in the transactions costs (brokerage fees, transport costs, incon-venience) in the conversion of money into bonds and back again. All information regarding interest rates and transactions costs is known with certainty.

The model seeks to determine how often it is worthwhile switching between money and income-earning assets within a single payments period. From this, we can calculate the optimum stock of money to be held on average over the period. The model assumes that income is received at a steady rate and is all spent during the period.

Let the transactions costs of buying a financial asset be called a. Switching from money into bonds and back into money costs $2a$. Let i_b be the annual yield on the bond. Let income $Y = £1000$ per month, n is the total number of transactions undertaken. Income is spent evenly through the month at £250 per week. Assume firstly that the transactions costs are zero.

In week 1, £250 (Y/n) is held as money and the remaining £750 is used to acquire interest-bearing assets. Then, in each of weeks 2, 3 and 4, £250 worth of the securities is cashed to finance expenditure. Thus, four transactions are involved ($n = 4$). The formula for the initial holding of the asset is:

$$\frac{(n-1)}{n}.Y = \left[\frac{(4-1)}{4}\right].£1000 = £750 \qquad (3.16)$$

To find the return from holding bonds over the month we need to find the average holding of bonds over the period. Given our assumption of equal expenditure in each week, this is always half of the initial bond holding $\{[(n-1)/2n].Y\}$. In our simple example here, the holding of bonds is £750 in week 1, £500 in week 2, £250 in week 3 and zero in week 4, an average of £375. The profit (π) from holding bonds over the period can be expressed as:

$$\pi = \left[\frac{(n-1)}{2n}\right].Yi_b \qquad (3.17)$$

Now, allow for transactions costs. If a is a fixed cost, the total costs of n transactions $= na$ and the net profit from holding assets becomes:

$$\pi = \left[\frac{(n-1)}{2n}\right].Yi_b - na \qquad (3.18)$$

$$= \left[\frac{Yi_b}{2}\right] - \left[\frac{Yi_b}{2n}\right] - na \qquad (3.19)$$

$$= \left[\frac{Yi_b}{2}\right] - \left[\frac{Yi_b.n^{-1}}{2}\right] - na \qquad (3.20)$$

The next problem is to find the number of transactions (n^*) that maximises the net return. To do this, we differentiate (3.20) with respect to n and set the resultant derivative equal to zero:

$$\frac{\partial \pi}{\partial n} = \frac{\left(n^{-2}.Yi_b\right)}{2} - a = 0 \tag{3.21}$$

$$\frac{Yi_b}{2n^2} - a = 0 \tag{3.22}$$

and

$$\frac{Yi_b}{2n^2} = a \tag{3.23}$$

$$n^2 = \frac{Yi_b}{2a} \tag{3.24}$$

Therefore

$$n^* = \sqrt{\frac{Yi_b}{2a}} \tag{3.25}$$

This gives the formula for the optimum holding of cash balances (M_T). On the assumption that expenditure occurs smoothly over each week, the average holding of money is half that held at the beginning of each week ($Yi_b/2n$) and:

$$M_T = \frac{Y}{2n^*} = \frac{Y}{2.\sqrt{\frac{Yi_b}{2a}}} = \sqrt{\frac{Ya}{2i_b}} \tag{3.26}$$

Thus, the transactions demand for money is inversely related to the interest rate. Further, the demand for money increases less than proportionately to increases in Y. That is, there are economies of scale in holding money, and to return the economy to equilibrium following an increase in the money stock (assuming that there is only a transactions demand for money), income must increase more than in proportion to the increase in money supply. It follows that an exogenous increase in the money stock (if it were to happen) would have a greater impact on economic activity than it would if there were no economies of scale in holding money.

However, the extent of economies of scale depends on the nature of the costs involved. If we assume costs to consist of a fixed and a variable element ($a + bE$) where E is the amount withdrawn each time, the formula becomes:

$$\sqrt{\left[\frac{Ya}{2i_b}\right].\left[1 + \frac{2b}{i_b}\right] + 2Y.\left[\frac{b}{i_b}\right]^2} \tag{3.27}$$

This considerably reduces the economies of scale involved. With fully proportional costs, they disappear altogether.

In general, the model predicts:

(a) a (real) income elasticity of demand for money between 0.5 (fixed transactions costs) and 1.0 (proportional costs);

(b) an interest rate elasticity between -0.5 (fixed costs) and -2.0 (proportional costs); and

(c) nominal money balances increasing proportionately with prices.

The principal ways in which the basic model has been qualified are listed in box 3.3.[8]

Pause for thought 3.8:

If the transactions demand for money is interest elastic, how does an increase in interest rate affect the demand curve for active balances in figure 3.1?

The empirical relevance of the model has often been questioned. The earliest attacks were in relation to the demand for money of firms.[9] It has also been argued that the possible gains for an individual are so small relative to the costs (especially if the value of time is taken into account) that the rational individual would not bother switching into bonds and back again.[10] In general, there seems little doubt that the relationship between money, interest rates, and transactions is more complex than in the Baumol/Tobin model. Nonetheless, it retains theoretical significance because of its generation of an inverse relationship between interest rate and the demand for money despite the assumption of perfect certainty.

3.5   Introducing uncertainty into transactions-models of the precautionary motive

Inventory models have been modified to allow for uncertainty in the form of a known probability distribution of receipts and payments. These models introduce the possibility of net payments exceeding money holdings (illiquidity). Results vary a good deal depending on how likely this is assumed to be but, as in transactions models, mean holdings of money are inversely related to interest rates and directly related to the brokerage fee. Miller and Orr's version (1966, 1968), contains thresholds, with people only changing from money to bonds or vice versa at upper or lower thresholds of money balances. This is an idea we shall return to in section 3.8 when we look at the buffer stock theory of the demand for money. Milbourne (1986) took the Miller-Orr framework and considered within it the impact of financial innovation on monetary aggregates.

Box 3.3: The principal variations on the inventory-theoretic model of the transactions demand for money

(i) With fixed or partly fixed transactions costs, a person does not hold securities at all unless the interest income is greater than the transactions costs of converting money into and out of bonds. Then, a change in interest rate may not cause any change in the demand for money. The inverse relationship between interest rate and the demand for money that the model seeks to demonstrate disappears at low rates of interest.

(ii) The frequency of pay periods and the timing of payments may be influenced by institutional and technical changes (for example, the use of credit cards) and by economic factors such as high and variable interest rates.

(iii) Only the interest rate on bonds is included in the model; but if a firm can use an overdraft facility to obtain money, the relevant rate is the difference between the rate charged on borrowings on overdraft and the rate paid on bonds. Again, the demand for money depends on the relative interest rate if the model is extended to include an interest rate or an implicit interest rate (in the form of bank services provided below cost) on holdings of money.

(iv) The transactions demand for money may be modelled such that money holdings are only deliberately adjusted when they reach upper or lower thresholds.

(v) Individuals can be allowed to save part of their income, acquiring interest-bearing assets for holding long-term as well as for short-term reasons.

(vi) Once it is accepted that some people but not others make money/bonds/money conversions with transactions balances, aggregation problems arise. It can then be shown that almost any elasticity is possible depending on the propensity to save and the proportion of income earned by those who do not make any conversions.

The formal inclusion of interest rates into the precautionary demand for money adds further to the case for an inverse relationship between interest rate and the demand for money, without suggesting that the demand for money function might be unstable.

3.6   Tobin's portfolio model of the demand for money

Tobin's model (1958, 1969) can be seen as a response to the common criticisms of the speculative demand model. It introduces a wider range of assets including equities and real assets. Where, in his 1958 article, Tobin limits himself to the same choice as in Keynes, that between money and bonds, he seeks to remove the apparent dependence on the assumption of regressive expectations and to have each individual holding a mixture of money and bonds. Thus, the model is very much concerned with microeconomic choice behaviour. It is generally regarded as a Keynesian model because the model preserves the possibility of an inverse relationship between the rate of interest and the demand for money and because the transmission link between money and nominal income is indirect — money only influences nominal income through changes in interest rate, rather than directly. However, it also produces a demand for money function that is very likely to be stable and so removes the third of the characteristics of the speculative demand model listed above. For this reason, it can be argued to be a misrepresentation of Keynes's ideas (Chick, 1977; Dow and Earl, 1982).

To consider the nature of the demand for money in Tobin's model, we need to concentrate on the choice between money and bonds. This depends on a trade-off between the net income receivable on bonds and the degree of risk associated with the total portfolio of bonds and money (which is assumed to be perfectly liquid and non-interest-bearing). The trade-off arises because Tobin assumes people in general to be risk-averse, although it is possible to investigate the effect of an assumption that people are risk-lovers. However, because the general uncertainty prevalent in Keynes's model has disappeared, interest rates are thought to be equally likely to rise or fall, irrespective of both the current level of interest rates and what has happened to them in the recent past: expectations regarding future interest rates are neutral. In these circumstances, the risk associated with bond holding is much more manageable than in Keynes. Now, for any given level of wealth, we can calculate mathematically the impact of a change in interest rate on both the interest income and the capital gain or loss associated with the holding of different quantities of bonds and money. The capital gain/loss becomes a random variable that is normally distributed around the mean, μ. The total return from bond holding (interest payments + capital gain/loss) is also normally distributed around μ. The standard deviation is used as the measure of risk. The various assumptions are reflected in figure 3.3.

In the upper part of the diagram, the vertical axis shows the expected return on portfolios while the degree of risk associated with the portfolio is on the horizontal axis. The ray from the origin shows the relationship between risk and return for a given level of interest rate on portfolios composed of different proportions of bonds and money. Thus, a portfolio consisting entirely of money is located at the origin, with a zero return and no risk. As the proportion of bonds in the portfolio increases, so do both the degree of risk and the expected return from the portfolio.

Figure 3.3: Possible composition of portfolios

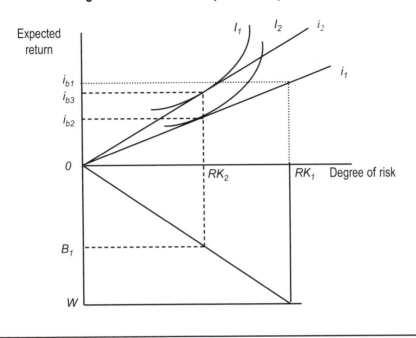

The possible compositions of the portfolio are shown in the lower part of the diagram where $0W$ is the total (fixed) value of the portfolio. The proportion of bonds held in the portfolio is measured down from the origin along the vertical axis. Thus, at the origin, the portfolio contains no bonds, at W no money. The ray from the origin indicates the amount of risk associated with each possible composition of the portfolio, with the extreme positions of all money and all bonds placing us at 0 and RK_1 respectively along the horizontal axis. We can then see from the upper part of the diagram that, at an interest rate of i_1, an all bonds portfolio produces an expected return of i_{b1} along the vertical axis. A mixed portfolio of, say, $0B_1$ bonds and B_1W money involves risk as shown by RK_2 along the horizontal axis and an expected return of i_{b2}. We can see that an increase in the interest rate to i_2 leaves the risk associated with this portfolio unchanged but raises the expected return to i_{b3}.

To investigate the choice of the optimal portfolio and the way in which this will be affected by changes in the rate of interest, we need to show the trade-off of the market agent between expected return and risk. We do this through the indifference map in the upper part of the diagram, which shows the trade-off of a risk-averse agent. Utility increases as we move up to the left from I_2 to I_1 since on I_2 the same degree of risk produces a higher expected income than on I_1. Utility is maximised where the ray from the origin is tangent to an indifference curve (at P). Since this determines the chosen degree of risk associated with the portfolio, it also determines the division of the portfolio between bonds ($0B_1$) and money (B_1W).

Figure 3.4: The effect of a fall in interest rates

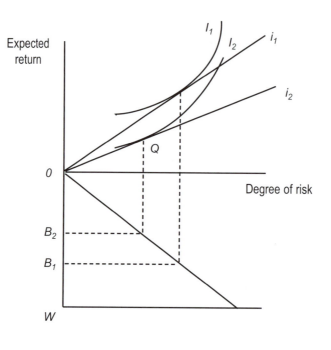

Now we are in a position to consider the impact of an exogenous increase in the money stock. People use excess money balances to buy bonds, causing bond prices to rise and the interest rate to fall: the expected income from any given quantity of bonds falls. The ray in the upper part of the diagram shifts down to the right and (as shown in figure 3.4) the portfolio-holder maximises utility at Q on the lower indifference curve I_2. The outcome depends on the relative strengths of the income and substitution effects of the fall in interest rate. Income falls for each degree of risk of the portfolio. To preserve the previous income level, more bonds must be held (increasing the degree of risk of the portfolio).

The substitution effect operates in the opposite direction since an acceptance of a given amount of extra risk now produces a smaller increase in expected income, making it less worthwhile to choose a higher degree of risk. In figure 3.4, we make the usual assumption that the substitution effect outweighs the income effect so that a fall in interest rate produces a fall in the holding of bonds and an increase in the demand for money. Thus, part of any increase in the money stock is held in the form of idle money balances, reducing the possible impact on nominal income and causing monetary policy to be weaker than it would be otherwise.

Since the outcome for each individual depends on the relative strengths of income and substitution effects and since there may be some risk-lovers in the economy, there is no reason to believe that the demand for money will be highly interest-elastic; nor that the aggregate demand for money curve will be unstable. The curve will only move if there is a widespread change in people's attitude towards the risk associated with holding bonds. However, since the model does not assume any general uncertainty in the economy and since risk is defined as the standard deviation of a normal distribution, this is unlikely. Certainly, there is no possibility of the demand for money curve shifting in response to an increase in the stock of money.[11]

Pause for thought 3.9:

When interest rates rise, is it the income or the substitution effect that causes the demand for money to fall? Why?

Keynesian developments of *The General Theory* helped to restore the view that monetary policy through changes in the money supply (continuing to assume an exogenous money supply) might be useful since, if the demand for money were stable, the monetary authority would at least have a good idea of the likely effectiveness of monetary policy. Nonetheless, Keynesian economics continued to give considerable importance to fiscal policy.

3.7   Monetarism and the demand for money

The term 'monetarism' was first used by Brunner (1968) and has since been defined in a variety of ways. Mayer (1978) identifies twelve propositions associated with monetarism, but we shall be content with his 'narrow meaning' — *the view that changes in the money stock are the principal cause of changes in nominal income.* In line with this, we continue to assume an exogenous money supply and concentrate on Milton Friedman's demand for money. Money is demanded by two groups:

(a) ultimate wealth holders (for whom money is simply one way in which they may hold wealth); and

(b) business enterprises (for whom money is a productive resource).

The theory concentrates on ultimate wealth holders. Their demand for money can be analysed in the same way as the demand for any asset. We can consider the demand for money as a whole rather than needing to consider separate 'motives' for holding money. Thus, the demand for money function contains:

(i) a budget constraint (either permanent income or wealth);

(ii) the prices of the commodity itself (money) and its substitutes and comple-ments (Friedman sees the counterparts of these as being the rates of return on money and other assets);

(iii) other variables determining the utility attached to the services rendered by money relative to those provided by other assets (these may include the degree of economic stability, the variability of inflation, and the volume of trading in existing capital assets);

(iv) tastes and preferences.

When Friedman refers to 'wealth' as the budget constraint, he intends total wealth — the sum of *human* and *non-human* wealth (see section 1.2). Since this is impossible to measure, Friedman suggests the use of permanent income (the expected future stream of income generated by the stock of human and non-human wealth) as a constraint. There is also a theoretical complication with the use of total wealth as a budget constraint since there are institutional restrictions on the conversion of human into non-human wealth and so human wealth is less liquid than non-human wealth. Friedman explains this by saying that it is only possible to buy or sell the services of human wealth, not the wealth itself. Another way of thinking about it is to compare the relative ease of obtaining a bank loan using as collateral: (a) non-human wealth — a portfolio of government bonds, say; and (b) human wealth such as a university degree expected to allow the holder to earn a higher salary in the future. This difference in liquidity between the two forms of wealth means that the composition of wealth influences the demand for money. An increase in human wealth relative to non-human wealth reduces the overall liquidity of wealth and will cause people to hold the non-human proportion of their wealth in a more liquid form than previously. In other words, the demand for money will increase.

Pause for thought 3.10:

Why is it possible only to buy or sell the services of human wealth, not human wealth itself?

Friedman's demand for money function

Putting all this together, we arrive at Friedman's 1970 version of his revised quan-tity theory:[12]

$$\frac{Md}{P} = f\left(Y_p, w, i_m, i_b, i_e, \left(\frac{1}{P}\right)\cdot\frac{dP^e}{dt}, u \right) \qquad (3.28)$$

where:

•P is the price level. It is included because the demand for money is a demand for real balances and a change in P changes the real value of money holdings. Thus, P is positively related to M_d.

•Y_p is permanent income, introduced as a proxy for wealth because of the difficulties involved in measuring wealth. As in Friedman's consumption theory, permanent income was taken as an exponentially weighted average of past and current levels of income. Y_p is positively related to the demand for money.

• w is non-human wealth/wealth and is negatively related to the demand for money.

•i_m is the rate of return on money itself and is positively related to the demand for money.

• i_b is the rate of return on bonds, abstracting from the possibility of capital gains and losses. It is negatively related to the demand for money.

• i_e is the rate of return on equities, abstracting from the effects on equity prices of changes in interest rates and the rate of inflation. It is negatively related to the demand for money.

• $(1/P).dP^e/dt$ is the expected rate of inflation, included as the rate of return on real assets. It is also *negatively* related to the demand for money. Note that the demand for money is positively related to the price level, but negatively related to the expected rate of inflation.

• u is a portmanteau symbol standing for other variables affecting the utility attached to the services of money and also includes tastes and preferences. It may be either negatively or positively related to the demand for money.

The rates of return in the above equation are expected variables. Although we have indicated the likely signs to be attached to the variables in the above equation, in Friedman's view the signs should be determined principally by the data.

Although this is a theory of the demand for money and we have seen that the original Quantity Theory (as distinct from the Cambridge version) was not a theory of the demand for money, Friedman regarded his theory as a 'restatement' of the Quantity Theory.[13] We can show why with some assumptions and a little manipulation. Let us first multiply both sides of (5.27) by $1/Y_p$. This gives us:

$$M_d/(PY_p) = g[i_b,\ i_e,\ i_m,\ (1/P).dP^e/dt,\ w,\ u] \qquad (3.29)$$

Next, assume that the demand for real balances is stably related to the small number of variables we have on the right hand side and replace the whole expression by k. Then we re-arrange to produce:

$$Md = kPYp \qquad (3.30)$$

As we did with the Cambridge version of the Quantity Theory, we can define k as the inverse of velocity and arrive at:

$$MdV = PYp \qquad (3.31)$$

With the money market in equilibrium, we have:

$$MV = PYp \qquad (3.32)$$

This looks very similar to the Fisher version of the Quantity Theory. Of course, $1/k$ in this model is quite different from Fisher's V. The factors determining Fisher's V appear only as one element in u in Friedman's model. Friedman's theory can be defended as a restatement of the Quantity Theory if the money supply is exogenous, causality runs from left to right, the demand for money is a stable function of the small number of variables summed up in k, and Yp, as a long-run measure of real income grows steadily over time. Then, the price level is explained by changes in the stock of money. We could easily, as we did with the Quantity Theory itself, express this in terms of rates of change and say that Friedman's theory supports the view that the cause of inflation is a too-rapid growth in the money supply.

Friedman made use of permanent income in the above equation to explain apparently conflicting long run and cyclical tendencies. His historical studies of money in the US economy suggested that in the long-run as income rose, V fell but that over the business cycle, there was a tendency for V to rise in booms and fall in recessions. The argument rested on the proposition that if the demand for money were a function of permanent income, it would fluctuate less ceteris paribus than if it were a function of current income. As income rises in the boom of a business cycle, people continue to base their demand for money on their permanent income, which is now lower than current income because part of current income is positive transitory income. The demand for money falls in relation to current income and V rises. In the trough of the business cycle, transitory income is negative, the demand for money rises in relation to current income, and V falls.

We have not said anything about the demand for money of business enterprises. Friedman himself says little except to point out some differences from that of ultimate wealth holders. Thus, he notes that:

(i) The constraint is different; it is not permanent income or wealth since firms can influence the total amount of capital in the form of productive assets by borrowing through capital markets. Not much work has been done on the best scale variable for firms. Friedman suggests three possibilities: total transactions, net value added, and net worth.

(ii) The distinction between human and non-human wealth is not relevant for firms.

(iii) The rates of return relevant to firms are different from those for ultimate wealth holders, for instance, bank loan rates may be more important for firms than for households.

Despite these differences, Friedman treats the equation for ultimate wealth holders as the aggregate demand for money function for the economy, while observing that the inclusion of firms makes problems of aggregation more difficult. The problem of aggregation, however, causes little difficulty. This is because of Friedman's methodological approach. Having indicated a number of variables likely to be of importance in an aggregate demand function, he argues that the ultimate test of theories is their ability to predict accurately. Since he believes the demand for money to be a stable function of a small number of variables, the variables to be included in the equation, the form that they take and the relationship between them may be changed in order to produce the desired result. Testing, in effect, takes over from theory, although the aim of the testing is to demonstrate that the basic theory is correct.

Despite this importance attached to the testing of demand for money functions, Friedman's approach to the demand for money suggested that it should be a stable function of real income and interest rates and that the interest elasticity of demand for money should be expected to be low. As we shall see in section 8.4, when combined with other aspects of his model of the economy, Friedman's approach to the demand for money provided support for the view that the monetary authority should control the price level by adopting a medium- to long-term monetary rule, setting a target for the rate of growth of the money supply. It aimed to undermine the Keynesian belief in the short-term management of the economy and was an important part of the general attack on fiscal policy.

Thus, we can see why the arguments about the nature of the demand for money were thought to be so important, as long as economists continued to assume an exogenous money supply.

3.8　　Other developments in the theory of the demand for money

Before the middle of the 1950s, there had only been a small amount of empirical work on the demand for money. Since Friedman's formulation of his demand for money function, however, relatively little attention has been paid to the theory of the demand for money. Indeed, much of the theory that has been explored has developed in an attempt to explain problems that have arisen in the testing of the demand for money function. Perhaps the most important has been the development of the buffer stock approach to the demand for money.

The buffer stock approach grew from the need to explain time lags in the face of the standard expectation of low transactions costs and short time lags in financial markets. The need for an explanation grew in the 1970s when there appeared to be evidence that time lags in money demand functions were lengthening. The best known buffer stock attempt to explain why the adjustment of the demand for money to return the system to equilibrium following a change in the money supply may be subject to long and variable lags was provided by Laidler (1984).[14]

The idea derives from the notion that, given risk and uncertainty, not all events are correctly anticipated and so, following a shock, at least one variable won't be equal to its planned value. However, one can arrange one's affairs so that the shock will fall on a predetermined variable — the buffer. In the buffer stock approach to the demand for money, people accept deviations in money holdings around their equilibrium levels. Assume, as an example, that a long-run equilibrium is disturbed by an expansion of the money supply, causing money holdings to be temporarily greater than the demand for money. To return portfolios to equilibrium, agents would seek to move out of money into other financial or real assets. However, in the short-run, they might choose instead to absorb the shock by holding excess money balances. There are two clear reasons for behaving in this way:

(a) monitoring money balances continuously requires both time and information, and

(b) the adjustment of portfolios is not costless and so agents wait until they are convinced that the change in the money supply is not merely transitory.

Money thus becomes a substitute for information. It is only when money holdings deviate too much from the equilibrium level (they hit a ceiling), that the excess money holdings are used to buy other assets, taking money balances back to their long-run equilibrium level. In the case of a monetary contraction, money balances would be allowed to fall until they hit a floor. Only then would other assets be sold.

Money is assumed to act as a buffer in this process because it is liquid and the costs of adjusting money balances are likely to be less than the cost of adjusting holdings of other assets. If it is relatively easy to borrow, credit might also act as a buffer; but if borrowing is inflexible, money will be the only buffer and money balances can be expected to fluctuate more than holdings of non-money assets.

It remains that if transaction and information costs in the financial sector were relatively low, there should not be a great need for a buffer stock asset. However, it was argued that adjustment might be spread over a number of months or even quarters because of stickiness in both interest rates and goods prices. Buffer stocks would then be willingly held during this gradual process of adjustment. This can be seen as a formalisation of the idea that money is needed in the process of exchange to cope with lack of information and to economise on the use of time (see section 1.2). The existence of money provides an asset holdings of which people allow to vary rather than constantly striving for an exact value of their money holdings as in the deterministic demand for money models such as the

Baumol/Tobin inventory-theoretic model. Rather, they wish only to keep their money holdings within a band, monitoring them only at intervals. Modifications of the buffer stock approach included the development of forward-looking buffer stock models which employ rational expectations. Cuthbertson and Taylor's (1978) add a cost function measuring the cost both of being away from equilibrium and of changing money holdings to a conventional money demand function. To minimise this cost function, agents form expectations of future values of real income, the interest rate and the price level. The model distinguishes between expected and unexpected changes.

Whereas an expected future increase in price level or real income or an expected fall in interest rate will produce an immediate increase in money holdings, unexpected changes of this type will not initially do so unless they represent news about a change in the process generating the variable in question. An exogenous increase in the money stock will be communicated only slowly through the money demand function to the price level, real income and the interest rate. This is all of some theoretical interest but, as we have said, its origins lay in attempts to explain difficulties encountered in testing and it has, in turn, been difficult to establish empirically the quantitative significance of buffer-stock money.

All of the theory we have looked at in this chapter has been concerned with the demand for money in the aggregate even if there has been a quite strong underlying feeling that aggregate models should be built on microeconomic foundations.

However, we should mention the relatively small amount of work on microeconomic transactions models given that these have sought to provide an answer to a problem we pointed out in section 1.2— the difficulty of justifying the holding of money for transactions purposes within general equilibrium models. The most prominent models of this kind (McCallum, 1989; McCallum and Goodfriend, 1992; Dowd, 1990) analyse the demand for money in terms of the shopping time saved in carrying out transactions through the use of money (as distinct from barter). Shopping time saved has value since it can be used to earn income or to obtain utility from other uses. In McCallum and Goodfriend's (1992) version, an agent maximises present and future utility from the consumption of goods and leisure. He currently holds a stock of bonds and money (the purchasing power of which is eroded by expected inflation); and the economy provides a stream of opportunities for the earning of further income by selling labour services and for rearranging consumption over time through a capital market in which bonds may be bought and sold. Consumption goods can be obtained in exchange for income only by shopping for them.

The amount of time required for shopping increases with the quantity of consumption goods bought, but is negatively related to the size of real money balances carried on shopping trips. It follows that a decision to hold more money now, ceteris paribus, reduces shopping time, leaving more time for current leisure and/or increased labour supply and future real income. Equations can be derived from the model for current and future demands for consumption, leisure, bond holding, money holding, and the supply of labour.

The demand for money function that can be derived from these can be compared with Friedman's. In McCallum and Goodfriend, the demand for money is related to inherited assets; expected unearned income (non-human wealth); current and expected future wage rates (human wealth); interest rates and inflation rates. Since decisions about current money holding are part of a utility-maximising strategy governing future plans as well as current behaviour, the demand for money depends on expected future values of interest rates and inflation as well as current values. The model also implies that the current volume of market transactions is chosen simultaneously with the demand for money — real income does not determine the demand for money: both are simultaneously influenced by deeper underlying forces.

3.9 The theory of the demand for money: a conclusion

The central issue dealt with in this chapter has been the question of the stability of the demand for money function. This has long been seen as crucial in relation to economic policy because it determines whether the authorities can hope to influence the rate of growth of nominal income by controlling the rate of growth of the money supply. All of the writers we have dealt with here, with the exception of Keynes, have proposed theories that support the idea of stability. Although there are important differences between the views of, say, Tobin and those of Friedman, strictly from the point of view of the relevance of demand for money theory to economic policy, the important distinction is between Keynes and the others; and a large proportion of that debate rests on the dispute over the speculative demand for money.

We have seen that the major criticisms of Keynes's theory arise from its claimed lack of microfoundations. The problem with theories based upon microeconomic reasoning is that they provide us with individual demand for money functions and leave aside the problem of aggregation, even if difficulties involved in it are mentioned from time to time. This becomes a genuine difficulty when we arrive, as we have done with Friedman, at the proposition that theories can be best judged by their ability to predict. Clearly, if we are to say anything at all meaningful about policy, it is the aggregate demand for money that we need to predict. This leads to the opening up of a gulf between the theories discussed here and the empirical work, and casts doubt on both.

There is, of course, an even more serious problem. All of the reasoning about the importance of the demand for money is based upon the importance of knowing what factors in the economy will change in order to cause the demand for money to return to equality with an exogenously determined money stock. We have seen in chapter 2 that this is at odds with reality. We shall see in chapter 5 that this can cause serious differences to arise in the approach taken to the transmission mechanism of monetary policy.

3.10 A note on the testing of the demand for money

Almost all of the large number of empirical studies of the demand for money over the past fifty years have been concerned to demonstrate that the stability of the demand for money function[15] — generally regressing the demand for a measure of money on measures of income and interest rate. Specifically, the studies have aimed to discover whether the independent variables (interest rates, a measure of income or wealth) have significant and stable coefficients and whether most of the variation in the demand for money is accounted for by variations in interest rate and income. There have been some subsidiary aims including attempts to estimate the interest elasticity of the demand for money. Most studies have used highly aggregated time-series data. Functions have been estimated for both the long-run (using annual data over periods ranging from around 30 to over 100 years) and the short-run (mainly with quarterly data, mostly over time periods between 5 and 20 years). Most short-run studies have incorporated time lags, with equilibrium assumed to occur only in the long run.

This type of testing faces several problems. In particular, the demand for money is not a directly observable variable. We can observe the quantity of money currently being held but not whether it is being willingly held. If the money market is in disequilibrium, with people, on average, attempting to increase or decrease their money holdings, measuring the quantity of money does not measure the demand for money. If we assumed the money market is always in equilibrium and the money supply exogenous, we could allow the measured money supply to stand for the demand for money in demand for money equations. On the other hand, with an endogenous money supply, the supply of money is no longer independent of the demand for money — the same variables influence both the supply of and the demand for money. Then, the demand and supply curves move together and we cannot be sure that, as the supply of money changes, the money supply curve is moving along a single demand for money curve. There is an identification problem. Investigators attempt to overcome this problem by employing techniques that enable supply and demand functions to be fitted simultaneously, but there is clearly a serious problem.

Other problems emerge if we drop the assumption of equilibrium, even if we assume an exogenous money supply. Indeed, it can be argued that econometric analysis can not easily be applied at all to economies characterised by disequilibrium and uncertainty of the kind suggested by Keynes.

Other difficulties include:

- the lack of an agreed definition of money for testing purposes;

- problems in the choice between income and wealth as the scale variable and difficulties in the measurement of wealth;

- problems with the selection of the interest rates;

- possible correlations among the independent variables, making it difficult to isolate the specific relationship between each variable and the demand for money;

- the inability to measure easily or measure at all some variables that the theory of the demand for suggests should be included in a testing equation;

- problems in the choice of time period.

One result of these problems is that the standard regression equation used in demand for money testing makes relatively little use of theory beyond taking as a starting point the need to include both an income term and an interest rate term. It is hard, therefore, to argue that it is the theory being tested. Rather, we start with a view of the world that leads to a belief in a stable relationship between the demand for money and real income and we seek to confirm this. Failure to do so does not produce a re-evaluation of the theory or a change of world view but a determination to change the equation and try again.[16]

Even so, the results have not been particularly convincing. Until the early 1970s, the studies in general produced the sort of results that researchers had expected and it was claimed that they provided support for the propositions that the demand for money was a stable function of income and interest rate and that interest rate elasticities were relatively low. However, in the 1970s, problems appeared in both the UK and the USA with the existing equations seriously over-predicting or under-predicting the demand for money. Equations also broke down in several other OECD countries.

Further problems became evident in the 1980s. This led to a great deal of work attempting to explain these problems through improvements in econometric techniques such as the development of error correction models and cointegration techniques.

Other economists attempted to save the hypothesis of a stable long-run demand for money by looking for causes of once-and-for-all shocks to the demand for money function. The principal candidates were financial innovations associated with institutional change in the financial sector; uncertainty about the rate of inflation as a result of the large swings in inflation rates in the 1970s and 1980s; and currency substitution, especially following the movement away from fixed exchange rates in the early 1970s. Changes investigated as possible causes of financial innovation included the deregulation of financial markets, the introduction by banks of interest-bearing demand deposits, the impact of technological change on financial services, the liberalisation of international capital flows and the imposition or removal of controls on bank lending. Policy measures specific to particular economies also played an important role in the discussion, notably, for the UK, the relaxation of lending controls over the period 1971-73. This approach, however, assumes that financial innovation is exogenous and is undermined to the extent that institutional change within the financial sector is influenced by the existence of high or low interest rates brought about by changes in monetary policy.

We can thus conclude by saying:

(a) in a world of endogenous money, the importance of the demand for money, stable or not, becomes difficult to defend;

(b) economic theories of the demand for money that lead to an expectation of a stable long-run demand for money are dependent on a belief that economies can best be analysed in equilibrium;

(c) the existence of endogenous money poses particular problems for the standard form of testing used in empirical work on the demand for money.

3.11   Summary

In a world of endogenous money, the aggregate demand for money is of little importance in any attempt to understand the nature of monetary policy and its impact. However, for much of the history of monetary economics, most economists have assumed the money supply to be exogenous. Consequently a great deal of work has been done on the theory of the demand for money.

The Quantity Theory of Money (QTM) provides a good starting point for the study of this material — even though it is not a theory of the demand for money — because it has been very influential and can be related to later theories of the demand for money. The QTM contained a number of variations and was far from the simplified model based upon the equation of exchange and assuming a constant transactions velocity of income that most students now study. Still, the simplified version provides the important policy messages that lie at the heart of one of the major approaches to monetary economics — that changes in an exogenous money supply produce proportional changes in the general level of prices and that money is neutral in relation to real income. The replacement in the expression of the Quantity Theory of transactions by income undermined the logic of the original theory but brought it more closely into line with the first major theory of the demand for money, the Cambridge cash balances approach, which was being developed at the same time.

The Cambridge approach introduced important changes because the demand for money was treated at a microeconomic level and was, like other demand functions in economics, subjective. However, most proponents of the Cambridge approach accepted the policy conclusions of the Quantity Theory. This was not true of Keynes who, in 1936, proposed a radically different theory of the demand for money based upon the motives for holding money. This gave interest rates a much more important role in the theory and raised the possibility that the demand for money function might be unstable. This led to the view that monetary policy might be relatively weak, especially when the economy was in a depression. It also raised the question of whether the authorities could hope to control the rate of inflation through changes in the rate of growth of the money supply. In doing this, it elevated the role of fiscal policy in the management of the economy.

Keynes's theory was heavily criticised, particularly because it was said to be overly concerned with the short run and lacked microfoundations. There followed a series of attempts to explain the demand for money so as to retain some of Keynes's propositions (notably that the demand for money was interest-elastic) but to do so in a less controversial way. These included the incorporation of interest rates into transactions and precautionary models of the demand for money and the reformulation of the speculative demand as an asset demand for money. Even the notion of interest-elasticity was reduced greatly in importance in Friedman's demand for money theory. Friedman saw his theory as a return to the spirit of the Quantity Theory in the sense that he sought to re-establish the importance of controlling the money supply as the means of controlling inflation. This required a return to the acceptance of a stable demand for money function. Although Friedman's initial approach was theoretical, he suggested that the form of the demand for money function could only be determined by empirical testing. Thereafter, apart from some developments that grew out of general equilibrium theory, the focus of academic work on the demand for money shifted away from theory to econometric testing or to attempts to explain why econometric tests did not always produce the stable demand for money in which most economists believed.

Key concepts used in this chapter

Quantity Theory of Money	active money balances
equation of exchange	idle money balances
transactions velocity of money	disequilibrium
income velocity of money	liquidity trap
stability of the demand for money function	inventory-theoretic model
motives for demanding money:	portfolio models of the demand
transactions motive	for money
precautionary motive	human wealth

speculative motive	buffer stocks of money
finance motive	financial innovation
the Cambridge k	human wealth
normal rate of interest	non-human wealth

Questions and exercises
Answers at the end of the book

1. Economics generally tells us that one must analyse the factors influencing both the demand for and supply of important variables. Why, then, might the demand for money not be of great importance from the point of view of economic policy?

2. Why is the Quantity Theory of Money not a theory of the demand for money? What is it a theory of?

3. Both the precautionary and the speculative motives for holding money arise from the existence of uncertainty — uncertainty about what in each case?

4. Why did the testing of the demand for money grow rapidly at the expense of theorizing about the demand for money after Friedman published his theory?

5. Why was the speculative demand for money so controversial?

6. Both the inventory-theoretic model of the transactions demand for money and Tobin's portfolio model are commonly called Neo-Keynesian models. Why?

...and also to think about

7. Given the various points mentioned in box 3.1 as influencing the velocity of money, would you expect the long-term velocity of money to have increased or decreased over the past fifty years?

8. In the light of Keynes's view about the difference between risk and uncertainty, explain each of the following ideas from Keynes:

(a) it might be rational (rather than simple money illusion) for workers to make labour supply decisions based on relative money wages rather than real wages;

(b) households base their consumption and savings decisions on current income rather than wealth.

Does the second of these lead you to think differently about the choice of scale variable in the demand for money function?

Further reading

A great deal has been written about the theory of the demand for money. For a quite different approach to the historical approach taken here, see Howells and Bain (2002). Other good textbook treatments can be found in Laidler (1993) and Gowland (1991). For more detailed treatments than is found here see Lewis and Mizen (2000) or Handa (2000). For an essay on the demand for money that manages to dismiss Keynes in a few lines as a victim of money illusion see McCallum and Goodfriend (1992). Post-Keynesian explanations of Keynes's finance motive for holding money are in Rousseas (1986) and Wray (1990).

4 Money supply and control

'Virtually every monetary economist believes that the CB can control the monetary base and...the broader monetary aggregates as well. Almost all of those who have worked in a CB believe that this view is totally mistaken...'

C A E Goodhart, 'What should central banks do? What should be their macroeconomic objectives and operations?', *Economic Journal*, vol. 104, (1994) p.1424.

4.1   Introduction

In chapter 2 we looked at two models of money supply determination, one of which focused upon stocks (of broad money and the monetary base) and the other on flows (of bank credit). In our comparison of the two we stressed that while either could be used to analyse the money supply process in any particular regime, the insights of each were more relevant to, or more helpful in, under-standing a particular type of regime and therefore we should not be surprised to discover that the flow of funds FoF approach has been the preferred way of look-ing at the money supply process in the UK. The simple reason for this, we said, is that the Bank of England has, for many years, chosen to set the level of interest rates and then allow private sector preferences to determine the growth rate of money and credit. In fact, as Borio (1997) shows, operating procedures are now very similar across most central banks (and changes to the Bank of England's money market operations in 2006 have increased this convergence).

In this chapter we want to show, firstly (in 4.2), that setting interest rates while letting market forces determine quantities, effectively makes the quantity of money a demand-determined or *endogenous* variable. In Mervyn King's words:

> In the United Kingdom, money is endogenous - *the Bank supplies base money on demand* at its prevailing interest rate, and broad money is created by the banking system (King, 1994 p.264. Our emphasis).

We shall see that the link to the rest of the economy lies in the demand for *loans* or credit. Essentially, banks are quantity-takers. They set the price of loans, in the light of the official rate, and then endeavour to supply all demands from credit-worthy customers. As we saw in table 2.2, loans create deposits.

In section 4.3 we shall look at how the central bank can set a rate of interest. We shall note that setting an official rate is one thing, but the *effect* of that official decision depends initially upon the extent to which the official rate is transferred to market rates. We shall report research which says that the link between official and market rates is not a simple one-to-one relationship, nor is it instantaneous. However, it is generally true that a change in the official rate is accompanied by a change in market rates (eventually) in the same direction. In 2007, however, we saw a major shock to this relationship when the conventional premium of inter-bank rates over the official rate widened dramatically and remained stubbornly wide for a while. In section 4.4 we shall show how the setting of the the official rate of interest and its effect on the rest of the monetary system can be modelled using a diagram and some simple algebra.

We have commented several times already, and especially towards the end of chapter 2, that the image of a money supply *exogenously* determined by a central bank expanding as a multiple of the monetary base on which the bank acted directly, dies hard. For this reason, it seems worth looking at the wide variety of reasons which lie behind the comprehensive rejection of monetary base control as a practical strategy. We do this in section 4.5, before summarising in section 4.6.

4.2   The endogeneity of the money supply

The debate over whether the quantity of money is ultimately imposed by some external agency or may somehow depend upon the values taken by other variables within the economic system, has a long history. Schumpeter (1911) and Wicksell (1898) both recognised that endogeneity was inevitable once central banks decided to impose a regime of stable interest rates — a situation that had emerged by the 1890s in the UK (Sayers, 1976, ch.3). In the 1930s, historians were arguing over the extent to which the 'great inflation' of the sixteenth century could be explained by the importation of gold from the New World (an exogenous increase in the money supply) or by the debasement of the coinage (an endogenous response to a chronic shortage). Furthermore, the same scholars were aware that the same debates had taken place amongst contemporaries of that inflation, and possibly even earlier still.[1]

Confining our attention to more recent times, however, we owe the recognition of money's endogeneity to three main sources. With no significance to the ordering, these are firstly the post-keynesian economists to whom, since at least Davidson and Weintraub (1973) 'Endogenous money theory is one of the main cornerstones.' (Fontana, 2003 p.291).

We have already seen, in section 2.3, that Paul Davidson (1988) attached the expression 'interest-endogeneity' to the base-multiplier model if it was presented properly with a positively-sloped money supply curve, resulting from banks' reserve-economising behaviour as interest rates on non-reserve assets changed. Except for this very limited case, the endogeneity has usually been understood by post-keynesians in Davidson's other sense, that is to say 'base-endogeneity', referring to the fact that, in practice, central banks do not attempt quantitative control over reserves, but, having set the price, let market forces determine the quantities. This is the process being described by Mervyn King above, and if we persist in thinking in terms of a money stock diagram draw in interest-money space, then the picture is one of the intercept continually shifting to the right, rather than any question of slope. Since nominal incomes are generally rising and the demand for credit is a demand for nominal credit, at any given rate of interest the curve will naturally be shifting to the right. A change in the rate of interest influences the rate at which the curve shifts. In these circumstances it is the rate of *flow* (of new money) that is of interest rather than the stock itself. A positive flow is the norm and *expansion* of the stock will continue at its current rate will continue unless the authorities intervene (by changing the level of interest rates). It should now be clear why the FoF model is more helpful than one which concentrates on stocks.

Notice that it is the demand for loans or credit which is the proximate determinant of the rate of monetary expansion. Given the importance of loan demand in credit and money creation, therefore, it seems mildly curious that empirical work on the demand for bank loans is so sparse while studies of the demand for money abound (as we saw in the last chapter). Of course, one can argue that credit demands cannot create money unless the resulting deposits are willingly held and thus the demand for money is the ultimate constraint on its creation. But this is an equilibrium argument.[2] Buffer stock models of money demand (see section 3.8) were developed precisely to cope with the possibility that the quantity of money could, at least in the short-run, differ from what agents ultimately wish to hold.[3]

Within the post-keynesian tradition, the common practice has been to locate the critical demand for credit in the behaviour of firms. 'Production takes time'. This means that a firm planning to increase output (or faced with rising costs) must undertake the additional expenditure before it can recoup the additional outlays through sales revenue. During the intervening period, the firm requires additional working capital which it gets in the form of loans from banks. In this view, money is endogenous because 'loans create deposits' and the demand for loans originates with the 'state of trade'. A clear exposition of this argument can be found in Basil Moore's seminal text, *Horizontalists and Verticalists* (1988, ch.9) where there is also some empirical evidence. Much of this is based on a study by Moore and Threadgold (1985).

It is less clear today that firms and the production process should be singled out in this way. With respect to non-financial firms, their demands for bank credit have been surpassed by households' demand for some years as table 4.1 shows.

Furthermore, households (and maybe firms too for that matter) borrow to finance all sorts of expenditure, not simply expenditure related to production or 'trade'. In the UK, data on *all* transactions, including financial transactions, intermediate payments, the purchase of secondhand goods and assets and more, is available from APACS.[4] We should naturally expect such a magnitude to dwarf GDP but it is quite common to assume a stable relationship between the two,[5] in spite of Keynes's warning:[6]

Table 4.1: Bank lending to selected sectors (amounts outstanding, £m)

End:	Lending to financial firms	Lending to non-financial firms	Lending to households, secured on dwellings	Consumer credit
Nov. 1997	171,327	179,582	394,199	63,785
Nov. 2002	274,138	252,624	569,198	120,065
March 2008	388,324	638,013	812,801	145,666
2008 values as % of total 2008 lending	20	32	41	7

Source: http://www.bankofengland.co.uk/statistics/ms/2008/May/tabc1.2.xls

[Speculative and financial transactions] need not be, and are not, governed by the volume of current output. The pace at which a circle of financiers, speculators and investors hand round to one another particular pieces of wealth, or title to such, which they are neither producing nor consuming but merely exchanging, bears no definite relation to the rate of current production. The volume of such transactions is subject to very wide and incalculable fluctuations…(1930/1971, vol.V p.42)

For the UK, the APACS data shows a dramatic increase in the multiple during the 1980s from c.20 to c.50. There have been violent fluctuations since, but no sign of a return to the levels of the 1970s. The message is clear: spending on non-production dwarfs spending on output and is highly variable. Some of this, no doubt is borrowing on mortgage to buy (largely secondhand) dwellings. Some reflects the comparatively rapid growth of the financial sector in the UK. The point is that some, if not all, of this expenditure is capable of generating a demand for credit. Howells and Hussein (1999) used the APACS data to estimate an otherwise fairly standard demand for credit equation and found that on most tests an equation containing a measure of total transactions performed better than one based on GDP. Other researchers have also found that estimates are improved by including variables which might be regarded as proxies for what is happening to total spending. What all this means is that we should perhaps be careful in ascribing the origin of loan demand to the 'state of trade' alone. However, this does not alter the central point that the demand for loans and ultimately the quantity of money are being driven by events *within* the economic system.

The second source of evidence on money's endogeneity comes from those in the forefront of policy design and operation — the central bankers and their economist-advisors. We have seen the view of Charles Goodhart, quoted at the head of this chapter suggesting something of a rift between economists with and without experience of central banking. More recently, Michael Woodford has commented rather similarly: 'It is true that the conceptual frameworks proposed by central banks to deal with their perceived need for a more systematic approach to policy were, until quite recently, largely developed without much guidance from the academic literature on monetary economics' (Woodford, 2003 p.3). In section 4.1 we noted Mervyn King's statement that the banking system creates the broad money supply. This is very similar to the earlier statement by a senior vice-president of the New York Federal Reserve '…in the real world banks extend credit, creating deposits in the process, and look for the reserves later ' (Holmes, 1969). More recent evidence on just how firmly attached central banks are to setting interest rates and the lengths to which they are prepared to go in varying levels of liquidity in order to maintain that control was shown during the so-called credit crunch that emerged in the late-summer of 2007.

Central banks have been forced to inject massive doses of liquidity in excess of $100bn into overnight lending markets, in an effort to ensure that the interest rates they set are reflected in real-time borrowing....The Fed is protecting an interest rate of 5.25 per cent, the ECB a rate of 4 per cent and the BoJ an overnight target of 0.5 per cent. (*Financial Times*, 11/12 August, 2007)

Given that, in practice, the policy instrument was an official rate of interest while the flow of new money and credit was demand-determined, it is not surprising that economists working within and close to central banks found themselves investigating the responsiveness of these flows to changes in interest rates. We have already noted the Moore and Threadgold (1985) estimation of a demand for bank lending equation. This had an antecedent in work done by Moore while he was at the Bank of England and subsequently published as a (1980) working paper. In 1981, a major review of monetary policy techniques decided yet again that a short-term interest rate was the only feasible policy instrument (see section 10.2). This decision provoked a further flurry of interest in the demand for bank lending. In the UK, HM Treasury, the National Institute of Economic and Social Research (NIESR) and the Bank of England all had well-developed models of the demand for bank lending and their main characteristics were compared by Cuthbertson and Foster (1982). The Bank of England model was essentially similar to the model estimated by Moore and Threadgold (1980) and carried through Moore's subsequent work: the dependant variable was the flow of nominal lending to ICCs. Firms' costs were important and there was a low elasticity on the real cost of borrowing. By contrast, the HMT model was expressed wholly in real terms (except the interest rate) and sought to explain the stock of bank loans while the NIESR model focused, like the Bank of England, on flows but in real terms (but again with nominal interest rates). Only the Bank of England refers explicitly to firms' costs; the NIESR model had the change in manufacturing output as its activity variable while the HMT model had (the level of) real GDP. Nonetheless, taken together the models all seemed to indicate that, given the level of interest rates, the flow (and/or stock) of credit depended upon prices and real economic activity, or, as we called it above, 'the state of trade'.

Finally, and most recently, the so-called 'New Consensus Macroeconomics' has come to accept that the policy instrument is a short-term interest rate administered by the a central bank which has little, if any, interest in monetary aggregates. On monetary policy within this consensus the seminal work is Woodford's (2003) *Interest and Prices*. What is especially notable about Woodford's work is that it pushes monetary aggregates firmly out of the picture. What matters about the rate of interest does not depend upon what is happening to the resulting money supply: it is not just an equivalent way of expressing the behaviour of quantities.

It is often supposed that the key to understanding the effects of monetary policy on inflation must always be the quantity theory of money... It may then be concluded that what matters about *any* monetary policy is the implied path of the money supply... From such a perspective, it might seem that a clearer understanding of the consequences of a central bank's actions would be facilitated by an explicit focus on what evolution of the money supply the bank intends to bring about - that is by monetary targeting... The present study aims to show that the basic premise of such a criticism is incorrect. One of the primary goals ... of this book is the development of a theoretical framework in which the consequences of alternative interest-rate rules can be analysed, *which does not require that they first be translated into equivalent rules for the evolution of the money supply*. (Woodford, 2003, p.48. Second emphasis added).

There are encouraging signs now that the emergence of this consensus is leading at last, to the demise of the *LM* curve with its assumption of exogenous money shocks working their way through the economy via real balance effects. (See Carlin and Soskice 2006 and section 5.2 below).

4.3   Interest rates as the policy instrument

In conventional accounts of monetary policy the monetary base is an exogenous variable determined by the central bank. The quantity of broad money is then determined through a multiplier process of the kind we set out in chapter 2. Given the demand for money, equilibrium is maintained by the rate of interest — an endogenously-determined variable — which influences the demand for loans. Letting B stand for the monetary base, M for the broad money stock, i for the rate of interest and L *for* loans, we can represent the process thus:

$$B \to M \to i \to L$$

The analysis of the previous section, however, should have made it clear that a better representation of what happens in practice is:

$$i \to L \to M \to B$$

Here, the rate of interest is the exogenous variable (or at least the 'policy-determined' variable to use Goodhart's preferred description) while broad money is endogenous and reserves or base money are supplied as required. In this sequence, the ability of the central bank to set interest rates is obviously critical and so, in this section, we look at how the central bank can impose a decision about the general level of interest rates and what limits there might be to this power.

Our starting point is that banks must be able to guarantee the convertibility into cash of customer deposits.[7]   For this purpose they hold 'reserves' of notes and coin and deposits at the central bank, Cb and Db in our symbols of chapter 2. (A glance back at box 2.2 and the surrounding text may be useful here). In the UK these reserves are very small (around 1 per cent of customer deposits) and are supplemented by loans to the money market which are not quite so liquid but have the benefit that they pay rather better interest. Other things being equal, the demand for loans (and the demand for deposits) expands over time since both are related to nominal income and this increases as a result of both increases in real income and in the price level. (This is why, when the UK authorities have been concerned about the size of the monetary aggregates — after 1973 and most obviously between 1980 and 1985 — it has been the growth rate and not the absolute size which has been the focus of attention). It is thus a fairly simple task for the central bank to ensure that the quantity of monetary base (of which reserves are a part — see equation 3.2) grows slowly enough that at the end of each day the banks involved in the settlement process are short of funds (Bank, 1997a). In addition to this, a large fraction of banks' liquidity consists of previous short-term borrowing from the central bank. When these loans mature ('unwinding of official assistance' in the jargon) they need to be refinanced. Provided that the shortage is system-wide, interbank lending and borrowing cannot resolve the shortage and the central bank is then in the position to exploit its monopoly position in the supply of reserves.

Like any monopolist, the central bank can set either the price or the quantity of reserves which it supplies. In choosing to set the rate of interest at which is supplies or refinances reserves, central banks are choosing to set the price. Therefore it is, in effect, the 'lender of last resort rate'. Analytically, it is, i_d or what we called the rediscount rate in section 2.3. However, the precise rate in question may vary from regime to regime, depending upon the manner in which the central bank chooses to provide liquidity. The ECB literature refers to it as the 'refinancing rate', because as we said the shortage that we have been imagining can and does often arise from the maturing of loans of reserves that the central bank has made in the recent past as well as from the system's expansion. In the UK it was for some years called 'minimum lending rate' and was in practice the rate at which the Bank of England was prepared to discount (i.e. buy) 14-day ('band 1') treasury bills offered by the discount houses when there was a cash shortage. Several changes in money market operations arrived shortly before the Bank of England's independence in 1997 (Bank 1997). One of these was a dramatic widening of the 'counterparties' with which the Bank was willing to deal in smoothing the supply of reserves. Where previously it had confined its dealings to discount houses, since then it has been willing to deal with banks, building societies and securities houses (though each must be registered for the purpose). Furthermore, instead of providing assistance by the outright purchase of treasury and sometimes commercial bills, since 1997 assistance has been provided by the use of repurchase agreements ('repos'), in a manner very similar to that of the ECB.

As box 4.1 explains, repos are agreements to sell an asset for cash and then to buy it back at a higher price at a specified time in the future. The difference in the two prices is the 'interest' paid from the borrower to lender. Repos are in effect collateralised loans and in money market operations the collateral is government bonds. Thus the rate of interest set by the Bank of England is often referred to as 'repo rate'.

Notice that this official rate is the *only* rate that the central bank can influence directly.. Furthermore, as we have been at pains to stress, it is a very special rate with very limited application. Hence, when it comes to the question of limits to central bank influence over interest rates, the first place that we must look is the transmission of interest changes from the official rate to market rates. When the central bank changes its official dealing rate, it is reasonable to suppose that this affects many other short-term market rates quite quickly — pushing them in the same direction and by similar amounts.

It does not follow that all changes will be identical, however (i.e. that existing differentials will be preserved). Depending on the competitive nature of the system, banks may find it possible to change deposit rates by more than loan rates or *vice versa*. The transmission of these effects occurs mainly by convention but arbitrage would bring it about very quickly anyway. Banks price many of their products by mark-ups on or discounts on what are called 'interbank rates' — the rates at which they lend to each other. Since a bank which is short of reserves can borrow either from other banks or from the central bank, these are very good substitutes for one another with the result that interbank rates rarely differ from official rates by more than a few basis points. (A basis point is 1/100 of a percentage

---

Box 4.1: Using gilt-repos to raise interest rates

A repurchase agreement (repo) is an agreement to buy a number of specified securities from a seller on the understanding that they will be repurchased at some specified price and time. In the UK, there is an established market for repos in government bonds ('gilts'). Since the repos are usually for very short periods, three months at most, repos are classified as money market instruments (even though the maturity of the underlying gilts may be quite long). The difference between the selling and buying price represents interest paid to the repo buyer by the seller. The formula for finding the interest rate is:

$$i = \frac{(R-P)}{P.n} \tag{4.1}$$

where R is the redemption or repurchase price, P is the price at sale and n is the length of the repo deal in fractions of a year.

Suppose that the Bank enters into a repo for £1m of government bonds for repurchase at £1,001,900 in fourteen days. From Equation 4.1 we can calculate that it will be setting a price for borrowed reserves of:

$$\frac{(1.0019-1.0)}{1.0\,(0.038)} = \frac{0.0019}{0.038} = 0.05 \text{ or } 5\%$$

Suppose now that the Bank wishes to raise interest rates by 25 basis points. Rearranging Equation 4.1 we can find the new repurchase price for future deals in the same securities.

$$R = (i.P.n) + P = (0.0525 \times 1m \times 0.038) + 1m = £1,001,995$$

Raising the repurchase price of £1m-worth of bonds for fourteen days by £95 is equivalent to raising the rate of interest by 25 basis points.

point). Hence, when changing the official rate, a central is normally looking to change interbank rates as the first step. This change in the most fundamental of market rates will then be communicated to other short-term commercial rates.

Box 4.2 describes recent changes in Bank of England money market operations designed to tie interbank rates more closely to its official rate; box 4.3 shows that the conventionally close link between interbank and the official rate can sometimes break down.

Box 4.2: Recent changes in Bank of England money market operations

In April 2006, after extensive consultation, the Bank of England made a number of changes to the way it conducts money market operations in order to set interest rates.

As described in box 4.1, the Bank supplies liquidity through repo deals. These are conducted every Thursday and are of 7-day maturity. The price reflects the official rate of interest set by the MPC. The deals are intended to supply banks with the reserves they require to meet their self-imposed target. The innovations involved expressing the target as an *average* over the month between MPC meetings and, providing the target is met, the earning of interest on those reserves at the MPC rate.

Standing deposit and borrowing facilities with the Bank were introduced for the first time. These are available to all members of the scheme. The deposits/loans are priced at MPC rate -/+ 100bp.

The main objective of the changes was to keep interbank rates close to the official rate and to keep the interbank yield curve flat at the very short end. The first would follow from the standing facilities since the moment that interbank loans cost MPC+100bp, it would be cheaper to borrow from the Bank. This would be reinforced by the remuneration of reserves (which meant that banks holdings of reserves were significantly larger than in the past) and the expression of the target as an average over the period since this meant that as interbank rates (say) began to rise, banks would run down reserves and lend in the interbank market, knowing that they could meet the target by holding 'excess' reserves later. Much the same applied to the yield curve. If (say) 3-week interbank rates showed a tendency to rise, banks could lend from their reserves until the incentive was eliminated.

Given that it is market rates (not the official rate itself) which affect agents' behaviour, it is not surprising that the transmission of interest rate changes through the money markets and beyond has received quite a lot of empirical attention over the years. In the UK, for example, Spencer Dale examined the link between the Bank of England's 'band 1 stop rate' (the treasury bill rate which was for many years the rate which the Bank set) and market interest rates at maturities of 1, 3, 6, and 12-months and 5, 10 and 20-years, for 30 changes in that stop rate between January 1987 and July 1991 (Dale 1993). His findings were that:

• The response of market rates was generally positive but often 'overshot' the change in official rate (i.e. changed in the same direction by more than 100 per cent of the official change);

- The effect decayed with term to maturity;

- The effect was greatest at turning points of the interest cycle.

- The examination consisted of estimating the equation:

$$\Delta MR(i)_n = \beta(i)\Delta stop_n + \varepsilon_{in} \tag{4.2}$$

where:

$\Delta MR(i)_n$ is the change in the market rate of maturity i on the day of the nth change
$\Delta stop_n$ is the n-th change in the Bank's band 1 stop rate
$i = 1, 3, 6$ months...20 years
$n = 1,2,3...30$
ε_{in} is an error term.

The first two results were what one would expect. Furthermore, assuming that short-rates are generally below long-rates, the second result tells us something about long-short spreads: they narrow when official rates rise and increase when official rates fall.

Dale and Haldane (1993) also looked at the effect of a change in official rates on market rates. The independent variable was UK banks' base rate (set by reference to the Bank's official rate) changes between March 1987 and October 1992. Market rates were differentiated by type of asset/liability rather than term, as in Dale 1993. The method used was the event-day study, familiar in studies of financial markets' response to news but used also in this context by Cook and Hahn (1989). The findings this time were:

- The mean response of all the market rates to a base rate change is positive but significantly less than 100 per cent.

- The responsiveness of market rates is lower, the lower is the degree of substitutability for the non-bank private sector. Thus, the response to an official rate change is about 30 per cent for personal loans and credit card debt, 38 per cent for corporate loans, above 50 per cent for mortgage and deposit rates.

It is worth noting their conclusion that:

As market rates are sticky, the marginal impact may be less and potentially much less, than suggested by a given base rate change. Moreover, this stickiness suggests that such spreads may contain useful information about the effective stance of monetary policy and hence future movements in activity following a monetary policy shock. (Dale and Haldane, 1993 p.21).

The stickiness of market rates has also been extensively investigated by Shelagh Heffernan (1993, 1997). Following anecdotal evidence of bank and building society failure to pass on interest rate cuts to loan customers Heffernan (1993) showed that the retail banking market was one of complex imperfect competition with sluggish loan and deposit rate adjustment, with LIBOR, the London Interbank Offer Rate, proxying the official rate.

Pause for thought 4.1:

Suppose that the central bank is quoting a repurchase price of £20,100,000 for 7-day repos based on £20m of UK gilts.

Find:

a) the rate of interest that the central bank is setting

b) the price that it needs to quote if it wishes to change interest rates to 3%

More recently (Heffernan, 1997) used an error correction approach to explore the short- and long-run responses of rates on a number of banking products to changes in official rates. The model was initially estimated for seven different retail bank products using data from four large clearing banks, a number of smaller banks and five large building societies, covering the period (at longest) May 1986-January 1991.

On average, adjustments of chequing accounts and mortgages were 37 per cent complete within a month, but much slower for personal loans. The imperfect competition, noted in the 1993 paper was one reason for the slow response, reinforced by administrative costs. Interestingly, Heffernan makes a comparison with the pre-1971, pre-Competition and Credit Control, era when banks operated an interest rate cartel. In these circumstances, she notes, prices adjusted much more quickly because banks linked their product costs/returns directly to official rates by a conventional mark-up. Changes were mechanical and instantaneous.

Other factors might also influence the speed at which changes in the official rate are translated into changes in longer-term interest rates. For example, the administrative costs to the banks in making interest rate changes might cause them not to respond immediately to relatively small changes in the official rate, although much again depends on whether they expect a further change in the official rate in the near future and on what they expect their competitors to do. Banks are in competition with each other for both assets (for example, in the house mortgage market) and for liabilities (in the market for bank deposits). To maintain their spread between borrowing and lending rates (the source of their profits from lending), banks that cut lending rates must also cut deposit rates. An intensification of the competition for bank deposits might, for example, make banks unwilling to lower the rates of interest they were offering on deposits. They might be prepared temporarily to reduce their spread between borrowing and lending rates but even so, they might not follow fully a cut in official rates under these circumstances.

Box 4.3: Official and interbank rates — the Northern Rock affair

As we have seen, the first target of any change in the official rate of interest must be interbank rates since these form the basis for the setting of many other market rates. In normal circumstances the official rate and interbank rates will be close together because they represent the price of very close substitutes. In practice, we have come to expect interbank rates to show a premium of about 20bp over the official rate.

In the late summer of 2007, however, this spread widened quite sharply in many financial centres (in the UK and USA in particular) to around 100bp. The immediate cause was that banks, particularly in the USA, had lent large amounts to borrowers with a poor credit history and, to make matters worse, these loans had often been securitised and were subsequently being held throughout the financial system. This made it very difficult for one financial institution to assess the riskiness of another. Very quickly, banks became reluctant to lend to each other and interbank rates rose sharply. SInce interbank rates form the basis of most other market rates, it was as though the central bank had tightened monetary policy by about 75bp, *in one go*. Central banks tried a number of devices to bring the spread down to normal levels without much success. Eventually, they had to cut official interest rates so as to bring down the whole structure of rates.

In the UK, there was an additional problem. We have seen in box 4.2 that the Bank of England had recently taken steps to ensure that interbank rates would stay close to the official rate. But in August 2007, the Northern Rock Bank found itself in difficulties because it relied heavily on the interbank market to fund its mortgage business. With the interbank market drying up, it had to borrow from the Bank of England. This caused a panic amongst depositors which was eventually calmed by official action. But it sent a strong signal to banks that there might be serious reputational risk in using the Bank of England's standing facilities and that it might be safer to stick with the interbank market even if interbank rates were very high. We say more about this in section 9.2 and appendix 2.

This implies that banks have some choice in deciding whether or not to respond to the prompting of the central bank. In addition to varying the spread between borrowing and lending rates, banks are able to change the conditions under which they are prepared to lend (for example, in the collateral they require for loans). Banks engage as a matter of course in the rationing of credit — not everyone is able to borrow the amount they wish (or at all) at existing bank interest rates. Thus, to some extent at least banks may choose to respond to tighter monetary conditions by restricting their lending in the hope of reducing the risk associated with their loans. After several years of relaxed lending criteria, leading to the development of the so-called 'sub-prime' loans market, banks became very restrictive indeed in their lending policies during 2008.

It should be more difficult for banks to resist attempts by the central bank to push interest rates up since, as we have seen earlier in this section, the central bank has the power to induce a genuine shortage of liquidity in the economy. If banks hold their assets in a more liquid form than is needed, all they are doing is forgoing potential profits. If they hold their assets in a less liquid form than is needed, they ultimately face the possibility of a loss of confidence by the depositors and hence of collapse. Even here, however, there are some limits to the power of the central bank since it would be a very risky policy for central banks to squeeze liquidity to such an extent that the banks genuinely feared collapse. Indeed, for such a policy to be effective, the authorities would have to accept reasonably frequent bank collapses. This, in turn, would reduce the confidence of depositors in the banking system — a result that modern governments do not desire.

So far as *monetary growth* is concerned, what matters most is the responsiveness of bank loan rates. If an increase, for example, in official rates is quickly communicated to bank loans, then we move up a downward sloping demand curve for (the flow of) new loans. Consequently, loans and, through the flow of funds identity, deposits grow more slowly. If it is also the case that the rise in official rates can cause changes in spreads such that there is a relative cheapening of non-bank sources of credit then better still. This cheapening of the cost of a substitute causes the bank loan demand curve to move inward. In these favourable circumstances, changes in the official rate have the effect of the proverbial 'double whammy'. A change in rates moves us along a curve which simultaneously shifts in a reinforcing direction. This mechanism is quite complicated and we return to it in section 10.3 where we suggest that various financial innovations in recent years have dismantled these favourable circumstances, so much so that changes in official rates are probably very blunt instruments for controlling monetary growth, supposing that the authorities ever wished to do such a thing.

Pause for thought 4.2:

Why might market interest rates not change instantly and exactly in line with changes in official rates?

In the last few pages we have explored a number of reasons (and some evidence) for a degree of elasticity in the relationship between the official rate and market rates, such that the central bank may not always be able to get the change in market rates that it wants, or at least that there may be some delay.

There are two further constraints on the rate of interest as policy instrument, albeit of a rather different kind. The difference is that these are constraints on the adjustment of the official rate itself. The first concerns the level and change in official rates in other major financial centres. This constraint is usually imposed by foreign exchange markets which will quickly make it clear if they think that a central bank is pursuing an interest rate policy which is inconsistent with the current exchange rate. A classic example for the UK is provided by the occasion of the pound's exit from the European exchange rate mechanism in September 1992. No one doubted the Bank of England's ability to raise interest rates (which it did, to

15 per cent), but the forex markets judged that the political will would fail to raise them sufficiently unless other central banks (notably the Bundesbank) cut their rates to help sterling. Massive sales of sterling occurred until the exchange rate parity was abandoned. We look at market constraints on policy in section 9.4.

In years gone by, a further constraint was imposed by conflicts of policy objectives. From 1945 until the mid-1970s, governments, for whom central banks acted in effect as monetary policy agents, were inclined to list their policy objectives as stable prices, full employment and economic growth — often with a stable exchange rate and balance of payments equilibrium thrown in. The problem is that four goals are not simultaneously consistent with one instrument (in the imperfections of a real world, at least). Hence interest rates might be raised to protect the exchange rate (as was often the case in the UK) but would be reduced at the earliest opportunity when growth stagnated and unemployment rose. This experience of inconsistency underlies some of the arguments for giving central banks independence. 'Independence' is usually taken to mean independence from government. But there is little point in freeing the central bank from political interference if its anti-inflation strategy is to be constrained by other, conflicting, policy objectives. Hence when we find a genuinely independent central bank, we will usually find that it has only one objective to maximise — price stability.

4.4   The rate of interest and the banking sector

In this section we construct a simple model to show how, in the system we've just been describing, the central bank sets interest rates and how this affects the behaviour of commercial banks. We begin with a summary of the system we are trying to model (on the assumption that the system is functioning under normal conditions). In a paraphrase of Goodhart (2002):

1. The central bank determines the short-term interest rate in the light of whatever reaction function it is following;

2. The official rate determines interbank rates on which banks mark-up the cost of loans;

3. At such rates, the private sector determines the volume of borrowing from the banking system;

4. Banks then adjust their relative interest rates and balance sheets to meet the credit demands;

5. Step 4 determines the money stock and its components as well as the desired level of reserves;

6. In order to sustain the level of interest rates, the central bank engages in repo deals to satisfy banks' requirement for reserves.

Figure 4.1 embraces these characteristics in its four quadrants.[8] In QI the central bank sets an official rate of interest, r_0.[9]

$$r_0 = \overline{r_0} \tag{4.3}$$

In normal circumstances, this official rate determines the level of interbank rates on which banks determine their loan rates by a series of risk-related mark ups. We make two simplifications. The first is (*pace* the discussion in the previous section) that interbank rates are conventionally related to the official rate so that the mark-ups are effectively mark-ups on the official rate. The second is that we can represent the range of mark-ups by a single, weighted average, rate. This is shown as m.

$$r_L = \overline{r_0} + m \tag{4.4}$$

In QII (and again in normal circumstances) banks supply whatever volume of new loans is demanded by creditworthy clients at the loan rate r_L. Notice that the loan supply curve, L_S, denotes *flows*, consistent with what we have said about the flow of funds being positive at the going rate of interest. This is further confirmed by the downward-sloping loan demand curve, L_D, showing that the effect of a change in the official rate is to alter the *rate of growth* of money and credit. At r_0, loans are expanding at the demand-determined rate L_0.

$$L_S = L_D \tag{4.5}$$

$$L_D = f(\Delta \ln P, \Delta \ln Y, r_L) \tag{4.6}$$
$$+ \quad\quad + \quad\quad -$$

QIII represents the banks' balance sheet constraint (so the $L=D$ line passes through the origin at 45°). In practice, of course, 'deposits' has to be understood to include the bank's net worth while 'loans' includes holdings of money market investments, securities etc. At r_0 the growth of loans is creating deposits at the rate D_0.

$$L_S = L_D = L_0 = D_0 \tag{4.7}$$

The *DR* line in QIV shows the demand for reserves. The angle to the deposits axis is determined by the reserve ratio. In most developed banking systems, this angle will be very narrow, but we have exaggerated it for the purpose of clarity.

$$DR = \frac{R}{D}(D) \tag{4.8}$$

In a system (like that in the UK, see box 4.2) where reserve ratios are prudential rather than mandatory, the *DR* line will rotate with changes in banks' desire for liquidity. Even in a mandatory system, the curve may rotate provided that we understand it to represent *total* (i.e. required + excess) reserves.

Finally, in QI again we see the central bank's willingness to allow the expansion of reserves at whatever rate (here R_0) is required by the banking system, given developments in QII-QIV.

$$R_0 = \frac{R}{D}(D_0)$$ (4.9)

$$R_S = R_D$$ (4.10)

Figure 4.1: Interest rates, money and credit

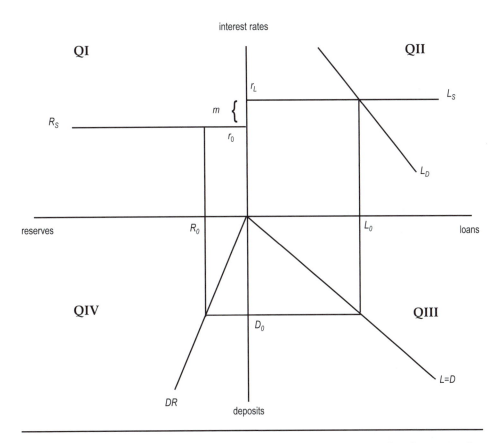

It is a fairly simple task to trace the effects on the system of a change in the official rate of interest, or in the banks' mark up. Indeed, by increasing m, we can illustrate the effect of the jump in interbank lending rates and the crisis referred to in box 4.3. The increase in m causes an upward shift of L_S in QII. The flow demand for loans is decreased, leading to a lower rate of monetary expansion. As we said above, it is *as if* the central bank had increased the official rate, even though in fact r_0 is unchanged.

In section 5.2 we shall see how this model can be integrated with the IS/PC/MR model of the macroeconomy in order to enrich the discussion of monetary policy.

4.5   The rejection of monetary base control

The message of this chapter so far is that, under current operating arrangements the money supply is endogenously determined and it is the rate of interest that is exogenous. In fact, under current trends, even that may be questionable since many central banks have opted to make the policy-making process as open as possible on the grounds that policy is less destabilising if agents can anticipate it. The ultimate case is where a central bank sticks rigidly to a Taylor rule and broadcasts this fact to all and sundry. In these circumstances, even the policy rate has become endogenous and it is the inflation target that is the strictly exogenous term. We shall return to this in chapter 8.

However, the idea that the money supply is exogenously determined by the central bank using open market operations to control the monetary base dies hard, especially in macroeconomic textbooks. So, in this section we take a few pages to explain why central banks, without exception, have turned their back on this approach.

The problems, as Goodhart explained in 1994, all stem from the fact that banks must be able to provide *undoubted* convertibility between currency and deposits at par,[10] combined with the fact that reserves pay zero interest or at least interest rates which are below money market rates and with fluctuations in flows of funds between the public and private sectors which cause sharp fluctuations in banks' operational deposits. From the first it follows that the demand for reserves is extremely inelastic; from the second it follows that reserve-holding acts as a tax on banking intermediation and so banks will hold minimum reserves. Putting the two together means that money market interest rates would be extremely volatile given net flows in and out of the banking system. Since any interest is better than none, an end of day excess of bank reserves will be dumped in the money market until rates are driven down virtually to zero while a shortage will drive rates up to the penal rate at which the central bank does step in or the banks are prepared to face the penalty for reserve deficiencies.

Tinkering with the details can introduce some smoothing. Specifying the reserve target as an *average* over a period will eliminate day to day fluctuations but will leave rates volatile at the end of the maintenance period. Paying interest on reserves will reduce the distortionary tax effect of reserve holding and lead to larger holdings on average. But a new element is introduced into the demand for reserves as money market rates fluctuate relative to the rate on reserves.

Why banks are not reserve constrained in practice is a question that has received a number of answers over the years, but they all stem from this fundamental dilemma that targeting the quantity of reserves would produce disruptive interest rate fluctuations. We look briefly at the development of these arguments and provide a summary in box 4.4.

The earliest claim that central banks have little choice but to supply reserves on demand rests upon the conflict of policy objectives that would follow from the behaviour of interest rates under reserve targeting. One version appears explicitly in Weintraub (1978) and is linked ultimately to his wage theorem. The growth of nominal income (due to a rise in unit labour costs, or in the mark-up on those costs) results in a rise in the demand for active balances. If the level of real output is to be maintained, the supply of money must increase. If it does not, or does not do so sufficiently, interest rates will rise and this will reduce the level of output and employment. In Weintraub's view, political considerations make this intolerable. Ultimately, the political authorities will instruct the central bank to accommodate the extra demand for money. Similar views, that central banks could, if they chose, restrict reserves but choose not to do so for reasons of policy conflicts, appear in Myrdal (1939) and Lavoie (1985). The accommodating behaviour of central banks, seen from this angle, is essentially political in origin and the interpretation has a distinctly 'Keynesian' flavour. In the UK, however, the level of interest rates has always been an issue of political sensitivity. In the early-1970s, for example, when broad money growth touched 30 per cent p.a. the government of Edward Heath pressed the Bank of England to introduce the supplementary special deposits scheme and return to direct controls rather than raise interest rates to the necessary level (see section 11.2). Goodhart also relates how Margaret Thatcher in the UK, leading a government in the early 1980s which rejected any responsibility for output, growth and employment, and stressed the importance of controlling the monetary aggregates, nonetheless baulked at the prospect of raising interest rates to the levels suggested by the Bank (Goodhart, 2002, p.17).

Pause for thought 4.3:

Explain why non-interest bearing reserves act as a tax on banking intermediaries.

Given the manifest readiness of governments from the 1970s onwards to sacrifice full employment for low inflation, the accommodating behaviour of central banks needed another explanation. According to Moore (1988a chs. 5-8) and Kaldor (1982, 1985) such pressures can be found in the structure of modern banking systems. The starting point is that central banks, in addition to their role as managers of monetary policy, bear a heavy responsibility for ensuring the stability of their domestic financial systems. This role is commonly referred to as their 'lender of last resort' (LOLR) function and reminds us again of a central bank's monopoly position. Since financial intermediation always involves an element of maturity transformation, intermediaries are always subject to the risk that they may have calls on their liabilities which they cannot meet from their relatively illiquid assets. In the case of an individual institution in difficulties, borrowing within the system is a realistic solution but in the event of a system-wide shortage of liquidity the general sale of assets will be self-defeating as regards the raising of liquidity but it could easily cause a collapse of asset prices with the threat of insolvency and a general debt deflation. The only safeguard against disaster is the central bank's willingness always to provide liquidity (Moore, 1988a pp.57-65;

Kaldor, 1985 pp.20-25). It needs to be emphasised: this is not a discretionary function. If confidence in the financial system is to be maintained, the public needs to
be convinced that this assistance will always be forthcoming. Such reassurance
requires an unquestioning response, not a response which is hedged around with
conditions (Goodhart, 1984, p.212).

Box 4.4: The difficulties of monetary base control

One implication of the B-M analysis of money supply determination is that the central bank can control the size of the monetary base and that this will produce a predictable and multiple change in
the broad money stock. In each major review of the operation of UK monetary policy (1958, 1971,
1980) however, the authorities have rejected such an approach and, indeed, it is difficult to find
examples of its use in any developed country. Although policy makers have sometimes stressed
the importance of monetary aggregates and the need to control their growth, the chosen instrument
has almost always been the short term rate of interest. The reasons for this universal rejection of
MBC are many. We give just a brief list below.

If the authorities were able to fix the base, any shock (to the demand for reserves) would have to
be accommodated by changes in very short-term interest rates. Because of the convertibility
requirement, the demand for reserves is extremely inelastic and these interest rate fluctuations
would be very violent.

• While it is true that the authorities know the size of the base *ex post* it is very difficult to control it *ex ante* because it is very difficult to predict the market flows that cause changes. In its
daily money market operations, the Bank of England has frequently to intervene more than
once because its morning forecasts turn out to be wrong.

• Even if it could forecast accurately, it does not follow that the central bank could undertake
the operations necessary to hit the target. If it were necessary to offset a predicted expansion,
for example, a sale of bonds or other government debt to the non-bank private sector would be
necessary and this cannot be carried out at short notice without major changes to the debt markets. Continuous auctions would be required and once again interest rates (on bonds this time)
would become very unstable.

• MBC would probably be inconsistent with other institutional arrangements. For example, it is
difficult to see how banks could make overdraft-type commitments to clients if they might suddenly find it impossible to obtain the reserves to cover the additional lending.

• Banks' response to the risk that there might be shortages of reserves would be to hold
'excess' reserves. Since these are non-interest bearing this imposes a tax on all institutions
subject to reserve requirements. Such a tax would raise the price and reduce the quantity of
bank intermediation.

• Experience shows us that any direct control of quantities will stimulate innovation designed to
evade the constraint. Lending via offshore subsidiaries seems one obvious possibility in a
world with free capital movements.

A second structural feature of modern systems explains why such assistance might often be required. Most textbook discussion of the lender of last resort tends to focus upon the shortage of liquidity caused by net withdrawals of cash ('runs on the bank'). However, the same shortage of liquidity, a fall in the R/Dp ratio, will occur when banks increase their lending and in many banking systems banks are contractually committed to make additional loans on demand. This arises from the 'overdraft' facility where banks agree to meet all demand for loans up to a ceiling. Customers then use that proportion of the facility that they require on a day to day basis. Typically, the proportion of the facility that is in use at any one time is about 60 per cent of total commitments. Thus it follows that if the state of trade requires an increase in working capital to bridge the time gap between firms' additional outlays and the receipts from increased sales, requests for loans will always be met. '...if bank loans are largely demand-determined, so that the quantity of bank credit demanded is a non-discretionary variable from the viewpoint of individual banks, this then implies that the money supply is credit driven.' (Moore, 1988b, p.373). If the state of trade[11] means customers demand more advances, banks have no choice (unless they are to break contractual agreements) but to expand their lending. Advances (and deposits) will rise relative to reserves, interest rates will rise and security prices fall, reducing the value of bank assets. Faced with a general shortage of liquidity, the central bank must, as we said above, provide assistance. Essentially the same argument is put by Wray (1990, pp.85-90).

There are two further structural features which make it impossible for central banks to resist the demand for reserves. The first is the structure of banks' assets which are overwhelmingly non-marketable loans (rather than marketable securities). Moore highlights the problem by posing a reduction in the monetary base brought about by open market operations of the textbook type. Bank reserves are reduced but banks cannot reduce their balance sheets because calling in loans will bankrupt their customers. This illustration is easily modified to reflect a more realistic state of affairs. Recall that expansion of bank balance sheets is the norm. We must imagine banks making new loans, in response to demand, expecting the additional reserves to be forthcoming, only to find that they are not because of a change in central bank stance. From this point, Moore's argument follows as before. Banks cannot unwind this position without causing chaos.[12]

Lastly, it is worth noting that most monetary regimes which pay any attention to the base/deposits relationship require banks to report on their holding of base at time t, and their holdings of deposits at some earlier period, t-1, the system of lagged reserve accounting. The current level of required reserves is thus predetermined by the past level of deposits (Moore, 1988a; Goodhart, 1984 p.212). In these circumstances, there is plainly nothing that banks can do to accommodate deposits to reserves. Any desired ratio can only be met by the central bank supplying the reserves.

For all of these reasons, some a matter of choice, others decidedly non-discretionary, central banks accommodate the demand for reserves and confine their policy gestures to setting the price.

Given the ability of banking systems to innovate products and practices in response to regulation (see section 11.3 for some examples) it is worth considering what might be the outcome if central banks did take a less accommodating position.

Suppose, for example, that central banks, under pressure from financial markets perhaps, were forced to impose quantity constraints on reserve availability. Some have argued that this might still matter little since the structure of modern financial systems enables banks to engage in a number of activities which enable them to avoid the consequences of reserve shortages. In this view it is sometimes said that banks can 'manufacture' reserves though this is a little misleading since most of the practices are aimed at reducing the quantity of reserves that are required. If reserves are defined appropriately as the liabilities solely of the central bank then banks can do nothing to avoid a system-wide shortage. What, perhaps, they can do is to economise on reserves so as to avoid the effects of the shortage.

Central to this argument is banks' management of their liabilities. For example, in a period where the central bank is consciously seeking to restrain the growth of reserves, and presumably also the money supply, banks will attract funds out of sight deposits which have a high reserve requirement, into time deposits, CDs and other instruments which have lower requirements. The result is that a given volume of reserves will support a higher volume of lending (and a higher volume of total deposits). It also follows that periods of reserve shortage and consequent liability management will be periods of rising interest rates. Such periods will also be conducive to financial innovation as banks try to find cheaper ways of adjusting to the shortage. An obvious example of this is the development of certificates of deposit where the superior (liquidity) characteristics of the product enables banks to raise funds for a fixed term more cheaply than they could through traditional time deposits.[13]

To date, the only attempt to establish empirically which of the two descriptions (complete accommodation or reserve-economising) is the more accurate was carried out by Pollin, looking at the Federal Reserve. The criteria used were threefold. Firstly, Pollin argued, if 'accommodation' were the rule, then we would expect stationarity in the ratio of loans (L) to reserves (R); secondly, if the Federal Reserve were to provide reserves 'willingly' then borrowed (from the Fed) and non-borrowed reserves would be very close substitutes and there would be no need to develop circumventory products and practices; thirdly, market interest rates would not move independently of official rates (official rates would 'cause' market rates). Formal tests of stationarity in the L/R ratio, of elasticities in the demand for borrowed and non-borrowed reserves and of causality between official and market rates, were all claimed to lend support to the structural view (Pollin, 1991).

The controversy remains, however, since some of the results are open to alternative interpretation (Palley, 1991). For example, the discovery that the L/R ratio is subject to an upward secular trend is advanced by Pollin as evidence that reserves are constrained. On the other hand, as Palley points out, the need to hold reserves against deposits has been recognised for years in the standard banking literature as acting as a tax upon banking intermediation — limiting the amount of each deposit that can be lent out. The fact that the L/R ratio rises over time could merely be evidence that banks are profit seekers wishing to reduce the burden of reserve requirements even when reserves are readily available. Rather similarly, the discovery that there appears to be two-way Sims (1972) causality between Federal and market interest rates (where the logic of complete accommodation would require uni-directional causality from Fed to market rates) could be accounted for by market rates embodying expectations about future Fed rates.

The truth may lie somewhere between the two views, and be heavily dependent on time horizon. It is difficult to see how innovatory behaviour could act quickly enough to alleviate a sudden shortage of reserves but, if only because of their tax-like effects, certainly banks have a long-run incentive to minimise reserve requirements.

4.6   Summary

A particular problem in defining money is that economists tend to think of 'money' in different ways depending on the general view they hold of how the economy works. An economist who essentially thinks of the economy as an equilibrium system is likely to stress the importance of the aggregate supply of money and to define it narrowly, concentrating on the medium of exchange role of money. On the other hand, an economist who emphasises disequilibrium and uncertainty is likely to regard credit as a more important concept than the money supply.

In seeking to produce a precise definition of 'money' amongst all these difficulties, economists have attempted to do so both descriptively, usually starting from the medium of exchange role, and prescriptively, being willing to adjust the definition of money to produce the desired stability in the demand for money function. There have been many official definitions of money and these have changed frequently over the years.

Key concepts used in this chapter

lending ceilings	spreads
qualitative guidance	convertibility
direct controls	monetary base control
repurchase agreements	endogenous money

refinancing rate   buffer stocks

counterparties   interest-endogeneity

basis point   base-endogeneity

Questions and exercises
Answers at the end of the book

1. Distinguish between 'interest-endogeneity' and 'base-endogeneity'.

2. Why, in practice, are commercial banks unconstrained in their access to reserves?

3. Explain briefly the disadvantages of attempting to regulate monetary growth by non-price methods.

4. Why is the demand for reserves by commercial banks highly interest-inelastic?

...and also to think about

5. Explain what is meant by a repurchase agreement and work an example to show how, by changing the terms of a repo deal, the central bank can raise and lower short-term interest rates.

6. Go to the statistical section of the Bank of England's website (www.bankofengland.co.uk/statistics/statistics.htm), look for the publication 'Bankstats', find table G1.1 and look at the relationship between interbank rates and the Bank of England 'base rate' in the last few years. The 4-digit codes at the top of each column can be used to extract longer time series from the Bank's interactive database.

Further reading

The use by central banks of short-term interest rates as the sole monetary policy instrument is documented by all the sources below. The reasons for choice of this instrument (as opposed, for example, to the monetary base) and the central bank's ability to impose its choice are explained in Goodhart (1994). Blinder (1998) provides a central banker's view of monetary policy making and ch.2 especially looks at the choice of the interest rate as policy instrument.

The procedures by which rates are set are explained in a box in *Bank of England Quarterly Bulletin* (1999) 'The Transmission Mechanism of Monetary Policy' (May), 161-70, which also explains how the Bank thinks a change in interest rates affects other variables. Although the principles described in the box remain broadly valid, the details need updating to take account of the 2006 money market reforms. The handbook (no.24) written for the Centre for Central Banking Studies, written by Gray and Talbot and titled *Monetary Operations* gives the most detailed account of the procedures (and choices) involved in setting interest rates. It can be found at:

www.bankofengland.co.uk/education/ccbs/handbooks/index.htm

Borio (1997) confirms the widespread similarity of these procedures across countries. The fact that these operating procedures have the effect of making the money supply endogenous is documented in Goodhart (*op cit* and 2002) and in Howells's essay in P Arestis and M C Sawyer (eds) (2001). This also surveys a number of issues arising from the endogeneity of money. H M Treasury (2002) provides the background to the conduct of monetary policy in the UK in recent years. Chs. 3-6 explain the monetary policy framework, the choice of an inflation target and the conduct of an independent Bank of England.

The 2006 changes in Bank of England money market operations can be found on the Bank's website: www.bankofengland.co.uk/markets/money/index.htm Further details are available in *The Framework for the Bank of England's Operations in the Sterling Money Markets* (the 'Red Book'). This also can be found on the Bank of England's website.

5 Monetary policy and aggregate demand

'Accordingly we find that in every kingdom, into which money begins to flow in greater abundance than formerly, everything takes on a new face; labour and industry gain life; the merchant becomes more enterprising, and even the farmer follows his plough with greater alacrity and attention...'

David Hume, 'Of Money', *Political Discourses,* (1752).

5.1   Introduction

There is now considerable agreement about the design of an optimal monetary policy and about the way in which monetary policy works. Indeed, it is now common practice to talk about the 'New Consensus Macroeconomics' (NCM) and the briefest examination shows that this consensus owes a great deal to the experience of policymaking. Charles Bean (2007) gives the following as the key features of the NCM:

- In the long-run, monetary policy has no real effects;

- In the short-run, nominal rigidities create a trade-off between output and inflation

- Monetary policy is the principal means of influencing aggregate demand;

- Policy outcomes are improved under an independent central bank;

- Ends (a specific inflation target) matter more than means (intermediate targets);

- The management of expectations is critical;

- The policy instrument is the short-run nominal interest rate set by the central bank.

This chapter and the next look at the way(s) in which the effect of a change in the policy instrument is linked to the ultimate target of policy, that is at the 'transmission mechanism of monetary policy'. We have divided the linkage into two phases (hence the two chapters), but with some degree of overlap. In the first phase (this chapter), our main interest lies in how a change in the nominal interest rate affects the level of aggregate demand. In the second phase (in chapter 6), we shall look at how a change in aggregate demand affects inflation, but we shall also go beyond the consensus and look at the (still) controversial question of whether the ultimate effect of monetary policy need be restricted in the long-run to prices, or whether there may be some lasting effect on output.

In section 5.2 we look at the linkages from the policy instrument to aggregate demand using a framework employed by the Bank of England, the ECB and almost certainly by many other central banks. Then in section 5.3 we shall show how this process can be modelled more formally, using the *IS/PC/MR* model. As we shall see, this model is constructed so as to capture the whole of the transmission mechanism from the policy rate through to the inflation target. To that extent, section 5.3 treats as resolved some issues which we shall re-open in chapter 6. In section 5.4 we shall extend the model to incorporate a banking or monetary sector along the lines of section 4.4. As we do that, we shall have in mind the test of whether the formal model enables us to capture the processes described in section 5.2.

5.2   The transmission mechanism

In this section, we look at the transmission mechanism of monetary policy in regimes where the rate of interest is the policy instrument. Interestingly, Bean's list of features of the NCM make no reference to the money supply but others have been quick to point out that the quantity of money plays no role in the widely accepted view of how the macroeconomy works nor, more relevantly for this section, does it play any part of the formal macromodels of the UK Treasury, the Bank of England (Arestis and Sawyer, 2002). Similarly, in the macroeconomic model of the US economy used by the Federal Reserve, shifts in monetary policy are fully captured by innovations to the Federal Funds rate, with no role for monetary aggregates (Federal Reserve Board, 1996; see also Fontana and Palacio Vera, 2004, pp.29-34).

It is the central bank's key interest rate that is now seen as the policy instrument for achieving the desired inflation rate through its effects on aggregate demand. The following diagram is an adaptation of a flow chart published a few years ago, to illustrate the way in which one should think about the transmission mechanism (Bank of England, 1999). The ECB uses a very similar chart (ECB, 2004, p.45).

Figure 5.1: The transmission mechanism of monetary policy

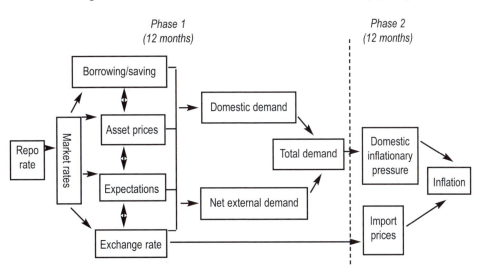

Source: Adapted from *Bank of England Quarterly Bulletin*, May 1999

We have made two modifications. The first is to insert a box marked 'market rates' between the repo or official rate and the rest of the transmission mechanism.[1] This recognises that the repo rate itself is of little interest to anyone outside the counterparties with which the central bank deals. The link between the official rate and private sector behaviour is entirely dependent upon the central bank's ability to change market rates. As a rule of thumb, we might regard this link as conventionally determined and secure but it is worth remembering, from section 4.3, that the pass-through from official to market rates is not simple, but contains lags which, while they work themselves out, must necessarily result in significant changes in *relative* rates. Furthermore, we should remember that one of the disturbing features of the 'sub-prime problem' and the resulting credit crunch was the sharp rise in market rates (in the UK, LIBOR rates) relative to the official rate. In September 2007, the LIBOR-repo spread in the UK reached about 110 basis points where 10 would have been more normal. Given that this spread had opened up within a few weeks, and that market rates are priced off LIBOR (and *not* the repo rate), the shock was rather as though the central bank had raised the policy rate four times in a month.[2] We return to this in section 5.4 and in appendix 2.

The second modification emphasises the distinction we have introduced between the two phases of policy for purposes of discussing it over two chapters. Phase one (this chapter) lies to the left of the dashed line; phase two (chapter 6) lies to the right. Conventional wisdom assumes that the full effects of a change in the official interest rate require about two years to materialise.

The central message of figure 5.1 is that changing the repo rate affects inflation if, and only if, it changes the level of aggregate demand.[3] In other words, inflation is determined by an expectations-augmented Phillips curve which we can write as follows:

$$\pi_t = \alpha_1 \pi_t^e + \alpha_2 (Y - Y^*) \tag{5.1}$$

where α_1 represents the degree of money illusion, α_2 is the slope of the PC and $Y\text{-}Y^*$ is a measure of the output gap. Assuming that there is no money illusion ($\alpha_1 = 1$) and that there is some inertia such that current inflation depends upon last period's inflation,[4] we can write

$$\pi_t = \pi_{t-1} + \alpha (Y - Y^*) \tag{5.2}$$

It is the final term, $\alpha(Y\text{-}Y^*)$, that is relevant to figure 5.1. As output deviates from its long-run equilibrium, this creates inflationary (or deflationary) pressure.

The principal components of domestic private sector demand are consumption and investment expenditure.

Consumption expenditure derives from current income but consumption decisions depend also on expected future income, the level of wealth and on the ability to borrow against existing wealth. Thus, monetary policy is likely to influence household consumption through several channels. For example, an increase in interest rates:

• makes saving from current income more attractive

• increases repayments on existing floating-rate debt and thus lowers disposable income

• increases the cost of borrowing and thus increases the cost of goods and services obtained on credit

• lowers the price of financial assets and hence influences estimates of private sector wealth

• lowers house prices or, at least, slows the rate at which they are increasing and this, too, influences estimates of household wealth and lowers the value of the collateral against which households seek to borrow.

When discussing asset prices, it is important to stress that the policymaker's concern over asset prices is limited to their effect upon the demand for current output. The mere fact that asset prices may be rising, or falling, is not of itself a matter for policy. Nor is it the central bank's job to stabilise the housing market. In the last few years, research by Goodhart and Hofmann (2007) has shown that the behaviour of house prices, especially in the UK, has been a useful leading indicator, amongst others, of future inflationary pressure. But it is once again, the link between asset prices and aggregate demand that matters and not the move-ment in asset prices themselves that is at issue. That said, it has been claimed by some commentators, that central banks, led by the US Federal Reserve, have begun to take on a role as 'lender of last resort' to the whole of the financial sys-tem, being quick to loosen monetary conditions when financial markets have turned downwards. We look at this point again in section 9.3.

If households believe that the interest rate changes will lower aggregate demand, they might also become concerned about the impact on output and employment. Increased worries about future employment will cause households to lower their estimates of expected future income from employment and become more cautious about current expenditure. Any fear of an impending recession might, in addition, cause banks to tighten the conditions they apply to loan appli-cations, making it more difficult for people to obtain credit even if they remain willing to borrow credit.

Pause for thought 5.1

(a) why are equity prices likely to fall following an increase in interest rates?

(b) why might they not fall?

Of these various influences, changes in repayments on floating-rate mort-gages are particularly important in the UK since loans secured on houses make up about 80 per cent of personal debt, and most mortgages carry floating interest rates. All of these operate in the same direction — we expect an increase in inter-est rates to reduce consumption expenditure.

Yet, not everyone will reduce consumption expenditure as interest rates rise. The discussion so far has implied that interest rate rises reduce the disposable income of all households, but this will not be true for those consisting of people living off income from savings deposits. Nor is it true for people whose expected future income depends on an annuity to be purchased in the near future. In both of these cases, higher interest rates imply a higher income. Thus, interest rate changes have redistributional effects. When interest rates increase, net borrowers are made worse off and net savers better off. However, the groups made better off (net savers) are highly likely to be dominated by those made worse off (net borrowers) and so we continue to expect increases in interest rates to reduce household consumption expenditure.

The same applies to investment expenditure. An increase in interest rates:

• raises external borrowing costs for firms that raise funds through bank loans or from bills or bonds markets;

• increases the rate at which they discount back expected future returns from investment, making investment projects less attractive;

• increases the return from the savings of firms, retained from past profits, raising the opportunity cost of financing investment internally;

• increases the difficulty and cost of raising investment funds through the issue of new capital on the stock market;

• increases the costs of holding inventories of goods, which are often financed by bank loans;

• lowers asset prices, reducing the net worth of firms and making it more difficult for them to borrow.

The way in which firms respond to monetary policy changes also depends on the way in which those changes affect estimates of future aggregate demand since these are a major influence on their forecast future sales and hence on estimated future profits. Thus, if a change in the official interest rate — or, indeed, a failure to change it — reinforces a view that aggregate demand is likely to fall in the future firms may respond by 'restructuring' and cutting back employment by greater amounts than might be expected simply on the basis of the direct effects listed above.

As with households, not all firms will be affected in the same way or to the same extent. Much depends on the nature of the business, the size of the firm and its sources of finance. An increase in interest rates improves the cash flow of firms with funds deposited with banks or placed in the money markets, although this does not imply that they will make use of their improved position to increase investment. It is more likely, indeed, to encourage firms to hold greater quantities of financial assets or to pay higher dividends to shareholders. The cash flow of firms whose short-term assets and liabilities are more or less matched will be

little affected by changes in short-term interest rates but are still likely to be influenced by changes in longer-term rates. Further, despite the above list, the impact
of changes in the official interest rate on the cost of capital for particular firms is
difficult to predict, especially for large and multinational firms with access to
international capital markets. Nonetheless, it remains true that for firms taken
together increases in interest rates are highly likely to lead to reduced investment
expenditure.

Open economy influences also need to be taken into account. Other things
being equal, an increase in domestic interest rates should increase the attractive-
ness of the currency in foreign exchange markets, raising the value of the currency. This damages the international competitiveness of domestic firms since it raises the prices of their goods when expressed in foreign currencies and, in the short
run at least, they have little scope for reducing costs of production and lowering
domestic currency prices. Thus, they must reduce their profit margins, accept a
loss of market share in export markets or both. Problems arise in domestic markets also. Import-competing goods face increased competition from foreign
products because their prices are now lower in domestic currency terms.
Difficulties are likely to follow also for domestic firms that are not in direct competition with foreign firms because of changes in the composition of household
spending that results from changes in the relative prices of domestic and foreign
goods. For example, households may respond to a reduction in the domestic currency price of foreign holidays by cutting back on expenditure on books or CDs
in order to take a foreign holiday. Of course, it is only those changes in exchange
rate that are brought about by monetary policy changes or expected changes in
monetary policy that we are concerned with here. Exchange rates may be affected by many other factors.

Pause for thought 5.2

Can you think of situations in which an increase in domestic interest rates will not cause an
increase in the value of the domestic currency?

Again, different sectors will be affected in different ways by monetary policy
induced exchange rate changes. The manufacturing sector is the most exposed to
foreign competition and thus is likely to suffer most from increases in the value
of the domestic currency. Agriculture, financial and business services, and those
parts of the service sector heavily reliant on the arrival of foreign tourists are also
likely to be strongly affected.

Expectations and confidence about the future clearly play a major role in all
of this. It follows that the size of the likely fall in aggregate demand depends crucially on:

(a) whether the present increase in interest rates had been expected; and

(b) whether the present increase leads to expectations of further increases in future or quick reversals of policy;

(c) expectations regarding future inflation rates.

Inflationary expectations are particularly important since much of the influence of interest rate changes on the expenditure of households and firms relates to changes in real interest rates (the rate of interest adjusted to take into account the expected rate of inflation). Monetary policy operates directly on nominal interest rates. Much of the above discussion takes inflationary expectations as given, in which case a change in nominal interest rates is equivalent to a change in real interest rates. However, monetary policy may well have an influence on inflationary expectations. Indeed, it is commonly the intention of the monetary authorities that it should do so. Hence, if an increase in interest rates lowers market expectations of the future rate of inflation, the real rate of interest will increase by more than the nominal rate. Those areas of expenditure particularly influenced by real rates of interest (e.g. investment expenditure by firms and housing expenditure and expenditure on consumer durables) will be affected more than would have been the case had inflationary expectations remained unchanged.

Pause for thought 5.3

Why does the effect of monetary policy on expectations matter?

Can you think of cases where a change in interest rates might have a 'perverse' effect on expectations?

We can conclude from this section that:

- monetary policy influences aggregate demand in a variety of ways;

- the relationship between interest rate changes and changes in aggregate demand might be quite powerful;

- the relationship between interest rates and aggregate demand is inverse — increases in interest rates reduce aggregate expenditure; reductions in interest rates cause aggregate expenditure to increase

- nonetheless, the relationship between interest rates and aggregate demand is complex

- interest rate changes affect the distribution of income as well as the level of aggregate demand.

Pause for thought 5.4

Are the effects of a *reduction* in interest rates likely to be the exact reverse of the effects described above for an increase in rates?

Knowing the direction in which aggregate demand is likely to change when interest rates change is of very limited use. We need to know how powerful a policy instrument monetary policy is, whether the size of the impact of a given change is predictable and how long it will take for the full impact of a change in interest rates to be felt in the economy. Clearly, the size of the impact of a monetary policy change and the length of the time lags involved in the process may well vary from one economy to another. Nonetheless, we can make some general points about time lags.

There are several different time lags involved in monetary policy. We can distinguish the following:

• the length of time it takes for the authorities to observe changes in the economy and to decide on a change in the official short-term rate of interest (policy decision lag);

• the length of time it takes for the change in the official rate to feed through to other interest rates in the economy (institutional lag);

• the length of time required for interest rate changes to affect the disposable income of households (income lag);

• the length of time required for changes in short-term and long-term interest rates to affect the expenditure of households and firms (expenditure lag);

• the length of time needed for changes in expenditure to be reflected in changes in the rate of inflation, output, and employment (real response lag).

Pause for thought 5.5

Why does it take so long for interest rate changes to affect the rate of inflation?

Evidence from industrial economies generally suggests that once the monetary authorities have changed the official rate it takes about twelve months for the full impact of the change to be felt on demand and production. It takes a further twelve months for the full effect on the rate of inflation to be felt. This in itself presents serious problems for the monetary authorities since it means that they must be constantly looking forward trying to assess the likely state of inflationary pressures two years ahead on the assumption of unchanged policies and then trying to estimate the impact of a policy change. Given that the interest rate is only one influence among many on expenditure, this is clearly very difficult.

Pause for thought 5.6

During the spring of 2008, the rate of inflation in the UK was above target and rising and yet the Bank of England was reducing interest rates and was expected to reduce them further. How might we explain this?

However, things are even worse because the time lags of twelve months and two years mentioned here are only approximate and are only averages. The time lags associated with any particular act of monetary policy may be much shorter or much longer — they are highly variable and will depend, among other things, on the state of business and consumer confidence, how this confidence is influenced by monetary policy changes, events in the world economy, and expectations about future inflation.

5.3   The *IS/PC/MR* model[5]

Formally speaking, the 'New Consensus Macroeconomics' (NCM) is usually represented by three equations. The first of these is an **IS equation**

$$Y_{t+1} = A - \phi r_t \tag{5.3}$$

where A is autonomous demand and r_t is the real rate of interest, in the previous period.

The second is the short-run **Phillips curve** we saw in eqn. 5.2.

$$\tag{5.4}$$
$$\pi_{t+1} = \pi_t + \alpha(Y_{t+1} - Y^*)$$

We then require a third equation which sets the interest rate r_t. This could take the form of a Taylor rule or it could be written more generally as the rate of interest that minimises a loss function of the kind:

$$L = (Y_{t+1} - Y^*)^2 + \lambda(\pi_{t+1} - \pi^T)^2 \tag{5.5}$$

subject to the Phillips curve in eqn. 5.4. Notice the significance of the term λ here. With $\lambda = 1$ the policymaker suffers equal losses when output or inflation deviate from target. With $\lambda > 1$, greater weight is given to inflation than to output losses. The policymaker is 'inflation averse'. By substituting the Phillips curve into the loss function and differentiating with respect to Y, we have:

$$\frac{\partial L}{\partial Y} = (Y_{t+1} - Y^*) + \alpha\lambda\{\pi_t + \alpha(Y_{t+1} - Y^*) - \pi^T\} = 0 \tag{5.6}$$

Substituting the Phillips curve back into this equation gives:

$$(Y_{t+1} - Y^*) = -\lambda\alpha(\pi_{t+1} - \pi^T) \tag{5.7}$$

This is the third equation of the model, known as the **MR-AD equation**,[6] where *MR* stands for 'monetary rule'. It shows the equilibrium relationship between the level of output (chosen by the policymaker in the light of preferences and constraints) and the rate of inflation.[7]

Finally, to find the rate of interest that the policymaker should set we need to go back to the *IS* equation

$$Y_{t+1} = A - \phi r_t \tag{5.3}$$

In order to write this in output gap form we need to introduce the concept of the 'stabilising' rate of interest — the real rate required to hold actual output at its equilibrium level ($Y_{t+1} = Y^*$). Then:

$$Y_{t+1} - Y^* = -\phi(r_t - r_S) \tag{5.8}$$

If we substitute for π_t using the Phillips curve in the *MR-AD* equation (5.7), we get

$$\pi_t + \alpha(Y_{t+1} - Y^*) - \pi^T = -\frac{1}{\alpha\lambda}(Y_{t+1} - Y^*)$$

$$\pi_t - \pi^T = -\left(\alpha + \frac{1}{\alpha\lambda}\right)(Y_{t+1} - Y^*) \tag{5.9}$$

and if we now substitute for $(Y_{t+1} - Y^*)$ using the *IS* equation (5.8), we have

$$(r_t - r_s) = \frac{\alpha\lambda}{\phi(1 + \alpha^2\lambda)}(\pi_t - \pi^T) \tag{5.10}$$

This is the **interest rate rule** and tells us how the real rate of interest needs to be set, relative to the stabilising rate, in response to a deviation of inflation from its target. Notice that if $\phi = \alpha = \lambda = 1$, then

$$(r_t - r_s) = 0.5\,(\pi_t - \pi^T) \tag{5.11}$$

If we rearrange this to find r_t, we have:

$$r_t = r_S + 0.5\,(\pi_t - \pi^T) \tag{5.12}$$

and if we assume that the stabilising real rate is two per cent, then we have a formula for setting the nominal interest rate that may look familiar:

$$i = \pi + 2.0 + 0.5\,(\pi_t - \pi^T) \tag{5.13}$$

This is two-thirds of the familiar Taylor rule — without any reference to adjustments necessary to take account of the output gap. We shall come back to the output gap and the Taylor rule again shortly.

One advantage of this framework, over the *IS/LM-AD/AS* model is immediately obvious. The policy instrument (eqn. 5.12) is the rate of interest set by the policymaker rather than the money stock. One might object that eqn. 5.12 requires the setting of a *real* interest rate, while the policymaker only has control over a *nominal* rate. But since the current (and expected) inflation rates are known and given at any moment (and since in practice the policy rate is reviewed at high frequencies) we can assume that policymakers are generally successful in setting the real rate that they desire. Crucially, this focus upon an instrument makes the model entirely consistent with the kind of monetary regime that we discussed in the last chapter (particularly sections 4.2 and 4.3). The policymaker sets the rate of interest and the broad money stock is endogenously determined. Furthermore, if the policymaker does nothing (leaves the interest rate unchanged) the stock of money and credit, far from being fixed, will continue to expand at the going rate.

Figure 5.2 sets out the model diagrammatically and helps us to illustrate the processes of adjustment. We shall illustrate adjustment to an *AD* shock which shifts the *IS* curve. In the lower panel, the economy is initially in equilibrium at *A*. Inflation is at its target rate of two per cent and output is at its natural rate, Y^* on the vertical long-run Phillips curve (*LRPC*). Furthermore, the economy has been at this position for long enough for lagged inflation to adjust to the current rate, so *A* lies on the short-run $PC\pi^I = 2$ per cent. The rate of interest, which is of course the stabilising rate, r_S, is shown in the upper panel with the *IS* curve.

The shock to the *IS* curve causes output and inflation to move to point *Z* in the lower panel ($Y = Y_0$ and $\pi = 4$ per cent). The policymaker forecasts that the Phillips curve will shift upward, as inertial inflation adjusts, until it cuts *LRPC* at 4. In order to return inflation to target, the policymaker must decide on the target level of output. This is where the new Phillips curve cuts the *MR* curve (at *B*). In order to know the rate of interest that it should set in order to achieve this level of output, the policymaker forecasts the position of the new *IS* curve (at *IS'*). Given this forecast, the policymaker can observe the rate of interest required to reduce the level of output to Y_1. This is at r_1. Notice that the combination Y_1/r_1 is chosen because it puts us at *B* in the lower panel, where $PC\pi^I = 4$ per cent cuts the *MR* line. This is the policymaker's preferred position, given the constraint of the short-run Phillips curve that it faces.

Following the increase in the interest rate, we move down $PC\pi^I = 4$ per cent, to the rate of inflation, 3 per cent, shown at *B* in the lower panel. In time, inertial inflation will catch up and the short-run Phillips curve will shift down to cut the *LRPC* at 3 per cent ($PC\pi^I = 3$ per cent), and the *MR* curve at *C*. With inflation now falling, the policymaker can reduce the rate of interest progressively until, by iteration, we return to point *A*. If the policymaker's forecast of the new *IS* curve is correct, that rate of interest will be at r_S'.

Notice that we described point *B* (lower panel) as the policymaker's preferred

Figure 5.2: The *IS/PC/MR* model

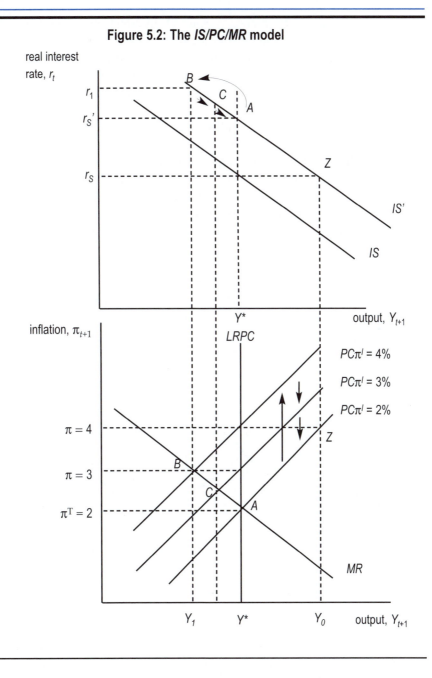

position, subject to a constraint and that this combination of preferences and constraints is responsible for generating the *MR* line. Figure 5.3 shows how we can represent these combinations by conventional reference to indifference curves.

In figure 5.2 we saw the policymaker responding to an inflation shock by choosing point *B*. In figure 5.3, we can represent this point as tangential to an indifference curve which at least approximates a segment of a circle. By contrast, the policymaker could have chosen point D. In effect, this would have been a decision to accommodate the rate of inflation rather than face the lost output and (increased unemployment) that would have followed from introducing a deflationary policy. Point C, shows the preference of a strongly inflation-averse policymaker, willing to sacrifice a large amount of output in exchange for a dramatic reduction in inflation.

In figure 5.3, we have drawn indifference curves for policymakers with different loss functions. Point B represents the position that would be taken by a policymaker with a loss function like eqn. 5.5, with $\lambda = 1$. Inflation and output losses are treated with equal concern. However, a policymaker with little concern about inflation ($\lambda \approx 0$) would be on an indifference curve like that at D, while a strongly inflation averse policymaker would be at C ($\lambda > 1$). Notice also that if the indifference curve at B resembles a segment from a circle, the indifference curves at C and D are taken from ellipsoids.

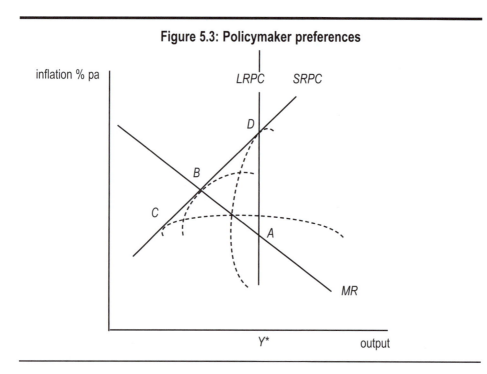

Figure 5.3: Policymaker preferences

More importantly still, all the curves, whatever their shape, are centred on A, *provided that positive and negative deviations are regarded equally*. In effect, this amounts to a requirement that the inflation target be set symmetrically, as in the UK. To quote from the annual 'remit' given to the Bank of England: 'The inflation target is 2 per cent at all times; that is the rate that the MPC is required to achieve and for which it is accountable...But if inflation moves away from the target by more than 1 percentage point *in either direction*, I shall expect you to send an open letter to me...' (Bank of England, 2007, emphasis added). We show this in figure

5.4, using a $\lambda = 1$, loss function. Since A is the target, A' is preferred to A'', and this is true for all points on the circles. Given the remit, π_0 is just as undesirable as π_1.

Figure 5.4: Indiifference curves and policy targets

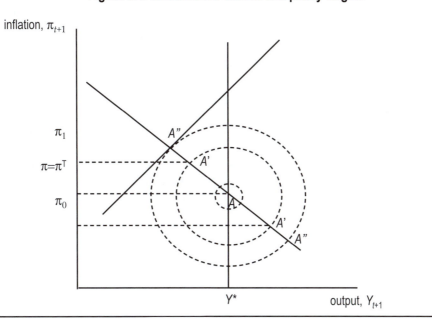

Pause for thought 5.7

'The ECB aims at inflation rates of below, but close to, 2% over the medium term.' (ECB, 2007).

How would you modify figure 5.4 to reflect the preferences implicit in the ECB's aim?

It might be argued that A' at π_0 is preferable to A' at π_1 since there is a gain in output. But careful inspection of the loss function, eqn. 5.5, shows that *any* output deviation from Y^* is treated as a loss. Loss functions which are tolerant of output above Y^* are one source of 'inflation bias'. We discuss this further in section 8.4.

5.4   Money and banking in an *IS/PC/MR* model

When it comes to analysing monetary policy as it is currently conducted in most OECD countries today, the *IS/PC/MR* model has overwhelming advantages over the traditional *IS/LM-AS/AD* framework. It treats the rate of interest as the policy instrument and the money supply as endogenously-determined. In this section we want to show how it can be linked to the model of the banking sector that we developed in section 4.4. Making the link is simple: we take the loan rate of interest, determined as explained in QI of figure 4.4, and treat it as the equivalent of the policy rate in the *IS/PC/MR* model. This should be unexceptionable; indeed, it might be regarded as an improvement. Earlier in this chapter we stressed that it is is not the official repo rate itself that matters for the transmission mechanism, but the vector of *market* rates to which it gives rise. To this extent, using the loan rate, which we've acknowledged may vary in its relationship with the policy rate, is rather more realistic. And we shall see very shortly that *allowing* a variation in the spread between the official and market rates is essential to our analysis of the 'credit-crunch'.

The challenge for the moment lies in showing that, once the models are combined, a disturbance in one part is transmitted to the other in such a way that it produces sensible outcomes in both the banking and real sectors. Thus, for example, we need to ensure that the *IS* shift in figure 5.2 has plausible effects on the

Figure 5.5: The banking sector and the *IS/PC/MR* model (a)

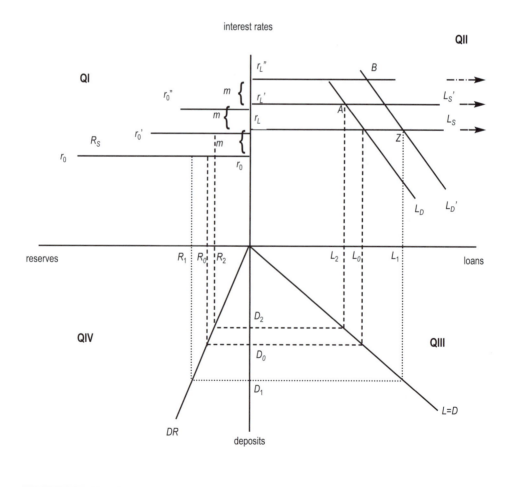

banking sector. As another, and highly topical, test we could see first of all whether our banking sector model can illustrate the effects of the credit crunch 2007-08 and then, when we link it to the *IS/PC/MR*, whether it produces the adverse effects on the real economy that caused so much anxiety to policy makers. Figure 5.5 brings the two models together across two pages, numbered in quadrants QI-QIV (the banking sector) and QV and QVI (the macroeconomy).

Figure 5.5 reproduces the shock to the *IS* curve (from figure 5.2) and traces the effects in our model of the banking sector. We begin in QVI, in equilibrium, with inflation at target (π^T, assumed to be 2 per cent) and a zero output gap (Y^*). Notice that the rate of interest is r_L and from QI we can see that this is the outcome of an official rate set at r_0 and a mark-up, m. (Notice that r_L is now equivalent to the stabilising rate, r_S of equation 5.12). At r_L we can see that the loan demand curve is generating new lending (and money) at L_0/D_0 and the central bank validates this expansion by making available the required reserves.

Figure 5.5: The banking sector and the *IS/PC/MR* model (b)

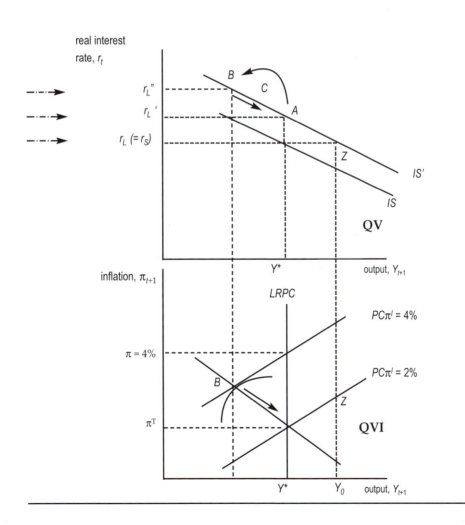

There is then an outward shift of the *IS* curve and we move, as before, to point Z (in QV and QVI). Notice that a point Z is also identified in QII. This reminds us that the loan demand curve depends upon the 'state of trade' — the level of output and the rate of inflation (eqn. 4.6). Hence, the curve L_d' shows what the rate of monetary expansion would be *if* the real economy were at Z (with $\pi > \pi^T$ and output at Y_0). However, we know from our earlier discussion that Z is not a sustainable combination of inflation and output (except in the very short-run) and that (in QVI) the short-run Phillips curve will shift upwards until it intersects *LRPC* at $Y=Y^*$ and $\pi=4$ per cent. During the adjustment process the π/Y combination is changing, with Y falling towards Y^* and inflation rising towards 4 per cent. In QII, the new loan demand curve, L_d', is to be taken as showing the demand for loans consistent with the π/Y at point Z, *and any combination of π/Y between Z and the long-run equilibrium* ($Y=Y^*$ and $\pi=4$ per cent). If we follow the dotted line from Z, then QII and QIII tell us the rate of credit and deposit expansion that will now occur if the policymaker does nothing, while QIV shows the resulting growth in required reserves which the central bank satisfies at the current official rate, in QI.

In our earlier discussion, we saw that the policymaker's response to the shift in the *IS* curve was to raise the real rate of interest by an amount which depended on the loss function, but for a moderate degree of inflation aversion might be represented by r_L'' in QIV, with the intention of depressing output and inflation to the combination represented by B, in QVI. Turning to the banking sector, we see that, *assuming an unchanged mark-up*, this involves raising the policy rate from r_0 to r_0''. Furthermore, we see that this has the effect of returning the rate of money and credit expansion to approximately its original rate (consistent with Y^* and π^T). This is shown as point B in QII and the essential point is that this rate of monetary expansion is deflationary. It is insufficient to support the Y/π combination at Z (QVI) or the Y/π combination at $Y^*/4$ per cent (or any of the combinations in between). As drawn, it generates roughly the same degree of money and credit as was necessary to finance the Y^*/π^T combination. Hence while $\pi > \pi^T$, this rate of monetary expansion is consistent only with $Y < Y^*$

After a period of $Y < Y^*$ at B (QVI) the *SRPC* shifts down. The policymaker reduces the policy rate (consistent with C in QV, but not shown) so that output expands from Y_1 at B (QVI) towards Y^* and we move down the *MR* line. Eventually, we return to the original equilibrium at Y^*/π^T. At this equilibrium, the new stabilising rate of interest (QV) is r_L. Notice that $r_L' > r_L$ because of the increase in autonomous components of spending, underlying the shift in the *IS* curve.

In the banking sector, the rise in interest rates to r_L'' produces deflationary pressure shown by the restriction of money and credit growth at point B (QII). But as soon as point B is reached (in QVI), the L_d curve in QII begins to shift left Again, this is because the demand for loans depends upon the 'state of trade' . L_d' was drawn for the $Y^*/4$ per cent combination but output and inflation are *both* below these levels at B. In fact, though it isn't shown in QII, once B is achieved, the L_d will shift to the left even of the original L_d curve. As the policymaker steers the economy down the *MR* line, the L_d curve will approach and converge on the original, *from below*. In QII, we are now at point *A*, with the position of the L_D curve fixed again in accordance with the restored state of trade (Y^*/π^T) but with a higher loan rate (r_L'), resulting in a rather lower rate of credit and monetary expansion ($L_2/D_2/R_2 < L_1/D_1/R_1$) than before the *IS* shock. This is the monetary consequence of having to run the real economy at higher real interest rate to off-set the shift in the *IS* curve.

We turn our attention now to a shock of a different kind. This originates in the banking system itself and we take the recent (2007-08) case of a so-called 'credit-crunch' induced by anxieties over sub-prime lending. If we are to judge the model's ability to represent these developments successfully we need to be clear on the main features of this episode. The following paragraph describes the key events as they developed from mid-August through to the spring of 2008.

By mid-2007, banks (especially in the USA) had built up a large portfolio of lending to so-called 'sub-prime' borrowers. In some cases these loans were securitised and sold on to various 'special vehicles' and hedge funds. In some cases banks had lent to these SPVs and hedge funds themselves. A downturn in the US housing market raised doubts about the value of some of this lending. However, compared with past housing market recessions, there were two novel problems. The first was that the securitisation obscured the ownership of the loans and thus the distribution of the associated risk; the second was that the extent of the risk was unknown because many of the collateralised debt obligations (CDOs) were never traded. The results, which we shall try to represent in the model, are shown in box 5.1. (A more detailed discussion of the crisis is provided in appendix 2).

Box 5.1: Features of the banking crisis, 2007-08

• the market for CDOs collapses

• banks cannot securitise further loans

• banks become nervous about their own liquidity position

• they are unwilling to lend to each other since they don't know the risk exposure of the counterparty

• the market rate (ie LIBOR, FIBOR, Fed Funds) premium over the official rate jumps by as much as 100 basis points

• central banks become concerned about likely effects on the real economy

• central banks reduce the official rate; and widen the range of securities that they are prepared to accept from banks in exchange for liquidity.

Throughout these difficulties, a major issue of concern to all central banks was the stability of the banking system itself. This was underlined in September

2007 in the UK by the collapse of the Northern Rock Bank and in March 2008 by the collapse of Bear Stearns in the USA. One of the major problems the crisis posed was one of accurate diagnosis. Clearly there was a liquidity problem, which central banks could try to alleviate in the normal way. But on the other hand, the drying up of interbank lending suggested that banks themselves were genuinely worried about counterparty risk — the risk of insolvency arising from effectively worthless assets. In fact, the episode rather called into question the continued relevance of trying to distinguish between liquidity and solvency risk.

From our point of view, however, the relevance of the credit crunch to monetary policy and to the real economy is rather more important than financial stability. Bearing in mind our discussion of the transmission mechanism in section 5.2, we can identify three concerns.

The first arises from the behaviour of interest rates. We have made the point several times that, under current arrangements, the policy instrument is the rate of interest but a change in the official rate affects aggregate demand and the real

Figure 5.6: The banking sector and the credit crunch (a)

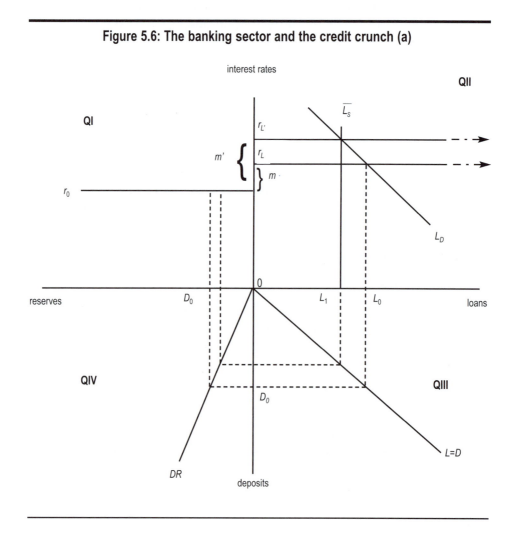

economy only in so far as it is reflected in market rates. In practice, market rates are generally priced as a mark-up over interbank rates. So, if the spread between the policy rate and interbank rates widens by 100 bp, that is approximately equivalent to a 1 percentage point increase in the policy rate. By modern standards, that represents a very severe (and involuntary) tightening of monetary policy.

Secondly, the lack of confidence that led to banks hoarding liquidity was rooted in concerns about the quality of bank assets that were directly tied to the housing market. Any default on the mortgage loans sufficiently widespread to damage banks' balance sheets was almost certainly going to be accompanied by a weakening of property prices as banks tried to sell the collateral property. For most households, the primary residence is the major asset and so any downward trend in values (and this would apply to all households, not just those in default) would have a wealth effect that could severely reduce aggregate demand.

Finally, aside from the generally unsettling effect that banking crises were bound to have on financial markets, there was the more tangible probability that

Figure 5.6: The banking sector and the credit crunch (b)

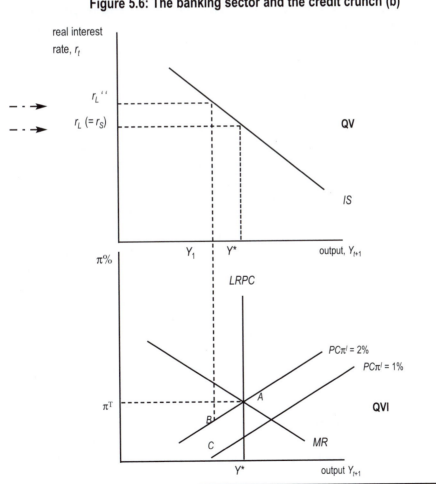

banks would have to strengthen their balance sheets by raising more capital. This would mean issuing more equity with a consequent downward pressure on existing values and a rise in the cost of capital.

The question is whether our model of the banking sector can incorporate the developments listed in box 5.1 and then whether, when the outcomes are translated to the *IS/PC/MR* model, we can see the potentially deflationary impact. As before, we shall have to examine the links across two pages, in figure 5.6.

We begin in equilibrium in QVI at point *A*, with inflation on target and output at Y^*. The required rate of interest can be read off the *IS* curve (QV) as r_L and this is produced by the central bank setting the policy rate at r_0 and banks adding a mark-up, m (QI). The flow of new lending is at L_0 (QII) and other monetary conditions can be read from the remaining quadrants.

The effect of the credit crunch can be seen firstly in QII where, instead of the flow of loans being demand determined, banks are rationing the flow of loans to $\overline{L_s}$. Restricting the flow enables them to increase the mark-up (from m to m'). This has the effect of raising market rates to r' (QII), even though the official rate is unchanged. As before, the other monetary conditions can be read from the remaining quadrants. Notice that we have left the *DR* line unchanged. This is done largely to maintain clarity in the diagram. It means that, with banks restricting their lending, their demand for reserves grows more slowly than before ($D_1 < D_0$ in QIV). However, it is one of the strengths of this representation of the banking sector that we can rotate the *DR* line to show shifts in banks' liquidity preference. In this case, we could add realism by rotating it in a clockwise direction to show banks wishing to hold more reserves at all levels of loans and deposits.

Notice that the official rate is unchanged but market rates have risen. This represents the increase in LIBOR rates. And it is this unplanned rise in interest rates that lies at the core of policymakers concerns about the effects of the credit crunch on the real economy. This can be seen in QV and QVI by translating the new market rate, r_L', to the *IS* curve. The effect then is to reduce the level of output to Y_1. This moves the economy down the short-run Phillips curve in QVI. Inflation and output are now both below target, at *B*. Assume that the rate of inflation at *B* is 1 per cent. With time, lagged inflation settles at 1 per cent, shown by a downward shift of the short-run Phillips curve to $PC\pi^I = 1$ per cent. So long as the rate of interest remains above r_S, there will be a negative output gap and the deflationary pressure will continue. If conditions in the credit market do not improve and r_L' is maintained, the real economy will move to point *C* in QVI. The nightmare implications are now clear. The *IS/PC/MR* model shows the real economy moving into a deflationary spiral which will continue for so long as market rates are above the stabilising rate. The urgency with which central banks have responded to the credit crunch is easily understood.

It is a further recommendation of our model of the banking sector that we can use it to illustrate each of the two central bank strategies mentioned in box 5.1. Firstly, we noted that central banks responded by cutting the official rate of interest. This was a course of action pursued most vigorously by the Federal Reserve, but also to a lesser degree by the Bank of England and the ECB. In QI we could show this by a lowering of r_0. Assuming that the mark-up remains at its elevated level, then this should bring market rates down by the amount of the official reduction. But, as QII shows, this will only happen if banks are prepared to increase the rate at which they make new loans. If loan supply remains fixed at $\overline{L_s}$, there will be an excess demand for loans which will have to be met by some form of rationing and/or a further rise in the mark-up. As box 5.2 reports, both of these features of bank behaviour were observable in March 2008.

Box 5.2: Credit rationing in practice

Borrowers with modest loan-to-values and clean credit records are being dragged into the centre of the current crisis, as it becomes increasingly difficult for existing homeowners to secure new mortgage deals.

Lending restrictions, which had until recently been largely confined to first-time buyers and borrowers taking on riskier loans, have now spread to the wider market.

Announcements that banks are pulling offers, scaling back loan-to-values or increasing interest rates for existing as well as new customers are emerging daily....

Banks and building societies that are still able to lend at reasonable rates are being overwhelmed with applications and are having to limit the number they can accept...

The mortgage securitisation market has completely dried up and Libor....has risen sharply again over the last week, making it harder for lenders to access funding...

The Bank of England's injection of £5bn injection of liquidity this week was almost five times oversubscribed, illustrating the lack of available funds in the market.

Adapted from, Sharlene Goff, 'Clamp on lending spreads to wider group of borrowers', *Financial Times*, ('Money' supplement), 22 March 2008, p.2

The second strategy adopted by central banks was to accept a wider range of securities as collateral for the repo deals through which they provided liquidity and to do deals for longer than usual periods. Prior to the crisis, the general practice was to accept only government bonds as collateral for repos deals with a maximum of seven days. In August 2007 the ECB announced a willingness to accept a wider range of collateral and to lend for up to three months — since it was 3-moth interbank rates which in particular were proving sticky. In December 2007, the Federal Reserve and the Bank of England also announced a widening of collateral and lengthening of term.

Looking at QII in figure 5.6(a), we have just observed that lowering the official interest rate cannot lower market rates unless banks can be persuaded to increase their lending, i.e. to shift $\overline{L_s}$ to the right. Suppose that in normal circumstances banks would be willing to lend L_0 at the interest rate r_L. Then we could remind ourselves (see p.110 above) that the 'loans', on the horizontal axis, should strictly-speaking be interpreted as standing for 'all assets' (just as 'deposits' includes all liabilities and capital). Hence, L_0, represents a flow of new lending in the form of overdrafts, personal loans and mortgages, but also in the form of securities and investments. Let us now suppose, still in normal circumstances, that the proportion of total lending that banks wish to undertake in conventional or traditional form, is shown by the distance $0\text{-}L_1$, while $L_1\text{-}L_0$ represents the proportion that banks wish to undertake by securitisation and similar innovations. Then we can view the collapse of the CDO market as meaning that all lending must be taken on to the asset side of the balance sheet in the form of conventional loans and since banks desire only $0\text{-}L_1$ in this form, they restrict lending to $\overline{L_s}$. In these circumstances, we could interpret the willingness of central banks to accept a wider (than government bonds) range of securities as collateral as an attempt to encourage banks to increase their holdings of such securities and thus to revive the CDO market. In QII, this is an attempt to shift $\overline{L_s}$ to the right and to bring down the interbank premium over the official rate.

5.5   Summary

In this chapter, we have seen that policy instrument in most monetary regimes is the short-term rate of interest at which the central bank is prepared to make additional reserves available to the commercial banking system and, just as importantly, to refinance existing borrowed reserves. Furthermore, we have seen that the immediate purpose in adjusting this rate is to bring about a change in market rates which will then affect the level of aggregate demand through a number of channels as shown by figure 5.1. Significantly, none of these channels makes reference to real balance effects arising from a disequilibrium in the supply and demand for money. Indeed, there is no apparent role for the money stock — its level or rate of growth. Thus we recall the point made by Woodford towards the end of section 4.2.

Although we want to come back to the question of policy targets in the next chapter, we know that price stability is the widely accepted long-run objective of monetary policy in practice. Given that the policy instrument is a rate of instrument and the money supply is endogenously determined, then when it comes to linking the instrument to target in formal way we must dispense with the traditional *IS/LM* model. We have shown in this chapter that the *IS/PC/MR* model produces useful insights while staying close to institutional realities. Furthermore we have shown how that model can be linked to a representation of the banking or monetary sector which also respects these realities. It is especially encouraging that when we combine the two we can show that a disturbance arising in either has effects in the other which are entirely congruent with what we think happens in practice. Hence an aggregate demand shock originating in the real economy has precisely the effect on monetary conditions that we would expect, *a priori*.

Equally, introducing a 'credit -squeeze' type disturbance in the banking sector can be shown to threaten precisely those effects that so concern central banks and policymakers at the time of writing.

The entire discussion in this chapter has taken place against a background of the received wisdom, namely that while aggregate demand can be strongly influenced by monetary policy, this has only short-run effects upon real variables; its long-run effects fall solely on the price level. In the next chapter, we take a critical look at the basis of this division.

Key concepts used in this chapter

New Consensus Macroeconomics	Phillips curve
expectations	money illusion
inflation inertia	monetary rule
IS/PC/MR model	Taylor rule
transmission mechanism	*MR-AD* equation
LIBOR	policy remit
output gap	credit rationing
time lags	securitisation
IS equation	

Questions and exercises
Answers at the end of the book

1. Focusing upon people's *wealth*, explain how a change in interest rates might affect the level of spending

2. We said in the text that a change in the official interest rate does not necessarily result in an instant and identical change in market rates. How might we explain this.

3. What difference would it make to the strength of UK monetary policy if all mortgages were fixed-interest-rate loans:

(a) in the short run; (b) in the long run?

4. How are interest rate changes likely to affect the distribution of income between:

(a) rich and poor; (b) borrowers and lenders; (c) old and young?

...and also to think about

5. In its discussion of the transmission mechanism, the Bank of England says that the effect of a change in interest rates on expectations is the most difficult to predict. Why might this be?

6. Imagine that a rate of inflation of 4 per cent p.a. becomes established in an economy with an inflation target of 2 per cent p.a. (say, because of a sustained rise in the prices of energy and commodities). Use the *IS/PC/MR* model to show how a policymaker brings inflation back to 2 per cent p.a. if (a) the policymaker is extremely inflation-averse and (b) the policymaker is concerned about the loss of output.

Further reading

A useful survey of the 'New Consensus' is the collection of essays in P Arestis (ed), (2007). This includes the essay (ch.9) by Charles Bean referred to in section 5.1. The flow chart in section 5.2 comes from Bank of England (1999). The ECB version can be found in ECB (2004). Section 3.2 discusses the ECB's view of the transmission mechanism. It is difficult to recommend any textbook account of the transmission mechanism. Ch.13 in M K Lewis and P D Mizen (2000) has this title, but only the final, and brief, section (13.3) is really about the transmission mechanism as we have understood the term here. Furthermore, two-thirds of the section is devoted to models of the transmission mechanism where the money stock is the policy instrument. The following chapter has a sub-section titled 'interest rate linkages' that is rather more helpful and contains a diagram which is a more detailed version of our figure 5.1. It is unfortunate that the accompanying discussion occupies little more than a page. Ch.12 of Handa (2000), *Monetary Economics* is the main policy chapter but the whole analysis is conducted from an *IS/LM-AS/AD* perspective whereby the instrument is the stock of money. Section 12.5 recognises that central banks are very concerned with interest rates, but interest rates are described as *targets*, determined of course by exogenous changes in the money stock.

The role of asset prices and the attention they should receive has been widely discussed. Four useful sources are K Aoki, J Proudman and G Vlieghe (2001); R Clews (2002); CAE Goodhart and B Hofmann (2007); G D Rudebusch (2005).

Students should also read D Laidler (2002) wherein he accepts that the rate of interest is the policy instrument and that the money supply is endogenously determined, but argues that the quantity of money may still play some part in the transmission mechanism.

The macroeconomic model used by the Bank of England for policymaking purposes is discussed in P Arestis and M Sawyer (2002). The version of the *IS/PC/MR* which we have used in this chapter, is set out in W Carlin and D Soskice (2005). The same model appears in their (2006) textbook.

The ECB's inflation target can be read at www.ecb.int/mopo/html/index.en.html; the Bank of England's remit is at www.bankofengland.co.uk/monetarypolicy/pdf /chancellorletter070321.pdf

6 Aggregate demand, output and prices

'But it is pretty to see what money will do.'
Samuel Pepys, *Diary*, 21.3.1667

6.1   Introduction

In chapter 5, we considered the impact of changes in short-term interest rates on
the macro economy, making use of a diagram of the transmission mechanism of
monetary policy (figure 5.1) and the *IS/PC/MR* model. The principal purpose of
the chapter was to examine the links in the first part of the transmission process
— that between the repo rate and total demand (that is, between the short-term
interest rate set by the central bank and nominal income).   However, the
IS/PC/MR model takes us a good deal further, postulating also relationships
between nominal income, output and employment, the relationships we are particularly concerned with in this chapter.

Figure 5.1 clearly shows that changes in short-term interest rates brought
about by changes in central bank monetary policy affect inflation. We need to consider here the extent to which short-term interest rate changes also affect output
(and employment), whether such effects persist into the long-run and whether
governments and/or monetary authorities can take advantage of any short-run
effects without causing damage to the economy. That is, we are interested in
whether money is neutral in the long-run (having no effect on output) and
whether there exists a short-term trade-off between inflation and unemployment
that can be exploited by the authorities.

We saw in chapter 5 that the *IS/PC/MR* model makes assumptions that give
us short-term and long-term forms of the Phillips curve with the short-term
showing a trade-off between output and inflation but with the long-term curve
being vertical at the long-run equilibrium level of output (Y^*). In our statement of
the NCM, the short-term trade-off is accounted for by nominal rigidities but it can
also be explained by the existence of money illusion and incorrect inflationary
expectations.

These assumptions about trade-offs in the short- and long-runs have been
controversial and it is important to understand how the consensus has been
reached. The NCM contains elements of both New Keynesian and New Classical
Macroeconomics. These, in turn, had their derivation in Keynesian and Classical
Macroeconomics, with Classical Macroeconomics being the term given by Keynes
to encompass the accepted economic ideas of relevance to the macro economy
prior to the publication of his own *General Theory*.

Classical Macroeconomics was essentially the preserve of the Quantity
Theory of Money. In all Classical economics, the term 'monetary policy' was used
to describe a change in the money supply or its rate of growth since interest rates
were thought to be determined on the real, rather than the monetary side of the
economy. The Quantity Theory, then, suggested that, in anything other than the
short-run, any increase in the rate of growth of the money supply would lead to
inflation. Real income (output) was assumed to be determined by the real forces
of saving (thrift) and productivity and not by monetary factors. This implied a

stable demand for money and hence a stable income velocity of money. There was, effectively, no transmission between changes in the money supply and output. Long-run real interest rates could not be influenced by monetary policy. Classical theory argued that they were determined by the behaviour of savers and investors, as set out in the loanable funds theory of the determination of interest rates. Both saving and investment decisions, and hence the real rate of interest, depended on long-term considerations. The monetary authorities could influence nominal interest rates, but these were of no long-run importance for the real economy. Their actions might have short-run effects on output and employment but these were simply indications of disequilibrium and, as such, of no great significance, especially since it was accepted that there were powerful forces at work in the economy to reverse any movement away from equilibrium. There was no idea that short-term fluctuations in output might allow governments or monetary authorities to trade off higher output (and lower unemployment) against higher inflation or *vice versa*.

This picture was disturbed by Keynes's *General Theory* (and by the interpretations made by Keynesians of this theory) in two ways. Firstly, Keynes thought that, without government intervention, the economic system could remain out of equilibrium for long periods of time and that this might involve continuing high unemployment. If this were so, macroeconomic policy might be able to reduce undesirable fluctuations in employment and output. Secondly, he held that the nominal interest rate was determined by the demand for and supply of money and provided a vital link between the real and monetary sectors of the economy. Changes in nominal interest rates could bring about changes in real interest rates and have an effect on the real variables of output and employment. Further, the demand for money was held not to be stable and hence control of the money supply would not have a predictable effect on nominal income. The interest rate became the accepted monetary policy instrument but it was thought to have only a weak effect on nominal income, especially when the economy was in recession. However, whenever the economy was operating at less than full employment, any impact on nominal income implied also an impact on output since inadequate demand was argued to be the major cause of unemployment. Before Keynes, fiscal policy had no role to play — the duty of the government was simply to do its best to run balanced budgets. After Keynes, it was thought that fiscal policy could be used to help pull economies out of depression.

This approach explained the standard Keynesian models in which the general price level was assumed to be constant and hence no distinction was made between nominal income and output. An increase in demand implied an increase in output and employment. It was always acknowledged that excess demand would cause prices to increase when the economy was at full employment as inflationary gaps (the gap between aggregate demand and aggregate supply at the existing price level) developed. In more detailed models, prices had to rise before the economy was at full employment because an increase in employment required a reduction in real wages and this could only occur through an increase in the general price level. There was thus an inherent notion of a trade-off between reductions in unemployment and increases in the price level. Despite this, there was little enquiry into this trade-off until 1958 when A W H Phillips first constructed the Phillips curve (Phillips, 1958). Section 6.2 deals with the original Phillips curve and the subsequent attack on the idea of the existence of a long-run trade-off between inflation and unemployment in the Friedman-Phelps expectations-augmented Phillips curve. This required a theory of expectations formation but the backward-looking approach to expectations employed by Friedman-Phelps was unsatisfactory.

The New Classical model which followed was more satisfactory at a theoretical level because it made use of forward-looking (rational) expectations, incorporating them into a market-clearing model of the economy. This caused the trade-off between inflation and output to disappear even in the short- run. Money, in this model, was neutral in both the short- and the long-run. The New Classical model had a powerful effect on the way in which people looked at economic policy. In particular, it led to the policy irrelevance proposition that the authorities cannot influence real variables by boosting or squeezing aggregate demand. This, in turn, led to the notions of credibility and time consistency in macroeconomic policy and the idea that the economy can only reach the optimum (zero) rate of inflation if the monetary policy of the authorities is held to be credible by market agents. These are considered in section 8.4.

Unfortunately for the New Classical model, it is clear that, in practice, there is a short-run trade-off between inflation and unemployment and this is accepted in the New Consensus Macroeconomics. A monetary policy shock does have real effects, at least in the short-run. Further, the impact of such a shock on unemployment precedes the impact on the rate of inflation. Thus, in section 6.4, we look at New Keynesian attempts to explain the inflation/unemployment trade-off not through incorrect expectations but through failure of markets to clear in the short-run because of price stickiness. section 6.5 brings these ideas together and considers whether there is any possibility that money is not neutral, even in the long-run. Section 6.6 summarises.

6.2   The Phillips curve and expectations

After World War II, the UK government accepted for the first time the obligation to try to run the economy as close to full employment as possible, although the term 'full employment' was never precisely defined. Keynes's *General Theory* had suggested that economies in deep recession could reduce unemployment by expanding aggregate demand and that, in such circumstances, fiscal policy was likely to provide a more powerful instrument than monetary policy. There appeared to be empirical support for these ideas. Unemployment had been high in the 1930s when demand was low; it was non-existent during the war years when demand for everything outstripped supply; and it seemed in the 1950s that expansionary demand management could reverse small increases in unemployment.

Pause for thought 6.1

What definitions have been proposed for the term 'full employment'?

After 1958, the idea that governments could effectively choose the level of employment and output up to some critical full employment level, enjoyed what appeared to be overwhelming empirical support from the work of A W H Phillips (1958). The Phillips curve plotted the relationship in the UK between the recorded level of unemployment, U, and the rate of change of money wages, $\dot{W}$, from 1861 to 1957. The rate of change of money wages was used as a proxy for inflation since price inflation data was not available for the early years. Figure 6.1 shows a Phillips curve fitted to this data, with wage inflation on the vertical axis. Phillips's research showed that the rate of wage inflation was a decreasing function of the level of unemployment and that the relationship had been a remarkably stable one, not changing to a significant extent over the whole period. The study also indicated that in years with the same level of unemployment, wage inflation had been higher when the unemployment rate was rising than when it was falling.

The implication seemed clear. The evidence suggested firstly that the economy could be run at various levels of employment and, consequently, output. Secondly, it suggested that the level of unemployment could be reduced without producing inflation until it fell to the level of unemployment at which the curve cut the horizontal axis, shown by A in figure 6.1. This was a level of unemployment of around 5.5 per cent in Phillips's original study.

Thirdly, the government appeared able to choose to run the economy at even lower levels of unemployment if it so wished but at the cost of inflation. It could, for example, choose point B in figure 6.1. The original study suggested that to have an acceptable rate of inflation of two per cent, the unemployment rate in the UK would need to be 2.5 per cent. Thus was born the idea of a stable trade-off between unemployment and inflation.

The Phillips curve was initially drawn in price inflation/unemployment space. To achieve this, we allow for increases in labour productivity and accept the rate of change of money wages as a proxy for the rate of price inflation. Then we can write:

$$\pi = \alpha . 1/U \qquad (6.1)$$

where π is the rate of price inflation and $1/U$ (the inverse of the rate of unemployment) measures the pressure of demand in the economy. As demand increases, unemployment falls, and the rate of inflation increases. The sensitivity of the relationship (the slope of the curve) is determined by the coefficient, α.

Figure 6.1: The simple Phillips curve

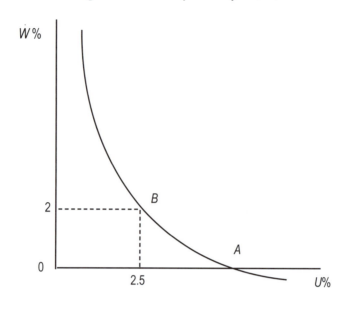

Empirical support for the Phillips curve trade-off was found in many economies in the early 1960s, but there were still questions about the theory underlying the statistical Phillips relationship. Much of standard Keynesian macroeconomics assumed constant prices. Where prices were introduced, the analysis was in terms of the price level rather than the rate of inflation. Samuelson and Solow (1960), Lipsey (1960) and others provided some support with Lipsey's study producing an equation in which the rate of wage inflation was a function of the level of unemployment and the rate of change of unemployment.

Nonetheless, the theoretical underpinnings of the curve were not strong. Neoclassical economists were concerned about the role being played in the analysis by the money wage rate. Until Keynes's *General Theory*, it had been assumed that, following a fall in aggregate demand, the real wage would need to fall to keep the labour market in equilibrium and that this would be achieved by a fall in the money wage. Keynes argued that because of imperfect information and lack of coordination in the economy, this would not happen. Groups of workers, not knowing what was happening to money wages elsewhere in the economy would resist cuts in their money wages — hence the need for price rises to bring about the required fall in real wages. Neoclassical economists were not convinced by this explanation of market failure and were also worried by some of the apparent implications of the Phillips relationship, notably why money wages should be rising over a range of positive unemployment rates. Still, while the Phillips relationship remained stable, it was difficult to challenge.

Then, in the late 1960s, inflation rates started to rise steadily and the points showing unemployment/inflation combinations began to appear well off to the right of the curve plotted by Phillips in 1958. Many attempts were made to explain the movement away from the original Phillips curve. Several of these depended on institutional changes and/or the existence of class conflict, identifying the higher rates of inflation with no increase in demand pressure in the economy as cost inflation. However, several American economists sought to bring the statistical evidence into line with the neoclassical theory of labour market behaviour. This led to the development of the argument that workers who kept their money wages high in the face of falling demand were doing so because they did not realize that prices would fall, causing the real wage to be above the equilibrium level and hence leading to unemployment. That is, the problem was simply that workers were making incorrect short-term forecasts of the rate of inflation. Once they understood what was happening to prices, money wages would fall returning the system to equilibrium. The problem was not one of lack of coordination, requiring a movement away from equilibrium analysis; nor was government intervention needed to cause prices to rise.

This led to the explanation that the original Phillips curve only applied if one assumed a zero rate of expected inflation. In other words, workers were being assumed always to take the existing money wage as equivalent to the real wage — a restatement of the existence of money illusion. In the face of rising inflation (as, for example, if demand pressure increased and the economy moved along the Phillips curve in figure 6.1 from point A to point B), this would clearly be irrational. As prices rose and real wages fell below money wages, workers would attempt to forecast the rate of inflation and build this into their wage negotiations. Unemployment would would only fall below 0A if these forecasts of inflation were incorrect. The trade-off between inflation and unemployment illustrated by the Phillips curve then could be seen to depend on incorrect inflation forecasts. The resultant model became known as the expectations-augmented Phillips curve.

It became common to express this theory in terms of the relationship between the rate of inflation and, rather than unemployment, an output gap, the gap between the existing level of output and a measure of full or high employment output. To achieve this, use was made of Okun's Law, a statement of the empirical relationship in the US economy between the percentage change in the unemployment rate and the difference between actual and potential real *GDP*. In 1968 Friedman introduced the notion of the 'natural rate of unemployment' — the level of unemployment at which unemployment is equal to job vacancies with unemployment determined by a variety of factors including the level of economic development and the various interferences with the labour market mechanism such as the existence of social security benefits for unemployed workers, collective bargaining by trade unions, restrictions on labour mobility and skill mismatches between vacant jobs and unemployed workers — a mixture of what Keynesian economists had called frictional and structural unemployment.[1]

Attempts to reduce the natural rate of unemployment were held to require labour market supply-side measures and would only have effect in the long-run. It followed from this that the output gap of relevance to an analysis of policies aimed to produce changes in aggregate demand was that between the existing output level and the natural or equilibrium level of output (Y^*) — that level of output associated with the natural rate of unemployment. The simple Phillips curve was then expressed as:

$$\pi_t = \alpha_2 (Y - Y^*) \tag{6.2}$$

where α_2 is the slope of the Phillips curve when drawn in output/inflation rate space, Y is actual output, and Y^* the natural level of output. There has remained some unhappiness about this reformulation of the Phillips curve since Okun's Law was a relationship postulated in the early 1960s within a Keynesian framework with the output gap seen as relating to full capacity output rather than to a measure of equilibrium output. Expressing it in terms of the natural level of output implies confidence in the stability of the natural rate of unemployment which presents problems we shall consider in section 6.3.

However, the use of Okun's law to substitute a measure of the output gap for a measure of unemployment allowed the expectations-augmented Phillips curve to be written, as we have done in equation 5.1 in setting out the *IS/PC/MR* model, as:

$$\pi_t = \alpha_1 . \pi_t + \alpha_2 . (Y - Y^*) \tag{5.1}$$

where $\alpha_1 \pi_t$ represents the expected rate of inflation in period t with α_1 measuring the extent to which workers take the expected rate of inflation into account.

In the original Phillips curve, α_1 was equal to zero — workers took no account of inflation in wage bargaining. However, this could only be temporary since rational labour market behaviour requires forecasts of the rate of increase of real wages and hence of inflation. If workers' estimates of the rate of inflation were correct ($\alpha_1 = 1$), there would be no money illusion, the labour supply decisions of workers would be based on the true real wage rate and there would be no trade-off between inflation and unemployment. Values of α_1 between zero and 1 would indicate that workers were attempting to take the rate of inflation into account but were making incorrect assumptions about its true rate. In the short-run, actual output could be above the natural level (workers underestimating the rate of inflation) or below it (workers overestimating the true rate of inflation) — but both of these states would be only temporary. This leaves the question of how long it takes for workers to forecast the rate of inflation correctly. An answer to this required that a theory of expectations formation be incorporated into the model.

The Friedman-Phelps expectations-augmented Phillips curve assumed that current expectations of inflation were based on a weighted average of past inflation rates (adaptive expectations). Expectations of this kind are said to be backward looking since past errors are built in to future forecasts (the errors are serially correlated). For ease, let us write the weighted average of past inflation rates as π_{t-1}. Then,

$$\pi_t^e = \pi_{t-1} \tag{6.3}$$

Substituting into Equation 5.1 we then have the rate of inflation given by

$$\pi_t = \pi_{t-1} + \alpha_2(Y - Y^*) \tag{6.4}$$

We illustrate the expectations-augmented Phillips curve in output/inflation rate space in figure 6.2. Assume that the economy is in long-run equilibrium at point A in figures 6.1 and 6.2. Both actual and expected inflation are zero and $\alpha_2.(Y - Y^*)$ is also equal to zero. Output is at the natural level (Y^*) and unemployment at the natural rate.

In this model, a government which mistakenly seeks to tackle unemployment by increasing aggregate demand, pushes the economy along the Phillips curve, creating inflation (let us assume 2 per cent p.a.). Unemployment temporarily falls (and output rises) but only because we now have:

$$\pi_t^e = \pi_{t-1} < \pi_t$$

Workers accept money wage increases below the rate of inflation and the real wage falls. At the lower real wage, employers hire more workers and expand production. Output and employment increase. If, however, we accept point B as a satisfactory trade-off between inflation and unemployment, the workers' forecast of inflation will steadily adjust towards the true rate. Money wages will be pushed up and the real wage will begin to rise towards the initial level. Unemployment (and output) will move back towards the long-run equilibrium position. In the long-run, the forecast of inflation will again be correct and in figure 6.1 unemployment will return to $0A$. In figure 6.2, we shall have moved to point C on a new short-run Phillips curve along which $\pi_t^e = 2$ per cent.

In the expectations-augmented model, there is a different short-run Phillips curve for every expected rate of inflation, on each one of which there will be one point at which expected inflation is equal to actual inflation. Each of these points will lie directly above A with output at the natural level ($0A$). Linking these equilibrium positions provides a vertical long-run 'Phillips curve' along which there is no trade-off between inflation and unemployment. Inflation is caused by excess demand but there is no long-run impact on output or employment. Short-run trade-offs between unemployment and inflation exist but only because the economy is out of equilibrium.

Further attempts by the authorities to reduce unemployment by expanding aggregate demand push inflation higher but, in the long-run, produce no increase in output. It follows that any level of output above the natural level (unemployment below the natural rate) and is associated with accelerating inflation. For this

Figure 6.2: The expectations-augmented Phillips curve

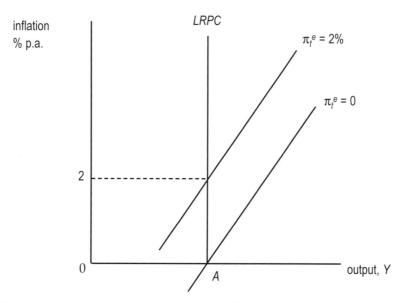

reason, the natural rate of unemployment became widely known as the NAIRU (the 'non-accelerating-inflation rate of unemployment').[2]

The expectations-augmented Phillips curve was bad news for governments wishing to control unemployment by managing aggregate demand. It implied that increases in aggregate demand could reduce unemployment but only in the short-run and only at the expense of accelerating inflation. Money was again, as in the Classical Model, held to be neutral in the long-run. Each attempt by the government to lower unemployment below the NAIRU would ratchet up the rate of inflation. In fact, the news was even worse since it was also argued that increasing inflation interfered with the operation of the price mechanism and reduced the efficiency of the economy. This would cause the NAIRU itself to rise. This view assumed that higher rates of inflation meant more volatile inflation and hence an increased chance of incorrect inflationary expectations. The argument against aggregate demand policies was supported by views that the costs of inflation to an economy were extremely high. Box 6.1 provides an exercise based on the expectations-augmented Phillips curve.

The most prominent explanation of the damage done to the price mechanism by volatile inflation came from Lucas (1972, 1973). He assumed that firms know the current price of their own goods but only learn what happens to prices in other markets with a time lag. When the current price of its output rises, a firm has to decide whether this reflects a real increase in demand for its own product or a general increase in prices resulting from random demand shocks. In the former case, the rational response would be to increase its output; in the latter case, it should not do so. That is, firms have to distinguish between absolute and relative prices. The signal that should be provided to producers by changes in rela-

Box 6.1: The expectations-augmented Phillips curve

The following table represents an economy in which the 'natural' level of output (Y^*) is 4,000. The actual level of output is given by $Y = Y^* + 10(\pi - \pi^e)$, while expected inflation is found as $(0.5\pi_{-1}) + (0.5\pi_{-2})$. Suppose that the policymaker decides to aim for $Y = 4,030$ and begins by increasing aggregate demand and raising inflation to 2% in t_1. Complete all the entries up to and including t_5. What is happening to inflation and why?

t	π	π_{-1}	π_{-2}	π^e	$\pi - \pi^e$	Y
0	0	0	0	0	0	4,000
1						
2						
3						
4						
5						
6						

Suppose that the policymaker decides to reduce the rate of inflation starting in t_6 by bringing the rate down to 8%. What happens to output and why?

tive prices is being confused by the possibility of inflation, especially by volatile inflation. Firms face a signal extraction problem. The greater the variability of the general price level, the more difficult it is for a producer to extract the correct signal, and the smaller the supply response is likely to be for any given change in prices. Far from there being a trade-off between unemployment and inflation, the accepted theory now suggested that inflation caused unemployment to increase. To reduce unemployment in the long-run, governments were required to keep inflation low and to attempt to lower the NAIRU through supply-side measures.

Pause for thought 6.2

Is it reasonable to assume that inflation is more volatile at higher average rates of inflation? Can the rate of inflation also be volatile if the average rate of inflation is low?

There was also bad news for authorities starting with a high rate of inflation and wishing to get it down. A deflationary monetary policy would push inflation down but workers would continue for some time to expect the previous high rate of inflation and would continue to push money wages up in line with their expectations. Real wages would rise, output would fall, and unemployment would increase beyond the NAIRU. The amount of output lost in order to bring about a fall in inflation was called the sacrifice ratio. Of course, in the long-run, workers would adjust their expectations and unemployment would fall back to the NAIRU. However, the short-term costs in terms of lost output and increased unemployment could be high, especially since the theory did not indicate how long it would take workers to adjust their expectations.[3] Indeed, it is perfectly possible to argue that the 'long-run' should not be interpreted as a statement about chronological time at all. Rather, it is a logical construct. We return to this at the end of the chapter. Thus, within the Friedman-Phelps model, monetary policy might have considerable and continuing real effects.

There are other objections to the theory. Firstly, the strength of the argument depended heavily on the proposition that even very low rates of inflation were a major problem for the economy. It had always been accepted that high rates of inflation could involve serious economic and social costs. The standard literature referred to hyperinflation or (more colourfully) 'galloping inflation' and referred to the great damage done by historically important episodes of rampant inflation such as that in Germany in 1922-23. We consider the modern example of runaway inflation in Zimbabwe in box 8.3. Arguments concerning the welfare costs of low levels of inflation were, however, less clear cut. We look at these arguments in box 6.2.

Secondly, unemployment might also have long-run impacts. It has been argued that increases in unemployment damage confidence leading to lower investment and economic growth and might lower the skill levels of workers causing reductions in labour productivity. That is, increased unemployment in the short-run could cause higher unemployment in the long-run and the long-run costs of unemployment might be greater than the long-run costs of low inflation. We return to this idea in section 6.5.

Pause for thought 6.3

The argument here implies that workers determine the rate of growth of money wages — they build the expected rate of inflation into money wages, so that if their expectations are correct, the real wage remains unchanged. Is this an accurate picture of wage bargaining?

The debate over the expectations-augmented Phillips curve thus led to many attempts to enumerate and compare the various costs of both inflation and unemployment. If the costs of unemployment were high relative to those of low rates of inflation and if economies never reached long-run equilibrium positions, there might still be a case for attacking unemployment by expanding aggregate demand when the actual unemployment rate remained above the NAIRU for significant periods. This led to the notion of using the NAIRU as a benchmark for the operation of monetary policy with the NAIRU being accepted as the result of real forces but cyclical variations around it being caused by monetary factors. This, however, required estimates to be made of the NAIRU for each economy.

Box 6.2: The welfare costs of inflation

The welfare costs of inflation are generally divided into menu costs and the resource and subjective costs associated with the impact of inflation on the choices made by economic agents.

Menu costs are simply the costs of changing price labels on goods and associated changes such as alterations in wage slips, adjustments to slot machines and revisions of advertising material. They do not make up a high percentage of the total costs attributed to inflation and inflation-prone economies are generally able to adjust their practices to keep menu costs relatively low. Menu costs have also fallen with computerisation and the widespread use of bar codes on packaged goods. Further, when inflation rates are low, many firms are able to absorb cost rises for extended periods, making only occasional fairly large changes in their prices. Consider the case of newspapers and magazines, the prices of which do not change a penny at a time but in discrete jumps of 10 pence or more.

Thus, most attention has been paid to the costs arising from the changes produced by inflation on the choices facing savers and consumers. These are widely known (following Milton Friedman) as the 'shoe-leather' costs of inflation. Inflation reduces the real value of money and of assets denominated in money terms. For interest-bearing assets, nominal interest rates adjust to reflect the rate of inflation but money itself, taken in the literature as carrying no interest, is particularly affected by inflation. Consumers still need to hold money balances for transactions purposes but will hold smaller and smaller balances as inflation increases. This led to the idea that they would need to go to the bank more often to replenish their cash balances and would, therefore, wear out their shoes more often.

This is misleading in two ways. Firstly, we know that cash represents only a small proportion of money and these days many people move funds around from one account to another by computer or telephone. Secondly, it concentrates attention on the monetary costs to consumers. In fact, the real cost to individuals is the extra time involved in the collection of information and the time and uncertainty in the decision-making needed to protect them against rising prices.

The real cost to the economy also includes the additional resources that are channelled into those parts of the financial sector that advise consumers and savers on how to protect themselves against inflation and create new financial products that help them to do so. In addition, there is also an arbitrary impact on the distribution of income since some groups of economic agents will always be able to protect themselves against inflation more effectively than others.

It is clear that the welfare costs associated with very high rates of inflation are likely to be very high, possibly involving economic collapse and social breakdown. The difficult question is, however, to calculate the welfare costs of steady, low inflation rates. Early attempts (Fischer, 1981; Lucas, 1981) concentrated on the impact of inflation on the demand for money and sought to estimate the costs by measuring the reduction in the area under the demand for money curve as interest rates rise with inflation and the demand for money falls. This, of course, assumes a known and stable relationship between the interest rate and the demand for money, a view which, as we saw in chapter 3, is not beyond dispute. In particular, estimates of the costs of inflation using this approach depend on the closeness of substitutes for money and hence the interest elasticity of the demand for money — the more elastic is the demand for money, the lower the measured costs of inflation will be.

A second problem with these studies is that they calculated the costs of inflation by comparing a zero inflation rate with a 10 per cent inflation rate. But, although 10 per cent inflation is a long way from hyperinflation, it is not a low rate of inflation. These studies suggested that the welfare costs of an inflation rate of say 2 to 3 per cent per annum might be quite low. Feldstein (1995) even suggested that the shoe-leather costs saved by reducing inflation from 2 per cent to zero might be outweighed by the loss of seigniorage revenue to the monetary authorities. This, we hardly need to say, follows from the view that the reduction in the inflation rate has come about through a reduction in the rate of growth of the money supply. We can reject this, however, while still noting Feldstein's views on the low welfare cost of low rates of inflation.

Other studies (Lucas, 1995; Pakko 1998; Chadha, Haldane and Janssen 1998) have made use of more elaborate general equilibrium demand for money models or shopping-time models to calculate the costs of inflation and have generally proposed higher costs. These models are highly theoretical and are heavily dependent on debatable assumptions and it is not possible to come to firm conclusions. Similar problems arise in theoretical attempts to calculate an optimal rate of inflation for the purposes of inflation targeting (see Buiter, 2007).

This is not to suggest that the control of inflation is not important but it does leave the debate about the relative importance of monetary policy targets open, especially to the extent that inflation-reducing policies are not costless. We deal with the question of monetary policy targets in Chapter 8.

When he introduced the term the 'natural rate of unemployment', Friedman (1968, p.10) did not claim that it could be estimated accurately and he also suggested that it would change from time to time. In doing so, he argued that the natural rate could not be established as a reliable benchmark for the monetary authorities, even if it were true that the actual rate might deviate from the natural rate for long periods of time. Nonetheless, if the NAIRU was to have any policy significance at all, estimates were needed. One approach was to treat the NAIRU as equivalent to the long run average unemployment rate in an economy. Other methods were tried to arrive at measures of a market-clearing unemployment rate but this has led to a variety of answers such that Mankiw (2001, p. C47) judges that the natural rate of unemployment 'is impossible to know with much precision'.

In one sense, this makes life more difficult for the monetary authorities and supports the notion that unemployment should not be tackled through expansionary monetary policy. However, it is also true that the theory attacking aggregate demand policies is weakened if the explanation is dependent upon a theoretical concept that has no policy content.

This contributed to a continuing general dissatisfaction with the Friedman-Phelps model. Another element in this dissatisfaction arose from the dependence of the model on incorrect expectations. It was hard to accept that major booms and recessions could be explained by frequent, large and persistent errors in the inflation expectations of market agents, especially given the quantity and quality of information that is available about current changes and likely future movements of the price level.

Nonetheless, the Friedman-Phelps model, together with the experience of stagflation in many developed economies in the 1970s, was influential in the increasing acceptance by governments of the limitations of demand management policies. The model was sufficiently accepted that economists who opposed Keynesian demand management policies sought to modify it. This was done principally by the rejection of the use of backward-looking expectations because they result in past errors being built into forecasts. With backward-looking expectations, when inflation is increasing, workers systematically underestimate the rate of inflation but this was held not to be rational. If the way in which expectations are formed consistently produces incorrect forecasts, rational agents would change their method of forming expectations until they reached a position in which errors were not systematically built into forecasts.

6.3   The New Classical model and policy irrelevance

The criticisms of the use of backward-looking expectations in the expectations-augmented Phillips curve model was tackled by the development of the New Classical model in which the rational expectations hypothesis was applied to a model of continuous market clearing. Rational (forward-looking) expectations are informed predictions of future events and are essentially the same as the predictions of the relevant economic model, which is assumed to be the correct model for the economy. It follows that the expected rate of inflation is an unbiased predictor of the actual rate of inflation. Mistakes may be made because the available information is incomplete but expectations are correct on average. That is,

$$\pi_t^e = \pi + \varepsilon_t \qquad (6.5)$$

where ε_t is a random error term, which (i) has a mean of zero and (ii) is uncorrelated with the information set available when expectations are formed. Thus, forecasting errors are not serially correlated. The assumption of rational expectations could be seen as a clear advance because they are compatible with all other aspects of the model in a way that adaptive expectations are not. Adaptive expectations require an additional hypothesis — how market agents adapt expectations to take account of previous errors. The assumption of rational expectations, however, means that the expectations of agents are always the values of the variables produced by the model itself.

The rational expectations hypothesis suggests that market agents make the best use of all available and relevant information in their forecasts of inflation — rather than simply taking account of past rates of inflation, as in adaptive expectations. New Classical economists applied the rational expectations hypothesis to a simple Monetarist model that employed a modified version of the Quantity Theory of Money in which the rate of growth of the money supply was seen as the principal factor in the determination of the inflation rate. Such models bypassed the problem of how monetary policy was practised by assuming an exogenous money supply. Within this framework, the policy intentions of the monetary authorities regarding the rate of growth of the money supply was important information for market agents seeking to forecast future rates of inflation. For New Consensus Macroeconomics, of course, it is the intentions of the central bank towards the repo rate that is crucial. In either case, market agents are assumed to consider the policy of the monetary authorities in making their forecasts. In other words, the application of rational expectations led to government being incorporated into the model. In all previous models, government had been exogenous.

Pause for thought 6.4

Compare the nature and formulation of the original Phillips curve with the PC curve in the IS/PC/MR model.

If we accept, solely for the purposes of explication, that the best available model for forecasting the rate of inflation is the Quantity Theory of Money, we can modify equation 6.5 as follows:

$$\pi_t = \alpha_1 \pi_{t-1} + \alpha_2.(\dot{M} - \dot{Y}_t^*) \tag{6.6}$$

where $\dot{M}$ is the current rate of monetary growth and $\dot{Y}$ is the natural rate of growth of output (that is, the rate of growth of output associated with the natural rate of unemployment). Expected inflation no longer depends on past inflation but on expected monetary policy.

The assumption of continuous market clearing implies that prices are free to adjust instantaneously to clear markets. It follows that anyone wishing to work can find employment at the market-clearing equilibrium wage and thus that all unemployment is voluntary. The combination of the rational expectations hypothesis and the assumption of continuous market clearing implies that output and employment fluctuate randomly around their natural levels. Thus, unemployment fluctuates randomly around the NAIRU. All we are left with of the Phillips curve is the vertical line at the NAIRU. Increases in aggregate demand do not produce systematic reductions in unemployment, even in the short-run. All they do is increase inflation. Acceptance of the New Classical model denies that there is any advantage to be had from demand management even in the short-run. Money is neutral in both the short- and the long-run.

Another way of making the same point is to say that rational market agents fully anticipate the actions of the authorities and incorporate this information in their expectations of the rate of inflation. That is, if the monetary authorities seek to increase the rate of growth of the money supply (or, more realistically, seek to cause short-term interest rates to fall) in the hope of reducing unemployment, market agents realize this and correctly forecast that the rate of inflation will rise. Workers then push wages up in line with the correctly forecast inflation and real wages, employment and output all remain unchanged. The level of unemployment does not fall. Thus, fully anticipated changes in monetary policy are ineffective in influencing the level of output and employment even in the short-run.

This is known as the policy ineffectiveness or policy irrelevance theorem. According to this theorem, the only way in which the authorities can influence output and employment through demand policies is to take market agents by surprise. For example, an unexpected increase in the money supply (or reduction in the repo rate) causes workers and firms to see the consequent increase in the general price level as an increase in relative prices. They react by increasing the supply of output and labour and the economy moves to a new short-run aggregate supply curve. Both employment and output temporarily increase. As in the expectations-augmented Phillips curve, once agents realize there has been no change in relative prices, output and employment return to their natural levels at the higher price level. However, there are two important differences from the expectations-augmented Phillips curve.

Firstly, market agents include the rate of money supply growth (or the repo rate) in the information they use to forecast inflation and quickly realize that inflation is about to rise. They thus adjust their inflation forecasts much more quickly than in the expectations-augmented Phillips curve case, where agents do not realize what is happening until inflation actually rises. Secondly, the authorities are unable to exploit the possibility of the temporary trade-off between inflation and unemployment. If they try to reduce unemployment through monetary shocks at all frequently, agents learn that this is what the authorities do when unemployment reaches undesirable levels. Workers and firms anticipate the monetary shocks and are no longer taken by surprise. In other words, any short-run trade-off between inflation and unemployment disappears if the authorities try to exploit it.

The more often the authorities try to engineer reductions in unemployment through monetary shocks, the less easily are workers and firms fooled and the closer the short-run Phillips curve is to the vertical. The incorporation of government into the model ensures the policy invariance result. If market agents believe that expansionary monetary policy has no real effects but only cause increases in the rate of inflation, government cannot have an impact on output and employment by following such a policy. When governments do so, market agents immediately respond by raising their inflationary expectations, the short-run Phillips curve moves out and the economy remains at the NAIRU.

However, as we have suggested above, the complete rejection of even a short-run trade-off between inflation and unemployment does not receive support from empirical observation and this has led to a number of adjustments to and criticisms of the model. We shall consider some of these under the following headings:

- Modifications to the continuous market clearing model

- Criticisms of the assumption of rational expectations

- Criticisms of the natural rate hypothesis

- The complete rejection of equilibrium models

Of greater importance to us have been the New Keynesian theories that can be grouped under the heading of price stickiness which have rejected continuous market clearing in the short-run and we deal with these separately in section 6.4.

Modifications to the continuous market clearing model

Relatively small changes to the model can restore the power of governments to reduce output fluctuations at the cost of an increase in price fluctuations, without attacking the principal assumptions of the New Classical model. These include:

(a) Progressive income tax structures push workers into higher tax brackets as inflation rises, affecting employment and output. Tax changes might also affect net-of-tax real rates of interest and, hence, influence borrowing and lending.

b) Changes in the rate of inflation might influence investment and, thus, the long-run rate of growth. For example, higher inflation makes holding real capital more attractive relative to money, and might stimulate investment.

(c) Higher inflation might have a positive impact on consumption as saving in the form of financial assets becomes less attractive.

(d) Price movements in a model with asset holdings might produce real effects:

(i) through changes in the real value of nominally denominated government assets provided they are considered to be net wealth; and

(ii) through distribution effects that might occur even with assets issued by the private sector, as creditors and debtors react asymmetrically to changes in the real value of debt. However, these are only likely to have real effects if the price level changes are unexpected and this conflicts with the forward-looking assumptions of the New Classical model.

(e) With fixed exchange rates in an open economy, the relative prices of tradable and non-tradable goods change in response even to expected changes in monetary policy.

However, although changes such as these would make the model a better reflection of real world relationships, they do not return us to the position implied by the original Phillips curve — that governments could choose an unemployment rate compatible with an acceptable inflation rate and could achieve this combination by manipulating aggregate demand through monetary and fiscal policy.

Criticisms of the assumption of rational expectations

There have been several criticisms of the rational expectations hypothesis. It has been argued, for example, that the form of learning applied in the rational expectations model is unrealistic. Acocella (1998) also suggests that the New Classical model is a model of a stationary society and that the 'rationality' of human beings in this system ignores 'creative rationality', which involves the attempt to transform society and the environment rather than just accepting what already exists. Akerlof, Dickens and Perry (2000) take a different approach in arguing that the way agents *form* expectations might not be as important as the way in which they *use* expectations. They may not make the best possible use of the information available to them. Rather, the authors follow models of psychologists in which agents make use of simplified abstractions from which mistakes might arise. They propose three ways in which the treatment of inflation by workers in the setting of wages might differ from that suggested by rational expectations — they might ignore low inflation, they might not take expected inflation fully into account and/or they might not fully appreciate the impact of inflation on the demand for their services. Consequently, they hypothesise that at low rates of inflation prices and wages might be set consistently lower relative to nominal aggregate demand than at zero inflation and thus that running the economy at a low rate of inflation might result in a higher level of output and employment than at zero inflation. This would mean that at zero inflation, a trade-off between inflation and output would be restored.

Criticisms of the natural rate hypothesis and the NAIRU

The full New Classical model rejects the existence of any attack on unemployment through expansionary monetary policy and so removes the idea that the natural rate of unemployment might be used as a benchmark for such policies. Nonetheless, the natural rate remains important as the unemployment rate associated with market clearing and, if supply-side policies are to be used to reduce the NAIRU, we need to know the causes of the NAIRU and to have some possibility of identifying the rate and the associated natural rate of output. We have already mentioned the difficulty of doing this. Other problems arise. Firstly, in the New Classical model, movements away from the NAIRU occur only when market agents are taken by surprise by the policy authorities but this cannot last long and, to the extent that it works, generates future inflation. Thus, a period of low and stable inflation suggests that the authorities have not attempted a surprise policy and should imply a stable level of unemployment close to the NAIRU. However, in the USA in the 1990s, low and stable rates of inflation coexisted with a wide range of unemployment rates (Akerlof, Dickens and Perry, 2000).

Secondly, it has been suggested that cyclical variations in unemployment around the NAIRU might be explained by real rather than monetary factors. Research in this area has led to a variety of proposals related to search theories of unemployment, patterns of the reallocation of jobs across, firms, industries and regions and of the advertising of job vacancies. In some cases, however, what appear to be real factors influencing cyclical unemployment might occur because

wages are much less flexible than are assumed in many labour market models
(Hall, 2005a). Indeed, Hall (2005b) suggests that it might be difficult to distinguish real from monetary factors as determinants of unemployment fluctuations.

Thirdly, the notion even of a stable, long-run Phillips curve at the natural rate
of unemployment has been questioned. Rowthorn (1999), for example, constructs
a model in which the equilibrium unemployment rate is affected by capital accumulation, technical progress and labour force expansion. He argues that these
forces are ignored in conventional models because they make use of the Cobb-
Douglas production function, which assumes that the elasticity of substitution
between labour and capital is equal to unity. Rowthorn suggests that an elasticity of substitution of less than unity has more empirical justification.

The complete rejection of equilibrium models

More extreme are criticisms that reject entirely the assumption of continuous
market clearing, arguing that real world prices are not perfectly flexible and markets do not continuously return to equilibrium. The neoclassical identification of
the long-run with equilibrium, which leaves disequilibrium as a short-run phenomenon based on imperfect knowledge, is replaced by a view of the world dominated by uncertainty in which disequilibrium is the norm. Equilibrium is a special case, unlikely ever to be reached. When markets do clear, it is often not
through the process of price adjustment. Lack of information about the future
leads to coordination failures among markets.

This certainly overcomes the policy ineffectiveness problem despite the introduction of rational expectations into the analysis, but there remains the problem
of explaining the transmission mechanism from monetary policy to prices and
output. A number of general disequilibrium models were produced in the 1970s
(Benassy, 1975; Barro and Grossman, 1976; Grandmont, 1977; Malinvaud, 1977).
These were fix-price models, although absolutely fixed prices were not required
for monetary and fiscal policy changes to produce real effects. However, the
models lacked plausible explanations of how prices are determined in an economy not at a market clearing equilibrium. Consequently, they had little long-term
influence on the debate.

Empirical work on the New Classical model

Two statements are made in response to criticisms that the assumptions of the
New Classical model are unrealistic: that markets act as if the assumptions were
true; and that the only way of judging a model is through testing its predictions
— if the model predicts well, the underlying theory must be a sufficiently good
representation of reality. We, thus, need to say a little more than we have so far
done about the empirical work done on the New Classical model.

Much of this empirical work involves testing one of the implications of the
policy irrelevance hypothesis — that deviations of real variables from trend result

from people being surprised by movements in the general price level. In other words, only unanticipated monetary policy has real effects. Anticipated monetary policy should be neutral. On this basis, early work (Barro, 1977, 1978) appeared to support the policy ineffectiveness proposition. Using annual data for the US economy from 1941 to 1976, Barro's study suggested that, while output and employment are significantly affected by unanticipated monetary growth, anticipated monetary growth has no real effects. However, subsequent studies (Mishkin, 1982; Gordon, 1982), found evidence that output and employment are affected by both anticipated and unanticipated monetary policy. By 1989, Goodhart (1989a, ch.13) was able to report 63 tests of the policy irrelevance hypothesis for seven different countries. Of these, 17 appeared to confirm the hypothesis that only unanticipated monetary shocks had real effects. The great majority suggested that monetary policy had real effects, whether it was anticipated or not.[4] More recent testing has not altered that balance.

It seems far more likely that monetary policy's impact on real variables is the result of one or more of the arguments critical of the New Classical model. The most likely candidate is the failure of real world markets to clear perfectly and instantaneously. This leads us, in particular, to the idea of price stickiness and New Keynesian attempts to explain it.

6.4   Price stickiness

As we mentioned in 6.1, a major problem for the New Classical model is that money is not neutral in the short-run, and no policymaker acts as if it is. It is widely accepted that a monetary shock does have an impact on output and unemployment and that this impact occurs before the shock begins to influence the rate of inflation. One of the more important attempts to return to the short-run Phillips curve's trade-off between output and employment while maintaining a belief in rational expectations have been the various New Keynesian models.

Pause for thought 6.5

How can markets clear other than through price changes? Does any other form of market clearing lead to a genuine equilibrium?

New Keynesian economics rejects the notion of continuous market clearing but accepts the existence of a long-run equilibrium and the tendency for economies to return to equilibrium positions. However, this may take a considerable time, not because of incorrect expectations but because of institutional features of the market and nominal price rigidities that exist because of these features. We expressed these in equation 5.2 in which current inflation depends on last period's inflation. Workers' expectations might be correct but these correct expectations may not be built into money wages in the current period.

The most prominent of the New Keynesian models are the sticky wage and price models. The best known of the sticky wage models assumes long-term overlapping wage contracts (Taylor, 1979). When trade unions enter into a contract in which wages are fixed for one or two years, even if workers form expectations rationally and are able to forecast the actions of the policy authorities, they are unable to react to new information. Thus, an inflationary monetary shock pushes up aggregate demand and prices rise but, during the life of wage contracts, money wages cannot rise. Real wages fall. Output increases above the natural level and unemployment falls below the natural rate. The economy moves up along a short-run Phillips curve as in figure 6.2. It is only as some wage contracts end that money wages are pushed up. Equally, following a disinflationary monetary shock, in the short term real wages are pushed up, output falls below the natural level and unemployment rises above the natural rate. In both cases, these movements are temporary since, once the contract period ends, money wages adjust to reflect the current rate of inflation and the economy returns to its long-run equilibrium position. However, there is a period in which money is not neutral, during which the authorities might exploit a trade-off between unemployment and inflation.

We can see that the outcome is the same as in the case of incorrect inflationary expectations except that:

(a)   we need only one short-run PC curve, not a separate curve for each expected inflation rate;

and, more importantly,

(b)   we have a different notion of the long-run. With expectations-augmented Phillips curves, the long-run is defined as that period of time required to bring about a return to equilibrium. There is no clear idea of how long that period might be. We need to incorporate additional theories (such as those relating to the formation of expectations) before we can say how long the short-run might be. In Neo-Keynesian models, the length of the short-run is determined by institutional factors such as the length of labour contracts. This means that institutional changes can bring about changes in the length of time in which an economy might benefit from lower unemployment at the expense of higher inflation. For instance, wage contracts might (and, indeed, do) tend to become shorter in periods of rapid inflation.

To support this model, we need an explanation of why workers and firms enter into long-term wage contracts. New Keynesian economists see these as the product of rational behaviour given the conditions in real world labour markets.

Pause for thought 6.6

What form might asymmetric information take in negotiations between employers and workers over labour contracts? Which side may be better informed about what?

For instance, the theory of implicit contracts assumes incomplete labour markets (workers do not have full access to insurance against risk). There is also asymmetric information and workers and firms have different degrees of risk aversion. The outcome is the standard labour contract in which the wage is held constant and the worker's job is guaranteed over the period of the contract, no matter how well or badly the firm is doing.

Another possible explanation of the failure of the labour market to clear continuously is provided by the insider-outsider model, in which workers already employed by firms have an advantage over unemployed workers. In neoclassical models, the real wage is kept at the market clearing level through competition between workers for jobs. Workers with jobs cannot push their wages above the equilibrium level because there are other workers willing to take their places at a lower wage rate. However, in real world labour markets, there is often no genuine competition between employed and unemployed. Employers know the abilities and attitudes of the workers they already employ, but must make judgements about unemployed workers based on limited information, such as the length of time the potential worker has been unemployed. Firms often assume that a long period of unemployment implies something personally unsatisfactory about the worker, or that the period of unemployment has reduced his potential productivity, or both. Again, the firm has spent time and money training its existing work force and would face costs in both getting rid of existing workers and hiring new workers. For these reasons, firms are willing to pay higher wages to existing workers than would be accepted by unemployed workers.

Pause for thought 6.7

Why might the insider/outsider model apply better to skilled than to unskilled workers?

Existing workers (insiders) take advantage of their position to push the wage above the market clearing level, causing employers to hire fewer workers than they would in a competitive market. The unemployed workers remain unemployed. In practice, unemployed workers seldom receive job offers and are not in a position to show their willingness to undercut the wage paid to the existing workforce. Equally, employers are seldom in a position to discover the wage at which unemployed workers might be prepared to do the job. Unfortunately, this theory conflicts with reality. If there is no competition from the unemployed, there is no reason for money wages to rise more rapidly in booms than in slumps. Since prices rise more rapidly in booms, we might expect real wages to move contra-cyclically — falling in booms and rising in slumps. This does not happen.

Consequently, attention has shifted to New Keynesian models of the price-setting behaviour of firms such as in the staggered price setting model of Calvo (1983). These assume monopolistic competition in goods markets and incorporate costs of adjusting prices. Each firm produces a differentiated product and, thus, has market power and are able to set prices above marginal cost. Thus, they always wish to sell more at prevailing prices. In each period some firms change price but others do not. The probability of a firm changing its price in any period is independent of whether it had changed its price in the previous period. A monetary shock changes both aggregate demand and the demand for labour and leads firms to adjust output and employment. Thus, it has real effects. In a recession, there is excess supply in both the goods and labour markets. This theory of the goods market is often combined with a model of the labour market that produces above-equilibrium real wages. Mankiw (2001) points out that this approach runs into difficulties when economists attempt to develop dynamic models of price setting. The most common approach to this assumes that price adjustment is costly and, hence, infrequent.

Box 6.3: Expectations, market imperfections, α_1 and the Phillips curve

Consider the equations we have used in explaining the Phillips curve. The original Phillips curve written in inflation/output space is:

$$\pi_t = \alpha_2. (Y - Y^*)$$

where α_2 is the slope of the Phillips curve. α_2 measures the sensitivity of prices and wages to changes in aggregate demand and may be influenced by the degree of competition in the economy, the strength of trade unions, the extent of regional or other imbalances and so on. However, we are concerned here with α_1.

Neoclassical theory concentrates on equilibrium in which employment and output are determined by the real wage and this, in turn, is determined by the demand for and supply of labour. By definition, in equilibrium, the economy is at the natural level of output and there is no output gap. The size of α_2 is irrelevant. If the economy is away from equilibrium, we are in the short-run. Why might this happen? We have several possibilities outlined in the text.

(a) Keynes's *General Theory* assumes an uncertain world in which workers cannot forecast the future inflation rate and hence the future real wage. They base wage bargaining and labour supply decisions on relative wages — the money wages of workers doing similar work. Thus, with falling prices, workers do not easily accept a cut in money wages because to do so would be to accept a lower money wage than other workers are currently being paid. This can be taken as an example of money illusion since workers are replacing the real wage by the money wage in their labour supply decisions but it may be sensible behaviour in an uncertain world. For neoclassical economists, taking equilibrium as the natural state of the world, it is irrational behaviour.

(b) In the Friedman-Phelps model, we have workers behaving rationally so that money wages rise by the expected rate of inflation. However, because they use backward-looking expectations, they make errors in their forecasts of future inflation rates, their forecasts being too low (when the inflation rate is rising) or too high (when the inflation rate is falling).

$$\pi_t = \alpha_1.\pi_t + \alpha_2.(Y - Y^*)$$

where $\alpha_1.\pi_t$ measures the expected rate of inflation

If expectations are correct, $\alpha_1 = 1$. For $\alpha_1 < 1$, expectations are incorrect. Thus, following an inflationary expansion of demand by governments, α_1 is initially low but steadily increases as workers realize that the inflation rate is changing. In the long-run, expectations are by definition correct, $\alpha_1 = 1$, and with no output gap, inflation is equal to the expected rate of inflation.

(c) In the New Classical model, rational workers also employ rational expectations, their inflation forecasts are on average correct and inflation is equal to expected inflation in both the short-run (unless the policy-makers succeed in creating an inflationary surprise) and long-run. α_1 is always unity, there is no output gap and the size of α_2 is of no importance.

(d) New Keynesian Economics accepts that workers base decisions on the real wage and employ rational expectations but are unable, in the short-run, to keep money wages rising in line with inflation because of institutional imperfections leading, for example, to overlapping wage contracts or staggered price setting. $\alpha_1.\pi_t$ plays the same role as in Friedman-Phelps but is not now an expectational variable but reflects the degree of price stickiness in the economy.

(e) For Tobin, we again have $\alpha_1 < 1$, but this time because unemployment is unevenly distributed across industries and in those industries with high unemployment, workers feel unable to defend their real wage for fear of putting their jobs at risk. Here there is no clear notion of moving from the short run to the long run.

(f) In Akerlof, Dickens and Perry (2000), α_1 may be less than one and remain so, not because workers form expectations inefficiently but because they choose, for a variety of possible reasons, not to make full use of the information they have about likely future inflation. The way people behave in practice may be more important than theories about the formation of expectations. The short run/long run distinction disappears because there is no suggestion that people change their behaviour in the long run. α_1 may remain below unity and the vertical long-run Phillips curve disappears.

Mankiw sets out an illustrative model in which the current inflation rate becomes a function of inflation expected to prevail in the next period and the deviation of unemployment from its natural rate. If expected inflation is held constant, higher unemployment leads to lower inflation, much as in the Friedman-Phelps model. Again, however, the model runs into trouble when confronted with evidence. Oddly, according to the model, credible monetary disinflations are likely to produce booms (Ball, 1994) whereas, in practice, monetary disinflations typically lead to recession. Mankiw also argues that the New Keynesian Phillips curve is incapable of producing empirically plausible impulse responses to monetary policy shocks. He assumes a plausible response of inflation to a monetary policy shock and then shows that the New Keynesian Phillips curve implies an implausible result for unemployment — a monetary contraction causes unemployment to fall!

Other models have been developed more recently but problems remain. Harrison, Nikolov, Quinn, Ramsay, Scott and Thomas (2005) produce a New Keynesian Phillips curve with a forward-looking profits function that includes the cost of price adjustment. Critical views can be found in Galí and Gertler (1999). Work, however, continues and New Keynesian Phillips curves continue to be incorporated into macroeconomic models as in Blanchard and Galí (2007).

6.5 The neutrality of money in the long-run

We have seen that all of the widely-accepted approaches later than Keynes's General Theory and the original Phillips curve express the view that money is neutral in the long-run and that this is accepted in the New Consensus Macroeconomics. All of these other than New Classical economics accept, however, a short-run impact of money on output and employment. The only issues that appears to remain in these approaches are the meaning of the 'long-run' and the relative costs to an economy associated with inflation and unemployment. These issues also appear to have been resolved to the satisfaction of mainstream economics with an acceptance of the view that inflation beyond a level of around two per cent per annum is highly damaging to an economy. Thus, even if a short-term trade-off exists between output and inflation, few economists are likely to approve of the exploitation of this trade-off deliberately to lower unemployment. On the other hand, it is widely accepted that monetary authorities seeking to lower inflation need to be aware of the output and employment costs of unexpected restrictive policies — hence the importance in the NCM of the management of expectations.

Yet there remain dissident voices. These may take one of two approaches. Firstly, as we have suggested in section 6.3 above, we might deny the relevance to economic policy of the concept of the long-run either by rejecting entirely equilibrium models or by arguing that the short-run is likely to be such a long period in terms of calendar time that the short-run costs of pursuing a policy that ignores the short-run trade-off between inflation and output might be highly damaging.

Secondly, arguments can be advanced for the existence of a long-run trade-off between inflation and output. An early case for this was made by Tobin (1972) who argued that, even in the long-run, workers in the aggregate would not take expected inflation into account (in eqn. 5.1, we would have $0 < \alpha_1 < 1$), not because of money illusion but because workers in high unemployment industries would not wish to endanger their jobs by strongly resisting cuts in real wages caused by rising prices. Only in industries with low unemployment or full employment will inflation be fully taken into account. In a multisectoral view of the economy, unemployment will be unevenly distributed across industries so that a1 will be less than one in some industries and in the economy as a whole. Even though the distribution of unemployment will change over time as workers become better informed and the composition of aggregate demand and the structure of the economy changes, Tobin argued that there would always be uneven distribution and that the long-term Phillips curve would be downwards sloping (upwards sloping in inflation/output space as in figure 6.2).

Another major proposition is based on evidence in support of hysteresis in labour markets—the notion that the current level of unemployment has an impact on future unemployment levels. We have suggested earlier, for example, that high levels of unemployment might lower the skill levels of workers and reduce labour productivity or might lead to a reduction in confidence in the economy leading to lower investment and economic growth. If this were true, there would be no single 'natural rate' of unemployment for an economy and increases in unemployment resulting from disinflationary monetary policy persist into the long term. Ball (1997) analyses the growth of European unemployment in the 1980s and shows that countries with larger decreases in inflation and longer disinflationary periods experienced larger increases in their natural rates of unemployment. In a 1999 paper, Ball shows that these larger increases in the natural rate of unemployment could be linked back to a failure to pursue expansionary monetary policy in the early 1980s. That is, monetary policy influenced both actual unemployment and the natural rate of unemployment. Shocks to US real GDP are also typically very persistent, offering support for the existence of hysteresis.

The hysteresis argument could be interpreted as simply one reason among many for changes over the long-term in the NAIRU — we could think of a vertical long-run Phillips curve associated with an increasing NAIRU. However, in this case, the increase in the NAIRU is being caused by restrictive anti-inflationary policies and so lower rates of inflation become associated with higher rates of unemployment in the long-run. Thus, we have a clear attack on one of the more beguiling aspects of New Classical Macroeconomics and New Consensus Macroeconomics — that inflation can be reduced at no long-run cost in terms of higher unemployment.

These arguments remain important because the theoretical nature of the concepts of the NAIRU and the natural level of output makes it extremely difficult to carry out effective empirical work on the slope, or lack of slope of the long-run Phillips curve. Economists have put forward ideas that could suggest a vertical long-run curve (monetary factors have no long-run impact on the real forces that determine output and employment), a negative slope in inflation/unemployment space (limited bargaining power of workers in some industries, higher unemployment in the short-run increases unemployment in the long run) or, indeed, a positive slope — higher inflation damages the operation of the market and increases the NAIRU. Difficulties in identifying the natural rate of unemployment not only mean that it cannot safely be used as a benchmark for monetary policy but also that the long-run slope of the Phillips curve can't be demonstrated empirically.

All that has really happened despite the great deal of work on the Phillips curve is that the 'money as a veil over the real economy' debate has been shifted to the long-run. Money is clearly not neutral in the short-run; in the long-run its neutrality remains an unresolvable theoretical issue.

6.6   Summary

The Quantity Theory of Money had suggested that, in the long-run at least, expansionary monetary policy (taken, as in all Classical economics, to mean an expansion in the money supply) led directly to increases in prices. Keynes's *General Theory* had analysed the way in which monetary policy could influence not only prices but also output and, hence, the level of unemployment. The Phillips curve showed the statistical relationship between rates of (wage) inflation and levels of unemployment, implying that governments could trade off higher inflation against lower unemployment or vice versa. The Phillips curve was criticised because it showed a relationship between money wages and unemployment whereas, according to the neoclassical theory of the labour market, labour demand and supply depended on real rather than money wages. Thus, when the Phillips curve relationship broke down in the late 1960s, it was quickly replaced by the expectations-augmented version of the Phillips curve in which there was a separate short-run Phillips curve for each expected rate of inflation. The original Phillips curve was converted into a relationship between inflation and an output gap between actual output and the natural level of output, that level of output associated with the natural rate of unemployment.

Whichever way the relationship was expressed, the inclusion of expectations into the model meant that, in the long-run, the trade-off disappeared — the long-run Phillips curve was vertical at the natural level of output and the natural rate of unemployment. Any attempt by the monetary authorities to reduce unemployment by increasing aggregate demand through monetary policy would have no long-run impact on unemployment but would cause accelerating inflation. This, in turn, would interfere with the efficiency of the market economy and cause the natural rate of unemployment to rise.

Attempts to reduce the rate of inflation by unanticipated restrictive monetary policy would cause unemployment to rise above the natural rate, where it would stay until workers' expectations of inflation adjusted to the lower level of inflation in the economy. This idea of the cost (in unemployment) of reducing the rate of inflation was named the sacrifice ratio. A major objection to this model was that the 'long-run' had no clear meaning in calendar time, indicating only the period needed for the economy to return to equilibrium. Thus, a monetary policy that expanded aggregate demand might succeed in reducing unemployment for quite a long period and might be seen as worthwhile. This would be particularly the case if there were hysteresis effects in the labour market, with the short-run reductions in unemployment producing longer-run gains in employment.

The opposition to the macroeconomic policy of aggregate demand was strengthened by the development of the New Classical model. In effect, it removed the short-run from the analysis by combining rational expectations with a market-clearing model of the economy. In this model, workers would correctly anticipate expansionary monetary policy and would increase their wages in line with the money supply increases. Real wages and employment would be unchanged. Aggregate demand policy could have no real effects even in the short-run. This was a full return to the neutrality of money. There are, however, a number of problems with both aspects of the New Classical model (rational expectations and market clearing) and a number of ideas have been explored to re-introduce short-run real effects from a monetary change. These include New Keynesian models based mainly upon price- or wage-stickiness. These, too, have their problems. Other authors have also continued to develop arguments for the existence of a long-run trade-off between inflation and output and employment.

Finally, as we have remarked twice already in this chapter (pp. 159, 173) there remains the question of how long the 'long-run' might be. Clearly, we need only assume a degree of rationality and self-interest on the part of individual agents to assume that they will want to correct errors as soon as possible, be they errors regarding expectations, the pricing of contracts or whatever. The 'long-run' is then easily interpreted as having a conventional, chronological meaning as the length of time that it takes for these corrections to take place. But there is another, and radically different, interpretation that one may place on the long-run. This is that it is only a *logical* construct. It refers to that state 'in which all those assumptions necessary to make the model work as described hold true'. And this could be a purely theoretical case which in practice, may never come to pass.[5] In a decentralised economy, for example, there will always be some contracts fixed at the wrong price even while others are being revised. Viewed like this, we are always in the short-run with consequences described many years ago by David Laidler:

> ...a little price stickiness goes a long way in macroeconomics...it is sufficient to enable us to explain not only why output fluctuates in response to monetary shocks and why such output fluctuations persist over time...(1988, p.153).

On this view, policymakers are always in the short-run and policy always has real effects.

Key concepts used in this chapter

Phillips curve

expectations-augmented
Phillips curve

natural rate of unemployment

non-accelerating-inflation rate
of unemployment (NAIRU)

adaptive (backward-looking)
expectations

money illusion

signal extraction problem

sacrifice ratio

policy ineffectiveness/policy
irrelevance

forward-looking expectations

price stickiness

Questions and exercises
Answers at the end of the book

1. Why is the natural rate of unemployment referred to as 'natural'?

2. Why was the 'shoe leather cost' of inflation so called? What other costs are there of anticipated inflation?

3. Why does 'the combination of the rational expectations hypothesis and the assumption of continuous market clearing' imply that output and employment fluctuate randomly around their natural levels?

4. The Chambers Twentieth Century Dictionary defined 'hysteresis' as:

  the retardation or lagging of an effect behind the cause of the effect: the influence of earlier treatment of a body on its subsequent reaction.

How then can hysteresis occur in labour markets? How can the existence of hysteresis in labour markets be used to argue against the neutrality of money?

5. How are the following arguments discussed in this chapter affected, if at all, by an assumption of endogenous money?
  (a) the expectations-augmented Phillips curve
  (b) policy irrelevance

...and also to think about

6. The model to which New Classical economists applied rational expectations is described in the text as 'market clearing' and 'monetarist'. How are these descriptions related? What must have been the principal assumptions of the model?

7. How useful do you think equilibrium models are in analysing a world that is never in equilibrium?

Further reading

The expectations-augmented Phillips curve, New Classical models, and the policy irrelevance theorem can be found in any recent intermediate macroeconomics text. A good account, together with criticisms, is provided by Acocella (1998). This also discusses public choice views and political business cycles. Carlin and Soskice (2006) cover the same ground and link it to the *IS/PC/MR* model model, used here in chapter 5. A summary of the New Keynesian approach can be found in Clarida, Galí and Gertler (1999). On the role of price stickiness, see Laidler (1990) ch.5. Empirical evidence of the effect of policy on output and prices is covered in Walsh (2003) ch.1. The theory is in ch.5.

7 International issues in policymaking

'The best money to take to the United States, is either guineas or Spanish milled dollars; Bank of England notes will not do'

Noble's *Instr. Emigr. U.S.* 107, 1860

'Money speaks sense in a language all nations understand'

Aphra Behn, *The Rover*, pt 2 1681

7.1   Introduction

In figure 5.1 in section 5.2, we showed the linkages between changes in the central bank's short-term interest rate (the repo rate) and inflation. We also looked at the relationship between interest rates and total demand in the economy but we made little of the distinction, clear in figure 5.1, between the domestic demand and external demand components of total demand. We said little more than that, other things being equal, an increase in domestic interest rates should increase the value of the domestic currency and that such a change would be likely to damage the international competitiveness of domestic firms.

The exchange rate appears in the diagram as one of the variables influenced by changes in short-term interest rates. This has not always been the case for the UK and is not now the position for countries that maintain fixed exchange rates or are members of a monetary union. Thus, to look fully at the impact of monetary policy across all countries, we need to look at the way it operates under different exchange rate systems. The effectiveness of monetary policy also depends upon the degree of mobility of international capital. These are the issues we seek to tackle in this chapter.

Before doing so, we need to say a little about the past role of exchange rates as a target of economic policy. From the end of World War II until 1973, most countries participated in a fixed exchange rate system, known as the IMF or the Bretton Woods system. A number of European countries then participated in fixed exchange rate systems for all or most years between 1973 and 1999, when monetary union was established in Europe. It is not surprising, then, that much of the, still widely taught, open economy monetary theory begins by assuming fixed exchange rates. The fixed exchange rate world, however, presented a quite different challenge to monetary authorities than does the world of today.

The obligation to maintain a fixed rate of exchange turned the exchange rate into one of the targets of economic policy, increasing the number of targets the authorities faced. Indeed, the exchange rate target was usually seen as in conflict with another accepted target of the times — the maintenance of full employment. An expansionary policy aimed at reducing unemployment would, *ceteris paribus*, cause the current account balance to worsen, possibly sending the balance of payments into deficit. The consequent outflow of capital would put downward pressure on the international value of the domestic currency. Thus, it was often argued, that the authorities should counteract this by an increase in short-term interest rates to attract a flow of capital into the economy. Short-term interest rates would then be set not in relation to the desired rate of inflation but to protect the fixed exchange rate. It was further argued by some writers that it was efficient to behave in this way because small interest rate changes could be expected to have a large impact on capital flows whereas it was widely believed at the time that quite large changes in monetary policy would be needed to have much impact on domestic variables.

All of this changed for currencies facing floating rates of exchange after March 1973. Although some governments have sought to influence the exchange rates of their currencies even within a floating rate system, by and large the exchange rate was no longer a target. The wide acceptance of the vertical long-run Phillips Curve removed full employment as a target and we were left with the rate of inflation as the single target of monetary policy. As figure 5.1 suggests, the exchange rate, no longer a target, became one of a number of variables influenced by changes in the repo rate and, in turn, influencing the rate of inflation through two channels — its impact on total demand and on import prices.

Pause for thought 7.1

Why does the acceptance of the vertical long-run Phillips curve mean that full employment can no longer be a target of macroeconomic policy?

The world of macroeconomic policy-making has changed in another way also. In the 1950s and 1960s, governments thought of themselves as having a number of potential policy instruments at their disposal, notably fiscal policy, monetary policy and direct controls such as incomes policies. The increased dominance of free market economics put paid to the use of incomes policies for economies as a whole from the beginning of the 1980s.[1] From the middle 1970s onwards, the use of fiscal policy became increasingly unpopular. With the limitations sought by the European Union on budget deficits within monetary union, the ability of many countries to pursue demand management through fiscal policy was greatly limited. This has left monetary policy, through the control of short-term interest rates, as the only remaining instrument of macroeconomic policy. Thus, figure 5.1 shows more than the links between changes in central bank interest rates and the rate of inflation — it shows the world of macroeconomic policy as it is now seen by the governments of developed economies.

7.2   Fixed exchange rate systems, the mobility of capital and the effectiveness of monetary policy

For many years, the analysis of the effectiveness of monetary policy was based upon the Mundell-Fleming model, a model that modified the *IS/LM* model to include a Balance of Payments equilibrium curve (*BP*). Our rejection of the *IS/LM* model, principally because of its dependence on the assumptions of an exogenous money supply and of constant prices, does not prevent us from looking at the lessons drawn from the model and from illustrating these with the help of the *IS/PC/MR* model we employ. We begin by looking at the basis of the Mundell-Fleming model and outline the conclusions it reached regarding monetary policy.

The Mundell-Fleming analysis was developed in the 1960s when most currencies were linked through the Bretton Woods fixed exchange rate system. Consequently, the *BP* curve is drawn on the assumption of fixed exchange rates and shows all combinations of income and interest rates at which the balance of payments is in balance. Equilibrium in the balance on payments required only that any deficit in the balance on current account was offset by a surplus on the capital account or *vice versa*. Thus:

$$B = B_C + B_K \qquad\qquad (7.1)$$

where B is the overall balance of payment, B_C is the balance on current account and B_K represents net capital inflow which may be positive or negative. In a simple version of the model, the current account is represented by the balance of trade (exports - imports), exports are a function of world income and the international competitiveness of home-country exports, and net capital inflow is a function of the difference between home-country interest rates and world interest rates and expected changes in the exchange rate. We can break these relationships down further to take into account our assumption of fixed exchange rates.

Pause for thought 7.2

What, other than the balance of trade, is included in the current account of the balance of payments.

Consider firstly the balance of trade. Both exports and imports are influenced by home prices for goods and services relative to those abroad, expressed through the exchange rate, in a common currency. Exports are influenced also by world income levels while domestic demand is an important influence on imports. However, since the model assumes both constant home prices and a fixed exchange rate, and since both world income and foreign prices are outside of the control of the home government, exports are written as an exogenous variable ($\overline{X}$). The net result is that domestic income (Y) is the only endogenous variable affecting the current account balance (B_C). Interest rates enter the picture through their effect on domestic demand. Remember that the upper panel in figure 5.2 is in interest rate/output space. Since we assume in the *IS/PC/MR* model that any deviation of actual output (Y) from the natural level (Y^*) results from changes in the level of total demand, we can easily substitute output for demand. Thus:

$$B_C = \overline{X} - IM(Y) \qquad\qquad (7.2)$$

where Y is the actual level of output and IM the marginal propensity to import.

As domestic demand increases, *ceteris paribus*, imports increase and the balance on current account worsens. The extent to which it worsens depends upon the country's marginal propensity to import. This has increased in most countries as international trade has steadily become more important. Nonetheless, we can assume it to be constant in the short run.

Net capital inflow (the capital account balance) depends on home interest rates relative to those in the rest of the world, the expected change in exchange rates and the degree of international capital mobility. In a fixed exchange rate model, the second term drops out and net capital inflow (B_K) is seen to depend on home interest rates (r) in comparison with the exogenous world interest rates (r^w) and the degree of capital mobility. Consequently, we have:

$$B_K = f(r - r^w) \tag{7.3}$$

As r increases, *ceteris paribus*, capital inflow increases. The extent to which this happens (summed up in the functional relationship between B_K and the interest rate differential) depends on the degree of international capital mobility. The more mobile capital is among countries, the greater is the change in net capital inflow following a change in relative interest rates. We can reasonably treat capital as highly but not perfectly mobile among developed countries.

By putting together information from (7.2) and (7.3) we can come to a conclusion about the general shape of the *BP* curve. Remember, that as income increases, *ceteris paribus*, the balance on current account worsens. Thus, for the overall balance of payments to remain in balance, the balance on capital account must be improving. But this only occurs if the domestic interest rate is rising relative to world interest rates. We can relatively easily translate interest rates into the form used is the *IS/PC/MR* model. Remember that in the *IS/LM* model, price changes were not taken into account and so there was no distinction between nominal and real rates of interest. Generally, when the external effects of interest rate changes are considered, it is nominal interest rates that are highlighted. Capital flows are affected immediately by a central bank change in short-term rates or expectations that such a change is about to occur. We can, however, accept the use of real rates of interest as in the *IS/PC/MR* model on the grounds that the foreign exchange market does take into account relative rates of inflation and that the central purpose of central bank adjustments to interest rates is to control the rate of inflation. Thus, we can accept the use of r and r^w above as real rates of interest and draw a *BP* curve in the real interest rate/output space that we employed in the upper panel of figure 5.2. Of course, there is a problem with time lags since short-term interest rate changes have an immediate impact on the capital account of the balance of payments but affect the current account only with a time lag.

It is clear that the *BP* curve has a positive slope in the general case since an increase in output creates a deficit on current account and must be matched, if balance of payments equilibrium is to be maintained, by a rise in the rate of interest to increase net capital inflow. We illustrate this in figure 7.1 as *BP*.

It is also clear that, other things being equal:

(a) the *BP* curve is more steeply sloped, the higher is the marginal propensity to import;

(b) the *BP* curve is less steeply sloped, the more mobile is international capital.

In practice, for developed countries at least, the degree of international capital mobility is the dominating factor and so the *BP* curve will be relatively flat as shown in figure 7.1. To consider how the inclusion of the *BP* curve affects the analysis of monetary policy in a simple case, consider the impact of a monetary expansion, making use of the upper panel in figure 5.2. We begin by assuming that the *BP* curve intersects the *IS* curve at the natural level of output (determined by the position of the vertical long-run Phillips curve in the lower panel of figure 5.2) and at the stabilising real rate of interest. We have drawn the *BP* curve to indicate highly mobile but not perfectly mobile capital. Now we assume an inflationary shock which shifts the *IS* curve out to IS^1. Following figure 5.2, the initial effect of the expansion takes us to point Z with output at Y_0 but, given the forecasts of the policymaker concerning the short-run Phillips curve, the interest rate is set at r_0 but can later (as the short-run Phillips curve adjusts) be lowered to the new stabilising interest rate of r_s^1, giving us a new equilibrium position at A. We return to the natural level of output.

Figure 7.1: Expansionary monetary policy and the balance of payments with fixed exchange rates

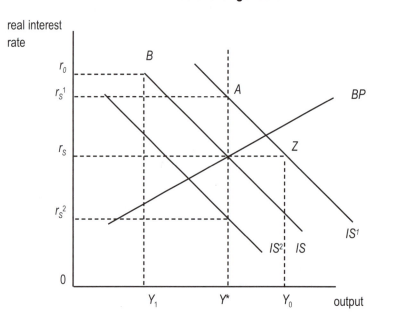

However, both B and A are comfortably above the BP curve — the high interest rate and the reduced level of output have both contributed to a balance of payments surplus. The consequent inflow of capital would put strong upward pressure on the value of the domestic currency. In a fixed exchange rate world, governments would be required to resist this but there would be little the authorities could do. Governments having generally rejected fiscal policy as a means of adjusting demand in the economy, the authorities would be left only with the short-term interest rate as a macroeconomic policy instrument and this is in use to tackle the inflationary effects of the initial expansion.

This problem arose for Japan, Switzerland and Germany in the late 1960s with the inflationary aggregate demand expansion resulting from the expansionary policies of the USA. They were concerned that the high domestic interest rate needed to counter the inflationary effects of the expansion would damage investment and, in time, would affect both employment and the rate of economic growth. Nonetheless, faced with the threat of imported inflation, they chose to act as is shown in figure 7.1.[1] With the international mobility of capital increasing steadily during the period, however, the countries had to try to deal with the problem that the high interest rates were attracting further capital inflows from abroad, compounding the initial balance of payments surplus problem. They sought to make the policy work by putting in place draconian capital controls to limit the inflow of capital.

The problem is worse in the case of a deflationary shock that shifts the IS curve back to IS^2. In this case, the stabilising interest rate (r_s^2) leaves us with a balance of payments deficit. The low interest rate leads to an outflow of capital that puts downward pressure on the value of the currency. Countries in this position would initially seek to borrow from the International Monetary Fund and from other governments but this could not overcome a persistent problem. They might also attempt to operate capital controls — to prevent the outflow of capital. In the longer term, they could seek to improve their international competitiveness by increasing productivity, switching their pattern of production to emphasise industries with greater export potential, encouraging domestic saving and changing the pattern of consumption. All of this might take a very long time and so such policies would need to be supported by measures that had some hope of more immediate results. Hence, a country might seek to overcome the balance of trade problem by increased protection — increasing tariffs, imposing quotas or employing other non-tariff barriers to trade. These actions might, of course, be against international agreements, although this does not prevent countries from practising them for as long as they can manage.

Pause for thought 7.3

(a) What forms of control did Germany use in the late 1960s to try to restrict the inflow of foreign capital?

(b) What longer-term policies might a country with a continuing balance of payments surplus follow, assuming it was unable to adjust its exchange rate?

If we assume that countries are prevented from following protectionist policies by international agreements and that capital controls are ineffective, the only solution left within the fixed exchange rate system is to accept a once-and-for-all change in the value of the currency. A country with a balance of payments deficit problem would need to accept a devaluation of its currency. This would immediately improve the competitive position of the country's exports and import-competing goods and would improve the trade balance. Countries are, thus, able to maintain a balance of payments balance for any given level of income at a lower interest rate.

In figure 7.2, the *BP* curve moves out from BP to *BP*[1]. With considerable judgement and a good deal of luck, the new *BP* curve might produce balance of payments balance at the stabilising interest rate and the natural level of output.

Figure 7.2: Short-term impact of devaluation of a fixed exchange rate

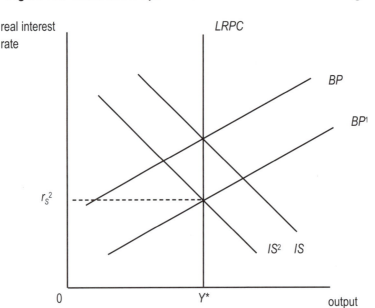

We should not, in practice, expect such rapid adjustment of exchange rates and balance of payments positions as is implied in our discussion of figure 7.2. since there are many time lags in the process. Trade volumes do not respond quickly to price changes and the process is further slowed down by the presence of a non-tradable goods sector. The goods market certainly adjusts much more slowly to the exchange rate change than the asset market. We should also note that the analysis above is simplified in other ways.

Firstly, a change in the exchange rate might not only cause the *BP* curve to shift. Indeed, an exchange rate change should also have an impact on the marginal propensity to import and hence on the slope of the *BP* curve. An exchange rate depreciation should improve the international competitiveness of a country's output and hence lower the marginal propensity to import. Thus, a fall in the value of a country's currency should flatten the *BP* curve; an exchange rate appreciation should make it steeper. However, in the normal case, we are assuming that the slope of the *BP* curve is influenced to a much greater extent by the degree of mobility of capital than by the size of the propensity to import. Consequently, allowing for changes in the propensity to import as the exchange rate changes does not make a significant difference to the analysis.

Secondly, we are discussing here only flows, implying, for example that a country's balance of payments is in equilibrium when a deficit in the current account is offset by a surplus on capital account (or *vice versa*). But this would require a steady increase in the holding of domestic assets in foreign portfolios. As these holdings increased, the risk for foreign countries of holding further quantities of domestic assets would increase and, sooner or later, domestic assets would need to bear higher rates of interest to attract foreign investors. A full equilibrium requires stocks to be in equilibrium as well as flows. The Mundell-Fleming model assumes that a capital outflow continues as long as domestic interest rates are below world interest rates. It is this that causes monetary policy not to work under fixed exchange rates. This implies that differences in interest rates provide the only basis for choosing among domestic and foreign bonds. If, however, we allow for the existence of exchange rate or default risk, in equilibrium people hold a mixture of foreign and domestic bonds. An expansionary monetary policy drives down the domestic interest rate and causes a switch from domestic to foreign bonds, but only until a new stock equilibrium occurs; and, to the extent that foreign bonds are regarded as more risky than domestic bonds, this happens with the domestic rate of interest below the world rate. Once the new stock equilibrium has been reached, the flow of capital ceases.

Pause for thought 7.4

Why might bond holders be likely to hold a mix of domestic and foreign bonds rather than all domestic or all foreign bonds?

Thirdly, and more importantly, the story does not end with the movement of the *BP* curve to BP^1. Consider figure 5.1. The change in the exchange rate affects net external demand and domestic demand as both exports and import-competing goods become more competitive. Total demand rises. As this occurs, the *IS* curve will move. Further, there is a direct link between the exchange rate and import prices. The increase in import prices consequent on a devaluation of the currency increases the costs of firms using imported raw materials or intermediate goods, and may encourage workers to seek higher wage rates. Over time, these changes undermine the gains obtained from the devaluation and the current account gain is likely to be only temporary. Further devaluations may well be needed to retain balance of payments balance. However, the possibility that one devaluation will be followed by others reduces the credibility of the existing fixed exchange rate and damages any reputation for an anti-inflation stance the government might have been trying to build up. Workers and firms build higher inflationary expectations into wage demands and price-setting formulae and speculators are likely to put pressure on the currency. Nonetheless, the competitive edge granted by a single devaluation may last over a sufficiently long period to be judged useful.

So far we have told a story of the problems faced by monetary policy within a fixed exchange rate system because policy makers face two targets (controlling the rate of inflation, maintaining the fixed exchange rate) and have only one instrument of policy (short-term interest rates). The difficulty is increased in the commonly assumed case of perfect capital mobility, represented by a perfectly elastic *BP* curve. This requires foreign and domestic bonds to be perfect substitutes and implies that domestic interest rates cannot vary from world rates — any slight movement of domestic rates above/below world rates causes immediate inflows/outflows of capital, which drive domestic rates back to the world rate.

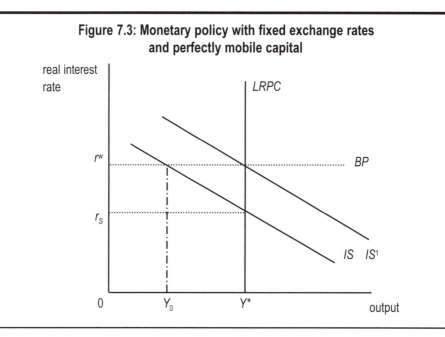

Figure 7.3: Monetary policy with fixed exchange rates and perfectly mobile capital

Consider the case of a country for which the stabilising interest rate (r_S) is below the world rate of interest (r^w). The stabilising rate of interest cannot be maintained and output is constrained to the level produced with an interest rate of r^w. Any attempt to lower domestic interest rates to r_S causes capital to flow out until interest rates are equal to world rates. There is no reason to believe that the output produced at r^w is the natural level of output. Indeed, if we assume Y^*, the natural rate level of output, to be above Y_0, as in figure 7.3, with perfect capital mobility, the economy will not be able to reach Y^*. Thus, we can easily understand one of the principal conclusions of the Mundell-Fleming analysis: *in a world* *of fixed exchange rates and perfect capital mobility, domestic monetary policy is complete-ly ineffective.*

We can also easily illustrate the concomitant proposition that a fiscal expansion shifting the *IS* curve to *IS*[1] would overcome the problem.

This leaves us to consider how the 'world' rate of interest within a fixed exchange rate system is determined. There will not, of course, be a single interest rate across the system as long as the possibility of changes in the currency pegs exist. Some currencies will always be judged more likely than others to be forced to devalue their currencies, and their interest rates will thus include higher exchange rate risk premiums. Nonetheless, there will be a rate, which we can call the system rate, movements in which have a powerful influence on the level of interest rates in all member countries.

In theory, the system interest rate and movements in it might be determined through the agreement of all member countries. It is much more likely, however, for the system rate to be determined by the most powerful economy within the system. This is known as asymmetric leadership since the leading country is in a different position from all other members. Only the leading country is able to determine its own monetary policy. We discuss the question of the factors influencing leadership below. For the moment, we assume that there is such a leader and make use of the ideas considered above to show how the leader's monetary policy is transmitted to the other member countries of the system. In figure 7.4, we keep the assumption of perfectly mobile capital and assume that, the stabilising interest rate is equal to the system interest rate ($r_S = r^{w0}$).

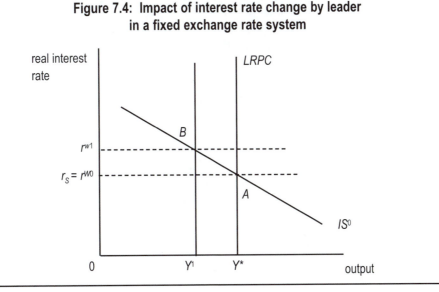

Figure 7.4: Impact of interest rate change by leader in a fixed exchange rate system

The strong country then tightens its monetary policy, raising its interest rate to r^{w1}. Capital immediately flows out of the domestic economy, putting downward pressure on the value of the domestic currency. The domestic monetary authorities act to protect the exchange rate by restrictive domestic open market operations (selling domestic bonds, forcing down bond prices and forcing domestic interest rates up to r^{w1}). We move from point A to B, at a lower level of output than previously. Domestic monetary policy is being determined by the strong country within the system.

Opponents of fixed exchange rates argue, rather, that the monetary policy forced on the domestic economy through the fixed exchange rate link may run counter to the interests of the domestic economy. This happens when the business cycles of the two countries are not synchronised or when the countries have different views of the desirable short-run relationship between inflation and unemployment. For example, a relatively small country within a fixed exchange rate system may have a level of income at which there is high unemployment and low inflation while, the strong economy is experiencing boom conditions and high rates of inflation. The strong country applies a tight monetary policy, forcing up interest rates just at the time when the smaller economy requires an easing of monetary policy. Clearly, a fixed exchange rate system (or a single currency covering a number of countries) is likely to face fewer problems if the business cycles of the member countries are synchronised and if external shocks to the economies are symmetric — that is, they effect all member economies in broadly the same way.

Another issue of importance is the extent to which monetary policy has real effects in the long run, an issue we considered in chapter 6. If the long-run Phillips curve is genuinely vertical and monetary policy does not have real effects in the long run, applying the incorrect monetary policy for a country's position on its business cycle causes short-run pain but does not damage the real economy in the long run. However, if there are hysteresis effects, then the application of a tight monetary policy during a period when the economy is already experiencing high unemployment both increases that unemployment in the short run and results in long term damage.

The strong country might take some account of the needs of the other members in choosing its policy. However, if it feels that it would, for political reasons, have to compromise its own policy preferences too much, the strong country would have little incentive to join the system in the first place. In any case, if the strong country does take account of the needs of the weaker countries in determining its policy, it may, by lowering the anti-inflationary credibility of its own monetary policy, damage the anti-inflation credentials of the system as a whole. This, in turn, would reduce the potential gains for the small countries from being a member of the system.

Pause for thought 7.5

Why might a country's anti-inflationary statements lack credibility in the eyes of market agents?

The strong country need not adopt an anti-inflationary stance. Expansionary policy is transmitted through a fixed exchange rate system just as is deflationary policy. Much depends on what gives the strong country its position within the system. The Bretton Woods adjustable peg exchange rate system was criticised because the macroeconomic policy of the USA in the later years of the system's operation was more inflationary than that desired by other major countries and US inflation was being transmitted to other countries through the fixed exchange rates.

US inflation made US goods uncompetitive, producing a deficit on the US current account and surpluses on the current accounts of their major trading partners. Any attempt they made to maintain higher interest rates than in the US to counter inflationary pressure led to a large inflow of capital, pushing up asset prices and forcing interest rates down to US levels. The trading partners found themselves with lower interest rates and higher inflation rates than they wished. One answer for them would have been to revalue their currencies within the system. This would, after a time lag, have removed the current account surplus and eased the inflationary pressure. The theoretical solution was for countries such as Germany, Japan and Switzerland to accept revaluations of their currencies but, as with devaluations, the gains would only have been temporary and each revaluation would have generated expectations of further revaluations, reinforcing the tendency for capital to flow in from the USA. There were also political arguments against taking the revaluation path since many countries thought that a longer term solution would have been for the USA to accept a general devaluation of the dollar against all other currencies in the system.[2]   In fact, Germany did accept some small revaluations but also, as we have mentioned above, attempted to solve its problems through capital controls.

An additional problem caused by allowing exchange rate changes within a fixed exchange rate system is that it opens up the possibility of countries seeking to gain advantage through devaluations. Thus, fixed exchange rate systems may be constructed on the principle that large changes in exchange rate parities should occur infrequently and should be allowed only if a country can show that its balance of payments is in 'fundamental disequilibrium'.[3] The ability to alter exchange rate parities within a fixed exchange rate system can provide only an escape route for economies in serious difficulties rather than granting monetary policy independence.

Pause for thought 7.6

Can you think of alternative ways of discouraging member countries of a fixed exchange rate from devaluing their currencies in order to obtain a terms of trade gain?

We have suggested, then, that within fixed exchange rate systems, countries, other than the leading country within the system, may have very little independence in the operation of monetary policy. We have said that some degree of independence may be obtained through changes in the currency pegs but have pointed out the limitations of these.   One problem we identified is that devaluations/revaluations in the system might well generate expectations of further such changes. But this is not always so. Consider a case in which a country maintains a fixed parity for an extended period but steadily loses competitiveness over that period. Its rate of inflation may be converging on that of the strong country within the system, but only slowly. Under these circumstances, many come to appreciate that the existing parity cannot be maintained and that devaluation is necessary to restore competitiveness. The secret is either to make small adjustments to the exchange rate when needed, such that each change does not engender significant inflationary expectations and/or to accompany the devaluation with other policies aimed at preserving the credibility of the government's anti-inflationary stance.

We have also pointed out that countries might seek some independence by operating controls over capital flows. We should not rule this out entirely since capital controls played an important role in the European Monetary System (EMS) up until 1991 and were resorted to in emergencies after 1991. However, they are widely regarded as undesirable and have become increasingly difficult to enforce with the development of offshore financial markets. In the modern world, they can probably only be enforced for short periods, at best. The difficulties caused to monetary authorities by the international mobility of capital has led to a call by some economists for a tax on international capital movements in the hope of slowing them down. We consider this in section 7.6.

We need to look briefly at two other possibilities for retaining some element of monetary independence within a fixed exchange rate system — fixed exchange rate systems usually allow some freedom for the exchange rate to move around the established exchange rate parities; there are normally, also, some limitations on the free international flow of goods and services.

Bands around exchange rate parities

All fixed (but adjustable) exchange rate systems maintain bands around the established central parities within which market-determined exchange rates may move. These bands may be narrow, as with the ± 1 per cent of the Bretton Woods system between 1945 and 1971, or broad, such as the ± 6 per cent for currencies within the broad band of the exchange rate mechanism of the EMS in operation until July 1993. Following the turmoil in the EMS in that month, an extremely wide band of ± 15 per cent was adopted, although this was intended to be only temporary and was not fully used.[4] Its sole purpose was to reduce the scope for profit-making attacks on currencies by speculators.

The rules of the system may prevent the full use of the band. In the EMS system, currencies were required to stay within their bands both against the European Currency Unit (Ecu) — a weighted currency basket consisting of the currencies of all members of the European Union (EU) — and against each other single currency. This meant in practice that the range of variation before July 1993 was limited to 2.25 or 6 per cent against the strongest or weakest currency in the system. Further, governments could not allow their currencies to fall to the bottom of the allowed band since this raised expectations of a possible devaluation and encouraged speculation against the currency.

Nonetheless, the existence of bands around parities can provide governments with a limited amount of short-run monetary policy freedom as long as the central exchange rates to which the bands apply are thoroughly credible. Any freedom granted will be greater the wider is the band.

Limitations on free trade

Some freedom may be retained also through the ability of a government to protect the current account of its balance of payments using commercial policy (tariffs, quotas and other non-tariff barriers). Although the capital account is a much more potent source of instability, expectations of devaluation are often triggered by current account weakness. Extra tension was caused in the EMS in the early 1990s because of the move (under the Single European Act of 1986) towards a unified market within the EU, severely limiting the ability of member governments to protect their current accounts through trade restrictions as well as leading to the removal of restrictions on capital movements within the EU.

The inconsistent quartet

To sum up this section, we can refer to the 'inconsistent quartet',[5] which states that governments cannot at the same time maintain all of the following:

(1) free trade
(2) full capital mobility
(3) fixed exchange rates
(4) national autonomy in the conduct of monetary policy.

This does not apply to the strong country of the system, which is able to determine its own monetary policy, as long as it is able to withstand the political pressure emanating from other members in cases where interests conflict.

Leadership of fixed exchange rate systems

We have so far been assuming that any fixed exchange rate system is characterised by asymmetric leadership — with a single country occupying a dominant position. This was certainly true of the Bretton Woods system and was widely held to be the case in the EMS, which was often referred to as a DM-zone. Yet, the two cases are notably different.

The USA owed its position as leader of the Bretton Woods system to its overwhelming strength at the end of the Second World War, which led the system to be constructed around the US dollar. Confidence in the system was provided by the large US gold holdings and the link established between the US dollar and gold by which the USA agreed to redeem any foreign holdings of dollars at a fixed gold price.

This, together with the strong demand for US goods in the period after the war, encouraged other governments to hold dollars in their international reserves, making the dollar the international intervention currency. Later loss of confidence in the US dollar destroyed the basis of the system. The nature of the system gave it an inflationary bias since the USA suffered no penalty from operating expansionary policies in both the economic and political fields. In addition, up until the late 1950s, other members wanted US expansion (in the economic field at any rate) to help post-war reconstruction. Tight US monetary policies in these periods would have been very unpopular. Indeed, the Bretton Woods treaty contained a scarce currency clause to discourage the USA from taking actions that would make its currency difficult to obtain in the amounts required by other members.

Leadership in the EMS developed differently. German leadership came from market confidence in the Deutschemark (DM). The strength of the DM relative to other currencies meant that agents required a risk premium to persuade them to hold other currencies. This confidence in the DM was a reflection of the anti-inflation record of the German government and of confidence in its future anti-inflationary stance. In theory, changing policies and performances of different governments could cause leadership to pass into other hands — what markets had delivered, markets could take away. Leadership based on a credible anti-inflationary stance has two side effects.

Firstly, it introduces a potentially deflationary bias to the system. To maintain its position and its apparent independence the leader must continue to operate strongly anti-inflationary policies. Then, as we have seen, these policies are transmitted through the fixed exchange rates to other members. This raises the question of exactly how 'independent' the leader is — it is free to determine its own monetary policy, but only as long as that policy is what the market expects.

Secondly, political pressures seem bound to ensure that the country able to deliver the most convincing inflation performance over a run of years, is the one with the best short-run unemployment-inflation trade-off. This means that the pain of convergence on the inflation rate chosen by the leader for the system is not only unequal across the system but also greater for followers than for the leader. This is likely to intensify the deflationary bias. However, membership of the system itself may have changed the German unemployment-inflation trade-off. Thus,[6] membership may have made the German short-term Phillips Curve less steep since part of the inflationary impact of any German monetary expansion was transmitted abroad through the fixed exchange rate system. Germany could then reduce unemployment at less cost in terms of domestic inflation than previously. If this were so, membership would provide an incentive for the German authorities to follow more expansionary policies than would be the case with floating rates.

On the other hand, it is equally plausible[7] that membership of the fixed exchange rate system made the German Phillips Curve more steep since the exchange rate could no longer adjust to compensate for any loss of competitiveness resulting from domestic inflation. In practice, German policy in the 1990s was influenced much more by the problems it faced in digesting the East German economy than by judgements as to what was happening to the unemployment-inflation trade-off in the West German economy.

Box 7.1: An attempt to reduce deflationary pressure within a fixed exchange rate system — the Basel-Nyborg agreement

The Basel-Nyborg agreement (1987) sought to introduce into the EMS two anti-deflationary devices. Firstly, when a currency fell to the bottom of its band against another currency, both central banks had to intervene, using the strong currency to buy the weak one (before 1987, most intervention in the system had been carried out in dollars). The weak currency country borrowed the strong currency through the Very Short Term Financing Facility of the EMS. Thus, in the short term, the weak currency country's reserves did not fall but the act of buying back its own currency reduced the domestic component of its money supply. The strong currency country issued more of its domestic currency, both to lend to the weak currency country and to buy the weak currency itself in the market. The net result was an increase in the money stock of the strong currency country.

Secondly, the agreement relaxed the terms of the Very Short Term Financing Facility by:

• extending the loan period, lengthening the period over which a more expansionary policy was forced on the strong currency country; and

• widening access to borrowing.

Before 1987, borrowing was only allowed for marginal interventions: those required because a currency had reached a prescribed intervention limit. After 1987, countries could borrow for intra-marginal interventions before a currency came under threat. Thus, theoretically, a government concerned about the tightness of the monetary policy in the system could apply a limited degree of short-term expansionary pressure on the strong currency country. However, the strong currency country could still sterilise the monetary effects of intervention through selling additional securities in open market operations. If it did this, the full burden of any adjustment was forced back onto the weak country and the deflationary bias of the system was preserved.

Systems can be designed to try to overcome tendencies towards deflation. In box 7.1, we set out an example of this taken from the operation of the exchange rate mechanism of the EMS. However, as is explained in the box, it is difficult to force strong currency countries to follow more expansionary policies than they wish to do. The only way out appears to be through cooperation among members to establish a monetary policy suitable to all. This requires all countries to make policy concessions and, as we have already noted, there is often little incentive for the strong country to do so. Of course, if the alternative is a floating exchange rate system characterised by conflict, the strong country may accept cooperation, even if it involves some sacrifice on its part in terms of policy choices. However, to the extent that this happens, the anti-inflationary stance of the whole system may be weakened.

For the world economy, the asymmetric leader path is no longer available. Although the US dollar remains the dominant world currency, the balance of economic power is more evenly spread across three economic power blocs than it was in the 1940s and 1950s. The issue of cooperation in monetary policy has thus become increasingly important. We say more about this in section 7.5.

7.3   Exchange rate pegs and monetary union

It seems a little strange to spend so much time on monetary policy in fixed exchange rate systems when there are currently no significant systems in which countries retain their own currencies, with currency values pegged, but with the possibility of adjustment to the pegs occurring from time to time. Indeed, the only example is ERMII — the exchange rate mechanism for member countries of the EU which either do not wish or are not yet permitted to join the euro area but who wish to peg their currencies to the euro. Present members are Denmark, Estonia, Lithuania, Latvia, Slovakia but all except Denmark have ambitions to join the euro area within the next five years and so it is rather a staging post for monetary union membership than a genuine fixed exchange rate system.

However, many countries have established links between their currencies and a major currency of importance to them — most obviously to the US dollar or the euro. At last count, 23 currencies (covering 30 countries were pegged to the US dollar), nine currencies (covering 27 countries) were pegged to the euro,[8] while small numbers of countries have pegged their currencies to the Indian rupee, the pound sterling and the Australian dollar. The Faroese krona is pegged to the Danish krona which is in turn pegged to the euro through its membership of ERMII. Thus, many countries cannot operate independent monetary policies. Their exchange rate pegs constrains them to the monetary policies followed by the country to whose currency their currency has been pegged. As in our discussion above, small amounts of independence may be squeezed out of the system but these must remain very limited if they are to avoid the serious problems faced by currencies such as the Argentine peso in 2001. This is set out in box 7.2.

The desire for a fixed exchange rate system covering most countries has also never entirely disappeared since the collapse of Bretton Woods in the early 1970s. Many proposals have been made to overcome the problems that led to the demise of that system. Principal among these were the dependence of the system on confidence in the US dollar, the fixed relationship between the dollar and gold, the narrow bands around the fixed pegs and the infrequency of adjustments to the currency pegs, which, when they occurred, were necessarily large. Thus, proposals have been made such as those for regular, small adjustments to pegs (the crawling peg). There has remained, however, a scepticism that any general fixed exchange rate system can survive in a world of such large and rapid international capital movements.

Box 7.2: A failed exchange rate link — the Argentine peso 1991-2002

Background

At the end of a period of military dictatorship (1976-83), Argentina had a large government debt and high unemployment. In 1983, the newly elected government established a new currency (the Austral) but continued to borrow. Ultimately, the government was unable to meet the interest on its debt, the economy collapsed and hyperinflation followed, the inflation rate surpassing 3,000% per annum in 1989. In that year, a new president began to follow a set of policies favoured by the IMF — trade liberalization, deregulation of the labour market, the privatisation of state enterprises and, from 1991, the establishment of a convertible currency with a fixed exchange rate with the US$. Initially the exchange rate was fixed at $1 = Austral 10,000 but the peso was soon restored as the country's currency and fixed at a rate of $1 = 1 peso.

The theory

Argentina was thus attempting to benefit from the low inflation rate in the USA — borrowing the US's low-inflation reputation. People should immediately have lowered their expectations of future inflation causing the exchange rate to fall. According to the New Classical model, inflation should have fallen at no cost, with output staying at its natural level. According to the Friedman-Phelps approach, adjustment to the lower inflation would have been fairly slow as, initially, expectations of inflation would have been too high. Real wages would have been too high during this period and unemployment would have increased. However, this would have been a short-run cost only and the economy should eventually have returned to the natural level of output at a low inflation rate.

The event

Inflation certainly fell sharply but as US dollar rose in value in the late 1990s, the Argentine economy became increasingly uncompetitive. The high value of the peso made imports cheap and exports dear, putting Argentine industry under great pressure. Initially, the balance of trade deficit was partly funded by foreign capital as state enterprises were privatized, but foreign capital flows soon dried up. The IMF continued to lend money to Argentina but problems were building up. Unemployment increased. Matters became much worse in 1999 when the Brazilian currency was devalued. This, together with the continued high value of the US dollar to which the peso was linked, meant a large revaluation of the peso against the currencies of its major trading partners. In 1999, Argentina's GDP fell by 4 per cent and a full-scale economic crisis developed.

The government sought to maintain the fixed exchange rate but it was clear to many people that it couldn't last. There was a run on the banks as people drew money from their bank accounts to convert it into dollars and send it abroad. The loss of faith in the peso led to the development of complementary currencies. The economic woes were accompanied by widespread political demonstrations and violence. Presidents came and went with indecent haste until the problem began to be treated seriously with the ending of the fixed exchange rate peg in January 2002. The peso fell sharply in value, reaching $1 = peso 3.95 late in June before beginning to strengthen again as the economy began to recover and confidence began to return. It rose in value to $1 = peso 2.74 a year later before settling at around $1 = peso 3.

in a world of fixed exchange rates and perfect capital mobility, domestic monetary policy is completely ineffective.

Pause for thought 7.7

Why do so many small countries link their currencies to one of the major world countries? What factors are likely to determine which major currency they link to?

There is a further reason to study monetary policy under fixed exchange rates. The theory of monetary policy under fixed exchange rates was the base upon which optimum currency theory was built and this was at the centre of much of the theory concerning the desirable size of monetary unions. We consider the question of monetary policy in a monetary union in chapter 11.

7.4   Monetary policy with floating exchange rates

We can easily see from our discussion in section 7.2 that monetary policy is more effective with floating exchange rates than with fixed exchange rates. We can think of the argument in either of two ways. The removal of the exchange rate as a target removes the problem faced by policymakers who have only one instrument at their disposal but two targets to attempt to achieve. With floating exchange rates, short-term interest rates can be used to tackle the inflation problem and the exchange rate floats to overcome the balance of payments problem. Alternatively, we can say that the floating exchange rate overcomes the problem of inflationary or deflationary pressures being passed on in a fixed exchange rate system and grants the economy monetary independence. This restores to the authorities the ability to choose and allows the authorities to choose the domestic inflation rate. Of course, if we accept the long-run vertical Phillips curve analysis, monetary policy remains neutral in the long run.

It is also easy to see that, with floating exchange rates, monetary policy is more effective in an open economy than in a closed economy. Consider our example from figure 7.1 where an aggregate demand expansion creates inflationary pressure in the economy which is countered by an upwards movement of the stabilising interest rate from rs to r_s^1. In a closed economy, our new equilibrium would be at point A with output at the natural level and the interest rate at r_s^1. In an open economy with fixed exchange rates, we saw that, at this position, we would have a balance of payments surplus. In an open economy with floating rates, the increased demand for the domestic currency associated with the balance of payments surplus would cause the domestic currency to appreciate in value. The BP curve would be pushed up from BP to BP^1. The appreciating exchange rate would cause the current account to deteriorate and remove the balance of payments surplus associated with point A. But now, there is a further effect. Remember figure 5.1. The deteriorating current account would reduce both net external demand and domestic demand and the appreciating currency would reduce import prices. Both effects lower the inflationary pressure in the economy, partially offsetting the initial expansion in aggregate demand. The *IS* curve moves back to, say, *IS²*. With a further adjustment of the *BP* curve, we might finish at point *C*, with a stabilising interest rate of r_s^2. In other words, the initial inflationary impulse will be countered by a smaller increase in the stabilising interest rate because of the impact of the appreciating currency.

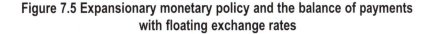

Figure 7.5 Expansionary monetary policy and the balance of payments with floating exchange rates

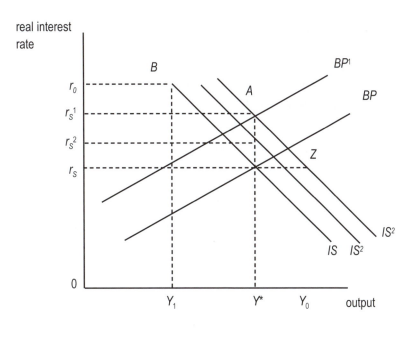

Expressed in this way, the argument for floating exchange rates over fixed exchange rate systems appears irrefutable. However, this analysis implies that the exchange rate changes smoothly to restore the goods and money markets and the balance of payments to equilibrium. This is an interesting idea but there is no evidence in practice to suggest that exchange rates do move to produce balance of payments equilibrium in individual countries. Indeed, movements in foreign exchange rates appear more likely to cause problems for economies than to overcome them. Foreign exchange rate movements among the major currencies since 1973 have been dominated by large swings in the value of the US dollar.

Consider the performance of the dollar against the German mark[9] and the Japanese yen since the floating of the dollar in March 1973, using monthly average exchange rate figures.[10] In March 1973, the monthly average DM/$ exchange rate was $1 = DM2.8133. Throughout the rest of the 1970s, the dollar generally fell against the mark, reaching $1 = DM1.7246 for January 1980, a decline of just under 40 per cent. However, the early 1980s witnessed a sharp and prolonged rise in the value of the dollar with the monthly average mark/dollar exchange rate reaching $1 = DM3.3025, not much short of double the figure at the beginning of 1980. A steep decline followed and the monthly average figure for August 1992 was down to $1 = DM1.4473. After a short period of recovery, the dollar dropped in value to reach $1 = DM1.381 in April 1995 but then picked up, especially during the first two years of the life of the euro so that by October 2000, the monthly average figure was $1 = DM2.2946. Since then, although there was a small increase in strength in 2005, the value of the dollar has been steadily falling. The monthly average exchange rate for April 2008 was $1 = DM1.2416. Much the same story can be told of the yen/dollar rate, with somewhat different dates for highs and lows. Table 7.1 shows the average yen/dollar exchange rate for selected months between March 1973 and April 2008.

Table 7.1: Yen/dollar exchange rate
(monthly averages, for selected months)

Month	Monthly average yen/dollar exchange rate
1973 March	$1 = Y261.904
1976 January	$1 = Y304.637
1978 October	$1 = Y183.633
1982 October	$1 = Y271.615
1988 November	$1 = Y123.203
1990 November	$1 = Y158.437
1995 April	$1 = Y 83.654
1998 August	$1 = Y144.585
2005 January	$1 = Y103.337
2007 January	$1 = Y122.697
2008 April	$1 = Y102.69

Source: taken from tables of the Pacific Exchange Rate Service of the Sauder School of Business, University of British Columbia at http://fx.sauder.ubc.ca/data.html

Again, the swings have been quite wide and wild. It is hard to fit such figures as these to a story of floating exchange rates adjusting smoothly to return economies to balance of payments equilibrium. Of course, it can readily be argued that this has not been a period of freely floating exchange rates. Individual central banks have intervened in the market to influence the value of currencies. Indeed, in the UK in the second half of the 1980s, monetary policy was used to target the DM/Sterling exchange rate rather than to target the rate of inflation directly. This was a prelude to the very short period of UK membership in the fixed exchange rate European Monetary System (EMS) and removed much of the independence of monetary policy that is in theory granted by a floating exchange rate. UK interest rates were pushed up sharply in this period. This episode is discussed in section 10.4 At times, also, there have been joint interventions by a number of central banks in a coordinated attempt to influence the values of important world currencies such as the dollar and the yen. On the other hand, it can be argued that joint interventions have only been thought necessary by the large changes in exchange rates, sometimes over quite short periods. Overall, it is hard to accept that government intervention can explain a high proportion of the exchange rate movements of the period since 1973.

Many models have been constructed to try to explain these exchange rate changes but none have predicted well. Early models (flow models) concentrated on the current account of the balance of payments and were concerned with factors influencing a country's competitiveness in international trade. We thus had real factors such as relative labour productivity across countries and rates of economic growth as well as purchasing power parity (PPP) — the idea that goods of the same quality should sell at the same price, when expressed in a common currency, in all countries. With the rapidly increasing importance of international capital flows from the late 1950s onwards, economists began to pay more attention to the capital account of the balance of payments and models started to stress the role of relative interest rates and the importance of expectations about future interest rates, future inflation rates and future exchange rates themselves. These are known as stock or asset models of exchange rate determination. They, in turn, can be divided into monetary models and portfolio models, distinguished by the acceptance of in monetary models of the assumption that foreign and domestic bonds were perfect substitutes — uncovered interest rate parity (UIRP) applies. Portfolio models assume that residents of the domestic economy think foreign bonds are more risky than equivalent domestic bonds and hence require a higher rate of interest on foreign bonds to be persuaded to hold them.

Monetary models assumed equilibrium, flexible prices and an exogenous money stock. They incorporated propositions such as PPP and the Fisher effect as well as uncovered interest rate parity, none of which have tested well in their own right. For example, the simplest model of exchange rate determination, the flexible price monetary model, assumes that capital is perfectly mobile (domestic and foreign bonds are perfect substitutes), markets are competitive, transactions costs are negligible, and investors hold exchange rate expectations with certainty. Uncovered interest rate parity (UIRP) and PPP hold, all prices are perfectly flexible and money markets clear continuously. The demand for money is stably related to real income and stably and negatively related to the rate of interest. In economics, simple models with grossly unrealistic assumptions do, from time to time, predict fairly well and can then be defended on the basis that markets act *as if* the assumptions were valid, even when we know them not to be. However, this does not occur often and the flexible price monetary model seemed to be taking this approach much too far. Nonetheless, the model was used to consider the impact of expansionary and contractionary monetary policy changes.

Pause for thought 7.8

What does 'uncovered' mean in the phrase 'uncovered interest rate parity'?

Unsurprisingly, given the other assumptions of the model, monetary policy was modelled as increases or contractions in the rate of growth of the domestic money supply although, as we have noted often, this is not how monetary policy is practised. Again, it is not unexpected that money is neutral in the model, with a 10 percentage point increase in the rate of growth of the domestic money supply causing the domestic currency to depreciate by ten per cent. The predictions of the model were never supported by evidence. Portfolio models suggested greater freedom for monetary authorities by distinguishing among exchange rate operations, open market operations and sterilised exchange rate operations but this was all based upon an assumption of monetary base control.

Working with generally more complex models which were, however, built upon the sort of assumptions underlying the flexible price monetary models, economists had great difficulty trying to explain what was happening to the value of the dollar in the 1970s. One approach to the problem was to allow for exchange rate overshooting in the short run. That is, the models continued to assume the existence of long-run equilibrium rates of exchange, to incorporate both UIRP and PPP and to assume rational expectations but produced exchange rates that overshot their long-run equilibrium positions by assuming the existence of sticky prices. One of the early sticky price models (Dornbusch, 1976) assumed that goods and labour markets were slow to adjust but that the asset market adjusted immediately. Exchange rates are determined in the asset market and, thus, exchange rate changes are not matched, in the short run, by price changes. That is, the model departs from PPP in the short run but returns to it in the long run. Again, monetary policy within the model is treated as an increase in an exogenous supply of money.

Such models at least acknowledged that floating exchange rates did fluctuate considerably and spent extended periods out of equilibrium. Greater realism could be obtained by dropping the assumption of rational expectations. If we assume instead that the market agents do not know the long-run equilibrium position and try to infer it from what other participants in the market are doing, we can produce much wilder movements in the exchange rate.

Another well-known model (Frankel, 1979) combines inflationary expectations with the sticky price element of the Dornbusch model. As in Dornbusch, the expected rate of depreciation of the domestic currency is positively related to the difference between the current exchange rate and the equilibrium exchange rate, but here it is also a function of the expected long-run inflation differential between the domestic and foreign economies. Yet again, we have exogenous money and the long-run equilibrium exchange rate is determined by the relative supplies of and demands for money in the two countries just as in the flexible monetary model. The gap between the current exchange rate and its long-run equilibrium value is now proportional to the real interest rate differential between the two countries. If the expected real rate of interest on foreign bonds is greater than the expected real rate of interest on domestic bonds, there will be a real depreciation of the domestic currency until the long-run equilibrium exchange rate is reached. When this occurs, real interest rates will be the same in the two countries and any difference in nominal interest rates must be the result of differences in inflation rates. As in the Dornbusch model, an unanticipated monetary expansion in the domestic economy causes the exchange rate to over-shoot its long-run equilibrium level.

Other similar models have been developed, distinguishing for example between the speeds of adjustment of the prices of tradable and non-tradable goods or of volumes and prices of exports and imports (known in the balance of payments literature as the J-curve). The central feature of these models is that they retain most of the assumptions of the standard approach to foreign exchange markets while attempting to produce results closer to the reality of volatile exchange rates. They also suggest that the monetary authorities can influence real variables in the short run, although not in the long run. The importance of the freedom granted to the monetary authorities depends on the length of time taken for prices and the nominal exchange rate to move to their long-run equilibrium positions. Expansionary monetary policy could obtain worthwhile reductions in unemployment for significant periods. If a sticky-price model were combined with a labour market model with hysteresis, these short-run employment gains could become long-run gains.

Sticky-price models also provide a justification for a gradual approach to monetary policy. For example, assume the monetary authorities wish to reduce the rate of inflation. When they push interest rates up sharply, prices do not change in the short run, the nominal and real exchange rates fall sharply (over-shooting the long-run equilibrium level), causing problems for exporters and import-competing industries. Unemployment results. With prices changing only slowly, these real problems would persist for a considerable time. The position would be worse if the short-run overvaluation of the currency caused bankrupt-cies of domestic firms and serious loss of market share in important industries. The short-run cost of reducing inflation could be high. This leads to the view that monetary policy should be applied gradually to allow the economy to adjust slowly.

Thus, although the treatment of monetary policy is unrealistic, it is possible to draw some interesting suggestions from them regarding the practice of mone-tary policy in an open economy. However, none of the models do well in testing, many performing worse than a simple random walk model. One study (by Meese and Rogoff, 1983) tested the predictions over the late 1970s of a monetary model, Dornbusch's overshooting model, and a stock model which added current account factors to the Dornbusch model together with those of a model stating simply that the exchange rate in the following period would be the same as in the current period. They found that the last model performed best! Models based on exchange rate fundamentals faced particular difficulties in the first half of the 1980s as the dollar continued its prolonged increase in value apparently against all economic logic. This led to a number of developments in exchange rate theories.

Models were developed which attempted to explain sudden and apparently inexplicable jumps in the value of a currency through the phenomenon of rational bubbles (bubbles in which all participants know the correct model for the determination of the exchange rate but nonetheless the actual rate moves sharply away from equilibrium until eventually the bubble bursts). Models that explain these jumps but which continue to assume that the market is characterised by rational behaviour, start in a disequilibrium position and show how rational decisions may cause the market to move further away from equilibrium rather than returning to it.

For example, in trying to explain the inexorable rise in value of the US dollar between 1981 and 1985, Dornbusch started with an overvalued exchange rate. Investors were assumed to be risk neutral, and so a strategy that has a risk of high losses if things go wrong but a potential for high profits if they go right is equivalent to one in which potential losses and profits are both low. Investors had to compare two probabilities: that the exchange rate would return to equilibrium and that it would go on rising. The further the exchange rate was currently above the equilibrium rate, the greater was the potential loss for investors if it fell back to equilibrium and the greater the required profits had to be if the rate kept on rising. To put it another way, the greater the risk of a crash, the faster the rate of appreciation had to be to compensate for potential losses. Investors were thus obliged to go on buying the currency, pushing the rate up further and further, although there was no economic justification for doing so.

Some models allowed for the existence of two kinds of forecasters in the market. In Goodhart's (1988) model, for example, dealers make their decisions on the basis of a weighted average of the forecasts of market efficiency theorists and modellers of fundamentals, with the weights determined by the relative past success of the two forecasts. An alternative approach has been to reject rationality in its narrow economic sense. It is argued that much trading in forex markets is based on 'noise' - information that is irrelevant to market price and only confuses market participants — rather than 'news' and that this results in excessive volatility. Frankel and Froot (1990) developed a model similar to Goodhart's, except that the bubble is not rational but speculative, being the outcome of self-confirming market speculations. Again there are two types of forecasters but this time they are fundamentalists and chartists. Fundamentalists (using an overshooting model) forecast a depreciation of the dollar which would be rational if there were no chartists. Chartists extrapolate recent trends based on an information set that includes no fundamentals. Portfolio managers base their decisions on a weighted average of the forecasts of fundamentalists and chartists. Later work attempted to set such models within the framework of chaos theory in which very small changes in a system can produce dramatic results.

Speculators are also sometimes divided into those who think short term (which in this context refers to one week or less) and those with long-run horizons (up to three months), with short termers holding extrapolative expectations and long termers regressive expectations. Much then depends on which group dominates the market at any particular time. Models such as these, together with attempts to incorporate psychological factors into the economic analysis of economic behaviour, are of some interest from the point of view of the analysis of exchange rate changes; but little use is made of them to analyse the effects of monetary policy in an open economy.

We have so far seen that with mobile capital the following applies:

(a) in fixed exchange rate systems, the target of monetary policy is the exchange rate — domestic inflation rates are determined by the monetary policy of the whole system;

(b) in floating rate systems, the monetary authorities can target the domestic rate of inflation. However, the notion that this grants full independence to monetary authorities is based upon simple exchange rate models in which the exchange rate changes to return the economy to equilibrium and purchasing power parity following a monetary policy change. In practice, economies are likely to be away from anything that might be recognised as an equilibrium exchange rate for long periods of time.

Under these circumstances, it is not surprising that exchange rates in floating exchange rate systems do not float freely. Central banks intervene to varying degrees to influence exchange rates. Sometimes the intervention is light, with the intention only of smoothing out fluctuations in exchange rates. On other occasions, central banks join together to intervene strongly in the foreign exchange market in the hope of influencing the direction in which exchange rates are moving or to try to keep rates within unspecified target ranges. In this case, monetary policy may be aimed either at internal or at external objectives. Problems under these conditions are discussed in section 9.5

7.5   Monetary policy coordination

We have seen that one of the standard arguments for floating exchange rates is that they isolate an economy from external shocks, allowing the authorities to pursue their own independent monetary policy. But this is never the case. All economies are to some extent interdependent even with freely floating exchange rates. All are subject to spillovers from the domestic monetary policies of other economies. Further, the degree of interdependence among countries has been growing. This happened particularly in the early 1970s because of:

(i)   increased capital flows after the collapse of the Bretton Woods fixed exchange rate system

(ii)   alterations in terms of trade following large changes in world oil prices

(iii) a greater degree of openness to foreign trade and

(iv) the development of offshore financial markets.

The interdependence among countries has continued to grow with increased cross-border movements of capital and labour and technological change that has integrated markets. Increased integration makes it more likely that monetary policy decisions in one country will affect other countries and also that macroeconomic shocks are transmitted more rapidly among countries.

Our particular interest here is in what has been called 'sensitivity independence', defined by Cooper (1985) as the amount of adjustment a country has to make to foreign events under conditions of normal economic activity. This is, of course, influenced by the exchange rate system but is also influenced by factors such as the marginal propensities to spend on foreign products or assets, the elasticity of substitution between foreign and domestic products or assets, the elasticity of substitution in production and the relative size of the economies in question. Given the existence of policy spillovers and their growing size, we need to know whether there are advantages in the coordination of monetary policies across countries. Let us begin with theory and then look at policy coordination in practice.

Pause for thought 7.9

Explain the significance from the point of view of the size of monetary policy spillovers of the elasticity of substitution between foreign and domestic products.

The theoretical approach to macroeconomic policy coordination calls upon a number of areas of macroeconomic theory, as well as making use of games theory. Game-theoretic models look at the effects of cooperative behaviour between countries, the likelihood of gains from cooperative behaviour and the likely distribution of the gains across countries. A coordinated game is one in which governments are assumed to maximize a weighted average of the welfare functions of all countries in the game whereas in an uncoordinated game each government is assumed to maximize its own welfare function. The models frequently seek to incorporate the notions of credibility and reputation, and the sustainability and time consistency of policy.[11]

The first stage in the analysis of macroeconomic interdependence among economies was the investigation of the channels along which influence flows from one economy to another. The beginnings of a case for some form of policy coordination can be derived from the simple open economy multiplier. For a small economy, it is clear that increased linkages with the rest of the world weaken the impact on domestic targets of domestic fiscal policy since some of the increased demand escapes into imports. Models can, however, be greatly complicated by dropping the small country limitation, by making different assumptions about the nature of the exchange rate regime, by introducing various forms of price or wage stickiness, or by considering the timing and nature of tax policy changes needed to pay for government expenditure increases.

In analysing monetary linkages, we may also make varying assumptions about the exchange rate regime, the degree of international capital mobility, and country size. Depending on the assumptions made, spillovers from domestic macroeconomic policy may be positive or negative. It has also been shown that it is possible both for an instrument's spillovers to change signs over time and for an instrument to have impacts of different signs depending on the target at which it is aimed.

The importance of spillovers became clearer, however, with the recognition of price spillovers operating through the terms of trade linkage (Hamada, 1976). This plainly meant the end of arguments that a country engaged in international trade could fully insulate itself from events and policies in the rest of the world. Even with perfectly flexible exchange rates, the terms of trade transmission works.

Cooper (1969) examined the impact of spillovers on domestic policy using a simple model with fixed exchange rates and constant prices. He argued that the greater is the degree of interdependence (and the stronger are spillovers), the less will be the effectiveness of policies in non-cooperating economies. Greater interdependence, in other words, leads to either worse results from domestic policies and longer periods away from equilibrium, or greater costs to restore targets to their desired values. In Canzoneri and Gray's (1985) model, the governments of two identical countries both attempt to achieve full employment output without increasing inflation. Both countries are subject to supply shocks. The paper is concerned with the monetary transmission mechanism, specifically with the impact of an expansion of the money supply in each country. Canzoneri and Gray consider three possibilities:

(a) beggar-thy-neighbour in which monetary expansion in one economy has a negative effect on output in the other economy;

(b) locomotive in which the spillover effects are positive; and

(c) asymmetric in which monetary spillovers have different signs, the result depending on the size of the exchange rate and interest rate changes following the domestic monetary expansion as well as the import content of the foreign price index. The outcome is an empirical question, depending on the structure of the economies involved.

Specific conclusions of theoretical models must, however, be treated with caution since many depend on the sign or relative size of particular coefficients while the models assume that the economy's behavioural parameters are unchanged under different conditions. They thus founder on the Lucas critique. In addition, there have not been enough empirical studies to produce clear ideas about the likely direction and size of spillovers in practice. We are only left, following Hughes-Hallett (1989), with a set of not very surprising theoretical conclusions:

1. Spillovers vary with the policies pursued in other countries

2. There are multiple transmission mechanisms that operate simultaneously

3. Net spillover effects depend on the particular circumstances of the economies concerned

4. The impacts of spillovers crucially depend on the size of the economy, the degree of asset substitutability, relative price and wage flexibility and exchange rate flexibility.

The use of games theory to analyze the desirability of policy coordination commenced with the development of models incorporating two simple forms of policy decisions by national governments in an international context — Nash non-cooperative games in which either governments act independently taking the decisions of other governments as given or one country acts as leader;[12] and cooperative games in which countries attempt to pursue some common interest, attempting to maximize the sum or product of the utilities of the national governments. The problem is to elucidate and, if possible, to quantify the gains from cooperative decisions.

Non-cooperative models suffer from a variety of defects. For example, they consider only static decisions and thus allowance cannot be made for predictable future effects of current decisions. Further, the restrictions on the assumptions regarding the behaviour of the other country's policy makers presupposes that policy makers already know the form of the equilibrium decision rule: but this can only be so in special circumstances. Despite these difficulties, the sub-optimality of non-cooperative decisions is accepted.

The presence of significant policy spillovers forms the basis of a well-known model (Hamada 1976, 1985) illustrating the case for international policy coordination between countries. It is a two-country model, with each country targeting its inflation rate and balance of payments position in a fixed exchange rate regime. Each country controls a single policy instrument — the level of domestic credit creation. Neither country can attain both objectives by acting alone except by coincidence. In one version of this model with demand-constrained output and price inertia, Nash non-cooperative behaviour gives the system a deflationary bias. Coordination is clearly preferable. This fits in with the general conclusion that non-cooperative decisions are socially inefficient except under special conditions.

However, it is one thing to argue for the inefficiency of non-cooperation, but quite another to accept the need for coordination. To begin with, one can produce cases where Nash non-cooperative behaviour is superior to cooperation. Perhaps the best-known example of this is Rogoff's international inflation game in which governments gain from unexpected inflation (Rogoff, 1985b). In Rogoff's model, governments fix exchange rates and then agree to raise their domestic money supplies. By cooperating, they are able to exploit the gains to be had from inflation surprises. Their citizens lose out. This assumes that the private sector can be taken by surprise. Most models rule this possibility out by assuming forward-looking expectations. Without surprises, the costs to the private sector of antici-pated inflation remain, but an understanding of the nature of government policy by the private sector leads to a rapid reduction in their willingness to hold gov-ernment debt except at interest rates that fully take government policy into account.

Pause for thought 7.10

Why might governments wish to cause inflation at the expense of their citizens?

One can also show that the degree of sub-optimality of non-cooperative deci-sions can be affected by the strength of preferences of national policy makers, by the economy's policy responses, and by capacity constraints. Some models (for example, Obstfeld and Rogoff, 2002) show that coordination does produce wel-fare gains but suggests that these are likely to be small. However, Sutherland (2002) stresses the importance in reaching this conclusion of restricting the elas-ticity of substitution between home and foreign goods to unity and of assuming that international financial markets do not exist. Changing these assumptions can change the results as can assuming international risk sharing. Different assumptions about the reputation of the governments in the model can also cause the results to change.

Again, even if we accept that there are significant gains to be had for the welfare of all countries considered together from cooperation, it does not follow that all countries will be happy to participate because the gains may be unevenly spread across countries. We can conclude that the size of net gains (or losses) from cooper-ation can only be determined by empirical analysis. A considerable number of empirical studies have been undertaken. These have produced mixed results regarding the benefits from macroeconomic policy coordination. On balance, where studies have shown gains from coordination, they have tended to be rather small, although the gains appear to increase with the persistence of disturbances that lead to coordination. They also appear to increase over time. In the long run, gains from cooperation in the face of permanent supply or demand shocks may be very consid-erable. Such studies are of some interest in themselves but the ability of researchers to vary the results by making relatively small changes in their models means that they can, at best, provide only lukewarm support for policy coordination. We can conclude that the results of research in this field have so far have not been sufficient-ly clear or robust to be likely to have much influence on policymakers.

In attempting to bridge the gap between theory and reality, economic theory has also paid attention to a different question from that of the size of welfare gains from cooperation — if governments succeed in reaching an agreement to coordinate macroeconomic policies, how can we be sure that such policies will be sustained in each country? There are two separate issues here.

The first deals with the relationship between the state and the private sector. If rational expectations are assumed and thus the private sector cannot be taken by surprise by the government, the effectiveness of macroeconomic policy depends on that policy being credible to the private sector. If this is not the case, macroeconomic policy is ineffective. One way out for governments is to pre-commit themselves to their stated policy. An obvious example is the pre-commitment of monetary policy through membership of a fixed exchange rate regime as long as the exchange rate parity is itself credible.

The second issue relates to the temptation felt by governments to renege on their agreements with other governments. The issue hardly arises in the Hamada two-country model since an attempt by one country to improve its position by reneging on the agreement will be met by a withdrawal of the other country from the agreement - both countries move back to the original sub-optimal non-cooperative equilibrium and are worse off. The threat of such action prevents either country from reneging. However, with more than two participants, the question of the credibility of threats becomes relevant. Where the incentive to renege on agreements cannot be removed by credible threats to retaliate, policy coordination cannot be sustained.

There are two ways out of this dilemma. The first is to concentrate on the notion of reputation. Governments may adopt a longer term view of coordination than is implied by the one-off bargains that dominate the world of policy models. Consequently, they may be willing to forgo potential short-term gains available from reneging on agreements in order to make future bargains possible. Yet again, the loss of reputation in the field of macroeconomic policy coordination might be thought likely to affect a country's standing in other international negotiations. This is an example of the problems involved in analysing macroeconomic policy in isolation. It is clear that the outcomes of G7 economic summits have been influenced by much more than narrow macroeconomic considerations.

The second possible escape is through developing arguments in favour of rule-based rather than discretionary policy coordination. The acceptance of rules means that all governments are pre-committed to agreed polices, removing the dangers apparent in cases where some parties are effectively pre-committed but others are not.

The obvious question that remains is why more has not come from the interest, at all levels, in increased policy coordination. There have been many meetings on economic issues of the heads of government of G7, supported by considerable academic lucubration. Yet very little of substance has resulted and what has resulted has been subject to much criticism. Perhaps the most substantial outcome has been the development of two major proposals for international macroeconomic cooperation: Williamson and Miller's target zone proposal[13] and McKinnon's currency substitution proposal. These have led to a good deal of argument and this has, in itself, underlined the difficulties involved in making serious progress towards macroeconomic policy coordination at a world level. A brief outline of the two proposals helps to make the point.

Williamson and Miller proposed that interest rate differentials between countries should be varied to keep real exchange rates within a given, wide band around the agreed equilibrium level for the real exchange rate (chosen so as to give medium-run to longer-run current account equilibrium). The target zone would have 'soft buffers' so that authorities would cease defending it in the face of large unexpected shocks. The zone would also be regularly adjusted in line with actual changes in exchange rates. Domestic fiscal policy should be used to achieve domestic targets for nominal demand growth. Although these targets should take account of the need to reduce inflation to zero, countries would be able to give greater or lesser weight to the inflation objective relative to capacity utilization.

Pause for thought 7.11

What is a soft buffer?

McKinnon, on the other hand, proposed fixing the exchange rates of the currencies of G3 (USA, Japan and the EU) approximately at purchasing power parity. G3 would then agree on a constant expansion rate for the combined money supply of the three members. We are clearly back again here in the world of exogenous money, but the story could be converted into one in which the monetary authorities of the different governments coordinated policy on relative interest rates. In McKinnon's version, if portfolio holders increased their demand for one of the currencies at the expense of another, the authorities would simply accommodate this at the existing exchange rates. The money stock of the country whose currency was in demand would expand more rapidly; the rate of growth of the other country's money supply would decline. Much academic work followed on target zones for exchange rates.[14]

Although it is worth noting that both Keynesians and monetarists may support some form of international coordination, the difference between the two proposals outlined above is pronounced. It is clear that there has been little, if any, convergence in the views of economists. If we add to these disagreements among economists, the many other issues likely to divide governments of the major industrial countries, as well as such problems as sustainability and time consistency, we cannot be very hopeful about the prospects for a rapid movement even to a simple rule-based regime.

Certainly, there has been no progress in recent years towards a more fixed exchange rate system at international level. The prospect of full discretionary coordination of macroeconomic policies is remote. Nonetheless economists continue to launch proposals for global policy coordination, the establishment of a global central bank or the return to a past world, such as a return to the gold standard.

Policy coordination in practice

We can talk about the practice of policy coordination at a number of levels. The most comprehensive proposals are at the world level. In the discussions that led up to the establishment of the IMF, Keynes proposed the establishment of a world currency (bancor) and central bank — ideas that were rejected by the USA at the time but which have continued to haunt the minds of international economists. However, the most that we can contemplate at present is policy coordination of monetary and fiscal policy among the large economies, say of G8, or monetary policy coordination among the central banks of the large countries.

The closest we have come to any form of international macroeconomic policy coordination since the collapse of the Bretton Woods adjustable peg exchange rate system was in the economic summit meetings of G7 countries in the 1970s and 1980s. At the level of central banks, we certainly have not had a global cooperative monetary policy as defined by Taylor (2008) — one in which there is a joint international choice of policy rule with all central banks agreeing on a global objective such as price stability and output stability. However, he argues that the gains from such a policy would be small in comparison with a global policy rule without cooperation where policy makers in each country take as given policy reaction coefficients in other countries and that a policy rule without cooperation is a big improvement on sub-optimal policies followed in the 1970s. In other words, there are gains to be had from:

(a)   all countries following a sound policy rule (which does not target exchange rates);

(b)   all countries building into their models a view of the policy rules being followed by other countries;

(c)   the development of empirical multi-country models taking into account the   spillovers generated by monetary policies.

This sounds, however, optimistic in comparison with the apparent reality - occasional joint actions by groupings of central banks usually spurred into action by the exchange rate performance of one of the major currencies.

Beyond this, we can discuss coordination among regional groupings of countries. The most important of these from the points of view of size and of the amount of literature generated has been the euro area. Here, we might be interested in coordination among member countries of the euro area, in which case we shall be concerned with fiscal policy coordination among countries with a common monetary policy; or in coordination between the euro area and EU members outside the euro area in which case we shall be dealing with monetary and fiscal policy coordination. There are also single currency areas among the ex-colonies of France in Africa and many other regional groupings of countries with varying degrees of integration. The question of monetary and/or fiscal policy coordination arises in all of these from time to time.

Policy coordination in practice since the 1970s

Let us concentrate on the G7 economic summits of the 1970s and 1980s. The first significant attempt at discretionary policy coordination was the setting up of the annual economic summit of the G7 countries in 1975, seen as an important new forum for policy coordination following the breakdown of the Bretton Woods system, which had been an example of rule-based coordination. Later meetings of some importance in terms of macroeconomic policy included the Bonn Summit of 1978, the Plaza Accord of 1985, and the Louvre Accord of 1987. Two problems arise in attempting to deal with these: that of attempting to judge their success or failure; and that of trying to account for that success or failure. The crucial question is whether failure is an indication that any such exercise is bound to fail; or whether there are particular lessons to be learnt that might allow more successful policy coordination to be undertaken in the future.

In 1974, the finance ministers of the industrial countries agreed not to have competitive devaluations. However, after 1975, the USA chose a policy of loose fiscal policy and tight monetary policy; while Europe and Japan used contractionary policies (largely, government expenditure cuts and tight monetary policy). The Bonn Economic Summit in 1978 endorsed the view that coordination at this time might have considerable benefits; the USA called for joint action to expand the major economies as a locomotive for the world economy. However, when Germany tried to carry out its part of the programme alone, it quickly ran into trouble. From 1980 to 1982, there were further calls for joint expansion but by then the USA were opposed to joint action. It has been argued that had the OECD countries other than the USA accepted fiscal expansion in return for reduced US budget deficits, US inflation would have been lower, while export demand would have increased via a fall in the value of the dollar. The other OECD countries would have grown faster and had less unemployment. Developing countries would have increased export earnings and reduced their indebtedness.

There was a start on this kind of programme with the Plaza Agreement (late 1985) between G3: it was agreed that monetary policies should be coordinated to manage worldwide reductions in interest rates. 1986 saw the fiscal counterpart to the Plaza Agreement: budgetary changes were to be coordinated to lower the value of the dollar together with fiscal expansions in Japan and Germany to compensate for any contractionary tendencies in US policy. Yet in practice, little happened although interest rates and the dollar did start to fall. In 1987, in the Louvre Accord, finance ministers decided to try to maintain exchange rates within agreed target zones, but the arrangement was abandoned after the 1987 stock market crash.

At one end of the spectrum of opinions on these attempts at policy coordination, are those who do not agree that the economic summits were attempts at policy coordination at all. In Kindleberger's presidential address to the 98th annual meeting of the American Economic Association in 1985, he asserted that '...the commitment to consultative macroeconomic policies in annual summit meetings of seven heads of state has become a shadow play, a dog-and-pony show, a series of photo opportunities ....with ceremony substituted for substance'.[15] Portes argues somewhat differently, questioning not their effectiveness but the motives behind them, seeing the global macroeconomic policy attitudes of 1979-85 as '...the very antithesis of policy co-ordination'.[16] In his view, the spirit behind policy coordination should be a desire to produce more efficient outcomes, but he saw the G7 summits as attempts to alter the balance of power within the existing economic system by bringing about changes in fellow-members policies in one's own interests.

Pause for thought 7.12

What is a 'dog-and-pony show'? To what aspects of such a show might Kindleberger be referring in the quote above?

At the other end of the spectrum lie the views of those who do, indeed, see G7 and G3 meetings as coordination but who believe that all such attempts are likely to do more harm than good. Such views are based on a central belief in the efficiency of markets, a Public Choice school interpretation of the aims and ambitions of bureaucrats who attempt to manage markets, and a feeling that economists are '...abysmally ignorant about the macro-economic processes and the dynamics of forces that determine the fate of national economies'.[17]

Horne and Masson (1988) provide a good example of the 'lessons to be learnt' approach to the summits. They distinguish between 'procedural' and 'substantive' achievements. At a procedural level, they suggest that the summits were a success, establishing '...an increased awareness of policy interactions, a recognition of the role of exchange rate factors in macroeconomic policy formulation, and the need for mutually consistent medium-term strategies'.[18] However, they argue that the record has been much less convincing at a substantive level. The 1978 Bonn economic summit, which endorsed the view that coordination at this time might have considerable benefits but which led to an apparent over-expansion of the West German economy, is selected particularly as an example of the pitfalls of international fine-tuning. Currie (1990) suggested, on the other hand, that criticism of the macroeconomic aspects of the Bonn summit may have been unfair and contrasts the '...detailed analysis and negotiation that took place prior to the Bonn summit with the sketchy and hasty preparations for the Plaza and Louvre Accords'.[19] He reserved his ire principally for the shortcomings of the Louvre Accord, which he saw as an example of stupid coordination since its targets for exchange rates were not supported by a willingness to adjust the underlying macroeconomic policies.

The failure of the Louvre Accord set back the development of international policy coordination. Very little happened at the level of the world economy after 1987, at least until the coordinated interest rate reduction of 8 October 2008. The notion of international macroeconomic policy coordination had seemed close to expiry. We were left with attempts by governments to exert pressure on other governments, although few of these had much effect. For example, in 2001, as the US economy headed into recession and as the Federal Reserve cut interest rates sharply, American economic policy advisers on several occasions expressed their unhappiness at the failure of the European Central Bank to follow suit. Again, in late 2007 and early 2008, the US government made their disappointment clear that the ECB did not respond to the cuts in taxation and the lowering of interest rates employed in the USA to try to offset the effects of the credit crunch. However, there was no suggestion at that stage that there should be an organised exercise in policy coordination to reduce the possibility of world recession.

An example of the small number of joint central bank actions occurred in September 2000 when, in response to the weakness of the euro, the ECB joined with the central banks of the USA, Japan and the UK to purchase euro. But exchange rate interventions of this kind certainly don't fit well with Taylor's global cooperative policy or the use of a global non-cooperative policy rule.

The 2007-8 credit crunch was of particular interest from the point of view of the monetary interdependence of countries. The spread of the US sub-prime problem to the rest of the world economy arose particularly because of the increasing ease with which capital flowed internationally. This had enabled the USA to continue to run long-term current account deficits - apart from two quarters in 1991, the USA has had current account deficits in every quarter since the third quarter of 1982. The deficits grew steadily to reach a then record of nearly $211bn. by the third quarter of 2006. They remained high, with a deficit of $183bn being recorded for the second quarter of 2008. These deficits were financed by the net foreign acquisition of US assets, particularly, the foreign acquisition of US financial assets. These included government securities and corporate bonds but also included securitised US mortgages. Before the credit crunch, the principal concern expressed about these large imbalances were about the impact on the value of the dollar whenever there was any tendency for foreign capital inflow to diminish. No thought was given to the quality of US financial assets appearing in the balance sheets of European banks.

The world imbalance in international trade provided a second element in the spread of financial crisis in 2008. The USA was far from the only country to become dependent on the inflow of foreign capital. The growth of European banks, in general, had been supported by funds obtained in international financial markets, flowing particularly from the major current surplus countries of Japan and China. Of course, those European banks that had become over-dependent on raising funds in wholesale financial markets, and had added to domestic housing market booms by issuing their own sub-prime mortgages were most vulnerable when credit markets froze. But there is no doubt that there was a major element of contagion in the rapid development of a global crisis.

It was in this context that we had the coordinated half-point cuts in interest rates by many of the central banks of the developed countries on 8 October. This was by meetings of finance ministers from many countries to consult on remedies to the crisis. The next question was whether the threat of a major financial collapse would produce serious long-term policy coordination or whether the general cut in interest rates would transpire to be a one-off action.

As we pointed out earlier, exercises in international policy coordination include regional cooperation. The EU's EMS was an example of rule-based policy coordination. The widening membership of the exchange rate mechanism in the 1980s, with most members moving into the narrow band, together with the increasing freedom of capital movements within the EC, ensured a high degree of coordination of monetary policy. Monetary union in 1999 replaced this with a single monetary policy for the euro area members. A high degree of monetary policy coordination also applies between the ECB's policy and those of the central banks of the ERMII countries. However, there has been no evidence of monetary policy coordination between the ECB and the central banks of the UK or Sweden.

The establishment of the Stability and Growth Pact and the Excessive Deficit Procedure was an attempt to limit the differences among fiscal policies of all EU members but it has been argued (von Hagen and Mundschenk, 2002) that the mechanisms for policy coordination in the EU are deficient, largely ignoring the interdependence of national economic policies.

7.6   Capital mobility and the Tobin tax

We have seen that internationally mobile capital reduces the freedom of policy makers to act independently. In a fixed exchange rate system, monetary policy is, at best, effective for only a short period. In a floating exchange rate system, rapid flows of capital cause fluctuations in exchange rates, which add to uncertainty and cause problems for policy makers. These problems are discussed further in section 9.4. Here, however, we wish to consider the application of a small tax to international capital flows. This was first proposed by the American Nobel Prize-winning economist, James Tobin (1978) and has become universally known as the Tobin Tax. The original plan was for a uniform tax on capital flows, levied by all countries, to make 'hot money' round trips unprofitable and to remove the dominance of capital account movements over exchange rates. Tobin originally proposed a tax of 1 per cent but as the volume of international capital flows has increased dramatically, the tax rate proposed by various supporters has been lowered, most commonly to 0.1 per cent. This was the figure suggested by Tobin in 2001 when he rejected the general views of the anti-globalization movement and their arguments for the tax, although he did not reject the idea of the tax.

There have been many criticisms of the proposal and, until recently, it languished in occasional journal articles. Following the Asian financial crisis of 1998, however, the proposal was taken up particularly by groups campaigning against the impact of globalization on developing countries. It has now attracted support from some governments. It was supported by the Canadian parliament in 1999 and a version of the tax, the Spahn tax, was approved by the Belgian parliament in 2004. In effect, both countries committed themselves to introducing the tax when everyone else did so, although in Belgium's case, the requirement was only that all other members of the euro area should also introduce it. Thus, there is no imminent prospect of the tax being introduced anywhere.

Some criticisms of the Tobin Tax have been practical. For example, it has been argued that capital flows for long-term investment are desirable and certainly should not be taxed. The aim should be to reduce, or at least slow down, speculative capital flows, but it would not be possible to discriminate accurately between the two types of flows. It has also been claimed that the proportion of international capital flows that are genuinely speculative in nature has been exaggerated. Another practical difficulty is that many international assets are not controlled by a single authority or group of authorities and this makes it difficult to keep track of all capital flows. Many already go unrecorded. The application of the Tobin tax would provide another incentive for investors to evade official attention and would lead to a large increase in unrecorded flows. In addition, there is the problem that the tax would need to be imposed by all financial centres but would provide an incentive for some centres not to charge the tax as a way of attracting new business.

Quite apart from the practical objections, neoclassical economists argue that the Tobin Tax is undesirable because it is not a first-best policy and would have undesirable side effects. It would favour inertia and local asset bias in portfolios and would infringe Pareto-efficiency conditions. From this viewpoint, the underlying problem should be identified and policy should be aimed directly at that problem. For example, if the problem were the slow adjustment of goods market prices (as in the Dornbusch overshooting model), the first-best policy would be one aimed at the rigidities in goods markets. Of course, if such policies were themselves impracticable, one could argue for the Tobin Tax as a second-best policy.

The tax has also been criticised by post-Keynesians. Davidson (1997) accepts that speculative flows create problems. He stresses the relevance of Keynes's beauty contest analogy to foreign exchange markets. This is the view that market behaviour largely consists of people guessing what other people in markets are likely to do. This easily leads to wild speculation and panics. However, he argues that the usual magnitude proposed for a Tobin tax would be a negligible deterrent to short-term speculation and would probably be a greater deterrent to real trade flows and arbitrage activities. He makes an alternative proposal for preventing speculation, based on Keynes's 1940s writings, suggesting a need for rules and structures to prevent crises, pointing out that when Keynes analysed this problem, he saw that a system of outright prohibition of international hot money flows would be required.

In recent years, the tax has been supported as a source of funds for sustainable development. It is argued that if the tax were applied and were to fail in its primary purpose of slowing down flows of hot money, it would provide large funds that could be used for the assistance of poorer countries. This assumes that countries could arrive at a decision as to how the funds would be best used.

7.7 Summary

The impact of monetary policy in an open economy depends on the nature of the exchange rate system. When a fixed exchange rate system is in force and capital is mobile, monetary policy is weak. If capital were perfectly mobile, monetary policy would be completely ineffective. In this case, a small country within the system could not determine its own monetary policy. The monetary policy of the system could be that of an asymmetric leader or it might be determined by the group of countries acting together. In either case, there could be problems for a small country whose business cycle was not synchronised with those of the other members of the system. This would be particularly the case if there were hysteresis effects, which caused an incorrect monetary policy to have a damaging long-run impact on the economy.

Countries may retain some freedom in monetary policy if the system has relatively wide bands around the fixed exchange rate parities or if governments are able to devalue or revalue their currencies within the system without damaging either the system or the anti-inflationary reputation of the government. The authorities also on occasions attempt to preserve monetary independence by engaging in open market operations to sterilise the impact of monetary influences from abroad. However, this cannot be effective for long in a world of highly mobile capital. This also applies to the attempt to preserve monetary independence with capital controls. The leadership of a fixed exchange rate system may be determined by the nature of the system or by the attitudes of governments and financial markets. In the latter case, the country most trusted to keep inflation low and to preserve the international value of its currency is likely to become the leader. Then, there is a possibility of the leading country following a tight monetary policy that could have a deflationary impact on other members.

Monetary policy is effective if exchange rates are allowed to float. The precise nature of the impact depends, however, on what determines exchange rate movements. In simple monetary models of the exchange rate an increase in the rate of growth of the money supply leads to a proportional change in the exchange rate, preserving purchasing power parity in both the short and the long run. That is, monetary policy is neutral. However, purchasing power parity certainly does not hold in the short run. Exchange rates are much more volatile than domestic prices. The overshooting exchange rate model attempts to explain the volatility of exchange rates. The best-known version of this approach makes use of the idea of sticky prices in goods markets. In this case, monetary policy has real effects in the short run, although it again becomes neutral in the long run. Monetary models suffer from the disadvantage that they preserve the assumption of perfect capital mobility and do not allow a distinction to be made between open market operations and foreign exchange operations. This is overcome in portfolio models of the exchange rate.

Floating exchange rate systems are sometimes defended because they allow countries to preserve independent monetary policies. However, even with floating exchange rates, the monetary policy of a country can have an impact on other countries. This possibility has increased as countries have become more and more interdependent economically. This raises the question of the desirability of international monetary policy coordination. Although a good deal of time has been spent developing policy coordination models, the size of any net benefits from policy coordination remains unclear. In practice, little progress has been made in discretionary monetary policy coordination among the major economies.

Key concepts used in this chapter

target ranges	exchange rate parities
spillovers	exchange rate bands
perfect capital mobility	intervention currency
synchronised business cycles	uncovered interest rate parity
devaluations/revaluations of the exchange rate	purchasing power parity
	overshooting exchange rates
sterilisation of monetary influences	macroeconomic policy coordination
capital controls	rule-based coordination

Questions and exercises
Answers at the end of the book

1. How is the deflationary policy of a strong country transmitted through a fixed exchange rate system?

2. Why might a revaluation of a currency only temporarily reduce a Balance of Trade surplus?

3. Why does a wide band around fixed exchange rate parities (as with the 15 per cent band in use in the EMS between 1993 and the end of 1998) make life more difficult for currency speculators?

4. What is the relationship between purchasing power parity and the neutrality of money?

5. What is the Lucas critique? What is its relevance to this chapter?

... and also to think about

6. What meaning or meanings might be attached to the notion of the equilibrium exchange rate?

7. In what senses is:

(a) the Williamson-Miller target zone model Keynesian?
(b) the McKinnon fixed exchange rate model monetarist?

Further reading

The Mundell-Fleming model is dealt with at length in most second level macro-economics texts. It is particularly well used and discussed in Acocella (1998). Textbooks that cover exchange rate economics well include the third edition of Copeland (2008) and the second edition of Pilbeam (2005). Most of the material on policy coordination dates from the late 1980s and early 1990s, when it was rather more popular as a topic than it has been recently. Recommended are the essays by Currie in Llewellyn and Milner (1990) and by Hughes-Hallet in Greenaway (1989). Open economy issues are discussed in Walsh (2003) ch.6

8 Issues in the design of monetary policy

'The best thing undeniably that a government can do with the Money Market is to let it take care of itself.'

Walter Bagehot, *Lombard Street* (1873)

8.1   Introduction

In section 5.1, we claimed that much of the 'new consensus' in macroeconomics (NCM) has grown out of a consensus about the best way to design and operate monetary policy. This in turn means that at least a number of major issues of the recent past in regard to design and operation must have been resolved. The main purpose of this chapter is to see *how* they have been resolved and what remains for debate. But first of all, in order to support our claim that 'consensus over theory' owes a great deal to 'consensus over policy' we look at the main features of what most economists would regard as a well-designed monetary policy. The following list can be compared with the list of NCM features on p.122 above:

- In the long-run, monetary policy has no real effects;

- In the short-run, nominal rigidities create a trade-off between output and inflation;

- Monetary policy is the principal means of influencing aggregate demand and policy is linked to inflation through its ability to influence the pressure of demand;

- Policy outcomes are improved under an independent central bank and further improved if the central bank operates in an open and 'transparent' manner;

- Ends (a specific inflation target) matter more than means (intermediate targets);

- The policy instrument is the short-run nominal interest rate set by the central bank in supply and refinancing of banks' reserves.

We use section 8.2 to clarify some of the terms that arise in connection with policy design, including: targets, instruments, objectives, goals (and others) and we shall illustrate the categories by reference to examples. (A fuller history of monetary policy in the UK, with its evolution of targets, objectives and instruments is provided in ch.10). In section 8.3 we look at the recent preference for the adoption of a specific inflation target. This is followed by three sections (8.4 to 8.6) which are linked by the phrase 'inflation bias' — the belief that there are 'pressures' in the conduct of policy which give rise to a higher rate of inflation than the optimal unless the conduct of policy can be constrained in some way to avoid it. In section 8.4 we discuss (a) the origins of the inflation bias allegation and (b) the merits of imposing 'rules' which the policymaker must follow rather than allowing the use of complete freedom or 'discretion'. This links with the previous section in the sense that adopting an inflation target is sometimes described as a form of 'constrained discretion' — a sort of half-way house.

In section 8.5, we look at a more recent argument that policy might contain an inflation bias. This is the notion that policy may be 'time inconsistent' meaning that whenever low inflation is achieved there are gains to be made from boosting aggregate demand.

This is followed by section 8.6 where we examine the trend towards placing policy in the hands of a central bank which is 'independent' of government. We look critically at the theory behind it and at some of the empirical literature which appeared to support the argument that 'independence was best' in the early 1990s.

Finally, we shall look at the latest enthusiasm in the design of monetary policy — the idea that central banks should be as open as possible about the way in which they make decisions so that private sector agents can, more or less, anticipate how central banks will respond to a given macroeconomic situation. As with the section on independence, we shall take a critical look at the theory and at the empirical work which is claimed to support it.

8.2   Policy goals and instruments

We begin with some terminology. **Targets** are **quantified objectives** (or **quantified 'goals'**, the achievement of which increases the material well-being of the population. As we shall see in chapter 10, the choice made by governments among the objectives of macroeconomic policy has varied considerably over the past sixty years. Throughout the 1960s and 70s governments were often described as trying to achieve multiple objectives, including 'low' inflation but by 1990 the low inflation objective had been widely replaced by a (quantified) target — commonly around 2 per cent p.a. — which was to be achieved as a first priority (i.e. before any other objectives were considered). This shift was based on the argument that a low rate of inflation was a *sine qua non* for the achievement of low unemployment and high rates of economic growth.

There are two issues here. Firstly, we have the debate over the Phillips curve that we considered in chapter 6 — the question of whether lower unemployment can be traded off against higher inflation. Secondly, if we conclude that the authorities can indeed succeed in reducing unemployment through macroeconomic policies,[1] we need to know the economic and social costs of both inflation and unemployment. A particular problem arises over the distinction between the short-run and the long-run. If inflation acts to increase the long-run equilibrium rate of unemployment, but policies aimed at reducing inflation produce an increase in unemployment in the short-run, how do we decide between short-run and long-run costs and benefits? The answer depends on the extent of the short-run and long-run effects as well as on the length of time it will take for the long-run to come to pass. Bear in mind that the people unemployed in the short-run as a result of anti-inflationary policies will be different from those who might obtain jobs in the long-run as a result of these policies. Arguments based on the notion of improving the welfare of the economy as a whole frequently conceal judgements about the distribution of income and other benefits both among various social groups and between present and future generations.

We must also accept that long-run impacts of policy are often difficult to judge because of the possibility of change in many of the factors influencing the economy. Thus, we might accept the proposition that inflation produces inefficiencies within the market economy and, in this way, increases the natural rate of unemployment in the long run, but argue also that anti-inflationary policy has hysteresis effects in labour markets, resulting in long-run costs. For example, the skill levels of workers may be seriously affected by increased spells of unemployment.

Pause for thought 8.1:

What sort of 'inefficiencies' might inflation cause that affect the level of employment in the long-run? How do these inefficiencies vary with the rate of inflation?

The operation of policy naturally requires rather more than a general statement of goals such as 'the control of inflation'. At some point, numbers must be attached to goals, converting them into targets.[2] Even if there is general agreement over the nature of policy goals, there may be discord over the precise targets that are desirable or practicable, in the light of the available instruments and the associated costs. For instance, attitudes towards inflation may change with its level. At modest rates, inflation may seem no more than an irritant and, possibly, a constraint on the achievement of other objectives. Rampant inflation may, on the other hand, seriously undermine both economic and social relationships and become a major source of welfare loss. It follows that, even if we are willing to accept the control of inflation as the dominant macroeconomic objective, we may well require strong justification for propositions that it should take precedence over all other policy goals, irrespective of the existing rate of inflation and level of unemployment.

An **instrument** of policy is a variable that the policy authorities control directly, being able to determine its value independently of other variables in the system. What constitutes an instrument is partly a technical question. For example, we have seen (in section 4.3) that the monetary authorities effectively have direct control over only the very short-term rate of interest at which they make reserves available to the commercial banking system But as events of late-2007 and early-2008 showed they have little direct control over other short-rates. As a generalisation, the longer the term of interest, the less influence the central bank has and, by contrast, the greater the role played by market forces. Alternatively, we have seen that they might have direct control over the monetary base, but this is not the same thing as having direct control over the quantity of money. As a general rule, discussions about the appropriate instrument for a given set of circumstances tend to be rather optimistic in their view of what constitutes a feasible instrument of policy. The genuine list is frustratingly short.

Further, a government may technically have a policy instrument under its control but be prevented by practical and/or political considerations from using its full range of values. The freedom a government has to change interest rates, for example, may depend on the need to defend a fixed exchange rate or on the proximity of the next election.

Pause for thought 8.2:

Why might the pattern of home ownership be a constraint on the rate of interest as a monetary instrument?

Additional problems are produced by the existence of uncertainty. There may be uncertainty over the structure of the economy or over which is the best model of its operation as well as over the effects of instruments. In this regard, it can be demonstrated that performance is improved by using more instruments than targets. Each instrument may be imperfectly used but weaknesses may to some extent be offsetting. If one instrument is given the wrong value, other instruments may also need to be given sub-optimal values in order to produce the best available result.

The relative effectiveness of instruments in achieving particular targets is also of considerable importance. Even if the authorities have instruments sufficient in number and in flexibility to achieve their targets, there remains the question of which policy to apply to which target. One approach to this problem is to direct each policy instrument at that target over which it has the greatest relative influence. Robert Mundell (1962) referred to this as the *principle of effective market classification*. He chose as targets external balance (balance in the balance of payments) and internal balance (full employment with low inflation) and, as instruments, the interest rate (monetary policy) and the budget balance (fiscal policy). He then showed that in a fixed exchange rate system, using fiscal policy to achieve internal balance and monetary policy to achieve external balance would move the system towards equilibrium, while the reverse would send the economy further and further away from equilibrium.

Another possible approach is to allocate each instrument to a separate authority, giving each authority the responsibility for hitting one well-defined target as nearly as possible (Meade, 1978). For such decentralisation of policy to be successful, we require each instrument to have a strong impact on one policy goal and relatively little impact on all other goals. One obvious example of this is to allocate monetary policy to an independent central bank, which is given the responsibility for controlling inflation (considered in section 8.6).

A problem of particular relevance to monetary policy stems from the fact that the relationship between instruments and final policy goals is far from direct. Furthermore, it takes a long time to work itself out and (worse still) the time lags may even be uncertain. Figure 5.1 shows both the complexity of the linkages and the possibility that it takes a year for a change in the instrument to affect aggregate demand and then another year for that change in demand pressure to have its full effect upon inflation. This makes it extremely difficult for the policymaker to make the right instrument setting at time *t*, since so much can change between setting the instrument and the two year horizon. Furthermore, it will be a long time before the policymaker receives any sort of feedback (confirmation or otherwise) that the instrument decision was correct. In the circumstances, it is hardly surprising that policymakers have been on constant alert for variables which, while having no great welfare significance in themselves, nonetheless react quickly to the policy instrument and then *have a reliable connection to the final target*. A variable that met these conditions would at least give the policymaker early-warning that the instrument settings were (or were not) keeping the economy on the right track. Thus lying between *instruments* and *targets* there might be **proximate** or **intermediate targets**: a set of variables that the authorities cannot control directly and that do not have a direct impact on economic welfare but that may be important determinants of final goals and that we may thus wish to target.

Pause for thought 8.3

Using our classification of target/intermediate target/instrument, where would you place each of the following:

unemployment   a mandatory reserve ratio
the budget deficit   bank lending to the non-bank private sector
the exchange rate   output *per capita*

The most obvious example of an intermediate target in monetary policy is the rate of growth of the money supply. We shall see in section 8.4 that one of the earliest monetary policy rules was one recommended by Friedman (1959) whereby the policymaker was required to maintain a steady growth in the money stock calculated at a rate which would match the acceptable rate of inflation plus the long-run growth of output. This was attempted explicitly in the UK during the period known as the 'Medium Term Financial Strategy' between 1981 and 1985. At the outset of the strategy, a declining target range for money growth was published in the hope that this would bring down the rate of inflation. But the scheme was abandoned in 1985 because the money supply proved impossible to control with sufficient precision and the rate of inflation fell sharply anyway. As an intermediate target, the money supply seemed to tell us nothing useful.

Other variables may act as indicators or intermediate targets. After the failure of the monetary rule experiment, UK monetary policy 'targeted' the UK:Deutschemark exchange rate. The argument here was that the principal determinant of exchange rates is the rate of inflation in the two countries concerned. Therefore if the UK operated a monetary policy which kept stable the value of the pound sterling against the Deutschemark, this would tell the policymakers that foreign exchange markets at least believed that policy in the UK would deliver the same rate of inflation as policy in Germany. And since foreign exchange markets were regarded as notoriously sensitive, it was believed that any deviation of policy from what was required would be noticed instantly. Both of these episodes are discussed in more detail in section 10.3.

8.3   Targets in monetary policy

Since the early 1990s the monetary authorities in a large number of countries (25 in March 2008) have adopted an explicit inflation target. A notable exception is the US Federal Reserve which makes no formal announcement of a target, though it is widely believed to be targeting a rate of 1.5 to 2 per cent in practice. However, as events of 2008 have shown, the absence of an explicit inflation target, had made it easier for the Fed to relax monetary policy in an attempt to counteract the first signs of recession. In this section we look at some of the issues surrounding inflation targeting (the pros and cons and some difficulties) and towards the end we look more briefly at some other possible targets.

8.3.1 Inflation targeting

Inflation targeting refers to the practice, as the name suggests, of setting an *explicit* numerical target for the rate of inflation over some future time horizon. When this is done, it is usually within a context in which it is understood that the policymaker gives some degree of priority to achieving that objective. In addition, the context normally assumes that the policymaker is a central bank with some degree of independence of government.

Although the widespread shift towards inflation targeting is a product of the 1990s, inflation targeting is not new. Alfred Marshall (1887) advocated a monetary system which would fix the purchasing power of the currency closely to an absolute standard; while Knut Wicksell advocated an explicit price-level standard for monetary policy (Wicksell, 1898). Sweden even operated such a price-*level* target in the early 1930s. In the UK, an inflation target was adopted in the autumn of 1992 following the pound sterling's exit from the ERM. Having lost the peg to the Deutschemark, some alternative way was required to express and to judge the stance of monetary policy. In its original form, the target was specified as a 2.5 per cent p.a. increase in the retail prices index (after excluding mortgage interest payments), the so-called RPI-X

Five points are generally made in favour of a monetary policy which embraces inflation targeting:

- Inflation targeting (IT) focuses attention on what the policymaker can actually achieve rather than diverting attention across a number of objectives, some of which may conflict and/or be unfeasible. This argument is strengthened where the target comes with some clear statement about its overwhelming priority over any other objectives.

• Perhaps most importantly, specifying an IT means that agents know what to expect and can make decisions accordingly. This brings the general advantage that decisions made with superior information are better than decisions made with inferior information. But there are also some specific advantages. Recall that when we discussed the policymaker's reaction to an inflation shock in figure 5.3, we noted that an increase in the rate of interest pushed the economy *down* an upward-sloping *SRPC*. This involves a real loss since output (and employment) are below their potential levels. The loss continues for so long as we are to the left of the *LRPC*. How long this will be depends upon how long it takes for the *SRPC* to shift downwards. In chapter 5 we simply *assumed* a degree of inertia in the adjustment process and in chapter 6 we said that this might be the result of expectations needing to catch up with reality or it might be due to 'stickiness' in the adjustment of wage contracts. The argument for an IT is that *whatever it is* that takes time to adjust, the adjustment time will be lessened if agents know what rate of inflation the policymaker is aiming at. This, of course, carries the assumption that the policymaker is believed or is 'credible'.

• We return to the issue of credibility in section 8.6, but we might just note that the publication of an inflation target is itself sometimes argued to increase credibility. This is because publishing a clear target, makes it easy for others to judge the policymaker's performance. The loss to the policymaker's reputation is therefore greater in the presence of IT and therefore, it is argued, the policy-maker will try harder to meet the target. Furthermore, with a clear yardstick for measuring performance, it would, in principle, be possible to link success/failure to a system of rewards/punishments and further increase incentives to achieve the target.

• Related to this third, or 'commitment' argument is the idea that specifying an IT might force the policymaker to adopt a more 'conservative' monetary policy than would otherwise be the case. The idea here is that the policymaker is seeking to minimise a loss function (eqn. 5.5 is a good example) in which deviations of inflation from a target are just one component. One monetary policy may be said to be more conservative than another if, either the weight attached to the loss from inflation deviations is greater or if the inflation target is itself lower (or of course both). The argument that IT leads to a more conservative policy therefore consists of saying that an explicit target is likely to involve a lower rate of inflation than is a vaguely formulated objective of 'low inflation'. But this raises tricky questions of where the target comes from and how the loss function is formulated. Since both are connected with central bank independence we shall deal with them there.

• Finally, there is a strong argument in favour of IT that has rather limited relevance to economic outcomes. This is that having an explicit IT makes it easier to judge the performance of the policy maker (as we said in point 3 above). and is part of the deal regarding 'accountability' that has to be done with the electorate when policymaking is handed to a non-elected body.

We turn now to some of the difficulties associated with operating an inflation targeting regime.

The first of these is the choice of the target. In practice, most IT regimes use a target in the area of 2 per cent p.a. increase in the general price level. At first sight this might seem odd since, if inflation gives rise to the negative effects that we have earlier described, then eliminating it altogether would seem preferable to accepting a low but positive level. The arguments are essentially pragmatic and are due to a strong desire to avoid *negative* inflation (see Sinclair, 2003). The first is that however hard the policymaker tries, the policy outcome will always be affected to some degree by 'shocks'. This means that the best that can be hoped for is that over a period of time the average outcome has a mean equal to the target and a very small variance. However, given that there will be *some* variance, it is important to ensure that we do not trigger a general fall in the price level. Hence the decision always to target a *positive* inflation rate.

Related to that is the possibility that the way in which we measure changes in the price level tends to overstate the actual rate of inflation. So, if we set the target too close to zero, then actually achieving the target on paper could mean that prices are generally falling. This tendency to overstate the rate of inflation comes from the way in which we update the selected price index. The prices of goods and services contained in the index are monitored continuously and updated at pre-determined intervals (commonly one month). But the weights assigned to each good or service are updated less frequently (typically annually). This means that if there is a sharp rise in the price of a group of products (wheat-based food-stuffs provide a current example) the impact on the cost of living depends upon the weight prior to the price rise. However, elementary economics tells us that consumers will endeavour to lessen the impact by switching to some alternative. So the weight (and the impact) is automatically reduced even though this is not reflected in the index until the next update.

Another argument focuses on sticky prices (especially in the labour market). If a fall in nominal wages is impossible in practice there is the risk that that labour markets could get stuck with a disequilibrium real wage — one that it too high to clear the market. The only way this can be eliminated is for other prices to rise. A low level of positive inflation enables this to happen. On this basis, we should expect to see some persistent and *positive* link between inflation and employment as we suggested in section 6.3. Recent work by Akerlof, Dickens and Perry (1996 and 2000) for the USA and Wyplosz (2001) for Germany, Switzerland, France and the Netherlands, appears to bear this out.

Finally, we have the argument that positive inflation allows the policymaker to set a *negative* real rate of interest. Since there is a zero nominal bound to interest rates, the main instrument of monetary policy could become ineffective if prices were falling. In precisely those circumstances, e.g. a deep recession, where negative real rates were required, they would be unavailable.[3]

Another issue, which is inseparable from the question of what rate to choose, is the question of which index to use to measure inflation. Since no two indices are likely to show the same rate of change, choosing the index is as important as choosing the rate. One obvious requirement is that it should be as representative as possible of the change in the overall level of prices as experienced by most people. But no index can be fully representative for all groups which is why most offices of national statistics publish a range of index numbers. Closely related to the question of representativeness is the question of credibility. If the purpose of adopting an inflation target is encourage bargains to be struck *in anticipation* of the achievement of the target, the strategy will fail if negotiators feel that a corresponding change in the targeted index grossly understates (for example) the rate of inflation to which they are subject. This is more than an academic issue. It has become problematic in the UK since a change in the targeted index was made in January 2004.[4]

Pause for thought 8.4:

If the objective of policy is price stability, why are positive rates of inflation always chosen as targets?

In the UK, the inflation target, which began as a 2.5 per cent p.a. increase in the RPI-X, was changed to a 2 per cent p.a. increase in the consumer price index, CPI. The arguments in favour of the switch were threefold. Firstly, it was argued that the use of a geometric (rather than arithmetic) mean for the aggregation of individual prices reduced the substitution bias we mentioned a moment ago. Secondly, the CPI is a more comparable measure of inflation internationally and represents international best practice. Thirdly, the coverage is different, and it was said that coverage of the CPI is preferable because it is more consistent with national accounts principles of consumer expenditure. Herein lay the problem. For some years before the change was made, the two indices were monitored closely in order to establish any differential that they might show in charting the rate of change of prices. It was eventually established that the CPI tended to record a rate of inflation which was approximately 0.5 percentage points lower than the RPI-X. Hence, when the changeover was announced, it was accompanied by a lowering if the target. But since the changeover, and especially since 2006, the RPI-X has been recording rates of inflation nearer to 1.5 percentage points higher than those recorded by the RPI-X. Thus while the private sector has been asked to plan on the basis of official inflation rates in the range of 2-2.5 per cent, the 'unofficial' rate has been running at some 3.5 to 4 per cent. Understandably, this has created some degree of resentment and a reluctance to accept the official rate for negotiating purposes, making the policy-maker's task harder.

A further question is whether it is better to specify the target as a point or a range. On the one hand a point is easier to understand — and much of the argument for an inflation target, as we have seen, comes from its ability to communicate clearly with the private sector. On the other, we know that a point target will be hit only infrequently and that missing the target carries reputational costs. The ECB resolves this dilemma by aiming for a target of '...below but close to 2 per cent.' At the same time, the Bank of England is often quoted as pursuing a target of between one and three per cent, though strictly speaking this is based on a mis-readng of the remit. The first page of the remit states quite clearly that 'the inflation target is 2 per cent at all times'. The second page then goes on to explain the consequences that follow if the target is missed by more than one per cent in either direction (including the writing of an open letter of explanation) but it goes on to say 'The thresholds do not define a target range.' One per cent and three percent are simply values which trigger certain consequences regarding accountability.

The way in which the ECB and Bank of England targets are framed raises another issue — the issue of symmetry which we first encountered in connection with figure 5.4. The Bank of England faces the same sanctions if it undershoots the target by one percentage point as it does if it overshoots. There is no such pressure on the ECB to avoid an undershoot. The result of this, it is widely argued is that the formulation of monetary policy at the ECB is subject to a downward bias. Alternatively, one might say that it has, in practice, a lower inflation target than the Bank of England.

We now look briefly at some other possible targets that have been considered in the design of monetary policy regimes, beginning with one which has a close connection with inflation targeting.

8.3.2 The inflation forecast as target

Svensson (1997) suggests that, because of the long lags in the monetary transmission mechanism, inflation targeting is actually inflation forecast targeting. That is, instead of altering the instrument to ensure that a specific target is hit in m-quarters time, the monetary authorities might form an optimal sequence for the policy instrument derived from a forward-looking policy rule based on a forecast horizon for expected inflation. The forecast horizon (n) need not necessarily coincide with the target horizon (m). Unless the target horizon is chosen carefully, the use of an optimal forecast horizon that is model-specific may result in a missed target at a time $t + m$. If different authorities choose the different horizons, the central bank may be held responsible for missed targets even though it is optimising using an acceptable loss function to derive n. In the UK, the Bank of England is free to specify the policy horizon and thus to equate n and m. This gives the Bank of England a degree of goal independence since it is able to choose the horizon *ex ante* (currently set at around eight quarters) over which it will be judged on its performance *ex post*. However, the choice of the optimal horizon is not easy.

It is also hard to forecast inflation. Over the period 1971-96, average errors in the forecasting of inflation by HM Treasury were 0.71 for four quarters ahead and 3.31 for eight quarters ahead. Over the shorter period from 1993 to 1996 (during which inflation rates were lower), the errors were -0.45 and -1.04 respectively, indicating that forecasts had been too high. Forecasts also understate inflation volatility. Thus, the Bank of England questions the value of setting a target for forecasts in terms of a single measure and stresses the role of judgement. They prefer the use of fan charts and probability distributions from the Bank's own model, private sector forecasts and cross-sectional information. This brings into question the transparency of MPC decisions since they are based on a forecast of inflation two years hence, which is influenced by subjective information not in the public domain. There is also the question of whether the Bank's forecast should be subject to outside checking — for example, by comparison with private sector forecasts. However, these are usually unconditional forecasts that incorporate the Central Bank's own reaction function as seen by the Bank forecasters. This can lead to problems of multiple equilibria or even non-existence.

In the USA, the Fed has always outperformed the private sector forecasts. This raises the question of what private sector forecasts tell us. If the private sector believes that the central bank's target is credible, it will publish the target as its forecast and no one will learn anything. This implies that the divergence between the forecast and the target is a measure of the bank's credibility. That, in turn, gives the bank an incentive to produce the target in its own forecast in order to suggest that policy is correctly set. That is, if the central bank regards proximity of inflation forecasts to target as a measure of its own credibility, it may seek to create (self-fulfilling) expectations of falling inflation over the two-year horizon.

Svensson (1997) thus argues for an independent body charged with producing strictly conditional forecasts based on present policies given by constant short rates or market expectations. The central bank would then be required to deposit its own forecast models with the independent body, reducing the opportunity for covering tracks. The independent body could assess which mistakes were avoidable and which were likely to be made by any good forecaster.

8.3.3 Nominal income targets

An alternative to targeting the rate of inflation, one could target the rate of change of nominal income — the rate of change of prices and real output combined. But nominal income targets also have a number of disadvantages. Firstly, national income data is generally quite long delayed, of uncertain accuracy and subject to minor revisions. This means that policy makers could only react to new information about the target variable on a quarterly basis rather than on the monthly basis possible with price data. Further, nominal GDP figures represent the lagged consequences in the economy of previous policy decisions rather than giving a reasonable indication of where the economy may go in the future if no policy action is taken now.

Secondly, moving to nominal income targets involves giving exactly equal weight to a percentage deviation of real output from its desired level as to a divergence of prices from the price level target. Hall (1986) proposed placing weights on output and price level deviations so as to reflect more closely some social welfare function weighting of unemployment on the one hand and price level instability and uncertainty on the other. This would be a considerable improvement on a simple nominal income target.

Thirdly, there would be a possible conflict between an independent central bank and the government over the nominal income target. Fourthly, other instruments (for example, fiscal policy) that influence nominal income are not under the control of the central bank. Finally, it is difficult to combine a good thing and a bad thing in a single target. For example, one may want to react to a shock to prices by encouraging through policy measures a (partial) offset to output, in pursuit of stability. However, the attainment of a nominal income target might require the authorities to seek to raise prices in order to offset a fall in output due, say, to a bad harvest.

8.3.4 Targeting an index of monetary conditions

Targeting an index of monetary conditions allows the formal incorporation of a number of variables relevant to the monetary policy decision, rather than leaving various elements to be included subjectively by the policy makers, as in the case of the Bank of England's emphasis on the judgement of the policy makers. Targeting an index is more open and, to the extent that a satisfactory index could be established, would make the monetary authorities more accountable.

Making monetary policy decisions on the basis of a number of important variables rather than just the rate of inflation or nominal income also might have specific advantages. For example, one component of any monetary conditions index would be the exchange rate. Taking the exchange rate into account would ensure that the external consequences of a tight monetary policy were taken into account, avoiding the achievement of a low inflation rate through excessive exchange rate appreciation. The incorporation of the exchange rate in the index would also address the question of who should take care of the exchange rate in a world of delegated responsibility for monetary policy.

However, there would be severe problems with the choice of the components of a monetary conditions index and the establishment of the weights to be attached to each component. It seems unlikely at present that a reliable and broadly acceptable index of monetary conditions could be established.

8.4   Rules and discretion

At the beginning of the last section we noted that one of the arguments sometimes advanced in favour of inflation targeting is that it may encourage the policymaker to follow a more conservative monetary policy than would otherwise be the case. 'Conservative' here means 'likely to yield a lower rate of inflation'. In section 5.3 we introduced the idea that the policymaker was trying to minimise a loss function of the kind:

$$L = (Y - Y^*)^2 + \lambda(\pi_1 - \pi^T)^2 \qquad (5.5)$$

Where $\lambda=1$, the policymaker places equal weight on the losses from inflation deviations as on the losses from output deviations. A more conservative loss function would have $\lambda>1$. We shall see shortly that other modifications to the loss function could also result in more or less conservative policies.

During the last thirty years or so, there has developed a widely-held view that monetary policy, especially if it is operated by an authority which is subject to popular election, is prone to suffer from **inflation bias**. Inflation bias refers to a situation where the rate of inflation, in equilibrium, is higher than the optimal rate. In theory one can make a case for an optimal rate of zero (Friedman (1959) argued that the optimal rate should be *negative*).[3] But we noted in the last section that there were practical reasons for choosing a low, positive, rate, usually around 2 per cent. This has led to two recommendations for improving the design (and operation) of monetary policy. The first is that the policymaker should be constrained in some way, such that it cannot react to the pressures for higher inflation. The other is that policymaking should be taken out of the hand of an elected authority, since it is the ballot box that is ultimately responsible for the inflationary pressure. The two strategies are not exclusive of course. In section 8.6 we shall see that many independent central banks are also subject to constraints.

Pause for thought 8.5

Which of these two loss functions is likely to produce the more conservative monetary policy and why?

(i) $L = (Y - Y^*)^2 + (\pi - \pi^T)^2$ and   (ii) $L = (Y - Y^P)^2 + (\pi - \pi^T)^2$, where $Y^P > Y^*$

8.4.1 Rules: the pros and cons

In this section we shall look at the case for rules which would constrain the behaviour of the policymaker. As we have just noted, the arguments in favour of rules derive largely from the inflation bias supposition. However, there is an additional argument, quite unrelated to the political context, that rules are required because of the technical difficulties involved in operating a successful monetary policy. It makes sense to consider that argument here as well. In summary, the arguments for rules can be viewed as shown in box 8.1.

The origin of the inflation bias supposition lies in the upward-sloping short-run Phillips curve. As we know, this creates a trade-off between higher output and low inflation. Higher output may be available (at least for a while) but only if the policymaker is prepared to accept higher inflation. The first of our arguments in box 8.1 says that governments feel under pressure, perhaps to maximise electoral support and improve their chances of remaining in office, if they aim for a higher level of output than the long-run equilibrium. Recall that this is likely to be associated with lower levels of unemployment, and so it may be this rather than higher output that is motivating voters. However, whether it is output or unemployment that is driving the policymaker, the result is the same and is shown in figure 8.1.

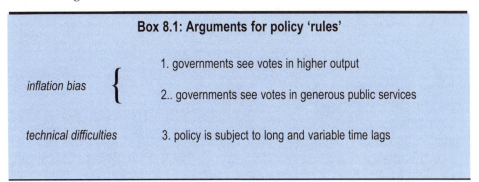

Box 8.1: Arguments for policy 'rules'

inflation bias $\left\{ \begin{array}{l} \\ \\ \end{array} \right.$ 1. governments see votes in higher output

2.. governments see votes in generous public services

technical difficulties   3. policy is subject to long and variable time lags

Figure 8.1 is based on the lower quadrant of figure 5.1 so, as drawn, it shows *A* as the optimal and sustainable combination of output and inflation. Inflation bias is created by assuming that, instead of aiming at *A*, the policymaker actually prefers *A'* and relaxes monetary policy with this purpose in mind. Enthusiastic students may like to refer to the six-quadrant diagram (figure 5.6) in order to trace out the full monetary consequences of this easing of monetary policy.

Figure 8.1: Inflation bias

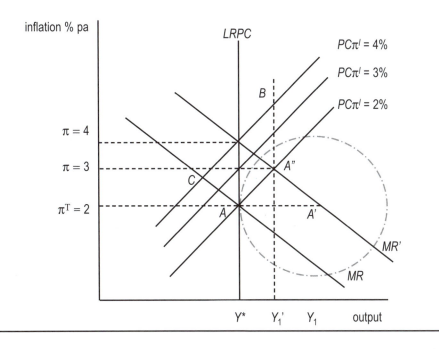

Note that if we were looking at a conventional AD/AS diagram we would draw a downward-sloping AD curve passing through A'. In the $IS/PC/MR$ model, however, we have to show it by moving the MR curve to MR'. This is because the MR curve shows the combinations of inflation and output that the policymaker chooses. This shift in the MR curve recalls our discussion of the similarity between the MR curve and a conventional AD curve in chapter 5, note 7. Notice also that while A was the centre point of a series of indifference curves, A' is the centre point of a new, different set of curves.

In terms of loss functions the policymaker has abandoned the familiar:

$$L = (Y - Y^*)^2 + \lambda(\pi_1 - \pi^T)^2$$

in favour of:

$$L = (Y - Y^P)^2 + \lambda(\pi_1 - \pi^T)^2$$

where $Y^P > Y^*$ and is 'politically inspired'.

The problem with aiming at A', however, is that it is unattainable. Firms are not willing to supply Y_1 at $\pi = 2$ per cent. The excess demand raises the rate of inflation and $PC\pi^l = 2\%$ tells us that firms will be willing to supply Y_1' when $\pi = 3\%$ (at A''). However, once we have settled at $Y_1'/\pi=3\%$, the $SRPC$ shifts upward to incorporate the new rate of inflation. With this adjustment, what firms are willing ti supply returns to Y^*. With actual inflation at 3%, we have the same excess demand that we had before and so inflation rises further. Eventually lagged inflation adjusts and the $SRPC$ shifts again. Provided the policymaker holds the real rate at its lower level in pursuit of a level of output higher that Y^*, the rate of inflation will accelerate.

Suppose now that the policymaker stops to reconsider when the economy is at point B. If, in figure 8.1 , we were to draw additional indifference curves it would be clear that B lies on an indifference curve which involves a bigger loss than the policymaker was originally experiencing at A. If we rank the losses from each of our positions (largest loss first) then we have:

$$B > A > A'' > A'$$

Unfortunately, only B and A are feasible.

Consequently, starting from B, the policymaker's preferences revert to MR. and A becomes the target of choice once again. Monetary policy is tightened and we move down the short-run $PC\pi^l = 4\%$ to point C. As lagged inflation adjusts (and the $SRPC$ shifts downwards), the policymaker eases monetary policy and allows some expansion of output. Eventually we return to point A through the sequence described in more detail in section 5.3. Depending upon the political pressures, the policymaker may repeat the experiment. The outcome, as is clear from figure 8.1, is that the rate of inflation will oscillate between the points A and B (between two and four per cent, in our example). Since A represents what we earlier called the optimal rate of inflation, it follows that the *average* rate will exceed the optimal. Policy suffers from an inflation bias.

Although the idea that political pressures can give monetary policy an in built inflation bias is quite widespread, there are some problems with the proposition that need at least a brief mention. The first is one of evidence. The notion of an inflation bias stems from the early 1970s and was the product of rising inflation in the late-1960s and high inflation through most of the 1970s. Set in a historical context, this is a very short period of time when compared with the existence of popularly-elected governments. If inflation bias is the *inevitable* result of pressures that are endemic in a democracy, then how do we account for the long periods of price stability before, and since, this brief inflationary interlude? One might, perhaps, explain the more recent period by reference to changes in institutional structures (especially independent central banks, inflation targeting etc) since the diagnosis of inflation bias, though even this overlooks the fact that the decline in inflation during the 1980s predates most of these changes. It is worth remembering that there is no shortage of alternative explanations for the upturn in inflation after 1965: the Vietnam War, two OPEC oil shocks, the end of Bretton Woods.

The second issue relates to the use of the term 'the optimal rate of inflation' to describe that rate of inflation which forms the lower bound of the inflation bias. We defined it very pragmatically as a rate close to zero but leaving a small positive margin as protection against a number of practical problems. And we noted that in most discussions it hovered around two per cent. But if, in a democratic system, the pressure is on to elect governments that deliver a higher and fluctuating rate of inflation we have to ask why the electorate, which is usually assumed to be blessed with quite remarkable foresight and access to information, makes this error *repeatedly*. At the very least we have to consider the uncomfortable possibility that the electorate does not see a low single digit inflation rate as 'optimal' at all. This is not altogether surprising if we stop to think that the meaning of 'optimal' in this debate has a very narrow foundation. It is based, of course, on the view that there are various costs or inefficiencies associated with higher rates of inflation — costs and inefficiencies which can be identified by economists even if they are not readily apparent to the population at large. This may or may not be an acceptable use of the term 'optimal' but the idea that this optimal rate is preferable to all other rates in some moral or political sense is clearly false. It is simply the rate that economists would choose.

Our inflation bias argument so far has been based upon the notion that the policymaker, especially if it is an elected government, might have incentives to run the economy at unsustainable levels of output. In box 5.1 we noted a second argument which makes reference to public services. The starting point here is rather similar to our earlier discussion. Governments are seen as short-sighted, self-interested maximisers whose main objective is to hold on to power. In this they are aided by large public sector bureaucracies whose members wish to increase the size and importance of their organisation so as to increase the number of higher paid posts and their own prospects of promotion. The way to succeed here though is slightly different. It is not so much an attempt to seduce voters with promises of higher output, lower unemployment and so on as to offer them increasingly generous and better quality public services. This line of argument is an offshoot of public choice theory which applies standard microeconomic analysis to the behaviour of the public sector (Buchanan and Wagner, 2000).

Once made, such promises have to be financed and since the promises are linked to the search political support, funding them by matching increases in taxation is unattractive. Only marginally more attractive is to fund them by the issue of government bonds, since this tends to raise medium- and long-term interest rates. This leaves governments with the temptation to finance the projects by borrowing from the central bank ('monetary' or 'residual' financing). The consequence of this method of financing is that there is an increase in the money supply, equal to the amount borrowed (as there always is — recall the principle that 'loans create deposits' from chapter 2). But potentially more serious, the loan creates additional bank reserves, also equal to the size of the loan thus increasing the liquidity of the banking system and facilitating further money/credit expansion. The process is illustrated in box 8.2. In short, monetary financing of public deficits has the potential for rapid increases in the money supply. As we know, there is considerable scope for debate over the detailed effect of this expansion upon aggregate demand, but the direction of the effect is unambiguous. We can use figure 8.1 again to illustrate the consequences. As drawn, figure 8.1 show the policymaker expanding aggregate demand in order to achieve the level of output associated with A'. In the present case, there is no focus upon an output target. Rather, aggregate demand expands as a result of the monetary financing. Nonetheless, the consequences hereafter are the same *as if* the policymaker were aiming at A', as before. Fear of the potentially inflationary consequences of monetary financing lay behind the decision in the clauses of the Maastricht Treaty that established the European System of Central Banks (ESCB) to prohibit central bank financing of government deficits. This prohibition is not normally cited as an example of a monetary rule, but it was put there in order to constrain the conduct of monetary (and fiscal) policy.

Once again, there is something of a problem in this argument with the way that the voting public is treated. It is assumed that high rates of inflation are undesirable and yet voters are assumed to vote *repeatedly* for governments that behave in this monetarily reckless fashion. This suggests either that voters do not understand what they are doing, and moreover do not learn. Or, that they are perfectly well-informed but acting rationally in voting for their own preference. This suggests again that the overwhelming merits of low inflation may be more apparent to economists than to the general public.

Be that as it may, the idea that governments are subject to pressures which encourage inflationary policy is quite widely established and, as we said at the beginning of this section, it gives rise to the argument that policy might be improved if the policymaker's freedom of action could be constrained in some way — maybe the requirement to follow a rule.

A rather different case against discretionary monetary policy has been made in terms of its feasibility: that an activist policy is too difficult to operate and is bound, in practice, to make things worse rather than better. There are several strands to this argument.

Box 8.2: The monetary consequences of residual finance

The stylised balance sheets below are taken from box 2.2.

Central Bank

Assets		Liabilities	
BLcb	central bank loans to the banking system	Db	commercial banks' deposits with central bank (+)
GLcb	central bank loans to government (+)	Cb	notes and coin with commercial banks
Gcb	central bank holdings of government debt	Cp	notes and coin with the non-bank public
		Dg	government deposits (+) (-)

Commercial banks

Assets		Liabilities and capital	
Cb	banks' holdings of notes and coin	Dp	customer deposits (+)
Db	banks' deposits with the central bank (+)		
MLb	banks' holdings of loans to the money market	Fs	capital and shareholders' funds
Gb	banks' holdings of securities		
Lp	loans (advances) to the general public		
Lg	loans to the government or public sector		

Suppose that the deficit = £1bn. The central bank lends £1bn to the government and credits government deposits accordingly. The loan is an asset to the central bank (it makes no difference whether it is a conventional loan or a purchase of new government securities) and the new deposits are an additional liability. So on each side we show the change as (+).

But the government has borrowed only to finance the deficit and so it spends the new deposits on purchases from the private sector adding to customer deposits in commercial banks. So we now have (-) against government deposits at the central bank and (+) against customer deposits. This leaves both balance sheets unbalanced but the resolution is achieved when the central bank credits the commercial banks deposits with the funds spent by government. In both balance sheets we have Db (+).

Since the money supply is defined as notes and coin (Cp) and bank deposits (Db) held by the M4PS, the money supply has plainly increased (by £1bn). But consider banks' liquidity. Suppose that reserves (Cb + Db) = £1bn while customer deposits = £100bn, so that the reserve ratio is 1 per cent (= £1bn/£100bn). We have just seen that this method of funding the deficit involves adding £1bn to both sides of the ratio. So we now have £2bn/£101. The ratio is now 1.98 per cent, a virtual doubling.

Firstly, a beneficial application of discretionary policy requires that the authorities know with some precision how different policies are likely to affect the economy. There are many problems here. To begin with, there are costs involved in the collection, preparation, presentation and analysis of statistics. Some statistical series are notoriously inaccurate and figures may be changed retrospectively. Definitions may also change over time, as we have seen in chapter 2 with definitions of the money stock. Hence, it is arguable that governments do not know what is happening currently to many important variables, let alone what is likely to happen to them in the future.

It is plainly vital for the successful practice of discretionary policy that forecasters, at the very least, are able to forecast turning points in economic activity: when, for example, an economy is likely to move out of recession if governments continue with their present policy. Unfortunately, the history of macroeconomic forecasting has not been a happy one. Forecasters failed, for instance, to forecast correctly the size of the 1987 boom in the UK and the timing, size and duration of the subsequent recession. Governments also need to know how the economy is likely to respond to policy changes — but this implies a much greater knowledge of the structure of the economy than currently exists.

These problems are exacerbated by the existence of time lags in the policy process. Even if policy makers were able to recognise when action should be taken and decide quickly and correctly on the nature of that action, there would be administrative limitations on the speed with which it could be taken. Worse, a policy change may not have the desired effect on target variables for a considerable time. Obviously, the longer the time lags are, the more difficult it is to forecast the nature of other changes that will have been happening in the economy independently of the policy action. Everything becomes more difficult if the lags are not only long but also variable.

Pause for thought 8.6:

Make a list of all the lags that may be involved between a development in the real economy (say a fall in GDP growth below trend) and the earliest appearance of any evidence of the effect of a change in instrument(s) designed to correct it. Note that you are being asked to consider the time between actual *occurrence* (of event) and *recognition* (of results of policy).

Once a policy action has been taken, there is a clear need to consider how the outcome relates to the policy targets and whether it is possible to say why things have gone right or wrong. If things have gone wrong, has it been because of inadequate knowledge of the system, wrong choice of instruments, incorrect information regarding the performance of the economy, or exogenous shocks that would have been difficult or impossible to allow for adequately? Again, the achievement of objectives does not necessarily mean that the policy pursued was the best one available. It may have been possible to do better (the objectives set were, under the circumstances, too modest). Again, policy goals may have been achieved for reasons that had nothing much to do with the policy followed (for example, there was considerable disagreement about the true causes of the fall in inflation in the UK in the early 1980s and of the rapid rates of growth in the United States in the same period). Yet again, the objectives may have been achieved at too high a price in terms of the impact of the policy on other variables (such as the distribution of income).

All of these problems raise doubts about the feasibility of discretionary policy and lead us by a different route to the proposition that all governments can do is to set fixed medium-term or long-term policy rules that will provide a stable framework within which the private sector can act. Such rules are said to reduce both the costs of acquiring information and uncertainty about current and future government policies. This was the basis of the Medium Term Financial Strategy (MTFS) introduced by the UK government in 1981 (discussed in section 10.3).

This second form of argument against discretionary policy is not, however, absolute. Models have been developed showing that active monetary policy may be stabilising even in the presence of lags. Empirical estimates of the actual effects of policy in the UK have produced conflicting judgements regarding its success. Defenders of discretionary policy, while acknowledging the difficulties, are able to claim that knowledge of the working of economies has increased over the years and that better forecasts will be made in the future.

8.4.2 Some suggested rules

In any case, the argument for a rule leaves open the question of the nature of that rule: evidence is needed that there is a rule that will work better than discretionary policy. Most arguments by supporters of a fixed monetary rule have been for a money supply rule. The simplest form of monetary rule proposed is one that requires the central bank to set the rate of growth of the money supply equal to the rate of growth of real income plus the desired rate of inflation, π. A slightly more complex rule, taking account of changes in velocity, would be:

$$\dot{M} = \dot{Y} - \dot{V} + \pi \tag{8.1}$$

where $\dot{Y}$ and $\dot{V}$ are long-run equilibrium values of output and velocity (Tödter and Reimers, 1994).

Preference for a money-supply rule has been based largely on the view that a fixed-interest rate rule would be unworkable. For example, Friedman argued that it is the nominal interest rate that is observable whereas concern should be with the real interest rate, which is not observable because of problem of modelling price expectations. Stable nominal rates of interest only indicate a stabilising monetary policy if real rates of interest are constant and inflationary expectations are not changing. Maintaining a stable nominal interest rate in the face of rising inflationary expectations would involve a declining real rate of interest and hence would be expansionary; the reverse would be true if inflationary expectations were falling.

It was further argued that interest rates were very sensitive to exogenous influences and could only be kept within a target range if that range were very wide. Any attempt to keep them within a narrow band against the dictates of the market would be destabilizing. Wicksell (1898) and Sargent and Wallace (1975) argued that if monetary policy attempted to set the interest rate and not the money supply then the price level would be indeterminate, but this proposition has since been qualified (Sargent and Wallace, 1982).

Fixed rules need not be simple but may involve feedback in which rules depend on what is happening to the goals of policy and the specification of circumstances (contingent rules) under which policy actions will change. However, once feedback is included in rules, the distinction between fixed rules and active policy becomes blurred. It is for this reason that supporters of rules generally preclude the inclusion of feedback in the rule, though it is precisely because it *does* contain such feedback that the Taylor (interest rate) rule has overcome much of the scepticism noted above about interest rate rules. We look at the Taylor rule below.

The choice of a money supply rule presents a problem since, on our definitions, the money supply is at best an intermediate target rather than an instrument, since it cannot be controlled directly by the authorities. To control the money stock, they would have to adopt the monetary base as the policy instrument and we know that central banks have always rejected this approach. Consequently, raising the money supply to some sort of target status while using the interest rate as the policy instrument was bound to invite problems. As we shall see in section 10.3, in relation to the Medium Term Financial Strategy of the British government in the first half of the 1980s, it is one thing to propose a rule, it is another thing entirely to be able to comply with it.

The argument in favour of rules against discretion in economic policy has taken an entirely different form over the past twenty years through the application of rational expectations to the question of the effectiveness of government policy. The rational expectations hypothesis sees economic agents as efficiently applying all relevant knowledge to the best available model in order to predict future values of economic variables. Strictly speaking, economic agents need only act as if they know the best model of the economy. That is, it is sufficient if they derive their expectations from someone who does know the best model. However it is achieved, the forecast of a rational agent is the forecast generated by the model itself. It follows that if government policy is relevant, it too will be fully taken into account. If the best model of the economy were the neo-classical market-clearing model, government policy would not be able to move the economy away from those values determined by the operation of markets. Monetary policy would have no effect on real variables in either the short- or the long-run. This is the strong policy invariance proposition examined in section 6.3. The hypothesis of rational expectations has also been used to criticise forecasting with the aid of large econometric models of the economy (the Lucas critique). The structural parameters in such models are invariant with respect to policy changes, but if policy changes are fully taken into account in private sector decisions, these parameters will change with alterations in the policy regime. Consequently, econometric models produce errors when used to forecast beyond the period over which the data was collected in order to estimate the model. If forecast errors are inevitable, the chances of stabilisation policy making things worse (rather than just having no effect) increase considerably. Much depends in practice on how different the new policy is from the old one. A small change in policy may not change the parameters sufficiently to undermine seriously analysis based upon the model.

There are a number of ways of re-introducing the possibility of government being able to affect real values. This will be so, firstly, if the government has an informational advantage over the private sector, although in this case an argument has to be made as to why the government should not make available to the private sector all the information it has. Such an argument may be based on the resource costs involved in collecting and distributing information — it may save resources if the government collects information and then chooses its policies to produce the same results as would have transpired had information been costless and fully available to the private sector.

A second counter-argument depends on the existence of labour contracts of more than one period in length. This prevents workers from adjusting immediately to changes in rational inflation-rate expectations and introduces a fixed-price element into the model. Models may thus be partly rational, for example with full market clearing in asset markets but with 'sticky prices' in goods and labour markets. Much work has been done in recent years in developing models in which price and wage stickiness is derived from rational behaviour (see section 6.4). Other modifications may be introduced to the model that allow government to be able to reduce output fluctuations at the expense of higher price fluctuations.

Thirdly, the government may also be able to influence real values in the short-run if it succeeds in taking the private sector by surprise by reneging on its policy promises. As we'll see in the next section, Kydland and Prescott (1977) demonstrated that there may be welfare gains for the government from such behaviour. The problem for governments is that agents will quickly adjust once they realise the true nature of government policy and so the welfare gains will be limited to the short-run. Worse, the credibility of future government statements will be damaged.

Assume that the government announces a strong intention to bear down on inflation and a determination to keep the rate of growth of the money stock at a low level; but the markets do not believe that the government is prepared to push interest rates up sufficiently high to achieve its monetary growth targets and thus believe that inflation will be above the government's aim. Workers will make high wage claims to preserve their real wage in the face of the expected high inflation; employers will be prepared to make high wage settlements and will push up prices to allow for the expected increases in both wage and other costs. High inflationary expectations will cause the rate of inflation to remain high, for some time at least, irrespective of what the government actually does.

These arguments lead to the claim that governments should pre-commit themselves to fixed policy rules rather than engaging in discretionary policy. In addition to the general questioning of the rational expectations hypothesis itself, there have been two main criticisms of this approach to economic policy. Firstly, questions have been raised about the process by which agents arrive at knowledge of the best model of the economy. This is a particular problem following major changes in the economy, for example from fixed to floating exchange rates. The rational expectations hypothesis does not allow for the possibility that agents will take time to learn what the best model is under the new circumstances. Secondly, much of the strength of the criticisms of discretionary policy derive not from the assumption of rational expectations, but from its application to the neo-classical market-clearing model (Laidler, 1990, ch.5). Discretionary policy again becomes feasible when rational expectations are applied to non-market-clearing models.

An intermediate notion in the rules versus discretion debate is that there is a continuum of rules and discretion, not a clear-cut distinction between them. The 'extent' of the discretion left in any monetary arrangement is determined by:

- the nature and precision of the targeted variables;

- the immediacy of the link between policy actions and the attainment of the targeted variable;

- the transparency of the policy strategy.

The idea of imposing rules on the policymaker's behaviour is to make policy actions predictable and to hold the authorities accountable for their performance. At one end of the continuum, the authorities' objective function is precisely specified and is directly attainable through policy actions, and the public is fully informed about the policy strategy. The degree of discretion then rises with reductions in each of the three areas above.

Bearing in mind the consensus amongst central banks that the appropriate policy instrument is the rate at which they supply reserves to the banking system it is hardly surprising that recent years have ween much discussion about the design of a rule for the setting of this rate. The best known example is the rule suggested by John B Taylor (1993):

$$i_t = \pi_{t-1} + \theta_1(\pi - \pi^T)_{t-1} + \theta_2\left(\frac{(y - y^*)}{y^*}\right)_{t-1} + (i - \pi_t)^* \qquad (8.2)$$

where i_t is the official rate set by the central bank, π_{t-1} is the inflation rate in the previous period, $(\pi - \pi^T)_{t-1}$ is the deviation of inflation from its target rate in the previous period and $\left(\frac{(y - y^*)}{y^*}\right)_{t-1}$ represents the deviation of output from its natural rate. Notice that output is expressed in logarithmic form (y) so that the deviation is expressed as a percentage. ($i_t - \pi_t$)* is the target real rate of interest. θ_1 and θ_2 are constants and were set by Taylor at 0.5. The interpretation is that, in an ideal world, the official (nominal) rate would be set at a level consistent with the inflation target and 'natural' rate of output growth, i.e. the 'stabilising' rate that we met in chapter 5. To maintain this real rate, the nominal rate must be adjusted by adding the current rate of inflation. Further adjustments are then made as follows. If the current rate of inflation is above the target rate, then the nominal rate should be increased by 50 basis points for every 1 per cent of the deviation. The effect is to raise the real interest rate above its long-run 'neutral' level. At the same time, a similar adjustment (50 basis points per unit) is made in respect of the extent to which actual output differs from potential. This imparts a forward-looking character to the rule in so far as current demand pressure is thought to have some bearing on the future inflation rate.

Pause for thought 8.7:

Suppose that an economy is at its target rate of inflation and there is no output gap. The rate of inflation then increases by one per cent. What does the Taylor rule recommend regarding (a) the nominal and (b) the real rate of interest?

'Taylor-type' rules are similar in that inflation and the output gap (or some other measure of demand pressure) are the key variables in the reaction function, but the coefficients and/or the lags differ from those in Taylor's original specification.[5] One modification is to replace the first term on the right hand side by a forecast of the future path of inflation (giving rise to Svensson's (1997) observation that 'inflation targeting' is better described in practice as 'inflation forecast targeting').

No central bank admits to setting interest rates in this way. If it did, then a central bank would have no need of a committee and no need of a meeting (with minutes, voting records etc.) in order to take a decision. (Though it would not prevent a committee appearing to be making a discretionary decision while in practice, and covertly, using a rule). In Svensson's memorable words:

> Thus, if a central bank wants to commit itself to a simple instrument rule, it should announce the simple instrument rule and then mechanically follow it. This has the further implication that once the decision about the instrument rule is made, the decision process of the bank is exceedingly simple and mechanical. For the Taylor rule, it just consists of regularly collecting data on inflation and output, collecting either external estimates of potential output or constructing internal estimates, and then calculating the output gap. (Estimating potential output is a nontrivial matter, though, and a major challenge in practical monetary policy.) Once these inputs in the Taylor rule are available, calculating the instrument-setting is completely mechanical. In particular, there is no room for judgment (except that judgment may enter in the estimation of potential output). As McCallum (2000) has expressed it, policy decisions could be turned over to

'a clerk armed with a simple formula and a hand calculator.' (Svensson, 2003, p.3).

However, while the central bank may not explicitly follow such a rule, its exercise of discretion could still lead to results which are very similar to those that would follow from such a rule. Indeed, this becomes quite likely if both the rule and the model framework within which discretionary policymakers were operating share the same fundamental view of the inflationary process. As we saw in chapter 5, the Bank of England's view of the transmission mechanism from policy instrument to inflation (figure 5.1) is based upon an expectations augmented Phillips curve (equation 5.1). Briefly, therefore the rate of inflation depends upon what agents expected, modified by the pressure of aggregate demand, represented by the output gap. By comparison, the Taylor rule effectively says that the policymaker should set the rate of interest taking into account the past rate of inflation (as a proxy for expected inflation) modified by the size of the output gap.

There is now an extensive literature on the extent to which the Taylor rule describes the conduct of monetary policy by central banks in recent years. For the USA, for example, Clarida, Galí and Gertler (1998) and Judd and Rudebusch (1998), have found that variants of Taylor-type rules fit the data reasonably well, once we allow for the Fed's policy of 'interest rate smoothing' (making a series of small adjustments when the rule might suggest a single larger one). Rudebusch and Judd's (1998) study interestingly divides the data for 1970 to 1997 into three periods corresponding to the leadership of the Federal Reserve by, in turn, Burns, Volcker and Greenspan. The rule fits the data quite well in the Greenspan era while under Burns it tends to overpredict and under Volcker to underpredict. Carlstrom and Fuerst (2003) bring the data up to 2003. This reveals that official rates were above those dictated by the rule from 1995 to 1999 but that the close fit was subsequently re-established.

For the UK (1972-97), Nelson (2000) finds that the rule fits the data quite well since the switch to inflation targeting in 1992. For the 1970s, the estimated long-run response of the nominal interest rate to inflation was well below unity. Moreover, the real interest rate was permitted to be negative for most of this period. In the 1980s, control of inflation was more successful and the estimates suggest a tighter monetary policy. This tightening was manifested in an increase in the average prevailing level of real interest rates, though the estimated response to the domestic inflation rate was lower than a Taylor rule would require. Indeed, the estimates in the paper suggest that the long-run response of nominal interest rates to inflation remained below unity until the period of inflation targeting, 1992- 97. For this most recent period, the long-run estimated responses of the UK nominal interest rate to inflation and the output gap are remarkably close to the values of 1.5 and 0.5 respectively, found by Taylor (1993) to be a good description of recent US monetary policy.

Clarida, Galí, and Gertler (1998) looked at the record of the Bundesbank from 1970 to 1996 and found that its interest rate decisions were 'encompassed' by the parameters in the original Taylor rule. It typically pushed up nominal short-term interest rates by about 130 to 160 basis points (and thus the real rate by some 30 to 60 basis points) for every 1 percentage point rise in expected inflation one year ahead, holding the output gap constant, and that it reduced the nominal (and real) short rate by about 25 to 50 basis points for every 1 percentage point shortfall in output relative to potential, holding expected inflation constant. There are significant differences, however, between the rules based on Bundesbank behaviour and the original Taylor rule with respect to the equilibrium real interest rate which appeared to vary between 3.25 per cent and 3.75 — while in the original Taylor rule the neutral rate was assumed to be 2 percent.

In a 1999 paper for the Bank for International Settlements, Gerlach and Schnabel showed that a conventional Taylor rule captured the behaviour of average interest rates in the EMU area in the 1990-1997 period, with the exception of the period of exchange market turbulence in 1992-93, extremely well. Inevitably, this gives us very little guide as to what may have happened after the major discontinuity represented by the formation of EMU and the passing of responsibility for policy to the ECB. regards the ECB, the jury is out.

8.5　Time inconsistency

In the previous section, we looked at three arguments that monetary policy outcomes would be improved if the policymaker were to follow a rule. These were summarised in box 8.1 as political pressures for higher output and more generous public services and also that a successful discretionary policy was very difficult to operate for a variety of practical reasons.

In this section, we look at another argument that could be used to support the case for rules, though in practice it is more often used in support of transferring the conduct of monetary policy to an independent central bank (see section 8.6). The argument is similar to those we saw in section 8.4, in that the policymaker is tempted to expand output beyond its natural level. But in this case, the pressures to do so are not restricted to a desire to be re-elected. They are more deep-seated and apply to *any* policymaker whose loss function incorporates benefits from higher output. The foundations of the time inconsistency argument were laid by Kydland and Prescott (1977) and Barro and Gordon (1983). Before we begin we should note two things about the original argument. Firstly, the policymaker's loss function included inflation and unemployment rather than inflation and *output* as we have done up to now. This makes no difference to the theoretical argument since we know that changes in output are associated with changes in unemployment through Okun's Law (see section 6.2). Secondly, in the standard tradition of the macroeconomics of the day, the policy instrument was assumed to be the money *stock*. But this also is of little significance. We can simply talk of a loosening or tightening of monetary policy, knowing by this that we mean lowering or raising the real interest rate.

We begin with the New Classical position and the policy irrelevance proposition that we left in section 6.3, and to the idea that the expectations of market agents regarding the rate of inflation depend on their view of the likely behaviour of the authorities, specifically the expected conduct of monetary policy. In such a world, the monetary authorities could assist market agents in the formation of expectations by following a clear monetary rule or, at least, announcing targets for the rate of growth of the money supply or some other indicator of the policy stance. There would be no point in attempting to mislead market agents because, to be effective, they would need to do so in a consistent direction. That is, if the authorities wanted to reduce unemployment they would always need to adopt a policy which was more expansionary than agents expected. However, market agents would soon realise that the authorities were always trying to spring a monetary policy surprise and would adjust their inflation expectations accordingly. In other words, agents would make a judgement regarding the credibility of the policy announcements of the authorities.

The credibility of a particular policy statement would depend on:

(a) the performance of the policy authorities in the past (their reputation) and

(b) the nature of the policy institutions.

Even if the policy authorities were not to be trusted, institutional arrangements might prevent them from attempting to mislead the public. For example, the authorities might be pre-committed to following a particular policy. This might make their policy statements credible in the view of market agents. This is related to the notions of **time consistency** and inconsistency. Kydland and Prescott introduced these terms in 1977, although the ideas behind them are not new. A time consistent equilibrium is another version of long-run equilibrium. A time inconsistent equilibrium is one that, for one reason or another, cannot be sustained.

In Kydland and Prescott's model, the policymaker is engaged in a strategic dynamic game over a period with sophisticated forward-looking private sector agents (agents who employ rational expectations). They argue that, in such circumstances, '...discretionary policy, namely the selection of that decision which is best, given the current situation, does not result in the social objective function being maximised' (Kydland and Prescott, 1977, p.463). What this means is that if a government formulates and announces an optimal policy and private agents believe this, in subsequent periods the policy may not remain optimal. This is because, in the new situation, the government has an incentive to renege on the previously announced optimal policy. This change in the optimal policy over time is known as time inconsistency. More formally, the optimal policy computed at time t is time-inconsistent if re-optimization at time $t+n$ produces a different optimal policy. The fact that policies may be time-inconsistent significantly weakens the credibility of policy announcements by the authorities since market agents are always aware that the authorities might not carry out the promises made in the first period.

Kydland and Prescott employ the New Classical version of the Phillips curve to illustrate this view that discretionary policies are incapable of achieving an optimal equilibrium. Assume that the monetary authorities can control the rate of inflation perfectly, that markets clear continuously and that economic agents have rational expectations. Then:

$$U_t = UN + \psi(\pi_t^e - \pi_t) \qquad (8.3)$$

where UN is the natural rate of unemployment and ψ is a positive constant. In section 6.2, we wrote the Phillips curve in output form as:

$$\pi_t = \pi_{t-1} + \alpha_2.(Y - Y^*) \qquad (6.4)$$

where π_{t-1} could be interpreted as expected inflation. We can rearrange equation 6.4 to to give an alternative version of equation 8.3, as:

$$Y_t = Y^* + \frac{1}{\alpha_2}(\pi_t - \pi_t^e) \qquad (8.4)$$

Kydland and Prescott assume that there is a social welfare function of the form:

$$S = S(\pi_t, U_t) \qquad (8.5)$$

where $S'(\pi_t) < 0$ and $S'(U_t) < 0$. That is, both inflation and unemployment are undesirable and so a reduction in either or both increases social welfare. This is a very general description of the social welfare function. If we try to write this in terms of the loss functions with which we are familiar, there are many specifications which will satisfy these conditions. All that is required is that utility increases with a reduction in inflation and a *rise* in output. The following meets those requirements:

$$L = \pi^2 - Y^2 \qquad (8.6)$$

or, if we wish to target a specific rate of inflation:

$$L = (\pi - \pi^T)^2 - Y^2 \qquad (8.7)$$

We shall see that the time inconsistency problem arises because the loss function is written in such a way that there are *always* gains to be made from increasing output (or, of course reducing unemployment). A consistent policy seeks to maximize (8.7) subject to the Phillips Curve constraint in (6.4).

Pause for thought 8.8:

Why should games between market agents and the government be non-cooperative?

The form of game proposed by Kydland and Prescott is a dynamic non-cooperative Stackelberg game in which the dominant player (the government) acts as
leader and the remaining players react to its strategy. Both market agents and the
government seek to maximize their own objective functions subject to their perception of the strategies adopted by the other player. Thus, the government, as
leader, decides on its optimal monetary policy taking into account the likely reaction of the followers. The response of market agents, in turn, depends on their
expectations of the future behaviour of the government.

Figure 8.2: Time inconsistency

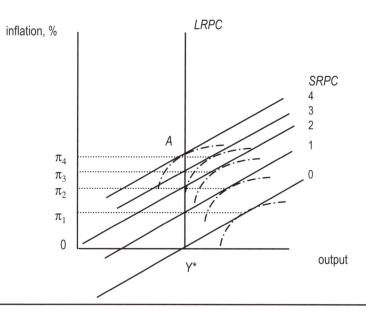

Barro and Gordon (1983) constructed a model to illustrate the ideas of
Kydland and Prescott. This represents equations 8.3 and 8.5 by an expectations-
augmented Phillips curve and a set of indifference curves showing the willingness of the community to trade off inflation against unemployment. We do the
same in figure , but it is drawn in output form and so it is based on equations 8.4
and 8.7.

If the economy is at the natural rate of unemployment (on the vertical Phillips
curve) with zero inflation, it is always possible for the government to expand the
economy along the short-run Phillips curve associated with an expectation of
zero inflation. In doing so, it reaches a superior indifference curve. Welfare is
temporarily increased. The reduction in unemployment is at the expense of higher inflation but the combination is thought preferable to the existing one. If we
think of the social welfare function as indicating electoral popularity, democratically elected governments will always opt to expand the economy in this way.
Hence, the position with zero inflation and the natural rate of unemployment is
time inconsistent in a democracy because a democratically elected government

always seeks to expand the economy. But the same will be true of any policymaker who regards an increase in output (reduction in unemployment) as desirable. The point of tangency between an indifference curve and the short-run Phillips curve associated with an expectation of zero inflation yields the highest level of utility the policymaker can achieve, *given the it is starting from zero inflation.*

We know from the expectations-augmented Phillips curve analysis that the economy cannot remain at this point since points to the right of Y^* imply mistaken expectations or sticky prices. The policymaker has brought the economy to this point by causing a higher rate of inflation than that expected by market agents. As soon as market agents realise this, they adjust their inflation expectations. Money wages rise to restore the original real wage and unemployment moves back to the natural rate — we return to a point on the vertical Phillips curve but now at a positive rate of inflation.

Although we are now worse off than when we started, there appears once again to be a welfare gain to be had by expanding the economy along the *new* short-run Phillips curve ($SRPC1$). The process continues, generating a higher rate of inflation with a matching $SRPC$ until we reach a point at which the existing short-run Phillips curve is tangent to an indifference curve on the long-run Phillips curve (A). At that point, there can be no welfare gains from expanding the economy since any move up $SRPC4$ would take us to an indifference curve further away from the origin, which no rational policymaker would want as a matter of choice. Thus, this point is time consistent. It is on the vertical Phillips curve, with the expected and actual rates of inflation equal (there is no money illusion). The policymaker can obtain no advantage from seeking to move the economy away from this position. However, the position is sub-optimal since the economy could have the same level of unemployment with a zero rate of inflation.

This time consistent rate of inflation varies from country to country depending on the form of the social welfare function and on the level of the natural rate of unemployment. Countries in which governments can increase their popularity markedly through short-term reductions in unemployment have high equilibrium inflation rates. Countries in which people are more concerned about inflation have lower equilibrium inflation rates.

The addition of rational expectations to the analysis removes all intermediate steps. Starting from zero inflation and the natural rate of unemployment, the economy moves up the vertical Phillips curve to the time consistent position at the equilibrium rate of inflation. This occurs because rational market agents understand that the government is always seeking to expand the economy and they immediately build the expected (equilibrium) inflation rate into their price- and wage-setting behaviour. The Barro-Gordon model (drawn for inflation and output) is shown in figure 8.3. A government from a high inflation country cannot easily lower the equilibrium inflation rate. Any announcement of a tighter monetary policy than that followed in the past will not be credible to market agents. We begin at E. The monetary authorities announce a target rate of inflation of zero, to be achieved by a dramatic tightening of monetary policy. If this announcement is credible to market agents, they revise downwards their expected rate of inflation, causing the Phillips curve to shift down from E to Y^*. However, market agents are aware that if this occurred, the authorities would renege on their promise and cut interest rates in order to move to S, with the result that the economy would finish at E. Consequently, the announcement of a zero target rate of inflation is not credible. As a result, market agents continue to

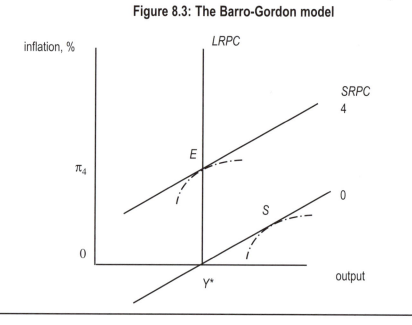

Figure 8.3: The Barro-Gordon model

build into their wage-setting behaviour, the old, higher rate of inflation.

What then happens if the monetary authorities do follow the announced policy? The rate of inflation falls and now lies below the expected rate of inflation. Real wages and unemployment rise (we are now to the left of the vertical Phillips curve with output below and unemployment above the natural rate). The economy could remain in this position for a prolonged period, at a high cost in terms of lost output and additional unemployment. If, after some time, market agents begin to believe the government has changed and lower their expectations regarding the equilibrium inflation rate, we temporarily reach Y^*, only for the process to begin again.

Thus, only unanticipated increases in nominal income have an effect on real variables. All of the transmission channels from money to nominal income lead to the same result: no impact on real variables either in the long- run or the short-run. One escape route from this position is provided by the policymaker accepting pre-commitment to a tight monetary policy. However, policymakers can improve the situation by building up a reputation for keeping the inflation rate low. If they were to act always according to their announcements, the long-term equilibrium could occur at zero inflation and the natural rate of output. In macro-economic policy terms, governments might pre-commit by the acceptance of fixed or *a priori* rules. Hence, as we said at the outset, the time inconsistency proposition can be seen as another argument in favour of the policy rules in the preceding section. If the policymaker is an elected government, then a popular alternative to pre-commitment is to transfer power over macroeconomic policy from elected governments to non-elected bodies such as independent central banks, which are assumed not to face the temptation to re-optimise because they do not face elections. This is where we go in the next section.

The Barro-Gordon model has also been applied to the foreign sector in relation to the choice between fixed and floating exchange rates. Governments whose monetary policy announcements lack credibility with their own citizens might seek to borrow credibility by tying the domestic currency to a country whose central bank has greater anti-inflationary credibility. Then, as we shall see in chapter 10, the issue becomes the credibility of the fixed exchange rate system. This, in turn, can be used to support a move to full monetary union — on the assumption that the central bank of the union is independent and takes over fully the anti-inflationary stance and credibility of the central bank of the low inflation economy.

The Barro-Gordon model has been subject to various criticisms in addition to those arising from the underlying assumptions of rational expectations and market clearing. For example, Driffil (1988) argued that private agents do not know what type of government behaviour they face because they have incomplete information. They analyse the various policy actions and announcements and attempt to determine whether the government is strongly anti-inflation ('hard-nosed') or relatively soft on inflation ('wet'). However, life is made difficult for them because they are aware that 'wet' governments have an incentive to masquerade as 'hard-nosed' and may engage in 'the dissembling actions of an impostor' (Blackburn, 1992). This might mean that hard-nosed governments face a high sacrifice ratio when they follow disinflationary policies because agents mistakenly regard them as wet. The 1997 decision of the newly elected Labour government to hand over monetary policy to an independent Bank of England can be

Pause for thought 8.9:

Why might 'wet' governments have an incentive to masquerade as 'hard-nosed'?

interpreted in these terms (Milesi-Ferrettti, 1995; Bain, 1998).

8.6   Central bank independence

The dynamic time inconsistency theories were widely regarded as providing a strong case for independent central banks as a pre-commitment device. Rogoff

(1985c) suggested that the appointment of conservative, inflation-averse, central bankers would prevent the excessive use of discretionary stabilisation policies and the inflationary bias that they imply.

This provided support to the anti-discretionary policy view that had been developed over many years by public choice theorists and others. Public choice theory applies the methodology of neoclassical economics to the political process and assumes that governments seek to maximize the utility of individual members of the government by retaining power. Politicians act to maximize votes. Since elections occur frequently, governments are principally interested in the short-run impact of their policies. This implies that voters are shortsighted and judge the position of the economy only at the time of elections, forgetting what happens between elections. This leads to a number of different types of argument suggesting that democratically elected politicians are likely to favour policies that are more inflationary than is desirable for the economy in the long run.

For instance, voters can be divided into smaller groups, each of which seeks increased government expenditure in a particular area — health, education, roads, defence etc. Politicians seek to win votes by promising higher expenditure in all these areas. Thus, government expenditure rises inexorably. Governments are then faced with the problem of financing this. Beyond a certain level, it becomes politically unpopular to raise taxes. If taxes are not increased, government borrowing must increase. However, if governments borrow by selling increasing quantities of bonds to the non-bank sector of the economy, interest rates are pushed up. In a modern economy, with large numbers of voters burdened by mortgages, interest rate rises are also unpopular. Thus, vote-seeking politicians increase government expenditure and finance this by borrowing through the banking sector, thus increasing the money supply and causing inflation.

Another approach has been to consider the government as a unit, which seeks to gain advantage for itself at the expense of its citizens. It can do this by creating inflationary surprises because any expansion of the money supply provides seigniorage to the issuer of money.

Pause for thought 8.10:

Memory test: Define 'seigniorage'.

This may take a number of forms. For example, by causing inflation the government reduces the real value of the national debt. In effect, an expansionary monetary policy acts as a tax on the savings of the citizens. Recall, the expectations-augmented Phillips curve suggests that each time the government creates an inflationary surprise, it ratchets up the rate of inflation while achieving no long-run increases in employment or output.

This, in turn, fits in with the view that governments create political business cycles — unnecessary cycles with real costs for the economy, which are generated by the need for governments to face elections. Governments expand the economy in order to win elections, only to be forced to deflate the economy after the election as the inflationary impact of the expansionary policy is fully felt. This makes governments unpopular between elections but puts them again in a position to expand the economy in time to win the next election. This does not, in itself, produce ever-increasing inflation but involves real costs for the economy, as inflation falls following each election only at the expense of high, albeit short-term, unemployment. The economy faces a regular and unnecessary stop-go cycle, which creates uncertainty and interferes with longer-term growth prospects.

These arguments, too, face problems. Attempts to find evidence for the existence of political business cycles have not, on balance, been successful. Studies that find no evidence of electoral cycles outnumber those that do. All theories depend on the shortsightedness or limited vision of the voter in contrast with the rational and well-informed market agent. In any case, all these arguments have a rather dated feeling since elections in the 1980s and 1990s in most countries were won, in the main, by political parties promising low taxation and low inflation rather than high government expenditure and low unemployment as suggested by the anti-discretionary policy theories.

This reflects an over-simple view of the political process in many public choice models, in which all citizens are assumed to have similar preferences. However, since unemployment (especially long-term unemployment) is heavily concentrated among unskilled workers and poorer sections of the economy, the chances of becoming unemployed are much greater for some people than for others. Equally, the losses arising from inflation vary widely depending on household indebtedness and holdings of financial assets. In general, middle income households with mortgages and significant holdings of financial assets, but whose workers have a lower than average risk of becoming unemployed are likely to be more worried by inflation fluctuations than by output fluctuations. The reverse is likely to be true for working class households. In addition, elections are often decided by changes in the voting behaviour of relatively small groups of floating voters in swing constituencies. In the UK, the great majority of these swing constituencies have been in the suburbs of cities and in small towns and have been predominantly middle class. Consequently, in order to be elected, political parties have needed to signal a greater concern with inflation than with unemployment (Bain, 1998).

Pause for thought 8.11:

Mortgages are a debt. The real value of debts falls with inflation. Yet, the text suggests that holders of mortgages might be particularly worried by fluctuations in the rate of inflation. Is this likely to be the case? If so, why?

This is not to say that there are no cases where central banks can be unduly influenced by governments with an agenda that may be far removed from price stability (or any kind of stability at all).

Box 8.3: The money supply and inflation - the case of Zimbabwe

In this book we do not discuss the causes of inflation in detail; we are more concerned with the monetary policies used to overcome them. It is clear from the transmission diagram in figure 5.1 that the Bank of England feels that domestic inflationary pressure arises from a variety of sources but that there is no direct role for the money supply. This is typical of policymakers in most developed economies: increases in demand (from whichever source) lead (at the existing interest rate) to increases in the demand for bank loans which, when met, cause an increase in bank deposits, the principal component of the money supply. Money supply figures might, then, act as a useful indicator of an increase in demand but changes in the money supply are a consequence of changes in demand rather than a cause of them. Excessive government spending generally leads to high government borrowing which pushes interest rates up. However, while all this is true for developed economies at the moment it need not be true for all places at all times. Indeed, it may even be possible, somewhere to find a regime in which the money supply is exogenously determined and where changes in the quantity affect the level of aggregate demand in a way that is similar to that envisaged in the Quantity Theory.

An interesting case at the moment is provided by Zimbabwe, though even this is not the same as the (still) commonly told story of a developing country causing inflation by printing money, accompanied by the simplest possible version of the quantity theory of money.

By July 2008, Zimbabwe had an official inflation rate (almost certainly an underestimate) of 231 million per cent. One cause of that almost incredible rate of inflation is one we have not hitherto considered - a significant fall in the economy's output. In normal circumstances, output only falls in response to a fall in the demand for goods and services and we are not, then, in an inflationary environment since demand and supply contract together. In Zimbabwe, on the other hand, the commercial farming sector had been badly damaged by a poorly operated and violent land reform programme. Production fell sharply and unemployment increased greatly. The collapse in domestic production turned Zimbabwe from a net exporter to a net importer of food at a time when the value of the currency was falling fast as the country's foreign exchange reserves were diminishing rapidly. This had been partly caused by the country's involvement in the 1998-2002 war in the Democratic Republic of the Congo but was later aggravated by high world oil prices as well as by the deterioration in Zimbabwe's balance of trade. The rising prices of domestic food and the increasing cost of imported food helped to push up the inflation rate. The loss of international reserves removed the possibility of the government meeting interest payments on loans from the IMF which, for this and other reasons, suspended its support for Zimbabwe. Unemployment spread to other sectors of the economy. The shortage of international reserves and high oil prices caused fuel shortages that damaged all industries. We should note that the government of Zimbabwe and the Governor of the Reserve Bank of Zimbabwe also blamed sanctions imposed by the EU and the USA for the country's economic problems.

However, there can be little doubt that the major inflationary stimulus came from the subsequent actions of the government which increased government expenditure, partially to prop up the economy but also to finance the election campaign of the governing party, ZANU-PF, and of the President, Robert Mugabe, and to continue to pay the army, the support of which was vital to the government. The budget deficit increased hugely. Funding this by conventional government borrowing was not possible either domestically or internationally and so the government borrowed from the central bank which lent to the government with the inevitable consequence (see box 8.2) that the money supply and the liquidity of the banking system dramatically increased. Inflation took off, public sector salaries and payments to the army had to be constantly increased, the deficit continued to grow and so did the money supply. By 7 March 2008, 42 per cent of total government domestic debt was in the form of advances to the government by the Reserve Bank. By the end of June 2008, the government overdraft with the central bank had reached $Z83.6 quadrillion ($Z83,600,000,000,000,000) . There were other reasons for the growth of the money supply. For example, the Reserve Bank effectively acted as a division of the Treasury and provided grants directly to the agricultural and other sectors. This was just a disguised form of central government spending. As a result of these actions, broad money supply grew by 420,867 per cent in April 2008 alone.

None of this conflicts with any of the arguments of this book, although it is clear that it is not possible to counter an inflation of the Zimbabwean size and type by the conventional method of pushing up interest rates since the inflationary push is coming principally from government expenditure supported by the central bank rather than from an increase in demand by the private sector. It remains true, however, that in this example also the money supply is not exogenous (it is still the by-product of a demand for credit) and the growth of the money supply is not in itself the cause of the inflation.

Finally, it is worth noting that, with inflation of this extent, short-term interest rates do extraordinary things. Despite its best efforts, the Zimbabwe central bank could not always print money fast enough to meet the demand for it - on at least one occasion this was because of the refusal of a German firm to supply the necessary paper (an example given by the Reserve Bank of the damaging effects of sanctions). Daily cash withdrawal limits were imposed but despite actions of this type, the money market experienced periods of liquidity of shortage and short-term interest rates fluctuated wildly. In the first half of 2008, the interbank rate varied between zero and 1000 per cent.

For further details of the Zimbabwe inflation see the Reserve Bank's Monetary Policy Statement of 30 July 2008 and earlier statements. These are available on the bank's web site: http://www.rbz.co.zw

Unfortunately, for the countries concerned, this often occurs where the economy is at an early stage of economic development or has been badly affected by war or severe social upheaval. In these circumstances, the institutions of government are often weak, with little accountability and this allows unscrupulous, and usually undemocratic, politicians to exploit the central bank and its influence over the banking system for their own ends. This is illustrated in box 8.3 by reference to the case of Zimbabwe. In the case of the Zimbabwe central bank, the Governor, Deputy Governors and all the directors are appointed by the President in consultation with the Minister of Finance. Furthermore, the appointments are renewable. This breaches two of the fundamental requirements for independence as we shall see below. (Funding government deficits breaches a third). A flavour of the attitudes to economic management that can result when the central bank is deeply politicised can be gleaned from the Governor's six-monthly report in June 2008.

The divisions have not only sapped our energies but they have also created destabilizing opportunities to many among our erstwhile enemies who do not want to see us succeed as a nation of talented citizens to which God has given amazing natural resources.

The crisis in Zimbabwe is interesting in another respect. We have stressed in our early chapters that in modern economies, the central bank sets the rate of interest and the money supply is endogenous — driven proximately by the demand for credit. And we have contrasted this with notions that can still be seen in many macroeconomic textbooks that the money supply is exogenously determined by the central bank manipulating the seize of the monetary base. What the Zimbabwe cases illustrates is that 'circumstances alter cases'. Exactly how the money supply changes (and how policy is conducted) depends to some extent on the institutions and structure of the monetary system since ultimately the stock of monetary assets is the outcome of the combined portfolio preferences of the banking system, government and private sector agents. One could, conceivably, imagine a monetary system where the stock of money really was delivered by helicopter. So we should not generalise too far in our account of how monetary systems work. In Zimbabwe, and other less-developed countries, the situation is often very different from what we see in the West and other developed countries.

Box 8.4 : The Bank of England's remit

The remit sent each year to the Bank of England from the Treasury is published on the Bank's website (http://www.bankofengland.co.uk/monetarypolicy/remit.htm). The following are some extracts from the March 2007 remit.

...the objectives of the Bank of England shall be:
   (a) to maintain price stability; and
   (b) subject to that, to support the economic policy of Her Majesty's Government, including its objectives for growth and employment

...the inflation target is 2 per cent at all times: that is the rate which the MPC is required to achieve and for which it is accountable.

...if inflation moves away from the target by more than one per cent in either direction, I shall expect you to send an open letter to me...

The thresholds do not define a target range. Their function is to define the points at which I expect an explanatory letter from you because the actual inflation rate is appreciably away from its target.

However, the fact that the central bank in Zimbabwe is obliged to fund government deficits in a most extreme manner, does not alter the fact that the theoretical arguments in favour of central bank independence, in general, are open to criticism and therefore its supporters have sought to add strength to their argument through empirical studies. These have looked at the degree of independence of central banks and attempted to find correlations between this and the rates of inflation in the respective countries. These studies have largely claimed to find such correlations within developed economies as well as failing to find correlations between the independence of central banks and rates of economic growth. The implication is that countries with politically independent central banks can maintain lower rates of inflation with no loss in terms of economic growth.

In one of the earlier major studies, Alesina and Summers (1993) examined 17 OECD countries over 35 years. They used a composite index of central bank independence based on a number of indicators of independence, the chief of which they identified as:[6]

(a) the ability of the central bank to select its policy objectives without the influence of government and the frequency of contacts between the government and bank officials

(b) the selection procedure for choosing the governor of the central bank, including the length of tenure of the governor

(c) the ability to use monetary instruments without restrictions

(d) the requirement of the central bank to finance fiscal deficits.

When they examined the correlation between this index of independence and some major economic indicators, they found that more independence was accompanied by lower inflation. On the other hand, more independence was not associated with real variables — the level employment, the stability of the economy, the rate of economic growth or the volatility of economic growth rates.

Thus, Australia and the UK had more stable rates of growth than Japan, the USA and Germany, all of which had central banks that were more independent; and Spain, Australia and Italy had higher average annual rates of growth over the period 1955-87 than did Germany despite having less independent central banks and higher average inflation rates. There was a puzzle here since one of the reasons generally given for wanting to have low rates of inflation was that lower inflation would, in the long run, produce higher rates of economic growth and this did not seem to be true. Still, we can put this to one side and simply look at the correlation between central bank independence and lower inflation and the absence of a correlation between independence and real variables. Alesina and Summers, and many others, interpreted this as support for the view that central bank independence could produce lower inflation at no real cost.

This seemed sufficiently clear to Issing, then the chief economist of the Bundesbank, that he felt able to argue that '...as regards the relationship between monetary stability and employment, the findings are pretty unambiguous, and, except in the very short-term, the hypothesis of an alleged conflict in the sense of a trade-off between inflation and unemployment may be considered quite refuted' (Issing, 1993, p.14). There were, however, several difficulties with these studies.

Firstly: the index employed. While there was general agreement on the characteristics associated with independence, they had to be weighted to produce a composite index of independence. Different researchers could use different sets of weights and, hence, rank central banks differently in terms of independence. There were also problems in deciding whether central banks fulfilled the various criteria, especially when there were differences between the constitutions of the banks and their performance. For example, the average length spent by governors in office might, in practice, be rather different from the term of office specified in the constitution. Again, Issing (1993), in distinguishing between functional independence (related to the legal framework) and personal independence asked how the courage, steadfastness, and skill of the members of the decision-making body could be measured. Crawford (1993) suggested that Alesina and Summers had either overlooked differences in customs and traditions among countries or handled them arbitrarily. Overall, although it was accepted that the Bundesbank ranked highly on any index, there was sufficient doubt about other central banks to query the apparent correlations between independence and inflation rates.

Secondly: correlation is not causality. The existence of a correlation between central bank independence and low inflation does not necessarily indicate a causal relationship from degree of independence to inflation rates. Any correlation could be accidental or a third factor might be responsible for both the independence of a central bank and the low rate of inflation. For example, the low rates of inflation in Germany may have been due principally to a strong anti-inflationary attitude among German people following politically and socially damaging episodes of inflation. This meant that there was, for a long period, little or no disagreement among the major political parties over the need to keep inflation rates low. This made it easy for the government to accept the conduct of monetary policy by an independent central bank. German governments may well have followed much the same monetary policy as that chosen by the Bundesbank. Even Alesina and Summers acknowledge that the excellent anti-inflationary performance of Germany might have had more to do with the public aversion to inflation than the existence of an independent central bank.

Thirdly: regional diversity. In the cases of both the USA and Germany, a major reason for establishing an independent central bank was to limit the extent to which regions of the countries were dominated by distant financial and political centres: both the Federal Reserve and the Bundesbank have strong regional representation on their central governing boards. It can be argued that this kept the central banks in touch with the real economies in the regions and led to some tempering of monetary policy. Thus, while control of inflation may have remained the central aim of policy in Germany (reflecting a national consensus), there has been little feeling that the interests of the financial sector of the economy have dominated the central bank. Any reading of the reports of the US and German central banks shows them to have been highly pragmatic institutions. Thus, it seems clear that any relationship between the nature of a central bank and inflation performance within its economy is a highly complex one and that simple correlations between them do not advance the argument far.

Finally: the distinction between types of independence. One might argue that the studies failed to follow up the distinction between 'full' independence and 'operational' independence — where the central bank was free to set the policy instruments but was obliged to set them to achieve a target set by government. In those cases where central banks with limited, operational, independence achieved low inflation outcomes, this could clearly be due to the 'remit' or instructions given to the bank by government. In this case, it is not independence that is responsible for the low inflation but the remit. And if this is imposed by government then we have the rather curious case that the low inflation outcome depends upon the government having issued instructions for a low inflation outcome. One is bound to wonder, why, if government can impose a low inflation target on a central bank, it cannot operate a low inflation policy for itself. Box 8.4 shows extracts from the remit given by the UK government to the Bank of England.

Other writers sought explanations for differences in monetary policy in the other functions central banks were required to carry out. For example, Issing (1993) stressed the importance of the German decision to separate the monetary policy role (given to the Bundesbank) from that of responsibility for bank supervision (given to the Federal Banking Supervisory Office).

Again, changes during the period in the degree of independence of central banks and in rates of inflation presented difficulties. Inflation rates had tended to converge, which might have been due to increased central bank independence, but might also have been influenced by other factors such as changing government views of the possibility of exploiting a trade-off between inflation and unemployment or changes in labour market organisation. Indeed, Campillo and Miron (1997) argued that the empirical correlation between inflation and central bank independence disappeared once other potentially explanatory variables that might account for cross-sectional variations in average inflation rates were incorporated into the analysis. Such factors included a measure of political instability, the ratio of imports to GDP, the ratio of debt to GDP, and income.

Despite these doubts, the 1990s saw a widespread acceptance among economists and politicians of the desirability of politically independent central banks. This was translated into action in many countries. In Europe, the Maastricht Treaty on European Union (1992) required that the national central banks of all members of the future monetary union should be politically independent while the European Central Bank itself would be independent of all governments and of the European Commission. This was largely responsible for the increased independence granted to the central banks of France, Spain, and Italy. This requirement of economic and monetary union was needed to help to persuade financial markets that monetary policy after monetary union would be as determinedly anti-inflationary as Bundesbank policy had been. Market confidence in the future single currency was needed, in turn, to convince the low inflation countries, notably Germany, to give up their domestic currencies.

This need to persuade financial markets was part of the acceptance, in a world of highly mobile capital, of the dominance of financial markets. It is now taken for granted that a country's long-term interest rates might fall if only, and only if, governments can convince the financial markets of the credibility of their expressed determination to keep inflation low. Handing control of monetary policy over to the central bank was seen as one way of achieving this, since financial markets have more trust in the anti-inflationary credentials of central banks than in those of elected governments.

We, therefore, have a classic example of self-fulfilling beliefs. We have suggested that the theoretical arguments in favour of taking the control of monetary policy out of the hands of elected governments are not strong and that the empirical evidence is rather weak. It remains that, so long as these views are accepted in financial markets, it is in the interests of governments to accept them also. Strength is added to this proposition by the view that governments are not, in practice, giving up a great deal since the increased mobility of international capital has made it increasingly difficult to operate national monetary policies markedly different from those being followed in other countries.

Despite the widespread support for central bank independence, there has been much concern over the question of accountability. 'Accountability' has been defined (ECB 2001 p.126) as 'the principle that an institution with decision-making authority is held responsible for its actions'. Clearly, the bank should ultimately be accountable to the public since it administers monetary policy on behalf of the economy as a whole. The only way this can happen is through accountability to parliament and/or the government in power. However, the political system in operation in developed countries is representative democracy. Thus, for accountability to the public to have any meaning at all, it must be clear to the public what the bank is trying to achieve and what it is doing in order to meet its objectives. If this is not so, members of parliament will not be able to represent the views of their constituents over the behaviour of the bank. This introduces the different but related (and often confused) issue of transparency. The European Central Bank defines 'transparency' narrowly as requiring the provision of information about the internal decision-making process and more broadly as 'explaining how monetary policy is used to achieve the mandate assigned' (ECB, 2001, p.57). We shall return to both issues when we consider individually the Bank of England, the ECB and the Federal Reserve. Here, we are concerned particularly with the issue of accountability.

Concern over accountability has been expressed in a variety of ways. For public choice theorists, members of boards of independent central banks, like everyone else, seek to maximize their own utility and it is not clear that this coincides with the maximisation of social welfare. For example, Milton Friedman preferred the idea of a monetary rule to central bank independence partly because he was worried that central bankers might be strongly influenced by particular inter-est groups, notably by the banking sector. Forder (2002) takes a rather similar view in his analysis of the ECB. He argues that its behaviour shows many of the signs that one would expect from a bureaucracy trying to maximise its own inter-ests and that it is completely unaccountable in the sense that no consequences, in the form of sanctions, follow from its failure to achieve its targets. Many on the left of the political spectrum have deplored the loss of democracy involved in allowing important economic decisions to be made by unelected people. Even Rogoff (1985c), who was strongly in favour of monetary policy being put in the hands of an independent conservative[7] central banker , accepted that there might need to be a clause in the central bank constitution allowing policy makers to overrule the central banker when the economy was hit by large shocks.

The analysis of the behaviour of independent central bankers has sometimes been cast in the form of a principal/agent problem, with the government (on behalf of the society) as the principal and the central bank as the agent. The difficulty lies in ensuring that the agent acts to achieve the goals of the principal. In terms of the theory earlier in the chapter, any doubt about the behaviour of the agent results in a time consistency problem, even in the case of independent central banks. Thus, much has been written on the question of the constitution of central banks, includ-ing attempts to design an optimal incentive contract for the central banker, which would leave him with full flexibility but avoid the time inconsistency problem (Walsh, 1995). Blinder (1997), however, rejects this approach because the principal (the government) may not have an incentive to enforce the contract on the central banker (the agent). That is, even if an optimal contract were designed for the cen-tral bank, the time inconsistency problem would still remain but would be shifted from the central bank back to the government.

Lohman (1996) takes a rather different line. She suggests that monetary authorities able to grant independence to a central bank in order to bring about lower inflation should, logically, also be able to operate directly a monetary poli-cy that would ensure lower inflation. All that is needed is for the public (now regarded as the principal) to be able to punish the monetary authorities (now the agent) for failing to deliver the low inflation that we are assuming the public ulti-mately want. This requires policy decisions to be made visible so that the public can easily monitor what the authorities are doing. Thus, visibility and accounta-bility are the best guarantees for monetary stability in a democracy. There might still be a case for delegating monetary policy to an agent with clear responsibili-ties at arm's length from the government to increase the possibility of monitoring by the public and parliament by distinguishing one public task from others. However, she sees this as quite different from independence.

We can relate this argument to an earlier point — the idea that central bank independence can only be achieved when there is general public agreement (as shown by election results) on the overriding importance of controlling inflation. In this case, the independence of the bank might not be the cause of low inflation but simply the institutional arrangement chosen to deliver it. It also raises another issue — the distinction between goal independence (freedom to set the goal of monetary policy) and instrument independence (freedom to set the value of instruments in order to achieve the goal). A central bank (such as the Bank of England) that has instrument independence but not goal independence could be judged to fall into Lohman's second category of a delegation of monetary policy, which is quite different from full central bank independence. Much depends on the sanctions available to the government if the central bank fails to deliver the goal set by the government.

8.7   Transparency in policymaking

Alongside the benefits of independence, it has often been argued in recent years, that policy outcomes are improved if the central bank operates with a high level of 'transparency'. This is a rather curious word to use to describe something which is 'clearly visible to all', nonetheless it is in widespread use. There are three lines of argument here.

Firstly, transparency and credibility. In so far as being open about the inflation target and operating methods makes it easier for agents to hold the central bank to account, 'transparent' central banks have more incentive to deliver. And we have already met some of the benefits of credibility. With greater credibility, the sacrifice ratio is reduced. In figure 5.2, for example, where the policymaker is trying to reduce inflation by moving the economy down a given *SRPC* to point *B* (in the lower panel), there is a loss of output (and a rise in unemployment). As figure 5.2 shows, some loss is involved for the whole period that the economy lies to the left of the *LRPC*. How long this is, depends on how long it takes for the *SRPC* to shift down (to *A*) and this depends in turn upon how quickly expectations (or price-setting behaviour) adjust to the policymaker's intentions. If these intentions are recognised and believed, then the adjustment should be quicker and the losses smaller. This is the basis of the paper by Chortareas *et al.*, (2003).

Secondly: transparency reduces noise. This in turn reduces the possibility for error in private sector decision-making. Important here is that private sector agents understand the model of the economy with which the policymakers are operating. This helps anchor the public's expectations about future policy moves (Bean, 1998 p.1796) and is the main argument behind the Bank of England's ambition to make monetary policy 'boring' (King, 1997, p.440). If agents understand how the central bank's mind works, then they can anticipate the next policy move, as though they were making policy for themselves. In these circumstances, the 'news' is in current economic developments and not in any subsequent interest rate change that the central bank might initiate in response. If this can be achieved, then monetary policy actions themselves no longer risk adding to the noise and general instability in the economy.

Thirdly: the structure of interest rates. This argument follows from the break-down of the policy ineffectiveness proposition that we discussed in section 6.3. This is that monetary policy actions do have an effect upon the real economy but that the transmission mechanism often involves medium or long-term interest rates, while the policy instrument is invariably a very short-term rate. What links the two is often said to be 'expectations' and from this it is argued that agents' expectations are more likely to be correct if they fully understand the thinking behind the authorities' actions. If all this is true, then policy transparency enhances the effectiveness of stabilisation policy. (Blinder *et al.*, 2001; De Haan and Amtenbrink, 2002; Woodford, 2001; Freedman, 2002).

Table 8.1: Central bank transparency - rankings by study

	Fry et al. (2000)	Eijffinger & Geraats (2002)	De Haan & Amtenbrink (2002)	Bini-Smaghi & Gros (2000)	Goldman Sachs* (2000)	Waller & De Haan* (2004)
Australia	15=	7=	-	-	-	-
Canada	13=	4	3	-	-	-
D Bundesbank	25=	-	6	5	2	5
Eurozone	-	5=	4	2	4	6
France	40=	-	-	-	-	4
Italy	12	-	-	-	-	1
Japan	5	7=	-	-	-	3
New Zealand	4	1	1	4	-	-
Sweden	1=	3	-	-	-	-
Switzerland	8=	9	-	-	-	-
UK	3	2	2	1	3	2
US	1=	5=	5	3	1	7

Sources: see text. Note: * = survey of market opinion

Attempts to measure the degree of monetary policy transparency have taken three broad forms. The first, very reminiscent of the central bank independence literature of the last section, might be called the 'characteristics approach' since it lists the characteristics which seem necessary a priori for transparency (in all its dimensions) and then checks them against individual policy regimes. Such characteristics include:

- a fixed schedule of policy decision dates;
- the publication of the minutes of the meeting at which the decision is taken;
- publication of the voting record (where a committee is involved);
- a quantified inflation target;

- publication of the macroeconomic data underlying the decision (e.g. an *Inflation Report*);

- and an explanation of the macromodel used by the policymakers.

A second approach is to use survey evidence. Since money market traders have a powerful commercial incentive to anticipate central bank interest rate changes, it seems reasonable to assume that such agents will be particularly well-informed as to the principles guiding central bank decision-making and will hold strong views on how easy it is to understand those principles.

Thirdly, some studies have looked at the behaviour rather than the opinion of professional traders to see what this reveals about their ability to understand central bank thinking. Although there are many ways of doing the empirical tests, the central logic is to look at the extent to which market rates (determined by traders) anticipate the subsequent decision of central banks regarding the official rate. This is the ultimate and most direct test of the King ambition that the 'news' should be in the macroeconomic news and not in the central bank's decision.

It also addresses Daniel Thornton's (2003) reservations about the tendency to pursue transparency as an end in itself. Thornton issues a number of cautions. Prime amongst these is the argument that economists should view transparency as beneficial only if it enhances monetary policy outcomes and the possibilities for this are dependent upon the objectives of policy. If, for example, stabilisation were a major objective of monetary policy, then secrecy and surprise would more likely be outcome-enhancing than transparency. Transparency can only be relevant if price stability is the paramount objective. Even then, it is not clear that transparency is a necessary condition for success. 'For years, the Swiss National Bank and the Bundesbank had credibility for keeping inflation low and steady. This occurred despite the fact that neither central bank was a model of transparency'. (Thornton, 2003, p.485). If the principal objective of policy is price stability, then the ability of agents to understand and anticipate central bank decisions is one aspect of transparency that should be helpful.

Table 8.1 shows the rankings of a range of central banks as determined by a variety of the 'characteristics' studies and by two surveys. Some caution is needed in interpreting the results since the studies vary considerably in size and range. But it is apparent that, within each study in which it appears, the Bundesbank comes low in the rankings (except for the Goldman Sachs survey) and the ECB ('Eurozone') comes low in the rankings (except for the survey by Gros and Bini-Smaghi). The low ranking of the ECB is echoed, of course, in the debate between Buiter (1999) and Issing (1999) where the former laments the ECB decision not to publish minutes or voting records of meetings, or an inflation report.

As we said above, the third approach, focusing upon the behaviour of short-term market interest rates, offers a more direct test of transparency particularly if we see transparency as meaning the ability of agents to anticipate central bank decisions. Examples of this approach include Kuttner (2001) and Poole, Rasche and Thornton (2002) who have all documented the ability of US money markets to anticipate monetary policy change., the latter showing that anticipation has improved since the Federal Reserve began announcing its target for the Federal Funds rate in 1994.

The remarkable feature of those studies which shed light on anticipation in the case of the Bundesbank and the ECB, however, bearing in mind variations in data, time periods and methodologies, is the extent of their agreement that agents understand the Bundesbank/ECB decision-making process at least as well as they do in regimes noted (in the other evidence) for their transparency. Typical is the paper by Perez-Quiros and Sicilia (2002) which makes explicit comparison between the ECB and the Federal Reserve and finds '…that markets do not fully predict the ECB decisions but the lack of perfect predictability is comparable with the results found for the United States Federal Reserve.' (2002, p.4). In their study of Norway's central bank, Bernhardsen and Kloster (2002) found that market anticipation of policy was inferior to that of the Eurozone, but that the latter was higher than in the UK and USA. Coppell and Connolly (2003), looked at market anticipation in Australia using a methodology similar to that of Haldane and Read, 2000 (see below) and compared it with other regimes including the USA, UK, Canada and Germany. The data covered the period 1996 to 2002 and thus for Germany covered a period of both Bundesbank and ECB policy-making. They found '…it [was] not possible to reject the hypothesis that the level of anticipation by the markets of a rate move in each country [was] equal'. Daniel Hardy's (1998) study for the IMF rather pre-dates the interest in transparency and is a rather oblique test of anticipation. It focused directly on the Bundesbank, without comparisons, but nonetheless shows evidence of German money markets having little difficulty in anticipating Bundesbank interest rate decisions. Ross (2002) is another IMF study, this time of the ECB after three years of operation. This too makes comparisons with the Federal Reserve and the Bank of England and concludes 'That all three central banks are relatively predictable institutions with a high degree of credibility'. The study did though find that markets have had some difficulty in anticipating large changes and especially cuts in ECB rates.

The study by Haldane and Read (2000) is interesting because it decomposes monetary 'surprises' into news about policy variables and news about policy preferences. But its immediate relevance here is that it compared the response of the yield curve to 'surprises', in the UK, USA, Italy and Germany. News about policy variables shows up in movements at the short end of the yield curve and is evidence of imperfect transparency. The sample period is March 1984 to January 1997 (so for Germany it covers only the Bundesbank regime). The results are worth quoting at some length.

Looking first at surprises at the short end … these are significantly larger in the UK and Italy than in the United States and Germany. For example, in Italy the percentage surprise is between 40-80 per cent at the short end, while in the UK it is between 30-60 per cent. This compares with between 5-15 per cent in the United States and Germany, pointing towards a much better defined reaction function in the latter two countries. *This seems intuitively plausible.* (Haldane and Read, 2000 p.29. Our emphasis).

So, there is something strange here. On the basis of visible operating procedures, the Bundesbank and the ECB score relatively low on the transparency index. And yet the Bundesbank by reputation was the model of a successful central bank. Furthermore, tests of agents' ability to understand and anticipate central bank policy actions both perform relatively well. A clue to the paradox may be found in Biefang-Frisancho Mariscal and Howells (2007) which used money market data (along the lines of Haldane and Read, 2000) to look at the transparency of policymaking at the Bank of England. This found that most of the improvement in transparency in recent years dated from the decision in 1992 to announce an explicit inflation target. Little additional transparency was provided by the increase in publications (or by the move to operational independence). What this suggests is that a perfectly good route to transparency may be to make the objective clear and then behave consistently with regard to achieving that objective. Provided the policymaker does that, it can be pretty sure that financial market traders, with millions at stake, will work out what the policymaker is likely to do in any particular circumstances. They do not need a deluge of official publications. Consistency of behaviour is a large part of Thornton's (2003) explanation for the success of the (decidedly secretive) Bundesbank and the Swiss National Bank.

8.8   Summary

n the course of this chapter we have looked at all those features that have been identified in recent years as essential to the 'good' conduct of monetary policy. Firstly policy needs a clear and dominant goal which should ideally be expressed as a quantitative target for the rate of inflation. Secondly, the instrument should be the rate of interest at which the central bank supplies liquidity to the banking system. The remaining sections were then concerned with the question of inflation bias and ways to eliminate it. We noted, first of all, that there have long been arguments that democratically elected governments might be prone to being rather half-hearted in the pursuit of low inflation because there might be electoral benefits to be had from periodically expanding demand to an excessive degree. The earliest attempts to deal with these temptations focused upon rules These were also favoured in some quarters because of what were argued to be the technical difficulties of operating a discretionary policy. We then saw that these arguments have come round again in the modern guise of time inconsistency, where it is argued that *all* policymakers face an incentive to expand demand as soon as inflation is under control. The modern solution to this more recent difficulty is to place monetary policymaking in the hands of an independent central bank even though it is not immediately apparent why an independent central bank, *of itself*, should have a more conservative approach to monetary policy, nor why an independent central bank should not have its own self-interested agenda like any other large bureaucracy.

Key concepts used in this chapter

Medium Term Financial Strategy	policy instruments
Taylor rule	inflation target
loss function	intermediate targets
inflation bias	nominal income targets
residual finance	policy rule
time inconsistency	monetary conditions index (MCI)
Stackelberg game	indicators
instrument independence	discretionary policy
full independence	Medium Term Financial Strategy
policy goals	policy transparency

Questions and exercises
Answers at the end of the book

1. Distinguish between 'goals', 'targets', 'instruments' and 'indicators'.

2. It is often said that 'in the long-run' inflation reduces output and employment. What costs might be incurred in the short-run and why might these fall upon those who may not benefit from a long-run reduction in inflation?

3. Outline the arguments against discretionary macroeconomic policy.

4. Explain the problems associated with the choice of the money supply as an intermediate target.

5. Why does the ability of the MPC of the Bank of England to set its own policy horizon give it some goal independence?

...and also to think about

6. Why do you think inflation targeting in practice means the targeting of the central bank's inflation forecast rather than the rate of inflation itself?

7. Why do you think central banks have not adopted an instrument setting rule of the Taylor type?

8. Go to the Bank of England website (www.bankofengland.co.uk), find and read the latest annual remit given to the Bank of England. Identify the key phrases that:

(a) specify the current inflation target
(b) specify the priority to be given to it amongst the Bank's other responsibilities

9. Compare and contrast the merits of inflation and nominal income as monetary policy targets.

Further reading

A collection of essays which discusses most of the issues raised in inflation targeting is in Haldane (1995b). Amongst them, Bowen explains the thinking behind inflation targets in the UK while Yates discusses issues involved in designing inflation targets. Useful on UK experience also is Haldane (1995a) in the *Bank of England Quarterly Bulletin.* The authoritative source on all aspects of inflation targeting is Bernanke and Woodford (eds) (2006). A useful discussion of targets and rules for the conduct of policy is Cecchetti *et al* (2000) while Gerlach and Schnabel (2000) show that the setting of interest rates in the EMU has in practice approximated what would have followed from a Taylor rule. For an elaboration of the idea that inflation targeting amounts in practice to the targeting of central bank inflation forecasts see Svensson (1999). Targets, goals and instruments are discussed in the first part of Walsh (2003) ch.9.

For a discussion of the issues involved in choosing an inflation target see Sinclair (2003).

Two essential articles for any study of the conduct of monetary policy are provided by Goodhart in the *Economic Journal* (1989b and 1994) and a very readable account of central banking in theory and practice was written a few years ago by Alan Blinder (1998).

The issue of time inconsistency is dealt with in many macroeconomic textbooks. The two foundation papers in this debate were by Kydland and Prescott (1977) and Barro and Gordon (1983). Three papers which are very critical of the arguments in favour of independent central banks are by Forder (1998, 1999 and 2003). Discretionary policy, time inconsistency and solutions to inflation bias are in Walsh (2003) ch.8.

9 The monetary authorities and financial markets

'...little confidence can be attached to the determination that an asset bubble exists except in the most extreme of circumstances ... even less confidence can be attached to predictions of the effects of policy on asset prices.'

Donald Kohn, US Federal Reserve

9.1   Introduction

The relationship between monetary policymaking and the financial markets is complex and interesting. And if anything, it has become more complex, and certainly more interesting, in recent years. To understand why, consider the following:

- The policy instrument is a very short-term interest rate applied to the refinancing of bank reserves. The effect on the economy depends upon the response of *market* interest rates;

- the policymaker sets a short-term rate but many decisions depend upon long-term rates;

- if markets think the current (official) interest rate is inappropriate they will anticipate a change and this will be sufficient to change market rates;

- the present value of financial assets varies inversely with interest rates;

- if a low-inflation policy is credible, this will be reflected in market rates;

- a shock to asset prices has wealth effects which may enter the transmission mechanism and change the level of aggregate demand;

- investors with a choice between short-term and long-term lending must take a view about what is going to happen to future interest rates.

For all these reasons (and more) monetary policymakers have to be acutely aware of what is happening, and likely to happen in financial markets. It is no coincidence that each issue of the *Bank of England Quarterly Bulletin* begins with a section on 'markets and operations'.

In the next section we look at why it is the case that central bank money market transactions, which are usually quite small in relation to total money market flows, can have such a powerful effect on domestic interest rates. In effect we are asking the question: 'how do markets help to transmit the effects changes in the official interest rate?'. In section 9.3 we take a first look at how policymakers should react to a change in asset prices in a regime of inflation targeting. We shall see that there is a case for responding to asset price movements if there is reason to think that the change in prices will affect aggregate demand. In section 9.4 we look at a second reason for taking asset prices into account. This is where the change in asset prices may convey useful information about the future. In 9.5 we look at other possible constraints on policymaking, in particular the question of whether central banks have started to accept some responsibility for supporting financial markets at critical times. Finally, as a variation on the theme of markets as a source of information, in section 9.6 we ask whether market reactions suggest inflation targeting and instrument independence have increased the credibility and openness of the Bank of England's monetary policymaking.

9.2   Central bank leverage

In section 4.3, we saw how the Bank of England sets interest rates through its operations in UK money markets, mainly through deals in gilt repos, and that the approach of other central banks was essentially similar. Furthermore, we also looked at a number of studies of the way in which a change in the official rate was communicated to market rates. Some rates changed more quickly than others, and by differing amounts, creating temporary changes in interest rate spreads that could nonetheless last for some time. In this section we are more concerned with 'why' the central bank should be able to influence money market rates than the 'how'. At the end of the section we shall notice that this influence may occasionally break down.

The term 'money markets' refers to a range of markets for short-term loans. 'Short-term' in this context means an original maturity of less than one year, though in practice most money market instruments have an even shorter initial maturity while the average residual maturity is much less, between two and three months. The term 'money market' is usually used in the plural to denote the existence of a number of different instruments and markets. These range from what is sometimes called the 'traditional' or 'discount' market wherein bills are issued at a discount to their maturity value and have their yields quoted as a rate of discount rather than a conventional interest yield, to the interbank market which is a 'market' in which banks lend and borrow between themselves, the resulting deposits being non-negotiable. Other money markets include the CD market (in which time deposits can be made negotiable by trading the certificates of ownership) and the gilt repo market. The latter is a market for what are in effect collateralised loans, the collateral being government bonds. Note that government bonds themselves are normally thought of as capital market instruments, having much longer initial (and in most cases residual) maturities than money market instruments. The fact that repos are classified as money market instruments reflects the fact that the repo is for a short period, while the residual maturity of the underlying bonds can be anything, provided only that it exceeds the maturity of the repo deal. The pricing of repos, with an illustration of how a change in price causes a simultaneous change in yield was given in box 4.1.

The participants in money markets are banks, other financial institutions, large corporations and, critically, the central bank. Money markets are, in other words, wholesale markets dominated by professional institutional traders. The minimum denomination of the instruments is large and the personal sector has little if any direct access. Some banks offer money market accounts, offering money market but restricted as to the number of withdrawals/transfers of deposits per period of time and subject to a high minimum threshold for each transaction. Some mutual fund managers also offer unitised investment facilities for individuals wanting to get access to money market instruments indirectly. Given that the markets are dominated by professional, well-informed traders and that the instruments are close substitutes for each other (short-term, minimal risk), it is not surprising that spreads across the market are small and that rates usually move closely together. Changes in yields and spreads are often reckoned in 'basis points' (1bp = 0.01 per cent) because they are so small. Table 9.1 shows the yields on a range of UK money market instruments in May 2008.

Table 9.1: UK money market rates, %

(Bank of England official rate = 5.0)

	Overnight	1-month	3-months	6-months
Interbank sterling	5.08-4.98	5.46-5.38	5.86-5.78	5.96-5.88
Sterling CDs		5.45	5.82	5.94
UK gov't bonds				4.95
UK Libor	5.09	5.46	5.85	5.96

Source: Adapted from the *Financial Times*, 28.5.08 *http://markets.ft.com/ft/markets/*

Notice, as one would expect, that rates on assets for which Bank of England loans are the closest substitutes are closest to the official rate. Overnight rates on interbank lending are only a few basis points away from the official rate. Rates on one month money are noticeably higher and rates on three month money are around 80bp above the official rate. This may also seem small but this differential is substantially larger than its historic value of around 20bp and reflects the fall-out from the sub-prime crisis that we discussed in section (and box) 4.3.

Pause for thought 9.1

How would you explain the interest differentials shown in table 9.1?

But money markets are very large and the scale of Bank of England operations in relation to total transactions is very small, even after the reforms of 2006. (The weekly repo deals usually amount to less than 2 per cent of sterling money market operations on that day). So, as we said at the opening of this section, the big question is not 'how?' do central banks influence market rates, it is 'why?'. Why should decisions by central banks to change their official lending rate have so much leverage in these markets that many of the market adjustments are instantaneous, or even anticipated, when the volume of funds in which they deal directly is a minute fraction of the total funds flowing through these markets? To the extent that there is an analogy between central bank intervention to set interest rates and central bank intervention to deliver a desired rate of exchange the analogy is not encouraging. Central banks, and the Bank of England more than most, have often failed to defend a particular rate of exchange.

The beginnings of an answer can be found in section 4.2. In a system wide shortage of liquidity, the central bank is the monopoly supplier while the demand for central bank money is extremely inelastic (Goodhart, 1994 p.1424). The next step involves recognising that while the central bank may act only on a small fraction of money market flows, relying a great deal on convention to do the rest of the work, it could if it wished impose its will by the sheer scale of its operation if it so chose — and markets know this. This is because, although their proportion of total flows looks small, central banks are much bigger players in domestic money markets than they could ever be in foreign exchange. The creation of central bank money is virtually costless and the central bank can create as much as it needs to buy whatever quantity of securities (repo deals) is necessary to force or keep down market rates. Conversely, when it comes to imposing a rise, its power is limited only by the quantity of securities it is prepared to sell. Provided that markets know this, there is no need for an everyday demonstration. Recall too the recent changes that we noted in box 4.2. Part of the reason for offering interest on bank reserves and creating the standing loan/deposit facilities, was to increase the arbitrage impact of banks switching funds between accounts at the Bank of England and the commercial money markets — in effect, ensuring that the Bank was a sufficiently large competitor in the money markets that its decisions would have some effect.

An alternative (but not exclusive) explanation was offered by Dow and Saville (1988). This is that without central bank stabilisation, it would be very difficult for money market participants to know what the 'correct' day to day risk-free rate should be. In many monetary systems, government banks with the central bank and thus transactions between government and private sector could have big daily effects upon money market rates and they would be very hard to predict (since their timing — critical if the banking system requires end of day settlement — arises as much from administrative decision as from any economic 'fundamentals'). In these circumstances, where relevant information is very scarce, market participants are easily swayed by official statements. Provided that there is some action to back up the official announcement, the announcement itself is the key. Viewed like this, the setting of short-term interest rates relies less on open market operations and more on what has become known as 'open mouth operations'.

Until 2008, the proposition that central banks can influence a constellation of money market rates by setting just one, fairly remote, rate would have been taken as read. Because of their potential monopoly powers, we thought, central banks have immense leverage. However, recent events have shown that there may be circumstances in which central bank influence is much reduced.

To understand this, we can begin with some facts. One of these is emerging in table 9.1. There we can see that the spread between the official rate and 3-month LIBOR is 85bp. What the table does not show is that the 'normal' spread for many years was around 25bp. What the table also does not show is that by October 2008 this spread had widened to 170bp. Nor does it show that when the Bank of

England engaged in an internationally coordinated reduction in interest rates of 50bp on 8th October, LIBOR scarcely moved. In other words, the corridor arrangement described in box 4.2 was clearly not working. Recall that this arrangement provided for a standing loan facility available to banks at 'policy rate + 1 per cent'. The idea was that if banks could borrow from the Bank of England at this rate then they would not borrow in the interbank market at rates above this. Arbitrage, in other words, would prevent LIBOR rates rising above the rate on the standing facility. Since this looks foolproof, the obvious question is why did it fail. The answer lies in the experience of the Northern Rock Bank in the UK which experienced a liquidity crisis in September 2007 and, when it drew on the loan facility, found that this information was immediately released to the market and was enough to start a panic. Consequently, the standing loan facility became stigmatised and banks preferred to borrow more discreetly in the interbank market. Unfortunately, and for reasons which are explained in appendix 2, the interbank had largely seized up during 2008 and LIBOR rates were well-above the policy rate.

One final point we might make on the subject of the central bank's power over market rates is that in the consultation document that the Bank published in October 2008 on methods to revive and destigmatise the standing loan facility (Bank, 2008), the Bank was at pains to point out why it still preferred to find a solution that restricted its direct impact to the shortest possible rate at which it was supplying reserves, rather than dealing directly in a range of markets and maturities which would have allowed it to determine a whole range of rates directly. The primary reason is the belief that markets no best. Once we move away from overnight rates and rates involving only the central bank and a carefully defined list of counterparties, rates must incorporate risk and other premia as well as reflecting expectations of future rates. These calculations are best left, it insists, to private sector agents. We discuss the 2008 'credit crunch' and some related problems in appendix 2.

9.3   Inflation targeting and asset prices

We are all familiar with the volatility of prices displayed in many asset markets. At various times in the last twenty years equity and housing markets in the USA and UK have both been described as showing the signs of a price 'bubble' (and both have been the subject of sharp corrections). In the first half of 2008, commodity prices — particularly the price of wheat and oil — rose by nearly 50 per cent.[1] Given that monetary policy's principal objective is price stability, it seems natural that monetary policy should be sensitive to asset price behaviour. However, it is not a straightforward case of assuming that movements in asset prices are part of the general price level and therefore part of the inflation that policy is focused on. But inflation targets are normally expressed as movements in a consumer price index and consumer price indices record the prices of goods and services, not the price of assets.

The starting point in understanding the relationship between asset prices and monetary policy is that both policy and asset prices share the characteristic that *they are forward-looking*. Assets are held because they yield a future stream of benefits (indeed this is part of the definition of an asset) and in pricing assets markets are trying to put a value on that future benefit stream. Monetary policy, as we already know from chapter 5, involves setting the policy instrument now, with a view to its impact on changes in the price level some eighteen months to two years hence.

In practice, this forward-looking quality of assets creates two reasons for policymakers to pay attention to the behaviour of asset prices:

- A change in asset prices is likely to change the level of aggregate demand through an effect on saving, borrowing, consumption and investment;

- a change in asset prices tells us that the markets have anticipated some change relating to the future benefit stream. It may be possible to extract information about what these changes are and this information might be useful to the current formulation of policy.

We look at the first of these — the 'aggregate demand case' — in the rest of this section. The second — the 'information case' — is dealt with in the next section, 9.4.

To understand how a change in asset prices may affect aggregate demand is might be useful to look again at figure 5.1. We saw there that a change in the official interest rate, if it is communicated to market rates, will tend to move asset prices in the opposite direction. The effect will be strongest for long-dated fixed-interest assets but will apply to a greater or lesser extent to all assets since their present value is arrived at by discounting the future stream of benefits and the discount rate incorporates market rates. However, asset prices do not change only as the result of policy decisions. They may change as a result of spontaneous market events. For example, markets may anticipate an increase in the future flow of benefits, as in the case of improved profits and dividend payments. Other things unchanged, asset prices will rise. Or they may reappraise the level of risk associated with the income stream. The discount rate incorporates a risk premium and a reduction in the perception of risk produces a lower discount rate and a rise in asset values.

Staying with a *rise* in asset prices as an example, we can identify four channels whereby asset prices may affect aggregate demand.

- A rise in asset prices adds to people's perceptions of their wealth and leads to an increase in consumption (reduction in saving) at all levels of income;

- A rise in asset prices increases the wealth that agents can use as a form of collateral to underwrite new borrowing. So-called 'mortgage equity withdrawal' is one way in which households can exploit this. They borrow against the value of their house in order to finance additional consumption.

• For firms, there is the advantage that a rise in equity prices (the value of the firm), *ceteris paribus*, lowers the cost of capital. This is because shares now sell at a higher price for a given level of dividend payments and therefore a new issue of shares raises more funds for a given commitment to dividend payments.

• The exchange rate is set in an asset market — the forex market. A rise in the value of the domestic currency increases the costs of a country's exports (and lowers the cost of imports). The reduction in net exports, other things equal, is a reduction in aggregate demand. Recall too, that regardless of the fall in net exports through aggregate demand, there is a direct effect on inflation through the reduction in the cost of imports.

What all of this suggests is that the authorities reaction to a change in asset prices should be conditioned on the extent to which price changes will be communicated to aggregate demand through one or more of these channels. It is only if a rise (for example) adds to aggregate demand pressure and may therefore feed through to future inflation that the policymaker should react.

Pause for thought 9.2

How might a fall in asset prices affect the level of aggregate demand through its effects on:

a) collateral

b) the cost of capital

Looking at figure 5.1, we can now understand a number of ways in which asset price behaviour may have some influence upon aggregate demand. Where this seems likely, we would expect the policymaker to react by taking this into account in the setting of the policy instrument. This might be described as the 'normal' case — a movement in asset prices changes demand pressure and the interest rate decision reflects this. But there remain two questions relating to the policymaker's response to asset prices, not just when they are changing over some 'normal' range but when the price change is sudden and, above all, large.

The first of these is whether the monetary authorities should be willing to 'prick' asset price bubbles as they see them emerging. If we accept (as all policymakers do) that changes in asset prices can influence aggregate demand, then we have to accept that *major* instabilities in asset prices could at some point translate into major instabilities in the real economy. The UK house price booms of the late 1980s and early 2000s, together with the boom in world equity markets in the 1990s are obvious examples of plausible cases. And if these bubbles, where prices depart from their fundamental values, can destabilise the real economy they must therefore be capable of destabilising the inflation rate. If bubbles grow when left unchecked, this might be an argument for using policy to deflate them early on. The problems are twofold. Firstly there is a problem of identifying bubbles at an early stage. Since there is always scope for debate over the nature of *future* fundamentals, there will always be debate over whether prices are misaligned or whether there has been some change in risk or future profit prospects (Bernanke and Gertler, 2001). There is then the question of how such bubbles might be arrested. The famous 'open mouth operation' by Alan Greenspan when he referred to 'irrational exuberance' in 1996 produced only a momentary pause in equity prices which rose by a further 35 per cent before a major 'correction' in 2000.

The second is the question of how the authorities should react when a large change in selected asset prices threatens to feed through to higher inflation through a direct effect on costs rather than on aggregate demand pressure. This is a particularly topical issue at the time of writing (May, 2008) where the prices of oil and wheat (and consequently energy and food) have risen rapidly over a six month period. This has led to strikes and street protests in a number of European countries about the effect on the cost of living for many groups. More relevant here are the predictions that these rises, even if they go no further, could add 1 per cent to the rate of inflation at a time when that rate, in the eurozone and in the UK, is already above target.

When it comes to the question of how the authorities should respond, the first thing to note is that we get little guidance from our theory of inflation in chapter 5. As the Phillips curve equation 5.4 reminds us, this is that the rate of inflation depends upon the expected rate (or some rate otherwise inherited from the past) plus some allowance for the pressure of demand, measured by the output gap.

$$\pi = \pi_{t-1} + \alpha(Y - Y^*)$$

In other words, we have a purely demand side explanation of inflation in which costs play no part.

Pause for thought 9.3

Suppose that energy related products make up 3 per cent of the CPI and energy prices and the CPI are rising at 5 per cent p.a. in t_0.

In t_1, the cost of energy rises by 25 per cent while everything else continues as before.

In t_2, the energy price rise reverts to 5 per cent p.a. while everything else continues as before.

Calculate the rate of inflation in t_1 and t_2.

At first glance this may seem a serious shortcoming since no one doubts the ability of a sharp rise in energy costs (for example) to raise the price level. But the price level and the rate of inflation are not, of course, the same thing. Let us assume that a rise in the energy price is a one-off adjustment (which may nonetheless be spread over a number of months). This raises the price level, as measured by the CPI) by an amount which depends upon the change in the energy price and the weight of energy and energy-related products in the CPI. While the energy price is adjusting, this also adds to the rate of inflation. But once the adjustment is complete (let us assume the energy price stabilises completely) then the contribution to inflation is zero. The impact on inflation is self-terminating.

Alternatively, we can remind ourselves of the distinction between absolute and relative price. Inflation is the rate of change in the absolute level of prices. The rise in energy costs is a change in relative prices which has the usual income and substitution effects. Energy uses suffer a loss of real income as the latter is redistributed towards energy suppliers. This is how market economies work and one would not normally expect central banks to devise a monetary policy to offset relative price changes. The only issue with which the central bank should be concerned is whether the inflation created during the period of relative price adjustment gets 'built into' the first term in equation 5.4 — expected (or lagged) inflation. If it does, the rate of inflation is raised 'permanently', that is to say until the policymaker can eliminate it by increasing interest rates, widening the output gap and steering the economy precisely along the route described in figure 5.2. Many years ago, in evidence to the UK's Treasury and Civil Service Committee's (TCSC) enquiry into monetary policy, the Bundesbank distinguished between the relative price change and the *subsequent* effect on inflation. When asked by the Committee's chairman what the bank meant in its written evidence by 'unavoidable inflation' Hermann-Josef Dudler replied:

> If a situation is coming up where we feel external cost pressures such as resulting from higher raw material prices .... we do not have the illusion that we can fully offset these by a decline in domestic prices. Nevertheless, we would, in these circumstances, set a monetary target and publish a price objective which would not allow for any *secondary* domestic inflation effect in response to such external pressures...(TCSC, 1980-81, p.300. Our emphasis).

We return to the question of how the authorities should react to violent asset price fluctuations again in section 9.5 when we look, not at pricking bubbles, but at what the response should be if markets fall sharply. We shall consider whether policymakers have been rather quick to react to sharp price *falls*. This is the argument that central banks have started to become lenders of last resort to financial markets and not just to banks or, in other words, whether central banks have begun to offer free, universal, put options. If indeed it is the case that policymakers are starting to look over their shoulders for signs of financial weakness, then this market behaviour has the potential to become a serious constraint on monetary policymaking.

9.4   Asset markets as a source of information

The second role for asset prices is the potential supply of information about the future. The starting point here is that in their *current* pricing of financial assets, agents must be taking a view about future states of the world. Then it is argued that if these views are well-founded, or at least contain no systematic bias, and if those views can be derived from the current prices (or yields) then markets may be able to tell us something useful, on average, about the future. The unstated implication of the argument is that the disaggregated pursuit of self-interest by large numbers of agents, combined with their ability to learn quickly from mistakes, is likely on balance to produce a better forecast of the future than the painstaking construction of mathematical models embodying relationships estimated from past data. Indeed, the enthusiasm for extracting information from asset prices coincides with a period (the mid-1980s) when the Lucas critique (see section 6.2) combined with the poor forecasting record of large-scale structural models, to produce a disenchantment with this traditional approach to anticipating the future.

Pause for thought 9.4:

Why should markets know anything about the future?

One example of the use of financial markets for this purpose is discussed in Appendix 1 and involves the term structure of interest rates in the government bond market. Ignoring, for the moment, any term-varying risk premium that might be involved in the return on bonds of longer maturities, the term structure of interest rates should be such that current long rates reflect current expectations of future spot rates. Restricting the discussion to a 'two-period' yield curve and assuming all yields are equilibrium yields, then:

$$(1+i_2) = (1+i_1) \times (1+E^2 i_1) \tag{9.1}$$

which says that agents must be indifferent between investing for two periods at the current two period (i.e. 'long') rate, i_2, and investing for one period at the current one period (i.e. 'short') rate, i_1, and reinvesting in a year's time in the one year rate expected in the second period, $E^2 i_1$. Since we know the *current* long and short rates then from this we can solve for the *expected* future one year rate, $E^2 i_1$, as follows:

$$E^2 i_1 = \frac{(1+i_2)^2}{(1+i_1)} - 1 \tag{9.2}$$

Since the future one year rate, $^2 i_1$ is only *expected*, it is likely in practice that:

$$^2 i_1 = E^2 i_1 + \varepsilon \tag{9.3}$$

but provided that ε is a normally behaved error term, then E^2i_1 will be an optimum forecast of $^2i_1$ and the current relationship between short and long rates tells us something useful (i.e. correct on average) about future short rates.

Further more, if we now introduce the so-called Fisher hypothesis which says that the nominal rate of interest, i, is composed of a stable real rate, r, and an inflation premium, $π$, then:

$$E^2i_1 + ε = r + {}^2π \qquad (9.4)$$

Again, provided that ε is well-behaved (and provided that we know the stable real rate), then E^2i_1 contains an optimum forecast of inflation.

In practice, the picture is further complicated by the need to estimate a term premium which has to be extracted from our expectations of future rates, and as we say in Appendix 1 even more fundamentally compromised by the empirical evidence that the current difference between long and short rates does not forecast the path of future short rates particularly well. Nonetheless, while we may be sceptical of the ability of the term structure to forecast the absolute level of future short rates (and future rates of inflation) it might still be the case that changes in the shape of the yield curve (a steepening, for example) tells us something about the future direction of changes in short-term interest rates and inflation (upwards, in this case). Methods for estimating the term structure and the useful information that the Bank of England draws from such estimates is discussed in Anderson and Sleath (1999).

One reason why the Bank wishes to know the markets' expectations of future interest rates is that it wishes to know whether or not a given change in its repo rate is likely to surprise markets or not (we discuss the importance of this issue in section 9.5). In this case, the Bank wishes to know market expectations of two week repo rates for dates in the near future. With the exception of very short-dated gilts, bond yields are less than ideal since bonds are much longer term instruments than 7-day repos. But guidance may be possible from money market yields. The Bank of England currently makes judgements about market expectations of official repo rate movements from a range of market ('general collateralised' or 'GC') repo deals, interbank loans, short sterling futures contracts, forward rate agreements and swap contracts involving six month LIBOR and the sterling overnight interbank average rate (Brooke, Cooper and Scholtes, 2000). The approach is very similar to the one that we described for estimating future interest and inflation rates from the gilt yield curve and the difficulties and limited results illustrate well some of the points we made above.

Firstly, yields have to be collected from instruments which are strictly homogeneous in all respects but term. The advantage of the gilts market is that it contains a large population of bonds with varying terms to maturity but with absolutely identical risk. Money market instruments all carry a degree of risk which is greater than gilt repos with the central bank (GC repo probably comes closest). Hence estimates of future central bank repo rates derived from, for example, interbank rates, are found to have a systematic upward bias when their predictions of official rates are compared with the actual outturn. Unsurprisingly the bias increases with the length of forecast horizon, rising to about 100bp at two years. Brooke *et al* estimate that interbank rates probably contain a credit risk premium of around 25bp. But this leaves the conclusion that the remainder of the bias is due to some unknown term premium or systematic expectational errors. Similar considerations (albeit with different values) apply to the whole range of money market instruments. 'No particular money market instrument is likely to provide a "best" indication of Bank repo rate expectations at all maturities' (Brooke *et al*, 2000 p.398). In practice the Bank estimates two forward curves, one based on CG repo and the other on a combination of instruments based on LIBOR (London interbank offer rate) but subjects both to a degree of *ad hoc* adjustment.

Pause for thought 9.5:

If the central bank were to announce an *unexpected* increase in its forecast of inflation in one year's time, how would this affect the shape of the yield curve?

If the higher forecast were *expected* would your answer be any different and why?

With the development in recent years of markets for financial derivatives designed explicitly to allow agents to take positions regarding future events, the range of potential market information has expanded dramatically. In 1995 and 1997, for example, Malz showed how information in options prices might be used to indicate the probability of exchange rate realignments in the ERM (Malz, 1995, 1997). Options are contracts which give agents the right to buy or sell an asset at a given future date for a given price (the 'exercise' or 'strike' price). 'Call' options are options to buy and will be exercised if the market (or spot) price is above the strike. Thus the price of a call option is telling us something about the market's perception of the probability that the spot price *will* be above the strike price. Since the lower the strike price, the greater the probability that it will be exceeded at a given future time, the price of the call varies inversely with the strike price. Clews, Panigirtzoglou and Proudman (2000) show how an implied risk-neutral probability density function (pdf) can be extracted from a short sterling call option. A series of pdfs (from a series of calls) then tells us the probability (as seen by the market) that the sterling three month interest rate will fall within a particular range on a future date. These estimates often appear as a fan chart in the Bank's quarterly *Inflation Report*.

Given that the flow of benefits from financial assets lies in the future and thus that current price must incorporate something of agents' views of the future, scarcely any class of assets is immune from the search for potentially useful information. So far, we have considered the possibility of uncovering markets' expectations of future interest rates (of different kinds) and possibly of inflation. More ambitiously, it has been suggested in recent years that financial markets might be made to yield information about future developments in the real economy.

As with many fundamental insights into the working of financial markets, Irving Fisher (1907) was amongst the first to point out that changes in the spreads between the returns on different fixed income securities might foreshadow changes in the macroeconomy. The idea was further explored by Merton (1974), since when the growth in confidence in market wisdom has led to a near-explosion of empirical studies. The basic idea draws on the inverse relationship between risk and return. Thus, in any given economy, government paper will have the lowest rate of return, followed by 'AAA' bonds issued by the corporate sector and so on up to the returns available on 'junk' or sub-investment grade bonds. The spreads represent compensation for different degrees of risk and, provided the risk is correctly priced, must function simultaneously as an index of the risk contained in each security. It is a short step from here to assuming that changes in the spread are indicating changes in the degree of risk. The principle is familiar, indeed crucial, to investors making a choice between fixed interest securities on the basis of relative prices and yields. Hence we saw the collapse in Marconi's bond price and quadrupling of its yield after the disastrous profits warnings in 2001. What Fisher was pointing out, however, was the possibility that aggregate movements in corporate bond yields and thus in the corporate-gilt spread might tell us something not about changes in the riskiness of individual firms but about the degree of risk facing the corporate sector as a whole. If it did this, then it might be telling us something about the proximity of recession (the spread widens) or boom (the spread narrows).

Why should there be a connection between the economic cycle and the corporate-gilt spread? There are essentially two arguments which are mutually reinforcing. Firstly, the perception of the future possibility of recession causes investors to revise downward their estimates of firms' future cashflows out of which bond interest (and eventually the principal) have to be paid. The risk of default increases and so prices fall and yields rise. Secondly, the rise in yields represents an increase in the cost of capital for firms. Faced with a test that they cover this higher cost, fewer investment projects will pass. Firms will reduce the quantity of real capital demanded and this reinforces the recession. Notice that, since we are interested in spreads, nothing here contradicts the wisdom that faced with the prospect of a recession there is a 'flight to quality' or certainty by investors — from equity towards bonds. This undoubtedly happens and means that bond yields in the aggregate fall relative to the return on equity. But within the range of bond yields corporate yields will widen relative to government yields because there will be a 'flight' from both equity and corporate bonds toward government paper.

As we noted above, studies of bond spreads and their forecasting ability are many. Surveys include Stock and Watson (1989), Bernard and Gerlach (1996) and Dotsey (1998). Specific applications to the UK include Davis (1992) and Davis and Henry (1993) who found that including financial spreads in VAR models of output and prices improve our ability to anticipate turning points. The theory, and its application to monetary policy making at the Bank of England is explained by

Cooper, Hillman and Lynch (2001). One interesting feature of the recent work carried out at the Bank is that it suggests recent developments in these spreads are harder to link to the economic cycle than earlier episodes, say in the early 1990s. This is because the widening of spreads during 2000 was much more concentrated and was dramatic in particular sectors of the economy (notably in telecom and technology firms). This widens the average corporate-gilt spread but may be more indicative of sector- or firm-specific difficulties than a general downturn. On the other hand, the widening of these specific spreads will not be irrelevant to the broader picture if the firms concerned had previously been responsible for a large fraction of aggregate investment which they are forced to abandon by the sharp increase in the cost of capital.

The most recent efforts to extract information about macroeconomic trends from financial market data involves profit warnings. In the UK London Stock Exchange and the Financial Services Authority require firms to disclose to the Company Announcements Office without delay any change in the company's condition which might lead to substantial movement in the price of its listed securities. Recent work at the Bank has examined the response of returns on a company's securities to trading statements in general and to negative trading statements ('profits warnings') in particular. Two notable results, though not especially relevant to policy, are that returns begin their response to the warnings up to two days before they are made and the adjustment is complete on the day of the announcement (lending support to the semi-strong version of the efficient market hypothesis) and that the response to negative statements is much stronger than the response to positive statements. More relevant to the question of whether company news can provide useful leading information about the state of the macroeconomy is the correlation between the number of profit warnings per month and subsequent GDP growth. Preliminary results suggests that it may be (Clare, 2001).

So far we have argued that the authorities have a legitimate interest in asset prices (a) because of a possible link to aggregate demand which they endeavour to influence as part of their stabilisation policy and (b) because of the information potentially contained in asset price movements. Only if the behaviour of asset prices leads alerts the policymaker to a future change in the path of inflation is an official response called for. This is the conclusion to be found at the opening of Bernanke and Gertler (2001, p.253) where they argue that changes in asset prices should affect monetary policy only to the extent that they affect the central bank's forecast of inflation. In other words, once the predictive content of asset prices for inflation has been accounted for, there should be no additional response of monetary policy to asset-price fluctuations. To do anything else would imply that the policymaker has some responsibility for (and influence over) relative prices.

Clearly, what we have *not* argued at any point is that the authorities are (or should be) concerned about asset prices because of the changes in prices themselves. To put it bluntly, policymakers do not see the stabilisation of the housing market (or the equity market) as part of their responsibility. Whatever the media may think about the hardships facing young families who feel excluded from the housing market, questions of social equity are not the concern of monetary policy. Neither are asset prices of much concern in the measure of inflation itself. The CPI, which currently measures changes in the general level of prices in the UK, records the price of a basket of goods and services, not assets. Indeed by excluding conveyancing and estate agents' fees, insurance and council tax, it pays even less attention to housing-related costs than did the earlier official measure, RPI-X, which it replaced in January 2006.

9.5   Market constraints

The precise nature of central bank independence varies across regimes but minimally it includes freedom from political interference in the setting of interest rates and a requirement that the chief objective in the setting of such rates is price stability. This obligation actually adds to central bank powers in the pursuit of price stability. This is because it removes any dilemma that might arise from trying to pursue several incompatible objectives at once. Such 'conflict of objectives' was commonplace for policymakers (governments and/or central banks) for 30 years after 1945 as they tried simultaneously to achieve 'full employment', 'high' growth, a balance of payments equilibrium and low inflation. In the UK, the oscillation between these objectives was christened 'stop-go' policy.

   Given that central bank interest decisions have a major effect on market interest rates, given that they are free to set interest rates without political interference and given that they have a single objective, one could draw the conclusion that central banks have unlimited powers to set interest rates at whatever level they choose. This would be a major exaggeration (even before the banking crisis of 2008 – see section 9.2 above) and in this section we consider some of the constraints under which central banks have always had to work. One such constraint arises where monetary policy involves intermediate targets. Even with a single (inflation) objective conflicts can be reintroduced if policy is guided by more than one intermediate target. Such targets might be some combination of exchange rate, money growth, credit expansion and so forth. Finding an interest rate which enables a central bank to hit simultaneous intermediate targets could be as difficult as finding one which achieves multiple final objectives. But we are more interested here in constraints which arise from financial market behaviour. Many of these can be seen to be related to the credibility of central bank behaviour: they appear as the result of partial or incomplete credibility (Treasury, 2002, ch.2). One simple, but recent, example is provided by market reactions to the succession of cuts in repo rates that the Bank of England instigated during 2001. The main purpose, in a low inflation environment, was to limit the effect on the UK economy of what looked like a developing world recession. However, as we stressed in section 4.3, the central bank only has direct control over a current and very short-term nominal interest rate while it may be other rates which matter to spending decisions. These may be longer-term rates, and/or real rates or even expectations of future short-rates. These rates were much less influenced by the Bank's relaxation of monetary policy. In February 2002, the price of short-term interbank interest rate futures suggested a strong belief on the part of market participants that short-term rates were about to rise again and such expectations naturally worked against the efforts of the Bank to loosen monetary policy.

On February 19th, the Governor felt forced to make an announcement that this was not likely and markets 'reacted fast and furiously' to price in lower interest rate expectations (*Financial Times*, 20.2.02). This was another triumph, at least temporarily, for 'open mouth operations', and it is arguable that it would not have had the effect that it did in the early 1990s when Bank of England policy statements lacked the credibility that they have now (see section 9.6 below). Even so, it still shows how the effects of central bank policy can be modified by market reactions.

We are used to defining an open economy as one in which exports plus imports exceed a certain fraction of its GDP. For open economies thus defined, developments in the real economies of its trading partners will always be important. Typically, these developments involve divergent productivity trends which eventually have their effect upon competitiveness and show up in balance of trade trends and maybe eventually the exchange rate. This familiar concept of openness and its implications we might call 'real economy openness'.

Since the 1970s, under pressure from the World Trade Organisation and national governments (especially in developed economies) this openness has been promoted as policy. Alongside it, however, has been the growth of 'financial openness' with the progressive liberalising of capital markets. The result, predictably, has been a rapid growth in international capital flows, in relation to real GDP, and in relation to international trade flows. Much of this capital, therefore, is mobile in pursuit of the best returns and will respond to quite small differences in perceived risk/return combinations. In the absence of a fixed exchange rate regime, such flows inevitably cause fluctuations in exchange rates and since the monetary authorities usually have an exchange rate 'preference' (even if there is no explicit target) they can hardly be indifferent to these flows.

Frequently, therefore, it is foreign exchange flows and the reaction of forex markets that central banks must anticipate. The most dramatic example, applying to the UK in recent years, is provided by the end of the UK's membership of the ERM in 1992. The Bank of England was endeavouring to maintain an exchange rate of DM2.95:£1 at a time of rapidly rising unemployment and against background information that the UK was seriously uncompetitive with other ERM members at that exchange rate. In that particular case, the forex market took the view not so much that interest rates were 'wrong' but that the appropriate interest rates were simply unattainable. The situation was made worse by existing interest differentials between sterling and the DM and the reluctance of the Bundesbank to reduce its rates despite pressure from other EU partners. With unemployment climbing into double figures, the market gambled that the authorities (remember that the Bank of England was not then independent) would not tolerate the level of interest rates necessary to maintain DM2.95. Bearing in mind that forex dealers themselves had a great deal of influence over what level of interest rate would be necessary to achieve this, it was perhaps a reasonably safe bet. A simpler way of looking at the episode is to say that markets simply did not see DM2.95 as a credible rate of exchange, given the state of the real economy. It also shows how the choice of appropriate interest rate can be heavily influenced by the level of rates being set in other major centres. On any interpretation, it was the reaction of forex markets which brought the policy to an end.

As a paper by Cornford and Kregel (1996, p.2) shows, the breakdown of fixed exchange rates in the 1970s and the increase in international capital flows has been accompanied by a step increase in volatility, particularly of exchange rates. The standard deviation of percentage monthly changes has rose from 0.4 in the 1960s to about 1.7 since the 1980s. Their explanation for this is that the bulk of such flows now are asset flows, largely unrelated to trade and represent the application of standard capital asset pricing model principles to an ever increasing portfolio of risky assets. Under the CAPM, rational investors are assumed to diversify across the whole market of risky assets. As barriers to capital flows are reduced, additional currencies and assets become part of the whole market portfolio. Portfolio managers are then required to hold these additional currencies and assets with effects on their price which is analogous to the effect on the price of a stock which becomes a member of the FTSE-100, for example. The job of fund managers (to continue the analogy) is to earn the best returns by exploiting return differentials. Many of the newcomers to the whole market portfolio, 'emerging' markets for example, have very high yields. This may reflect a higher level of risk but if the fund manager is ill-informed about the level of risk then funds will flow to these markets, pushing up their exchange rates. Exchange rates (and asset prices and returns generally, for that matter) are no longer determined by fundamentals. Not only do these circumstances make it more difficult for central banks to pursue the single price stability objective (because of effects on import prices), they are simultaneously bound to consider the exchange rate effects of interest changes. Such difficulties have spawned a substantial literature on possible means for limiting international financial flows (see section 7.6).

More specific examples of markets constraining central bank behaviour are provided by the short history of European monetary union. In section 7.2, we refer to the difficulties for the ECB in setting an appropriate rate of interest caused by forex markets steadily marking down the value of the euro against the US dollar (from about US$1.18 in January 1999 to US$0.86 when notes and coin went into circulation in January 2002). A more interesting example, since it involves market sentiment in the design even of the institutions of policy, occurred in the spring of 2002 when the French government commissioned a report on the functioning of the ECB with a view to possible reforms. One such reform was the suggestion that the inflation target should be changed from 'between 0 to 2 per cent' to 'between 1 and 3 per cent' to remove the alleged deflationary bias which arises from setting zero as the lower limit and thus risking falling prices. Another proposal was for the ECB to publish more information about how its decisions are arrived at and to be open to examination about the decisions. In deciding upon the wisdom of these proposals, much discussion centred on the reaction of financial markets. It was argued against raising the inflation target that this would alarm financial markets and lead to further weakness in the euro while, on the other hand, markets would respond positively to suggestions to make ECB policy-making more transparent.

On 19 October 1987, the UK stock market declined very sharply, losing about 30 per cent of its value over two days. The collapse followed a large fall on Wall Street at the end of the previous week. In both cases the central banks, the Bank of England and Federal Reserve responded by cutting interest rates and indicating their readiness to create liquidity to meet the borrowing needs of financial institutions whose stability might be threatened by the fall in asset values. In the UK case at least, it was widely argued (e.g. Goodhart, 1989b) (after the event) that the Bank's willingness to ease monetary conditions was excessive, lasted for too long and helped to fuel what became known as the Lawson boom. The UK was subject to strong inflationary pressures from the beginning of 1988. The cut in interest rates began to be reversed in June and eventually reached a peak (of 15 per cent) in October 1989. This incident was the first of several in which central banks acted to support financial markets. Another was the liquidity crunch associated with the dramatic falls in South East Asian stock markets and exchange rates in 1998. Here again, central banks, led by the Federal Reserve cut interest rates and made clear their readiness to provide liquidity. And, whether as a result or not, the S E Asia 'crisis' was limited in its effects to less than commentators feared. This apparent new role for central banks eventually gave rise to the remark by the Financial Times which we quote at the beginning of this chapter. We are familiar with the role of central banks as lenders of last resort to financial institutions. If central banks have become lenders of last resort to markets as well then the effect is rather like giving investors access to a free, market wide, put option. The 1987 and 1998 incidents suggested that stock markets had acquired limited downside risk. Unsurprisingly, prices eventually reflected this. Though US shares fell sharply in the stock market crash of 1987, they then appreciated at a record-breaking pace into the new millennium. The broad-based S&P 500 index of top US companies, for example, increased 360 per cent from its pre-crash peak of about 330 in August 1987 to its recent peak of just over 1,500 in August 2000, an average annual growth rate of about 12 per cent. This asset price boom implied that, relative to the past, estimated dividend growth rates had risen, the risk premium had fallen, or there was a bubble. (Miller *et al*, 2002 p.C172)

Shiller (2000) explains the behaviour of stock prices in the 1990s as an example of a 'bubble' — driven ultimately by psychological factors which encouraged the view that rising prices would go on rising. Cecchetti *et al* (2000) first drew attention to the possibility that the price trend may have something to do with reduced risk by carrying out a small survey of major fund managers and chief economists in London and New York in early 2000. 'The results are quite clear. All respondents believe that the Fed reacts more to a fall than a rise, and all except two believe that this type of reaction is in part responsible for the high valuations on the US market.' (Cecchetti *et al.*, 2000, p.75). To see by what order of magnitude perceptions of stock market risk would have to change in order to justify the price levels of the late 1990s, they computed a long-run equity risk premium for the period 1926-97 of 4.3 per cent p.a. They then took the actual level of dividend yield on the S&P500 in early 2000 and added a dividend growth rate for three different assumed rates of growth ('low', 'medium' and 'high'). Comparing these three different equity returns against the long run real rate of interest suggested actual equity risk premia for early 2000 ranging from -0.1 (assume slow dividend growth) to 1.8 (the fast scenario) (Cecchetti *et al.*, 2000, table 3.1). As Miller *et al.* subsequently pointed out (2002, p.C173), the dividend yields required to restore the risk premium to 'normal' levels needed to be some 2-3 times higher than they actually were. Another way of expressing this is to say that, given the actual dividend yields, stocks were overvalued by the order of 50-67 per cent.

Could it be then that the long price boom was largely due to a reduction in the equity risk premium brought about by central banks acting as lenders of last resort to securities markets? This is the issue tackled by Miller *et al.* (2002). The paper shows how the belief that the Fed can prevent market prices from falling by more than 25 per cent from a previous peak reduces the equity risk premium from its long-run normal level of 4.3 per cent to about 2.6 per cent. The motivation for this piece of research was the rapid series of cuts in US interest rates following the collapse of the Long Term Capital Management hedge fund in 1998 which appeared to have been made in order to protect financial markets and asset prices from the loss of confidence that the collapse would cause. The cuts were held partly responsible for the continued book in stock process which continued to rise until the collapse of 2000. The reductions still do not justify the stock price levels of 2000, and the effect is weakened still further if agents perceive the insurance as only partial credible. But Miller *et al.* do not claim this is the only source of market overvaluation. Shiller's argument that the late 1990s represent a classic price bubble is almost certainly true for technology stocks; there may well be genuine reasons for a lower risk premium to do with better risk management and/or distribution. What they show is that beliefs in the stabilising effect of central bank behaviour may have played a substantial part in the stock market boom.

The Federal Reserve's actions in 1998 gave rise to the allegation that there was a 'Greenspan put' — in effect a put option given to investors for free to protect against a serious fall in equity prices. The term emerged again in 2007 when the Fed embarked on a series of aggressive interest rate cuts when stock prices fell in the wake of the sub-prime lending crisis. The problem with such allegations is that they are claims about *motivation*. As we have seen in section 9.3, there are perfectly good reasons for expecting asset price fluctuations to affect the level of aggregate demand and thus the level of inflationary pressure. A response to this by a compensating adjustment in interest rates is entirely appropriate for a policymaker with an inflation target. Box 9.1 contains some remarks from a speech by Donald Kohn, a Vice-President of the Fed, when rejecting the put allegation.

Box 9.1: The Federal Reserve denies supporting markets

The second [issue] — whether central banks should lean against possible asset price bubbles--was the key topic in my discussion here eighteen months ago, at Otmar [Issing's] festschrift. My answer then is my answer now. A central bank should focus on the outlook for the macroeconomy and generally relegate asset prices to the subordinate role of inputs to the forecast process. Although economic theory provides no settled answers to any topic, its predictions are especially imprecise with regard to asset pricing, which has two implications for central bankers. First, little confidence can be attached to the determination that an asset bubble exists except in the most extreme of circumstances. Second, even less confidence can be attached to predictions of the effects of policy on asset prices, and in particular on any speculative element in those prices. Moreover, monetary policy actions addressed at a perceived bubble in one sector may have undesirable effects on other asset prices and the economy more generally.

Donald L Kohn, Remarks at the conference 'Monetary Policy over Fifty Years', Deutsche Bundesbank, 21 January 2007

The problem for policy-makers, and central bankers especially, has always been how these *beliefs* about free stockmarket insurance could be unwound without causing a major market collapse. A dramatic collapse, through its effects on wealth and the cost of capital, would have a major deflationary effect. This is especially true in the United States where the direct ownership of stocks is much more widespread.

In October 2008, as major banks became insolvent and governments and central banks rushed to prevent a systemic collapse, the issuewas resolved in a rather brutal way. World stockmarkets fell by 30 per cent in the course of the month, some intra-day changes breaking all records. By the middle of the month, expectations of a major recession, stemming from the credit crunch itself but also based on falling house and stock prices, had replaced any concerns about inflation that had so concerned central banks when commodity prices were rising in the early summer (see section 9.3 above). Although central banks rushed to cut their official interest rate (to 1 per cent in the USA; to 0.3 per cent in Japan) prices continued to slide. The put option, if there was one, was spectacularly ineffective.

9.6   Markets as a test of credibility

In section 8.5, we explored the Kydland and Prescott argument that policymakers are always be faced with the problem of time inconsistency in their formulation of appropriate monetary policy. Knowing this, private sector agents are unlikely to believe governments whose stated aims are to reduce high rates or maintain low rates of inflation. This lack of credibility then means that if governments do try to carry out such policies, inflation expectations lag behind the declining (actual) rate of inflation with the result that the economy lies to the left of the vertical Phillips curve (in figure 5.2) with high unemployment and low output — a situation that may have to persist for some time. Various ways of gaining credibility were noted, including linking the exchange rate to that of a low inflation country and/or removing monetary policy from the hands of government altogether and handing it over to an independent central bank. Credibility matters to the monetary authorities then because it means that agents will incorporate policy statements more quickly into their own plans and any necessary adjustment in market behaviour will be carried out at lower cost.

An optimum monetary policy does not just require that the monetary authorities are believed, however. It also requires that their actions can be seen and understood. Thus in addition to credibility, policy also requires what has come to be called transparency (see section 8.7). In policy design, transparency is often linked to 'accountability' since accountability requires having to account for one's actions and thus to explain and justify. The argument for accountability is that private sector agents can learn and then anticipate what the authorities' reactions will be in any given set of macroeconomic conditions. We shall see in section 11.4 that the ECB's lack of accountability has had the effect of making its thinking obscure and that this has confused financial markets. By contrast, with a high degree of accountability, policy actions themselves contain little 'news' since markets would already know what the authorities were going to do. Since the ideal monetary policy is one in which prices can be stabilised without increasing instability elsewhere (in growth, output, unemployment etc), the best the monetary authorities can achieve is a predictable monetary policy. In principle, this could be achieved by having a simple rule, for example one which linked interest rates to the money growth rate. The rule could then be built into a policy reaction function so that agents could observe actual money growth trends and anticipate monetary policy changes. Experience has told us, however, that money growth rates do not contain sufficient information about the likely course of future inflation. It is the failure of any single indicator to provide adequate information about future inflation rates that has led to the direct targeting of inflation itself, with forecasts being based upon a wide range of variables. Once the forecast is known it could then be fed, along with a measure of the output gap into a well-publicised version of the Taylor rule and agents could read off the next change in interest rates. Beyond accepting the general principle that its interest rate decisions involve paying some attention to trends in both inflation and real output the Bank of England uses a more judgmental approach. This means that if private sector agents are to learn about the setting of interest rates, they have to learn alongside the Bank, or more specifically the Monetary Policy Committee, and this requires a great deal of openness on the part of the Bank. As we saw in section 8.7 the Bank of England first adopted an inflation target in 1992. Since then it has worked to create transparency by scheduling and announcing the dates of the monthly monetary policy meetings, issuing press releases immediately following each meeting, publishing minutes of the meeting together with a record of the votes (since 1997) and, most importantly perhaps, publishing the quarterly *Inflation Report* which contains the information on which the decisions are based. It may be hard work, but this should make it possible for analysts to learn over time how interest rates are likely to move in the face of given macroeconomic trends.

Pause for thought 9.6:

Two central banks increase their refinancing rates by 50bp. The consequence in country A is that the whole yield curve shifts upward by c.50bp. In country B, the yield curve is unchanged at the short end and falls at the long end by 30bp. What conclusion do you draw about the credibility and openness of the two banks?

Given the importance of credibility and accountability, therefore, it is not surprising that central banks should look for evidence on their performance and financial markets are an obvious place to look. For example, if policy is 'transparent' then changes in short-term interest rates should generally be anticipated and the prices and yields of short-dated assets should show little response on the day of the announcement. If policy is credible, and if the central bank is promising lower inflation (for example) in the future, then the yield curve should slope downward, after allowing for any term premium. Attempts to use information from financial markets in this way in recent years are many and varied. In the case of the UK where there have been two major changes in the monetary policy framework in the last ten years — the adoption of inflation targeting in 1992 and the independence of the Bank of England in 1997 — several of the studies have been of the 'before and after' variety.

In 1998, for example, there was much comment to the effect that the UK yield curve changed its shape after the announcement of Bank of England's independence. Long-term yields fell by about 40bp in response to the announcement, suggesting that the bond market took the promises of a low inflation environment in years ahead more seriously from an independent Bank of England than they did from its predecessor. Independence, even when limited to instruments, did indeed seem to add to credibility.

Haldane (1999) looked at changes in the shape of the yield curve in response to changes in official rates for the period 1984 to 1997 and for the two sub-periods

1984-1992 and 1992-1997 by calculating the average change in yields at various maturities in response to a one per cent change in official rates. The results suggested (a) that yield-curve 'jumps' in response to an official change were significantly different from zero over the whole period; (b) that the 'jump' was largest at short-maturities (up to two years) where it seemed that about one-third of the official change was not fully-anticipated and (c) that the jumps were very much smaller for the later period than for the earlier one, suggesting that the switch to inflation targeting and the information that went with it had reduced the news content of monetary policy announcements.

More recently, Clare and Courtenay (2000) have updated these findings by looking for evidence of the news content in monetary policy announcements before and after the movement to independence, studying the minute -by-minute change in price in a variety of interest and exchange rate contracts. Their findings seemed to suggest that the immediate impact of the announcement was generally greater after May 1997, though the total impact when cumulated over the day was less. The latter is some evidence that the news content of announcements has fallen since independence. The former, they suggested, may be due to 'pre-positioning'. Traders now know exactly when the announcement will come and are waiting for it.

9.7   Summary

As far as policymakers are concerned, there are two reasons for being interested in the behaviour of financial markets.

The first is that fluctuations in asset prices may have an affect upon aggregate demand which is a central component of the policy transmission mechanism. In normal circumstances, this requires the policymaker to take market trends (and the associated wealth effects) into account when setting interest rates. However, financial markets can sometimes show a high degree of volatility and this raises the question (linked to the role of markets as a constraint on policy) of whether central banks should be seeking to 'smooth' fluctuations in asset markets — becoming lenders of last resort to markets as well as to the banking system.

The second is that asset prices may be useful sources of information about future developments in the economy. Since one of the major difficulties in the formulation of monetary policy is the setting of instruments *now* with a view to delivering an outcome in eighteen months to two year's time, knowing what markets currently expect to be happening at that horizon is *potentially* very useful.

From our point of view, however, the behaviour of financial markets is interesting for three other reasons. The first is that financial markets are critical right at the beginning of the transmission mechanism when a change in the official rate of interest has to be translated into a change in market rates. Although this is traditionally regarded as a quasi-automatic and trouble free process, policymakers received a sharp reminder in 2007-08 that it should not be taken for granted when interbank rates broke away from official rates and proved very resistant to attempts to bring them back into line.

Secondly, financial markets may impose constraints on what the policymaker can achieve. This is a more general statement of the last point about official and market rates, but it covers the case where markets do not think that policy is credible and react so as to make it unsustainable.

Thirdly, and this combines the last role with the information role referred to earlier, markets can be used as a *test* of policy credibility. And again this serves to underline the importance of market reactions since it may be that the grounds for credibility are weak. But if markets *believe* a policy may work, then this in itself increases the chances of success.

Key concepts used in this chapter

money markets	futures
basis points	stockmarket insurance
conflict of objectives	leading indicators
volatility	term structure of interest rates
capital asset pricing model	yield curve
fundamentals	probability density function
call options	policy credibility
put options	accountability

Questions and exercises
Answers at the end of the book

1. Why do money market rates move so closely together?

3. Why do international capital flows make the conduct of monetary policy more difficult?

5. Why might central banks be concerned about major price fluctuations in asset markets?

4. Why might the yield on corporate bonds fluctuate relative to the yield on government bonds? What assumptions would you have to make in order to draw information about the economic cycle from these yields?

5. You observe a yield curve which slopes upward for maturities up to two years and then slopes gently downward levelling off at 10 years and beyond. What might this tell you about market expectations of future interest rate developments. State explicitly any assumptions you have to make.

...and also to think about

6. What useful forecasting information might there be in (a) company profit announcements and (b) corporate-government bond spreads. Explain how you might go about trying to extract that information.

7. Why do central bank repo deals have such a large impact on money market interest rates?

8. What are 'open mouth operations'? On what does their influence depend?

Further reading

On the Bank of England's view of how financial market disruption affects policy-making see Gieve (2008). A broader survey, including the 'aggregate demand' and 'information' cases is in Clews (2002). Bernanke and Gertler (2001) also summarises the arguments for and against reacting to asset price movements. A brief description of the UK's RPI-X and the CPI, which confirms their lack of attention to asset prices can be found at:
http://www.statistics.gov.uk/cci/nugget.asp?ID=665

On the economic information which may be contained in current financial market prices and yields see Bernard and Gerlach (1996); Brooke, Cooper and Scholtes (2000); Clare (2001); Cooper, Hillman and Lynch (2001);

Useful sources on central bank support for financial markets are Cecchetti, Genberg, Lipsky and Wadhwani (2000); Miller, Weller and Zhang (2002) and Bernanke and Gertler (2001).

Haldane (1999) shows how changes in the yield curve may indicate something about the credibility of central bank policy.

A comprehensive survey of the problems caused for monetary policy makers by international capital flows is provided by Cornford A and Kregel J (1996). For more detail of specific incidents including sterling's exit from the ERM and the crises in Mexico and Thailand, see H M Treasury (2002).

The Bank of England's (2008) consultation paper on how to revise its money market operating procedures is available at:
http://www.bankofengland.co.uk/markets/money/publications/condococt08.pdf
This begins by setting out the 2006 arrangements in a clear and helpful way before explaining what went wrong and making suggestions for further reform.

10 The evolution of monetary policy in the UK

'In the United Kingdom, money is endogenous - the
Bank supplies base money on demand at its prevailing interest rate, and broad money is created by
the banking system'

Mervyn King, 'The Transmission Mechanism of
Monetary Policy', *Bank of England Quarterly
Bulletin* (1994) p.264

10.1   Introduction

In this chapter, we are going to look at how monetary policy in the UK has evolved over the years, at what factors have caused policy to change and thus at what lessons have been learned. Here we shall start, in the next section, by looking at the conduct of monetary policy in circumstances where the authorities think that changes in the quantity of money matter. We should stress at the outset that the UK authorities have always been rather half-hearted in their commitment to this view. For most of the period from 1950 to 1985 monetary policy was conducted with at least some vague idea that the quantity of money probably did matter, but that other things — the level of interest rates, the exchange rate, the availability of credit, overall 'liquidity' — were also important. It was only from 1967 to 1985 that specific targets for monetary growth were set (but not always publicly) and only between 1980 and 1985 that the pursuit of these targets took clear precedence above all else. Section 10.2 ends in the mid-1980s with the final abandoning of monetary targeting.

The reasons for its end are various but many of them had to do with changes in the monetary and financial system which made the behaviour of monetary aggregates less important and also less controllable. We shall see that there is a certain irony here, since many of the innovations which undermined monetary targeting sprang from a policy of financial deregulation introduced by the same government which was at the same time insisting on the importance of hitting its monetary targets. Therefore, in section 10.3 we look at the process of financial innovation and how it undermined both the rationale and the feasibility of monetary targets during the 1980s.

In section 10.4 we look at how monetary policy has evolved since the demise of monetary targeting. This takes us through a period in which the authorities targeted the exchange rate (against the Deutschemark) and then targeted the rate of inflation itself. In these circumstances, and in contrast with those outlined in 10.2, money and credit growth rates are demoted, firstly to being a subsidiary target and then to, at most, one of many possible indicators of the future trend in inflation. We close section 10.4 by looking at how monetary policy in the UK has evolved since the Bank of England gained operational independence in 1997. Section 10.5 summarises.

10.2   UK monetary policy before 1985

Adopting a monetary policy in which control of the monetary aggregates is the main objective must obviously be based upon some theoretical notion of how monetary variables affect the rest of the economy and specifically upon the idea that the aggregates themselves are capable of having an independent, causal effect. The thinking is broadly that which we saw in section 3.2. Beginning with the equation of exchange and converting it to growth rates (since this is what usually interests us) we have:

$$\dot{M} + \dot{V} = \dot{P} + \dot{Y} \tag{3.5}$$

As in 3.2, this identity is turned into a theory by placing some restrictions on the following variables:

Y: that it grows at a 'natural rate' determined by population and productivity growth;

V: that it reflects custom and usage of money in the payments system and evolves very slowly;

M: that it is determined independently of other variables in the system.

In its pragmatic version, these restrictions are held to apply only in the long-run; short-run deviations are allowed. Notice three important conclusions that follow from these restrictions:

• Causality runs from left to right as a result of money's independence

• The monetary arrangements implied by the B-M approach (see section 3.3) would do very nicely as an explanation of this independence

• $\dot{P}$, the rate of change in the general price level, is the residual variable which will adjust to accommodate any tendency for the rate of growth of money to vary from the rate of growth of output.

The message, of course, is that the rate of monetary expansion determines the rate of growth of nominal spending $(\dot{M} + \dot{V})$ and if, in the long-run, this differs from $\dot{Y}$, the rate of growth of real output, the difference will be reflected in the rate of inflation.

As we shall see now, such ideas played little part in the first phase of post-war monetary policy. In fact, it took quite a long time for such ideas to gain what was a rather fleeting hold over policy.

Pause for thought 10.1:

In 2008, the Bank of England was content to observe the M4 money stock growing at an annual rate of about 6 per cent, while being confident that inflation would be close to 3 per cent. If real output was expected to grow at 1.5 per cent, what was the Bank assuming about the likely behaviour of velocity?

As we shall see now, such ideas played little part in the first phase of post-war monetary policy. In fact, it took quite a long time for such ideas to gain what was a rather fleeting hold over policy.

Monetary policy from 1945 to 1971

For these twenty-six years, British monetary policy was effectively determined by a theoretical approach, an institutional imperative, and membership of the Bretton Woods fixed exchange rate system. The theoretical approach was Keynesianism, an interpretation of the ideas of Keynes in which his strong views about the ineffectiveness of monetary policy in a depression were generalised to cover all phases of the business cycle. In terms of the *IS/LM* model, which was a popular if not always accurate exegetical device for Keynes's ideas in this period, the *LM* curve was believed to be flat and the *IS* curve steep. Thus, monetary policy was believed to be weak and fiscal policy strong.

Although Keynesian theory of the day did not reject monetary policy out of hand, it was certainly not thought possible to conduct it through controlling the stock of money. While accepting that planned expenditure was the key to behaviour of nominal income, the ability to carry out these plans was held to depend on the 'liquidity' of the economy, rather than on the narrower concept of the stock of money. For example, the ease with which people borrow from any source (not just banks) would affect their ability to spend. Secondly, the existence of many close substitutes for money meant that it was difficult to define the supply of money let alone to measure it. The existence of close substitutes (including non-bank borrowing) meant that spending could vary independently of changes in the money stock which was just another way of saying, in Quantity Theory terms, that velocity was highly variable. All of this was powerfully expressed by the Report of the Radcliffe Committee which deliberated for two years over the working of the UK monetary system.

> It is possible…to demonstrate statistically that during the last few years the volume of spending has greatly increased while the supply of money has hardly changed: the velocity of circulation has increased. We have not made use of this concept because we cannot find any reason for supposing, or any experience in monetary history indicating, *that there is any limit to the velocity of circulation*. (Radcliffe, 1959, para 391 our emphasis).[1]

This left monetary policy preoccupied with the general level of liquidity. Interestingly, Radcliffe opted for changes in the cost of borrowing (the rate of interest) rather than direct controls (lending ceilings) as the best way to influence liquidity. In practice, however, the level of interest rates was largely determined by the general tenor of macroeconomic policy. The principal objective of policy throughout the period was full employment, constrained by the need to achieve a balanced balance of payments within a fixed exchange rate system. The full employment target, combined initially with the need to reconstruct the economy following the war, led to a policy of low interest rates, punctuated by an occasional rise to protect the value of the pound sterling.

The institutional imperative derived from the dual role of the Bank of England as a central bank with responsibility for monetary policy and the country's international reserves, and as banker to the government with the responsibility for marketing government debt issues. The domination of fiscal over monetary policy was reflected in the priority given to the debt marketing responsibilities among the Bank of England's tasks. The generally accepted view of the UK market for government debt at the time was that it was dominated by capital risk aversion. This led naturally enough to the view that the size of the market could be maximised by keeping bond prices steady and this in turn meant a combination of stable interest and a policy of 'leaning into the wind' by the Bank, buying and selling debt as the market weakened or strengthened. However one looks at money supply determination, the Bank's position in these circumstances is severely compromised. In the flow of funds identity for example (see equation 2.18) it has to take any fiscal deficit as given. Its ability to sell debt to the non-bank private sector is inhibited by views about the debt market with the result that residual financing (ΔLg) broadly follows the deficit. Equation 2.20 puts it in B-M terms. Ignoring the external position, the monetary base expands to the extent that sales of government debt do not fund the PSBR. Worse even that this, interest rates were already serving two masters — the needs of the government debt market and the exchange rate. In these circumstances, giving primary attention to the rate of money and credit expansion would have been a practical impossibility.

Pause for thought 10.2:

Why does the presence of capital risk aversion in the bond market discourage frequent changes of interest rates?

This lack of access to both the monetary base and interest rates as instruments of monetary control meant that when, occasionally, the rate of money and credit expansion did reach the policy agenda as in the 'credit squeezes' of 1956 and 1964-5, control could only be conducted through the use of direct controls over bank behaviour . This fitted neatly with the needs and spirit of the immediate post-war period which reflected the very weak position of the economy following the war as well as a general Keynesian suspicion of unregulated markets. National indebtedness and fears regarding the scarcity of US dollars meant that controls over capital flows were inevitable.[2] In an economy in which rationing of consumer goods also existed for many years and in which a number of industries had been nationalised,[3] controls over the behaviour of banks hardly seemed alien.

Controls over banks, however, remained well after they had begun to be dismantled in other areas of the economy. They continued to be used in the 1960s, even though this was against the advice of the Radcliffe Committee. Borrowers, with the clearing banks unable to meet their requirements, sought other sources of funds. This contributed to the rapid growth of non-bank financial intermediaries, greatly weakening the effectiveness of direct controls. The first response of the authorities was to widen their application, with lending ceilings being extended in the late 1960s to secondary banks and hire purchase finance companies.

Apart from major devaluations of sterling in 1948 and 1967, balance of payments balance was sustained through macroeconomic policy. This was largely achieved through stop-go fiscal policies although interest rates had to be raised from time to time to protect sterling from speculative pressures. This was particularly true in the period before 1967 during which the government battled to avoid devaluation.

Controls over banks, however, remained well after they had begun to be dismantled in other areas of the economy. They continued to be used throughout the 1960s, even though this was against the advice of the Radcliffe Committee. Borrowers, with the clearing banks unable to meet their requirements, sought other sources of funds. This contributed to the rapid growth of non-bank financial intermediaries, greatly weakening the effectiveness of direct controls. The first response of the authorities was to widen their application, with lending ceilings being extended in the late 1960s to secondary banks and hire purchase finance companies.

Apart from major devaluations of sterling in 1948 and 1967, balance of payments balance was sustained through macroeconomic policy. This was largely achieved through stop-go fiscal policies although interest rates had to be raised from time to time to protect sterling from speculative pressures. This was particularly true in the period before 1967 during which the government battled to avoid devaluation.

By the end of the 1960s, all of the elements which had contributed to the formation of monetary policy in the previous 25 years were being called into question. Inflation rates had risen and the term 'stagflation' had been invented to refer to the periods of 'stop' which combined low rates of economic growth and rising unemployment with stubborn rates of inflation. Keynesian confidence that the macroeconomy could be managed at or near full employment had begun to wilt. Furthermore, conditions attached to an IMF loan in 1967 included requirements that the government restrict lending to the private sector and reduce the budget deficit in order to reduce domestic credit expansion (DCE).[4] Although it was expressed in terms of credit rather than money stock, this was the first statement that the aggregates must themselves be directly targeted, though the method was unspecified.

In brief, monetarism began to elbow Keynesianism aside and this was associated with a strengthening of belief in the efficiency of markets. From the point of view of the operation of monetary policy, this was doubly significant. Firstly it stressed the importance of targeting the monetary aggregates and it also hinted at methods. As we saw a moment ago, direct controls had always suffered from the ability of market participants to find their way around them and something of a game of cat and mouse had emerged between the authorities who made a rule, ingenious financial institutions which found a way round it, and the authorities who revised the rule to block the loophole and so on. However the monetary aggregates were to be restrained, direct, or non-market, controls should play no part.

To reinforce the theoretical shift, there was also a partial change in the institutional constraints. As we saw in equation 2.18, the money supply will change when the central bank uses exchanges between domestic currency and foreign assets as it is obliged to in a fixed exchange rate regime. This can severely hamper any attempt to target the domestic money supply and is one widely recognised source of money supply endogeneity. By 1970, however, the Bretton Woods fixed exchange rate system had begun to unravel and powerful claims were being made for floating exchange rates. In future, monetary authorities would have more freedom to target the domestic money stock.

1971-79: 'Competition and Credit Control'

By the end of the 1960s the authorities were becoming increasingly concerned at the effect of the accumulation of controls on the structure and in particular the competitiveness of the banking system. The objections to the battery of 'requests', 'guidelines', 'ceilings' and other forms of direct control were set out by the Governor of the Bank of England in 1971 (Bank 1971). The objections were those which routinely apply to all non-price methods of rationing: they encourage inefficiency, inequity and evasion.

Inefficiency arose, it was alleged, by diverting funds (priced below the market clearing level) into projects (typically in exports and manufacturing) which were favoured by government policy but whose return was less than that on other projects (often connected with property development or consumer goods). Inequities arose at many points. For example, the regulations discriminated against those institutions to which they applied, in favour of those to which they did not. Typically the burden of control fell most heavily upon the clearing banks to the benefit of existing non-bank financial intermediaries and of newly created secondary banks whose characteristics were designed to keep them just outside the reach of the controls.

The growth of new markets and institutions exempt from the controls yields a wealth of examples of regulation-induced innovation.[5] More importantly here it was a demonstration of the classic black market effect of non-price regulation. As soon as controls frustrate both sides of the market (banks and their clients) they create a market incentive for evasion. This in turn requires new regulation, and expenditure upon the resources required for enforcement. Furthermore, it also distorts the meaning of existing indicators and deprives the authorities of valuable information. It was this experience of seeing controls imposed at one point countered by circumventory innovations elsewhere ('squeezing the balloon' as it became known in Bankspeak) that eventually led to an extensive review of operating procedures in 1970.

At the same time, controlling the volume of bank credit was starting to emerge as a potential intermediate target of monetary policy partly, as we have seen, under pressure from the IMF, but also as the state of monetary economics itself came to link monetary aggregates with nominal income more directly through a stable demand for money function. In the terms that we adopted at the beginning of this section, the discovery of a stable demand for money function was tantamount to confirming that, contrary to the Radcliffe Committee's contention, velocity was subject to very little change. The quantity of money that people wished to hold (M) was a stable fraction of total spending (PY). Velocity changed only slowly and thus the effect of changes in P would be predictable changes in PY. (Notice that stability in V only creates a predictable association between M and PY. It says nothing about causality, but this was assumed, with little debate, to run from M). What emerged from a period of extensive discussion and consultation was a set of proposals known ever after as Competition and Credit Control (CCC). These proposals were introduced in September 1971 and the title is significant since the package was trying to achieve two objectives which did not necessarily fit easily together. On the one hand, the 'competition' part of the proposals was designed to reduce the discrimination between institutions — banks, secondary banks and finance houses — and to foster competition between banking firms. The principal targets here were an interest rate cartel operated by the banks which kept deposit rates down and made them 'sticky' or unresponsive to changes in other short-term rates, and bank charges, which were higher than in other countries with developed banking systems. On the other hand, the CCC proposals were intended to provide a more satisfactory method of controlling the expansion of money and credit than the market-distorting interventions of the past. The details of CCC are reported in many places,[6] but briefly:

- all quantitative restrictions on lending by banks and finance houses were to end

- all agreements and conventions on interest rates were to end

- the Bank would no longer support the gilts market by buying bonds with more than one year to maturity

- 8 per cent cash ratio reduced to 1.5 per cent and extended to all banks

- 28 per cent liquid assets ratio replaced with a reserve asset ratio of 12.5 per cent for banks and 10 per cent for finance houses with assets over £5m

- the Bank to be able to call for 'special deposits', with interest payable at treasury bill rate, from all banks.

The removal of directives and requests naturally raised the question of what form control of credit or monetary aggregates should take in future. Given the disillusion with direct controls, it is not perhaps surprising that the emphasis was to be on 'market methods', that is to say on price. Changing the market price of credit, it was argued, would be indiscriminate between institutions and would remove the incentives to collusion between borrowers and lenders that inevitably arose when interest rates were held at non-market-clearing levels. The intention was, therefore, to vary short-term interest rates which, it was hoped would cause changes in the demand for loans and the demand for the deposits which the loans created. The details of CCC have thus to be seen as a way of giving the authorities the ability to make those changes quickly and predictably, and to make them in a non-discriminatory way. The history of the initial failure and the subsequent patching up of CCC reflects the progressive discovery that these demands were not particularly responsive to interest changes, especially in periods of rapid inflation.

Pause for thought 10.3:

Why might the demand for bank loans be interest-inelastic?

Given the prevalence of official ratios in the history of UK banking, and the prevalence of bank deposit multipliers in textbook accounts of money supply determination (see section 2.3), it is important to emphasise that the reserve asset ratio (like all ratios before and since) and the calls for special deposits were never intended to operate as part of a monetary base control system where the Bank would seek to change the quantity of deposits by changing the supply of reserve assets. The objective was stated by the Governor in an often quoted passage:

> It is not to be expected that the mechanism of minimum reserve asset ratio and Special Deposits can be used to achieve some precise multiple contraction or expansion of bank assets. Rather the intention is to use our control over liquidity, which these instruments will reinforce, to influence the structure of interest rates. The resulting change in *relative rates of return* will then induce shifts in the current portfolios of both the public and the banks (Bank, 1971, p.10, our emphasis).

The key phrase is 'our control over liquidity'. This refers to the Bank's position as a monopoly supplier of funds in times of a general shortage (lender of last resort). In times of shortage the Bank can make funds available at a rate of its own choosing and this rate then sets the floor for other lending rates. In these circumstances the role of the reserve asset ratio (and a call for special deposits for that matter) is solely to speed up the process of interest rate adjustment. Essentially, the reserve asset ratio was intended to force banks with a reserve shortage to meet the problem by withdrawing call money from the discount market where the Bank could immediately put pressure on short-term rates by its response to the discount houses' requests for help. By classifying a wide range of bank liquid assets as reserves the authorities hoped to deter banks from meeting the shortage by disposing of these assets. Of course, a significant disposal — of gilts, for example — would eventually cause interest rates to rise with similar implications for the cost of bank advances and the flow of lending. But the interest rates affected, and the length of time required for the effect, would be more diffuse and less certain.

Clearly, and it is worth repeating, the reserve asset ratio was not intended and could not be used as the centrepiece of a fractional reserve-multiplier system and was there only to help in the manipulation of interest rates. It is the Bank's lender of last resort function and its willingness to vary interest rates which is crucial. Reflecting on the conduct of monetary policy as it was envisaged under CCC, the Bank later said 'Importance was now attached to the monetary aggregates; their rate of growth was to be controlled by the market instrument of interest rates. (Bank, 1978). It is easy to see the FoF approach at work here.

As regards debt management the authorities can adopt one of two attitudes. They can emphasise a support function giving priority to maintaining stable debt prices, buying and selling debt so as to smooth market fluctuations, and accepting whatever monetary consequences, via residual financing, may follow from that. The alternative is to emphasise the control (of money supply) function — selling whatever volume of debt is necessary to limit residual financing to whatever is consistent with monetary targets, and accepting whatever price/yield fluctuations follow from that. Each approach carries a number of detailed implications for the way in which the authorities operate in the market.

As we saw in the last section, in the pre-CCC period the authorities saw the support function as more important than control. This was consistent with the Keynes-Radcliffe scepticism about monetary aggregates and the consequent emphasis on interest rates. It also reflected some of the Bank's (often unsupported) views about the nature of the government debt market in the 1950s and 1960s as we saw in the last section, namely, that the market was dominated by capital risk aversion and that frequent changes in price might diminish the market for debt as a whole by driving large numbers of potential investors away.

The announcement, slightly predating CCC, that the Bank would no longer be willing to buy stock with more than one year to maturity obviously signalled a major shift in the direction of the control function. This was consistent with a desire to give more attention to the growth of money and credit arguments, though it is worth emphasising again that this priority itself emerged only from 1973 onwards. The arguments in the preparation of CCC reflected a wider range of growing doubts about the policy of 'leaning into the wind'. The first questioned the ability of the tactic to deliver its fundamental objective. While stabilising debt prices may maximize present demand it does not follow that long-term demand is similarly affected. It may be that a policy which gave more variable yields and more monetary control now, would do more for demand in the long term if the greater degree of monetary control produced lower and more predictable inflation rates. Furthermore, the ability of the tactic to maximize present demand could be called into question since there was no real evidence that the market was dominated by sceptics. Thirdly, the policy was contradictory. 'Leaning into the wind' involved selling debt and then buying it (or some other debt) back if the market weakened. The argument that supporting the market must conflict with the need to vary interest rates for monetary control purposes was therefore only one of several objections.

Allowing prices/yields to fluctuate more gave the authorities more potential control over residual financing of the government deficit, but left them with the problem of how to sell debt on a falling market. In the early years of CCC when, as we shall see, monetary and fiscal policy were both expansionary, this was not a problem. Indeed, in 1972 and 1973 the Bank provided support for the market for short periods. The situation became pressing in 1975, however, when large public sector deficits combined with a desire to control monetary growth required large sales of gilts. The response was twofold. The most dramatic part of the strategy was to raise short-term interest rates sharply in order to bring them down later and encourage investors to join the market to benefit from capital gains. This amounted to treating the demand for gilts as a function not just of the level of interest rates but as a (negative) function of changes, a fall in rates from their peak causing the demand curve to shift outward. The first use of the device, subsequently christened the 'Duke of York tactic' for obvious reasons, was in October 1975. Between then and March 1976 over £3bn of central government debt was sold to the non-bank private sector. The tactic was used on a further nine occasions before 1979. [7]

The other element in the authorities' attempt to increase the marketability of debt was to experiment with new types of stock and new methods of issue. In March 1977, the Bank invited the first subscriptions for part-paid stock and followed this with two issues of stocks with variable interest rate payments linked to treasury bill rate, offering holders some compensation for declining capital values when interest rates were rising. Although the possibility of moving away from the fixed price/tap system of issue was widely discussed in 1975 and 1976, the first experiment — with a partial-tender issue — had to wait until 1979.

Finally, amongst the changes often associated with CCC was the change from bank rate to minimum lending rate (MLR). The switch was not part of the provisions but may have followed necessarily from the change in debt management which allowed greater fluctuations in interest rates. Bank Rate had functioned both as the 'last resort' rate and as the basis on which many other rates were set by conventional mark-ups. Its level for the coming week was announced each Thursday though, during years of interest rate smoothing, the announcement consisted most frequently of 'no change'. With many rates linked to it by convention, changes in Bank Rate became increasingly momentous events which acquired a corresponding amount of inertia. When interest rates, were allowed to fluctuate more freely, it became inevitable that market rates sooner or later would move out of line with a sticky Bank Rate. Like most things, this was easily predictable with hindsight but it took experience to learn. In October 1972, bank rate was replaced by what later became known as minimum lending rate (since that is what it was). MLR was determined as treasury bill rate plus 0.5 per cent rounded up to the nearest 0.25.

As we said earlier, the dominant theme of monetary policy until 1973 was expansion. A succession of tax-cutting budgets and, as it turned out, easy credit led to a rapid rise in the PSBR, a dramatic deterioration in the balance of payments and unprecedented increases in money supply. In the four quarters of 1972 M3 grew by 4¾ per cent, 7½ per cent, 4¼ per cent and 5 per cent; equivalent to 27 per cent at a year-on-year rate. In the 1972 Budget Statement Chancellor Barber had indicated that not even the sterling exchange rate would hinder recovery. Predictably, the existing exchange rate immediately became difficult to maintain and sterling was floated on 23rd June. Until 1973, therefore, there was still a recognisable Keynesian flavour to monetary policy: unemployment still topped the list of potential economic problems and it was still believed that a combination of monetary and fiscal measures could deliver (sustained) changes in the level of output and employment. Nonetheless, in the background, views about the influence of monetary aggregates were beginning to change.[8] By the spring of 1973 unemployment had fallen by over 200,000 on the figures of a year earlier. Furthermore, from a small but rapidly declining surplus in 1972, the current account of the balance of payments was sent into deficit in the first quarter of 1973 and by summer was clearly headed for a very large deficit for the year. Inflation was 9 per cent and rising and unfilled vacancies were at a record level. The first tentative steps towards restraint came in July with a 1.5 point rise in MLR and a call for special deposits equal to 1 per cent of eligible liabilities to be made in August. In November, MLR was raised again (to 13 per cent) and a further 2 per cent call for SDs was made. Between the two calls, further lending guidelines were issued and the general drift away from CCC gathered pace with an official interest ceiling on deposits (for the first time in the UK), the reintroduction of hire purchase term controls in December and the appearance of a completely new device, the Supplementary Special Deposit scheme (or 'corset'), for imposing quantitative limits on the growth of deposits.

Under the SSD scheme, the Bank of England would issue target rates of growth of interest bearing liabilities (IBELs) for banks. Growth rates in excess of these targets were taxed in a steeply progressive manner by requiring banks to make non-interest bearing SSDs with the Bank of England. The scheme operated on five occasions between December 1973 and June 1980 with variations in the target rates and in the scale of penalties.

Once begun, the most interesting feature of the retreat from CCC was its speed and extent. As we have just seen, within the second half of 1973 monetary policy came once again to be firmly based on direct controls in spite of CCC's high hopes. There are various possible interpretations: the interest rate mechanism was ineffective or too slow. Alternatively, the mechanism was sound but the authorities declined to use it. 'Willing the end but fearing the means?' is Gowland's interpretation[9] and this is supported by an inside view from the Treasury. Browning (1986, p.284) admits that it was Government pressure that forced the Bank to find some alternative to further interest rate increases in the second half of 1973, because of the special circumstances of the energy and industrial crises. For the Bank, this is confirmed by Goodhart[10] though he stresses also the unexpected technical problems which confronted interest rate methods as a result of liability management and the consequent difficulty of.creating the appropriate relative interest rate changes. It is very significant for Goodhart's case that the two most dramatic innovations in the second half of 1973, interest rate ceilings on deposits and the corset, were both intended to limit the rise in deposit rates when other interest rates were increased, thus restoring some of the authorities' ability to influence the key relativities.[11] In 1972 and 1973 annual growth rates of M3 had reached 25 and 27 per cent respectively. The effect of the corset was to bring this down quite sharply during 1974 to 6 per cent in 1975. But by then, the annual rate of inflation, assisted by the first oil crisis, had reached 24 per cent.

The symbolic end of Keynesian monetary policy came in 1976 when Prime Minister Callaghan, addressing the Labour Party Annual Conference against a background of a collapsing pound and rumours of forthcoming cuts in public spending, announced that it was impossible for governments to spend their way out of recession, efforts to do so having only a temporary effect before being replaced by higher prices. Within three months the rejection of fiscal policy was accompanied by the first publication of monetary targets.

In 1976 inflation had begun to moderate but by then the major focus of attention was the PSBR, at £10bn equivalent to almost 10 per cent of GDP. Repeated speculation about the need for large cuts in public spending and splits in the governing Labour Party, helped by the misinterpretation of government policy toward the exchange rate, led to a thirty per cent depreciation between February 1975 and September 1976. The year ended with the government negotiating a loan from the IMF of $4bn over two years to support sterling. In exchange, the government agreed to major cuts in public spending and increases in revenue through to 1978 and agreed also to limit domestic credit expansion (DCE), the counterpart of sterling M3 (£M3), to a target range of 9-13 per cent. Money supply targets were at last out in the open.

The experiment with monetarism

The 1980 Budget speech announced the Medium Term Financial Strategy (MTFS) which projected declining target rates of growth for £M3 and for a PSBR forming a declining proportion of GDP. With inflation at 21 per cent it was always going to be difficult to hold monetary growth to its target (7-11 per cent) and interest rates were raised to 17 per cent in November. Even at this level, real rates were negative but this did not prevent an outcry from the personal and corporate sectors. Scepticism about both the ability of interest rates to constrain monetary growth and about the connection between monetary growth and nominal incomes had already been expressed. The arguments in favour of such a hostage to political fortune were essentially to do with information. Published targets, especially if the accompanying rhetoric made them sound credible, would give the private sector a framework of financial stability within which it could plan more effectively; publicised targets were an indication that negotiators who tried to thwart their implications by raising prices or wages excessively would know they would encounter heavy costs — in bankruptcies and unemployment — and would modify their behaviour more quickly and without the need for a costly learning process. It was also argued that target growth rates, published for some years ahead, would impose a discipline on governments which might otherwise be tempted to depart from the counter-inflationary objective for reasons of short-run political expediency .

The level of interest rates and the UK's new role as a major oil producer pushed the (nominal and real) exchange rate to very high levels and it was this which exerted the major deflationary pressure and caused the dramatic rise in unemployment (from 1.3m to 2.2m) during 1980.

By the turn of the year there was some evidence that inflationary pressures were easing (helped to some degree by external events) and interest rates were reduced to 14 per cent. The 1981 Budget was sharply deflationary, however, and inflation continued to fall in spite of rapid monetary growth (14.5 per cent) distorted by a Civil Servants' strike. Exchange rate worries reversed the interest rate trend in the autumn but rates declined again through 1982.

The overwhelming commitment to monetary targets in this period, combined with a desire to remove the direct controls on credit which had crept back into use after the failure of CCC, provoked an extensive review of monetary control techniques. The result was a rejection of the arguments for monetary base control. Instead, the authorities opted for a return to the spirit of CCC but with a number of institutional changes which, they hoped, would make interest rates more effective than they had been ten years earlier.

The starting point was the identification of institutions to whom the arrangements should apply. These were described as the 'monetary sector' (a term later substituted by 'banking sector' after the Banking Act, 1987) and comprised all banks 'recognised' under the Banking Act, 1979. By including also 'licensed deposit takers' it abolished the two-tier structure of recognition established in CCC. It also included the Trustee Savings Banks, the National Girobank, the Banking Department of the Bank of England, and such banks in the Isle of Man and the Channel Islands as chose to join.

Members of the monetary sector were required to maintain ½ of one per cent of their eligible liabilities as *non-operational deposits* at the Bank of England in order to provide resources and income for the Bank. In addition, banks were required to hold such *operational balances* as they thought prudent. Notice, this was not mandatory but a matter of judgement for banks, though banks were required to notify the Bank of England of any significant change which they proposed to make to this prudential ratio.

The most significant provisions concerned banks' relations with the discount market where the Bank wished to strengthen its leverage over short-term interest rates. The new arrangements extended the range of banks whose bills were eligible for discount at the Bank of England. Eligibility required an agreement to maintain at least four and an average of six per cent of eligible liabilities as secured call money with discount houses, money brokers and gilt-edged jobbers. This was intended to achieve two things. Firstly, it ensured an adequate supply of bills in which the Bank could conduct the open market operations by which it intended to provide liquidity and indicate its interest rate preferences; secondly it would ensure that banks would have significant assets subject to the change in interest rates which the Bank could engineer.

All other ratios were abolished along with the continuous posting of minimum lending rate although the possibility of announcing a rate in special circumstances was retained. The Bank instead committed itself to maintaining interest rates within an unpublished band. The possibility of calling for special deposits, however, was retained.

The disinclination to publish an official dealing rate was part of the desire, observed with CCC, to depoliticise interest rate changes — to make them seem more market determined. Without a pre-announced dealing rate, discount houses would have to offer bills to the Bank at a price of their own choosing. This could, at least in theory, be held to reflect the scale of the shortage 'in the market'. Nonetheless the Bank retained the right to reject the offers if it was unhappy with the corresponding discount rate. The impression that interest rates were market determined was to be further promoted by the Bank's preference for dealing only in 'band I' bills (those maturing within 14 days), seemingly leaving longer-term rates to be determined by the market.

Faced with the desire to slow the rate of monetary expansion, the mechanism envisaged the Bank pushing up band 1 rates by buying bills at a larger discount than had hitherto been the case, if necessary rejecting offers of bills from discount houses until the shortage of liquidity produced the appropriate rate of discount at the houses' initiative. Convention, though ultimately market forces if necessary, would ensure that all short-term rates would rise in response to reports of the Bank's action: amongst these would be bank base rates and thus the rate on advances. Assuming some negative interest-elasticity, a movement up the curve would slow the flow of new bank lending and therefore the rate of increase of the money stock. If the rise in the level of absolute rates meant also a widening of the bank lending-money and non-money-asset — money differentials, then the slowdown would be reinforced by an inward shift of the curve. We look at this process in more detail when looking at liability management later in this chapter.

By 1982, evidence that £M3 velocity was declining had become irresistible. For this reason, and with their confidence in monetary targets beginning to waver, the authorities extended the range of indicators they were prepared to consider (while maintaining public targets for broad money). From 1982-85 additional evidence on the deflationary stance of policy came from employment, output, various measures of inflation, asset prices and also, by 1983, two additional monetary aggregates — M1, a narrow definition and PSL2, a very broad definition (see table 1.1).

Bank lending, however, continued to grow very rapidly (at around 20 per cent p.a.) suggesting, without some drastic action, a similar growth in bank deposits. Some of the growth came from the banks' aggressive entry into the mortgage market. There was plenty of evidence from earlier periods that the demand for bank lending was interest inelastic but the demand for 'home loans' appeared particularly insensitive to high interest rates. Houses had proved the one successful hedge against inflation in the 1970s and prices were rising very rapidly again in the early 1980s. Capital gains on dwellings in the UK are generally tax-exempt and there were at the time quite widespread tax subsidies on mortgage interest payments.

By the end of 1982, base rates were just above 10 per cent and, with a general election not far away, the authorities were not willing to use interest rates to tackle this explosion in lending. Instead, they resorted to 'overfunding' the PSBR, introducing a number of novelties in the form of government stock that they issued but also putting some upward pressure on long-term interest rates. As a means of reconciling the rapid growth of private sector borrowing with much lower monetary targets, this device was entirely successful but had the inevitable effect that the UK banking system was regularly short of liquidity. This was remedied initially by the Bank buying treasury bills from the banking system and, when the stock of these ran out, buying large quantities of commercial bills. In effect, the Bank was lending short to the corporate sector, selling gilts in order to do so: a practice which was always open to the criticism that the corporate sector should have been able to borrow in the bond market on its own behalf. The practice ceased in 1985 when worries about distortions (to relative yields) combined with increasing scepticism about the value of money stock targets.

By the mid-1980s, therefore, it was clear both that the authorities' ability to target the broad money stock with any degree of accuracy by using interest rates, had been severely undermined, and that the rationale for monetary targets had itself broken down in the face of sharply falling velocity.[12] Both were recognised by the Bank of England when the Governor announced the end of formal targets from 1986.

10.3   Financial innovation and monetary policy

We have just seen that the policy of using interest rates to target the rate of growth of the money stock has a history going back to 1971, reaching its most explicit form after 1980 before ending suddenly in 1985. Its demise was brought about by a coincidence of circumstance. Firstly, interest rates became ineffective in controlling the aggregates while falling velocity removed most of the point of targeting the aggregates. Ironically, there was a certain amount of good luck here: the instrument failed just when the policy became pointless. The explanation often given for this state of affairs commonly makes reference to 'financial innovation' and 'liability management', and we need to look in more detail at just how it is that changes in financial products and processes can have such a major impact on the conduct of monetary policy.

Since financial innovation is a continuous process, it is unlikely that events of the period 1980-85 are unique in having some impact on the monetary system. This means that we should be prepared to look rather more broadly at the topic and recognise a number of developments which have caused major monetary changes with at least potential relevance to policy. We want obviously to look at the falling velocity episode but we will look at three others as well. The first is 'regulation Q' and the growth of eurocurrency markets; the second is the 'bill-leak' and the Supplementary Special Deposit scheme; the third is off-balance sheet activity. We will then look at liability management and the 1980s. We take them in chronological order.

Regulation Q and the eurocurrency markets

Under the Bretton Woods system the US$ functioned as an intervention currency, an international means of payment and store of value. The worldwide demand for dollars to which these roles gave rise was met by a combination of US balance of payments deficits and dollar borrowings from US banks, the resulting deposits being held until the early 1960s, mainly with US banks. In the mid-1960s, however, the US authorities began to impose controls on currency outflows which limited access to these deposits for overseas holders. This combined with two further, long-running, disadvantages. The first was 'regulation Q' which limited interest payments on deposits. The second problem, mainly relevant to Eastern bloc countries, was that cold-war tensions created the risk that dollar deposits might be impounded for political reasons. The result was the growth of dollar deposits placed with European banks and, later, with European subsidiaries of US banks.

Since reserve, deposit insurance, capital and other regulatory requirements are usually imposed with respect to banks' holdings of deposits in the domestic currency and act as a tax on deposit business, a further contributory factor to the long-term growth of eurocurrency business was the ability of Eurobanks to offer their services at more competitive rates than domestic institutions.[13]

At the end of 1990, estimates of the growth of the eurocurrency market, put it at over \$5,000bn, having increased three-and-a-half-fold during the 1980s. 'Eurobanks' (and 'eurocurrencies') are misnomers. Most such banks are departments or subsidiaries of major banks with a clear national identity. Most major countries are involved, although the largest shares lie with banks whose headquarters are in Japan or the USA. Equally 'eurocurrency' may refer to currencies with no european connection whatsoever. In this context, the prefix 'euro-' simply means a deposit held in a bank outside the country in whose currency the deposit is denominated. Hence dollar deposits in a Tokyo bank are eurodollars. The use of the term 'euro-' is a reminder that the practice of holding deposits outside their country of denomination began with the holding of US$ in 'european' banks.

From an economic point of view, there is nothing fundamentally different between a bank which specialises in eurocurrency business and a bank which concentrates on domestic deposits and lending. Both engage in maturity transformation, and in so far as they create assets and liabilities which are more attractive to end users than would be the case if the latter dealt directly with each other, then they help to mobilize funds which might otherwise have lain idle. However, there are two possible consequences of eurobanking activity which have attracted considerable attention.

The first is the effect upon world money supply and liquidity. If, as we said above, eurobanks are able to mobilize funds which would otherwise lie idle (through the usual processes of maturity and risk transformation) then private sector liquidity is increased. Furthermore, if we introduce into the banking system a further layer of institutions whose liabilities are money, as is plainly the case with any eurocurrency, then we introduce the possibility of further multiple deposit creation against a limited quantity of reserves. Most eurobanks hold reserves with major US banks or with major banks operating in the domestic monetary system. Imagine, for example, that a US resident moves dollars from a domestic US bank to a eurodollar bank which holds reserves with the domestic bank. In the domestic bank, there is no loss of deposits but there is a rearrangement of ownership of deposits (from a non-bank to the eurobank). In the eurobank, there is an increase in customer deposits matched, of course, by an increase in reserves. However, the bank's liquidity has increased on the assumption that its reserve:deposit ratio is less than one. (The effect is the opposite of the sale of government bonds in table 2.1). If its response is then to increase its advances and if those advances are redeposited, then a further expansion of the eurobank's balance sheet is possible. Numerically at least, the significance clearly depends upon two ratios, the reserve ratio and the redeposit ratio. Estimates of the size of the eurodollar multiplier are very uncertain and have a wide range, mainly because it is difficult to identify dollars in a US bank which are being held as reserves against eurodollars in a eurobank which is a branch of the domestic US bank.

A second consequence, or group of consequences, arises from the increasing difficulty of operating an independent domestic monetary policy in the absence of exchange control (i.e. post-1979 for the UK). Clearly, any attempt to control domestic monetary expansion can be partially thwarted at least by frustrated UK borrowers taking out eurodollar (for example) loans and exchanging the proceeds for sterling in the spot market. Such would be a predictable response whatever form the domestic monetary restrictions took. Furthermore, high UK interest rates, which would be part of a restrictive monetary policy, may attract an inflow of eurocurrencies which could then be exchanged for sterling at a guaranteed price (under fixed exchange rates), increasing both the money supply and UK banks' cash reserves. In principle such an inflow can be sterilised by sales of securities but there is the obvious danger that security sales themselves widen the gap between domestic and eurocurrency interest rates, leading to an increased inflow.

With floating exchange rates the impact falls upon the exchange rate itself rather than on the money supply.

The 'bill-leak'

We saw in section 10.2 that the CCC arrangements envisaged the use of interest rates to limit monetary growth but that this commitment faltered in the period of rapid growth after 1973 when it became clear that interest rates would have to rise to levels that were considered politically unacceptable. The emergency measure was the Supplementary Special Deposit scheme ('the corset') which allowed the Bank of England to specify growth targets for interest-bearing eligible liabilities (roughly speaking interest-bearing deposits) and then to impose steeply progressive penalties on banks whose IBEL growth exceeded the target. The object was to discourage banks from raising deposit rates when the Bank raised minimum lending rate. This enabled the Bank to open up a differential between deposit and other market rates and the thinking behind this was twofold. Firstly, making deposits relatively less attractive than other assets reduced the tendency for borrowers to hold the proceeds of loans as bank deposits (preferring government securities, for example). Since balance sheets must balance, the inability to attract deposits itself made it difficult for banks to lend. Secondly, the change in relative interest rates made borrowing less attractive. By widening the loan-deposit spread, using existing liquid assets (i.e. deposits) to finance a deficit, becomes marginally more attractive than taking out new loans. (Other relativities are also involved in what is quite a complex story — see 'liability management' below).

Pause for thought 10.4:

Can you give some examples of the relative interest rates that might affect (a) the demand for deposits and (b) the demand for bank loans?

The point about all this is that during the periods when the corset was in force, banks were deterred from increasing their lending. Nonetheless, firms still needed credit and banks were fretting at the loss of the interest income from loans unmade. One partial solution which quickly surfaced was the guaranteeing of commercial bills of exchange. Given the most highly developed discount market in the world, it had long been possible for firms to raise short-term funds in London by the sale of bills at a given discount for a specified period. Indeed, for large corporations this had been a standard method of short-term finance since the early nineteenth century. The disadvantage for smaller firms, or at least for firms with no established reputation in the discount market, was the rate of interest (discount) they would have to offer on the bill. This was bound to be greater than the cost of a bank loan, since the firm would have an established relationship and a credit record with the bank, while in the discount market it was asking buyers to hold the bills of an unknown debtor. The cost of bill finance was bound to contain a significant risk premium.

For firms in this position, one solution was to 'buy' reputation from their bank by getting the bank to guarantee the bill. With the bank's guarantee the bill would trade at the finest rates of interest since the risk of default was virtually eliminated. The bank, of course, would charge for this service, but provided that the guarantee fee was less than the interest saving, then the firm would gain from a reduction in the cost of bill finance while the bank would earn fee-income which would provide some compensation for the interest foregone on loans that it was unable to make. By the end of the 1970s the 'bill-leak' was very large indeed.

In effect, the corset introduced a form of non-price rationing. Non-price rationing almost always has two consequences. The first is that it encourages evasion. Such evasion often takes place in what is often called a 'black market' in which both sides, buyers and sellers, try to find a form of behaviour which allows them to achieve the results the authorities wish to prevent while appearing not to do so. The bill-leak was typical of behaviour of this kind. Firms could borrow and spend pretty much as they originally planned; buyers of the bills acquired assets which had almost the same liquidity as bank deposits; and banks received income from arranging loans. The second, less obvious consequence of non-price rationing but one which follows directly from evasion, is that the authorities lose information. In the present case, they no longer knew what the size of the loan market was or what volume of liquid assets agents were holding. The statistics which they regularly collect are those for bank loans and deposits. When the corset was in force, these statistics suggested that spending should be under control, but the reality was very different.

For UK banks, the bill-leak was their first experience of a larger category of activity known as 'off-balance sheet operations'. They learned quite quickly.

Off-balance sheet operations

It is a curious characteristic of traditional banking business, that the size of the business is directly reflected in the balance sheet. As more loans and deposits are 'produced' the balance sheet expands. Compared with the balance sheets of other types of enterprise, a bank's balance sheet is much more informative about the business. Hence, when the authorities wish to monitor banking activity it is hardly surprising that they focus upon the structure of bank balance sheets and when they wish to impose controls, these controls are specified in terms of balance sheet components (notice the growth rates for IBELS referred to in the last section). Avoiding these constraints, or at least minimising their impact often, therefore, involves engaging in income-earning activity which has no direct, corresponding, balance sheet entry.

'Off-balance sheet' operations are activities which generate income for banks without creating assets or liabilities which normal accounting procedures would place in their balance sheets. As with most other innovations, the interest in off-balance sheet operations lies not in their novelty but in their recent rapid expansion and increasing variety. Lewis (1988) listed some 60 off-balance sheet activities. These were divided roughly equally between 'financial services' and those giving rise to 'contingent claims'. The former included activities such as tax and financial planning, investment advice, portfolio management, insurance broking, credit/debit card services and (most recently) estate agency. The latter included the issuing of guarantees of many kinds, securities underwriting, market-making in securities and arranging swap and hedging transactions. One of the themes running through the growth of off-balance sheet operations, and much discussed in the financial innovation literature, is 'securitisation'. This refers both to the increasing use by ultimate lenders and borrowers of capital markets, in preference to bank intermediation, and to the practice by banks themselves, more especially in the US, of selling off loans from their asset portfolio, turning them into marketable securities — shifting them off the balance sheet.

Clearly, at an institutional level, one can view this growth of off-balance sheet activities as representing a significant change in banking operations. On a more theoretical level, however, one should take seriously the argument that off-balance sheet activities are essentially the same as the '...traditional on-balance sheet lending and borrowing operations of banks [which] can be seen to be packages of information and risk-sharing (or insurance) services' (Lewis, 1988, p.396). By taking a customer's deposit a bank (traditionally) creates a very secure, very liquid asset, repayable at par and turns it into a long-term liability for a borrower. The bank protects both from risk by its superior information and by its size. The interest rate 'spread' is the price that lenders and borrowers pay for this service. Nothing is fundamentally different when a bank accepts a bill or issues a standby letter of credit. The holder of the bill (or letter) enjoys a transfer of risk to the bank for which s/he pays by accepting a lower interest rate on the loan than would have been the case without the bank's guarantee; the borrower pays a fee to the bank for the benefit of the lower interest charge required by the market. Furthermore the bank is willing to accept the risk in the guarantee because it has information which enables it to make a reasonable assessment of the individual default risk and to price it bearing in mind the average default rate on the total pool of guarantees.

When it comes to identifying the consequences, actual and potential of the expansion of off-balance sheet activity, one can say as with the growth of Euromarkets, that by supplying services which customers want, banks are helping to mobilize funds which might otherwise have lain idle and are generally adding to the liquidity of the financial system. However, the consequences which are of more concern to the authorities are rather different. The first is the one that we saw in connection with the bill-leak. It opens up a range of opportunities which may well be used in response to regulations which are specified in terms of balance sheet size or composition.

The corset was a specifically UK regulation and one which the authorities applied intermittently during the 1970s to deal with a specific problem. Of more widespread and durable significance have been the regulations governing the capital adequacy of banks, laid down, amended and refined since 1988 by the Basel Committee and known as the 'Basel Accords'. The basic principle involves the use of 'risk-asset ratios'. Bank assets are divided into five categories, each of which is given a risk-weighting. For example, 'cash' has a weight of 0 while, at the other extreme, commercial loans have a full weight of 1. The approach is, broadly, to take the market value of assets in each category and multiply by the risk-weighting, to give a risk-adjusted value for each. These are then aggregated to give an overall value for the bank's risk-adjusted assets. This is then compared

---

Box 10.1: Capital adequacy ratios as a tax

Imagine a bank which has the following, simplified, balance sheet.

Assets £bn		Risk weights	Risk adjusted value	Liabilities £bn	
Loans	80	1	80	Time deposits	100
Bonds	30	0.4	12	Sight deposits	36
Bills	32	0.25	8	Capital	8
Cash	2	0	0		
Total	144		100		144

Suppose that the prime loan rate = 6%, while deposit rate = 4% and the cost of capital (the required return on the bank's equity) = 15%

Notice that the bank is operating at the limit of its capital adequacy ratio (= 8%). In these circumstances, additional lending (e.g. of £1bn) requires a matching increase in capital of £0.08bn if the ratio is to be maintained, accompanied by £0.92bn of additional deposits. The net income effect of this expansion can be calculated as:

	Expenditure	Income
£1bn of additional loans at 6% =		£60.0m
£0.08bn of additional capital at 15% =	£12.0m	
£0.92bn of additional deposits at 4% =	£36.8m	-£48.8m
Profit		£11.2m (= 1.12%)

Without the capital adequacy constraint, the bank would have been able to finance the additional loan solely by additional deposits, which are much cheaper than new capital. The effect of this can easily be compared with the situation above.

	Expenditure	Income
£1bn of additional loans at 6%		£60.0m
£1bn of additional deposits at 4%	£40.0m	-£40.0m
Profit		£20.0m (= 2%)

The effect of the capital adequacy requirement is to reduce the return on additional lending from 2% to 1.12%. The bank may feel that such a return is inadequate. In these circumstances, it has a number of choices. It can abandon its expansion plan. Alternatively, it can charge more for the loans and/or pay less for deposits. The result will depend upon the elasticities of deposit supply and loan demand but it is likely that the expansion will be smaller than the £1bn envisaged. Or, it can securitise the loans, avoiding the capital adequacy requirement but having to meet the costs of the securitisation deal. In all of these cases the outcome will be some combination of a lower volume of additional lending and a higher price — exactly as if a tax had been placed on bank lending.

to the bank's capital base, which itself is carefully defined and subject to rules of composition. The Basel Committee set a lower limit of eight per cent for the ratio of capital to risk-adjusted assets, though national bank supervisors have discretion to set higher limits.

The effect of such ratios for a bank operating near the limit is to make the further expansion of its loan portfolio very costly and may indeed make it unprofitable. Box 10.1 illustrates this and makes the point again that regulation has the effect of acting like a tax. In the circumstances, some banks have responded by the practice of securitisation. This involves setting up a separately capitalised 'special vehicle' whose job it is to buy bundles of loans from the bank. It does this by issuing bonds whose interest payments are guaranteed by the income from the loans (after deductions by the originating bank and the special vehicle). The result is that the sale of the loans frees up an equivalent amount of capital (assuming that the loans' risk-weighting was 1), lowering the risk-asset ratio, while leaving the bank with some income from the loans — the fees for setting up the loan and a small fraction of the interest.

Liability management

The last of these illustrations bring us to the circumstances which were widely regarded as being responsible for the demise of monetary targets in the UK in the mid-1980s.

Given a decision to make monetary targets the centre of monetary policy, there exists, in principle, a wide range of techniques which can be used in an attempt to control the aggregates. Box 10.2, which draws on Gowland (1984 pp.9-10) lists 14.[14] Bewildering as the range may look, however, the chosen technique (or techniques) must either restrict banks' ability to lend, restrict clients desire to borrow or reduce the community's willingness to hold the resulting deposits. In each case the restriction may come in the form of quantity ('direct') control or price ('market') incentive. Control of the monetary base, as implied by the B-M analysis is an example of a quantity restraint on a bank's ability to lend. As we have already seen, quantity controls (at any of the three pressure points) had been widely rejected by the time monetary targets became a serious feature of monetary policy and the plan was to use price (interest rates) to deter borrowing and deposit holding. Unfortunately, just when the techniques were applied in their purest form, institutional changes undermined the strategy in a fatal manner.

We recall that one aspect of the CCC arrangements was the ending of the bank's interest rate cartel and the beginning of competitive bidding for deposits to fund the rapidly growing demand for bank loans after lending ceilings were removed. At this stage the competition involved banks competing between themselves for wholesale deposits, that is to say large time deposits held mainly by the corporate sector. The effect, however, was to raise the level of interest paid on wholesale deposits relative to other rates and also to make it more sensitive to market movements. Taking the Bank of England's treasury bill rate as a benchmark, 7-day deposit rates were approximately half that rate at end-1971; ten years' later the proportion was 0.87.[15]

The 1980s saw the extension of this competition to retail deposits. Once again, deregulation played its part. The starting point was the entry of banks into

---

Box 10.2: Monetary control techniques

Variable	By price	By quantity
Deposits of the M4PS	Y	Y
Bank lending to public and private sectors	Y	Y
Non-bank lending to the public sector	Y	Y
Variations in the PSBR	N/A	N/A
Variation in the size of the base	N	Y
Variation in the size of the reserve ratio	Y	Y
Tax on banking	Y	N
Licensing	N/A	N/A

---

the mortgage market in 1981. From this stemmed the break up of the building societies' interest rate cartel in 1983, the rise in building society deposit and advances rates to market clearing levels and the consequent demise of mortgage rationing. As building societies moved onto the offensive, they entered into money transmission services by issuing chequebooks. But these were of limited attraction without the benefit of cheque guarantee cards and these in turn were impossible to issue under the Building Societies Act, 1962, which prevented societies from granting unsecured loans. To remove this and other restrictions the societies set about lobbying the government for a change in the legislation.

Pushing on an open door where deregulation was concerned, the societies were quickly rewarded with the Building Societies Act, 1986, which broadened both the sources and destinations of societies' funds. In particular, large societies were permitted a limited amount of unsecured personal lending. This apparently minor change had momentous results. Since societies could now legally permit customers to be overdrawn, they could, for the first time, issue cheque guarantee cards. This made building society cheque accounts indistinguishable from those of banks except for the considerable advantages that societies paid interest on all positive balances, stayed open longer and were generally seen as more user-friendly by the public. The change in building society regulation, therefore, ensured that banks which had, since 1983, grudgingly paid interest on selected cheque accounts with restricted use, would have to follow. The first announcement came from Lloyds Bank in December 1988. The increasing tendency to pay interest on sight deposits has a number of possible consequences. Firstly it raises money's 'own rate' by increasing the weighted average return on deposits. This in turn narrows the spread between lending and deposit rates, and is one way by which the cost of bank intermediation may fall. Borrowing to finance spending becomes cheaper relative to using existing liquid assets; at the same time, money's own rate increases relative to other assets. In short, money and bank credit both become more attractive at all levels of income and at any level of absolute rates. Looking at it in terms of a conventional money demand diagram, the demand curve shifts out as money's (interest) services increase.

Table 10.1: Broad money targets and outturns, and inflation, 1980-87 (%p.a.)

£M3 targets announced	outturns						
	1980/1	1981/2	1982/3	1983/4	1984/5	1985/6	1986/7
March 1980							
March 1981	7-11	(6-10)	(5-9)	(4-8)			
March 1982		6-10	(5-9)	(4-8)			
March 1983			8-12	(7-11)	(6-10)		
March 1984				7-11	(6-10)	(5-9)	(4-8)
March 1985					6-10	(5-9)	(4-8)
March 1986						5-9	(4-8)
Outturn							11-15
Inflation rate	18.5	13	11.5	10	12	15	20

Created from data in: Artis and Lewis (1991) p.136; www.statistics.gov.uk
Figures in parentheses are targets set for the second and subsequent years.

Nowhere was the effect more obvious than in a comparison between the targets and outturns for monetary growth and the rate of inflation. Under the Medium Term Financial Strategy (MTFS) starting in 1980, targets for £M3 were set, for usually the next three years, as a series of declining ranges. Table 11.1 shows the large, frequent overshoots in broad money growth rates. It also shows how targets had to be frequently revised: the target for 1983/4 was 4-8 per cent when first set in March 1980, but was revised to 7-11 per cent in 1982. It also shows the steady decline in inflation, the overshoots notwithstanding.

The consequence of increasing the range of deposits on which interest is paid (as well as bidding up the rate itself) raises the weighted average return on money relative to all other assets and liabilities. Broad money becomes more attractive as a savings medium. Velocity falls and the link with spending is broken.

The rise in money's own rate led to a decline in velocity and undermined the main rationale for monetary targets. But this was not all. The tendency for deposit rates to become more market-sensitive and to follow changes in official rates quite closely made it simultaneously more difficult to hit the target. The reason for this lies in the way in which a change in official interest rates affects the flow of new loans and new deposits. Briefly, the flow of new loans and deposits depends to some degree upon relative interest rates and these are increasingly difficult to influence when all rates move in sympathy with changes in official rates.

Pause for thought 10.5:

Imagine a family with a monthly income of £2000 and annual expenditure of £24,000. It spends the whole of its income each month at a constant rate. In addition it holds a minimum precautionary balance of £800. Deposits do not pay interest.

1)   Calculate the household's average money holding over the year;

2)   Recall that 'velocity' is the relationship between money holdings and total expenditure, calculate an annual velocity figure for this household;

3)   Suppose now that banks begin to pay interest on positive balances of £1,000+ and our household increases its precautionary balance to £1000, all else remaining the same.

Recalculate the velocity figure.

Three rates (and thus three relativities) are involved: money's own rate, the rate charged on bank loans and the rate on short-dated non-money assets (NMAs). To understand how this works, it is simplest to assume firstly that money's own rate is fixed and that the central bank raises its official dealing rates. This increase is followed, through a mixture of convention and arbitrage, by an increase in all other rates — closely in the case of short rates, more flexibly in the case of medium and long rates — with the notable exception of the rate on money. At this point, therefore, bank lending rates and rates on short-dated non-money assets have risen relative to money's own rate and by the same amount. This rise in the opportunity cost of holding money predictably induces some switch from money to NMAs with the result that the price of the latter is bid up and yields fall back from the level to which they initially adjusted in response to the rise in official rates. (This process is being described as taking time and proceeding in steps but this is a logical sequence, necessary only for exposition. In practice, adjustment is very rapid). We now have a change in two relativities. NMA rates have risen relative to money, while bank lending rates have risen even further (and therefore relative to NMAs as well as relative to money). We can now see that the rise in official rates affects the demand for bank loans through two channels. Firstly, the absolute rise in loan rates pushes us up a downward sloping (flow) demand curve for bank loans. But just as important, in raising the cost of bank loans relative to the return from NMAs, the change has, in effect, cheapened the cost of a (partial) substitute for bank credit. Issuing short-dated bonds and even shorter money market instruments is an alternative to borrowing from banks for firms at least (recall the episode of the bill-leak). In our virtual diagram, not only do we move up the curve, but the curve simultaneously shifts inward. In these circumstances, change in official rates have considerable influence over the demand for loans, and this influence is to some degree independent of the elasticity of demand for bank loans with respect to loan rates themselves.

While explaining what happens in an ideal world is necessarily complex, it is a relatively simple task to see what happens when circumstances move against the authorities as they did in the 1980s. Suppose now that money's own rate adjusts instantaneously to a change in official rates. All short-rates now move together. This means that there is no increase in the opportunity cost of holding money, no switch to NMAs and no change in the money-NMA-bank loan relativities. In the diagram again, an increase in rates (for example), pushes us up the loan demand curve, but the position of the demand curve is unchanged. The elasticity of the bank loan demand curve becomes critical to control of the monetary aggregates.

Pause for thought 10.6:

The possibility of a 'liquidity trap' is usually associated with very low interest rates. If, however, the demand for money depends upon relative interest rates, do we need to revise this view?

The importance of being able to influence relative interest rates in order to achieve control of the monetary aggregates has been stressed by a number of commentators (Gowland, 1978, 1984 pp.8 and 67; Goodhart 1984). It was also part of the rationale behind the corset episodes of the 1970s as we saw towards the end of the last section. By giving banks a disincentive to accumulate interest bearing deposits, it was hoped to drive a wedge between deposit and other short-term rates. Regulation Q had a similar effect. With deposit rates sensitive to market rates, it is very doubtful that the growth of monetary aggregates could again be targeted successfully by the use of interest rates. With direct controls ruled out because of their distortionary effects and control of the monetary base ruled out for reasons we come to in the next section, it is doubtful that monetary targeting will ever be attempted again.

It is time now to look at UK monetary policy after the demise of monetary targets.

10.4   Monetary policy after monetary targets

Ceasing to pursue impossible targets which were anyway becoming irrelevant, was clearly a sensible decision. However, the authorities remained convinced that the main objective of monetary policy was to minimise inflation and achieve an approximately stable price level. The danger in abandoning money supply targets was that agents would be left without any means of identifying the stance of monetary policy and thus of any way of anticipating future movements in the price level. Since one of the major objections to inflation is that it makes price signals harder to interpret and increases the chance of agents making allocation errors, uncertainty was clearly unacceptable.

The initial solution to the problem was to focus attention on the exchange rate. The argument here was that a 'lax' monetary policy — defined as one which was likely to produce a future inflation rate above that of the UK's major competitors — would lead to a declining value of the pound against other currencies. Conversely, a rising exchange rate indicates a 'tight' monetary policy and a lower (than competitors') rate of inflation. The argument was not wholly convincing, partly because it placed a great deal of confidence in financial markets' ability to interpret events correctly. This required that they operated with the 'correct' model of how current official interest rates were linked to future inflation, a level of modelling sophistication which the authorities themselves had failed to achieve in years gone by, and then that this prediction of future inflation would be fully and instantly incorporated in exchange rate movements. This amounted to saying that forex markets were both rational (in the choice of model) and efficient (in the use of the resulting information). These are characteristics of financial markets which many commentators would be reluctant to credit, but it ushered in a period, continuing to the present, in which feedback from financial markets became quite influential in monetary policy making, as we saw in section 9.4.

In the circumstances, the obvious step might have been for the pound to join a fixed exchange rate regime which would have compelled the authorities to adjust the policy stance whenever the pound deviated from its specified value. But the only show in town, for this purpose, was the European Monetary System and Mrs Thatcher's opposition to Britain's joining the EMS (and the more general euro-scepticism of a large section of her party) made it impossible. This left the UK's Chancellor (Lawson) to operate a monetary policy in which the pound was linked covertly to the Deutschemark. From the autumn of 1985, UK short-term interest rates came to be determined almost entirely by movements in the £:DM exchange rate. The choice of the DM as the basis of an exchange rate target made some sense in terms of trade flows but the most compelling reason was that the DM had historically been a strong currency, German inflation had been low (since the reform of the monetary system in 1948) and much of the credit for this, rightly or wrongly, was attributed to the Bundesbank. In effect, the UK authorities were 'buying' credibility for their monetary policy from an institution which had plenty to spare.

At the same time, and presumably to mitigate the *volte-face* involved in dropping monetary targets entirely, the UK authorities began publishing 'guidelines' for the growth of M0. It was emphasised at the time that this was not a precursor to a shift to monetary base control but was rather because its relationship with nominal GDP had been subject to less disturbance than that of other aggregates and because it would function as a leading indicator of future changes in nominal GDP. From the spring of 1987, the exchange rate target became more overt, though still unannounced.

The pound was held in a very narrow range against the DM, its upper limit was clearly 3.00DM though its lower limit was uncertain. The strength of the pound throughout 1987 allowed scope always for a cut in interest rates (as indeed occurred after the stockmarket crash in October) but not for a rise. By 1988 this was becoming a problem since further surges in bank and non-bank credit, a rapidly deteriorating trade balance and rising house prices suggested a return of inflationary pressures and the need for a rate rise, even though the pound remained strong. So long as markets believed the 3.00 DM exchange rate was secure, the German-UK interest differential caused capital inflows which then required intervention by the authorities which itself caused increases in broad money. The dilemma was resolved by a rise in interest rates in the second quarter of 1988. By the autumn, foreign exchange markets caught up with the deterioration in the UK's position and short-term interest rates rose steadily (to 13 per cent by December) while the pound became weaker. Base rates reached a peak of 15 per cent in October 1989 and remained there for the following year.

In the hope that formal membership of the European exchange rate mechanism would persuade forex markets of the authorities' long-run commitment to reduce inflation and secure the pound sufficiently to allow some easing of interest rates, the UK joined the ERM in October 1990 with 2.95DM as the central rate of the wider, 6 per cent, band. Interest rates were cut by one percentage point. At the time of joining, doubts were raised both as to the wisdom of the move in principle (by Sir Alan Walters, a long-run opponent of ERM membership) and of the chosen rate (by opposition political parties). In the event, the sceptics received some support as the authorities struggled to hold the pound above its lower limit (effectively set at DM2.87 by the strength of the Spanish peseta). Further evidence of the deepening recession and a decline in the headline rate of inflation, and a reduction in Spanish interest rates in February 1991, allowed the UK authorities' the tentative step of a half-point cut.

We have seen that the main reason for the UK's entry to the ERM was to gain credibility for its anti-inflationary policy by 'buying' some of Germany's reputation for financial prudence. To begin with, the policy showed some signs of success in so far as interest rates were reduced steadily by a series of half-point cuts through 1991, reaching 10.5 per cent by September, while sterling slipped only slightly from its DM2.95 target to end the year at DM2.89. Helped by the progressive cuts in interest rates, the lagged response of inflation to stagnation in the real economy was very sharp when it came. From 10.9 per cent in September 1990, the headline rate fell to 4 per cent by September 1991. Ironically, this contributed as much as anything else to sterling's difficulties in the ERM in 1992.

By the spring of 1992, credibility was once again the problem. With inflation running between 3 and 4 per cent and base rates around 10 per cent, *ex post* real rates fluctuated between 6 and 7 per cent. Even at these levels the DM:£ exchange rate slumped repeatedly to 2.85 while the real economy showed increasing signs of being in very serious recession. By the summer of 1992, non-oil output had fallen for six consecutive quarters — to nearly 5 per cent below its peak in 1990(2). Amongst the novelties of this particular slowdown was the sharp fall in output from services as well as manufacturing. The rise in unemployment (from 5.6 per cent in spring 1990 to 10.1 by autumn 1992) was thus spread geographically more evenly so that London and the South East were badly affected. It was in this region that the highest levels of personal sector floating-rate indebtedness had developed during the property boom of the mid-1980s and it was here, therefore, that the more dramatic cases of personal sector gearing and indebtedness were to be found. By the middle of the year the concern with falling house prices had crystallised in the problem of 'negative equity', preventing people from moving house and threatening banks and building societies with insolvency if they repossessed property from defaulting borrowers.

By the summer, opinion was widespread that, faced with a choice of even higher interest rates or abandoning the exchange rate, the government would have to choose the latter. The UK was not alone with this problem. The lira, the Irish punt, the peseta and escudo were all subject to speculative pressure as their weak economies suggested the need for interest rate reductions. The only way of avoiding widespread realignments within or defections from the ERM seemed to lie with a cut in German interest rates. The Bundesbank, however, was concerned about rapid monetary growth, domestic inflationary pressures and the costs of reunification and used the occasion to enhance even further its own credibility, by demonstrating its total independence of the general clamour. The crisis came in September 1992 when doubts about the willingness of some countries to ratify the Maastricht treaty called into question the durability of the ERM itself. Sterling, which had been very weak throughout August, came under heavy selling pressure in the middle of the month. The Bank used its powers to announce an MLR of 12 per cent (in effect raising base rates from 10 per cent) on the 16th September, accompanying it with a statement of intent to raise it to 15 per cent from the following day. This, plus large-scale intervention buying, failed to stop the pressure and sterling was withdrawn from the ERM on the evening of the 16th September. On the 18th, interest rates were reduced to 10 per cent, beginning a steady decline that continued through the first half of 1993.

Leaving the ERM in 1992 left UK monetary policy with the same problem that it had in 1985: how to find a target which would enable agents to judge the policy stance. The new monetary policy framework announced in October 1992 contained two features. The first was the adoption of an explicit inflation target. Instead of adopting an intermediate target in the hope that it had some reliable connection with the ultimate objective of policy, the ultimate objective itself would be directly targeted. Interest rates were now set with a view to their effects upon inflation some eighteen months ahead. One way of interpreting inflation targeting is to see it as an encompassing case of monetary targeting or exchange rate targeting. In the latter cases, the authorities are setting interest rates with a view to achieving a low inflation rate, using just one source of information (monetary growth, exchange rate etc.) disregarding all else. In an inflation targeting regime, interest rates are still set with the same objective but the decision draws upon all relevant variables. These include money and credit growth, the exchange rate, wage trends, asset prices, employment figures, the 'output-gap', surveys of 'confidence' etc. and these may change over time.[16]

The second feature was a much greater degree of openness and transparency in policy making represented by two innovations. Firstly, a quarterly *Inflation Report* would be published showing the information on which the Bank was making its interest rate decisions. Secondly, the minutes of the meetings between the Governor of the Bank of England and the Chancellor of the Exchequer at which interest rates were set were also published. This second novelty was especially interesting since it could be seen as part of the bid for credibility and a first step on the road to independence in the sense that the minutes would reveal any gross and inappropriate attempt to influence interest rates for political reasons. Any such revelation would survey have been harshly punished by financial markets as well as by public opinion.

The rate of inflation, which had been running at over 9 per cent in 1990, fell to 2 per cent in 1993 and remained in the 2-3 per cent range until 1997 when the Bank of England was given formal independence. The observation that countries with an independent central bank tended to have better inflation records than those without had been made for some years. We examined the arguments behind this alleged superiority in section 8.6. But we might note here that one of the reasons advanced was the increase in 'credibility' that we met earlier when UK monetary policy was linked to the £:DM exchange rate. In this case, an unelected and independent central bank is less likely to be subject to political pressure if and when it has to make unpopular interest rate decisions.

The decision to grant some degree of independence to the Bank of England was announced in May 1997 by the new Labour Government and confirmed by the Bank of England Act in 1998. The Act lays down many of the details regarding the operation and obligations of the Bank. For anyone interested in the question of 'how independent is the Bank of England?' a reading of the Act and a checking of details against the list given in box 11.4 is essential. The most obvious point to make is that 'independence' relates only to the setting of interest rates. The choice of policy *target* remains with the government and is specified in an annual 'remit' which can be read on the Bank's website. Thus the Bank has operational or instrument independence rather than the full independence enjoyed by the US Federal Reserve and the ECB.

With the coming of this independence, the responsibility for setting interest rates passed to a Monetary Policy Committee. This consists of nine members. Five of these are Bank staff (the Governor, the two Deputy Governors and two Executive Directors — with responsibility for monetary policy analysis and for monetary policy operations). Hence they are members of the MPC by virtue of their roles at the Bank (where, with one exception, they are permanent employees) and so provided they discharge their obligations to the Bank satisfactorily, their position on the MPC is completely secure. In fact, the only Bank member whose position is not potentially permanent is the Governor whose appointment *to the Bank* is subject to renewal every five years. In the 'independence stakes' this loses points since there is the obvious possibility that the Governor's decisions could be influenced by the desire for reapppointment. (We should stress that no such allegation has ever been made). The other four ('external members') are appointees of the Chancellor of the Exchequer. The notion of 'appointment' here is interesting since, as part of the accountability requirements (see below) the UK's House of Commons Treasury Select Committee (TSC) was allowed to interview individual members of the MPC about the Committee's work and thus, in effect, to pass judgement on the performance of the individual member. There have been occasions where the TSC has expressed reservations about an appointment but this has never amounted to an overt suggestion that they should not have been appointed. Nonetheless, the process may serve to constrain the Chancellor's choice of appointee and thus scores another point on the scale of independence. 'External' members of the MPC are appointed for a period of three years. The appointments are renewable in theory but this unusual. Voting is by simple majority and the Governor has a casting vote in the event of a tie. The Treasury also sends a representative, in order to brief on fiscal policy and other issues which the Treasury thinks the MPC may like to consider. This provides for some degree of policy coordination but the representative plays no part in the discussion (except to answer factual questions) and does not vote. The Committee meets according to a regular monthly schedule, though the facility exists for additional meetings and one was in fact held on 18 September 2001. Meetings are usually scheduled for the first Wednesday/Thursday after the first Monday of the month, with the policy decision being announced at 12.00 noon on the Thursday. The making of policy thus follows a monthly cycle and contains three elements:

- Briefings in advance of the policy decision meeting

- A two-day meeting at which decisions are made and implemented immediately

- Production and publication of the minutes.

We can begin the cycle with the circulation of briefing material to committee members. This is mainly material relating to data releases and market developments, prepared by bank staff. On the Friday prior to the decision meeting, there is a half-day meeting at which senior Bank staff present reports on major features of the economy under a set of standard headings such as 'demand and output', 'the labour market', 'monetary and financial conditions' etc. Members of the committee may ask for further information or analysis and this is done by the Bank staff on the Monday and Tuesday following. The policy meeting begins on Wednesday afternoon when members identify the key issues (broadly, the same headings as used in the Friday meeting) and their likely implications for inflation. Following discussion on each issue, led by the Deputy Governor, members are left to reflect overnight. On the Thursday morning the Governor summarises the discussion of the previous day and asks members to confirm or amend his summary. Each member is then asked to state his or her view of the present situation and the appropriate stance of policy. The Governor then puts a motion which he hopes will command a majority. In all cases, members who are in a minority are asked to confirm their preferred level of interest rates. These will be published in the minutes so that the weight of opinion and sentiment in the MPC can be clearly observed by the public. A press statement is prepared for release at 12.00 noon and where a change in interest rates is decided upon the statement will normally give a brief indication of why the MPC made the change.

The final part of the cycle involves the preparation of the minutes of the meeting. A first draft is circulated for comment in the week after the meeting and a final version is agreed on the following Monday for publication on the Wednesday two weeks after the meeting. Although the minutes show the voting decisions of individual members, their comments and arguments are unattributed. The purpose of this is to encourage the freest discussion in the meetings.

Alongside its routine of monthly decision meetings the MPC is also engaged in a detailed inflation forecasting exercise. This follows a quarterly cycle and culminates in the publication of the Bank's *Inflation Report*, normally in the week following a policy meeting of the MPC. The work normally takes about eight weeks (thus beginning about seven weeks before a policy meeting). The cycle begins with a review of any research commissioned by members at the end of the previous forecast cycle. It then moves to an examination of the latest trends as projected by Bank staff. These are based upon the Bank's suite of econometric models, on information extracted from current financial market prices and yields and on inputs from independent forecasting bodies like the National Institute of Economic and Social Research (see Bean and Jenkinson, 2001). Over the following weeks there is a series of meetings in which particular issues are the subject of discussion between MPC members and Bank staff. A week before publication the forecasts are put together, data and trends updated by Bank staff and a final view of risk and plausibility of the forecast is taken and added to the *Report*. The full text of the *Report* is published in hardcopy and is also available on the Bank's website at: www.bankofengland.co.uk/inflationrep/index.html

At the same time that it was granted operational independence, it was decided to relieve the Bank of England of two functions which it had carried out for centuries. These were the management of government debt and supervision of the banking system. In both cases, the intention was to increase further the Bank's sense of independence and to increase its freedom to set interest rates as required by the inflation trend with as few distractions as possible. There is little point in giving the policymaker freedom from government pressure if its hands are tied in other respects. The responsibility for debt management passed to a newly created 'debt management office' or DMO, an agency of the Treasury, in 1998. This

was a recognition of the occasions, referred to above, where the Bank had sometimes felt it necessary either to resist changes in interest rates in order to stabilise
bond prices or to adjust them to counter trends in bond prices (the episodes of
'leaning into the wind'). From now on, the state of the gilts market would be ultimately a Treasury responsibility. Similar thinking played a small part in the decision to transfer banking supervision to the Financial Services Authority. A decision had already been taken to centralise the regulation of all types of financial
activity in the FSA, but the advantage from a monetary policy point of view was
that the Bank would no longer be in possession of detailed information about the
state of individual bank balance sheets. It would not know, therefore, which, if
any, banks might be threatened by poorly performing loans and consequently it
would not be deterred from raising interest rates by the knowledge that such an
act might cause a bank failure. We return to this in a moment.

In return for the limited independence that it granted to the Bank, the 1998
Act laid out a number of mechanisms whereby the Bank could be held accountable for its conduct of policy. We have already seen that representatives of the
Bank and the MPC can be called to give evidence on their conduct to the Treasury
Select Committee. This creates a degree of *political* accountability — but to
Parliament as a whole and not to the government of the day. The MPC is also
required to report regularly on its activities to the Court of the Bank of England
and the Court in turn must submit an *Annual Report* to Parliament. In addition,
the MPC itself would argue that the decision to conduct policy with such a high
degree of openness (minutes, voting records, *Inflation Report* etc) is part of being
accountable to a much wider public. In addition, we have seen the occasional
need for the open letter. The annual remit to the Bank (though not the 1998 Act
itself) requires the Governor (as Chairman of the MPC) to write an 'open letter'
to the Chancellor of the Exchequer in order to explain the reasons for the deviation and the horizon over which it is intended to bring inflation back into the target range (in effect, making explicit the policy reaction function).

In addition to the argument that a policymaking body must be accountable to
the community in some way, there was the additional argument that openness,
over time, would help private sector agents 'learn' how the MPC decided on the
appropriate interest rate and would eventually be able to anticipate the Bank's
next decision. Eventually, changes in interest rates would cease to be 'news' since,
by the time they were announced, they would already be incorporated in private
sector decisions. The economic advantage of this, rather like the advantage of low
and stable inflation rates, is that another source of 'shocks' to the economy would
be eliminated and fewer incorrect decisions would be made by private sector
agents. It is worth noting that the lack of comparable openness has been a source
of recurrent criticism of ECB operating procedures (see section 11.4). Evidence
from financial markets suggests that both the introduction of inflation targeting
(and most of these arrangements) in 1992 and again the switch to central bank
instrument independence in 1997 had positive effects on credibility and openness
(see section 9.5).

Table 10.2: Bank of England repo rate and inflation, 2000-2008

Date		Repo rate %	Inflation %*	Real interest rate %	Inflation target %*	Inflation gap %
2000	13 Jan	5.75	2.1	3.65	2.5	-0.4
	10 Feb	6.00	2.2	3.80	2.5	-0.3
2001	8 Feb	5.75	1.9	3.85	2.5	-0.6
	5 Apr	5.50	2.0	3.50	2.5	-0.5
	10 May	5.25	2.4	2.85	2.5	-0.1
	2 Aug	5.00	2.6	2.40	2.5	-0.1
	18 Sept	4.75	2.3	2.45	2.5	-0.2
	4 Oct	4.50	2.3	2.20	2.5	-0.2
	8 Nov	4.00	1.8	2.20	2.5	-0.7
2003	Feb 7	3.75	3.0	0.75	2.5	0.5
	Jul 10	3.50	2.9	0.60	2.5	0.4
	Nov 8	3.75	2.5	1.25	2.5	0.0
2004	Feb 5	4.00	1.3	2.70	2.0	-0.7
	May 6	4.25	1.5	2.75	2.0	-0.5
	Jun 10	4.50	1.6	2.90	2.0	-0.4
	Aug 5	4.75	1.3	3.45	2.0	-0.7
2005	Aug 4	4.50	2.4	2.10	2.0	0.4
2006	Aug 3	4.75	2.5	2.25	2.0	0.5
	Nov 9	5.00	2.7	2.30	2.0	0.7
2007	Jan 11	5.25	2.7**	2.55	2.0	0.7
	May 10	5.50	2.5	3.00	2.0	0.5
	Jul 5	5.75	1.9	3.85	2.0	-0.1
	Dec 6	5.50	2.1	3.40	2.0	0.1
2008	Feb 7	5.25	2.5	2.75	2.0	0.5
	Apr 7	5.00	3.0	2.00	2.0	1.0

* Annual percentage change in RPI-X until December, 2003. CPI thereafter.
** 3.1 per cent in March 2007
Sources: www.bankofengland.co.uk/statistics and *Inflation Reports* (various)

Finally, in this review of the 1997 innovations, we should note one further thing. We should remember that by 1997 it was clear that some form of European monetary union would occur in the near future and plans were already underway for the creation of a European Central Bank modelled on the Bundesbank. If the UK were to join at some point in the future, then the Bank of England would need to adopt a number of procedures consistent with ECB operations. The movement towards independence, of course, was part of this recognition, but the opportunity was taken also to change the way in which the Bank of England imposed interest rate changes through its money market operations to bring them into line with European practice. This involved the greater use of gilt repurchase agreements (strictly reverse repos) and less reliance on the outright purchase of treasury and other eligible bills.

Given the novelty of these arrangements, it was inevitable that they would be subject to a great deal of scrutiny and subsequent review. The first of these was carried out by Donald Kohn of the US Federal Reserve in 2000, three years after the arrangements had been put in place. The Report (Bank, 2001) focused on four main themes including research, forecasting, arrangements for briefing the MPC on the state of the economy and the relationship between the MPC and other Bank staff. It was broadly supportive of existing arrangements but made a number of detailed suggestions for improvements, particularly in the forecasting of inflation and the way in which those forecasts could be best presented to the general public. More recently, in 2006, the TSC launched an enquiry which it chose to call 'The MPC of the Bank of England: ten years on'. The Bank of England's submission (2007) provides an interesting summary of the main monetary policy decisions, their background and the results over the period. In particular, while stressing that outturns had been generally satisfactory to date, it recognises that the world economic context since 1997 had been very benign and that it was unlikely that favourable conditions would continue forever. Table 10.2 shows the changes in repo rate made by the MPC since 2000 and the annualised rate of inflation measured by RPI-X (later CPI) at the time. Given our earlier discussion of the need for the policymaker to be aiming for a real rate of interest (in section 5.2), and of the Taylor rule in section 8.5, we have also calculated the real rate of interest and a contemporaneous inflation gap.

What is immediately apparent from the table is that the period of operational independence at the Bank of England has been one of low and stable inflation. The deviations of inflation from target have been generally less than one per cent and undershoots have been as frequent as overshoots. The figures conceal the one occasion, so far, on which the Governor has had to write an open letter to the Chancellor explaining why the rate of inflation departed from target by more than 1 per cent. This occurred in April 2007 when the annualised rate of inflation in March 2007 was 3.1 per cent. The table suggests that another such letter might be required before the end of 2008.

Some of the TSC's subsequent recommendations are interesting since they touch on the issue of independence. One of these was that external MPC members should be appointed for six years, with no possibility of reappointment. They should serve a minimum of three years, the extension depending on their choice and on the *Court's* review of their performance, thus ensuring their '...continuation was not at the discretion of the Chancellor of the Exchequer.' The TSC also endorsed planned changes that had already been announced. The first of these was that recruitment of external members of the MPC would be by public advertisement and the second was that the TSC itself would be allowed to subject new members to an appointment hearing *prior* to their taking up the post (though the decision of the TSC would be non-binding). It also recommended more flexibility in the timing of MPC meetings.

The TSC enquiry took place before the crisis at the Northern Rock Bank occurred. This began as a liquidity crisis in September 2007 and was finally 'resolved' in February 2008 by the Northern Rock being taken into public ownership. The way in which the crisis was handled, and the length of time that was needed to bring it to a conclusion, attracted a great deal of criticism. Much of this was focused on the so-called 'tripartite agreement' of responsibility for financial stability between the Bank of England, the FSA and the Treasury, the view being widely expressed that the division of responsibility between the Bank and the FSA was at the root of the problem. The Memorandum of Understanding between the three authorities made the Bank of England responsible for the stability of the financial system as a whole while giving the supervision of individual institutions to the FSA. As we know from our earlier discussion above, there were sound reasons for transferring prudential supervision away from the Bank when it became independent. But clearly it did increase the risk of communication failures. (The FSA also admitted after the crisis that it had insufficient staff and insufficiently qualified staff in its banking supervision department).

It may be partly a comment on the success of the MPC that the government's solution to problems caused by this division of responsibilities has focused on changes at the Bank where it is proposed to create a 'Financial Stability Committee' which will be chaired by the Governor and consist of Bank insiders but also external members appointed from financial institutions in the City of London and from the FSA. Like the MPC it will have statutory powers and obligations.

10.5 Summary

The theory and practice of monetary policy in the UK have both changed dramatically since the end of World War II. Until the late 1960s, policy was based on the 'Keynesian' thinking of the day. This was that that aggregate demand was not much influenced by monetary conditions. Furthermore, the Bank of England's hands were somewhat tied, when it came to operating an independent monetary policy, by the need to maintain a fixed parity with other currencies under the Bretton Woods agreement. The instruments of policy were largely direct controls over the amount and direction of bank lending.

The collapse of fixed exchange rate regimes in 1972 removed the constraint on an active monetary policy. This coincided with a shift in theoretical thinking towards monetarism and the demand of the IMF for more restraint of the growth of money and credit. It also coincided with a dissatisfaction with the distorting effect of direct controls on money and credit and so the switch in policy towards more restraint of the monetary aggregates was accompanied by a simultaneous shift towards a 'market' instrument — the official rate of interest — as outlined in the Competition and Credit Control arrangements of 1971.

This makes 1971 a turning-point in UK monetary policy since it establishes the rate of interest as *the* instrument of monetary policy and ensures that money and credit are endogenously determined. The interesting developments thereafter are the struggle to control money and credit during the 1970s using this single instrument, when very high rates of cost inflation were boosting demand. Real interest rates were frequently negative, since the authorities balked at nominal rates which would have been over 25 per cent. In the circumstances they preferred emergency recourse to the 'corset' and a step back toward direct control.

In 1980, the first Thatcher government announced a determination to restrict monetary growth and published a target range in order to give credibility to this commitment. In the event, the interest rate instrument proved insufficient (or alternatively its operators proved unwilling) to the task, but the rapid growth of money and credit was accompanied by a sharp decline in inflation and this clear demonstration that the rate of monetary expansion was neither a necessary nor sufficient condition for the determination of the rate of inflation led to the end of monetary targets. From 1986 to 1992, the 'target' of policy was informally and then formally the exchange rate.

With sterling's exit from the ERM in 1992 we enter what might be called the current phase of monetary policy wherein it is thought that the most appropriate target of policy is the inflation rate itself which can be influenced, with a rather long lag, by the pressure of aggregate demand. The instrument remains the official rate of interest but the link to inflation comes through the link of interest to aggregate demand and not to any particular money or credit aggregates(s).

Key concepts used in this chapter

liquidity	Medium Term Financial Strategy (MTFS)
equation of exchange	
Quantity Theory of Money	overfunding
velocity of circulation	off-balance-sheet operations
capital risk aversion	risk-asset ratios
domestic credit expansion	securitisation
leaning into the wind	monetary base control
Duke of York tactic	inflation targeting
special deposits	credibility
supplementary special deposits	openness

Questions and exercises

Answers at the end of the book

1. Explain why policy makers have generally come to the conclusion that the only effective instrument of monetary policy is the short-term rate of interest.

2. Why might giving the central bank responsibility for banking supervision make it more difficult for the bank to pursue an independent monetary policy with price stability as the primary target?

3. Explain how capital adequacy requirements impose a tax on banking.

4. Why might the presence of capital risk aversion in the bond market make the conduct of monetary policy more difficult?

5. Why does a rise in money's own interest rate, *ceteris paribus*, tend to increase the rate of monetary growth?

6. Explain briefly why 'credibility' and 'openness' are desirable properties in the conduct of monetary policy.

...and also to think about

7. What features of the UK's monetary policy framework contribute to credibility and openness?

8. Why might responsibility for the government debt market inhibit a central bank's conduct of monetary policy?

9. 'It is not that the demand for lending has become less sensitive to changes in relative interest rates. If anything, it has become more so. The problem lies in the increasing inability of the authorities to cause changes in relative rates by changing the level of absolute rates.' (Goodhart, 1984). Explain how this situation has come about.

10. From August 2007 to April 2008, the Bank of England reduced interest rates even when it was forecasting that the inflation target would be breached in 2008. How would you explain this action?

Further reading

The history of monetary policy in the UK since about 1971 is dealt with in Artis and Lewis (1991) and in Hall (1983). Goodhart (1989b) brings the story more nearly up to date. Later developments can be followed in H M Treasury (2002) and in the regular 'markets and operations' section of the Bank of England Quarterly Bulletin. A critical view of policy in earlier years is in Dow and Savile (1988).

Bank of England (1999) 'Monetary Policy in the United Kingdom' Bank of England Fact Sheet, (available at www.Bankofengland.co.uk) gives a succinct explanation of the way in which monetary policy is formulated and carried out. A detailed explanation of the way in which the MPC works is in Bean (1998 and 2001) while Lambert (2005) provides an insider's view of the way in which the MPC works. Details of the Bank of England Act, 1998, which gave the Bank independence, are discussed in Rodgers (1998). The thinking behind the setting up of the MPC and the movement towards independence at the Bank of England is in Bean (1998). The 'Kohn Report' on the work of the MPC and the Bank's response is in *BEQB* (2001). The Bank's submission to the Treasury Select Committee is in *BEQB* (2007).

The 'Memorandum of Understanding' between HM Treasury, the Bank and the FSA can be accessed at the Bank's website:

http://www.bankofengland.co.uk/about/legislation/mou.pdf.

A classic work on financial innovation and its relevance to monetary policy is Podolski (1985) though this focuses mainly on the implications for money supply. Goodhart (1986) gives a broader account. More recent work includes Lewis and Mizen (2000) ch.12, though their linking of financial innovation solely to the demand for money must be read in the light of our remarks about the potential irrelevance of the demand for money in chapter 3. Chapter 24 in Howells and Bain (2008) takes a broad look at the implications of financial innovation.

11 Monetary policy in the European Union

'The Mony of this kingdom is of a good Alloy'

Morland, *Geog. Rect., Asiat. Tartaria* (1685) 396

11.1   Introduction

In the lead up to the establishment of monetary union in Europe and since the establishment of the euro as a single currency in January 1999, the issue of monetary union has been much debated. Some economists continue to argue that the European single currency project will produce many problems and eventually fail. To others, the euro has so far been a great success although remaining an experiment.

There has also been much argument over future membership of the euro area both for present members of the EU which have so far rejected the single currency — the UK, Denmark, and Sweden — and for newer EU members which expect to embrace it over the next five years. The issue of the desirable membership of a single currency area is considered in section 11.2. Section 11.3 deals with the particular case of UK membership of the euro area. In 11.4, we move on to look at the existing monetary policy institutions of the euro area, while 11.5 examines the form of monetary policy and the way in which it has been influenced by the movement towards monetary union. Section 11.6 considers monetary policy as practised by the European Central Bank since January 1999 and looks particularly at the relationship between monetary policy and the value of the single currency. The chapter concludes with a comparison between the practice of monetary policy in the UK since June 1997 and that of the ECB and asks whether reforms of the ECB institutions or approach to policy are desirable.

11.2   The membership of monetary unions

In principle, there is no difference between the operation of monetary policy in a single nation state such as the UK and in a monetary union consisting of a number of nation states. In each case, a central bank operates a single monetary policy for the whole country or group of countries. In these times of independent central banks and the dominance of price stability as a policy goal, the constitutions and practices of the central banks are likely to have much in common. In no case are monetary policy decisions of the central bank likely to suit all regions or all economic sectors. Much of the debate over the European single currency has been of the 'one interest rate does not suit all' variety — that a policy decided by the ECB in Frankfurt might be helpful for some member states but not for others. Yet it is also true that an increase in interest rates by the Bank of England that suits the City of London or the south east of England generally might not please manufacturing industry in Scotland or Northern Ireland. A difference between the two cases only arises if it is more likely that a central bank decision will be wrong for some parts of the euro area or that it will do more damage to some parts of the area than is the case for the UK. We are talking about questions of degree rather than principle.

We could, thus, express the issues at the heart of the debate through the following questions:

- How likely is it that the interest rate set by the central bank of a monetary union will be unsuitable for some member countries?

- How much damage is the wrong interest rate likely to do to those economies that it does not suit?

- Are there other types of flexibility in the economy of the monetary union that will help the disadvantaged economies to cope with interest rate decisions that are wrong for them?

- Are the likely costs of interest rate decisions which do not suit some parts of the area likely to outweigh the benefits expected from the single currency?

The usual theoretical approach to these questions is known as optimum currency area theory. This seeks to determine the optimum size and composition of a single currency area. The logic is clear. Start with a very small single currency area. Then, as the area is enlarged, the costs increase and the net benefits (benefits - costs) of having a single currency decline. At some point, the benefits and the costs become equal and we have reached the optimum size. For areas of greater size than this, it would be advantageous to retain more than one currency. However, the question is more complex than this for two reasons.

Firstly, the composition of the area is important. In practice, we are not concerned with the idea that an existing single currency area (such as the UK or Sweden) should introduce additional currencies, even if this seemed justified by a strict application of optimum currency area theory.[1] Rather, we are interested in which existing nation states should give up their currencies and join a single currency area. Thus, we ask which countries should be members and this introduces considerations other than the geographical area of the union. That this is the question we are asking is a clear indication that decisions over monetary union almost always involve important political as well as economic issues.

Secondly, the size of both the costs and benefits of a group of countries moving to a single currency and a single monetary policy is uncertain and strongly disputed. This is true of the economic costs and benefits considered alone and is true, *a fortiori*, when one acknowledges that the movement to a single currency is inevitably a political as well as an economic project. This is especially true in the case of Europe where integration has always been expected to deliver dividends in terms of lasting international peace and harmony. Here, we shall largely endeavour to keep to economic arguments, but the political issues cannot be forgotten.

Pause for thought 11.1

Do peace and harmony deliver economic benefits? Is it ultimately possible to distinguish clearly between economic and political factors?

We cannot, then, be precise about the size of an optimum currency area. All we can do, at most, is to ask whether the benefits of a single currency appear to outweigh the costs for a specified set of countries — for example, the current membership of the euro area,[2] the EU 27 or some subset of the 27 other than the existing membership. To do this, we start by enquiring about the characteristics of groups of countries for which the costs of adopting a single currency are likely to be low. These are based on the idea that the principal costs are:

(a) the loss of the ability to adapt to changing economic circumstances by altering the exchange rates between the currency of the domestic economy and those of the other member countries; and

(b) the loss of an independent monetary policy.

Box 11.1 sets out the most important of these characteristics.

Box 11.1 Characteristics of an area in which the costs of adopting a single currency are likely to be low

1. The economies should be sufficiently similar that:

(a)   shocks affect them symmetrically and do not create balance of payments imbalances among member countries;

(b)   business cycles are synchronised so that all member countries want interest rates to be moving in the same direction;

(c)   monetary policy changes affect them in similar ways.

2.   Where balance of payments imbalances arise among the countries, there should be sufficient labour market flexibility and capital mobility to keep the costs of adjustment relatively low.

3.   There are fiscal mechanisms that automatically transfer resources within the single currency area from rich regions with low unemployment to depressed regions with high unemployment.

The conditions listed in point 1 in box 11.1 are seldom, if ever, fully met amongst groups of countries. Adopting a single currency across a number of countries introduces an element of rigidity into macroeconomic policy and there are costs associated with doing so. However, the extent to which countries fail to meet these conditions varies. Further, flexibility in other areas of the economy might keep the costs associated with the adoption of a single currency relatively low. We need to estimate how large these costs are in particular cases. Unfortunately, this is extremely difficult to do and is complicated by the possibility that closer integration of the European economy might either increase or decrease the likelihood of future shocks affecting member countries symmetrically.

Pause for thought 11.2

Does it follow that, because of the operation of economies of scale, there will be greater specialisation within member countries after joining a monetary union? Alternatively, might geographical areas in which industries specialise overlap national boundaries?

On the one hand, to the extent that the growth of the market allows greater specialisation through economies of scale, member countries might diverge and shocks become less symmetrical. On the other hand, to the extent that production is driven increasingly by consumer preference for variety and trade is increasingly intra-industry in nature, production patterns are likely to converge and shocks to become more symmetrical.

It is also difficult to be certain about the impact of wage flexibility and capital mobility. Wage flexibility requires money wages to fall to allow countries to recover from slumps in the economy. Where the slump is caused by an external demand shock and the immediate problem is a lack of demand, wage flexibility hardly provides an efficient adjustment mechanism. Labour market flexibility requires labour to be able to move easily between jobs and between member countries of the single currency area. It is unlikely that this is always beneficial since one possible outcome is that young and skilled workers move leaving depressed regions to become more depressed.

In any case, even if we were to accept wage and labour flexibility as unmitigated advantages, we might have to admit that neither exists in practice. For example, wages and labour markets are certainly not flexible across the euro area. The numbers of people moving from employment to unemployment and *vice versa* are much greater in the USA than in the euro area. The risk of employees becoming unemployed is smaller in the euro area, but those who become unemployed have much less chance of getting back into work quickly than have their American equivalents. In the 1990s, about half of the unemployed in Europe had been out of work for more than a year. In the USA, this was true of only about an eighth of the unemployed. In addition, the adoption of a single currency might reduce wage flexibility by increasing wage transparency, encouraging trade unions to push for greater equality of nominal wages across the single currency area.

A good deal depends on the level of economic and financial integration. Clearly, where there is a high level of economic integration, the conditions in point 1 of box 11.1 are more likely to be met and the benefits of a single currency would be higher. Further, the provision of fast, cheap and reliable financial services across an internal market should allow that market to function more effectively, increasing the level of economic integration. Again, the higher is the level of financial integration the more mobile capital becomes. Only small interest rate differentials are required to produce large capital movements and, as we saw in section 7.2, independent monetary policies become impossible to sustain in the absence of frequent and, perhaps, large movements in exchange rates. This would mean that a country wishing to be part of an economically and financially integrated area but to retain its own currency might have to accept a high risk premium in its domestic interest rates to offset potential fluctuations in the value of the currency in the minds of international investors. This leaves open the question of whether increased capital mobility might itself cause convergence or divergence among member economies. There are arguments in support of both sides of this issue, but the evidence in Europe so far suggests that it is more likely to favour convergence.

When the costs of the single currency have been estimated, they need to be compared with the benefits from its adoption. The most important benefits are listed in box 11.2.

Box 11.2: Benefits from membership of a single currency area

1. Transactions costs associated with the exchange of currencies and of keeping records in multiple currencies are reduced.

2. There is greater price transparency across the single market, which might increase competition and raise the level of efficiency across the market.

3. Welfare gains result from the reduction of uncertainty:

   (a)   the variation of profits around the mean is likely to be smaller;

   (b)   real exchange rate uncertainty is likely to fall, reducing uncertainty about the future prices of goods and services and allowing better investment and consumption decisions to be made; and

   (c)   real interest rates should be lower because the risk premium built into interest rates falls with the removal of exchange rate risk.

4. There are possible benefits from having a major international currency:

   (a)   countries whose currency is used by other countries obtain seigniorage in the form of additional revenue to the central bank (in Europe's case, the ECB) as the issuer of the money;

   (b)   the international use of the euro might also help domestic financial markets.

These, too, are difficult to judge and, indeed, might not all be positive. There is no doubt that there are some savings on transactions costs. However, there are differences of opinion over the size of these savings in particular cases. By any measure, the gains under this heading for the euro area are absolutely large but only small in relation to GDP. There is also plenty of evidence that price discrimination occurs across national markets in Europe. However, we cannot easily know how much of this discrimination is removed by the greater price transparency produced by a single currency. After all, there are other barriers to the free movement of goods and price discrimination remains in national markets that have long shared a single currency such as that of the UK.

There is little evidence that the use of multiple currencies greatly impeded trade and the efficient allocation of resources in Europe. Trade grew rapidly across the EU in relation to GDP throughout the period 1957-1999, before the introduction of the single currency. The evidence about the impact of reduced uncertainty on profits and investment is also mixed. Overall, it is extremely difficult to come to clear conclusions about whether the loss of the exchange rate instrument in the euro area might result in net benefits or net costs in the long run. This is likely to be the case in any ambitious single currency project.

Pause for thought 11.3

Why might a reduction in uncertainty lead to better investment decisions and an increase in the efficiency of the market? How do market agents normally protect themselves against uncertainty?

11.3   The UK and membership of the euro area

The above arguments have been highlighted by the debate over UK membership of the euro area. The single currency was established in January 1999 with 11 members. Greece had applied but was excluded at that point because it did not meet the requirements of convergence established in the Maastricht Treaty of 1992. However, Greece became the twelfth member of the area on 1 January 2001. This left three EU members outside of the single currency area.

Denmark and the UK had negotiated opt-outs for their acceptance of the Maastricht Treaty which had settled the arrangements for the establishment of the monetary union. Denmark had met the convergence conditions for euro area membership in 1999 but chose not to join following the rejection of membership in a national referendum. This decision was confirmed in a second referendum conducted on 28 September 2000. At the second referendum, the margin against was the quite large one of 53.1 to 46.9 per cent. The Danish currency remains linked to the euro through the fixed exchange rate mechanism known as ERMII but Denmark has not accepted the single currency. Although there are occasional discussions about the possibility of membership, parties opposed to giving up the national currency performed well in elections at the end of 2007 and there is little immediate prospect of a third referendum.

Sweden joined the EU in 1995 and does not hold an opt-out from euro area membership. Thus, under the conditions of its accession to the EU it is obliged to become part of the single currency as soon as it meets the convergence conditions for membership included in the Maastricht Treaty. However, one of those conditions is membership for two years of the ERM and so, as long as Sweden refuses to join ERMII it does not formally qualify for membership of the euro area. A referendum conducted in 2003 rejected euro area membership and Sweden shows every sign of maintaining its present position outside ERMII for some time. The European Commission has not been happy about this but has not insisted on Sweden joining, effectively granting Sweden a *de facto* opt-out.

The UK obtained an opt out from membership of the euro area in the Maastricht Treaty and the British government has chosen to exercise its option to remain outside. The question has always been whether the UK would join in the future and, if so, when. In 1998, the government indicated its willingness to join in principle but said that it would not recommend UK membership until the economic case for doing so was 'clear and unambiguous'. The factors to be taken into account in making that decision were expressed in the 'five economic tests' set out by the Chancellor of the Exchequer, Gordon Brown, in July 1997. In October of that year, H M Treasury published an assessment of the tests.[3] The government also committed itself to seeking the people's permission to join through a referendum.

The five economic tests were:

(1) Are business cycles and economic structures compatible so that we and others could live comfortably with euro interest rates on a permanent basis?

(2) If problems emerge is there sufficient flexibility to deal with them?

(3) Would joining EMU create better conditions for firms making long-term decisions to invest in Britain?

(4) What impact would entry into EMU have on the competitive position of the UK's financial services industry, particularly the City's wholesale markets?

(5) In summary, will joining EMU promote higher growth, stability and a lasting increase in jobs?

The first question relates to point 1 in box 11.1. We have identified three separate issues there, although 1(a) and 1(b) are closely related. 1(a) asks whether external shocks are likely to affect the UK economy in the same way as they do the present member countries of the euro area. 1(b) concerns the issue of timing. We have the general argument that the UK economy might require interest rate cuts when the German economy, say, requires interest rate increases or vice versa. In both cases, the debate centres on the level of convergence of the UK economy with the rest of the euro area.

Opponents of UK membership of the single currency often still hark back to UK experience as a member of the EMS between 1990 and 1992. In 1992, the UK economy was heading into recession and there was a strong argument for interest rate cuts. However, the Bundesbank increased German interest rates and this required the UK government to keep interest rates up in order to defend the exchange rate of sterling against the DM. Of course, in 1992, the UK government could have devalued but that would not be an option within the single currency and so is not relevant to the present debate. This 1992 example is commonly taken to be evidence of incompatible business cycles, but is better thought of as an example of an asymmetric shock.

The Bundesbank decision to push German interest rates up stemmed from its fear of rising inflation in Germany as the German government attempted to assimilate the East Germany economy following German reunification without raising tax rates. That is, the Bundesbank chose to keep monetary policy tight because it was worried that fiscal policy was becoming too loose. Thus, this was to a significant extent a special case. Shocks of the size of the reunification of Germany do not occur often. In any case, even if we take this as evidence of incompatible business cycles, we are now over 15 years on and it is possible that business cycles are no longer incompatible. What more recent evidence do we have?

The 1997 Treasury tests stressed the crucial nature of business cycle convergence and argued that the timing of the UK business cycle remained significantly different from that of the rest of the EU. In support of this proposition, it mentioned that official UK interest rates at the time were 7 per cent in comparison with rates of just over 3 per cent in Germany and France. Further, it argued that forward-looking measures indicated that significant differences would remain into 1999 and beyond. The particular worry was that had the UK joined the euro area at the beginning of 1999, euro interest rates would have been too low for the UK, resulting in an inflationary boom in the UK.

Pause for thought 11.4

Does a consideration of the difference between nominal interest rates provide a conclusive test of business cycle incompatibility? What factors other than different positions on the business cycle might have caused UK interest rates to be above those of Germany and France in 1997?

In 2002-3, H M Treasury was again charged with making an assessment of the degree of UK convergence with the euro area with the report being published in June 2003.[4] It concluded that significant progress had been made on convergence between 1997 and 2003 and that UK business cycles were more convergent with the euro area generally than was the case for some other euro area countries. However, concern over structural differences, notably in the housing market led to the conclusion that, on balance, the first of the five tests was not being met.

This concern over structural differences relates to point 1(c) in box 11.1 and constitutes another part of the 'one interest rate does not fit all' argument. That is, it is argued that the UK economy is different from the European economy in other ways than in possibly having incompatible business cycles. There may be differences between the UK and other members in production, tax, financial and wage setting systems and other differences in institutional structures, which would cause a change in a common European monetary policy to have a significantly different impact on the UK economy from that experienced by other members. For example, in financial markets, floating interest rate mortgages have been much more common in the UK than in other euro area economies. This raises the possibility that interest rate changes have a more powerful impact on household income and consumption in the UK than in the other economies.

This also can be viewed as an extension of what happens in any single economy. British interest rate decisions are often criticised for not taking into account the needs of some sectors of the economy, for example manufacturing industry in the Midlands and the North. It is possible that the problem with a single monetary policy for Europe is as much a regional problem as a national one - that is, that if the UK were a member of the single currency area, a particular interest rate decision might suit, say, the regions centred on Paris, Hamburg, Madrid and London but cause unhappiness in the south of Germany, north-east France, the Basque country of Spain and France and Scotland. In the debate about UK compatibility with the rest of the euro area, there is probably a tendency to overstate the extent to which all parts of the UK economy are similar. It is clear that there is a strong element of judgement here. It is also possible that membership of the single currency from 2003 would have sped up the process of integration and have led to a reduction in structural differences.

Question two concerns the flexibility of the labour market and of fiscal policy (points 2 and 3 in box 11.1) — that is, with possible escape routes if the UK economy were affected differently from other euro area countries by economic shocks or monetary policy decisions and its exchange rate with these countries could no longer change.

There are two fiscal policy issues. The first relates to the lack of automatic fiscal stabilisers across the euro area because tax and government spending decisions remain largely in the hands of national governments. Thus, regions that are badly affected by shocks to the euro area economy or by monetary policy decisions are not automatically supported by transfers from well-off regions through the budget. All that is left are discretionary disbursements from the structural and cohesion funds of the EU. These are very small relative to the euro area GDP and must deal with the large, existing regional disparities. The second fiscal policy issue concerns the attempt by the European Commission to constrain the fiscal policy freedom of euro area member countries by the application of the Stability and Growth Pact. We deal with this under the fifth test.

The role of labour market flexibility is also controversial. Again, we have two concerns here. The first is with the ability of the euro area as a whole to recover from negative economic shocks because of labour market inflexibility arising from government regulations regarding wages, working hours, employer rights to fire workers, and, in general, the 'freedom of management to manage'. The EU's concern with social policy and workers' rights is often pointed to as a basic reason for slow EU growth in comparison with growth rates in the USA.

The second issue is the lack of labour market mobility across the euro area. It is normally argued that the much greater degree of labour mobility in national economies such as the USA provides a safety valve for regional pressures as labour moves from high to low unemployment areas, helping to balance the unequal impact of asymmetric shocks or policies. Labour mobility might be hampered again by labour market regulation as well as by other aspects of social policy and regulations governing the housing market and pensions.

Pause for thought 11.5

Should the EU be prepared to weaken social policy and reduce the rights of workers if that is what seems to be needed to have faster rates of economic growth?

It is not clear that the weakening of employment and social policy would have much effect on euro area labour mobility, given the continuing language and cultural differences and lack of information regarding employment opportunities and living conditions across national boundaries. It is also not clear, as we have suggested above in 11.2, whether greater labour market mobility always has a positive impact.

The Treasury 2003 evaluation concentrated on UK labour market flexibility arguing that the slower is the progress on flexibility within the rest of the EU, the more important it is to have a high level of labour market flexibility in the UK. It concluded that, although labour market flexibility had increased considerably in the UK between 1997 and 2003, it was not certain that it had sufficiently increased. Again, this is a matter of judgement.

Theory can tell us very little about the third test. Euro interest rates are lower than those in the UK, in part because of the continued presence of an exchange rate risk premium on sterling. It is likely, therefore, that entry into the euro would reduce the cost of capital for UK firms. Small and medium-sized enterprises might also benefit from greater financial integration consequent on membership of the euro area. It is further possible that as foreign direct investment (FDI) in the euro area increases with the single currency, the UK's share of this would fall were it to remain outside for a prolonged period. Indeed, the UK's share of FDI flows into the EU did fall in the years after 1999 but the investment decisions of firms are influenced by many factors and we cannot definitely know what would have happened to incoming investment had sterling joined the euro area in 1999.

Nonetheless, the Treasury evaluation concluded that the quantity and quality of investment in the UK would very likely increase with euro area membership. The Treasury, however, hedged its bets by making this judgement dependent on the assumption that sustainable and durable convergence had been achieved before membership. Thus, the third test became subject to the first one, which then assumed greater importance.

The impact of entry into the euro area on the UK's financial services industry is also hard to know in advance and would be difficult to judge in retrospect. The only reason suggested in financial markets for the City of London benefiting from the UK remaining outside the single currency was that the UK's financial regulatory system and the Bank of England's monetary performance were regarded more highly than their euro area equivalents. Still, the question was generally considered the other way around — whether continued failure to join the euro area might cause the City to lose business to Paris or Frankfurt. There is no evidence that this has occurred since January 1999 and it seems likely that the City of London would remain strong in wholesale financial markets whether the UK joined the euro area or not. Nonetheless there are probable additional benefits for the financial services industry from membership of the euro area as European financial markets become increasingly integrated through the EU's Financial Services Action Plan. The Treasury, therefore, concluded in 2003 that this test had been met. Yet it remains difficult to quantify the potential gains here in order to weigh them against other possible losses.

The final test is even more difficult than the others. Indeed, ultimately, it cannot be answered. The UK's failure to join at the beginning of the EEC in 1957 may well have contributed to the relatively poor performance of the economy in the subsequent years, although we cannot know for certain that this was so. Equally, some past monetary unions have failed. However, arguments of this kind do not provide much guidance for the future. This really is a catchall condition and answering it would involve an attempt to weigh up all of the possible economic advantages and disadvantages, none of which can be quantified with any degree of precision, if at all.

The Treasury 2003 evaluation notes the increase in intra-euro area trade in recent years and attributes this to the single currency. It concludes, on this basis, that membership of the single currency could lead to a significant increase in UK trade within the euro area and that this, in turn, could lead to a small but sustained increase in potential output. This suggests that membership could help promote higher growth and a lasting increase in jobs. However, this potential growth is outweighed in the Treasury view by the concerns over macroeconomic stability, in particular that it would be harder to maintain stability within the euro area than outside it. Two particular worries are expressed.

The first of these relates to the monetary policy of the European Central Bank (ECB). As we shall see in section 11.7, the ECB has been accused of lack of clarity regarding its policy objectives and this, together with more general concerns about lack of transparency in ECB monetary policy has translated into worries that monetary policy may be inconsistent and difficult to anticipate.

The second issue raised by the Treasury in relation to the maintenance of macroeconomic stability concerns the Stability and Growth pact. Article 103 of the Treaty on European Union specifies that where the European Council finds economic policies of a member state that endanger the proper functioning of economic and monetary union, it may make policy recommendations to that member's government and may publish them. In all areas other than that of fiscal deficits, members need not accept these recommendations. Article 104c forbids member states from having excessive budget deficits and charges the European Commission with the task of monitoring the budgetary situation and the stock of government debt of member states. The Commission may report to the Council

that an excessive deficit exists. The Council may then make policy recommendations that the member state in question is obliged to follow. Failure to do so may
ultimately lead to the imposition of financial sanctions in the form of a non-interest-bearing deposit or a fine.

Detail was added to this clause by the agreement of the Stability and Growth
Pact of 1997, which set out rules for government borrowing of euro area members
after January 1999. These rules converted the 3 per cent of GDP limit on budget
deficits in the Maastricht convergence conditions into a permanent ceiling that
might only be breached under exceptional circumstances. These were defined as
a natural disaster or a fall in GDP of at least 2 per cent over a year. This would
only occur in a severe recession. In cases where GDP has fallen between 0.75 per
cent and 2 per cent in a single year, EU finance ministers have discretion over
whether to impose penalties.

Members who break the 3 per cent barrier in other circumstances are required
to make heavy non-interest bearing deposits with the European Central Bank.
These deposits would be converted into fines should the member's budget deficit
remain above the 3 per cent limit. Since there is discretion in the application of
fines, it is still unclear to what extent the Stability and Growth Pact will ultimately be enforced. Member countries have been warned and threatened with action
but nothing more has yet occurred. Nonetheless, the threat remains.

From a macroeconomic stabilisation point of view, the firm application of the
Pact would make little sense since the fines would make it more difficult for governments to get their borrowing back below 3 per cent of GDP and would very
likely require a higher level of unemployment to achieve it. The restriction of fiscal policy in this way thus removes another element of flexibility in the management of national economies and would increase the costs associated with the loss
of freedom to change exchange rates. The UK would like two changes to the
interpretation of the pact.

Firstly, it does not see a problem with public sector deficits produced by
increases in government investment since successful investment should contribute to future economic growth and permit the repayment of government debt
without forcing interest rates up. It would also allow the UK government to continue its current heavy investment programmes in health and education to overcome underinvestment in these areas over many years. Allowing this freedom to
break the 3 per cent deficit limit would be in accord with the British government's
'golden rule' of public finance — that over the economic cycle, the government
should borrow only to invest and not to fund current spending. Secondly, the UK
argues that governments that do not have a high public debt/GDP ratio should be
allowed greater freedom in fiscal policy than those countries that do. That is, the
rules should be applied strictly only to member countries with a debt problem.
The Treasury concluded in 2003 that if the macroeconomic framework were to
change in the direction favoured by the UK, the fifth test would also be passed.

There has been little indication that these views will be accepted. However,
after the operation of the Stability and Growth Pact had been effectively suspend-

ed in late 2003 when it became clear that France and Germany were unwilling to take the actions needed to return their budget deficits below the required 3 per cent of GDP, the rules were relaxed in March 2005 and an attempt was made to make the pact more enforceable. In 2007, excessive deficit procedures were still continuing against 7 of the 27 EU members but sanctions had yet to be taken against a member country.

Pause for thought 11.6

Is there a general problem with the enforcement of supranational rules within the EU? What powers of enforcement does the European Commission have short of expelling or suspending members?

We thus have some tests passed and some not. As one would expect, joining a single currency area at any time would carry with it some economic advantages and some disadvantages. However, the Treasury plainly does not see the exercise as one of weighing these up. One of the five tests — the first, relating to economic convergence — turns out to be more important than the others. We have seen that the Treasury's view that the UK failed this test in 2003 was one of judgement, rather than of clear-cut fact. It follows that there is little possibility that at any time in the future membership will be 'clearly and unambiguously' to the UK's economic advantage. This is hardly surprising since little economic analysis of future events produces 'clear and unambiguous' support for anything.

There has been no test of convergence since 2003 and no suggestion that a new assessment of the five economic tests be undertaken in the near future. Indeed, there has been no Treasury statement on the issue since the publication of the 2003 report. European issues and the question of UK membership of the euro have now disappeared from the home page of the Treasury's web site and have, instead, been incorporated under the broad heading of 'International Issues'. By 2008, though, a surface examination of the main items mentioned in the Treasury tests would suggest that the UK is now close to convergence with the euro area economies — over 50 per cent of UK trade is now with euro area countries, UK inflation rates are close to the euro area average and growth rates have been similar since 2004. A problem remains with real interest rates — these are still considerably higher in the UK than in the euro area. Supporters of UK membership of the euro area claim that this reflects a lack of credibility of Bank of England monetary policy and that membership of the euro area would allow the UK to have the same rate of inflation with lower interest rates. However, it can be still argued that the interest rate differential arises from still asynchronous economic cycles. As far as the City of London is concerned, any suggestion that the UK might lose from membership of the euro area through the loss of the superior financial and monetary framework provided by the FSA and the Bank of England has largely disappeared as criticism of the FSA and the Bank of England has increased.

We may also note here that one of the early arguments, not mentioned above, against UK acceptance of the euro has now disappeared. This was that sterling was too highly valued against the euro and that entry into the euro area at such a rate of exchange would have caused long-term competitive problems for UK industry. This worry now hardly applies. From an exchange rate of €1 = £0.71 in January 1999, sterling strengthened against the euro, reaching €1 = £0.58 in October 2000, clearly an exchange rate that much of British industry would have found difficulty with but in May 2008, the strength of the pound was well below its 1999 level at around about €1 = £0.80. Indeed, in 2008, the DM/£ exchange rate was 16 per cent below its level in 1992, when sterling was forced out of the EMS's exchange rate mechanism.[5] Supporters of British membership were, thus, likely to point out in 2008 that it would be a favourable time to join.

Quite apart from the five economic tests, there is a severe political problem associated with UK membership of the euro. The UK has always been the member country most sceptical of the benefits of deeper integration across the EU and the most fearful of the ideas of federation and political union in Europe. This has been strongly translated into opposition against UK membership of the euro area and it seems very unlikely that any referendum put to the British people in the foreseeable future on the subject of membership of the euro area would be passed. Indeed, it is sufficiently improbable to discourage UK governments from holding a referendum on the question. In addition, the current Prime Minister, Gordon Brown, the inventor and long-time custodian of the five economic tests, has always seemed personally very dubious about the benefits of euro membership for the UK. The Conservative Party, the principal opposition party, has despite strong internal differences of opinion in the past, remained opposed to UK membership and so UK membership seems an increasingly distant prospect.

Pause for thought 11.7

Should UK membership of the euro area be decided solely on economic grounds?

11.4   Monetary policy institutions in the euro area

The euro area was formally established on 1 January 1999 and trading in the euro commenced on 4 January. Box 11.3 sets out euro area developments from immediately before the establishment of the single currency area until February 2002. Monetary policy in the single currency area is conducted by the European System of Central Banks (ESCB), which consists of the European Central Bank (ECB) and the national central banks of the member states. The ESCB is under the control of the Governing Council and the Executive Board of the ECB. To ensure independence of the ESCB from the European Commission and the governments of member states, the national central banks, although continuing to be owned by their governments, were made to become independent of the political process in their own countries.

Article 105(2) of in the Treaty on European Union set the ESCB four basic tasks:

(a) to define and implement monetary policy of the Community;

(b) to conduct foreign exchange operations;

(c) to hold and manage the official foreign exchange reserves of the member states; and

(d) to promote the smooth operation of payments systems.

Article 105(1) of the Treaty established the primary objective of the ESCB as the maintenance of price stability. The ESCB was also required, without prejudice to the goal of price stability, to support the EU's general economic policies and to act in accordance with the principle of an open market economy with free competition, favouring an efficient allocation of resources.

The general economic policies of the EC are stated in Article 2 of the Treaty as being to promote throughout the Community:

• a harmonious and balanced development of economic activities

• sustainable and non-inflationary growth respecting the environment

• a high degree of convergence of economic performance

• a high level of employment and social protection

• the raising of the standard of living and quality of life and

• economic and social cohesion and solidarity among Member States

Article 3a further requires that in attempting to achieve all of this, member states and the Community should comply with the guiding principles of stable prices, sound public finances and monetary conditions, and a sustainable balance of payments. This gave it a set of objectives similar to those of the Bundesbank, which had been obliged by law to safeguard the currency while supporting the general economic policy of the German federal government.

Although pursuit of general economic policy objectives is not meant to prejudice the achievement of price stability, there is clearly scope for interpretation under circumstances in which an apparent conflict exists between tightening monetary policy and one or more of the general objectives. 'Price stability', after all, does not necessarily mean the lowest possible level of inflation. Indeed, with a central bank composed of people from a number of countries with different economic conditions and problems, one might expect a range of interpretations of it. Nonetheless, control of inflation was intended to be central. Further, the objective of low inflation is statutorily protected since the ESCB's objectives can only be changed by the unanimous decision of the Council of Ministers. The European Parliament has no influence on the objectives of monetary policy.

Box 11.3 Monetary developments in the euro area 1998-2008

Jun 1 1998   Establishment of ECB and ESCB

Sep 26 1998   Denmark and Greece agree to participate in ERMII with fluctuation bands around parity of 2.25% and 15% respectively

Oct 13 1998   ECB announces a target inflation rate for the euro area of less than 2%

Dec 1 1998   ECB announces a reference value for monetary growth (M3) of 4.5%

Dec 22 1998   ECB sets its main refinancing interest rate at 3%

Dec 31 1998   Conversion rates of the 11 participating currencies into the euro established from Jan 1 1999

Jan 4 1999   Trading begins in euros and ERMII commences operation

Dec 3 1999   Euro falls below parity with the US dollar for the first time

Jun 19 2000   Greece granted membership of the single currency from Jan 1 2001

Jun 28 2000   ECB changes refinancing operations from fixed to variable interest rate system

Sep 22 2000   ECB is joined by the US, UK Japanese central banks in intervention in the currency markets to support the weakening euro

Sep 28 2000   Danish referendum decides against membership of the euro area

Oct 25 2000   The euro falls to US$0.8250 - the lowest level of the euro against the dollar

Jan 1 2002   Euro notes and coin become legal tender in the 12 euro area countries

Sep 14 2003   Swedish referendum rejects membership of the euro area

Jan 1 2007   Slovakia becomes the thirteenth member

Jan 1 2008   Cyprus and Malta join taking euro area membership to 15

The possibility of the system's objectives being interpreted in different ways makes the composition of the ECB extremely important and raises the question of how the political independence of the decision-makers within the system can be ensured. Box 11.4 lists factors widely accepted as relevant to the degree of political independence of a central bank.

Pause for thought 11.8

What do you think 'price stability' means?

The ECB does well under the headings listed in box 11.4. The Executive Board of the ECB, which runs the bank, comprises a president, vice-president and four other members appointed by the Heads of State on a recommendation from the European Council after consultation with the European Parliament and the Governing Council of the ECB. All six members are required to be of recognised standing and professional experience in monetary or banking matters. In other words, they should be representatives from the world of finance, making it likely that their interpretation of 'price stability' will be conservative.

Box 11.4 Features important in determining the independence of a central bank

1. The existence of statutory guarantees of independence;

2. The nature of the statutory objectives set for the central bank;

3. Methods of appointment and removal of senior officers, the board of directors and the President

4. The length of the President's term of office;

5. The presence or absence of government officials on the bank's board;

6. The extent to which the bank is bound by instructions from the government and the range of instruments at the bank's disposal;

7. The limits on central financing of the government;

8. The ease with which any of the above features can be altered by government.

The term of office for Executive Board members is eight years and is non-renewable. Members of the Executive Board may be compulsorily retired but only for misconduct, which is defined to include the taking of instructions from a member government. To compulsorily retire an Executive Board member, the Governing Council or the Executive Board must apply to the European Court of Justice. Governors of national central banks must be appointed for at least five years and may end their terms prematurely only for serious cause, notified either by themselves or the ECB council. That is, they cannot be removed by their own national governments. The long and non-renewable term is meant to reduce the possibility of Board members following the wishes of governments in the hope of being reappointed to their positions.

Pause for thought 11.9

Why might representatives of the world of finance be expected to have a conservative view of 'price stability'? What is a conservative view of price stability?

The Governing Council consists of the Executive Board plus the governors of the national central banks. Thus, the membership rose to 21 with the entry of Cyprus and Malta to the monetary union at the beginning of 2008. Voting, on all issues except those related to the bank's capital, is on a one-person one-vote basis, with decision by simple majority. This makes it possible for the representatives of the national central banks to outvote the Executive Board members and for smaller members of monetary union to outvote large members such as Germany on all issues other than those related to the ECB's capital. This provided an extra reason for the insistence that the national central banks be politically independent.

The number of members of the Governing Council with voting rights will be capped at the present number of 21: six permanent voting rights for the members of the Executive Board and 15 voting rights for the Governors of national central banks. When there are more than 15 member states and thus more than 21 members of the Governing Council, voting rights for the Governors will be allocated on the basis of a rotation system (see box 11.5). All members will have the right to attend and to speak.

Box 11.5: The voting rotation system for the ECB Governing Council

With more than 15 central bank governors, the votes of the governors is limited to 15. The six Executive Board members always retain their independent votes. The allocation of votes to the central bank governors requires them to be divided into groups. With the number of governors between 16 and 22, there are two groups, the central bank governors of the five largest member states form the first group with country size being determined by the member state's share of the euro area's aggregate GDP at market prices (given 5/6 weighting in the calculation) and the member state's share of the euro area's total aggregated balance sheets of the monetary financial institutions (given 1/6 weighting). The remaining governors form group 2. Thus, if there are 20 member states, 5 are in group 1 and 15 in group 2. Group 1 governors have 4 votes and thus each group 1 governor is able to vote at 4 of every five meetings. Group 2 governors have 11 votes. Thus, with 20 governors on the Governing Council, 4 miss out at each meeting. Each governor votes at 73.3 per cent of all meetings. There is a problem when there are 16-18 number of governors as following the rules above would mean that the five biggest countries would vote less often than the smaller ones — and the five biggest countries would not like this at all. Indeed, it is specified in the amendment to Article 10.2 of the Statute of the ESCB and the ECB approved in March 2003 that the 'frequency of voting rights of the governors allocated to the first group shall not be lower than the frequency of voting rights of those of the second group'. Thus, if Slovakia succeeds in joining the euro area in 2009, bringing the number of governors to 16, there will need to be an adjustment to the rules.

With the number of governors above 22, things become more complex. Then there are three groups: Group 1 with the 5 largest countries as members as before; Group 2 with a membership of half the total number of governors (rounded up); Group 3 consisting of the remaining governors (of the smallest countries).

With 23 member states and therefore 23 governors on the Governing Council, there are 5 members in Group 1, 12 in Group 2 and 6 in Group 3. With 24 governors, the numbers are 5, 12 and 7. Group 1 has four votes, group 2 eight votes and group 3 three votes.

For a discussion of this method of rationing votes and of various alternatives see:

Katrin Ullrich, 'Decision-making of the ECB: reform and voting power', Discussion paper no. 04-70, ZEW, Centre for European Economic Research, September, 2004, http://opus.zbw-kiel.de

Where the bank's capital is involved, voting power is proportional to the member states' subscribed capital and the Executive Board has no votes. The subscribed capital, in turn, is determined by equal weighting of (i) the member states' shares of the population and (ii) GDP at market prices, averaged over the previous five years. Subscriptions are revised every five years.

The ECB is responsible for the note issue, open market operations, the setting of minimum reserve requirements and other aspects of monetary control and supplies liquidity to the banking system. It can make use of the national central banks to carry out open market operations. However, the ESCB is not permitted to lend to governments except through the acquisition of their paper in the secondary market. Article 104 of the Treaty explicitly prohibits the provision of overdraft or other credit facilities by the ECB or national central banks to any EU member state public body.

As we saw in 11.3, to strengthen the control of high-spending member governments, the Maastricht treaty forbad excessive government deficits and the 'bailing out' of indebted member governments by EU governments or institutions. Thus, in theory, member governments continue to face different degrees of default risk with the consequence that bond issues of different governments should continue to carry different rates of interest to reflect the market's assessment of the default risk associated with each government's debt issue. It was being suggested in bond markets in early 1997 that the formation of monetary union could see the dramatic downgrading of the debt of countries such as Belgium and Italy because of their high levels of public debt as a proportion of GDP. In practice, this has not occurred.

The Maastricht Treaty separated the operation of monetary policy from the prudential supervision of credit institutions and the stability of the financial system. The latter remains the responsibility of the member states, although the ESCB is expected to ensure the smooth conduct of policies relating to prudential supervision and the ECB may, with the unanimous approval of the European Council and the approval of the European Parliament, be given specific tasks in this area (Article 105.6). This conforms to the German model in which prudential supervision was not carried out by the Bundesbank but by the separate Aufsichtsamt (the Federal Banking Supervisory Office). The UK also changed to this arrangement with the independence of the Bank of England in 1997 when the supervisory role was taken away from the Bank and given to the Financial Services Authority (FSA), although this arrangement has been subject to much criticism since the failure of Northern Rock Bank in 2007.

Any attempt to place significant power in the hands of an unelected body such as the ECB raises the question of the accountability of that body to governments and, ultimately, to the citizens of the member states. Accountability under the Maastricht Treaty is weak. This is not surprising since:

- the aim of making central banks independent is to prevent as far as is possible the contamination of monetary policy decisions by the attitudes and actions of the democratic political system and

- there is a general problem of accountability within the European Union.

What accountability there is, takes the following forms:

1. The ECB is subject to audit and is under the jurisdiction of the Court of Justice;

2. The President of the European Council and a member of the European Commission are allowed to attend meetings of the Governing Council of the ECB but are not allowed to vote;

3. The ECB is required to report annually on its activities to the Council and the European Parliament, and the President and other members of the Executive Board are heard by the relevant committees of the parliament at either side's request.

None of this gives any genuine power to anyone to call the ECB to account. Disapproval can, of course, be expressed but there is no provision beyond this. There is another difficulty, which we shall come across below. Accountability requires transparency, in the sense that people should be able to know what the ECB is doing in order to fulfil its mandate. This, in turn, requires full knowledge of what that mandate is. Of course, we do know this in a general sense — the achievement of price stability. But this requires interpretation.

The aim of these regulations was to create a strongly independent central bank. Indeed, it is, in a sense, more politically independent than the Bundesbank itself. One argument given for this view is that when the Bundesbank and the German government held different views regarding economic policy, the Bundesbank had a single and united opponent which was able to point to its electoral support. Within the monetary union, the counterpart of the German government is a group of governments which may have different political persuasions and whose countries may be experiencing different economic problems. Consequently, there is unlikely to be a single united political view to contrast with that of the Executive Board of the ECB.

In addition, the Bundesbank central council included the 11 presidents of the German Länder (regions) and this regional representation probably kept the Bundesbank more in touch with the real problems of the economy than is the case with the General Council of the ECB.

The aim of all of these regulations was to create a strongly independent central bank. Indeed, it is more politically independent than the Bundesbank used to be. When the Bundesbank and the German government held different views regarding economic policy, the Bundesbank had a single and united opponent that was able to point to its electoral support. Within the monetary union, the counterpart of the German government is a group of governments that may be of different political persuasions and whose countries may be experiencing different economic problems. Consequently, it is less likely that the ECB Executive Board will confront a united political view than was the case with the Bundesbank.

And yet, despite all of the attempts to preserve the political independence of the ECB, to enforce strict convergence conditions for membership and forbid loose budgetary policies, the view of both the financial markets and leading economists before the establishment of the single currency was that the euro, in the long-term, would be a weaker currency than the DM had been. One reason for this view stemmed from the high proportion of intra-EU trade of monetary union members. This makes the EU a relatively closed economic area with its external trade making up only a small percentage of GDP. This, it was held, would cause the ECB[7] to be less concerned about the external value of the euro than the Bundesbank was about the DM and to behave like the US Federal Reserve — pursuing internal price stability but being largely indifferent to the impact of the exchange rate on foreign trade. This would make it more open to pressures for weaker monetary policy to stimulate economic growth, particularly given the slow growth and high rates of unemployment in much of the EU in the late 1990s. A supporting argument was that the euro would be a broader-based reserve currency than the DM and, thus, would be less likely to be driven artificially high on occasions.

11.5   The form of monetary policy in the euro area

Several issues relating to the operation of policy needed to be settled in advance of 1999. There were three principal issues:

- The determination of a target rate of inflation;

- Whether to target the inflation rate directly or to target an intermediate variable such as the rate of growth of the money supply;

- The choice of the policy instrument.

The target rate of inflation

The ECB, unlike the Bank of England, makes its own interpretation of price stability, referring to it as a 'quantitative definition of price stability' rather than as a target because the ECB denies that it is engaged in inflation targeting (ECB 2001). However, we are also told that the quantitative definition 'provides a yardstick against which the public can hold the ECB accountable' (ECB, 2001, p.38) and that:

> The ECB is required to provide an explanation for sustained deviations from this definition and to clarify how price stability will be re-established within an acceptable period of time (ECB, 2001, p.38).

This makes it sound close enough to a target for us to use the word. The Governing Council of the ECB announced a definition of price stability as a 'year-on-year increase in the Harmonised Index of Consumer Prices (HICP) for the euro area of below 2 per cent'.[8] This was qualified to make clear that 'prolonged declines in the level of the HICP index, would not be deemed consistent with price stability'. From this it was inferred that the ECB was being set a medium-term range of 0 - 2 per cent but left open the possibility of the rate of inflation falling below zero in the short-run and of being very close to zero even in the medium term. This caused concern that the policy might be too strict, particularly given the problems surrounding the use of price indexes in general and the HICP in particular. According to Eurostat, the statistics bureau of the EU, the HICP takes account of the latest economic research. However, national price indexes are probably more likely to overestimate inflation than the reverse (see section 8.3); the same is likely to be true of the HICP. Early practice with, from June 2000, the inflation rate spending much time at or above 2 per cent calmed these worries and then in May 2003 the ECB's Governing Council eased its statement of the meaning of price stability to:

> The primary objective of the ECB's monetary policy is to maintain price stability. The ECB aims at inflation rates of below, but close to, 2 per cent over the medium term.

This is the statement one now finds on the monetary policy page of the ECB's website. It differs from the 2 per cent target faced by the Bank of England in two ways. Firstly, inflation rates slightly below 2 per cent are clearly regarded as preferable to those slightly above 2 per cent. Secondly, the use of the phrase 'over the medium term' introduces an element of doubt regarding the judgement of current performance. The arrangement in the UK is straightforward — an inflation rate more than 1 per cent above or below the target is regarded as a failure requiring the Monetary Policy Committee to explain what has gone wrong and what it intends to do about it. The ECB is under no such pressure to explain deviations from the 'near 2 per cent inflation' definition of inflation it faces.

This greater vagueness in the ECB's case is understandable for two reasons, the first deriving from the problems of operating a monetary policy for a large number of countries. Plainly, a low inflation calculated across a number of economies might well involve falling prices in some national economies and this needs to be taken into account in making an assessment of the meaning of the measured inflation rate for all economies. An inflation rate for the euro area of, say, 1.8 per cent is not likely to be acceptable if it is associated with deflation in some member states. This problem is complicated by any doubts attached to the accuracy of the HICP.

The HICP is a measure of headline inflation. That is, it uses a consumer price index (CPI) and the measure is influenced by all factors including external shocks, even if these have only short-term effects, and policy changes, although they might be intended to reduce longer-term inflationary pressure. This contrasts with the idea of framing the inflation target in terms of core or underlying inflation (such as the RPI-X previously used in the UK), which seeks to measure

sustained domestic inflationary pressure. Although the use of a CPI rate of inflation for the framing of inflation targets has become standard practice for central
banks, it leaves an element of uncertainty as to how the central bank is likely to
react to an external shock such as increased world oil and food prices (see section
8.3 for other arguments regarding the choice of a price index for inflation targeting).

The ECB has argued that it retains a degree of flexibility because its concern
is with medium-term inflationary trends — but this leaves open the question of
the length of the medium term. The ECB defends the choice of a quantitative definition of price stability as a means of providing both transparency and accountability. However, this is not achieved if the meaning of the definition is unclear.
In other words, the form of the target reduces the transparency of ECB decision-
making and leaves the financial markets uncertain about the basis of ECB decisions.

The use or not of an intermediate target

The ECB had to decide whether simply to target the ultimate objective — the
achievement of a low inflation rate — or to choose an intermediate target through
which it would hope to control the rate of inflation. The likely intermediate target was some measure of the money supply. We have seen earlier, that there is no
possibility of, or justification for, using the money supply as an instrument of policy, but the use of a money supply intermediate target was defended by a number of economists at the time of the establishment of the ECB and its approach to
monetary policy.

The argument related to the length of time lags. The full effects of a change
in short-term interest rates on the rate of inflation might not be felt for two years
or longer. If we add in the numerous exogenous influences on the rate of inflation, it is easy to see the difficulties facing central banks. As we have seen in section 8.3, the central bank seeks additional information about the performance of
the economy and the inflationary pressure present in the economy to help it make
its judgements regarding adjustments in the interest rate. One idea still popular
in Europe in 1998 was that of establishing an intermediate target which responded more quickly to interest rate changes than the rate of inflation itself and which
had fewer external influences upon it. An intermediate target is only useful, however, if it is stably related to the instrument and to the final target.

A variety of intermediate targets have been proposed including the rate of
growth of the money supply. Clearly, the time lag between changes in short-term
interest rates and changes in the rate of growth of the money supply are relatively short and there are fewer exogenous influences upon the money supply than
on the inflation rate itself or on other intermediate targets proposed such as
changes in the level of aggregate demand. However, the use of an intermediate
money supply target would only make sense if there were a stable short-run
demand function for money. In the UK, the short-run money demand function

had been manifestly unstable over the 20 years before 1998 and the use of a money supply target in the UK had been abandoned very quickly. Germany, on the other hand, had continued to specify a target for broad money. Although, in practice, the Bundesbank had appeared to pay at least as much attention to the rate of inflation itself as to the broad money target, it had continued to recommend the use of a broad money target for the ECB. This was despite the existence of evidence that in the second half of the 1990s, the German demand for money function was starting to become unstable because of financial liberalisation and increased financial innovation in Germany. As well as causing short-term instability in the demand for money function, financial liberalisation had made it harder for central banks to control the money supply because it had become harder to influence relative interest rates between money and other financial assets.

This meant that there were sufficient uncertainties to make it inadvisable to depend on a single measure of the money supply as an intermediate target. A money supply target could have been based on past relationships between the money supply and inflation or on the basis of a model of the economy of the monetary union but there was a serious possibility that it would be of little use in making monetary policy decisions. In addition, a failure to achieve the single money supply target would have added to the uncertainty regarding the strength of the ECB's monetary policy.

Thus, instead of a money supply target, the ECB set a monetary growth reference point for a broad measure of the money supply, M3. M3 consists of currency in circulation plus certain liabilities of monetary financial institutions (MFIs) resident in the euro area and, in the case of deposits, the liabilities of some institutions that are part of central government (such as Post Offices and Treasuries). These liabilities included in M3 are:

- overnight deposits;
- deposits with an agreed maturity of up to two years;
- deposits redeemable at notice up to three months;
- repos;
- debt securities with maturity of up to two years;
- money market funds and money market paper (net).

The monetary growth reference value was established as the first pillar of the ECB's monetary stability strategy. The second pillar of the strategy is a broadly based assessment of the outlook for price developments and the risks to price stability, using other available indicators. These other indicators include the output gap, forecasts of economic growth and a forecast of the rate of inflation itself.

The monetary growth reference value was set at 4.5 per cent per annum and has been left unchanged. This figure was based on what the ECB referred to as the plausible assumptions of a medium-term rate of growth of 2 to 2.5 per cent per annum and an annual decline in the velocity of money of 0.5 to 1 per cent, together with the target rate of inflation of less than 2 per cent. The ECB made it quite clear from the beginning that the figure of 4.5 per cent for monetary growth was not a target and that figures above 4.5 per cent would certainly not automatically trigger interest rate rises. The reference value is also described as a medium-term concept. In the view of the ECB, temporary deviations from it are not unusual and do not necessarily have implications for future price developments.

Pause for thought 11.10

Why did the ECB forecast an annual fall in the velocity of money?

The choice of policy instrument

The ECB had first to decide upon its system for providing liquidity to the banking system. This is done principally through the main refinancing operations, weekly open market operations that provide liquidity to the banking system through repurchase agreements (repos) with a maturity of two weeks. Initially, this operated through a system of fixed rate tenders, with the fixed rate known as the main refinancing rate — 'refi' for short. This rate became the focus of attention at the regular announcement of the interest rate decision of the ECB's Governing Council.

In a fixed-rate tender, when the total amount for which banks bid is greater than the amount the central bank is prepared to lend, each bank receives the same proportion of the amount for which they bid. This encourages banks to bid for more than they really want since they know they are unlikely to receive all that they bid for and they know the interest rate they will have to pay on the funds they receive. This gives an advantage to large banks, which have the collateral to be able to support large bids for funds. It also makes it difficult for the central bank to judge the true demand for money in the system.

Thus, it quickly became clear that the ECB would prefer a variable rate tender in which banks indicate how much they are willing to borrow from the central bank at various rates. A cut-off rate of interest is then declared. Bids above this cut-off rate are fully filled while bids at the cut-off rate are filled proportionately. This gives the central bank a better idea of the state of demand in the market and of market expectations about future interest rates. The official refinancing rate is then simply a minimum rate of interest — no funds are provided by the central bank below this rate but it is possible for funds to be lent to the banks above this rate. For this reason, the ECB was wary about changing to the variable rate system. This was particularly the case because the large euro area economies were in recession during the first year of the ECB's operation. This had led the bank to cut the refinancing rate from 3 per cent to 2.5 per cent on 9 April 1999 and it had a clear desire at this point to keep interest rates low. During this period only about 5 per cent of total bank bids for funds were being met by the ECB and there was little doubt that the interest rate at which funds were actually provided under a variable rate system would be higher than the minimum rate.

The change to a variable rate tender was made on the 28 June 2000. By then, the main refinancing rate was on its way up as the ECB became more concerned about inflation. Nonetheless, the ECB wished to keep interest rates as steady as possible under the new system and so moved to variable rate tenders just after it had increased the refinancing rate by a half percentage point — a larger increase than many in the market had expected. Changing the system at that time made it less likely that the rates at which funds would actually be provided to the banks would be much above the official refinancing rate, which from that point became the minimum rate.

The main refinancing operations of the ECB are supported by two other types of open market operations: longer-term refinancing operations and fine-tuning operations. Longer-term financing operations are conducted monthly through repurchase agreements with a three-month maturity. The purpose of these is to prevent all liquidity in the money market from having to be rolled over every two weeks and to provide access to longer-term refinancing. As their name suggests, fine-tuning operations are conducted irregularly with the aim of smoothing the impact on interest rates of unexpected liquidity fluctuations in the money market. Structural operations are also possible - these are intended to adjust the structural liquidity of the Eurosystem in relation to the banking system.[9]

When the refinancing rate is announced by the ECB's Governing Council, two other rates are also declared. These are the ECB's rates on its marginal lending facility and on its deposit facility. The marginal lending facility provides the possibility of emergency overnight borrowing to meet liquidity needs. The rate of interest for such borrowings is always set above the refinancing rate. On 22 January 1999, after a brief adjustment period, the marginal lending interest rate was set 150 basis points (1.5 per cent) above the main refinancing rate. From 9 April 1999, this difference was reduced to 100 basis points (1 per cent) and the gap between the two rates has remained unchanged from that date. The deposit rate applies to overnight deposits and is always set below the refinancing rate. The gap between these two rates has also stayed steady at 100 basis points (1 per cent) since 9 April 1999. The main refinancing rate (refi) is by far the most important of the ECB's rates.

Another question was whether to support the control of short-term interest rates with the requirement that banks hold mandatory minimum reserve ratios. Before monetary union, this was practised in the majority of EU member countries in the belief that it allowed the central bank more easily to manage short-term interest rates by creating a predictable demand for reserves at the central bank under circumstances in which bank balance sheets were growing rapidly in response to increased demand for credit. However, because reserves at the central bank usually do not receive interest, the ratios act as a tax on banks and, as the required reserves grow, banks push up loan rates to make up for the lost interest and to restore overall rates of profit. This in turn puts downward pressure on the demand for credit.

The Bank of England argued that minimum reserve ratios were not required in deep and liquid financial markets since the central bank could achieve its objectives in such markets solely through open market operations. It was also suggested that the use of minimum reserve ratios conflicted with the Maastricht Treaty requirement that policy should be conducted in accordance with the principle of an open market economy with free competition, favouring an efficient allocation of resources.

Despite these objections, the ECB settled for a minimum reserves system with banks required to hold with the national central bank members of the ESCB a reserve ratio of 2 per cent of the liability base. This was defined to include: overnight deposits; deposits with agreed maturity up to two years; deposits redeemable at notice up to two years; debt securities issued with agreed maturity up to two years; and money market paper. A lump-sum allowance of €100,000 may be deducted from an institution's reserve requirement. The Governing Council argued that without the use of a minimum reserve system, the ESCB would be faced with a relatively high volatility of money market interest rates and would need to engage frequently in open market operations. This could undermine the operational efficiency of monetary policy as markets have difficulty in distinguishing policy signals made by the ECB from technical adjustments necessary to reduce the volatility of interest rates. It argued, too, that a reserve ratio system would safeguard the role of national central banks as providers of liquidity to the banking system. However, the Council acknowledged the burden that such a system places on banks if reserves at the central bank do not earn interest. It thus decided to pay interest on the required minimum reserves holdings at the main refinancing interest rate.

11.6   ECB monetary policy since 1999 and the value of the euro

It is difficult to judge the effectiveness of ECB monetary policy. Firstly, we must allow for the time lags in monetary policy and accept that the performance of the euro area economy in 1999 and perhaps a good proportion of 2000 had more to do with the monetary policies of the central banks of the member countries before 1999 and with the attempt by various governments to meet the Maastricht convergence criteria. Secondly, despite the setting of an inflation target and a monetary growth reference value, it has not been easy to know precisely what the ECB has been attempting to do.

In practice, the interest rate decisions appear to suggest that a medium-term average rate of inflation of 2 per cent would be perfectly acceptable and that monthly figures between 2 and 3 per cent per annum do not, in themselves, suggest a failure of policy. Thus, the Governing Council appears to become concerned when the monthly rate moves above 2 per cent per annum only if there is evidence of growing inflationary pressure that would continue in the medium-term, pushing the rate higher. However, it is difficult to know how long the medium term is in the minds of the members of the Governing Council. It has also been difficult to determine the attitude of ECB members towards the desired value of the euro.

We have mentioned the doubts that surrounded the likely policy of the ECB and hence the likely strength of the euro following its launch in January 1999. The constitution had been designed partly to convince the markets that the euro area would be a low inflation area with a strong currency. However, the ECB was a new institution and new institutions ultimately only establish a reputation through their behaviour over a number of years. In January 1999, no one knew precisely how the ECB would behave.

Despite these doubts, no one forecast the dramatic fall that took place in the value of the euro, particularly against the US dollar and the Japanese yen, in its first two years of life. The extent of this fall is shown in table 11.1 which provides exchange rates for the US$, yen and pound sterling principally on those days on which the ECB announced a change in its main refinancing rate.

The euro, having begun trading on 4 January 1999 at a rate of €1 = $1.1743 rose slightly on the first two days but from then until the 26 October 2000 (when it seemed to have finally reached its low), fell 30 per cent against the dollar, 33.2 per cent against the yen, and 18.4 per cent against the pound sterling. It then recovered briefly but soon fell back to below a rate of €1 = $0.90 in March 2001. In the first half of 2002, however, it began a steady climb, rose above parity towards the end of 2002 and reached new highs in late 2003. In February 2004, the euro reached a peak of $1.2858 before again falling back. The rate then remained remarkably stable for much of 2004 before another upward swing took the euro up to another new high of $1.3621 on New Year's eve of that year. A fairly steady but slow weakening of the euro took it back down to €1 = $1.1797 on the last day of trading of 2005, virtually the same as its rate on the opening day of euro trading seven years earlier. The euro was generally stronger in 2006 and ended that year at €1 = $1.16, a rate which held steady for the first part of 2007. Then, as the dollar weakened against all major currencies, the euro rose again.

In a little over nine years the value of the dollar against the euro had swung between $0.8252 and $1.594 (the exchange rate on 23 April 2008). The value of the yen against the euro had moved between €1 = Y89.3 (October 2000) and €1 = Y168.68 (July 2007). At 30 April 2008, the $/€ rate was 31.8 per cent higher, the Y/€ rate 21.6 per cent higher and the £/€ rate 10 per cent higher than they had been at the beginning of January 1999. We then need to ask what exactly had happened. Why did the euro fall so sharply and quickly in the first two years of its life.

The fall in the value of the euro was clearly partly a reflection of the strength of the US dollar as the US economy continued to grow rapidly and European firms invested heavily in the USA. This is reflected in the final column in table 11.1 which shows the difference on the date in question between the Federal Reserve's target Fed Funds rate and the ECB's main refinancing rate. This stood at 1.75 per cent when the euro was established but rose above that as the Fed engaged in a series of interest rate rises in 1999 and the first half of 2000. Simply on interest rate parity grounds it seems unsurprising that the dollar was strengthening against the euro.

Table 11.1 Exchange rates of the euro against the dollar, the yen and sterling, 1999-2008

Date	$/€	¥/€	£/€	refi (% rate)	Fed Funds - refi (%)
4 Jan 99	1.1789	133.73	0.7111	3.0	+1.75
9 Apr 99	1.0778	130.75	0.6724	2.5	+2.25
5 Nov 99	1.0408	109.79	0.6397	3.0	+2.25
4 Feb 00	0.9835	105.99	0.6195	3.25	+2.5
17 Mar 00	0.9672	102.31	0.6146	3.5	+2.25
28 Apr 00	0.9085	97.48	0.5794	3.75	+2.25
9 Jun 00	0.949	101.42	0.631	4.25	+2.25
1 Sep 00	0.8902	94.77	0.6135	4.5	+2.0
6 Oct 00	0.8703	94.82	0.6014	4.75	+1.75
26 Oct 00	0.8252	89.3	0.5807	4.75	+1.75
11 May 01	0.8773	107.35	0.6181	4.5	0
31 Aug 01	0.9158	108.65	0.6285	4.25	-1.0
18 Sep 01	0.9256	108.5	0.6304	3.75	-0.75
9 Nov 01	0.893	107.47	0.6144	3.25	-1.25
6 Dec 02	1.0006	125.02	0.6377	2.75	-1.5
7 Mar 03	1.1039	128.68	0.6867	2.5	-1.5
6 Jun 03	1.1813	139.28	0.7093	2.0	-1.0
31 Dec 04	1.3621	139.65	0.70505	2.0	+0.25
5 Jul 05	1.1883	133.03	0.67735	2.0	+1.25
6 Dec 05	1.1783	142.64	0.67905	2.25	+1.75
8 Mar 06	1.1914	140.35	0.68605	2.5	+2.0
15 Jun 06	1.261	144.84	0.68225	2.75	+2.25
9 Aug 06	1.2879	148.17	0.6753	3.0	+2.25
11 Oct 06	1.2543	149.96	0.67575	3.25	+2.0
13 Dec 06	1.3265	155.34	0.6728	3.5	+1.75
14 Mar 07	1.3183	153.66	0.68535	3.75	+1.5
13 Jun 07	1.3287	162.52	0.6745	4.0	+1.25
29 Jan 08	1.4773	158.02	0.74295	4.0	-1.0
30 Apr 08	1.554	162.62	0.79015	4.0	-2.0

Source: European Central Bank, Statistical Data Warehouse, http://sdw.ecb.europa.eu/ (20 May 2008)

In addition, because the markets had no clear no notion of how low the ECB were prepared to see the euro fall before they took action, market agents frequently 'tested the market' — they sold euro to see if falls would produce some indication of likely future action by the ECB. This doubt about the policy likely to be followed by the central bank was increased by the tendency of members of the Executive Board to make conflicting statements about the euro. The markets did not like this apparent lack of leadership. Nor were they convinced that the ECB would, despite its constitution, be truly immune from political pressure. This concern was strengthened by the confusion over the length of the term of office of the first President of the ECB, Wim Duisenberg of the Netherlands.

Duisenberg was appointed in 1998 to serve an eight-year term. However, there had been conflict over his appointment because of the fear of some member states, notably France, that Duisenberg's approach to policy would be too conservative and that monetary policy might be deflationary. It was generally understood that there had been a behind-the-scenes agreement that Duisenberg would not serve his full term of office and would be replaced by a French nominee, although the exact terms of the agreement were unclear. There was a widespread view that Duisenberg would serve only four years, although he consistently denied this. In the event, in February 2002, he announced that he would be retiring from the job on his 68th birthday, on 9 July 2003. By then, he will have served just over five years of his term of office.

As well as the worry about leadership, because the euro was a new currency, there was no firm view as to the long run exchange rate indicated by economic fundamentals. The starting exchange rate of the euro was simply a weighted average of the values of the 11 participating currencies at the end of December 1998. There was no reason to believe that the new currency would behave in the same way as this weighted average had done before 1999. Indeed, it was probably the case that recessions in the major economies would have a more depressing impact on expectations about the future of the European economy than was suggested by the weights applied in the old ERM.

Under these circumstances, other factors that might normally not have had much impact on the currency provided additional excuses for selling the euro. These included the resignation of the president and members of the European Commission and the NATO bombing of Serbia and Kosovo. The feeling was that only genuine news about improved fundamentals of the currency would push the value of the euro up, whereas it would fall merely because of rumour and political uncertainty. Thus, the fall resulted from a mixture of genuine economic news, the existence of uncertainty about the attitudes of the authorities and a variety of short-term political factors. The doubts about when the euro would 'bottom out' encouraged speculators to continue to sell the euro.

For most of 1999, the ECB was able to take a relaxed view of the value of the euro since the major European economies were in deep recession with high levels of unemployment and low rates of growth. And the HICP showed inflation rates well within the ECB's target range of 0 - 2 per cent.

Table 11.2 Inflation and unemployment rates, money growth rate and official interest rate for the euro area, January 1999-March 2008

Date		Inflation rate[1]	Money growth rate[2]	Unemployment rate[3]	refi rate[4]
1999	Jan	0.8	6.2	9.6	3.0
	Apr	1.1	5.3	9.4	2.5 (9 April)
	Nov	1.5	5.8	8.9	3.0 (5 Nov)
2000	Feb	1.9	5.9	8.6	3.25 (4 Feb)
	Mar	1.9	6.0	8.6	3.5 (17 Mar)
	Apr	1.7	5.9	8.4	3.75 (28 Apr)
	Jun	2.1	4.6	8.3	4.25 (9 Jun)
	Sep	2.5	4.2	8.2	4.5 (1 Sep)
	Oct	2.4	4.2	8.0	4.75 (6 Oct)
2001	May	3.1	4.4	7.8	4.5 (11 May)
	Aug	2.3	5.9	7.8	4.25 (31 Aug)
	Sep	2.2	6.9	7.8	3.75 (18 Sep)
	Nov	2.0	7.8	7.9	3.25 (9 Nov)
2002	Jun	1.9	7.2	8.2	3.25
	Sep	2.1	7.2	8.4	3.25
	Dec	2.3	6.9	8.5	2.75 (6 Dec)
2003	Mar	2.5	8.2	8.7	2.5 (7 Mar)
	Jun	1.9	8.6	8.7	2.0 (6 Jun)
	Dec	2.0	7.1	8.7	2.0
2004	Mar	1.7	6.2	8.8	2.0
	Jul	2.3	5.4	8.9	2.0
	Dec	2.4	6.6	9.0	2.0
2005	Mar	2.1	6.5	9.0	2.0
	Sep	2.6	8.3	8.8	2.0
	Dec	2.2	7.4	8.7	2.25 (6 Dec)
2006	Mar	2.2	8.4	8.6	2.5 (8 Mar)
	Jun	2.5	8.4	8.3	2.75 (15 Jun)
	Aug	2.3	8.2	8.1	3.0 (9 Aug)
	Oct	1.6	8.5	8.0	3.25 (11 Oct)
	Dec	1.9	10.0	7.8	3.5 (13 Dec)
2007	Mar	1.9	11.0	7.6	3.75 (14 Mar)
	Jun	1.9	11.0	7.5	4.0 (13 Jun)
	Dec	3.1	11.5	7.2	4.0
2008	Mar	3.6	10.3	7.1	4.0

1 Annual rate of growth of Harmonised Index of Consumer Prices, euro area (changing composition)
2 Annual rate of growth of M3, euro area (changing composition)
3 Unemployment as a percentage of the labour force; euro area 12 (fixed composition)
4 ECB's main refinancing (refi) rate at the end of month (date of interest rate change in brackets)

Source: European Central Bank, Statistical Data Warehouse, http://sdw.ecb.europa.eu/ (21 May 2008)

This is shown clearly in table 11.2, which sets out changes in the ECB's main refinancing rate since January 1999, together with inflation, unemployment, and money growth rate figures over the period for the euro area. We should note that the base of 100 for the HICP represents average 1996 prices. At the beginning of the operations of the ECB in January 1999, the HICP stood at 102.8.

In the first half of 1999, there was little desire to invest within Europe and the ECB was able to keep interest rates low to help the recovery of the European economy. The HICP remained almost stationary for much of the year. The ECB's initial interest rate of 3 per cent was lowered in early April to 2.5 per cent and was then left unchanged for seven months. By November, however, although the inflation rate was still well within the target range, it had begun to rise. The monetary growth rate, having fallen in early 1999, was on the way up again and had reached 5.8 per cent, the euro was plunging towards parity with the dollar and unemployment, while still high, was beginning to fall. The ECB responded to what they saw as developing inflationary pressure by pushing the main refinancing rate back to 3 per cent.

The euro continued to fall, breaching parity with the dollar for the first time on 27 January 2000. The monetary growth rate remained well above the reference value and unemployment continued slowly to decline. The ECB responded with a series of quarter point interest rises in February, March and April and a half point rise in June. Under this pressure, monetary growth fell back towards the reference value and the euro picked up to some extent. This was misleading since it began to fall again sharply in August and September. Meanwhile the inflation rate continued to rise, reaching 2.5 per cent in September. The ECB appeared now to be genuinely concerned about the possible inflationary effects of the weakening currency. Interest rates were again increased in September and on 22 September 2000, the ECB joined with the central banks of the USA, Japan and the UK to purchase euro in the attempt to prop up the currency. This, together with a further interest rate rise in October, had no immediate effect and the euro reached a low of $0.825 during the day's trading on 26 October.

Nonetheless, the euro area economy appeared soon after to be responding to the ECB's rate rises. By January 2001, the inflation rate (at 2.0 per cent) had fallen towards the target range; the monetary growth rate had fallen below the reference value; and the fall in unemployment had virtually come to a halt. The ECB felt able to relax. Following the October 2000 increase, the main refinancing rate was left unchanged for seven months. During this period, however, the US economy had started to head toward recession and fears of a global recession had begun to emerge. The Federal Reserve had begun to slash US interest rates and the financial markets were expecting the ECB to follow suit. The problem for the ECB was that monetary growth was again starting to move up and the inflation rate was under pressure from rising world oil prices as well as the weak euro. The impact on the HICP of the temporarily high world oil price provides a good example of the problem of using a headline rate of inflation as the target of monetary policy. It is at least possible that the ECB was unduly slow to cut interest rates because of the high rate of inflation as shown by the HICP, which reached a peak of 3.1 per cent in May 2001.

Following the May cut, the ECB resisted pressure for further cuts until the end of August. In the period between May and August, the inflation rate began to decline but remained well outside the target range. Monetary growth continued to rise. The 11 September attack on the World Trade Centre in New York and the Pentagon in Washington DC led to increased worries about world recession and the ECB responded with a half-point cut in rates on 18 September and a further quarter-point cut in November. By this time inflation had fallen to 2.1 per cent, just outside the target range.

The monetary growth rate continued to climb but this was dismissed by the ECB. It argued that the relatively high growth of M3 was the result of people shifting into the liquid and relatively safe short-term assets that make up M3 because of the uncertainty following the September 11 attacks. Support for this view was drawn from the fact that the growth of private sector credit had been continuously falling over recent months. The ECB felt that the main refinancing rate, which stood after the November cut at 3.25 per cent, had been reduced sufficiently. There was some criticism that the ECB was not responding sufficiently to the threat of world recession. In 2001, the US Federal Open Market Committee had reduced the Federal Funds rate by 4.25 percentage points (from 6 per cent to 1.75 per cent) while the ECB had cut its main refinancing rate from only 4.75 per cent to 3.25 per cent. Even the UK's MPC had cut its repo rate by more (from 6 per cent to 4 per cent) despite the fact that the UK economy appeared to be better placed to withstand a world recession than the large economies in the euro area.

However, the ECB continued to feel that it had done enough and did not make another change until December 2002. Then, with the inflation rate still just outside the target range and with money supply growth still well above the reference range, the ECB felt able to cut the refi rate by 50 basis points. The key to this decision was the continued sluggishness of euro area economies, the stubborn refusal of unemployment to fall below 8 per cent and the upward movement of the euro above parity with the US dollar. This reduction appeared to have little effect. The euro continued to increase in value but this was hardly surprising since the Fed funds rate was by then 1.5 percentage points below the main refinancing rate, a large turn around from the beginning of 1999.

Further cuts in the refi rate followed in March and June 2003. By then, the refi rate had fallen 275 basis points from the peak reached in late 2000, more than the 250 basis points fall in the UK's repo rate. Of course, by this time the Fed Funds rate had fallen to 1 per cent and the euro continued to rise, threatening the exports of the large euro area countries. By 2004, talk was again of rising interest rates. Interest rates in the UK were already on the way up and were expected to rise in the USA if not before, then soon after the presidential election in November. The ECB, however, felt the need to resist the upwards movement. Inflation rose to 2.5 per cent in May and stayed above 2 per cent for the rest of the year. Monetary growth was above the reference level but unemployment remained high. Despite the Fed's rush of interest rate increases, the dollar was weakening against the euro. By December 2004, the Fed funds rate had risen above the refi for the first time for three-and-a-half years. Increases in the ECB's rate would only have put further upward pressure on the euro.

The ECB faced the same problem throughout 2005. Inflation remained a little above 2 per cent for much of the year and the monetary growth rate was well above its reference value but unemployment remained high. The $/€ exchange rate finally began to respond to the increases in the Fed funds rate, drifting down, especially from May onwards and spending much of the second half of the year not much above (or on occasions even slightly below) the rate at the beginning of January 1999. By September the pressure on the ECB to move interest rates up was growing. Inflation reached 2.6 per cent over that month and the monetary growth rate had risen to 8.3 per cent, indicating the possibility of more inflation problems ahead. Unemployment had (if ever so slowly) started to come down and there was by then no immediate worry about an overvalued euro.

In the event, the ECB did not act until December and then it embarked on a steady series of interest rate rises, continuing through 2006 and lasting into 2007. Inflation and monetary growth remained above the ECB's desired levels until September but unemployment was continuing to come down. Although the Fed had continued its series of rate rises until late June 2006, the dollar had weakened a little against the euro but not sufficiently to cause any worry. Despite the fall in inflation rate to well below 2 per cent in September and October, the ECB continued with its rate rises, pushing the refi up in both October and December. After all, it could be argued that evidence from both the money supply figures and the labour market suggested the need for further tightening of monetary policy.

This remained the position during the first two-thirds of 2007. The ECB's policy of continuing interest rate rises appeared to be justified by the inflation rates which perfectly met the requirement of an inflation rate just below 2 per cent. The money supply and labour market figures could be held to justify the further interest rate rises of March and June 2007. Beyond June, the $/€ exchange rate was again beginning to become worryingly high especially following the Fed's half-point interest rate cut in September.

Then, in the second half of the year, the developed world was faced with the US sub-prime mortgage collapse and the crisis of the credit crunch. Fears emerged of recession in the USA and of the spread of this to Europe. The Fed began a dramatic series of cuts in its Fed Funds rate. It had been held at 5¼ per cent from June 2006 but from Sept 2007 to April 2008, a series of seven cuts of between 25 to 75 basis points took the rate down to 2 per cent. This put great pressure on the dollar and the value of the euro continued to rise sharply. The ECB was also being pressed to cut its interest rates. However, from September 2007, the HICP had started to record steadily higher inflation rates due to a significant extent to rising oil and world food prices. In November, inflation rose above 3 per cent, something it had done for only one previous month (May 2001) in the whole period from the beginning of 1999. In December 2007, money supply growth figures had gone above 10 per cent p.a. for the first time and had stayed there (reaching 12.3 per cent in October and November 2007). Unemployment fell slowly but steadily during the year and into 2008 and by March 2008 had reached 7.1 per cent, the lowest figure recorded in the single currency period.

These figures by themselves appeared to suggest continued interest rate rises; but faced with the fears of US-led world recession, the actions of the Fed, and the very high value of the euro, this was hardly an option. The ECB chose to sit and to leave the refi rate unchanged. By April 2008, the refi was 2 per cent above the Fed Funds rate, the highest it had been. This was seen as a conservative policy, with the ECB placing its inflation objective above all other possible concerns. Jean-Claude Trichet, the ECB president, confirmed this view by stressing the importance of central bank resistance to inflation. Even though the sources of the renewed inflation were external, he argued that it was important to prevent higher inflation rates from pushing up inflationary expectations and feeding through into wage bargaining. This, he claimed, was what had happened during the oil price rises of the 1970s leading to high rates of inflation for a long period and these, in turn, had caused high rates of unemployment.

Pause for thought 11.10

Relate the views of the president of the ECB and ECB policy in 2008 to the IS/PC/MR model in Chapter 5. In particular:

(a) if the policy is continued, what does the model show happening to output and unemployment in Europe in the short run.

(b) what is implied in the statement about the shape of the long-run Phillips curve and the causes of the NAIRU?

In the light of changes in the value of the euro and the performance of the euro area in terms of the objectives established by the ECB, what can we say about European monetary policy since 1999? Much depends on the interpretation of the 'medium term' element in the ECB's statement of its inflation objective. Up until the end of April 2008, the ECB had been responsible for monetary policy for 112 months but, given what we have said about time lags in monetary policy, it seems reasonable to judge its performance in terms of its price objective from, say, the beginning of 2001, a total of 88 months. In that period, using the ECB's figures, the annual rate of inflation has been below 2 per cent in 25 months and above it in 63 months. However, the difficulty of the task is such that any central bank must be allowed some leeway, especially if the aim is a medium-term one. Let us allow the ECB the same degree of freedom that the UK government allows the Bank of England's MPC (1 per cent above or below target), and interpret the 'below, but close to, 2 per cent' as a target of 1.9 per cent and consider the ECB's inflation performance in terms of the range 0.9 to 2.9 per cent. This seems reasonable particularly in the light of the problems associated with the HICP and the use of a headline rate of inflation. This leaves us with only one failure, a rate of inflation of 3.1 per cent in May 2001 before the period from November 2007, when inflation rose above 3 per cent and stayed there for a prolonged period. However, we have seen that the relatively high inflation in May 2001 and in the period from November 2007 were the result of high world oil and food prices. Strictly in terms of the inflation target, the ECB's monetary policy appears to have been fairly successful.

This is even more the case if one argues that a rate of inflation below 1.5 per cent would be too low given that very low rates of inflation across the area might well involve recession in some member economies. Taking this into account, one might suggest that the central bank should be less concerned with a rate of inflation above 2 per cent than with a rate significantly below 2. Given that the inflation rate has been below 2 per cent for less than a third of the time since January 2001 and that the lowest the HICP rate of inflation has been was the 1.56 per cent recorded in October 2006, this appears to be the attitude the ECB is taking.

We have said that the market was, at the beginning of the life of the euro, uncertain as to the ECB attitude to the desirable value of the euro. This seems to have become clearer over time. As a relatively closed economy wishing specifically to encourage intra-area trade, the euro area is able to take a relaxed view of the value of the euro in terms of its impact on both the balance of trade of the area and the rate of inflation. Nonetheless, external trade remains important for many member states and a very weak euro will ultimately become a problem from the point of view of inflation. The \$/€ rate clearly became too low for the ECB in September-October 2000 and has recently become uncomfortably high. The ECB's behaviour appears to suggest that for most values of the euro, the exchange rate is likely to provide no more than supporting evidence for an interest rate change indicated on other grounds. Of course, it is undesirable for a number of reasons to have large swings in the external value of the currency over relatively short periods but there is clearly a problem that the ECB can do little about associated with asynchronous US and euro area business cycles as indicated by the changing relationship between the refi and the Fed Funds rate.

This leaves us with the difficulty of the monetary growth monetary growth reference value of 4.5 per cent. Monetary growth has not been at or below this figure in any month since May 2001. The ECB has argued on several occasions that the rate of growth of M3 has been above the reference level for temporary and irrelevant factors. But if this happens frequently it is not easy to see the value of attempting to use the rate of growth of M3 as an intermediate target of monetary policy. It seems odd that monetary growth continues to be acknowledged as the 'first pillar' of policy when all that occurs is that 'developments of M3 are continuously and thoroughly analysed by the ECB in the broader context of other monetary indicators and information from the second pillar to assess their implications for the risks to price stability over the medium term'.[11]

To conclude, we need to mention two other possible concerns regarding monetary policy in the euro area. The first relates to the unevenness of inflationary pressures across the area. Table 11.3 sets out inflation and unemployment estimates for the then 13 member countries of the euro area in 2007.

Table 11.3: Inflation and unemployment estimates for 2007: euro area countries

Country	Estimated inflation rate	Estimated unemployment rate
Austria	1.9	4.3
Belgium	3.5	7.6
Finland	2.7	6.9
France	1.5	8.0
Germany	2.0	9.1
Greece	2.6	8.4
Ireland	4.7	5.0
Italy	1.7	6.7
Luxembourg	2.1	4.4
Netherlands	1.6	4.1
Portugal	2.4	8.0
Slovakia	2.7	7.6
Spain	2.4	7.6

Source: CIA World Fact Book. https://www.cia.gov/library/publications/the-world-factbook

Thus, some euro area countries have inflation rates well above the ECB's target range. These figures show a difference of over 3 percentage points between the lowest and highest inflation rates, ranging from 1.5 per cent (France) to 4.7 per cent (Ireland). Whether this is a problem depends on the extent to which above- or below-average inflation rates for individual countries are temporary or long-lasting. There are a number of factors including different patterns of consumption and weather conditions and variations in the timing and magnitude of government policies that can account for temporary deviations in inflation rates from the average. A problem only arises if the inflation rate in a country remains stuck well above or below the average for a significant period or if there is a clear lack of synchronisation of business cycles. If a country's inflation rate remained well above the euro area average for, say, two to three years and showed no sign of moving back towards the average, it would seem that the ECB's monetary stance was too weak to tackle the underlying inflationary pressures in the country. The higher rate of inflation would begin to undermine the country's competitiveness — and this can no longer be tackled by a devaluation of the national currency. Equally, a particularly low rate of inflation together with an above average unemployment rate might indicate that the centrally determined monetary policy was being too restrictive for the country in question.

On the evidence from table 11.3 alone, one would be forgiven for thinking that the ECB's refi was being set too low for Ireland and Belgium and too high for France and Italy. However, things are not so easy. A higher rate of interest would help to reduce Belgium's inflation rate but its unemployment rate is already relatively high. Plainly, to come to any conclusion as to whether some countries would do better if able to set their own interest rates, one would need a detailed study of the economic performance of individual countries. Table 11.3 does suggest, though, that some countries are in need of policies in addition to monetary policy to attempt to improve the relationship between inflation and unemployment.

The ECB's view regarding divergent inflation rates is that it needs to determine its monetary policy on the basis of average economic performance across the euro area and leave individual countries to deal with any excessive inflationary pressures that remain with fiscal policy. This, however, does not tackle the reverse problem of a country suffering the deflationary effects of an over-tight inflation rate since attempts to use fiscal policy to correct for this may run into difficulties with the Stability and Growth Pact.

11.7 Possible reforms of the ECB strategy and procedure

The ECB has faced criticism because of both its perceived lack of accountability and its monetary policy strategy. Svensson (2000) suggested that claims by the ECB that it was open and credible carried little weight when it was clear that it was less accountable than the central banks of New Zealand, Sweden and the UK. Most criticism has been based on the failure of the ECB to publish details of voting, the minutes of meetings at which interest rate decisions are made or forecasts of the future rate of inflation. The ECB also refuses to set a precise inflation target, leaving it open to arguments that this makes it difficult to judge how the Bank is interpreting its mandate. It has also been suggested that the lack of transparency of ECB monetary policy has made it more likely to take the financial markets by surprise but this seems to have been less of a problem in recent years as markets have become more familiar with the attitudes and behaviour of the ECB. Some adjustments have been made. For example, economic forecasts made by ECB staff are now published. The ECB shows that it is well aware of the importance of transparency on its web site[12] and clearly believes that it is sufficiently transparent. Box 11.5 compares the practices of the ECB and the Monetary Policy Committee of the Bank of England in terms of transparency and accountability.

Reform proposals other than those associated with transparency have concentrated on the inflation targets set, the role of the monetary growth reference value in the policy deliberations and the use of the Stability and Growth Pact although this derives from the EU as a whole rather than the ECB. Proposals regarding these have included the move to the use of a core rate of inflation in place of the headline rate provided by the HICP and a raising of the target rate to a range of 1 - 3 per cent. There have also been suggestions that the euro area should move to the UK system of having the inflation target set by the political system — for example by the European Parliament. Such proposals have generally been made in a political context such as in the French and Italian election campaigns in 2007 and 2008 respectively. For criticisms of all such proposals, particularly because they will cause the ECB (and other central banks) to lose their anti-inflation credibility, see Buiter (2008).[13]

Box 11.6: Accountability differences between the ECB and the MPC of the Bank of England

1.   The ECB sets its own inflation target (currently 0-2 per cent); the UK inflation target is set by the Chancellor of the Exchequer (currently 2.0 per cent). Thus, the Bank of England has instrument independence but not goal independence. The ECB has both.

2.   The Bank of England practices inflation targeting, setting its interest rate with the aim of meeting the inflation target set by the government. The ECB has two pillars of policy: (i) the monetary growth reference point (currently 4.5 per cent); (ii) a broadly based assessment of the outlook for price developments and the risks to price stability, using other available indicators. The ECB has an interest rate target but its intentions in relation to that target are not always clear.

3.   The Bank of England issues minutes of the meetings of its Monetary Policy Committee and voting records so that it is known whether the decision was closely contested and how individual members voted. The ECB publishes neither minutes nor voting records. Indeed, it is forbidden from publishing voting records. All that is issued after the meeting is a not-very-detailed press release.

4.   The Bank of England publishes a three-monthly inflation report that sets out the Monetary Policy Committee's inflation forecast together with an assessment of the factors likely to influence the rate of inflation over the following two years. The ECB does not publish an inflation forecast. It does publish a weekly financial statement, monthly and quarterly reports and an annual report, the last of which comments on its monetary policy over the last two years and also economic forecasts made by its staff.

5.   The MPC of the Bank of England is subject to biannual interrogation by the Treasury Select Committee of the House of Commons. The President of the ECB appears quarterly before the European Parliament's Committee on Economic Affairs and answers questions. Transcripts of these hearings are published on the ECB website.

6.   If it misses its target by 1 per cent or more in either direction, the MPC is required to write an open letter to the Chancellor of the Exchequer setting out the reasons for its failure and explaining what steps it will take to remedy the situation.

7.   The Annual Report of the Bank of England goes to parliament; the ECB's annual report goes to the European Parliament, Commission and Council.

11.8 Summary

In principle, the practice of monetary policy is the same in a monetary union as in a single country. However, the success of any monetary policy is strongly influenced by the size and composition of the area that it covers. Thus, when a single currency area is established across a number of nation states, we must ask whether this makes economic sense and must look at the costs and benefits associated with a country's giving up the possibility of changing its exchange rate. To do this, we must look at the characteristics of the countries involved. In particular, we must look at the extent to which the separate economies are coordinated and at the extent to which other elements in the economies are sufficiently flexible to cope with the loss of a traditional instrument of policy. In carrying out this exercise, we must realise that there are no precise answers and we must not forget that important political issues are also involved.

To help it to decide whether or not to join the euro area, the UK government set out 'five economic tests' based on a mixture of general principles about the membership of monetary union and specific issues of importance to the UK, notably the impact of the decision on the City of London and on inward foreign investment.

Monetary policy in the euro area is conducted by the European System of Central Banks, which consists of the European Central Bank and the national central banks of the member states. The constitution of the ECB was modelled as closely as possible on that of the Bundesbank. All constituent elements are required to be politically independent and the principal task of the Bank is to achieve low and stable inflation. The European parliament has no influence on the objectives of monetary policy. Because of the determination to convince markets that the ECB would be fiercely politically independent, it is now only weakly accountable to the governments and citizens of the euro area. This has sometimes resulted in the reasoning behind its decisions being opaque and has led to some uncertainty in financial markets about its likely future course of action. This has been particularly true in relation to its attitude towards the value of the euro. This was one factor behind the large slide in the value of the euro against the US dollar in the first two years of the euro's life.

The ECB, in its explanation of its policy, refers to two pillars of its inflation strategy — a monetary growth reference value, and an assessment of the outlook for the future using a range of other indicators. In practice, however, it is probably closer to being engaged in inflation targeting than anything else, although it has not always been clear how it has been interpreting its own inflation target range of 0 - 2 per cent.

Key concepts used in this chapter

optimum currency area

symmetric and asymmetric shocks

synchronised business cycles

labour market flexibility

convergence/divergence of
economies

Stability and Growth Pact

the main refinancing rate (refi) of
the ECB

monetary growth reference value

target inflation rate

European System of Central Banks

European Central Bank

Governing Council of the ECB

Executive Board of the ECB

political independence of central
banks

accountability of central banks

Harmonised Index Of Consumer
Prices (HICP)

fixed rate tender

variable rate tender

minimum reserve ratio

transparency

Questions and exercises
Answers at the end of the book

1. In 11.2, we suggest that wage flexibility does not always provide an efficient means of adjusting to external shocks. What is the basis of that argument?

2. Why might the business cycles of the UK not be synchronised with those of the 12 current members of the euro area?

3. What does the Executive Board of the ECB do? What does it not do?

4. In the text, we say:

'A supporting argument was that the euro, as a broader-based reserve currency than the DM would be less likely to be driven artificially high on occasions.'

Explain this statement. How did it relate to the question of the likely future strength of the euro?

5. When the ECB began operation at the beginning of 1999, how did it ensure that all members of the Executive Board would not end their terms of office at the same time? What would be wrong with the terms of all six members of the Board ending on the same date?

6. Outline the arguments for and against fixed and variable rate tenders as the instrument for the provision by the central bank of liquidity to the banking system.

... and also to think about

6. Why is the accountability of the central bank an important issue?

7. Do you think that the business cycles of Ireland are likely to be better synchronised with the rest of the euro area than are those of the UK? If so, given Ireland's long-standing economic links with the UK, why might this be so?

8. Look at the latest interest rate decision made by the ECB and explain it in terms of the first and second pillars of the ECB's monetary strategy.

9. Discuss the view that the second pillar of the ECB's strategy is redundant in the light of the first pillar.

10. Compare and contrast the ECB and the Bank of England in terms of:

   a) their independence
   b) the transparency of their policymaking
   c) their accountability

Further reading

For a good text book account of the economics of monetary integration, see P de Grauwe (2007). Among a wide range of other text books with useful material on European monetary policy, we would also recommend Eijffinger and de Haan (2000). The European Central Bank has published a detailed account of all aspects of its monetary policy as European Central Bank (2004). This is fully downloadable as a pdf file from the ECB's website: www.ecb.int

An extraordinary amount of material of all types and levels, from newspaper reports to difficult academic articles is available on the website of Giancarlo Corsetti of Yale and Bologna Universities at: www.econ.yale.edu/~corsetti/euro/,* although many of the pages are no longer updated.

Forder (2002) provides a critical view of the ECB's charter and behaviour, especially with respect to the issue of accountability. Many of the issues surounding the structure of monetary policy institutions in the euro area were first aired in a famous debate in 1999 between Willem Buiter and Otmar Issing in 1999.

12 Monetary policy in the USA

'The almighty dollar is the only object of worship.'

Anon. Philadelphia Public Ledger, 2.12.1836

'It is easy to conceive that great evils to our country and its institutions might flow from such a concentration of power in the hands of a few men, irresponsible to the people.'

Andrew Johnson, President of the USA in a speech to the US Senate, July 10, 1832

12.1   Introduction

The United States central bank, the Federal Reserve System, is widely regarded as the most powerful economic policy institution in the world. This is a testament to the size and strength of the US economy, the return to importance of monetary policy in the minds of economists, industrialists, and politicians and, perhaps above all, the dominance of financial markets in the modern imagination. We have indicated at several points in this book that the real power of the monetary authorities is rather less than this might suggest, but the Fed certainly has sufficient impact to mean that no account of current monetary policy could omit consideration of it. Thus, in section 12.2, we provide some necessary background historical information and look at the structure of the Federal Reserve System. We also look at the position within the system of the Federal Open Market Committee, the body responsible for US monetary policy. In 12.3, we consider the form of US monetary policy. In 12.4, we look at the independence and accountability of the Federal Reserve, while 12.5 discusses recent US monetary policy decisions.

12.2   The story of central banking in the USA

The US central bank, the Federal Reserve System (the Fed), was not established until the early years of the 20th century. Unlike the Bank of England, the Fed was set up as a central bank rather than evolving into one from a privately owned bank of discount, deposits and note issue. Two early attempts were made to set up a corporate central bank, chartered by the state, but owned by private investors.

The First Bank of the United States commenced business in 1791 and survived until 1811. The Second Bank of the United States also survived for twenty years (1816-36).[1] Both met with strong opposition. This came partly from banks given operating charters by state governments (state-chartered banks). The state-chartered banks wanted a share of the national government's banking business and did not like the attempts by the central banks to exercise control over them. For example, in 1791, the First Bank of the United States had attempted to control the number of bank notes issued by state banks.

However, not all the criticism was self-interested. There was a strong feeling that the central banks were too large and privileged and that this conflicted with the democratic ideals of the USA. This attitude is well illustrated by a statement made in 1832 by the US president, Andrew Jackson, that the Second Bank of the United States was a 'concentration of power in the hands of a few men irresponsible to the people'.[2] One problem was the private ownership of the bank, which included some foreign investors. A second was the geographical concentration of the bank.

From the beginning, the development of US banking was influenced by two major fears — of centralised authority and of domination by moneyed interests. These fears reflect the origins of the US nation state. Settlement from Europe had been by separate, relatively small groups often fleeing from religious or political domination — the first united action by settlers was the struggle against the distant authority of Britain. The two fears combined to produce a determination to prevent the financial system being controlled either by large institutions in the financial centre of New York or by political forces concentrated in Washington. The result was an idiosyncratic banking system that consisted of large numbers of small independent banks, restricted from opening branches across state boundaries.[3] In the 18th and 19th centuries, any attempt to control the operation of banks from the centre met with deep suspicion. The failure of the early central banks was one reflection of this.

In the absence of a central bank, for much of the 19th century the federal government had to act as its own banker. In doing so, Treasury officials gradually realised that funds might be added to or withdrawn from the private sector on a discretionary basis to prevent financial panics and as an element of macroeconomic policy. That is, the Treasury began to develop a central monetary policy. This also met with opposition since the Secretary of the Treasury was a political appointee, feeding the fear of the political control of money and finance and, hence, the economy. We find here, too, an early example of the view at the heart of much of the modern argument for independent central banks that the Treasury, because it was controlled by politicians, would have a long-run bias towards easy money and inflation. Perhaps more importantly, it was thought that the Treasury might favour particular financial, geographic, and economic interests.

Pause for thought 12.1

What was the point of stopping banks from opening branches in other states?

However, the extreme decentralisation of the banking system caused problems. In recessions, small banks regularly ran into problems and this frequently led to runs on banks, multi-bank panics, and the collapse of many banks. This was not helped by the absence of a central bank. There were nine multi-bank panics between the closure of the Second Bank of the United States and the end of the first decade of the 20th century. Consequently, following the panic of 1907, a commission of enquiry was set up and the Federal Reserve Act, which established the Federal Reserve System, was passed in 1913.

The form of the system was strongly influenced by the continuing fear of excessive control from the centre. Instead of setting up a single bank, the 1913 Act brought into being twelve regional Federal Reserve Banks overseen by the Federal Reserve Board in Washington D.C. The system was designed to provide a broad view of economic activity in all parts of the country. By the time the Fed was set up, US commercial banks consisted of both nationally chartered and state-chartered banks.[4] All nationally chartered banks were required to become members of their regional reserve bank. State-chartered banks could choose to become members, as long as they met standards set by the Fed. The regional reserve banks do not receive funds from the central government. They were individually chartered and required to raise their own capital, which is contributed by the member commercial banks in each district. They are profit making and twice a year pay their member banks a dividend on the subscribed capital at a fixed rate of 6 per cent. Earnings above those needed for operations and the payment of the dividends are paid to the US Treasury at the end of each year. The income of the district banks comes from fees paid for the services provided to commercial banks and from interest on their holdings of US Treasury securities and loans to the commercial banks.

Each district reserve bank has its own president and board of directors. Board membership should reflect the interests of the various sectors of the economy including business and industry, agriculture, labour, the financial sector and consumers. To this end, reserve bank boards consist of nine members: six representatives of non-banking enterprises and the public and three of the banking industry. Reserve bank presidents serve five-year terms while the members of the boards of directors serve for three years. Where there are branches of a federal reserve bank, each branch also has its own board of directors to try to ensure that local interests are always taken into account.

When the banks were set up in 1913, the regional reserve banks retained considerable power. They had a monopoly of the nation's note issue, acted as fiscal agents of the government, banks of rediscount and reserve for member banks, and lenders of last resort in their districts. They were involved in the regulation and supervision of the banking system although, because of the late establishment of the Fed, this had to be shared with already established state banking authorities and federal agencies. The intention of the decentralised structure was to ensure a sufficient supply of credit in each region. This was to be achieved principally by each reserve bank re-discounting commercial paper at rates set according to each regional its view of the needs of its region. Further, each bank was able to determine for itself which bills were eligible for re-discounting.

Member banks held legally prescribed reserves as deposits in their reserve banks and in return were entitled to rediscount their eligible commercial paper at the banks when in need of temporary liquidity. They were also able to use the Fed clearing facilities including electronic funds transfers and the currency and information services of the banks. It was anticipated that the availability of these services to members would encourage state-chartered banks to join the system.

The original Federal Reserve Board comprised five members[5] appointed to staggered ten-year terms by the US president with the Secretary of the Treasury and the Comptroller of the Currency as *ex-officio* members. The Board was required to oversee and supervise the operations of the reserve banks, coordinate their activities, and handle the System's relations with the federal government. At the beginning, the Federal Reserve Board had little authority to initiate policies and no power to coordinate monetary policy across the country. Indeed, the Board probably had less power than the unofficial Governors' Conference set up by the regional reserve banks under the chairmanship of the Governor of the Federal Reserve Bank of New York.

Pause for thought 12.2

Why might state-chartered banks have chosen not to join the Federal Reserve System?

The possession of the chairmanship of this unofficial body was merely one indication of the growing power of the New York bank. This arose largely because New York had by far the largest money and capital markets in the USA and the Federal Reserve Bank of New York soon started to act as agent for the other reserve banks in the purchase of securities. Following the entry of the USA into the First World War in 1917, government borrowing increased greatly and had to be financed. Government paper began to dominate commercial bills in the portfolios of the banking system. The principal objective of the Fed became, in effect, to finance the centralised needs of the Treasury. Since government securities were largely placed on the New York capital market, their prices were strongly influenced by the policies of the New York Reserve Bank.

Regional policy diversity began to decline. When, in 1921, the New York bank raised its interest rate to 7 per cent, the other reserve banks soon followed. In 1922, the New York Governor set up a committee of five governors to coordinate open market operations and between that year and 1928, the Fed began increasingly to act as a unified central bank.

However, in the late 1920s and again during the Great Depression, serious disagreements over policy resurfaced, both among the regional banks and between them and the Board. During the depression, the Federal Reserve Bank of New York favoured expansionary policies to stimulate the economy. Following the appointment by President Roosevelt in 1933 of a new Governor, the Board also favoured expansion, but this was opposed by several of the other district Banks and did not happen. This led to a campaign to increase the power of the Board. The behaviour of the Fed immediately before and during the depression is the subject of box 12.1.

In the early 1930s, multi-bank panics and collapses continued.[6] As a consequence of these problems, two major pieces of bank legislation were enacted — the Banking Acts of 1933 (the Glass-Steagall Act) and 1935. The Glass Steagall Act introduced the federal insurance of bank deposits and restrictions on the activities of insured banks, in an attempt to reduce the riskiness of the system. Among other things, the Act prohibited interest payments to owners of federally insured sight deposits and authorised the setting of limits on rates paid on federally insured savings deposits of various maturities. The regulation issued by the Federal Reserve in exercising its authority over deposit rates was known as Regulation Q.[7]

Box 12.1: The Federal Reserve and the depression of the 1930s

There are differences of opinion regarding the performance of the Fed in the lead up to the stock market crash of October 1929, although it is widely held that it did not perform well. There are two issues:

- to what extent did Fed policy in 1927 fuel the speculative boom in equity prices of 1928 and 1929;
- was the Fed responsible for the financial crash and the conversion of that crisis into a general, deep, and long-lasting economic slump.

In the spring of 1927, the Fed cut its rediscount rate from 4 to 3½ per cent and sold government securities, adding liquidity to the banking system. Did the provision of liquidity cause the speculative fever that followed? Or was the Fed at this point acting as a passive supplier of liquidity? The Fed raised interest rates in August 1929. In nominal terms, the money supply steadied and then fell. It did not grow during 1928, fell by 2.6 per cent from August 1929 to October 1930 and continued to fall until March 1933. Was this the cause of the stock market crash in October 1929?

Friedman and Schwartz blame the Fed on both counts, particularly for the collapse. As believers in exogenous money, they argue that the restrictions on liquidity brought about the crisis. Other economists reject both propositions. Galbraith (1955, p. 15) rejects the view that the Fed's actions encouraged speculation in the early stages of the boom as 'formidable nonsense' as, in his view, the interest rate was relatively high. Temin (1976) rejects the Friedman and Schwartz argument about the causes of the crash on a number of grounds, one of which was that interest rates fell rather than rose. If the fall in money supply had been the cause of the crash, that part of the transmission process that worked through the interest rate should have been:

$\downarrow$ money supply $\rightarrow$ $\uparrow$ interest rate $\rightarrow$ $\downarrow$ investment and consumption $\rightarrow$ $\downarrow$ income.

A standard monetarist argument, of course, requires that the exogenous reduction in the money supply does not have real effects in the long run. To explain these, Friedman and Schwartz depend on the banking collapses that followed the Wall Street crash. 8,812 banks collapsed between 1930 and 1933 and total bank deposits fell by 42 per cent between 1929 and 1933. These clearly had a large impact on the real economy. Thus, money is not neutral in this case because of institutional failures brought about by the Fed's actions.

Temin, however, argues that the problem had begun with consumption. A fall in consumption would have caused a fall in the transactions demand for money, causing interest rates to fall. The falls in the money supply would have occurred as a result of the decline in demand for bank loans. In fact, most interest rates declined sharply after the 1929 crash.

Kindleberger (1996) worries, however, that this still leaves the fall in consumption to be explained and finds none of the several explanations convincing. He also worries that neither the monetarist nor the Keynesian view explains the fact that industrial production had started to fall in advance of the financial crash. It fell in September 1929 and then continued to fall sharply so that an index of industrial production that had stood at 127 in June 1929 had fallen to 99 by December. Kindleberger relies on the instability of the credit system to explain the facts. He quotes the view of Simons (1948) that changes in business confidence led through an unstable credit system to changes in liquidity and effects on the money supply — which is again seen as endogenous here. Whether the Fed was responsible or not, however, no one has a good word for them in this period. Galbraith, indeed, describes them as 'a body of startling incompetence' (1955 p.33).

The 1935 Act replaced the Federal Reserve Board with the Board of Governors of the Federal Reserve System. The new Board comprised seven members, each appointed by the President with the advice and consent of the Senate. Membership of the Board should provide 'a fair representation of financial, agricultural, industrial and geographic divisions'[8] again indicating concern about the concentration of power in the centre and the possible neglect of the needs of industry. The new Board was given additional powers, including the authority to adjust member-bank reserve requirements, order the Federal Reserve Banks to change their discount rates, restrict discount window loans to member banks deemed to be making excessive loans for speculative purposes, and limit the volume of loans made by member banks. The term of Board members was lengthened to fourteen years.

The Federal Open Market Committee (FOMC) was set up to conduct monetary policy. The FOMC comprises the seven members of the Board of Governors, the president of the Federal Reserve Board of New York and four other reserve bank presidents, serving one-year rotating terms. The district banks are grouped for this purpose to ensure that all areas of the country are always represented on the FOMC. For example, the presidents of the Cleveland and Chicago Federal Reserve Banks alternate since they come broadly from the same part of the country. The presence of the seven Board members gives the Board a permanent majority on the FOMC.

Box 12.2: The Functions of the 12 district Federal Reserve Banks

Although monetary policy has, since 1935, been centralised and rests with the Board of Governors of the Federal Reserve System, the 12 district Federal Reserve Banks continue to play a number of important roles.

- They provide 5 of the 12 members of the FOMC and have the specific task of helping the Committee stay in touch with the economic conditions in all parts of the country;
- They supervise banks and bank and financial holding companies, helping to maintain the stability of the financial system;
- They provide financial services to depository institutions;
- They market and redeem government securities and savings bonds and conducts nationwide auctions of Treasury securities as well as maintaining the Treasury's funds account;
- They provide payments services – the safe and efficient transfer of funds and securities throughout the financial system;
- They distribute coins and currency;
- They are heavily involved in research and have an educational role.
- The Federal Reserve Bank of New York carries out open market operations and intervenes in foreign exchange markets on behalf of the Board of Governors.

The form of the Federal Reserve System established by the 1935 Act remains in place today. As the Bank of England did until its reform in 1997, the US central bank carries out all possible functions of a central bank, being:

- the bank to the banking system
- the bank to the US government
- the body responsible for monetary policy
- the operator of the payments system
- a major part of the system of supervision and regulation of depository institutions

It also has a responsibility for the protection of consumers' rights in dealing with banks and for promoting community development and reinvestment. The modern role of the 12 district Federal Reserve Banks is set out in box 12.2.

12.3   The aims and form of monetary policy in the USA

Policy objectives

The monetary policy goals of the Federal Reserve System were initially broad. They included the provision of an 'elastic currency' — ensuring sufficient liquidity in the banking system to guard against bank panics. Price stability was important, but so were the other standard goals of macroeconomic policy. In the 1970s, the Fed listed its broad objectives as 'to help counteract inflationary and deflationary movements, and to share in creating conditions favourable to sustained high employment, stable values, growth of the country, and a rising level of consumption'.[9]

As with other central banks, however, the goal of price stability has dominated since the beginning of the 1980s. The Fed now sums up its objectives as 'price stability and sustainable growth'. However, in practice, the two goals almost appear to become one. For example, in his testimony to the US Congress in July 2001, the then Chairman of the Board of Governors, Alan Greenspan, said, 'Certainly, should conditions warrant, we may need to ease further, but we must not lose sight of the prerequisite of longer-run price stability for realising the economy's full growth potential over time.'[10]

In other words, price stability is now seen as the *sine qua non* for the achievement of sustainable growth.

Pause for thought 12.3

What is an 'elastic currency?'

Nonetheless, the representative structure of the Fed appears to lead to greater attention being paid to the real economy and to economic performance across the country than is the case with many other central banks. Unlike the ECB and the Bank of England, the Fed does not specify the goal of price stability in the form of a target rate of inflation. The minutes of its meetings show that the FOMC heeds a wide variety of real and monetary indicators in arriving at its decisions and appears to pay considerable attention to anecdotal evidence of business conditions in diverse industries and regions. As we noted in section 8.3, the Fed is widely believed to be targeting an inflation rate of 1.5 to 2 per cent in practice although Buiter (2008) suggests that '[the Fed] may have "comfort zones" for the inflation rate of the PCE deflator (core or headline) or of the CPI (core or headline), but the exact location of these comfort zones is even harder to determine than the location of comfort stations in an American city'.[11]

At its January/February meeting each year, the FOMC establishes annual monetary growth ranges.[12] These are specified, on a fourth-quarter-to-fourth-quarter basis, for the broader monetary aggregates, M2 and M3. The aim is to identify monetary growth ranges that are consistent with the Committee's policy goals for inflation and economic growth. However, the FOMC is aware of the potential instability of money velocities and accepts that monetary growth rates have not recently been reliable guides for monetary policy. They are now just one indicator among many. The Committee also sets an annual monitoring range for the growth of aggregate debt of all nonfinancial sectors — allowing credit growth to be given at least an equal role in policy deliberations as that given to monetary growth.

Instruments and intermediate targets

The Fed, like all central banks, seeks to achieve its monetary policy targets by changes in short-term interest rates. In the case of the Fed, the interest rate that is central is the Federal Funds rate (the Fed Funds rate). This is the rate that depository institutions pay when they borrow reserves overnight from each other in order to meet reserve requirements set by the Federal Reserve, and to ensure adequate balances in their accounts at the Fed to cover cheque and electronic payments clearances. The Federal Funds rate often has a strong impact on other short-term rates.

Since the Monetary Control Act (MCA) of 1980, the Fed has set reserve requirements for all depository institutions, whether or not they are members of the Federal Reserve System. The MCA authorised the Fed's Board of Governors to impose a reserve requirement of from 8 to 14 per cent of sight deposits and of up to nine percent of nonpersonal time deposits, but not to impose reserve requirements on personal time deposits except in extraordinary circumstances. The reserve requirement on sight deposits is currently 10 per cent, although concessions apply for the first part of the total[13] while no reserves are required for time deposits. The lack of reserve requirements on time deposits means that important components of the broader money measures M2 and M3 can expand without any concern about reserve levels. In practice, reserve requirements now

play only a very limited role in monetary policy and the Fed's reserve requirements are changed only infrequently.

Pause for thought 12.4

The Fed has long wanted to pay banks interest on the reserves that must be held with them,
but the US Congress has refused to allow this. Why do you think the Fed would like to pay interest? Why does the Congress say no?

Reserves may be held as vault cash or as deposits at the Fed. Banks that fail
to meet their reserve requirements can be subject to financial penalties. Required
reserves are calculated on net sight deposits, using 'contemporaneous reserve
accounting'. That is, they are based on deposits more or less concurrently held.
This is not fully contemporaneous but is calculated as a daily average[14] over a
two-week period: a bank's average reserves over the period ending every other
Wednesday must equal the required percentage of its average deposits in the two-
week period ending Monday, two days earlier. Thus, banks can work out how
much they must hold in the last two days to raise their average reserves over the
period to the required average.

Banks short of reserves can borrow in the Federal Funds market or from the
discount window of the Fed. Reserves borrowed from the discount window are
referred to as borrowed reserves. Nonborrowed reserves constitute the bulk of
total reserves. They are supplied principally through Fed open market purchases of treasury bills in the secondary market.

A discount window is operated by each of the 12 regional reserve banks and
each decides its own discount rate (the rate that applies to borrowings at the discount window), although approval for changes to the discount rate must be
obtained from the FOMC. The discount window is usually held below the
Federal Funds rate. This means that, in theory, it provides the cheapest way of
acquiring reserves. Indeed, if the gap between the Fed Funds rate and the discount rate grew sufficiently large, there would be an opportunity for round trip-
ping — with banks borrowing from the discount window and lending at the Fed
Funds rate. However, the Fed's aim is to keep the discount window for lender-
of-last resort borrowing, after banks have exhausted other borrowing possibilities. Thus, the Fed discourages the use of the discount window, certainly for profit but also as a normal way of making up shortfalls in reserves.

To do this, the Fed operates rules governing the extent and frequency of borrowing and ultimately may turn away frequent borrowers through the discount
window. This means that banks realise that if they borrow too often from the discount window, they may be unable to do so when they have a genuine need. In
addition, too frequent borrowing by banks through the discount window creates
a bad impression in the financial markets. Thus, there are non-pecuniary costs
(commonly known as 'frown costs') in borrowing from the discount window that
more than balances the difference between the Fed Funds rate and the discount

rate. Banks, then, are only likely to borrow from the discount window for reserves purposes in emergencies. Rather, they seek to borrow reserves that they require initially in the Federal Funds market, despite the greater financial cost of doing so.

Under current arrangements, the FOMC, which normally meets eight times a year, sets a target for the Fed Funds rate and the Federal Reserve Bank of New York conducts open market operations on the Fed's behalf to try to ensure that the rate remains close to the target. To do this, the New York Reserve bank must forecast each morning the total reserves (the reserves required together with any additional reserves the banks might wish to hold minus those reserves that will be borrowed through the discount window). If it decides that the quantity of reserves available is too low or too high, it seeks to adjust this by direct intervention in the government securities market, making use of repos,[15] matched transactions[16] and outright purchases/sales of securities. Outright purchases of treasury bills are made when the Fed projects that commercial bank needs for reserves will last for a period of several weeks; repos and matched transactions when it projects only a temporary shortage or surplus of reserves. When the FOMC wishes to influence the Fed Funds rate, it does so by directing the New York Fed to vary the supply of reserves through its open market operations. A purchase by the Fed reduces available reserves relative to demand and tends to push the Fed Funds rate up. A sale puts downward pressure on the rate. Some details of the process of open market operations are provided in box 12.3.

This system clearly makes the money supply endogenous. Once the target interest rate has been set by the FOMC, non-borrowed reserves are supplied by the Fed through open market operations on demand from the banking system. As we have said above, no use is made of reserve ratios to control the rate of expansion of the banks' balance sheets. We have a straightforward attempt to control the public's demand for loans through interest rate control as practised by both the Bank of England and the ECB. The Fed has, however, attempted to introduce some control over the rate of growth of the money supply from time to time over the past 30 years.

Pause for thought 12.5

If reserve ratios are not used to control the rate of expansion of bank balance sheets, why are they set?

From 1970 to 1979, the FOMC tried to achieve this by specifying at each meeting both a target rate for Fed Funds and a target range for the rate for the period up to the next meeting. Then, if the money supply was judged to be rising too rapidly, the New York Reserve adjusted the supply of reserves to allow the Fed Funds rate to drift up towards the top of the target range. Nevertheless, once the top of the target interest rate range was reached, additional demands for reserves would be met and the stock of money would be allowed to rise. That is, the

money supply again became endogenous. Although it was true that extra pressure could be applied by raising the top of the target range at the next FOMC
meeting or, indeed, between meetings,[17] the Fed was not controlling the money
supply effectively during this period.

Box 12.3: Federal Reserve Bank of New York Open Market Operations

At the end of its regular meetings, the FOMC issues a directive to the New York Federal Reserve,
which indicates the approach to monetary policy considered appropriate in the period until its next
meeting. This guides the day-to-day decisions regarding the purchase and sale of securities by the
manager of the System Open Market Account at the New York Fed. Each working day, information is gathered about the market's activities from a number of sources.

- Discussions are held with the primary dealers in government securities;
- Discussions are also held with banks in the large money centres about their reserve needs
  and plans for meeting them;
- Data is received on bank reserves for the previous day;
- Projections of factors that could affect reserves for future days are received from reserve fore-
  casters;
- Information is received from the Treasury about its balance at the Federal Reserve

Forecasts of reserves are then made and a plan of action for the day is developed and reviewed
with a Reserve Bank president currently serving as a voting member of the FOMC. A summary of
this discussion is sent to members of the FOMC later in the day to allow the FOMC to monitor
closely the implementation of its directive. Conditions in financial markets, including domestic
securities and money markets and foreign exchange markets are also reviewed each morning.
The Trading Desk of the New York Fed then enters the government securities market to execute
any temporary open market operations (repos or matched sale-purchase transactions) by sending
an electronic message to the primary dealers, asking them to enter bids (if the Fed is selling) or
offers (if the Fed is buying) within 10 to 15 minutes. The terms of the operation are stated but not
its size - this is announced after the operation is completed. The dealers' bids/offers are evaluat-
ed on a competitive best-price basis and the dealers are notified whether their bids/offers have
been accepted or rejected. This usually happens about five minutes after the bids/offers were due.
Outright sales and purchases are arranged at various times during the day, following a similar procedure.

A more wholehearted effort was made from October 1979, when the Fed
sought to engage in what Fazzari and Minsky (1984) referred to as 'practical'
monetarism — the use of the quantity and rate of change of a monetary aggregate
as the intermediate target of monetary policy. Interest rate targets were replaced
by targets for non-borrowed reserves. Increases in Fed Funds rates brought about
by increases in the demand for reserves would, then, not be limited by the target
range for interest rates. In theory, this was a move in the direction of monetary
base control. Yet, the Fed still failed to control reserve growth.

One reason given in the early 1980s for this continued lack of control was that from 1968 a system of lagged reserve accounting had operated for calculating the reserves required by banks. The current level of required reserves was thus pre-determined by the past level of deposits and there was nothing banks could do to accommodate deposits to reserves. The required reserve ratios could only be met by the Fed supplying the reserves.

Yet, when the change was made to contemporaneous reserve accounting in 1984, the Fed's ability to control reserves did not improve. This was because banks were able to respond to reductions in open market purchases of securities by the Fed (aimed at squeezing bank reserves) by seeking to economise on reserves and by increasing competition for other sources of them — the Fed Funds market, international sources and idle cash balances of firms.[18] When these sources failed, banks could still borrow from the discount window. Thus, interest rates were pushed up and the Fed was again seeking to control bank behaviour through prices rather than quantities.

Goodhart (2002, p.16) argues that this episode of 'experimental monetarism' was not a genuine attempt at monetarism at all, but simply a ruse to get Congress and the US public to accept higher interest rates than would otherwise have been politically possible, by persuading them that aggregates mattered and that the level of interest rates was an unfortunate side effect. If this is a correct reading of the situation, it shows again the political pressures to which interest targeting is subject.

In 1982, the Fed introduced another variant by targeting borrowed reserves, only to find that it was again, in effect, supplying reserves on demand. An increase in the demand for reserves would cause the Fed Funds rate to be bid up and, as it rose further above the discount rate, banks would increasingly turn to the discount window as a source of reserves. This would push the quantity of borrowed reserves above target. To avoid this, the Fed would engage in open market pur-chases to increase bank reserves because only in this way could they sufficiently discourage banks from using the discount window to enable the target for bor-rowed reserves to be met. We were back to interest rate targets. Nonetheless, Lewis and Mizen (2000) argue that the post-1982 system was more flexible than that in use before October 1979 because the Committee was more easily able to choose, depending on the source of the increase in the demand for reserves, between providing additional reserves through open market operations and allowing interest rates to be pushed up. The result was that the Fed Funds rate fluctuated much more. In other words, policy became more discretionary in nature — hardly likely to be approved by monetarists. During the 1980s, the focus of policy gradually shifted back toward targeting a specified level of the Fed Funds rate, a process that was largely complete by the end of the decade, taking the sys-tem back to simple interest rate control. From the beginning of 1995, the FOMC has announced its target level for the Federal Funds rate after each meeting. Overall, despite the changes in practice from time to time, there can be little doubt that the US money supply has been endogenous throughout the period discussed.

12.4   The Federal Reserve - independence and accountability

Independence

When it was established in 1913, the Fed was intended to be independent of:

(i)   private financial business interests;

(ii) duly constituted government authorities (executive and legislature); and

(iii) partisan political interests.

By the usual standards applied (see box 11.4), the Fed is highly independent politically and has been since its inception apart from a period during the Second World War and up to 1949. Although the seven members of the Board of Governors are political appointments, their long and staggered terms (even if the majority of Governors do not serve the full fourteen years) ensures that any one government cannot stack the Board with its own appointees in order to ensure the results it wants. The duties and powers of the Fed are not enshrined in the US constitution but are statutorily protected and difficult to change. The Fed has full control of its policy instruments and has the freedom to interpret the mandate given to it. The government has no direct representative with voting power on the FOMC.

This leaves us with the interesting question of independence from 'private financial business interests'. This is interesting firstly, because it is mentioned at all. The usual assumption in the modern literature is that 'independence' in connection with central banks means independence from politicians and governments. We have seen, however, why independence from financial and business interests was included as a requirement for the Fed — again the general concern over possible domination by 'moneyed interests' especially in New York. We have seen also that at every point in the constitution of the Fed, attempts are made to ensure representation of all industries and geographical areas. The representation of consumers of banking services is also considered in the membership of the Boards of the regional Reserve Banks. Yet, there remains a potent distrust of the Fed in parts of American society.

This can be found on both the right and left of US politics. On the right, it is part of the rejection of all big government and centralised institutions. On the left, it is often seen as over-concerned with the world of finance. For example, Greider (1987) sees the Fed as a non-elected body with an anti-inflationary bias that restrains economic growth in order to preserve the value of financial assets, most of which are owned by wealthy people. It may be that the Fed appears to pay considerable attention to the real economy in the regular deliberations of the FOMC. It remains that any politically independent policy-making body is bound to be strongly influenced, if not controlled, by experts from the field. For independent central banks, this means control by bankers and experts from other areas of finance, who may well share values that do not chime with those of the majority of the people, especially of workers and the poor.

Further, the very nature of the task that the FOMC performs brings its members into touch daily with the representatives of high finance. In this time of the partial eclipse of older democratic ideals, in which in all countries and all areas of life public decisions are being made increasingly by committees of unelected experts, the independence of the Fed from private financial interests is not an issue. However, it will continue to surface from time to time in the future.

Pause for thought 12.6

Do you think it would be possible to have a politically independent central bank that was also independent of the financial sector of the economy?

Accountability

The Fed's mandate has been changed by Acts of Congress over the years but, at any time, is clearly stated and known. The Fed's interpretation of its own mandate also changes as conventional economic wisdom changes. Thus, the objectives of price stability and economic growth, which were once thought to be conflicting, have now effectively become the single goal of price stability. Again, however, the Fed's general interpretation of its mandate is always clear. We have seen, however, that the Fed does not set an inflation target. Nor does it publish an inflation forecast or report such as that of the MPC of the Bank of England. This reduces transparency since we lack knowledge of precisely what the Fed regards as 'price stability'. And, indeed, this can be interpreted differently at different times. On the other hand, this is not greatly different from the case of the ECB, which has a quantitative target but still succeeds in leaving us unclear what its precise intentions are.

Furthermore, the Fed is a more open institution than is the ECB. The principal form of Fed accountability is through its twice-yearly reports to Congress — in February and July each year. The report is presented by the Chairman of the FOMC (who is also the Chairman of the Board of Governors). The Chairman is then subject to questions by Committees of Congress. The February report provides a comprehensive review of the economic and financial situation in the country and reviews a wide range of indicators relevant to monetary policy. It also includes specific annual growth ranges for money and debt aggregates, consistent with expectations for inflation and growth of employment and output. In July, the Chairman reports any revisions to the plans for the current year, along with preliminary plans for the following year. Questioning by Congress committees can be detailed and tough. The reports are published by the Fed.

The meetings of the FOMC are also quite open. Although there are only twelve voting members, attendance at the meetings is much wider. The seven presidents of the regional reserve banks who are not currently voting members of the FOMC are allowed to attend and to speak. At the April 29-30 2008 meeting, ten voting members, five alternate members of the FOMC, three other presidents of regional reserve banks and another 57 people were present,[19] including other representatives of regional reserve banks and economists and associate economists of the various divisions of the Office of the Board of Governors, several of whom provided reports to the Committee on the present state of the economy and the financial markets. The decisions of the FOMC meetings are published immediately after the meeting.

At its December 1998 meeting, the FOMC decided also to announce immediately major shifts in its view about prospective developments relevant to the likelihood of a future increase or decrease in the targeted Federal Funds rate. The aim was to communicate to the public more quickly the FOMC's assessment of the balance of risks and its policy leanings. The Fed became worried, however, about the impact that these statements were having on the markets and now releases a statement after each meeting, whether or not it feels that there have been changes affecting future developments. These statements choose among a set of standard phrases to express the Committee's view. Thus, throughout 2001, all post-meeting statements concluded with the phrase that, in the view of the Committee, 'the risks are weighted mainly toward conditions that may generate economic weakness in the foreseeable future'. Minutes of FOMC meetings are published a few days after the following FOMC meeting and full transcripts become available five years later. Minutes include voting records, although these are sometimes not very useful. This is because the FOMC attempts to reach consensus before motions are put to the vote and so, when the vote is taken, there is frequently no dissenting voice. At the April 2008 meeting, however, there was opposition to the FOMC's decision to lower by 25 basis points the target for the Fed Funds rate. There were two dissenting members, both of whom wanted the rate to be left unchanged. The reasons for both the decision and the opposition are given. In April 2008, the supporters were more concerned with the weakness of the economy and the financial problems associated with the credit crunch; the dissenters were more concerned with the prospect of higher inflation in the future.

The Fed's monetary policy is, then, fairly transparent and its reasoning well understood. The views of the people, on whose behalf the FOMC is meant to be acting, can be expressed through elected members of Congress twice a year. However, there is no political representation at FOMC meetings and a question we raised in relation to the ECB appears here also concerning the political remedy available if the people are unhappy with the Fed's actions.

This brings us back to the question of independence from the financial sector since financial markets can be seen to be the only part of the economy capable of damaging the Fed in response to the Fed's policies. Through their actions, the financial markets can make it much more difficult for the central bank to fulfil its mandate and can damage the reputations of central bankers. We have seen, in chapter 11, a good example of this in relation to the value of the euro. The result of this is that the central bank might well feel itself more accountable to financial markets than to the political system. It is of interest in this regard that, as we report above, the Fed changed the way in which it expresses its views about the future prospects of the economy because of concern over the way in which its comments were being interpreted in the financial markets. This, of course, provides another reason why the desire expressed in the constitution of the Fed when it was set up in 1913, that it should be independent of both private financial business interests and duly constituted government authorities might not, in practice, be possible.

12.5   The Federal Reserve — monetary policy, 2000-2008

Background 1991-2000

The decade of the 1990s had started with interest rates relatively high. At the beginning of July 1990, the target Fed Funds rate stood at 8.25 per cent. The early 1990s, however, saw a downturn in all developed economies and the Fed set out on a long series of interest cuts, which saw the target rate fall sharply. In 1991, the Fed was extraordinarily active, making 10 cuts in the intended Fed Funds rate, bringing it down from 7 per cent to 4 per cent. That is, the FOMC not only cut the interest rate at each of its eight regular meetings, but also made further reductions in two special telephone linkups. Three more cuts followed in 1992, bringing the rate to 3 per cent by September, but this was as far as the Fed was prepared to go and the rate was then left unchanged for seventeen months until February 1994, by which time the US economy had started on a long period of rapid growth. The Fed, worried now about developing inflationary pressure, then pushed the rate up sharply. It made six increases in the target rate in 1994, two of fifty basis points and one (November) by the unusually large amount of 75 basis points. A further 50-basis-point increase in February 1995 meant that the rate had doubled from 3 per cent to 6 per cent in just twelve months. Perhaps this had been too far and too fast. In the following twelve months, three 25-point cuts had restored the Fed Funds target rate to 5.25 per cent.

Then came a period of extraordinary calm. Almost nothing happened from January 1996 until September 1998. In a period of two and three-quarter years, there was only a small increase in March 1997 as the economy kept growing but without generating serious concerns of inflation. Towards the end of 1998, a crisis developed in Asian financial markets and spread to Russia and Latin America. An influential New York hedge fund, Long Term Capital Management, was caught up in the financial market turmoil and a rescue had to be organised. There were short-lived fears that the world was headed for a serious financial crash. The Fed responded by cutting the intended Federal Funds rate in its meetings in September, October, and November to leave it at 4.75 per cent by the end of 1998.

When the crash did not occur, the Fed turned its attention back to the US growth rate and the then Chairman of the Board of Governors, Alan Greenspan, became worried by what he saw as excessive speculation leading to the overvaluation of equities. The Fed cautioned calm and tried to bring this about through the Chairman's public statements and by steadily raising rates. Three increases in the intended rate in the second half of 1999, followed by three further rises in the first half of 2000, brought it up from 4.75 per cent to 6.5 per cent in a year. The changes from the beginning of 2000 are shown in table 12.1.

2000-2008

At its meeting of 19 December 2000, the FOMC noted the slowing down of the US economy but left the intended Fed Funds rate at 6.5 per cent. However, they had been sufficiently worried to signal the possibility of an emergency meeting before the regular meeting due at the end of January 2001. They took advantage of this and reduced the target rate by 50 points on January 3 and by a further 50 points at the regular meeting on January 31. Two interesting questions occur here:

1. To what extent was the FOMC looking ahead at its December 2000 meeting?

2. Were the two fifty-point cuts in January at all influenced by the fact that the Chairman's report to Congress was rapidly approaching?

We cannot know the answer to either of these questions but the minutes of the December 2000 meeting reported that the FOMC had, *inter alia*, been told that:

• economic activity, which had expanded at an appreciably lower pace since midyear, might have slowed further in recent months

• consumer spending and business purchases of equipment and software had decelerated markedly after having registered extraordinary gains in the first half of the year

• housing construction, though still relatively firm, was noticeably below its robust pace of earlier in the year

• inventory overhangs had emerged in a number of goods-producing industries with manufacturing production declining as a consequence

• initial claims for unemployment insurance continued to trend upward, and the civilian unemployment rate edged up to 4 percent in November, its average thus far this year

• the weakening of factory output in November was reflected in a further decline in the rate of capacity utilisation in manufacturing to a point somewhat below its long-term average and

• consumer spending appeared to be decelerating noticeably further in the fourth quarter in an environment of diminished consumer confidence, smaller job gains, and lower stock prices.

Table 12.1: Intended Federal Funds rate March 1997 to April 2008

Year	Date	New intended Fed Funds rate, %	Change, basis points	Inflation rate[1]
2000	February 2	5.75	+ 25	2.7
	March 21	6.00	+ 25	3.2
	May 16	6.50	+ 50	3.1
2001	January 3	6.00	- 50	3.4
	January 31	5.50	- 50	3.4
	March 20	5.00	- 50	3.5
	April 18	4.50	- 50	2.9
	May 15	4.00	- 50	3.3
	June 27	3.75	- 25	3.2
	August 21	3.50	- 25	2.7
	September 17	3.00	- 50	2.7
	October 2	2.50	- 50	2.7
	November 6	2.00	- 50	2.1
	December 11	1.75	- 25	1.6
2002	November 6	1.25	-50	2.0
2003	June 25	1.00	-25	2.1
2004	June 30	1.25	+25	3.1
	August 10	1.5	+25	3.0
	September 25	1.75	+25	2.7
	November 10	2.00	+25	3.2
	December 14	2.25	+25	3.3
2005	February 2	2.5	+25	3.0
	March 22	2.75	+25	3.0
	May 3	3.00	+25	3.5
	June 30	3.25	+25	2.8
	August 9	3.5	+25	3.2
	September 20	3.75	+25	3.6
	November 1	4.00	+25	4.3
	December 13	4.25	+25	3.5
2006	January 31	4.5	+25	3.4
	March 28	4.75	+25	3.6
	May 10	5.00	+25	3.6
	June 29	5.25	+25	4.2
2007	September 18	4.75	-50	2.0
	October 31	4.5	-25	2.8
	December 11	4.25	-25	4.3
2008	January 22	3.5	-75	4.1
	January 30	3.0	-50	4.1
	March 18	2.25	-75	4.0
	April 30	2.0	-25	4.0

[1]annual inflation rate for the month prior to the FOMC meeting; CPI-U index prepared by Bureau of Labor Statistics: ftp://ftp.bls.gov/pub/special.requests/cpi/cpiai.txt

Certainly not all the news was bad. The economy had grown very rapidly in the first half of 2000 and some slowdown was to be expected and possibly welcomed given the tight labour markets. However, inflationary pressures seemed to be declining quite rapidly. The Committee were told that one measure of inflation had 'remained at a relatively subdued level'. Another, it is true, 'appeared to be increasing very gradually' but this was attributed to the indirect effects of higher energy costs following earlier oil price increases.

Rather oddly, in making its statement regarding the assessment of risks, the Committee moved from 'risks weighted towards rising inflation' in November to 'risks weighted toward economic weakness' in December, not taking advantage of the intermediate balanced risks assessment. Despite this, no change was made to the target Fed Funds rate. Overall, the case for doing nothing on 19th December but then dropping the intended Fed Funds rate by 50 points 15 days later does not suggest that the FOMC was looking very far forward on 19th December.

The year 2001 saw the Fed principally concerned with weakness — as the US economy headed towards recession, there was no threat to the goal of price stability, and the Fed saw its task as cutting interest rates and providing generous liquidity to the banking system in the attempt to avoid recession. Concern about the future weakness of the economy intensified following the attack on the World Trade Centre and the Pentagon on 11 September. As table 12.1 shows, once the Fed settled into its rate-cutting mood, things started happening quickly. The intended Fed Funds rate was cut at each scheduled FOMC meeting between January 31 and August 21, as well as at another unscheduled telephone meeting on April 18. The first four of these cuts were of 50 basis points with the result that the target rate plummeted by 3 per cent in fewer than eight months. Although in the early part of the year, the financial markets remained confident that the Fed would through its sharp cuts in interest rates keep the US economy out of recession, the need to cut rates so quickly as the economy headed down again raised doubts about the ability of central banks to forecast sufficiently well ahead.

In his explanation of Fed policy to Congress on 18 July 2001, Alan Greenspan raised an interesting point about the length of time lags. He defended the rapid series of cuts in the intended Federal flows rate by arguing that the depth of the downturn had been increased by the 'especially prompt and synchronous adjustment of production by business utilising the faster flow of information coming from the adoption of new technologies'. This was expanded later in his statement in the following way:

> Because the extent of the slowdown was not anticipated by businesses, some backup in inventories occurred, especially in the United States. Innovations, such as more advanced supply-chain management and flexible manufacturing technologies, have enabled firms to adjust production levels more rapidly to changes in sales. But these improvements apparently have not solved the thornier problem of correctly anticipating demand.[20]

If all this is so, forecasts of turning points and depths of recessions, already difficult, will become more so. Monetary policy will have little choice other than to respond to events as they occur. Yet, we were told that in making the decision to cut rates by only 25 points in July (rather than the 50 points of the previous five reductions), the FOMC 'recognised that the effects of policy actions are felt with a lag'. If lags in the economy generally are changing and becoming shorter but time lags in monetary policy remain as long as ever, the practice of monetary policy becomes ever more precarious.

The direction of US monetary policy in 2001 may well have been changed by the events of September 11. Although on August 21, the FOMC had continued to see the risks 'weighted mainly toward conditions that may generate economic weakness in the foreseeable future', there may well not have been a further cut in the target interest rate at the next scheduled meeting on October 2. However, the attack on the World Trade Centre and the Pentagon changed that as it led to immediate fears of a further loss in consumer confidence and serious problems for industries associated with air travel. The prospect that the downturn would be deeper than previously thought led the FOMC to have an emergency meeting on September 17, at which rates were cut by 50 points and further 50-point cuts followed on October 2 and November 6. A 25-point cut on December 11 reduced the target rate to 1.75 per cent, 4.75 per cent below the rate of 12 months earlier.

Of course, the sharp cuts in interest rate in the aftermath of September 11 were also, probably principally, intended to provide support for financial markets. The New York Stock Exchange remained closed for a week after the attack on the World Trade Centre and there were considerable fears regarding the way the markets would respond when it reopened. We thus had here another example of a 'Greenspan put option' (see section 9.4).

The FOMC plainly then thought that it had done enough for the time being to save the US from recession and to help to restore confidence to financial markets. It took no action for nearly a year. Then, in November 2002, we saw an apparently renewed concern with economic weakness and another 50 basis points were cut from the Fed Funds target rate, bringing it down to 1.25 per cent. But things were not so simple. The FOMC's statement, released on November 6 2002 included the following:

> The Committee continues to believe that an accommodative stance of monetary policy, coupled with still-robust underlying growth in productivity, is providing important ongoing support to economic activity. However, incoming economic data have tended to confirm that greater uncertainty, in part attributable to heightened geopolitical risks, is currently inhibiting spending, production, and employment. Inflation and inflation expectations remain well contained. In these circumstances, the Committee believes that today's additional monetary easing should prove helpful as the economy works its way through this current soft spot. With this action, the Committee believes that, against the background of its long-run

goals of price stability and sustainable economic growth and of the information currently available, the risks are balanced with respect to the
prospects for both goals in the foreseeable future.[21]

There was no immediate worry about inflation, it is true, but the committee
felt that risks regarding inflation and economic growth were balanced for the
foreseeable future. On the surface, this does not read like a statement accompanying a quite large cut in interest rates. The clue to the Fed's action is in the
phrase 'heightened geopolitical risks' — the US and other armed forces had been
committed to Afghanistan in 2002 and we were in the lead-up period to the second Iraq war which finally began in March 2003. The Fed clearly did have spending, production and employment figures causing them some concern. On the
other hand, these concerns were not sufficient to alter its view of the prospects for
longer term growth. We have talked often enough in this book about the importance of expectations and central banks certainly need to take account of uncertainty and lack of confidence on the part of consumers, firms and financial markets — but one might not think of central bankers as the people to ask to obtain
an accurate estimate of the likely extent of uncertainty about geopolitical risks.
The 50-point reduction was unanimously passed by the FOMC.

Pause for thought 12.6

Are there advantages in the FOMC's approach of always seeking consensus in meetings so
that the voting figures rarely tell us anything about the attitudes of the different Committee members? What are the disadvantages?

Seven months later, in June 2003, the FOMC shaved another 25 basis points
off its target Fed Funds rate, bringing it to the very low figure of 1 per cent.
Again, the FOMC's comments are interesting. These included:

> The Committee perceives that the upside and downside risks to the attain-
> ment of sustainable growth for the next few quarters are roughly equal. In
> contrast, the probability, though minor, of an unwelcome substantial fall in
> inflation exceeds that of a pickup in inflation from its already low level. On
> balance, the Committee believes that the latter concern is likely to predom-
> inate for the foreseeable future.[22]

The annual inflation rate for 2002, calculated from the consumer price index (CPI-
U) prepared by the Bureau of Labor Statistics had been 1.6 per cent. The rate had
risen in the early part of 2003 but the index for June 2003 (183.5)[23] was slightly
below that for March 2003 (184.2) and so one can perhaps understand the
Committee's concern, given the preference of monetary authorities for low but
positive rates of inflation. However, prices started rising again from July and the
annual inflation rate for 2003 turned out to be 2.3 per cent. It subsequently rose
to 2.7 per cent in 2004 and 3.5 per cent in 2005. Again, the question of the forecast

horizon being used by the Fed is of some interest. It is clear, though, that whatever factors were being taken into account, everyone on the Committee agreed that the target rate should move down. The resolution to reduce the rate by 25 basis points was passed by 11 votes to 1. The one dissenter wanted a 50-point cut.

The FOMC was not convinced that the US had entered a period of sustainable growth for another twelve months for the target rate was left at 1 per cent until June 2004. These decisions to keep the Fed Funds rate very low were later to attract much criticism. Once the Committee began to think things were picking up sufficiently to start to move the balance of risks away from fears of low economic growth, it began a quite extraordinary series of small interest rate increases. The target Fed Funds rate was raised by 25 basis points in each of the next 17 Committee meetings, starting on June 30 2004 and taking the target rate to 5.25 per cent by 30 June 2006. Consensus ruled throughout the period and no dissenting votes were recorded. In the light of later events, it is worth noting that until June 2005 comments on the housing market dealt largely with the buoyancy of the market and the support which growth in the market helped to support the rest of the economy.

Then, the minutes for the June 2005 meeting reported:

At this meeting the Committee reviewed and discussed staff presentations on the topic of housing valuations and monetary policy. Prices of houses in the United States had risen sharply in recent years, especially in certain areas of the country, to very high levels relative to incomes or rents. In addition to local market factors, a wide range of influences appeared to be supporting home prices, including solid gains in disposable income, low mortgage rates, and financial innovation in the residential mortgage market. Prices might be somewhat above the levels consistent with these underlying factors, but measuring the extent of any overvaluation either nationally or in regional markets posed considerable conceptual and statistical difficulties. Meeting participants noted that the rise in house prices had been accompanied by a modest shift toward potentially riskier types of mortgages, including adjustable-rate and interest-only loans, which could pose challenges to both lenders and borrowers. Nonetheless, financial institutions generally remained in a comfortable capital position, such loans had performed well thus far, much of the associated risk had been transferred to other investors through securitisation, and valuations had risen more rapidly than mortgage debt on average so that loan-to-value ratios had fallen.[23]

We see here that financial innovation is mentioned as a contributor to high house prices. We have two small pieces of information on the types of financial innovation is being discussed - potentially riskier types of mortgages and securitisation. Although the potential risk of adjustable-rate and interest-only mortgages is noted, there is little apparent concern. Indeed, it was later suggested that financial regulators encouraged these developments. In a speech in March 2007 to the US Senate Committee on Banking, Housing and Urban Affairs, the Committee

Chairman, Chris Dodd said:

> Despite those warning signals, in February of 2004 the leadership of the
> Federal Reserve Board seemed to encourage the development and use of
> adjustable rate mortgages that, today, are defaulting and going into foreclo-
> sure at record rates. The then-Chairman of the Fed said, in a speech to the
> National Credit Union Administration, 'American consumers might bene-
> fit if lenders provided greater mortgage product alternatives to the tradi-
> tional fixed-rate mortgage'.[24]

Securitisation of mortgages was clearly regarded by the FOMC as an entirely
desirable development.

By August 2005, the Committee was noting 'somewhat tighter standards in
real estate lending and becoming more cautious in their promotion of nontradi-
tional mortgage products', but nothing further. By November 2005, a slowing in
house price gains in some areas was being noted and it was suggested that
declines in home equity lending at banks could be indicating 'that the long-
expected cooling in the housing market was near.' In December, the minutes
reported that activity in the housing market remained brisk despite a rise in mortgage interest rates but that 'other available indicators of housing activity were on
the soft side: an index of mortgage applications for purchases of homes declined
in November, and builders' ratings of new home sales had fallen off in recent
months. In addition, survey measures of home-buying attitudes had declined to
levels last observed in the early 1990s'. But there was certainly no alarm and the
Fed Funds rate kept being pushed up.

In March 2006, it was noted that mortgage applications had continued to
decline in the previous month and that survey measures of homebuying attitudes
had maintained their recent downward trend. The FOMC observed that 'housing demand was likely damped by rising mortgage rates, which moved up further in late 2005 and early 2006'. The Committee had commented over a long
period on the low mortgage rates. It could not have come as a surprise that now
they were rising as the steadily rising Fed Funds rate had an impact throughout
the economy. In the minutes for the May 2006 meeting, it was reported that in
March, the average price for new homes had fallen compared to a year earlier.
The housing boom appeared to be over but any growing weakness in the housing market was insufficient to persuade the FOMC to stop steadily increasing the
Fed Funds rate. The June 2006 meeting, which was to see the last of the 17 consecutive increases in the target rate, saw the gradual cooling of the housing market as just a contributing factor to growth being 'likely to moderate to a more sustainable pace'.

Having reached a high of 5¼ per cent for the target rate, the FOMC was
happy to leave things be for the following nine meetings. Minutes of meetings
continued to note the slowing of the housing market but with no foreboding of
what was to come. In October 2006, the minutes reported that:

In their discussion of the major sectors of the economy, participants noted that housing activity was likely to remain a substantial drag on economic growth over the next few quarters. Many participants drew some comfort from the most recent data, which suggested that the correction in the housing market was likely to be no more severe than they had previously expected and that the risk of an even larger contraction in this sector had ebbed.

The March 2007 minutes mentioned that 'a tightening of standards for subprime borrowers in recent weeks seemed likely to restrain home sales'. By May, the minutes were noting the 'turmoil in the subprime market' and the view that 'the correction of the housing sector was likely to continue to weigh heavily on economic activity through most of this year--somewhat longer than previously expected'. Nonetheless, the Committee thought that the economy as a whole would continue to grow at a moderate pace and so did not decide upon an interest rate cut. In late June, 'a number of participants pointed to rising mortgage delinquency rates and related difficulties in the subprime mortgage market as factors that could crimp the availability of mortgage credit and the demand for housing'.

The regular meeting on 7 August spent rather longer discussing the economy and the market's view of likely future interest rates. It noted that housing continued to be a drag on the economy and the tightening credit conditions in the subprime mortgage market. It was also reported that during the period before the meeting 'growing apprehension that turmoil in markets for subprime mortgages and some low-rated corporate debt might have adverse effects on economic growth led investors to mark down their expectations for the future path of policy considerably further'. In other words, the markets were now anticipating future interest rate cuts. Still, the Committee concluded that

> readings on core inflation had improved modestly in recent months but did not yet convincingly demonstrate a sustained moderation of inflation pressures, and that   the high level of resource utilisation had the potential to sustain inflation pressures. Against this backdrop, members judged that the risk that inflation would fail to moderate as expected continued to outweigh other policy concerns.

The target rate for the Fed Funds rate was left unchanged at 5¼ per cent. Just three days later, the Committee had an unscheduled conference call meeting and another followed on 16 August. They were clearly by then worried about the state of the financial markets and judged that 'downside risks to growth had increased appreciably' but again thought that no adjustment to the Fed Funds rate was needed. That didn't come until the next regular meeting of the Committee on September 18.

But then, as with so often in the past, when the FOMC finally acted, it acted with panache. Seven cuts of various sizes sent the Fed Funds target rate tumbling to 2 per cent by 30 April 2008. Throughout this period, the Committee continued to note that inflationary pressures remained but these were by then heavily out-weighed by concerns about growth and, particularly, about the uncertainty generated by developments in financial markets. The Fed also acted strongly to attempt to shore up liquidity in the economy. For example, on March 8 2008, it expanded its securities lending program by introducing a new lending facility, the Term Securities Lending Facility (TSLF), under which it would lend up to $200 billion of Treasury securities to primary dealers secured for a term of 28 days by a pledge of other securities, including specified types of residential-mortgage-backed securities (MBS). The FOMC also authorised increases in its existing temporary reciprocal currency arrangements (swap lines) with the European Central Bank (ECB) and the Swiss National Bank (SNB).

The sharp cuts in rates in this period are particularly interesting in the light of earlier discussion in this book. As table 12.1 shows, the cuts were being made at a time of rising inflation as measured by a consumer price index. We know that the increase in the rate of inflation was largely due to rising oil and world food prices. In the past, these were often held to be cost inflation outside the control of the central bank of a single country and, therefore, not likely to be much affected by rises in domestic interest rates, although the USA is such a large consumer of oil that a marked fall in demand there would affect world oil prices. Still, there has always been a temptation to treat such rises as different and perhaps temporary. Because the FOMC does not declare an inflation target, it does not indicate the type of price index it is referring to, but all discussion at FOMC refer to 'core inflation'. This is in contrast to those countries that do use inflation targeting, which have moved to the use of a consumer price index.

What can we say overall about the decisions of the Fed over the past ten years? It is clear from its actions and comments that the FOMC believes that monetary policy does have powerful real effects, at least in the short to medium term. This is despite the fact that interest rate changes have been generally well anticipated by the financial markets. Differences of opinion regarding likely cuts have largely centred on the size of the cut and on whether the cut would be this or next month. Even on these issues, the financial markets have generally anticipated the Fed actions correctly. The markets have never genuinely taken by surprise in recent years. Thus, it seems that monetary policy is thought by practitioners to have powerful real effects whether policy is anticipated or not. This does not, of course, refute the proposition that money is neutral in the long run, but market practitioners act as if:

- the long-run is quite distant and
- short-run gains in employment and output are well worth having.

We return in these circumstances to simple Keynesian truths:

- if unemployment is rising and people fear for their jobs, they will reduce their spending
- if consumers reduce their spending, profits will fall and firms will reduce their output

- as profits fall, firms will cut investment

- as output and investment fall, firms will lay off workers.

The role of monetary policy in these circumstances is to encourage people to spend and firms to invest by lowering the cost of doing so.

> ## Pause for thought 12.7
>
> Do you think that the ECB would ever cut its refi rate by 75 basis points at a time when its consumer price index was showing an inflation rate of 4 per cent?

We have seen that the Fed, much more than the Bank of England and the ECB, is prepared to take risks with the inflation rate because of concerns about growth and, increasingly, the state of financial markets.

We have also seen that the Fed is extraordinarily activist. In the 112 months from the beginning of 1999 to April 2008, the Fed made 43 adjustments to the target Fed Funds rate. This contrasts with 23 changes by the ECB to its refi rate over the same period and 31 changes by the MPC of the Bank of England to its repo rate. Of the Bank of England's 31 changes, 29 were by the minimum amount of 25 basis points, the other two by 50 basis points. The ECB has made seven changes of 50 basis points with every other change being by 25 basis points, although the larger changes were all in the early days of the bank. Twelve of the FOM''s changes have been by 50 basis points and two by 75 basis points. Thus, the Fed acts often and decisively.

Although there have been some relatively long periods of calm in the 1990s, there have been several periods when the FOMC has rushed the target Fed Funds rate down or up in a great hurry, notably, in 1990-91 (down) and in 1994-5 (up), 2000-2001 (down), 2004-2006 (up) and 2007-2008 (down). The question we need to ask is whether this suggests that monetary policy is safe in the hands of the Fed since it shows the Fed as being decisive in the face of rapidly changing economic conditions. Alternatively, does it indicate that, for all the sophisticated policy models and the placing of monetary policy in the hands of experts, central banks are still largely flying by the seats of their pants?

12.6   Summary

The US central bank, the Federal Reserve System is not a single bank but a set of twelve regional reserve banks coordinated by a board in Washington D C. This structure can be explained by a look at the story of the development of the US banking system. This was dominated by two fears— of centralisation with power concentrated in New York or Washington DC and of domination by the 'mon-eyed interests' of the financial sector. The result was a highly decentralised banking system with very large numbers of small banks. Two attempts in the late 18th and 19th centuries failed because of the fears of centralisation. Consequently, the Federal Reserve System was not set up until 1913. The bank was required to be politically independent and independent of the financial sector. Initially, much of the power rested with the regional reserve banks. However, continued multi-bank panics and the lack of coordination evident at the time of the Great Depression in the 1930s led to a number of changes being made. This replaced the old Federal Reserve Board with the Board of Governors of the Federal Reserve and placed monetary policy in the hands of the Federal Open Market Committee (FOMC), which consisted of the seven members of the Board of Governors and five representatives of the regional reserve banks. One of the regional bank representatives is always from the Federal Reserve Bank of New York because it carries out open market operations on behalf of the FOMC. Power now rests with the centre, with the regional banks largely acting as local agencies of the Board of Governors. However, the presence of regional representatives on the FOMC means that it still pays more attention to economic conditions in the different parts of the country than is the case with many other central banks.

The Federal Reserve (the Fed) was required to act against both inflation and deflation and to act to encourage high employment and economic growth. However, over the past 25 years, price stability has become dominant in the bank's set of goals. The Fed has neither a target rate of inflation nor a target rate of growth of the money supply, but pays attention to a wide range of real and monetary indicators. It is required by law to calculate monetary growth ranges for M2 and M3 consistent with its price stability objective but does not believe that these are a reliable guide to policy.

The Fed carries out its policy through open market operations that seek to keep the Federal Funds rate of interest — the interest rate that depository institutions pay when they borrow reserves overnight to meet reserve requirements. The reserve requirements are set to help the Fed control liquidity within the system but the ratios are seldom changed and are not used as a way of attempting to control the money supply. The Fed made half-hearted attempts to influence reserves in the 1970s and early 1980s (firstly through establishing a target range for the Fed Funds rate, allowing for variations in the interest rate; and secondly by targeting non-borrowed and then borrowed reserves). However, these did not succeed in making the money supply exogenous.

Borrowed reserves are borrowings through the discount window, through which the Fed lends to banks as lender of last resort. The discount rate is usually kept below the Fed Funds rate, but banks are discouraged from borrowing in this way except in emergencies.

The Fed is certainly politically independent but has in place a number of features that make it relatively accountable to the political system. However, the extent to which it can be said to independent of the financial sector is open to doubt. The recent performance of the Fed also raises questions regarding the extent to which it succeeds in looking ahead and adjusting interest rates sufficiently early to control problems that are developing in the economy.

Key concepts used in this chapter

bank charters

state-chartered banks

federal-chartered banks

multi-bank panics

elastic currency

Federal Open Market
Committee (FOMC)

monitoring ranges

lagged reserve accounting

contemporaneous reserve
accounting

discount window

Federal Funds rate

reserve ratios

matched transactions

frown costs (non-pecuniary
costs)

open market operations

central bank independence

transparency

accountability

Questions and exercises
Answers at the end of the book

1. How centralized is the US central bank system now? Do the regional Reserve Banks have more or less power than the national central banks within the European System of Central Banks?

2. If the Fed wishes to discourage banks from borrowing at the discount window except in emergencies, why does it keep the discount rate below the Federal Funds rate?

3. Why does the Fed feel the need to maintain a system of reserve ratios when the Bank of England does not (apart from the small prudential ratio)?

4. How useful are the phrases from which the FOMC chooses for describing its view of likely future developments in the US economy? What is the purpose of making statements of this kind?

5. Does the FOMC engage in:

(a) inflation targeting;
(b) money supply targeting;
(c) nominal demand targeting?

If you choose none of these, what does it do?

... and also to think about

6. Consider the extent to which the current structure of the Federal Reserve System is a product of

    (a) geography;
    (b) history;
    (c) planning.

7. A distinction is usually made between the 'transparency' of a central bank and its accountability. What is the difference? Consider the proposition that, while the monetary policy of the Fed is transparent, the FOMC is not genuinely accountable. Is it possible for a central bank to be accountable without being transparent?

8. Discuss whether the change in the balance of the objectives of the Federal Reserve over the years is a product of:

    (a) our greater knowledge of economics;
    (b) shifts in the balance of economic power within the country;
    (c) fashion (doing what other monetary authorities do).

Further reading

For a brief but good history of the Federal Reserve System, see *The New Palgrave Dictionary of Money and Finance*, (1992). A brief account of the whole US banking and financial system can be found in Howells and Bain (2008). A great deal of useful material is available on the web from the sites of the Federal Reserve System (www.federalreserve.gov) and the Federal Reserve Bank of New York (www.ny.frb.org). Wray (1990) and Moore (1988b) provide detailed evidence to explain precisely why the money supply in the United States is endogenous.

    Forder (2003) contains a detailed discussion of the origins of the Federal Reserve and the meaning of 'independence'. Although it's a few years old, Blinder (1998) remains the best account of the practice of central banking and touches on a number of issues raised in this chapter.

Appendix 1

The Term Structure of Interest Rates

The relationship between interest rates on assets differentiated solely by their term to maturity is known as the 'term structure of interest rates' and a graphical representation is known as a 'yield curve'. We look at this relationship here for two reasons. The first is that in section 4.3 we noted that changes in short-term interest rates might not be fully reflected in changes in medium and long-rates because other factors played a part. We look in a moment at these factors. Secondly, in section 9.5 we noted that the shape of the yield curve (and changes in its shape) have often played a role in policy-making. We explain the argument behind this use of the curve.

Figure A1: The yield curve

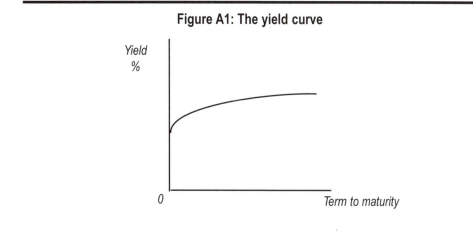

Figure A1 shows what is often referred to as a 'typical' or 'normal' yield curve. Notice that it is upward-sloping and thus shows yields increasing with the term to maturity. The idea that this is a 'normal' shape must be based upon an argument that there is something so systematically unattractive about long dated assets (bonds, for example), that people have to be paid an inducement (a premium) to hold them. It is tempting to jump to the conclusion that the premium must be due to the comparative illiquidity of long-dated bonds: if investors are to commit their funds for a long period there must be an additional reward. But this confuses 'term to maturity' with 'holding period'. An investor can buy short- or long-dated bonds today and sell them tomorrow. There is a large and active market for bonds of all maturities and she can hold a bond of any maturity for any period that she likes, up to the date of its redemption. The characteristic that is strictly speaking responsible for the positive term-premium is that long bonds show a greater price sensitivity to changes in interest rates than do short-dated bonds. If we define 'duration' as the weighted average length of time that it takes for an investor to receive the total cashflows from a bond, then it is pretty clear that duration increases with the term to maturity. Note also that, for a given term to maturity, duration is also inversely related to the size of the coupon since the effect of a high coupon is to bring forward the bulk of cashflows and thus to reduce the weighted average length of time that it takes to receive them. Now assume that a bond's market price equals the present value of the future cash-flows. The present value is arrived at by discounting and the effect of discounting depends upon both the size of the discount rate and the length of time that we have to wait for the payment. Consequently, long-deferred payments are more seriously affected by a change in discount rate than payments which accrue in the near-term. All of this can be demonstrated by the arithmetic of bond pricing and some further arithmetic can show that duration measures the elasticity of bond prices with respect to changes in interest rates (Howells and Bain, 2008, ch.16; Blake, 2000, ch.5)

Even this characteristic, however, is not sufficient on its own to explain a systematic upward bias to the yield curve. We need the further assumption that investors do not like this characteristic or, more strictly, that more investors dislike this characteristic of long-dated bonds than prefer the positive characteristic of long-dated bonds, namely that they provide an absolutely guaranteed income if held to maturity. We need the assumption that, on balance, the bond market is dominated by capital-risk averse, as opposed to income-risk averse investors. If this is true, the majority of investors in long-dated bonds need some additional compensation for the risk of price fluctuations. Other things being equal, the steepness of the curve indicates the strength of this aversion capital-risk aversion and thus it follows that changes in the degree of capital risk aversion will cause changes in the slope and thus in the relation between short and long rates.

Furthermore, the slope of the curve is likely to be influenced by expectations of future short-term rates. Imagine an investor who is prepared to invest in bonds for more than the shortest possible period, then he or she has the choice of making a single investment for the whole period or a series of shorter-term investments. In the simplest case we might take the investor who wishes to invest for two years and can thus buy now a two-year bond (which we shall call 'long') or a one-year bond ('short'), reinvesting the proceeds in another one-year bond in one year's time. Now let us assume that the current structure of interest rates (whatever it is) is an equilibrium structure. Investors are happy, in other words, with this structure (this is a reasonable assumption, since, if they were not, they could buy and sell bonds of different maturities causing yields to change until they were happy). Being happy with this structure means that investors (like ours) must be indifferent between holding a two-year bond and a succession of two one-year bonds. Formally speaking, the following must hold:

$$(1+i_2)^2 = (1+i_1) \times (1+E^2i_1) \qquad (A1)$$

where i_2 is the current two-year interest rate (the rate available now on a two-year) bond, i_1 is the current one-year rate and E^2i^1 is the one-year rate expected in the second year. Now suppose that $i_1 = 6$ per cent while $i_2 = 7$ per cent. It is a fairly simple task to calculate what investors must be expecting about the one year rate in one year's time, by rearranging A1.

$$E^2i_1 = \frac{(1+i_2)^2}{(1+i_1)} - 1 \qquad (A2)$$

Using our figures we have:

$$^2i_1 = \frac{(1.07)^2}{(1.06)} - 1 = \frac{1.1449}{1.06} - 1 = 1.0801 - 1 = .0801 \text{ or } 8.01\% \qquad (A3)$$

Thus, if the current one year rate is 6 per cent while the current two year rate is 7 per cent, it must be the case that investors expect to be able to reinvest in one year's time at slightly more than 8 per cent. Clearly, if current one year rates are 6 per cent and two year rates are 7 per cent, the yield curve is upward sloping. In these circumstances, it seems that investors must expect future short-term rates to be higher, and not just higher than current short term rates but higher even than current long rates (8.01 > 7). In short, an upward sloping yield curve implies higher short rates in future while a downward sloping yield curve implies lower short rates in future.

If there were no other influences on the yield curve (no capital risk aversion, for example) then expectations that current short rates were not going to change would produce a horizontal yield curve. But these influences are not mutually exclusive. If capital-risk aversion is generally present then all yield curve will have an upward bias added to whatever slope would result from interest rate expectations. If these were neutral, for example, then the yield curve would not be horizontal but would have an upward slope as a result of the risk premium; if investors expected interest rates to fall, then the yield curve might be downward sloping, but less steeply than it would have been if expectations were the only influence. If expectation about the future course of interest rates are normally distributed around a mean of 'no change', then capital risk aversion means that the curve will slope upwards more frequently than it will slope downwards. Hence the idea of the upward slope as 'normal'.

Now we can see why (in section 4.3) we suggested that the communication of changes in central banks' official interest rates, at the very short end of the maturity spectrum, to medium and long-term rates is complex. We can see that a rise (for example) in official rates could be modified at medium and long parts of the spectrum by changes in capital risk aversion. More likely the effect will be modified by expectations.

Thus, if financial markets believe that an increase in the official rate is the first of a series of rises (because they can see inflationary pressures developing), longer-term rates will follow short-term rates up. However, an increase in the official rate might persuade the markets that inflation will fall in future, allowing official rates to come down again. In this case, a rise in the official rate would produce expectations of lower future interest rates and long rates might even fall, while short rates go up. This is more likely to occur when short rates are moved to what appear to be historically 'extreme' levels in pursuit of policy objectives. Hence, downward sloping ('inverted') yield curves do sometimes appear when short rates are raised to counter inflationary pressure. As we note in section 4.3, much depends here on demand conditions in the other major economies, especially that of the USA, and the expected policies of other central banks, notably the Federal Reserve Board (the Fed).

The expectations theory of the term structure has been subjected to intensive empirical testing over the years (see Malkiel, 1992 for a survey). Generally, speaking, the tests have not been encouraging though it is not clear, strictly speaking, whether this is because interest differentials are not driven by expectations or whether they are driven by expectations but the expectations are incorrect. The testing continues, however, partly because the dataset is almost limitless (different definitions of short/long, different time periods etc); partly because changes in econometric techniques allow new tests to be carried out; and partly because it just is very hard to believe that agents make forecasts of interest rates which are frequently incorrect or that they are irrational and do not do the sort of calculations we have done above. There is another reason, however, for the reluctance to abandon the expectations theory and this is that there is a big policy prize at the end of this particular rainbow.

This can be most easily understood if we introduce what is frequently called the Fisher hypothesis which states that the nominal (risk-free, short-term) rate of interest is composed of a real rate of interest which is stable and an inflation premium which varies with inflation so as to maintain the stability of the real rate. In symbols:

$$i = r + \pi \tag{A4}$$

where i is the nominal rate, r is the real rate and π is the rate of inflation. Now, just suppose that the current term structure did enable us to make reliable forecasts of future short-term rates. We could take our earlier example which suggested that short-term rates would rise from 6 to 8 per cent in the near future. Then if we knew, from past observation, that the real rate was usually about 3 per cent, then our yield curve would enable us to forecast future inflation rates as well as future short-term interest rates. This would be immensely useful for central banks and other policy makers.

Unfortunately, as we have said, tests of the term structure's forecasting ability have not been very encouraging. Furthermore, the evidence suggests that real interest rates are not so stable as would be required for the simple kind of calculation that we have just done. At the moment, it does not seem possible to make accurate forecasts about either the level of future interest rates or the level of future inflation rates.

However, the fact that the term structure cannot be used to forecast a particular value, does not mean that it has no value to policy makers. Provided we think that expectations play some part in determining the shape of the curve and that an inflation premium plays some part in the nominal interest rate, then, with some degree of caution, we might be prepared to regard changes in the shape of the yield curve as indicating something about changes in inflationary pressures. A sudden steepening of the yield curve, for example, might be read as indicating that markets expect the rate of inflation to rise in future (even if it cannot tell us the actual rate). Similarly, a flattening of the curve might suggest a future reduction in inflationary pressure and serve as an indication to a central bank that it can reduce the official interest rate, especially if there is other supporting evidence of a moderation of inflation. In this limited role, the yield curve, and more especially changes in the shape of the yield curve has come to be one of the many information variables which central banks have come to use in setting interest rates. We look at attempts to extract information from the bond and other markets in section 9.5.

Appendix 2

The Banking Crisis and the Credit Crunch

Introduction

Since we began work on this edition (in the autumn of 2007) a great deal has happened. At times it has happened so quickly that it has been impossible to revise the text before the next development rendered the revisions out of date. It is clear now, with the benefit of hindsight, that future books about monetary policy are going to have to pay much closer attention to banks and the way in which they behave. This appendix is our attempt to show how recent events relate to, and should be interpreted in the light of, our earlier chapters.

We begin with a look at what we might call 'some principles of intermediation' or to put it informally 'how things are supposed to work, when all is well'. We then provide a summary of the key stages of the crisis before finishing with an examination of the implications for policy.

Some principles of intermediation

From the very first, we have stressed that money consists overwhelmingly of bank deposits and furthermore that those deposits expand as banks make net new loans. On the next page we have a balance sheet which is based upon the actual balance sheet of a UK high street bank in the middle of June 2007. It shows that the deposits ('customer accounts') dominate liabilities while the loans ('loans and advances to customers') are the largest item on the asset side. The abbreviations: *Dp, Lp, Sf* etc. are those that we use in the T-accounts in chapter 2 and later.

Since the average maturity of the loans is substantially greater than that of the deposits, we observe the first principle of financial intermediation, namely that of 'maturity transformation': banks 'borrow short' and 'lend long'. This inevitably exposes them to liquidity risk since depositors may wish to withdraw cash suddenly. If the net withdrawals are small, then they can be met from 'cash and balances at the central bank'. Clearly, these balances are critical and are sometimes referred to as 'reserves'. However, if the withdrawals are large, this is a serious threat since our balance sheet shows that the reserves are only 2.2 per cent of customer deposits (and only 1.8 per cent if we include deposits belonging to other banks). Notice that *if* depositors make large unexpected withdrawals and *if* the authorities do nothing the bank will fail. This is because, unlike the rest of us, a shortage of liquidity hits banks in a special way. While firms and households, confronted with an unexpected demand for payment, can usually delay for long enough to raise the funds by some means, approximately half of bank deposits are repayable *on demand*. Furthermore, they have a fixed nominal value (which is one reason why they function as money). Notice too that this risk is *inherent* in banking activity. It cannot be eliminated without abandoning the core banking function of maturity transformation.

In practice the reserve ratio is the first line of defence against liquidity risk, but we shall see in a moment that the externalities generated by a bank failure may be so large that additional protection is required. This is provided partly by the holding of other, near-liquid assets, on the balance sheet. This will include money market instruments of various kinds contained in the category 'available-for-sale- financial assets'. The ultimate protection in a crisis is provided by the central bank acting in its capacity of 'lender of last resort'.

In the next section we shall see that the banking crisis, in the UK, was first signalled by a liquidity crisis at the Northern Rock bank. This bank relied very heavily upon 'wholesale funding', shown in our balance sheet as 'deposits from banks'. When these (largely) time deposits matured they were not replaced by their bank owners, causing the equivalent of mass withdrawals from Northern Rock's perspective. In the circumstances the bank had no option but to ask the Bank of England for help, but once this was known, the retail clients of the bank panicked and began to withdraw their deposits as well.

Notice that liquidity risk is different from 'solvency' or 'bankruptcy risk'. The test of solvency involves comparing *total* assets with *total* liabilities (while liquidity focuses upon the relationship between a *subset* of assets and liabilities). Provided that there is a positive differential ('positive net worth' or 'capital' or 'shareholder funds') the bank is solvent. But, as Northern Rock showed, it is perfectly possible for a solvent and well-run bank to be hit by a liquidity crisis. This is partly why the authorities are willing to provide last resort assistance: a liquidity crisis can strike a perfectly solvent bank. There is, though, one potential link between liquidity and solvency. This will be triggered if a number of banks are simultaneously hit by withdrawals, in other words where there is a *general* liquidity crisis. In order to improve its liquidity position, a bank, like a household, may

Figure A2: Balance sheet of a typical UK high street bank

	Assets	£mn
'Reserves' R	Cash and balances at central banks	3,616
	Items in course of collection from banks	1,883
	Trading and other financial assets at fair value through profit or loss	52,037
Loans to the general public Lp	Loans and advances to customers	229,621
	Loans and advances to banks	29,319
Derivatives	Derivative financial instruments	9,914
including CDOs etc	Available-for-sale financial assets	25,032
	Investment property	3,366
	Tangible fixed assets	2,856
	Other assets	10,138
	Total	367,782

	Liabilities	
Interbank loans	Deposits from banks	40,207
Deposits of the non-bank private sector Dp	Customer accounts	162,129
	Items in course of transmission to banks	835
	Trading and other financial liabilities at fair value through profit or loss	3,572
	Derivative financial instruments	9,931
	Debt securities in issue	58,437
	Liabilities arising from insurance and investment contracts	52,111
	Unallocated surplus within insurance businesses	433
	Retirement benefit obligations	1,925
	Other liabilities	27,121
	Total	356,701

	Equity	
Equity/capital/ shareholder funds Sf	Shareholder funds	10,797
	Minority interests	284
	Total	11,081
	Liabilities + Equity	**367,782**

sell non liquid assets for cash. But recall that it must do this quickly. If several banks do it at once, there is likely to be a collapse of asset values because of the urgent sales. This will have the effect of reducing the value of bank assets and may drive them below the value of liabilities. This is another reason why the authorities are nervous about liquidity crises.

A second principle of financial intermediation is the reduction of risk. For the borrower, the risk of being asked for early repayment is reduced (compared with the risk if the funds had come direct from a lender). More obviously, there are reduced risks for the depositor. Firstly, the deposits being perfectly liquid, they are available to the depositor instantly if unforeseen events so require. Furthermore, the bank reduces risk to its depositors by holding a wide range of assets whose returns are imperfectly correlated. Thirdly, the bank employs some form of screening or evaluation of of the creditworthiness of borrowers. Finally, it holds capital or shareholder funds whose value fluctuates with changes in the value of the assets.   By way of example, we can see that our bank holds virtually £10bn of derivative financial instruments. If, say, these were to prove worthless, the bank must still honour its obligations under 'liabilities'. It does this by drawing on its capital. In this particular case, the bank would be almost insolvent (capital would fall to about £1bn). Given this role for capital, we can now see the importance of another ratio— capital to assets. In our balance sheet the ratio is about 3 per cent.

We now see another principle, namely that the risk of banking operations should be borne by the shareholders and not by the depositors or other creditors. This raises the question of what is an appropriate level of capital for a bank. The obvious answer is that it will depend not just on the total quantity of assets (reflecting the size of the bank's business) but also on the riskiness of the assets. International agreements (the 'Basel Accords') require banks to hold capital equal to a minimum of 8 per cent of 'risk-adjusted assets'. This recognises that some assets (cash and deposits at the central bank, government bonds) are risk-free, while others (domestic mortgages used to be a good example) have low but positive levels of risk. If we applied the Basel weights to the assets in our balance sheet, we should probably find that the risk-adjusted capital ratio was around 12 per cent.

As we shall see later, one of the most dramatic developments in the recent crisis has been the discovery that some assets were worth much less than had been thought (their risk was higher than anticipated). This has led to the depletion of bank capital and the banks concerned have had to raise new capital by issuing new shares. But some banks have found that investors do not want the shares at any reasonable price. These are the banks that have had to ask for government help and have been nationalised, in some degree or other.

What went wrong?

The first observation to make is that, prior to 2007, it was a very long time since anything had gone wrong at all. There had been problems with financial markets — the 1987 equity market crash and the ending of the 'dotcom' boom in 2000 but with the exception of BCCI (1991) and Barings (1995) both of which contained elements of fraud, we have to go back to the 1930s (pre-1914 according to the Governor of the Bank of England) to find an example of systemic bank failure. Seventy five years can breed complacency.

We noted earlier that banks reduce risk by screening borrowers for their creditworthiness. It is easy to suppose that banks are doing their best to reduce defaults and delinquencies to zero. But this is a misconception. Banks are prepared to accept a degree of default and this is reflected in their charges and their business plan. Without defaults, banks could not be sure that their lending criteria were not too strict and leading them to exclude risky but profitable opportunities. Furthermore, for a given set of lending criteria, the rate of default will vary with the economic cycle, and so it is reasonable to assume after fifteen years of prosperity, defaults in the new millenium were at historically low levels.

In these circumstances, it is not completely surprising that loan officers begin to wonder whether we are in 'a new era' in which there has been a permanent reduction in risk. Bear in mind too that screening and monitoring of loan applicants has resource costs and so it is not entirely foolish to ask whether the cost of caution might not be greater than the losses that would result from a default rate that might only be slightly higher in these benign circumstances. What we have here then is the beginning of what came to be known as the 'mis-pricing of risk' though it was not so much the *price* that was miscalculated as the amount of risk itself.

The relaxation of lending criteria could be seen most clearly in the home loans market where loan to value ratios rose to one hundred per cent (and even more in some cases). There was anecdotal evidence also that some lenders were prepared to lend up to six times income, where in the late 1990s three to four times would have been more normal. Extraordinary as it may seem, some lenders were prepared to accept claims about income that were 'self-certified' rather than backed by independent evidence. Given that mortgage brokers sometimes worked on commissions from lenders, it does not require a great deal of cynicism to imagine that some borrowers were being encouraged to make false claims and it is possible that prosecutions for fraud may yet emerge. As is often the case, these innovations were pushed to their furthest limits in the USA where the term 'NINJA-loan' (a loan to someone with 'no income, no job or assets') was coined in 2007.

So far, we have suggested that lenders were deliberately experimenting with higher risk assets, and that no doubt was true to some degree. But at the same time that these low-quality assets were being created, banks were finding ways of keeping risk (as they thought) off the balance sheet. This was done by 'securitising' some of the mortgages and selling them on. A glance at our balance sheet shows the benefits of this, and these pre-dated the reckless lending. A glance at the balance sheet shows that assets can be divided into 'tradable' and 'non-tradable'. The former can be acquired and disposed of through organised markets while the latter cannot. Traditionally, loans are non-tradable. If a bank wishes to 'dispose of' a loan to XYZ plc it has to ask the firm to repay, and this may have to be carefully negotiated if the firm is not to be pushed into bankruptcy. 'Securitisation' involved bundling together a number of loans of similar kind and selling them on to a third party who would also receive the interest, after a deduction of a fraction by the originating bank. Originally, these loans would be sold to a 'special vehicle' — a firm which was established by the originating bank but was a legally separate entity. This special vehicle would sell bonds in order to raise the funds to purchase the loans and, of course, some of those bonds might be bought by the originating bank. In more recent years, the securities found their way to a host of different types of financial institution including hedge funds, insurance companies, merchant banks etc. and again these purchasers would sometimes have financial links to the originating bank. The onward sale of these securitised mortgages had two major, but linked, advantages for banks. Firstly, if we ignore the fact that some of the purchasers were linked to the originating bank, the sale removed risky assets from the banks' balance sheets in exchange for cash. This lowered the capital that banks had to hold under the Basel regulations (or equivalently meant they could do more business for the same level of capital). And capital is expensive. In normal circumstances, assets would be funded by deposit liabilities which might cost say 4 per cent p.a. The return required by shareholders on capital invested in the bank could easily be 15 per cent. The other advantage is that the sale of these hitherto non-tradable assets enabled banks to raise money for further expansion. Just how much the sale of loans reduced the risk to the originating bank was obscure since the terms on which the buyer of the loans accepted them varied. In some cases they accepted the whole of the default risk, in others some, or even all, stayed with the bank. The critical issue that subsequently emerged is that these 'over the counter' (OTC) deals made it virtually impossible to know what level of risk a financial institution was exposed to, even if its holdings of the securitised debt (often referred to as 'collateralised debt obligations' or CDOs) could be identified. And, related to this, since the bundles were never traded it was impossible to know what their real value was.

Another development which added enormously to the general level of obscurity was the very rapid growth in 'credit default swaps' (or CDSs). Superficially, these looked like deals which offered insurance against a borrower defaulting. 'Swap' is a misleading term since the deal functioned more like an option, but in essence it was simple enough in that a lender, or holder of assets, could buy protection from default. The seller of the protection would receive a premium and would would then pay an agreed amount of compensation if the default (or some other 'reference event') occurred and would pay nothing if it did not. These, too were over the counter deals, so the terms and the quantities were not easily known. Furthermore, and in total contrast to conventional insurance, anyone could buy this credit protection *against events in which they had no material interest.* The law covering conventional insurance, requires that the buyer of the insurance have an 'insurable interest' in the event. Hence we can take out life insurance policies on close members of our family but not upon strangers. But in the CDS market anyone could take out protection against, say, the inability of Lehman Brothers investment bank to redeem its bonds, even though they held no Lehman bonds. This takes us across the line from insurance to straightforward betting. And the significance is that the obligations that were eventually triggered by Lehman's collapse in September 2008 were many times greater than the value of the bonds at stake. Some estimates put the payments triggered by Lehman's collapse at $400bn but bear in mind, since it is a feature of OTC deals, that no one really knows and furthermore no one knows who exactly is holding the liabilities.

Another trend, which really came to light only after the Northern Rock affair was the extent to which banks had come to rely on 'wholesale funding'. This is shown in our balance sheet by 'deposits from banks' and 'debt securities in issue'. In this case, deposits belonging to other banks make up about 20 per cent of total deposits, which was slightly below the norm for UK banks in mid-2007. Even so, this is a large proportion and for building societies and mortgage banks (ex-building societies) which had traditionally relied upon household savings, wholesale funding of 20 to 30 per cent represented a major shift in their funding. It also increased dramatically the level of systemic risk in the system. In the previous section we explained that banks (unlike other financial institutions) have access to a 'lender of last resort' and we justified this by reference to 'externalities'. These externalities refer to costs or damage inflicted upon third parties when a bank fails. These are potentially substantial because of the role of bank deposits as money. If a bank fails, people not only lose their wealth, they lose the means of payment. This means that they are bound to protect themselves by withdrawing any other deposits they may have with other banks — threatening the general liquidity crisis we mentioned — and by selling any near-liquid assets they may have. This threatens the collapse of asset values and widespread insolvencies. The speed with which one bank's problems are transmitted to another depends to a large degree on the degree of interbank lending. (One of the reasons that the Bank of England allowed Barings Bank to fail in 1995 is that it had a limited role in the interbank market and therefore was unlikely to trigger a systemic collapse).

Hence when the US and UK mortgage defaults began to increase in 2007, banks did what we all do in a crisis and rushed to build up liquidity. This involved their holding enlarged deposits with the central bank in place of the deposits that they previously held with other banks. With banks so heavily dependent on other banks' deposits this has made it very difficult for them to lend on the previous scale. The shortage of interbank deposits has, predictably, led to a sharp rise in the rate of interest on interbank deposits. Most empirical studies suggest that the 'normal' premium for 3-month sterling LIBOR over the Bank of England's official rate is about 20 bp. In October 2008, the premium was about 170 bp in spite of several initiatives by the Bank of England.

This unwillingness to lend is a powerful demonstration of how asymmetric information can lead to adverse selection. It is widely accepted that asymmetric information is common in financial contracts. Typically, the borrower has better information (about the likely risk and return attaching to the use of the funds) than does the lender. So, in a banking context, the ultimate borrower has an advantage over the bank and the bank has an advantage over the depositor. The nature of bank contracts (loans and deposits) — a fixed nominal value and a rate of interest unrelated to the position of the borrower — is a partial reaction to this, since it passes some of the risk back to the borrower and reduces the information disadvantage of the lender. (These characteristics also help make the deposits function as money). However, while this might work in normal circumstances (when information deficiencies fall within conventional bounds) we now know that it does not work where lenders have lost all confidence in their ability to appraise borrowers' creditworthiness. Take the case of the interbank market. Bank *A* has funds to lend which it might have lent in the past to bank *B*. But because of the general uncertainty banks are unwilling to lend except at quite a high rate of interest, to reflect the higher (unknown) risk. So bank *A* offers funds at a high rate of interest which bank *B* is prepared to pay. But how does bank *A* interpret this willingness to borrow at high rates? One obvious interpretation is that if bank *B* is willing to pay the high rate, then bank *B* must be in serious trouble and if bank *A* comes that conclusion it will not wish to lend to bank *B*, *at any rate of interest*. So *A* does not lend and *B* does not borrow, and this stalemate applies across the system and so banks sit on enlarged deposits with the central bank.

In addition to their understandable preference for holding cash rather than making new loans in a situation of severe asymmetric information, banks have faced further pressures on their ability to lend. These arose from the capital adequacy requirements that we mentioned in the opening section. Recall that capital adequacy is measured by the value of (strictly, risk-adjusted) assets to 'equity' or shareholder funds. This is because these funds are the first line of protection in the event of falls in asset values. Essentially (as we said) shareholder funds are used to plug the gaps so that the loss of asset value does not impair the bank's ability to meet its obligations under 'liabilities'. But as the losses lead to a reduction in shareholder funds they reduce the amount of remaining capital and this means that a bank may have to *reduce* its assets, and since the ratio of assets of assets to capital might be, say 10:1, this reduction is highly 'leveraged'. Running down the assets means not renewing loans when they fall due, or lending much less than borrowers require — another dimension of the credit crunch. At the end of the opening section we noted that a bank with insufficient capital could try to issue new shares, though this might be difficult in circumstances where confidence in the banking system has almost entirely disappeared. Another way forward is to suspend (or to drastically reduce) dividend payments to shareholders. In effect, this is asking *existing* shareholders to increase their stake in the firm. In fact, by far the largest part of what appears in our balance sheet as 'equity' is retained profit from previous years. Suspending dividends is equivalent to retaining all profits within the firm and thus helping to re-build capital. But the process takes time — especially if the bank's profitability is reduced at the same time.

It is easy to see from this account why governments and central banks needed to take a number of interlinked actions to try to overcome the credit crunch and to prevent a possible collapse of the banking system. Central banks (notably the Fed, the ECB and the Bank of England) had been pushing liquidity into financial markets for some months before the collapse of Lehman Brothers in September 2008, largely by accepting a much wider range of assets as collateral for short-term loans than had previously been the case. This had very little effect and interbank rates remained high. The impact of the Lehman Brothers collapse made it clear that everything possible had to be done to avoid the collapse of other large banks. Thus, we had the various guarantees to retail depositors to avoid the panic withdrawal of funds, together with the temporary bans on short-selling of banking stocks and the attempts to prevent particular collapses where damage had already been done (such as the British government's attempt to broker a takeover of HBOS by Lloyds TSB).

It also became obvious (first to the UK government) that several large banks had to be re-capitalised and that this could only be done in the existing market conditions by the government, leading to the acquisition of large government share-holdings in major banks in several countries. But even this would have done nothing for the mistrust among banks mentioned above and so had to be accompanied by government guarantees of interbank loans. Whether or not these dramatic actions would be sufficient to overcome the immediate problem was unclear by late October 2008 as was the likely impact in terms of increased government borrowing, increased taxation and, more generally, damage to the real economy. It was clear, however, that long-term changes would have to be made to the monetary and financial system and that these would require a level of international policy coordination certainly not seen since the collapse of the Bretton Woods fixed exchange rate system in 1971 (see section 7.5).

The implications for monetary policy and the regulation of the financial system

Consider, firstly, monetary policy itself and the nature of central banks. We have seen that part of the move to reduce the influence of governments in the economy had been the restriction of monetary policy to the use of a single policy instrument (short-term interest rates) in the hands of politically independent central banks to achieve a single target (control of inflation). This, combined with actions (notably by the European Union) to limit the size of government budget deficits and the deregulation of financial markets amounted to an acceptance of the pre-Keynesian proposition that the private sector could look after the real economy.

The present crisis plainly raises doubts about this whole model. This is particularly so given the considerable public unease that has accompanied the bailing-out by governments of delinquent banks and the many references to the present system as involving the privatisation of profit but the socialisation of risk. Several difficulties associated with the restriction of monetary policy to the control of inflation have become apparent. The low interest rates maintained for a long period by the Fed have been criticised as an element in the fuelling of the housing market boom in the US and the rapid increase in interest rates in 2005 and 2006 has been seen as aggravating the inevitable decline in house prices and triggering the crash in the market. There is always some element of hindsight in such criticisms but many people had expressed concerns about the rising levels of household debt and the low level of savings in all western developed economies over a number of years. It seems obvious that interest rate policy should not be entirely divorced from broader issues.

Recent events have also raised urgent technical questions about central banks' ability to set interest rates, in pursuit of whatever objectives they may have in mind. The 'one-club' interest rate instrument had always relied upon the assumption that a change in the official rate (which is of direct relevance only to handful of institutions that hold balances with the central bank) would be quickly and predictably dispersed through the vector of short-term market interest rates that the majority of agents actually pay. However, as noted above, the spread between the Bank of England's official rate and the key LIBOR rate increased more than fourfold during the crisis and has remained high, notwithstanding the Bank's dramatic widening and easing of its lending arrangements. It may well be that in future central banks will have to accept the need to lend at a wide range of maturities and on more varied collateral in the past. This will mean shifting the margin between officially-determined rates and 'market-determined' rates, reducing the range of the latter.

The crisis also sheds an interesting light on the 'rules v discretion' debate. In section 9.3 we cautioned against expecting monetary policy to combat the rise in raw material prices that was a feature of the time (June 2008) since it looked as though policymakers were teetering on the edge of raising interest rates. By October 2008, as we write this, the talk is entirely of recession, stockmarket valuations have fallen by 40 per cent in two months and we have seen an unprecedented, co-ordinated cut in interest rates of 50 bp., with more, it is widely assumed to follow. Within four months, the outlook for the world economy has changed beyond recognition. However, while no one doubts that we are entering what might be a very deep recession wherein inflation will fall rapidly (and may even turn negative, according to some commentators), the actual rate of inflation is not yet falling and (in the UK) remains well above target, at 5 per cent. Furthermore, although the statistics on retail trade have been universally gloomy for the last two months, we have only just begin to see the level of unemployment rising. So, if policy were to be guided by a rule of the Taylor type, it seems likely that interest rates would be much higher than they currently are. (If we assume that the output gap is zero, equation 8.2 would yield a nominal rate of 8.5 per cent, against the current 4.5 per cent). A crisis like the present, makes rules look too inflexible.

Again, the particular concern of central banks with inflation caused problems in Europe as the financial system tottered towards collapse in late 2007 and 2008. Inflation rates were rising everywhere because of high world oil and food prices

— inflationary pressures on which domestic interest rate policy has little purchase. Central banks could, however, only maintain high interest rates and justify this on the grounds that they had to prevent the development of higher inflationary expectations. The control of inflationary expectations remains important
but we shall certainly see the re-emergence of arguments that complex national
and international problems require the combined use of all the available policy
instruments rather then the hiving off of one important instrument and one relatively narrow goal to an independent authority. The problems with inflation in
the 1970s and 1980s together with the long period since the world economic
depression of the 1930s had convinced both governments and the private sector
that inflation was the only remaining macroeconomic problem. The revision of
this view will bring with it a revision of the role of monetary policy.

More immediately, the loss of faith in the banks and other sectors of the financial system will produce a significant increase in the quantity of regulation and a
change in the form of regulation. In the UK, there are two issues. The first relates
to the transfer in 1998 of control of the banking system to the Financial Services
Authority. Much of the criticism of this following the collapse of Northern Rock
involved hindsight since, at the time, the removal of control of the banking system from the Bank of England seemed to be just a logical part of the creation of
an independent central bank, aimed at avoiding any possible influence on monetary policy decisions of the state of individual banks or, indeed, the banking system as a whole - part, in other words, of the narrowing of the role of monetary
policy. Further, following the many conflicts of interest in the previous system of
regulation of financial markets, the creation of a single financial regulator
seemed, in 1998, to be a good thing to many people.

We can now easily see difficulties with this. Firstly, it placed the banking system on the same footing as all other elements of the financial system although, as
we have argued several times and as has now become blindingly obvious to
everyone, the banking system is different - the implications for the whole economy of a collapse of the banking system are far greater than for any other part of
the financial system. Placing banks under the control of a single financial regulator invites the regulator to treat each bank separately and to remove from consideration the notion of systemic risk. Secondly, the concern that a large single regulator would place too heavy a burden on highly successful and profitable financial firms led to the development of the idea of light-touch regulation — a model
of regulation that was increasingly praised in the period before the Northern
Rock collapse and, indeed, a model that seemed to be admired in other countries.
Yet it was also a form of regulation ill-adapted to observing the general increase
in the degree of risk going on within the banking sector of the economy. The
domestic regulatory problem was different from one country to another. For
example, in the USA, regulation of the banking system had always been ham-
strung by being spread across a number of bodies. Nowhere was the regulatory
system able to cope with the increasing complexity and opacity of the new financial instruments and systems of accounting. The future is certain to involve the

acceptance of banking as a special case, an increase in overall regulation and some limitation on the types of activities in which banks can engage.

The Basel Accord mentioned above was one example of international coordination but the capital asset ratio system discussed above was left behind by the movement of risk off the balance sheets of firms. An important element of the new Basel II was a movement towards the use of the risk assessment models of the banks themselves since the opacity of the system and the rapid changes in the risk faced by banks had begun to make it seem impossible to judge from outside the degree of risk faced by a large bank. This approach is now bound to be questioned. We shall see a period of many international conferences but it remains to be seen what these will produce. As in the case of domestic regulation, the most likely early response will be the restriction of the range and type of activities available to banks and other financial institutions combined with calls for much greater transparency. If banks are to be allowed to engage in so much over the counter business in future, some way will have to be found of showing accurately the scale and risk of this business, and it seems likely that much larger capital requirements will be imposed. In short, this kind of business will become much more costly for banks.

Answers to questions and exercises

Chapter 1

1. The text refers to the importance of the interest rate decisions of central banks. How often and when are interest rate announcements made by:

- the Bank of England Monetary Policy Committee?
- the European Central Bank?
- the Federal Reserve Board of the United States?

The MPC of the Bank of England — every month, usually on the Thursday after the first Monday of the month;

The ECB — every month, usually on the first Thursday of the month;

The Federal Reserve Board (Federal Open Market Committee) — after eight scheduled meetings a year but the FOMC also has unscheduled meetings that can produce interest rate changes.

2. For a short time, in the early years of the British settlement of Australia (the 1790s), rum was used as a currency. What advantages and disadvantages would rum have as a commodity money?

There are not many advantages. It is divisible but it is hard to think of much else in its favour. Since it is a manufactured product, there is no limit to its supply and its quality would be very difficult to control. In the short run, the supply might fall sharply during a heavy weekend. Rum is a liquid asset in the wrong sense of 'liquid'.

3. What limits currently exist on the amount of credit that can be obtained by households? Is there any attempt by the monetary authorities to control the amount of credit available?

There are effectively no limits other than those imposed by banks and finance companies themselves and, until very recently, credit was very easy to obtain. In the UK there is a requirement that five per cent of credit card bills should be settled each month but that appeared to have no practical impact on the amount of credit obtained. Following the credit crunch, the authorities sought to persuade banks to increase the availability of loans.

4. There is a distinction made in the economics literature between 'consumption''and 'consumption expenditure'. This distinction implies different definitions of 'saving'. What are these different definitions and how do they relate to the discussion in the text about information and uncertainty?

'Consumption' implies the use of the services of a durable consumer good. Thus, in the first year of the life of a new car, it is only partly consumed. Saving thus includes the increase in the value of real as well as financial assets over the period in question. 'Consumption expenditure' is the total expenditure on consumer goods. 'Saving' refers only to the increase over the period in the value of financial assets held.

5. Distinguish between:

(a) means of payment and medium of exchange;
(b) inside money and outside money.

(a) Frequently, the terms are used interchangeably. However, 'means of payment' is generally taken to cover all assets that can be used in the final settlement of debt and thus provides the basis for narrow definitions of money. Some writers use 'medium of exchange' more broadly to include credit.

(b) Iinside money covers assets both created by and held within the private sector, essentially bank deposits. Outside money (fiat money, high powered money) is issued outside the private sector by the monetary authorities.

6. Distinguish between 'monitoring' and 'targeting' in the context of money supply measures.

The use of the word 'targeted' indicates that the authorities have wished to achieve some specific rate of growth of the measure in question. (The target need not be publicly announced). 'Monitoring' simply means that the figures for the rate of growth of a money supply measure are closely observed, usually as one of a variety of types of information taken into account in the setting of interest rates. (See ch.8, Q.1).

Chapter 2

1. In the B-M approach, explain the effects of the following and show them diagrammatically:

   a) an introduction of a mandatory reserve ratio in excess of the prudential ratio currently in force;
   b) the development of new deposit liabilities with zero reserve requirements;
   c) a dramatic increase in the number and distribution of cash machines

a) The Ms curve makes a parallel shift to the left. This is because the increase in the reserve ratio requirements increases the value of r (eqn 2.10) and this reduces the value of the multiplier (eqn 2.7).

b) The Ms curve makes a parallel shift to the right. This is because a given value of reserves will support a larger volume of deposits. In effect, the reserve ratio has fallen and this increases the size of the multiplier (see eqns 2.10 and 2.7 again).

c) Easier access to cash machines means easier (and cheaper) access to notes and coin. Agents hold smaller cash balances resulting in a lower cash ratio, χ. A reduction in χ (eqn 2.7) reduces the numerator and denominator by equal amounts but this has a larger proportionate effect on the denominator. The Ms curve shifts to the right.

2. Using figure 2.1, show the difference in impact on money market equilibrium of a given reduction in reserve assets when (a) the money supply curve shows some positive elasticity with respect to the bond rate and (b) when the money supply curve is completely inelastic with respect to the bond rate.

The Ms curve shifts left. If we start with two Ms curves (vertical and sloped), starting from the same intercept and then we shift both to the left, being careful to make the shift the same for both (hint: make sure they still share a common intercept)we shall see that the initial equilibrium interest rate is lower where the Ms curve shows some positive elasticity and that when the curves shift, the interest rate rises by a smaller amount if the Ms curve has a positive slope. (You should now be able to show that a positively-sloped Ms curve gives a flatter *LM* curve. Normally, the slope of the *LM* curve is discussed solely with reference to money demand).

3. In the flow of funds analysis, explain the effect of an increase in the government's budget deficit, ceteris paribus.

The government's budget deficit is represented by the PSBR or 'public sector borrowing requirement in eqn 2.18. If nothing else changes, then an increase in the absolute magnitude of the PSBR leads to an increase in the increase in the money supply. Care should be taken not to see the increase in the PSBR as merely causing an increase in the money supply. The larger the PSBR, ceteris paribus, the more rapid the rate of monetary expansion. In effect, this is an example of residual or monetary financing. The process is illustrated in box 8.2.

Chapter 3

1. Economics generally tells us that one must analyse the factors influencing both the demand for and supply of important variables. Yet we have argued that the demand for money not be of great importance from the point of view of economic policy? Why not?

Demand and supply analysis is important when the price in question (here the interest rate) is market determined. Interest rates of importance from the point of view of expenditure are strongly influenced by the very short term rate set by the central bank. As we explain and as have seen during the credit crunch, central banks cannot fully control interest rates in the economy but, equally, they are not freely determined market prices. Since the rate of growth of money supply is largely determined by the demand for bank loans, it is this which is important rather than the demand for money.

2. Why is the Quantity Theory of Money not a theory of the demand for money? What is it a theory of?

The demand for money is not part of the quantity theory argument or any equation expressing it. The QTM is a theory of the relationship between the supply of money (or its rate of growth) and prices (or their rate of growth). It is possible to convert a quantity theory equation into one involving the demand for money but only in equilibrium.

3. Both the precautionary and the speculative motives for holding money arise from the existence of uncertainty — uncertainty about what in each case?

precautionary demand — uncertainty about the amount of expenditure necessary during a period;
speculative demand — uncertainty about the value of financial assets (notably bonds) other than money.

4. Why did the testing of the demand for money grow rapidly at the expense of theorizing about the demand for money after Friedman published his theory?

Because it was argued that the ability of an equation to predict reliably was more important than theoretical relationships. The important task was held to be the discovery of the form and content of an equation in which the demand for money was a stable function of a few variables.

5. Why was the speculative demand for money so controversial?

Because it developed a direct link between the interest rate and money and real sides of the economy through the interest rate. Classical theory had held that the real economy was affected only by real variables and that the money supply influenced only the price level. Keynes's theory implied, in other words, that the short run in which the economy was in disequilibrium was important.

6. Both the inventory-theoretic model of the transactions demand for money and Tobin's portfolio model are commonly called Neo-Keynesian models. Why?

Because they accept one of the central propositions of Keynes's *General Theory*, that the monetary and real sectors of the economy are related through the interest rate, even though they look for different explanations of the interest elasticity of the demand for money.

Chapter 4

1. Distinguish between 'interest-endogeneity' and 'base-endogeneity'.

'Interest-endogeneity' refers to a situation whereby the size of the money stock varies with the level of interest rates. This is usually arises in regimes here reserves do not pay interest and so a rise in interest rates induces banks to economise on reserves and make more interest-earning loans. The money supply has a positive slope (as in figure 2.1).

However, when economists talk about the money supply being endogenous, this is usually because because the central bank is willing to make reserves available on demand at the current rate of interest. In figure 2.1, this would be equivalent to allowing the curve to shift without limit. In the circumstances, the supply of reserves is perfectly elastic which is how we have drawn it in figure 4.1.

2. Why, in practice, are commercial banks unconstrained in their access to reserves?

Until the events of 2007-08, we would have said that *individual* banks are constrained in their access to reserves by virtue of the interbank market in which they could always bid for deposits from other banks. This source of reserves virtually dried up in the credit crunch. The main point of the question, however is to emphasise that central banks will always provide reserves rather than face the risk that the financial system might be jeopardised by a shortage of liquidity. This is obviously necessary when there is a system-wide shortage of reserves. The principle reason for fearing a liquidity shortage is the classic 'run on the bank' whereby depositors lose confidence and rush to withdraw deposits, causing a systemic collapse of the whole system. If anything this fear has increased during the credit crunch. Box 4.4 refers to some other consequences of a reserve shortage which also discourage the authorities from encouraging it.

3. Explain briefly the disadvantages of attempting to regulate monetary growth by non-price methods.

The disadvantages are those that inevitably follow attempts at non-price rationing:

• The 'black market'. Business is diverted into alternative channels. Hence we see the development of 'secondary banks' outside the regulations, loans being made by via offshore subsidiaries; the development of off-balance sheet business like the guaranteeing of commercial paper so that firms can borrow directly from the money markets. In monetary policy, a major drawback here is that it becomes difficult for the authorities to monitor what is happening. There is a high 'information cost'.

• Inefficiency. Loans no longer go to the borrowers who can pay most, so there's no guarantee that they flow to the most profitable projects. Instead, bank managers have to allocate loans to selected borrowers according to government guidance or some system of their own choosing — long standing customers, big borrowers, even corrupt inducements etc.

• The regulatory dialectic. As time goes by, banks (and their clients) find ways around the regulations. This requires new regulations (and increased supervision). Eventually, the new regulations are also avoided.

4. Why is the demand for reserves by commercial banks highly interest-inelastic?

As always, the answer is a lack of substitutes. Depending on the regime, banks will be required to hold a given level of reserves. At this point, there is no substitute for those assets that have been identified as reserve assets. If these are notes and coin and deposits with the central bank, then the central bank is the monopoly supplier and there are no alternatives at all. This is the usual case. Recall also that 'elasticity' will depend on timing. If banks have to meet a target on a daily basis, then the demand will be more inelastic than if the target allows for averaging over a week or a month. This inelasticity ensures that any attempt by the authorities to fix the quantity of reserves would result in extreme fluctuations in short-term interest rates.

Chapter 5

1. Focusing upon people's *wealth*, explain how a change in interest rates might affect the level of spending.

Recall that asset prices vary inversely with interest rates, *ceteris paribus*. Hence for households a rise in interest rates will reduce the value of their financial assets and may even reduce the value of their house.Households feel less wealthy and cut back on consumption in order to rebuild their wealth. The reduction in asset values also reduces the collateral that households can pledge against loans, making credit harder to get. This is most obvious when house prices fall since it reduces the size of the next mortgage.

The situation is much the same for firms. But there is an additional problem in so far as a reduction in value of a firm's assets is likely to lead to a reduction in its net worth and this will be reflected in its share price. This makes it more expensive to raise new capital for investment.

2. We said in the text that a change in the official interest rate does not necessarily result in an instant and identical change in market rates. How might we explain this.

Interest rates, like other prices, are determined by supply and demand. The central bank can set the interest rate on bank reserves because it dominates the supply side. What happens to other interest rates depends on the extent to which the loans are a close substitute for borrowing from the central bank. In normal circumstances, money market rates will follow the official rate very closely because money markets deal in very short-term lending between financial institutions many of whom can borrow from the Bank of England. But if, as in 2007-08, banks cease to trust each other, then interbank rates may rise relative to the official rate. Interest rates for longer term loans will be less closely connected so that when we come to long-term government bonds, yields may be higher or lower than the official rate, depending upon the supply and demand for long-term loans.

Furthermore, some interest rates are administered. These are mainly 'retail' rates offered/charged to households. Changing these involves administrative costs and banks and building societies may wait until several changes in the official rate have accumulated before making a change.

3. What difference would it make to the strength of UK monetary policy if all mortgages were fixed-interest-rate loans: (a) in the short run; (b) in the long run?

In the short-run, the effectiveness of monetary policy is likely to be reduced since the immediate change in official interest rates will not be passed on to borrowers. This will postpone the cut in households' discretionary income and the negative collateral effect that occurs if house prices fall. (See Q.1 above). In the long-run, however, some effect will be felt because the higher rates will be charged on new mortgages which will grow as a proportion of the total as old loans are paid off.

4. How are interest rate changes likely to affect the distribution of income between:

(a) rich and poor; (b) borrowers and lenders; (c) old and young?

(a) it is difficult to be absolutely certain about the redistributive effects of interest rates since it depends upon detailed questions of how people divide their wealth between assets which yield a fixed rate of return and those which pay a variable rate. It also depends upon the tax treatment of interest income on the one hand and the tax treatment of interest payments on the other. As a rule, however, we assume that a rise (for example) in interest rates makes a net redistribution in favour of the rich since it must involve a redistribution from borrowers to lenders (see (b) below) and we lenders in the aggregate inevitably have greater wealth than borrowers.

(b) a rise in interest rates redistributes income from borrowers to lenders.

(c) the caveats of (a) apply here too. But by virtue of (b) we would normally expect a net redistribution from young (households with mortgages and high levels of consumption) towards the elderly (who have paid off their earlier borrowing and have saved for retirement).

Chapter 6

1. Why is the natural rate of unemployment referred to as 'natural'?

It is the 'market clearing rate' — the rate that would be produced in equilibrium if the market were left to operate freely. In this view, government intervention is seen as 'artificial'. The market system is regarded by neoclassical economists as the best possible system for the allocation of scarce resources in an economy and so any intervention that might change the free market outcome is seen as a distortion to the natural state of affairs.

2. Why was the 'shoe leather cost"of inflation so called? What other costs are there of anticipated inflation?

It was short-hand for all the costs resulting from a decision to hold lower money balances than one would do if there were no inflation. The lower the money balances held by economic agents, the more often they would need to convert other financial assets into money in order to carry out their expenditure plans — hence, they would need to go to the bank more often and would more quickly wear out their shoes. In some ways it is quite misleading and appears to understate the problem. The only defence for its use is that it adds a little colour to the discussion. The other costs of anticipated inflation are grouped under the heading 'menu costs'.

3. Why does 'the combination of the rational expectations hypothesis and the assumption of continuous market clearing' imply that output and employment fluctuate randomly around their natural levels?

The natural levels of output and unemployment occur at equilibrium. The economy will not always be at equilibrium, although in the view of neoclassical economists it will always be tending towards equilibrium. Thus, sometimes output will be above its equilibrium and sometimes below but, on average, will be at its equilibrium level. Rational expectations implies that even if the government seeks to influence the levels of output and unemployment, it will fail to do so since market agents will always be able to anticipate government actions and will act in the market to neutralise them.

4. The Chambers Twentieth Century Dictionary defined 'hysteresis' as:

the retardation or lagging of an effect behind the cause of the effect: the influence of earlier treatment of a body on its subsequent reaction.

How then can hysteresis occur in labour markets? How can the existence of hysteresis in labour markets be used to argue against the neutrality of money?

The main idea is that spells of unemployment lower the skill levels of workers and thus affect labour productivity. In this way, high current unemployment could lower future output and employment levels. According to monetarist economists, higher than desired inflation can be tackled by a monetary squeeze with no no long run impact on real variables. There may be a short-run increase in unemployment as economic agents adjust their expectations but no long-run impact. However, if high short-run unemployment lowers future labour productivity, the monetary squeeze might have real effects in the long run.

5. How are the following arguments discussed in this chapter affected, if at all, by an assumption of endogenous money?
(a) the expectations-augmented Phillips curve
(b) policy irrelevance

Both theories assume that monetary policy occurs through changes in the rate of growth in the money supply brought about by the monetary authorities - that is, they assume exogenous money. However, this is not important in (a) since the usual assumption is that inflationary expectations are based on past rates of inflation irrespective of how that inflation has been caused. For the New Classical model (from which the policy irrelevance proposition derives), the ability to understand what the monetary authorities are likely to do to money supply growth is part of the standard explanation of the model. Nonetheless, the argument could be made in terms of the ability of economic agents always to forecast correctly what changes the monetary authorities will make in the repo rate of interest. Thus, an assumption of exogenous money is not essential to either theory.

Solution to the exercise in Box 6.1

t	π%p.a.	π_{-1}	π_{-2}	π^e	$\pi-\pi^e$	Y
0	0	0	0	0	0	4,000
1	2	0	0	0	2	4,020
2	4	2	0	1	3	4,030
3	6	4	2	3	3	4,030
4	8	6	4	5	3	4,030
5	10	8	6	7	3	4,030
6	8	10	8	9	-1	3,090

So long as the policymaker wishes to hold output above its natural rate, the rate of inflation must be made to *accelerate*. This is because output depends upon agents underestimating inflation. Since we've assumed that they form their expectations on the basis of *past* rates of inflation, the current rate has always to be higher in order to create the surprise. By the same token, since the expected rate is based on previous rates, the moment that inflation starts to fall it causes a negative surprise. Agents *over*estimate the inflation rate and output is pushed below its natural level.

Chapter 7

1. How is the deflationary policy of a strong country transmitted through a fixed exchange rate system?

An increase in interest rates in the strong currency attracts a flow of capital from other member countries putting downward pressure on the value of their currencies. Under the terms of the fixed exchange rate system, this has to be resisted and so other countries are forced to raise their interest rates also. Of course, if the market believes that the current exchange rate pegs cannot be maintained in one or more of the member countries, there will be strong speculative pressure on the weaker currencies which may force exchange rate realignments or even the collapse of the fixed exchange rate system.

2. Why might a revaluation of a currency only temporarily reduce a Balance of Trade surplus?

The revaluation lowers the price of imports and increases the price of exports causing the balance of trade surplus to fall or disappear. However, as the fall in import prices feeds through into wages and other costs, the domestic inflation rate of the revaluing country falls, counteracting the initial negative effect of the revaluation on the country's tradable goods.

3. Why does a wide band around fixed exchange rate parities (as with the 15 per cent band in use in the EMS between 1993 and the end of 1998) make life more difficult for currency speculators?

The big profits from speculating against a currency come from forcing a country to devalue a fixed exchange rate. Then speculators who have sold the currency forward at the original par value are able to buy it spot at a significantly lower price and take their profits. With narrow bands, a currency might with a relatively small amount of speculation be forced towards the bottom of its band. As this happens, there will be a large increase in speculative selling as a devaluation becomes more likely. With wide bands, the initial downward pressure might still leave the currency floating in the middle of the band with future upward movements in the value of the currency possible as well as downward ones.

4. What is the relationship between purchasing power parity and the neutrality of money?

They are different notions since PPP relates to the relationship between prices in different economies and the neutrality of money to the relationship between the domestic money supply and the price level in a single economy. However, in a simple monetary model of the exchange rate with an exogenous money supply PPP ensures the neutrality of money in an open economy.

5. What is the Lucas critique? What is its relevance to this chapter?

The Lucas critique is a criticism of the attempt to predict the impact of a change in economic policy making use only of the relationships observed in historical data. Lucas particularly criticised the use of highly aggregated macroeconomic models because he argued that the parameters of these models would themselves be altered by the policy changes. The reference in this chapter is in Section 7.5 on monetary policy coordination, specifically to the attempt to use models to predict the impact of a change in macroeconomic policy in one country on the economies of other countries (the size of spillovers).

Chapter 8

1. Distinguish between 'goals', 'targets', 'instruments' and 'indicators'.

'Goals' are what the policymaker ultimately wants to achieve. They might also be referred to as the 'objectives' of policy and should have some welfare significance. A target is a goal expressed in quantitative form. So, for example, if 'low inflation' is a goal, 'a inflation rate of 2 per cent p.a.' is a target. An instrument is a variable over which the policymaker has direct control and which is capable of influencing the economy towards the achievement of the chosen target. There are relatively few genuine policy instruments on this definition. For example, current thinking identifies an official rate of interest as the key policy variable. This is the rate at which the central bank supplies liquidity to the monetary system and strictly speaking this is the only rate over which the central bank has direct control. Therefore, it is not strictly accurate to describe the instrument as 'interest rates', since the connection between the official and market rates is not fixed as events through 2008 have demonstrated.

2. It is widely-accepted that the long-run benefits of low inflation exceed the short-run costs of dis-inflation. How would you defend that view?

If inflation is 'unanticipated' then agents find it difficult to read changes in relative prices correctly and resources are misallocated. Furthermore, real income and wealth are subject to arbitrary redistribution.

Even with anticipated inflation there may still be costs: 'shoe leather' and 'menu' costs. Box 6.1 explains. At very high rates of inflation these may be significant. Think for example of the effort that people have to go to to protect themselves against inflation. This is effort diverted from more useful activity. At very high rates of inflation, people lose confidence in the currency and normal trade becomes impossible.

However, at the moment we see inflation targets of 2-3 per cent and get alarmed when inflation exceeds 5 per cent. Since disinflation also involves costs — of lost output and higher unemployment — it is not an easy case to argue that this is preferable to, say, 5 per cent inflation, if we could be certain that inflation would stabilise at 5 per cent. There is a further difficulty, which is not often discussed. This is that the costs of inflation and disinflation fall on different social groups. Thus, telling unemployed, semi-skilled workers with small savings that they are better off if inflation can be reduced is rather unconvincing.

3. Outline the arguments against discretionary macroeconomic policy.

The arguments against discretionary monetary policy are, in effect, arguments in favour of following some rule. They fall into two groups (see box 8.1). The original argument was that monetary policy operated with such long and variable lags made it difficult if not impossible for the policymaker to choose the correct instrument settings. This was made worse by the inadequacies of economic forecasting. In the circumstances, 'activist' or discretionary policy could easily make the economy less stable than it would be if the policymaker stuck to a simple rule about which agents had full information.

More recent arguments stress an 'inflation bias' which arises from the political context in which policy decisions must be made. The older of the two focused on the pressures faced by democratic governments to provide public services without raising taxes to pay for them. This encouraged residual financing (see box 8.2).

More recently, the 'time inconsistency' argument is that voters want higher levels of output (or lower unemployment) and therefore governments are tempted to expand aggregate demand, especially when low inflation has been achieved. This expansion moves us up an upward-sloping short-run Phillips curve, but over time the curve shifts upward and eventually the 'natural' level of unemployment/output is restored but at a higher inflation rate. The government recognises this as sub-optimal and then deflates to bring inflation down before repeating the exercise. The result is an average rate of inflation that exceeds the optimal rate.

4. Explain the problems associated with the choice of the money supply as an intermediate target.

The money supply (strictly its rate of growth) has often been regarded as an intermediate target since theory has often assumed a close connection between the size of real money balances and the level of aggregate demand. This is the thinking behind the quantity theory of money.

The first problem is that, in practice, this relationship has proved to be very unreliable. Velocity has proved quite variable and not just in a predictable way in response to interest rates, but also in response to changes in expectations and to financial innovations which have changed the demand for money.

A second problem is that if we target one measure of money, agents change their behaviour by switching to other monetary assets destroying the relationship between the targeted measure and aggregate demand. This is known as 'Goodhart's law'.

Thirdly, targeting the money supply assumes that the quantity of money can be determined (exogenously) by some policy instrument. But in practice, central banks set interest rates and allow the money supply to be demand-determined.

5. Why does the ability of the MPC of the Bank of England to set its own policy horizon give it some goal independence?

'Goal independence' refers to the policymaker's ability to set the target or goal of policy. In the UK, the two per cent inflation target is formally set by the Treasury and the Bank of England's independence extends only to the setting of interest rates. However, we know that the Bank's view is that the transmission of effects from interest rates to inflation lasts from 18 months to 2 years, so its decisions today are targeting inflation in about 2 years time. This gives it some degree of independence regarding the target in the interim period. It could, for example, deliberately allow inflation to exceed its target in the interim (to stave off a recession) knowing it could tighten policy later. But even in this it is constrained by the requirement to stay within +/- 1 per cent of the target.

Chapter 9

1. Why do central bank repo deals have such a large impact on money market interest rates?

As always, when prices move together, we must look at the degree of substitutability between assets. Money market instruments (including repos) are all highly liquid, generally low risk, very short-term ways of lending and borrowing. This creates a high degree of homogeneity. Furthermore they are all traded by professional, well-informed traders. A small widening of a spread between two instruments would usually see a rapid and large flow of funds towards the higher-yielding instrument, pushing the spread back to its conventional size. However, since summer 2007, interbank loans been regarded as much more risky than other money market loans and so LIBOR rates in particular have risen relative to the repo rate and seem reluctant to respond to official rate changes.

2. Why do international capital flows make the conduct of monetary policy more difficult?

Assume a flexible exchange rate regime. An outflow of international capital will lower the value of the domestic currency and vice versa, *ceteris paribus*. So, for example, a central bank may set interest rates at what it feels is an appropriate level for monetary policy purposes, but foreign exchange markets may feel that policy is not tight enough and that inflation is likely to rise in future. In these circumstances an outflow of capital will push down the exchange rate, helping to bring the inflation that is feared. It is difficult for central banks to follow a policy which does not have the confidence of international capital markets.

3. Why might central banks be concerned about major price fluctuations in asset markets?

The main reason for concern is that the fluctuations may have an effect on aggregate demand and therefore on the level of inflationary pressure in the economy. Consider the case of a sharp fall (as in mid-October 2008). In this case:

- people's wealth is reduced and it is likely that they will cut back consumption in order to rebuild their wealth;
- the value of collateral that they can pledge for loans is reduced and makes borrowing more difficult;
- the fall in equity and bond prices increases firms cost of capital, so raising the cost of capital spending;
- the future flow of income from investment projects becomes more uncertain;
- there is likely to be rush to liquidity and a general unwillingness to lend.

The opposite is likely to follow from a sharp rise in asset values.

4. Why might the yield on corporate bonds fluctuate relative to the yield on government bonds? What assumptions would you have to make in order to draw information about the economic cycle from these yields?

Ceteris paribus, the yield on any bond depends upon its price and therefore upon the supply and demand for it. Thus if the yield on a corporate bond falls relative to the yield on government bonds, this is the result of a rise in the relative price of the bond and an indication that it has become, relatively, more attractive. Since its coupon and maturity are fixed, the most likely cause of this change is the level of risk, or at least the level of risk *as perceived by investors. Conversely a relative fall in price indicates a rise in perceived risk.* If investors regard corporate bonds, *in general*, as varying in risk relative to government bonds, this must mean that they see the issuers of the bonds — large corporations — becoming more or less risky. This in turn may indicate changes in the economic environment facing corporations.

5. You observe a yield curve which slopes upward for maturities up to two years and then slopes gently downward levelling off at 10 years and beyond. What might this tell you about market expectations of future interest rate developments. State explicitly any assumptions you have to make.

If we accept the expectations theory of the term structure then the shape suggests that agents expect the future short-term rate of interest to be higher than it currently is for the next two years. From two years ahead the situation will be reversed whereby people will be expecting the future short-term rate (say in years three to nine) to be below the current short rate. Eventually, around year 10, expected future rates will have settled in line with current rates. To draw this conclusion, we have to assume that there is no market segmentation (bonds of all maturities are perfect substitutes) and there is no term premium.

Chapter 10

1. Explain why policy makers have generally come to the conclusion that the only effective instrument of monetary policy is the short-term rate of interest.

Monetary policy instruments must come in one of three forms: setting the quantity of reserves (the monetary base) which restricts banks ability to *supply* loans; setting the price of reserves (the rate of interest) which restricts the *demand*; and direct controls. The arguments against the first are in box 4.4. The arguments against the last are standard arguments against rationing and fall into two groups. The first focuses upon *inefficiency*: there is no guarantee that funds go to the highest bidder; resources are required to ensure compliance; resources are devoted to avoiding the regulations which have to be revised increasingly frequently. The second focuses on *inequity*: potential borrowers with profitable projects are denied access to funds.

2. Why might giving the central bank responsibility for banking supervision make it more difficult for the bank to pursue an independent monetary policy with price stability as the primary target?

Banking supervision requires banks to make frequent (usually monthly) statistical returns of the state of their business. This is to ensure that the supervisor knows which banks may be taking undue risks or facing a dangerous level of poorly performing loans. If banks are faced with loans on the verge of default a rise in interest rates is likely to make matters worse and could even cause a bank to become insolvent. So, if the supervisor is simultaneously responsible for monetary policy and thinks that policy requires a rise in interest rates, it might hesitate if it knows that the rise could push banks into difficulty.

3. Explain how capital adequacy requirements impose a tax on banking.

The key to the answer lies in the cost of capital compared with the cost of deposits. For example, if banks can charge (on average) 12 per cent for loans which they can fund by deposits at 4 per cent, the net interest margin is 8 per cent. But if the bank is at the limit of its capital, *new lending* has to be funded in part by additional capital which may cost, for example, 10 per cent. This reduces the net interest income from the new loans to 2 per cent. If the profit margin is to be restored, the cost of loans has to be raised to 18 per cent. In a diagram, the loan supply curve shifts upward. This raises the equilibrium price and reduces the equilibrium quantity of loans: the standard result of imposing a tax on any activity.

4. Why might the presence of capital risk aversion in the bond market make the conduct of monetary policy more difficult?

'Capital risk aversion' means that investors dislike fluctuations in capital values. Consequently, if the fluctuations are frequent and severe enough, investors will leave the market altogether. With fewer potential buyers, this means that bonds will have to be offered with higher coupons which means that the cost of government borrowing is increased. If the policymaker is also responsible for government debt management, there is a clear conflict of interest.

5. Why does a rise in money's own interest rate, *ceteris paribus*, tend to increase the rate of monetary growth?

Other things being equal, a rise in money's own rate has two effects. Firstly it increases the demand for money. Secondly, it increases the demand for bank lending. This is because an agent with a deficit has a choice to make between using his or her savings or taking out a loan. The smaller the 'spread' the greater the incentive to borrow. Since loans make deposits, the increased demand for loans creates deposits at a faster rate, and these deposits are more willingly held.

6. Explain briefly why 'credibility' and 'openness' are desirable properties in the conduct of monetary policy.

'Credibility' means that a policymaker's statements are believed. The advantage is that if the policymaker announces the intention to reduce the rate of interest, agents believe this and build the lower rate of inflation into their plans and negotiations immediately. This has the effect of helping to bring down the rate of inflation. 'Openness' is assumed to be helpful because it helps agents to understand the policymaker's objectives and its thinking about how to achieve those objectives. This means that policy moves can be anticipated and consequently cause no shocks or surprises to the economy. There is also an argument that where the policymaker is independent of government, openness facilitates accountability and this is an essential part of the contract with society as a whole.

Chapter 11

1. In 11.2, we suggest that wage flexibility does not always provide an efficient means of adjusting to external shocks. What is the basis of that argument?

If the shock is a fall in external demand for important exports, leading to a fall in domestic production and an increase in unemployment, wage flexibility (here a fall in wages or, at least, a fall in the rate of wage inflation) will eventually lower costs in the industries affected and increase competitiveness but the adjustment will be very slow. However, the fall in wages or wage growth implies a fall in the rate of growth of domestic demand which will have an impact across the economy. Wage flexibility might help but it is hardly equivalent to an exchange rate adjustment as a means of preserving competitiveness.

2. Why might the business cycles of the UK not be synchronized with those of the 12 current members of the euro area?

The basic argument relates to the direction of the UK's trade. When the UK joined the then EEC in 1973, a much smaller proportion of UK trade was with the original six members than was the case for other members. Historically, much of UK trade had been with members of the British Empire/Commonwealth and the USA. Thus, the performance of the UK economy was more closely linked with those countries than with the rest of Europe. However, UK trade patterns changed quite rapidly following membership of the common market, have continued to change, and might change even faster following a decision to join the monetary union.

3. What does the Executive Board of the ECB do? What does it not do?

The Executive Board manages the day-to-day business of the ECB, prepares meetings of the Governing Council and implements the monetary policy of the euro area as determined by the Governing Council. This requires the Board to give instructions to and work with the national central banks of euro area members. The Executive Board does not decide the ECB's monetary policy but each of the six members have a vote in Governing Council meetings on all matters except issues related to the capital of the bank. Thus, they each have a vote on the interest rate decisions of the bank, the supply of reserves in the Eurosystem and other monetary policy matters. The Executive Board may also have other powers delegated to it by the Governing Council and reports to the European Parliament. The President and other members of the Board appear before the committees of the Parliament.

4. In the text, we say:

'A supporting argument was that the euro, as a broader-based reserve currency than the DM would be less likely to be driven artificially high on occasions.' Explain this statement. How did it relate to the question of the likely future strength of the euro?

This was used before the establishment of the monetary union in 1999 to support the argument that the euro would be a weaker currency than the DM had been on the grounds that the euro, because membership included countries with weaker economies,would be less likely to be viewed as a safe haven whenever the US economy and the dollar caused the markets concern, than the currency of the powerful German economy had been. In practice, this has not been the case.

5. When the ECB began operation at the beginning of 1999, how did it ensure that all members of the Executive Board would not end their terms of office at the same time? What would be wrong with the terms of all six members of the Board ending on the same date?

The first six members were appointed for variable terms of office. Only after the first round of appointments did the term of office revert to the eight years non-renewable specified in the ECB's constitution. Thus, members retire singly rather than all together. Currently, one of the five members (excluding the President) retires in each year from 2010 to 2014. This is intended to reduce the influence over the general attitude of the Board of any set of governments of member states in power at a particular time.

Chapter 12

1. How centralized is the US central bank system now? Do the regional Reserve Banks have more or less power than the national central banks within the European System of Central Banks?

Monetary policy is centralized, being in the hands of the Federal Open Market Committee of the Fed and, as we have seen in the September/October 2008 responses to the credit crunch, the Financial Secretary to the Treasury, both in Washington. The comparison with Europe is difficult. Seven of the twelve members of the FOMC are appointed centrally, a much higher proportion than in the Governing Council of the ECB. However, the central appointments are meant to provide a 'fair representation of financial, agricultural, industrial and geographic divisions' whereas the Executive Board of the ECB gives most weight to the larger countries. Current members (2008) come from France, Germany, Italy, Spain, Greece and Austria. In banking matters, as distinct from monetary policy, the regional reserve banks in the USA have more freedom of action than do the national central banks within the ESCB.

2. If the Fed wishes to discourage banks from borrowing at the discount window except in emergencies, why does it keep the discount rate below the Federal funds rate?

The intention is for the discount window only to be used for genuine lender of last resort borrowing. Banks are expected to meet normal shortfalls in reserves in the federal funds market despite the higher cost of doing so. The disapproval of the Fed and the loss of reputation of banks that over-use the discount window (the frown costs) are accepted as greater than the small differences between discount window rates and the Fed funds rate.

3. Why does the Fed feel the need to maintain a system of reserve ratios when the Bank of England does not (apart from the small prudential ratio)?

The Fed still appears to feel that the ratios play some role in helping to control the rate of expansion of banks' balance sheets and hence of the money supply although very little weight is now given to them — the ratios are changed very infrequently. This suggests an unwillingness to drop completely the idea of an exogenous money supply despite the fact that the monetary policy of the Fed effectively accepts the endogeneity of money. The Bank of England does not operate a reserve ratio system because it accepts fully that monetary policy should act through the impact of interest rate changes on the demand for bank loans rather than directly on bank balance sheets.

4. How useful are the phrases from which the FOMC chooses for describing its view of likely future developments in the US economy? What is the purpose of making statements of this kind?

The phrases themselves provide no detail, only a general indication as to whether the FOMC thinks that inflation or recession is a greater risk in the foreseeable future and, therefore, whether interest rates are more likely to fall or to rise. The purpose was to increase the accountability of the Fed by communicating more quickly the view of the Committee and thus to provide some explanation of their present and future actions. The use of a limited set of general phrases at each meeting, whether or not conditions have changed since the previous meeting, was intended to limit the immediate impact of the reports on the financial markets.

5. Does the FOMC engage in:

    (a) inflation targeting;
    (b) money supply targeting;
    (c) nominal demand targeting?

If none of these, what does it do?

None of the three. The Fed does not set specific targets except that for the Fed funds rate — the policy instrument. Rather, the FOMC takes into account a wide range of real and monetary indicators as well as anecdotal evidence of business conditions. Many economists believe that the Fed has an implicit target rate of inflation, but it certainly does not have an explicit one.

Endnotes

Chapter 1

1   It is perhaps revealing that Robinson Crusoe is male and that his servant, Man Friday, is ignored, avoiding any need to worry about employer-employee relationships.

2   This is modified in some models to allow the maximization of the utility of the family, although it is a mythical social construct in which roles are assumed to be frozen.

3   See Donald A. Walker, 'Walras, Léon (1834-1910) in *The New Palgrave Dictionary of Economics* online, http://cms.dictionaryofeconomics.com/ (2008)

4   Both of these methods of reducing search costs exist today — in the form, for example, of car boot sales and trade fairs. This shows that they are methods of organization that have no necessary relation with barter since they allow equally for monetary exchange.

5   The notion of 'information costs' can be considered in more detail. For example, Clower (1971) speaks of two types of cost associated with barter. These are transactions costs and waiting costs (storage costs, the interest foregone on the postponed purchase of an asset and the subjective costs in doing without a good or service).

6   We can easily see at this point why it is not easy to explain the presence of money in a Walrasian general equilibrium model with an auctioneer in which there are no information costs and trading only takes place with full information available on all relative prices.

7   Samuelson (9e, 1973) provided the following colourful list of forms that money has taken in past societies: 'cattle, tobacco, leather and hides, furs, olive oil, beer or spirits, slaves or wives, copper, iron, gold, silver, rings, diamonds, wampum beads or shells, huge rocks and landmarks, and cigarette butts'.

8   The term 'seigniorage' comes from the French word for a feudal lord. Seigniorage accrues to the issuer of the currency. In modern economies, the issue of bank notes provides a once-and-for-all gain for the monetary authorities of the country.

9   This led to Gresham's Law, stated by Sir Thomas Gresham in 1558 as 'bad money always drives out good'.

10   Essentially notes and coin.

Chapter 2

1   In many systems the expression 'non-bank private sector' is used to denote the general (non-government) public whose holdings of deposits are part of the money stock. In the UK, M4 includes building society as well as bank deposits and so the relevant deposit holders have to be identified as the 'non-bank, non-building society, private sector'. Fortunately, this is usually shortened to 'M4 private sector' or simply 'M4PS'.

2   The suggestion that deposits and loans (and changes in them) must match may seem strange. It does involve a small simplification in that it abstracts from shareholders' funds on the liabilities side. But this apart, the statement is correct since all bank assets are loans in some shape or form. Securities/investments are loans (mainly to government) backed by securities. Since notes and coin are issued by government, holdings of these are also in effect loans to the public sector as are deposits at the central bank — since the central bank is also part of the public sector. If necessary, changes in shareholders funds can be incorporated in the following derivations by the addition of a term, ΔNDL for changes in 'non-deposit liabilities'.

Chapter 3

1   For a brief but clear survey of pre-Quantity Theory views of the development of the Quantity Theory, see Visser (1974). More detail is provided in Harris (1985) and Humphrey (1974). For a discussion of the contributions of Alfred Marshall and earlier writers to the Quantity Theory tradition, see Eshag (1963)

2   Harris (1985) examines the pre-Keynesian Quantity Theory tradition in some detail and stresses the complexity of the body of thought surrounding it. He refers to the expression of the Quantity Theory in terms of a change in the quantity of money producing a proportional change in the absolute price level as the Crude Quantity Theory.

3   See Bain and Howells (1991)

4   The 'Classical model' was the name given by Keynes to the model in which the real and monetary sectors of the economy were held to be entirely separate with output, employment, relative prices and interest rates being determined in the real sector of the economy and the general level of prices being determined in the monetary sector through the QTM.

5   Patinkin (1965) argued that the Cambridge approach was quite different from the Quantity Theory because the Quantity Theory made no assumption as to why money was held. It operated through changes in the money stock influencing the goods market via a real balance effect. In this view, the Quantity Theory should be represented by a hyperbolic market equilibrium curve rather than a demand for money curve. For a full account of the real balance effect, the problems associated with it, and its significance, see Harris (1985)

6   Short but helpful explanations of the finance motive can be found in Chick (1983) and Rousseas (1986). Keynes's original article can be found in JMK, 1973, vol XIV pp 201-23

7 J M Keynes, 'The General Theory of Employment', *Quarterly Journal of Economics*, Feb. 1937 (JMK, 1973, vol XIV p 114)

8 For details of theoretical extensions and criticisms of the basic model see, in particular, Akerlof and Milbourne (1978, 1980). Gowland (1991) provides a good account of both the model and its defects.

9 Sprenkle (1969, 1972) claimed the theory to be useless in regard to large firms with multiple branches and accounts. See also Cuthbertson (1985a) and Cuthbertson and Barlow (1991).

10 For this criticism, see Fisher (1989) and Karni (1974). Gowland (1991) illustrates the point with some approximate calculations.

11 A number of other writers have produced risk aversion models based on the same broad premises as Tobin. For a discussion of these and later models see Cuthbertson and Barlow (1991).

12 The original (1956) version of the equation had the demand for nominal balances as a function of a similar set of variables plus the general price level (P). To produce the 1970 version, Friedman assumed the function homogeneous of degree one in both prices and permanent income, enabling him to divide throughout by P and Yp.

13 Much to Patinkin's displeasure.

14 Credit is also given, amongst others, to Darby (1972) who first used the term. Other writings on money as a buffer stock include those by Goodhart (1989a), Cuthbertson (1985a) and Cuthbertson and Taylor (1987b).

15 Before Keynes's *General Theory*, estimates were made of the velocity of circulation over long periods, with the aim of relating changes in long-run velocity to institutional changes (fitting in with the classical Quantity Theory of Money). After the publication of *The General Theory*, attempts were made to show a positive relationship between interest rates and velocity (and thus an inverse relationship between interest rates and the demand for money). Other studies sought to distinguish between idle and active balances and then to relate idle balances to interest rates. Friedman and Schwarzt's (1963) study dealt with long-term velocity rather than with the demand for money function.

16 A chapter on the testing of the demand for money in Handa (2000) contains the subheading, 'The desperate search for a stable money demand function'. This is an accurate description of much that has gone on.

Chapter 4

1. As in the debate between Jean Bodin and M de Malestroit. See Tudor and Dyson (1997). The origin of the quantity theory of money, of which money's exogeneity is essential, has been traced at least to the School of Salamanca (Grice-Hutchison, 1952) and even to Aquinas (Schumpeter, 1954).

2　Consider the flow of funds approach again. In this framework changes in the quantity of money are 'explained' by changes in the components of aggregate bank lending. As Cuthbertson pointed out '..the reader may be wondering what has happened to the demand for money in this analysis. There is an implicit demand for money in the model *but only in equilibrium*.' (1985, p.173. Emphasis in original).

3　In the 'Post-Keynesian' tradition it is sometimes argued that the demand for money is completely irrelevant: agents will hold whatever quantity of deposits are generated by loans. Where money creation is concerned, loan demand is everything. (See Kaldor (1982), and Moore (1997)). For an alternative view see Howells (1995 and 1997).

4　The Association for Payment Clearing Services (www.apacs.org.uk)

5　As in macroeconomic textbooks that argue that it does not much matter whether we write the Quantity Theory as $MV = PT$ or $MV = PY$. For example, 'Nonetheless, the dollar value of transactions is roughly proportional to the dollar value of output'. (Mankiw, 1992 p.83)

6　Irving Fisher also recognised this possibility. In his famous exposition of the Quantity Theory (Fisher, 1911), he divided nominal transactions into PT_1 and PT_2 where T_1 were income transactions and T_2 were financial transactions not related to the level of income.

7　They need also to be able to make transfers to other banks as payments take place between clients of different banks.

8　The basics of this model were first published in Fontana (2003).

9　Notice that we are using r (rather than i) as the symbol for interest rates. In many notations this would indicate the *real* rather than nominal rate. This is because we assume that the central bank is setting the nominal rate with a view to achieving a real rate for policy purposes. Furthermore, since the interest rate decision is made at frequent intervals (typically one month) the policy-maker has a frequent opportunity to correct any errors.

10　The damage that can be caused when these doubts arise, even when the doubts are ill-founded, were illustrated in the UK in July 2007 when depositors misunderstood the problems faced by the Northern Rock Bank.

11　Or, indeed, a tightening of monetary policy itself. Assume that this leads to a rise in price, increase in collateral requirements, and reduction in supply of credit from non-bank sources. The inevitable consequence will be a jump in overdraft utilisation and the liquidity problems described here unless the Central Bank relieves the shortage.

12　This illustration also draws attention to an asymmetry in the loan/deposit creation process. Central Banks can initiate a monetary expansion, through open market operations and expansion of the base; they cannot (at tolerable cost) initiate a reduction by reversing the process (see Moore, 1986, 1988a).

13　Supporters of the view that central bank behaviour matters little include Minsky (1982, 1986), Rousseas (1986), Pollin (1991) and Dow (1993, 1996). Niggle (1991) points out that the degree of (and the possibilities for) reserve-economising innovation will depend upon institutional features of the regime.

Chapter 5

1 On 11/12 August 2007, the *Financial Times* reported 'Central banks have been forced to inject massive doses of liquidity in excess of $100bn into overnight lending markets, in an effort to ensure that the interest rates they set are reflected in real-time borrowing....The Fed is protecting an interest rate of 5.25 per cent, the ECB a rate of 4 per cent and the BoJ an overnight target of 0.5 per cent.' (p.3).

2 The ECB version of the chart makes a very clear separation between the change in the official rate and the change in market rates.

3 This is a slight simplification. The figure shows a channel of influence running 'directly' from the exchange rate (dependent upon domestic interest rates) to import prices and thus to the rate of inflation. We discuss this further in chapter 6.

4 Because either inflation expectations are backward-looking or because while forward-looking there may be various frictions ('stickiness') which prevent contracts from adjusting instantly to expectations. For the rest of this chapter, we shall simply assume some degree of inflation inertia without further reference to reasons. Much of chapter 6 is devoted to different explanations for this inertia.

5 Based on Carlin and Soskice (2005). The same model is explained more briefly in Carlin and Soskice (2006) while a very similar model is in Bofinger, Mayer and Wollmerhäuser (2006). One of the first attempts to dispense with the *LM* curve and replace it with an interest rate set by the central bank was Romer (2000). Attentive readers will notice that the model incorporates only one lag, from the setting of the interest instrument to a change in the output gap. Unlike figure 5.1, therefore, the model assumes a *contemporaneous* link between the output gap and inflation.

6 So called because the curve links the rate of inflation with a level of output, it approximates an aggregate demand curve. But it is important to bear in mind that the relationship traced by the *MR* curve is *chosen* by the policymaker. This contrasts with the conventional aggregate demand curve that represents the behaviour of agents in general.

7 The *MR* curve will shift (and change slope) every time the policymaker has a change of preferences. This becomes an issue in section 8.4.

Chapter 6

1 Friedman (1968, p.8) more formally expressed the structural characteristics of labour and commodity markets that produced the natural rate of unemployment as including 'market imperfections, stochastic variability in demands and supplies, the cost of gathering information about job vacancies and labour availabilities, the costs of mobility, and so on'.

2 It could equally be called the non-decelerating-inflation rate of unemployment since any level of unemployment above the natural rate will also only be temporary and will be the result of inflation decelerating below workers' expected inflation rate.

3   In most formulations of adaptive expectations, much heavier weights are applied to recent experience but people give some weight to experience from many previous years. This causes workers' inflationary expectations to approach the new rate of inflation relatively quickly but it might be many years before the expectations are actually correct.

4   However, all rejections of hypotheses about expectations-determined events are hard to interpret since they may be rejections of the theory of expectations formation rather than of the hypothesis itself.

5   The idea that 'in the long-run' is a logical state that refers to the simultaneous occurrence of a set of assumptions rendered impossible by the facts of economic life sheds a new light on Keynes's objection to the optimism of his 'classical' critics that 'in the[ir] long-run, we are all dead'. (Keynes, 1923).

Chapter 7

1   These events occurred before the theory of the vertical LRPC became established as orthodox theory. Policy-makers were thought to be choosing a position along a short-run Phillips curve, trading off higher unemployment against lower inflation.

2   Under the Bretton Woods system, this would have required an increase in the value of gold in terms of US dollars.

3   'Fundamental disequilibrium' was the term used in the agreement governing the Bretton Woods adjustable peg fixed exchange rate system.

4   In the event, the 15 per cent band remained in force until the establishment of monetary union in January 1999.

5   Padoa Schioppa, 1988, p.373

6   Rogoff, 1985a; Fratianni and von Hagen, 1990

7   Mélitz, 1988.

8   not including the members of ERMII.

9   From January 1999, the exchange rate between the dollar and the mark is calculated through the euro/dollar exchange rate using the fixed exchange rate between the mark and the euro.

10   Monthly average exchange rates from the Pacific Exchange Rate Service of the Sauder School of Business, University of British Columbia at http://fx.sauder.ubc.ca/data.html.

11   These ideas are defined and discussed in section 8.5

12   Nash non-cooperative games are classed as either Nash-Cournot (actions by other countries taken as given) or Nash-Stackelberg (one country acts as leader and anticipates how the other country will respond to its actions).

13 Williamson and Miller, 1987; McKinnon, 1988

14 see, for example, Krugman, 1991

15 Kindleberger, 1988, p.137

16 Portes, 1990, p.226

17 Walters, 1990, p.54

18 Horne and Masson, 1988, p.273

19 Currie, 1990, p.144

Chapter 8

1 This omits other possibilities e.g. that, in periods of high unemployment, it may be possible to reduce unemployment without inflationary consequences.

2 A prior question is the standard of measurement to be used e.g. in the case of inflation, which price index provides the best guide to the success or failure of policy: the retail price index, the underlying rate of inflation, the wholesale price index, the GDP deflator, a deflator of value added in manufacturing industry, the rate of increase of private final demand .... This is in turn complicated by the regular changes in statistical series introduced by the authorities.

3 The situation that developed in Japan during the 1990s with official interest rates virtually at zero, gave rise to some interesting suggestions. See for example W. Buiter, 'Overcoming the Zero Bound: Gesell vs. Eisler' availiable at www.nber.org/~wbuiter/fukao.pdf

4 For further information on the changeover see: http://www.bankofengland.co.uk/monetarypolicy/pdf/annex031210.pdf

5 For further discussion of variations on Taylor's original specification, see Kozicki (1999) and Svensson (2003).

6 Compare this list with the points mentioned in box 11.4.

7 That is a central banker who is more concerned about the losses from inflation than from unemployment, than the public at large.

Chapter 9

1 One might argue that oil and wheat are not 'assets' in the strict sense. However, they are certainly traded in markets which resemble asset markets . The 50 per cent rise in less than one year was not the result of long-term changes in demand and supply. For a discussion of the role of speculation and futures trading in determining the oil price in this period see the article by Desai in the *Financial Times*, 6 June 2008.

Chapter 10

1 Lord Kaldor was one of several economists on the Radcliffe Committee and argued this particular case against monetary targets. As we shall see later, his rejection of monetary targeting strengthened over the years but the basis for rejection changed fundamentally.

2 Sterling, along with other major European currencies, became convertible for foreign holders of it in 1958. Full sterling convertibility for UK residents dates from 1979. Other European currencies moved towards full convertibility during the 1980s and early 1990s.

3 The Bank of England itself had been nationalised in 1946.

4 Domestic credit expansion is the sum of the domestic credit counterparts of the money supply. In Equation 3.18, for example, DCE is found by ignoring ± ext. The logic was that under a fixed exchange rate regime, there is little that government can do about the impact of external flows, but it could at least be asked to control the domestic sources of money.

5 This process was more eloquently christened 'the regulatory dialectic' by Kane (1984). More examples of regulation-induced innovation are given in section 4.3.

6 e.g. in Zawadzki (1981), Gowland (1984), Hall (1983). See also Bank 1971b).

7 Details of interest rate movements and volume and types of debt sold are in Hall (1983) pp.28-30.

8 See Hall (1983) ch..4.

9 Gowland (1982) p.109.

10 Goodhart (2002) p.17.

11 We return to the issue of relative interest rates and monetary policy in our discussion of liability management later in this chapter.

12 See Goodhart (1984).

13 See Lewis and Davis (1987) section 9.7.

14 See also Howells and Bain (2002) ch.12.

15 Bank of England, *Statistical Abstract*, 1997, vol. I, tables 19.3, 19.4).

16 '...monetary targeting is simply a limiting case of inflation targeting in which the policymaker assigns a weight of unity to money and of zero to all other variables'. M King (1997) p.440.

Chapter 11

1   A strict application of optimum currency area theory might, for example, lead to the conclusion that south-east and central England should share a common currency with northern France but that the north of England and Scotland should have a separate common currency.

2   Membership of the euro area stood at 15 after 1 January 2008 when Cyprus and Malta were admitted. Slovakia was due to become the 16th member in January 2009. Further increases in membership are not likely before 2011 or 2012.

3   H M Treasury (1997), UK membership of the single currency: an assessment of the five economic tests. See http://www.hm-treasury.gov.uk/media/4/C/single.pdf

4   H M Treasury (2003), UK Membership of the single currency: an assessment of the five economic tests (Cm 5776). For the Executive Summary of the report see http://www.hm-treasury.gov.uk/media/0/4/EMU03_exec_126.pdf

5   *Financial Times* (2008), 'Sterling and the Euro', May 21

6   Although we generally use the term European Union (EU) in this book, direct reference to the Treaty on European Union must use the term European Community (EC) because, according to the Treaty, the Economic Community is the economic and monetary pillar of the three-pillared European Union, the other two of which relate to common foreign and security policies.

7   Formally, the exchange rate strategy of the euro area rests with the European Council, not with the ECB. However, since the value of the euro has some impact on the future rate of inflation, the ECB must take it into account in making interest rate decisions.

8   European Central Bank, 'The stability-oriented monetary policy strategy of the Eurosystem', *Monthly Bulletin*, January 1999, pp39-50, p.46

9   For an outline of these, see European Central Bank (2001).

10 In an interview with the BBC 19 May 2008, as reported in the *Financial Times* of 20 May 2008: 'Trichet issues ECB warning on jobs', page 1. http://www.ft.com/

11 ECB, *Monthly Report*, December 2001, p.5.

12 See http://www.ecb.int/ecb/orga/transparency/html/index.en.html

13 Although Buiter thinks that the Fed, the ECB and the Bank of England have already lost much of the anti-inflation credibility they might once have had.

Chapter 12

1 In each case the bank was granted a 20-year charter that was not renewed.

2 Andrew Jackson, President of the USA in a speech to the US Senate, July 10, 1832 quoted in Davies (1994). The full text of the speech is available in several places on the internet, for example at:
http://infomotions.com/etexts/gutenberg/dirs/1/0/8/5/10858/10858.htm

3 Despite large falls in number of many years, there remained 7,350 commercial banks in the USA at the end of June 2007.

4 State governments have the power to charter banks under the US constitution. The National Banking Act of 1863 empowered a federal agency to issue bank charters also.

5 No two members were to come from the same Federal Reserve region.

6 Multi-bank panics occurred in 1914, 1930 and 1933 leading to widespread restrictions on the convertibility of deposits into currency. It is easier to see why fear of a bank failure in those times led to long queues of depositors seeking to withdraw their funds than it was in the case of Northern Rock in the UK in 2007.

7 See Section 10.3 for the part played by Regulation Q in the development of the eurocurrency system.

8 Federal Reserve Bank of New York, About the Fed, available on
http://www.ny.frb.org/aboutthefed/introtothefed.html

9 Quoted in Hamda (2000), p. 253

10 Testimony of the then Fed Chairman, Alan Greenspan, in the Federal Reserve Board's semiannual monetary policy report to the Congress before the Committee on Financial Services, US House of Representatives, July 18 2001

11 Buiter W (2008) 'Central banks, cheap talk and costly signals', *Financial Times*, May 21, http://www.ft.com

12 Indeed, the Fed is legally required to do this.

13 The MCA required that in 1980 the reserve requirement should be only 3 per cent of the first $25 million of a bank's demand deposits; another banking act in 1982 established a zero reserve requirement for the first $2 million of a bank's deposits. Both figures (the $2 million and the $25 million) are adjusted annually to reflect the growth in total demand deposits in the USA. These concessions were intended to reduce the burden on small banks of maintaining reserves.

14 As we explain in Section 4.3, the use of average deposits eliminates day-to-day fluctuations and leaves interest rates less volatile at the end of the maintenance period. That is, it is intended to smooth out interest rate fluctuations.

15 For an explanation of how repos (known in the USA as RPs) work, see box 4.1.

16 Matched sale-purchase transactions (MSPs) involve a contract for immediate sale of Treasury bills to, and a linked matching contract for subsequent purchase from, each participating dealer.

17 Although there are only eight FOMC meetings a year, decisions can be altered by special telephone link-ups — see below in relation to September 11, 2001.

18 Wray (1990) p.249.

19 For the list of people in attendance at FOMC meetings see the minutes of the meeting on http://www.federalreserve.gov/monetarypolicy/

20 Testimony of Chairman Alan Greenspan, *Federal Reserve Board's demiannual monetary report to the Congress* before the Committee on Financial Services, US House of Representatives, July 18, 2001

21 Quotations from Federal Reserve Press Releases are from http://www.federalreserve.gov/boarddocs/press/monetary; accessed in May/June 2008

22 base period 1982-84 = 100; all statistics taken from historical series of the Bureau of Labor Statistics ftp://ftp.bls.gov/pub/special.requests/cpi/cpiai.txt

23 This and subsequent quotations in this chapter from minutes of the FOMC are from http://www.federalreserve.gov/fomc/minutes; accessed in June 2008

24 US Senate, 'Opening Statement of Chairman Chris Dodd - Hearing on "Mortgage Market Turmoil: Causes and Consequences", March 22, 2007, http://banking.senate.gov/index.cfm?Fuseaction=Articles.Detail&Article_id=125&Month=3&Year=2007

References

Acocella N (1998) *Economic Policy*, Cambridge: Cambridge U P

Akerlof G A, Dickens W T and Perry G L (1996) 'The Macroeconomics of Low Inflation', *Brookings Papers on Economic Activity*, 1, 1-59

Akerlof G A, Dickens W T and Perry G L (2000) 'Near-rational wage and price setting and the long-run Phillips curve', *Brookings Papers of Economic Activity*, 1, 1-60

Akerlof G A and Milbourne R D (1978) 'New calculations of Income and Interest Elasticities in Tobin's Model of the Transactions Demand for Money', *Review of Economics and Statistics*, 60

Akerlof G A and Milbourne R D (1980) 'The short-run demand for money', *Economic Journal*, 90, 885-900

Alesina A and Summers L (1993) 'Central bank independence and macroeconomic performance: some comparative evidence', *Journal of Money, Credit and Banking*, 25, 151-62

Anderson N and Sleath J (1999) 'New estimates of the UK real and nominal yield curves', *Bank of England Quarterly Bulletin*, November, 384–92

Aoki K, Proudman J and Vlieghe G (2001) 'Why house prices matter, *Bank of England Quarterly Bulletin*, winter, 460-68

Arestis P (2007) *Is There a New Consensus in Macroeconomics?* London: Palgrave

Arestis P and Sawyer M C (2001) *Money, Finance and Capitalist Development*, Cheltenham: Edward Elgar

Arestis P and Sawyer M C (2002) 'The Bank of England Macroeconomic Model: its Nature and Implications', *Journal of Post Keynesian Economics*, 24 (4), 529-45

Artis M and Lewis M K (1991) *Money in Britain*, Oxford: Phillip Allan

Bain K (1998) 'Some problems with the use of "credibility" and "reputation" to support the independence of central banks', in Arestis P and Sawyer M (eds), *The Political Economy of Central Banking*, Cheltenham: Edward Elgar

Bain K and Howells P G A (1991) 'The income and transactions velocities of money', *Review of Social Economy*, XLIX (3), 383-95

Ball L N (1994) 'Credible disinflation with staggered price setting', *American Economic Review*, 84, 282-9

Ball L (1997) 'Disinflation and the NAIRU', in Romer C D and D H (eds), *Reducing Inflation: Motivation and Strategy*, Chicago: University of Chicago Press

Ball L (1999), 'Efficient rules for monetary policy', *International Finance*, 2, 63-83

Bank of England Quarterly Bulletin (1971) 'Key issues in monetary and credit policy — an address by the Governor', June

Bank of England Quarterly Bulletin (1997) 'The Operation of Monetary Policy', February, 5-20

Bank of England Quarterly Bulletin (1999) 'The Transmission Mechanism of Monetary Policy', May

Bank of England Quarterly Bulletin (2001) 'The Kohn Report', Spring

Bank of England Quarterly Bulletin (2001) 'The Kohn Report: The Bank of England's Response', Spring

Bank of England Quarterly Bulletin (2007) 'The Monetary Policy Committee of the Bank of England: ten years on', Spring

Bank (2008) *The Development of the Bank of England's Market Operations: Consultative Paper* (London: Bank of England)

Barro R J (1977) 'Unanticipated money growth and unemployment in the United States', *American Economic Review*, 67, 101-15

Barro R J (1978) 'Unanticipated money, output and the price level in the United States', *Journal of Political Economy*, 86, 549-80

Barro R J and Gordon D B (1983) 'Rules, Discretion and Reputation in a Model of Monetary Policy', *Journal of Monetary Economics*, 12, 101-21

Barro R and Grossman H (1976) *Money, Employment and Inflation*, Cambridge: Cambridge University Press

Baumol W J (1952) 'The transactions demand for cash: an inventory theoretic approach', *Quarterly Journal of Economics*, 66, 545-56

Bean C (1998) 'The new UK monetary arrangement: a view from the literature', *Economic Journal*, November 1998, 1795-1809

Bean C (2007) 'Is There a New Consensus in Monetary Policy?' in Arestis P (2007) *Is There a New Consensus in Macroeconomics?* (London: Palgrave)

Bean C R and Jenkinson N (2001) 'The formulation of monetary policy at the Bank of England'*Bank of England Quarterly Bulletin*, winter 2001, 434-41

Benassy J-P (1975), 'Neo-Keynesian disequilibrium theory in a monetary economy', *Review of Economic Studies*, 42, 503-24

Bernanke B and Gertler M (2001) 'Should central banks respond to asset prices?', *American Economic Review*, 253-57

Bernanke B and Woodford M (eds) (2005) *Inflation Targeting*, Chicago: University of Chicago Press

H Bernard and S Gerlach (1996) 'Does the term structure predict recessions? The international evidence,' BIS Working Papers 37, Geneva: Bank for International Settlements

T Bernhardsen and A Kloster (2002) 'Transparency and predictability in monetary policy', *Economic Bulletin*, 73 (2), 45-58

Bertocchi G and M Spagat (1993) `Learning, experimentation and monetary policy', *Journal of Monetary Economics*, 32 (1), 169-83

Biefang-Frisancho Mariscal I and Howells P G A (2007) 'Monetary Policy Transparency in the UK: the impact of independence and inflation targeting', *International Review of Applied Economics*, 21 (5), 603-617

Blackburn K (1992) 'Credibility and time-consistency in monetary policy', in K Dowd and M K Lewis (eds)

Blanchard O and Galí J (2007) 'Real wage rigidities and the New Keynesian model', *Journal of Money, Credit and Banking*, 39(1), supplement, 39-65

Blinder A S (1998) *Central Banking in Theory and Practice*, Cambridge MA: MIT Press

Blinder A S (1997) 'What central bankers could learn from academia – and vice versa,' Journal of Economic Perspectives, 11 (2), 3-19

Bofinger P, Mayer E and Wollmerhäuser T (2006) 'The BMW Model: a new framework for teaching monetary economics', *Journal of Economic Education*, 37 (1), 98-117

Borio C E V (1997) 'Monetary policy operating procedures in industrial countries', Bank for International Settlements, Working Paper no. 40

Brooke M, N Cooper and C Scholtes (2000) 'Inferring market interest rate expectations from money market rates', *Bank of England Quarterly Bulletin*, November, 392-402

Browning P (1986) *The Treasury and Economic Policy, 1964-85*, Harlow: Longman

Brunner K (1968) 'The role of money and monetary policy', *Federal Reserve Bank of St Louis Review*, 50, 8-24

Buiter W (2008) 'Central banks, cheap talk and costly signals', *Financial Times*, May 21, http://www.ft.com

Buiter W (1999) 'Alice in Euroland', *Journal of Common Market Studies*, 37 (2), 181-209

Burgess S and Jansen N (2007) 'Proposals to modify the measurement of broad money in the United Kingdom: a user consultation', *Bank of England Quarterly Bulletin*, Q3 402-414

Calvo G A (1983) 'Staggered prices in a utility maximising framework', *Journal of Monetary Economics*, 12, 383-398

Campillo M and Miron J (1997) 'Why does inflation differ across countries?', in Romer C D and D H (eds), *Reducing Inflation: Motivation and Strategy*, Chicago: University of Chicago Press, 335-57

Canzoneri M and Gray J A (1985) 'Monetary policy games and the consequences of noncooperative behaviour', *International Economic Review,* 26

Carlin W and Soskice D (2005) The 3-Equation New Keynesian Model: A Graphical Exposition, *The B E Journal of Macroeconomics*

Carlin W and Soskice D (2006) *Macroeconomics: Imperfections, Institutions & Policies*, Oxford: Oxford UP

Carlstrom and Fuerst (2003) The Taylor Rule: A Guidepost for Monetary Policy?, *Federal Reserve Bank of Cleveland Economic Commentary*, March

Cecchetti S G, Genberg H, Lipsky J and Wadhwani S (2000) *Asset Prices and Central Bank Policy*, Geneva Reports on the World Economy 2, International Center for Monetary and Banking Studies, Geneva; London: Centre for Economic Policy Research

Chick V (2nd ed 1977) *The Theory of Monetary Policy*, Oxford: Blackwell

Chick V (1983) *Macroeconomics after Keynes*, Oxford: Philip Allan

Chick V (1986) 'The evolution of the banking system and the theory of saving, investment and interest', *Économies et sociétés*, Cahiers de l'ISMEA, Série 'Monnaie et Production, 3, 111-26

Chick V (1993) 'The evolution of the banking system and the theory of monetary policy', in S F Frowen (ed) *Monetary Theory and Monetary Policy: New Tracks for the 1990s*, London: Macmillan

Chortareas G, Stasavage D and Sterne G (2003) 'Does Monetary Policy Transparency Reduce Disinflation Costs?', *Manchester School*, 71 (5), September, 521-40

Chrystal K (ed.) (1990) *Monetarism*, 2 Vols, Aldershot: Edward Elgar

Clare (2001) 'The information in UK company profit warnings', *Bank of England Quarterly Bulletin,* Spring, 104-09

Clare, A and Courtney R (2000), 'Assessing the impact of macroeconomic news announcements on securities prices under different monetary policy regimes', *Bank of England Quarterly Bulletin*, August 2000, 266-273

Clarida R, Galí J and Gertler M (1999), 'The science of monetary policy: a New-Keynesian perspective', *Journal of Economic Literature,* 37, 1661-1707

Clarida R, Galí J and Gertler M (1998) 'Monetary policy rules in practice: some international evidence', *European Economic Review,* 42, 1033-1067

Clarida R, Gali J and Gertler M (1997) 'Monetary policy rules in practice: some international evidence', NBER Working Paper 6254.

Clews R (2002) 'Asset Prices and Inflation', *Bank of England Quarterly Bulletin,* Spring, 178-85

Clews R (2005), 'Implementing monetary policy: reforms to the Bank of England's operations in the money market', *Bank of England Quarterly Bulletin,* Summer, pages 211–20

Clews R, Panigirtzoglou N and Proudman J (2000) 'Recent developments in extracting information from options markets', *Bank of England Quarterly Bulletin,* 40 (1), 50-59

Clower R W (1971) 'Theoretical foundations of monetary policy' in Clayton G, Gilbert J C and Sedgewick R, eds, *Monetary Theory and Monetary Policy in the 1970s,* Oxford: Oxford UP

Cook T and Hahn T (1989) 'Effects of changes in the Federal Funds rate target on market rates in the 1970s', *Journal of Monetary Economics,* 24, 331-51

Cooper R N (1969) 'Macroeconomic policy adjustments in interdependent economies', *Quarterly Journal of Economics,* 83 (1), 1-24

Cooper R N (1985) 'Economic interdependence and coordination of economic policies', in Jones R W and Kenen P B (eds) *Handbook of International Economics* II, Amsterdam: North Holland

Cooper N, Hillman R and Lynch D (2001) 'Interpreting movements in high-yield corporate bond market spreads', *Bank of England Quarterly Bulletin,* 41 (1), 110-120

Copeland L S (3e, 2008) *Exchange Rates and International Finance,* 5e, Harlow: Pearson Education

Coppell J and Connolly J (2003), 'What Do Financial Market Data Tell Us About Monetary Policy Transparency,' Reserve Bank of Australia, Research Discussion Paper 2003/05.

Cornford A and Kregel J (1996) 'Globalisation, capital flows and international regulation', Jerome Levy Institute, Working Paper no. 161

Crawford M (1993) *One Money for Europe? The Economics and Politics of Maastricht* (Basingstoke: Macmillan)

Currie D (1990) `International policy coordination', in Llewellyn D T and Milner C (eds) *Current Issues in International Monetary Economics,* Basingstoke: Macmillan

Cuthbertson K (1985) *The Supply and Demand for Money,* Oxford: Blackwell

464

Cuthbertson K and Barlow D (1991) 'Money demand analysis: an outline', in Taylor M P (ed) (1991) *Money and Financial Markets*, Oxford: Blackwell

Cuthberston K and Foster N (1982) 'Bank Lending to Industrial and Commercial Companies in Three Models of the UK Economy', *National Institute of Economic Review*, 102, 63-75.

Cuthbertson K and M P Taylor (1987),'The demand for money: a dynamic rational expectations model', *Economic Journal*, 97, 65-76

Dale S (1993) 'Effects of changes in official UK rate upon money market rates since 1987', *Manchester School,* Proceedings of the Money, Macroeconomics and Finance Research Group, 76-94.

Dale S and Haldane A G (1993) 'Interest rate control in a model of monetary policy', Bank of England, Working Papers Series no.17

Darby M R (1972) 'On economic policy with rational expectations', *Journal of Monetary Economics*, 3 (2), 118-26

Davidson P (1997) 'Are grains of sand in the wheels of international finance sufficient to do the job when boulders are often required?', *Economic Journal*,107 (May), 671-86

Davidson P (1988) 'Endogenous money, the production process and inflation analysis', *Economie Appliquée*, XLI (1), 151-69

Davidson P and Weintraub S (1993) 'Money as Cause and Effect', *Economic Journal* 81, 1117-32.

Davies G (1994) *A History of Money. From Ancient Times to the Present Day*, Cardiff: University of Wales Press

Davis E P (1992) 'Credit Quality Spreads, Bond Market Efficiency and Financial Efficiency', *Manchester School*, 55 (supplement), 21-46

Davis E P and Henry S G B (1993) 'The Use of Financial Spreads as Indicators of Real Activity', in P Arestis (ed) *Money and Banking: Issues for the Twenty First Century*, London: Macmillan, 261-286

De Haan, J and Amtenbrink F (2002) 'A non-transparent European Central Bank? Who is to blame?' Paper given at the conference on Monetary Policy Transparency, held at the Bank of England, 10 May 2002.

Diamond D W (1984) 'Financial intermediation and delegated monitoring', *Review of Economic Studies*, 51, 393-414

Dornbusch R (1976) 'Expectations and exchange rate dynamics', *Journal of Political Economy*, 84, 1161-76

Dotsey M (1998) 'The predictive content of the interest rate term spread for future economic growth', *Federal Reserve Bank of Richmond Quarterly Review*, 84 (3), 30-51

Dow J C R and Saville I D (1988) *A Critique of Monetary Policy*, Oxford: Oxford U P

Dow S C (1993) *Money and the Economic Process*, Aldershot: Elgar

Dow S C (1996) `Horizontalism: a critique', *Cambridge Journal of Economics*, 20 (4), 497-508.

Dow S C (1996) 'Regulation and differences in financial institutions', *Journal of Economic Issues*, 30 (2), 517-23 (with V Chick)

Dow S C and Earl P E (1982) *Money Matters: a Keynesian Approach to Monetary Economics*, Oxford: Martin Robertson

Dowd K (1990) 'The value of time and the transactions demand for money', *Journal of Money, Credit and Banking*, 22 (February), 51-64

Driffil J (1988) 'The stability and sustainability of the European Monetary System with perfect capital markets', in Giavazzi F, Micossi S and Miller M (eds) (1988) *The European Monetary System*, Cambridge: Cambridge U P

ECB (2001) *The Monetary Policy of the ECB* (Frankfurt: ECB)

ECB (2004) *The Monetary Policy of the ECB* (Frankfurt: ECB)

Eijffinger S and de Haan J (2000) *European Monetary and Fiscal Policy*, Oxford: Oxford UP

Eshag E (1963), 'The internal value of money: review of Marshall's work', reprinted in Chrystal K (ed) (1990)

European Central Bank (1999) 'The stability-oriented monetary policy strategy of the Eurosystem', *Monthly Bulletin*, January

European Central Bank (2e, 2004) *The Monetary Policy of the ECB*, Frankfurt: ECB available at: http://www.ecb.eu/pub/pdf/other/monetarypolicy2004en.pdf

Fazzari S and Minsky H P (1984) 'Domestic monetary policy: if not monetarism, what?', *Journal of Economic Issues*, 18 (1), 101-16

Federal Reserve Board (1996) *A Guide to FRB/US* available at: www.federalreserve.gov/pubs/feds/1996/199642/199642pap.pdf

Fisher D (1989) *Money Demand and Monetary Policy*, London: Harvester Wheatsheaf

Fisher I (1907) *The Rate of Interest*, New York: Macmillan

Fisher I (1911), *The Purchasing Power of Money*, New York: Macmillan. Reprinted (1963) New York: Augustus M Kelley

Fontana G (2003) 'Post Keynesian Approaches to Endogenous Money: a time framework explanation', *Review of Political Economy*, 15 (3), 291-314

Fontana G and Palacio-Vera A (2004) 'Monetary Policy Uncovered: Theory and Practice', *International Review of Applied Economics*, 18 (1), 1-19

Forder J (1998) 'Central bank independence - conceptual clarifications and interim assessment', *Oxford Economic Papers*, 50, 307-34

Forder J (1999) 'Central bank independence: reassessing the measurements', *Journal of Economic Issues*, 33 (1), 23-40

Forder J (2002) 'Interests and "Independence": the European Central Bank and the theory of bureaucracy', *International Review of Applied Economics*, 16 (1), 51-70

Forder, J. (2003) '"Independence" and the Founding of the Federal Reserve ', *Scottish Journal of Political Economy*, 50, 3, 297-310.

Frankel J A (1979) 'On the mark: a theory of floating exchange rates based on real interest rate differentials', *American Economic Review*, 69, 610-22

Frankel J A and Froot K (1990) 'Chartists, fundamentalists and trading in the forex market', *American Economic Review*, May, 181-5

Fratianni M and von Hagen J (1990) 'German dominance in the EMS: the empirical evidence', *Open Economies Review*, 1

Freedman C (2002) 'The Value of Transparency in Conducting Monetary Policy', *Federal Reserve Bank of St. Louis Review*, 84 (4), pp. 155-60

Friedman M (1957) *A Theory of the Consumption Function*, Princeton: Princeton U P (for NBER)

Friedman M (1959) *A Program for Monetary Stability*, New York: Fordham U P

Friedman M (1968) 'The role of monetary policy', *American Economic Review*, 58, 1-17

Friedman M (1970) 'A theoretical framework for monetary analysis', *Journal of Political Economy*, 78, 193-238.

Friedman M and Schwartz A (1963) *A Monetary History of the United States, 1867-1960*, Princeton: Princeton U P

Galbraith J K (1955), *The Great Crash 1929*, London: Hamish Hamilton

Galbraith J K (1975) *Money: Whence it came, where it went*, Harmondsworth: Penguin Books

Galí J and Gertler M (1999) 'Inflation dynamics: a structural econometric analysis', *Journal of Monetary Economics*, 44(2) 195-222

Gerlach S and Schnabel G (1999) 'The Taylor Rule and Interest Rates in the EMU Area', CEPR Discussion Papers 2271 (London: CEPR)

Gieve J (2008) 'The impact of the financial market disruption on the UK economy', *Bank of England Quarterly Bulletin*, Q1, 85-90

Goodhart C A E (1984) *Monetary Theory and Practice*, London: Macmillan

Goodhart C A E (1986) 'Financial innovation and monetary control', *Oxford Review of Economic Policy*, 2 (4)

Goodhart C A E (1988), 'The foreign exchange market: the random walk with a dragging ancho'', *Economica*, 55, 437-60

Goodhart C A E (1989a) *Money, Information and Uncertainty,* 2nd edn, London: Macmillan

Goodhart C A E (1989b) `The conduct of monetary policy', *Economic Journal*, 99 (396), June, 293-346

Goodhart C A E (1994) 'What should central banks do? What should be their macroeconomic objectives and operations', *Economic Journal*, 104, November, 1424-36

Goodhart C A E (2002), 'The endogeneity of money', in Arestis P, Desai M and Dow S (eds) *Money, Macroeconomics and Keynes: Essays in Honour of Victoria Chick,* Vol 1, London: Routledge

Goodhart C A E and Hoffman (2007) *House Prices and the Macroeconomy*, Oxford: Oxford UP

Gordon R J (1982) 'Price inertia and policy ineffectiveness in the United States 1890-1980', *Journal of Political Economy*, December, 90(6), 1087-117

Gowland D H (1978) *Monetary Policy and Credit Control*, London: Croom Helm

Gowland D H (2e, 1984) *Controlling the Money Supply*, London: Croom Helm

Gowland D H (2e, 1991) *Money, Inflation and Unemployment,* 2e, Hemel Hempstead: Harvester Wheatsheaf

Grandmont J (1977) 'Temporary general equilibrium theory', *Econometrica*, 43, 535-72

Gray S and Talbot N (n.d.) *Monetary Operations*, CCBS handbook no. 24, London: Bank of England

de Grauwe P (7e, 2007) *The Economics of Monetary Union*, Oxford: Oxford UP

Greenaway D (ed) (1989) *Current Issues in Macroeconomics*, Basingstoke: Macmillan

Greider W (1987) *Secrets of the Temple: How the Federal Reserve runs the Country*, New York: Simon and Schuster

Hagen J von and Mundschenk S (2002) 'Fiscal and Monetary Policy Coordination in EMU', Oesterreichische Nationalbank working papers 70

Haldane A G (1995a) 'Inflation targets', *Bank of England Quarterly Bulletin*, 35 (3), 250-9

Haldane A G (ed) (1995b), *Targeting Inflation*, London: Bank of England

Haldane A G (1999) 'Monetary policy and the yield curve', *Bank of England Quarterly Bulletin*, 39 (2) , 171-76

Haldane A G and Read V (2000) 'Monetary policy surprises and the yield curve', Bank of England Working Paper no. 102

Hall R (2005a) 'Employment fluctuations with equilibrium wage stickiness', *American Economic Review* 95, 50-65

Hall R (2005b) 'Separating the business cycle from other economic fluctuations', in *The Greenspan Era: Lessons for the Future, Proceedings of the Federal Reserve Bank of Kansas City Symposium*, August (available at: http://www.kc.frb.org/publicat/sympos/2005/PDF/Hall2005.pdf)

Hall M J B (1983) *Monetary Policy since 1971*, London: Macmillan

Hall R E (1986) 'Optimal monetary institutions and policy' in Campbell C and Dougan W (eds) *Alternative Monetary Regimes*, Baltimore: Johns Hopkins Press

Hamada K (1976) 'A strategic analysis of monetary independence', *Journal of Political Economy*, 84, 677-700

Hamada K (1985) *The Political Economy of International Monetary Interdependence*, Cambridge Mass.: MIT Press

Handa J (2000) *Monetary Economics*, London: Routledge

Hardy, D C (1996), 'Market Reaction to Changes in German Official Interest Rates', Deutsche Bundesbank Discussion Paper No.4/96

Harris L (1985) *Monetary Theory*, New York: McGraw-Hill

Harrison R, Nikolov K, Quinn M, Ramsay G, Scott R and Thomas R (2005), *The Bank of England Quarterly Model*, London: Bank of England

Heffernan S A (1993) 'Competition in British retail banking', *Journal of Financial Services Research*, 7, 309-32

Heffernan S A (1997) 'Modelling British interest rate adjustment: an error correction approach', *Economica*, May, 291-31

Hicks J R (1967) *Critical Essays in Monetary Theory*, Oxford: Clarendon Press

Holmes, A (1969) 'Operational Constraints on the Stabilization of Money Supply Growth', in *Controlling Monetary Aggregates*, (Boston MA: Federal Reserve Bank of Boston) 65-77

Horne J and Masson P R (1988) 'Scope and limits of international economic cooperation and policy coordination', *IMF Staff Papers*, 35 (2), 259-96.

Howells P G A (1995), 'The Demand for Endogenous Money', *Journal of Post Keynesian Economics* 18 (1), 89-106

Howells P G A (1997), 'The Demand for Endogenous Money: a rejoinder', *Journal of Post Keynesian Economics* 19 (3), 429-34

Howells P G A (2001) 'Endogenous Money', in P Arestis and M C Sawyer (eds) *Money, Finance and Capitalist Development*, Aldershot: Elgar, 2001

Howells P G A and Bain K (4e, 2008) *The Economics of Money, Banking and Finance*, London: Pearson Education

Howells P G A and Bain K (2e, 2002) *The Economics of Money, Banking and Finance*, London: Pearson Education

Howells P G A and Hussein K A (1999) 'The demand for loans and "the state of trade"', *Journal of Post Keynesian Economics*, 21 (3), 441-45

Hughes-Hallett A (1989) 'Macroeconomic interdependence and the coordination of economic policy', in Greenaway D (ed), *op cit.*

Humphrey T M (1974) 'The quantity theory of money: its historical evolution and role in policy debates', *Federal Reserve Bank of Richmond Economic Review*, 60, May/June. Reprinted in Chrystal K (ed.) (1990)

Issing, Otmar (1993) *Central Bank Independence and Monetary Stability*, Occasional Paper 89, London: Institute of Economic Affairs

Issing O (1999) 'The eurosystem: transparent and accountable, or "Willem in Euroland"', *Journal of Common Market Studies*, 37 (3), 503-19

Judd J P and Rudebusch G D (1998) 'Describing Fed Behavior', *FRBSF Economic Letter*, December

Kaldor N (1982) *The Scourge of Monetarism*, Oxford: Oxford U P

Kaldor N (1985) `How monetarism failed', *Challenge*, 28 (2), 4-13

Karni E (1974) 'The Value of Time and the Demand for Money', *Journal of Money, Credit and Banking*, 6, 45-64

Keynes J M (1923) *A Tract on Monetary Reform*, London: Macmillan, Vol. IV of Moggridge D and Johnson E (eds) (1973) *Collected Works of John Maynard Keynes*, London: Macmillan

Keynes J M (1930) *A Treatise on Money*, London: Macmillan, Vols. V and VI of Moggridge D and Johnson E (eds) (1973) *Collected Works of John Maynard Keynes*, London: Macmillan

Keynes J M (1936) *The General Theory of Employment, Interest and Money*, London: Macmillan, Vol VII of Moggridge D and Johnson E (eds) (1973) *Collected Works of John Maynard Keynes*, London: Macmillan

Keynes J M (1973) *The General Theory and After: Part II, Defence and Development*, Vol. XIV of Moggridge D and Johnson E (eds) (1973) *Collected Works of John Maynard Keynes*, London: Macmillan

Kindleberger C P (1988), *The International Economic Order:: Essays on Financial Crisis and International Public Goods*, Cambridge, Mass: MIT Press

Kindleberger C P (1996), *Manias, Panics and Crashes. A History of Financial Crashes* 3rd edn, New York: John Wiley and Sons

King M (1994) 'The transmission mechanism of monetary policy', *Bank of England Quarterly Bulletin*, August, 261-267

King M (1995) 'Credibility and monetary policy: theory and evidence', *Scottish Journal of Political Economy*, 42 (1), 1-19

King M (1997) 'The inflation target five years on', *Bank of England Quarterly Bulletin*, 37 (4), 431-42

Kuttner K N (2001) 'Monetary Policy Surprises and Interest Rates: Evidence from the Fed Funds Futures Market', Journal of Monetary Economics, June 2001, 47 (3), 523-44

Krugman P (1991) 'Target zones and exchange rate dynamics', *Quarterly Journal of Economics*, 106, 669-82

Kydland F and E Prescott (1977) ' "Rules rather than discretion": the inconsistency of optimal plans', *Journal of Political Economy*, 85 (3), 473-92

Laidler D E W (1984) 'The buffer stock notion in monetary economics', *Economic Journal*, Conference Papers Supplement, 94, 17-34

Laidler D E W (1988) 'Some macroeconomic implications of price stickiness', *Manchester School*, 1988, 56 (1), 37-54

Laidler D E W (1990) *Taking Money Seriously*, Hemel Hempstead: Philip Allan

Laidler D E W (4e,1993) *The Demand for Money*, New York: HarperCollins

Laidler D E W (2002) 'The transmission mechanism with endogenous money', in Arestis P, Desai M and Dow S C, *Money, Macroeconomics and Keynes*, London: Routledge

Lambert, R (2005), 'Inside the MPC', *Bank of England Quarterly Bulletin*, Spring, 56-65

Lavoie M (1985) 'Credit and Money: The Dynamic Circuit, Overdraft Economics and Post Keynesian Economics' in M Jarsulic (ed) *Money and Macro Policy*, Boston: Kluwer-Nijhoff

Leland H and Pyle D (1977) 'Information asymmetries, financial structures and financial intermediaries', *Journal of Finance*, 32, 371-87

Lewis M K (1988) 'Off balance sheet activities and financial innovation in banking', *Banca Nationale del Lavoro*, 387-410

Lewis M K and Davis K T (1987) *Domestic and International Banking*, Hemel Hempstead: Philip Allan

Lewis M K and Mizen P D (2000) *Monetary Economics*, Oxford: Oxford U P

Lipsey R G (1960) 'The relationship between unemployment and the rate of change of money wage rates in the U.K., 1861-1957: a further analysis', *Economica*, 27, 1-31

Llewellyn D T and Milner C, eds (1990), *Current Issues in International Monetary Economics*, London: Macmillan

Lohman S (1996), 'Quis custodiet ipsis custodes?', in Siebert H (ed) (1996) *Monetary Policy in an Integrated World Economy: Symposium 1995*, Kiel: J C B Mohr

Lucas R E (1972) 'Expectations and the neutrality of money', *Journal of Economic Theory*, 4 (1), 102-24

Lucas R E (1973) 'Some international evidence on output-inflation trade-offs', *American Economic Review*, 63, 326-34

Malinvaud E (1977) *The Theory of Unemployment Reconsidered*, Oxford: Basil Blackwell

Malz A (1995) 'Using options prices to estimate re-alignment probabilities in the European Monetary System' Federal Reserve Bank of New York Staff Reports, no.5.

Malz A (1997) 'Estimating the probability distribution of future exchange rates from options prices', *Journal of Derivatives*, winter, 18-36

Mankiw N G (2001) 'The inexorable and mysterious trade-off between inflation and unemployment', *Economic Journal*, 111 (471), C45-C61

Marshall A (1887) 'Remedies for fluctuation in general prices', *Contemporary Review*

Mayer T (1978) *The Structure of Monetarism*, New York: W W Norton

McCallum B T (1989) *Monetary Economics: Theory and Policy*, New York: Macmillan

McCallum B T (2000) 'The Present and Future of Monetary Policy Rules', NBER Working Papers: 7916

McCallum B T and Goodfriend M (1992) 'Demand for Money: Theoretical Studies' in Newman P, Milgate M and Eatwell J (eds)

McKinnon R I (1988) 'Monetary and exchange rate policies for international financial stability: a proposal', *Journal of Economic Perspectives*, 2 (1), 83-103

Meade J E (1978) 'The meaning of internal balance', *Economic Journal*, 88, 423-35

Meese R A and Rogoff K (1983), `Empirical Exchange Rate Models of the Seventies: Do they fit out of sample?', *Journal of International Economics*, 14, 3-24

Mélitz J (1988) 'Monetary discipline and cooperation in the European Monetary System: a synthesis', in Giavazzi F, Micossi S and Miller M (eds), *The European Monetary System*, Cambridge: Cambridge U P

Milbourne R D (1987) 'Re-examining the buffer stock model of money', *Economic Journal*, 97, supplement, 130-42

Milesi-Ferretti G (1995) 'The disadvantage of tying their hands: on the political economy of policy commitments', *Economic Journal*, 105 (433), 1381-1402

Miller M H and Orr D (1966) 'A model of the demand for money by firms', *Quarterly Journal of Economics,* 80, 413-35

Miller M, Weller P and Zhang L (2002) 'Moral hazard and the US stock market: Analysing the "Greenspan put"', *Economic Journal*, 112, C171-C186

Minsky H P (1982) *Can it happen again? Essays on Instability and Finance*, Armonk N Y: M E Sharpe

Minsky H (1986) *Stabilizing an Unstable Economy*, New Haven CT: Yale U P

Mishkin F S (1982) 'Does anticipated policy matter? an econometric investigation', *Journal of Political Economy*, 90, 22-51

Moore B J (1983) 'Unpacking the Post-Keynesian black box', *Journal of Post-Keynesian Economics*, 5 (4), 537-46. Reprinted in Sawyer M C (ed) *Post-Keynesian Economics* (Aldershot: Elgar, 1989)

Moore B J (1986) 'How Credit Drives the Money Supply: The Significance of Institutional Developments', *Journal of Economic Issues,* XX (2), 113-452

Moore B J (1988a), *Horizontalists and Verticalists*, Cambridge: Cambridge U P

Moore B J (1988b), `The endogenous money supply', *Journal of Post Keynesian Economics*, 10 (3), 372-85

Moore B J and Threadgold A R (1985), `Corporate Bank Borrowing in the UK, 1965-81', *Economica*, 52, 65-78

Moore B J and Threadgold A (1980) Bank Lending and the Money Supply: the Case of the UK, Bank of England DiscussionPaper no.10.

Mundell R A (1962) `The appropriate use of monetary and fiscal policy for internal and external stability', International Monetary Fund Staff Papers, IX

Myrdal G (1939) *Monetary Equilibrium*, London: William Hodge and Co

E Nelson (2000) 'UK monetary policy 1972-97: a guide using Taylor rules', Bank of England working paper no. 120.

Newman P, M Milgate and J Eatwell (eds) (1992) *The New Palgrave Dictionary of Money and Finance*, London: Macmillan

Niggle C J (1990) 'The evolution of money, financial institutions and monetary economics', *Journal of Economic Issues*, 24, June, 443-50

Niggle C J (1991) 'The endogenous money supply theory: an institutionalist appraisal' *Journal of Economic Issues*, 25 (1) 137-151

Obstfeld M and Rogoff K (2002) 'Global implications of self-oriented national monetary rules', *Quarterly Journal of Economics*, 117 503-536

Padoa Schioppa T (1988) 'The European Monetary System: A long-term view', in Giavazzi F, Micossi S and Miller M (eds) *The European Monetary System*, Cambridge: Cambridge U P

Palley, T I (1991) 'The endogenous money supply: consensus and disagreement', *Journal of Post Keynesian Economics*, 13, 397-403

Patinkin D (2e 1965) *Money, Interest and Prices*, New York: Harper and Row

Perez-Quiros G and Sicilia J (2002) 'Is the European Central Bank (and the United States Federal Reserve) Predictable?', ECB Working Paper Series, no.102

Phelps E S (1967) 'Phillips curves, expectations of inflation and optimal employment over time', *Economica*, 34, 254-281

Phillips A W (1958) 'The relation between unemployment and the rate of change of money wage rates in the United Kingdom, 1861-1957', *Economica*, 25, 283-99

Pigou A C (1949) *The Veil of Money*, London: Macmillan

Pilbeam K (3e, 2005) *International Finance*, Basingstoke: Palgrave

Podolski T (1985) *Financial Innovation and the Money Supply*, Oxford: Blackwell

Pollin R (1991) 'Two theories of money supply endogeneity: some empirical evidence', *Journal of Post Keynesian Economics*, 13(3), 366-396

Poole W, Rasche R H and Thornton D L (2002) 'Market Anticipations of Monetary Policy Actions', The Federal Reserve Bank of St Louis Review, 84(4), 65-94

Portes R (1990) 'Macroeconomic Policy Coordination and the European Monetary System', in P Ferri (ed) *Prospects for the European Monetary System*, London: Macmillan, 222-35

Radcliffe Committee (1959) Report of the Committee on the Working of the Monetary System, Cmnd 827, London: HMSO

Rodgers P (1998) 'The Bank of England Act', *Bank of England Quarterly Bulletin*, May, 93-99

Rogoff K (1985a) 'Can exchange rate predictability be achieved without monetary convergence? evidence from the EMS', *European Economic Review*, 28

Rogoff K (1985b) 'Can international monetary policy coordination be counter-productive?', *Journal of International Economics* 18, 199-217

Rogoff K (1985c) 'The optimal degree of commitment to an intermediate monetary target', *Quarterly Journal of Economics*, 100(4), 1169-89

Romer D (2000) 'Keynesian Macroeconomics without the LM curve', *Journal of Economic Perspectives*, 2 (14), 149-69

Rousseas S (1986) *Post Keynesian Monetary Economics*, London: Macmillan

Rowthorn R E (1999) 'Unemployment, wage bargaining and capital-labour substitution', *Cambridge Journal of Economics*, 23 (4) 413-25

Rudebusch G D (2005) 'Assessing the Lucas Critique in Monetary Policy Models', *Journal of Money, Credit, and Banking* 37(2), April 2005, 245-272

Samuelson P (9e, 1973) *Economics*, New York: McGraw-Hill

Samuelson P and Solow R (1960) 'Analytical aspects of anti-inflation policy', *American Economic Review*, 50(2) 177-194

Sargent T J and Wallace N (1975) 'Rational expectations, the optimal monetary instrument and the optimal money supply rule', *Journal of Political Economy*, April, 83, 241-54

Sargent T J and Wallace N (1982) 'The real bills doctrine versus the quantity theory: a reconsideration', *Journal of Political Economy*, 90, 1212-36

Sayers R S (1976) *The Bank of England, 1891-1944.* Cambridge: Cambridge U P

Schumpeter J (1911) *The Theory of Economic Development: An inquiry into profits, capital, credit, interest and the business cycle*, Cambridge MA: Harvard U P

Shackle G L S (1971), Discussion Paper in G Clayton, J C Gilbert and R Sedgewick (eds)

Shiller R (2000) *Irrational Exuberance*, Princeton: Princeton U P

Simons H (1948) *Economic Policy for a Free Society*, Chicago: University of Chicago Press

Sims C A (1972) 'Money, income and causality', *American Economic Review*, 62, 540-52

Sinclair P J N (2003) 'The optimal rate of inflation: an academic perspective', *Bank of England Quarterly Bulletin*, Autumn, 343-60

Smith A (1776) *The Wealth of Nations*, London

Sprenkle C M (1969) 'The uselessness of transactions demand models', *Journal of Finance*, 4, 835-47

Sprenkle C M (1972) 'On the observed transactions demand for money', *The Manchester School*, 40, 261-7

Sprenkle C and Miller M H (1980) 'The precautionary demand for broad and narrow money', *Economica*, 47, 407-21

Stiglitz J E and Weiss A (1981) 'Credit rationing in markets with imperfect information', *America Economic Review*, 71, 393-410

Stock J H and Watson M W, (1989) 'New Indices of Coincident and Leading Economic Indicators' in S Fischer and O Blanchard (eds) *NBER Macroeconomic Annual*, Cambridge: MIT Press

Stone C T and Thornton D L (1987) 'Solving the 1980s Velocity Puzzle: A Progress Report', *Federal Reserve Bank of St Louis Review*, Aug/Sept, 5-23

Struthers J and Speight H (1986) *Money: Theory, Institutions, Policy*, London: Longman.

Sutherland A (2002) 'International monetary policy coordination and financial integration', *International Finance Discussion Papers*, 751, Board of Governors of the Federal Reserve System available at http://www.federalreserve.gov/pubs/ifdp/2002/751/ifdp751.pdf

Svensson L (1997) 'Inflation forecast targeting: implementing and monitoring inflation targets', *European Economic Review*, 41, 1111-1146

Svennson L E O (1999) 'Inflation targeting as a monetary policy rule', *Journal of Monetary Economics*, 43, 655-79

Svensson L E O (2000), 'The first year of the eurosystem: inflation targeting or not?' *American Economic Review*, Papers and Proceedings, 95-99

Svensson, L E O (2001) 'Price stability as a target for monetary policy: defining and maintaining price stability', in Deutsche Bundesbank (ed) *The Monetary Transmission Process: Recent Developments and Lessons for Europe*, New York: Palgrave

Svensson L E O (2003) 'What Is Wrong with Taylor Rules? Using Judgment in Monetary Policy through Targeting Rules', *Journal of Economic Literature*, 426-77

Taylor J (1979), 'Staggered price setting in a macro model', *American Economic Review*, 83, 108-13

Taylor J B (1993) 'Discretion versus Policy Rules in Practice', *Carnegie-Rochester Series on Public Policy*, 39, 195-214

Taylor J B (2008) 'The impacts of globalization on monetary policy', presented at the Banque de France symposium on Globalization, inflation and monetary policy, March 7 2008 available at
http://www.banque-France.fr/gb/publications/telechar/seminaires/2008/colloque_mars_2008/Taylor.pdf

476

Temin P (1976) *Did monetary forces cause the great depression?*, New York: Norton

Thornton D L (2003) 'Monetary Policy Transparency: Transparent for what?', *Manchester School*, 71 (5), 478-97

Tobin J (1956) 'The interest-elasticity of transactions demand for cash', *Review of Economics and Statistics*, 38(3), 241-7

Tobin J (1958) 'Liquidity preference as behaviour towards risk', *Review of Economic Studies*, 25(1), 65-86

Tobin J (1969) 'A general equilibrium approach to monetary theory', *Journal of Money, Credit and Banking*, 1(1), 15-29

Tobin J (1972) 'Inflation and unemployment', *American Economic Review*, 62 1-18
available at: http://cowles.econ.yale.edu/P/cp/p03b/p0361.pdf

Tobin J (1978) 'A proposal for international monetary reform', *Eastern Economic Journal*, 4, 153-59

Tödter, K.-H. and H.-E. Reimers (1994), 'P-Star as a Link between Money and Prices in Germany', *Weltwirtschaftliches Archiv* 130, 273-289.

Treasury H M (1997) *UK membership of the single currency: an assessment of the five economic tests*, London: HM Treasury, October http://www.hm-treasury.gov.uk

Treasury H M (2003) *UK membership of the single currency: an assessment of the five economic tests*, London: HM Treasury, June   http://www.hm-treasury.gov.uk

Treasury H M (2002) *Reforming Britain's Economic and Financial Policy*, London: Palgrave

Treasury Select Committee (TSC) (2008) 'The Monetary Policy Committee of the Bank of England: ten years on: Government and Bank of England responses to the Committee's Twelfth Report of Session 2006-07' HC259

Treasury and Civil Service Committee (TCSC) (1980-1), *Monetary Policy*, vol.II, Minutes of Evidence

Visser H (1974) *The Quantity of Money*, London: Martin Robertson

Walsh C E (1995) 'Optimal contracts for central bankers', *American Economic Review*, 85, 150-67

Walsh C E (2e 2003) *Monetary Theory and Policy*, Cambridge MA: MIT Press

Walters A (1990) *Sterling in Danger. The Economic Consequences of Pegged Exchange Rates*, London: Fontana/Collins in association with the Institute of Economic Affairs

Wicksell K (1898) *Interest and Prices*, London: Macmillan

Williamson J and Miller M (1987) *Targets and Indicators: a blueprint for the International Coordination of Economic Policy*, Washington DC: Institute for International Economics

Woodford M (2001) 'The Taylor Rule and Optimal Monetary Policy', *American Economic Review* 91(2): 232-237

Woodford M (2003) *Interest and Prices: Foundations of a theory of monetary policy*, Princeton N J: Princeton U P

Wray L R (1990) *Money and Credit in Capitalist Economies. The Endogenous Money Approach*, Aldershot: Edward Elgar

Wyplosz C (2001) *How do we know how low inflation should be?* CEPR Discussion Paper 2722

Zawadski K K F (1981) *Competition and Credit Control*, Oxford: Blackwell.

Index